Sri Lanka

Richard Plunkett
Brigitte Ellemor

LONELY PLANET PUBLICATIONS
Melbourne • Oakland • London • Paris

JAFFNA
Be among the first to visit the newly reopened capital of the North, and witness the rebuilding of this bustling city

NILAVELI
Snorkel, dive or simply soak up the wide, fine-white-sand beaches and turquoise-coloured waters

ANCIENT CITIES
Anuradhapura, Polonnaruwa and Sigiriya – the magnificent relics of Sri Lanka's golden age

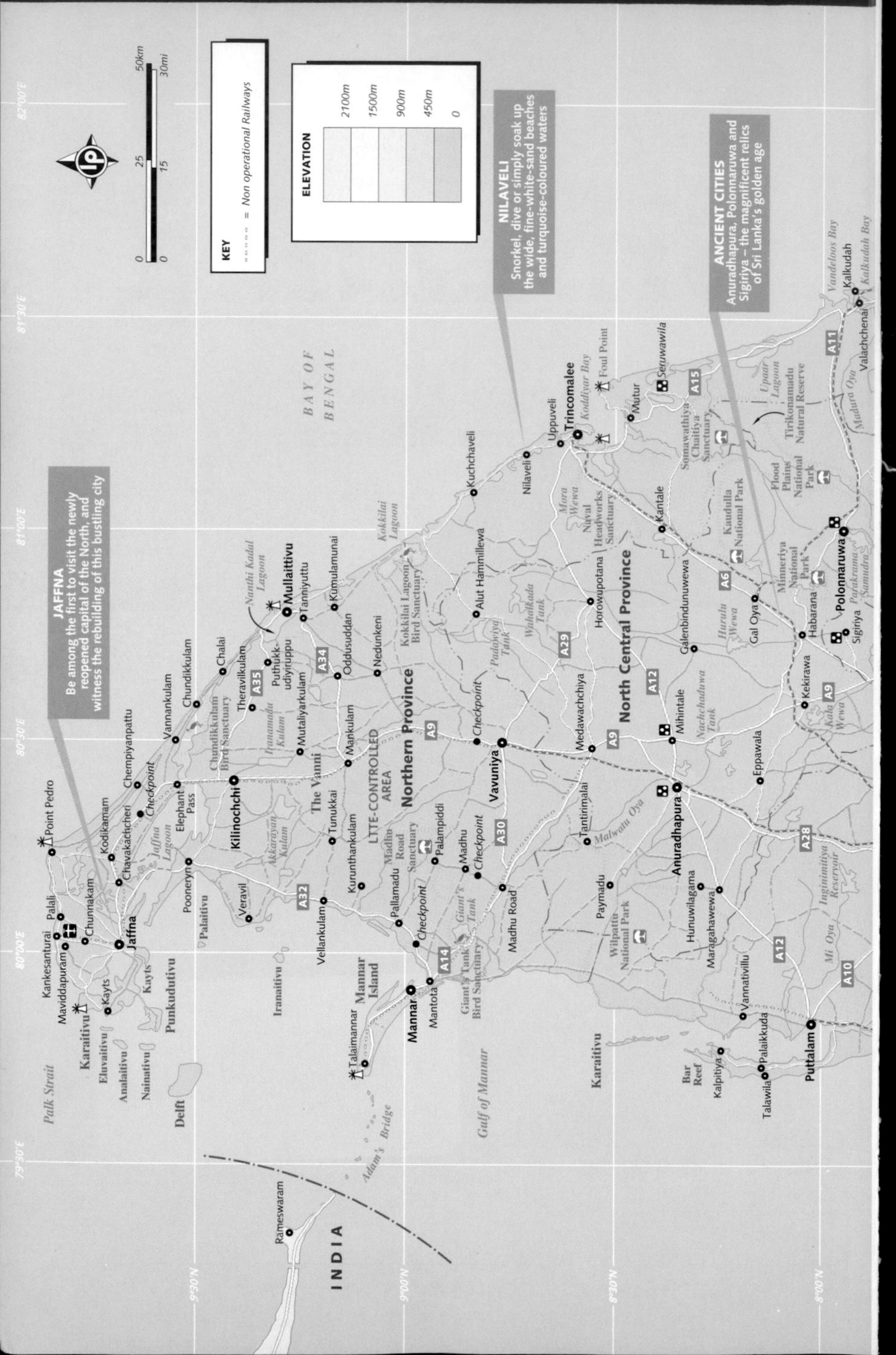

KEY
= *Non operational Railways*

ELEVATION
2100m
1500m
900m
450m
0

0 25 50km
0 15 30mi

79°30'E 80°00'E 80°30'E 81°00'E 81°30'E 82°00'E
9°30'N 9°00'N 8°30'N 8°00'N

INDIA
Rameswaram
Palk Strait
Adam's Bridge
Gulf of Mannar
BAY OF BENGAL

Point Pedro
Kankesanturai
Palali
Maviddapuram
Karaitivu
Chunnakam
Eluvaitivu
Kayts
Kodikamam
Analaitivu
Jaffna
Chavakachcheri
Chempiyanpattu
Nainativu
Kayts
Checkpoint
Jaffna Lagoon
Punkudutivu
Delft
Elephant Pass
Vannankulam
Pooneryn
Chundikkulam
Palaitivu
Chundikkulam Bird Sanctuary
Chalai
Kilinochchi
Veravil
Theravilkulam
A35
Nanthi Kadal Lagoon
Akkarayan Kulam
Iranamadu Kulam
Puthukk-udiyiruppu
Iranaitivu
Mullaittivu
A32
Mutaliyarkulam
Tanniyuttu
The Vanni
Vellankulam
A34
Tunukkai
Kumulamunai
Mankulam
Oddusuddan
Kurunthankulam
Talaimannar
Mannar Island
LTTE-CONTROLLED AREA
Nedunkeni
Madhu Road Sanctuary
Kokkilai Lagoon
Pallamadu
Northern Province
Kokkilai Lagoon Bird Sanctuary
Mannar
Checkpoint
A9
Mantota
Palampiddi
A14
Giant's Tank
Madhu
Giant's Tank Bird Sanctuary
Checkpoint
Checkpoint
Alut Hammillewa
Kuchchaveli
Padawiya Tank
Vavuniya
A30
Madhu Road
Wahalkada Tank
Nilaveli
Uppuveli
A29
Mora Wewa
Trincomalee
Koddiyar Bay
Tantirimalai
Medawachchiya
Naval Headworks Sanctuary
Karaitivu
Paymadu
Horowupotana
Foul Point
Malwatu Oya
Wilpattu National Park
A9
North Central Province
Mutur
A12
Kantale
Seruwawila
Anuradhapura
Mihintale
Galenbindunuwewa
Bar Reef
Nachchaduwa Tank
Somawathiya Chaitiya Sanctuary
Hunuwilagama
A15
Kalpitiya
Maragahawewa
Hurulu Wewa
A6
Kaudulla National Park
Vannativillu
Gal Oya
Upaar Lagoon
Palaikkuda
Eppawala
Talawila
Minneriya National Park
Flood Plains National Park
Tirikonamadu Natural Reserve
A12
Kekirawa
Habarana
Puttalam
A28
Mi Oya
Inginimitiya Reservoir
Kala Wewa
A9
Polonnaruwa
A11
Vandeloos Bay
A10
Sigiriya
Parakrama Samudra
Madura Oya
Kalkudah
Valachchenai
Kalkudah Bay

SRI LANKA
KANDY
History and culture, delightful old shops, lush green hills and a touch of urban buzz – all this and the country's most spectacular annual festival
ADAM'S PEAK
Take the night-time pilgrimage up this sacred mountain for the eerily magnificent sunrise view
SINHARAJA FOREST RESERVE
This untouched rainforest is a paradise for bird-watchers and jungle adventurers
GALLE
Join the locals in their sunset stroll around the old ramparts of this charming historic town
SOUTHERN BEACHES
From popular Unawatuna to sleepy Mirissa, you're sure to find a long stretch of white sand to suit your taste
HORTON'S PLAINS & WORLD'S END
Beautiful, silent and strange, these sweeping plains come to a breathtaking vertical drop – a classic sunrise walk
YALA WEST (RUHUNA) NATIONAL PARK
Take a wildlife safari – your best chance to spot the elusive leopard
ELLA
This sleepy village-with-a-view is the perfect base for walks through tea plantations to temples and waterfalls
ARUGAM BAY
Enjoy Sri Lanka's best surfing and an easy-going party atmosphere in the country's newest hot spot
INDIAN OCEAN
North Western Province
Central Province
Eastern Province
Province of Sabaragamuwa
Western Province
Southern Province
Province of Uva
COLOMBO
Sri Jayawardenepura-Kotte
Kandy
Kurunegala
Matale
Kegalle
Gampaha
Ratnapura
Kalutara
Galle
Matara
Hambantota
Badulla
Monaragala
Ampara
Batticaloa
Nuwara Eliya
Negombo
Chilaw
Dambulla
Cave Temples
Yapahuwa
Dimbulagala
Knuckles Range (1863m)
Pidurutalagala (Mt Pedro) (2524m)
Adam's Peak (Sri Pada) (2243m)
Kirigalpotta (2387m)
Totapola (2361m)
Namunukula (2035m)
Kokagala (687m)
Wadinahela (666m)
Bintenna (723m)
Gongala (1358m)
Horton Plains National Park
World's End
Peak Wilderness Sanctuary
Sinharaja Forest Reserve
Uda Walawe National Park
Yala West (Ruhuna) National Park
Yala East National Park
Yala Strict Natural Reserve
Bundala National Park
Gal Oya National Park
Lahugala National Park
Maduru Oya National Park
Wasgomuwa National Park
Hikkaduwa Marine Sanctuary
Wirawila Wewa Bird Sanctuary
Muthurajawela Marsh
Victoria Reservoir
Randenigala Reservoir
Senanayake Samudra
Arugam Bay
Weligama Bay
Dondra Head
Great Basses
Little Basses
Ratmalana Airport
Mahaweli Ganga
Walawe Ganga
Kumbukkan Oya
7°30'N
7°00'N
6°30'N
6°00'N

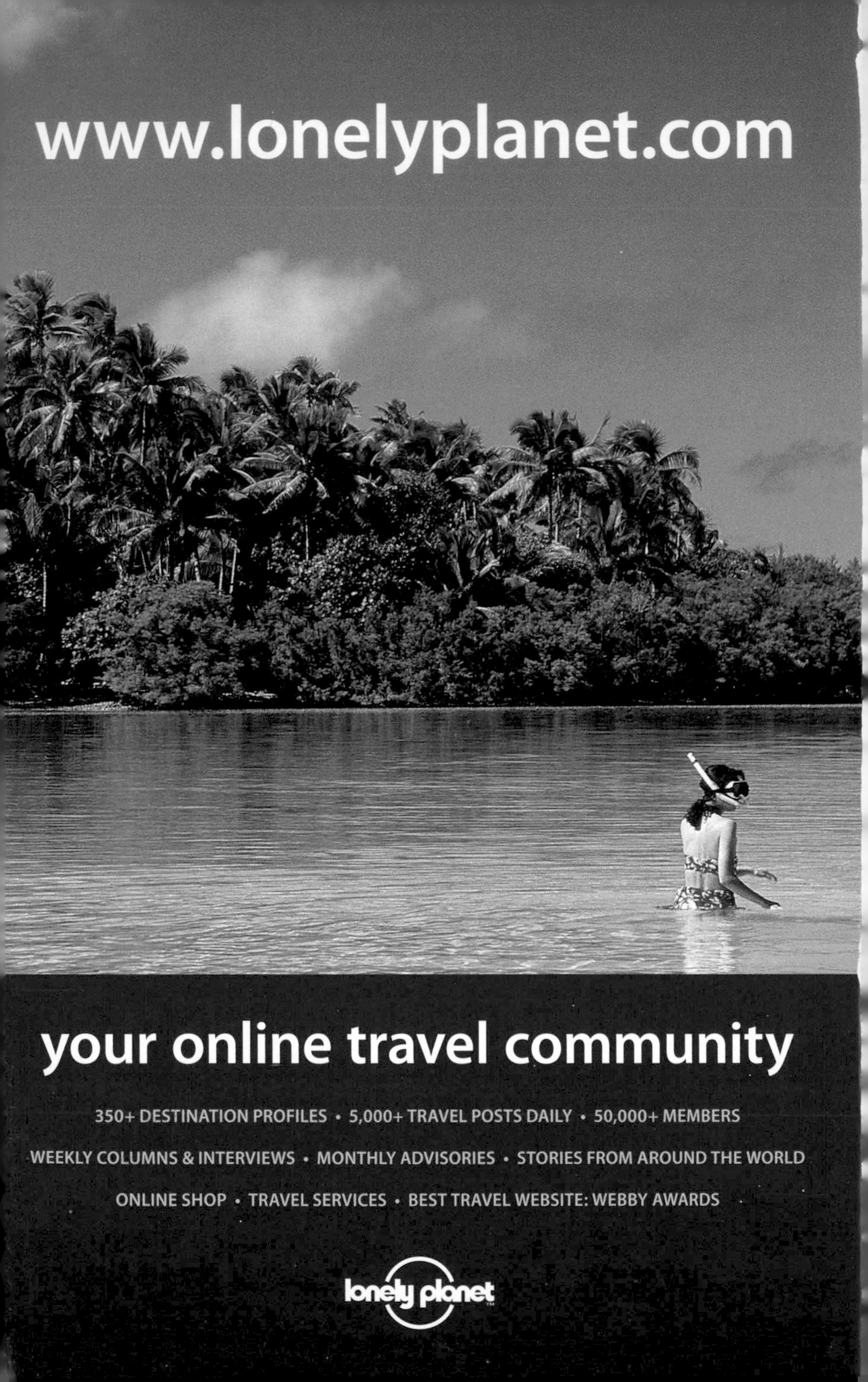

Contents – Text

Contents – Maps

MAP INDEX

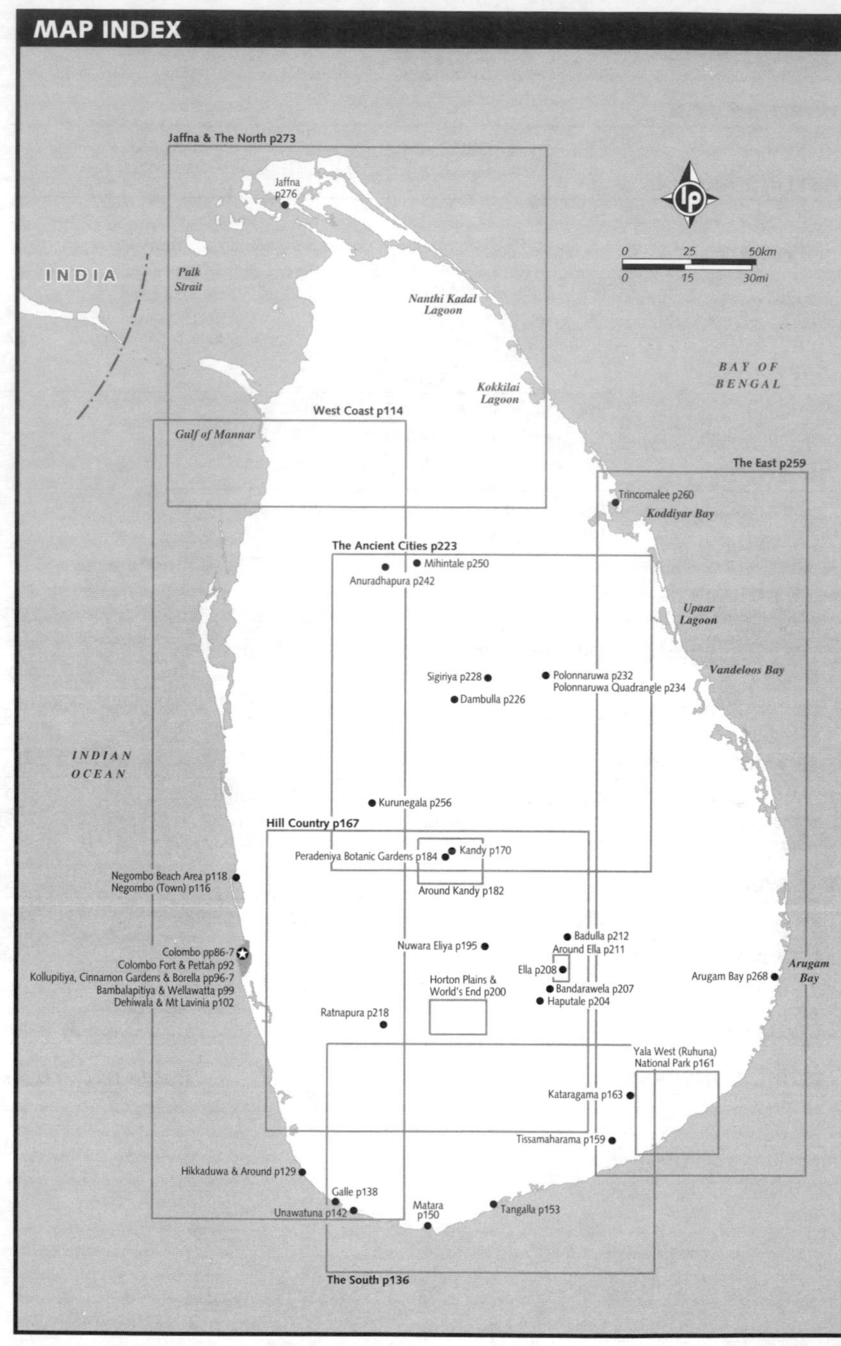
Jaffna & The North p273
Jaffna p276
INDIA
Palk Strait
Nanthi Kadal Lagoon
BAY OF BENGAL
Kokkilai Lagoon
West Coast p114
Gulf of Mannar
The East p259
Trincomalee p260
Koddiyar Bay
The Ancient Cities p223
Mihintale p250
Anuradhapura p242
Upaar Lagoon
Sigiriya p228
Polonnaruwa p232
Polonnaruwa Quadrangle p234
Vandeloos Bay
Dambulla p226
INDIAN OCEAN
Kurunegala p256
Hill Country p167
Peradeniya Botanic Gardens p184
Kandy p170
Around Kandy p182
Negombo Beach Area p118
Negombo (Town) p116
Badulla p212
Around Ella p211
Nuwara Eliya p195
Colombo pp86-7
Colombo Fort & Pettah p92
Kollupitiya, Cinnamon Gardens & Borella pp96-7
Bambalapitiya & Wellawatta p99
Dehiwala & Mt Lavinia p102
Ella p208
Horton Plains & World's End p200
Bandarawela p207
Haputale p204
Arugam Bay p268
Arugam Bay
Ratnapura p218
Yala West (Ruhuna) National Park p161
Kataragama p163
Tissamaharama p159
Hikkaduwa & Around p129
Galle p138
Unawatuna p142
Matara p150
Tangalla p153
The South p136
0 25 50km
0 15 30mi

The Authors

Richard Plunkett

Richard grew up on a farm and vineyard near Avenel, Australia. He's been a stockmarket reporter, rock concert reviewer, farm labourer, subeditor for the *Big Issue*, and once very briefly had the job of cleaning the mincer at a butchers. He has worked on various Lonely Planet books to the subcontinent, including *South India* and *Bangladesh*.

Brigitte Ellemor

Brigitte spent her school years living in different towns in north-western Victoria with her schoolteaching parents, before taking off on her journalism career in western Victoria. Punctuated by trips to Europe and Asia, her time in newspapers ended when she felt there was more to life than getting the local angle on every event and opinion. Brigitte became an Australian Volunteer Abroad and lived and worked in Sri Lanka, where life took unexpected twists and turns. She joined Lonely Planet as an editor after returning and is now a managing editor in the Melbourne head office.

Verity Campbell

A Melbourne-based writer, Verity jumped at the chance to visit Sri Lanka, after having thoroughly enjoyed extensive solo travels through India and Nepal. She researched and updated the eighth edition of *Sri Lanka*, and has worked on many other titles for Lonely Planet.

FROM THE AUTHORS

Richard Plunkett

I need to thank lots of people, but in particular Joseph, Palitha and Stephanie in Negombo, Yusuf Mohammed and Gamini Andrahennady in Anuradhapura, Faiesz Samad, Charles Carmichael and NG Jayasinghe in Kandy, Christopher J Worthington and Andrew Renton in Nuwara Eliya, WM 'Santha' Wijesinghe in the Adam's Peak area, Sampath Ekanayaka and Senadi Abeysuriya in Ella, SAR Perera in Bentota, Paola Sciarrini in Hikkaduwa and DM 'Goonie' Gunasekera in the Ratnapura area. In Colombo thanks to Rohan Balasubramaniam for three-wheeling me around and putting up with the odd burst of temper, and to the Samarasinghes and Settupathys for their hospitality. For unveiling the mysteries of domestic and international flights, thanks to George and Ashok at George Travel and Seraj Mohammed at Expo Aviation. Special thanks to John Mensing for his advice on the Buddhism section, and for his hospitality in Kandy. Thanks to Siri Basnayake and Asoka Samarakoon of Sri Lanka Telecom for the information on the new telephone numbers. Thanks also to co-author Brigitte and her husband Jagath for their advice and support. More thanks to all the people who wrote to LP about the last edition – those letters contained some real gems.

Back home, love and gratitude to Dr Rebecca Ryan.

Brigitte Ellemor

Numerous people made significant contributions to my research and writing. In Galle, thank you to Lal for expert guiding and to driver Sumeda for taking on additional roles as the trip progressed. Thanks also to the travellers and Sri Lankans who offered valuable tips and information along the way. Australian Volunteers Abroad, United Nations Volunteers, people from other nongovernmental organisations and international staff based around the country provided insight, on-the-ground advice and additional information. Thanks Kellie, Lee, Steve, Cat, Brendan, Martin, Sebastian, Tim and Dushi. In Jaffna a huge *nandri* to Joe, who made a town that had been distant and unfamilar, real and more fascinating than imaginable. In Colombo Linda provided the space and support for an exhausted researcher to write and rejuvenate, and Kelly and Mel filled just about all the above roles, as well as being great mates.

Back home, thanks to Lonely Planet for the opportunity to experience life on the other side of the editor's pen, and to visit Sri Lanka at such an exciting time in the nation's history. Many Sri Lanka-philes who had been much more adventurous much earlier than me helped me to prepare: thanks Max, David, Chris and John. Thank you to my family for putting up with another long absence, and to *mage mahattaya*, who reminds me daily of the potential of a peaceful Sri Lanka.

This Book

Tony Wheeler wrote and researched the first three editions of *Sri Lanka*. John Noble tackled the fourth edition and, together with Susan Forsyth, updated the fifth edition. Christine Niven updated the sixth and seventh editions, while the eighth edition was updated by Verity Campbell. Richard Plunkett and Brigitte Ellemor updated this ninth edition of *Sri Lanka*.

FROM THE PUBLISHER

This edition of *Sri Lanka* was was produced in Lonely Planet's Melbourne office. Evan Jones coordinated the editing with assistance from Stephanie Pearson, Katrina Webb, Danielle North, Daniel Caleo and Meg Worby. Jimi Ellis coordinated the mapping with assistance from Chris Thomas, who also supplied the map legend. Indra Kilfoyle designed the colour pages and Birgit Jordan laid out the book. Sally Darmody set up the index. James Hardy and Maria Vallianos designed the front cover. Quentin Frayne compiled the Language chapter. The layout checks were done by Adriana Mammarella and Kate McDonald.

Janine Eberle commissioned and developed *Sri Lanka* and Ann Seward helped with the manuscript assessment. Eoin Dunlevy was the project manager.

THANKS

Many thanks to the travellers who used the last edition and wrote to us with helpful hints, advice and interesting anecdotes. Your names appear in the back of this book.

Foreword

ABOUT LONELY PLANET GUIDEBOOKS

The story begins with a classic travel adventure: Tony and Maureen Wheeler's 1972 journey across Europe and Asia to Australia. There was no useful information about the overland trail then, so Tony and Maureen published the first Lonely Planet guidebook to meet a growing need.

From a kitchen table, Lonely Planet has grown to become the largest independent travel publisher in the world, with offices in Melbourne (Australia), Oakland (USA), London (UK) and Paris (France).

Today Lonely Planet guidebooks cover the globe. There is an ever-growing list of books and information in a variety of media. Some things haven't changed. The main aim is still to make it possible for adventurous travellers to get out there – to explore and better understand the world.

At Lonely Planet we believe travellers can make a positive contribution to the countries they visit – if they respect their host communities and spend their money wisely. Since 1986 a percentage of the income from each book has been donated to aid projects and human rights campaigns, and, more recently, to wildlife conservation.

Although inclusion in a guidebook usually implies a recommendation we cannot list every good place. Exclusion does not necessarily imply criticism. In fact there are a number of reasons why we might exclude a place – sometimes it is simply inappropriate to encourage an influx of travellers.

UPDATES & READER FEEDBACK

Things change – prices go up, schedules change, good places go bad and bad places go bankrupt. Nothing stays the same. So, if you find things better or worse, recently opened or long-since closed, please tell us and help make the next edition even more accurate and useful.

Lonely Planet thoroughly updates each guidebook as often as possible – usually every two years, although for some destinations the gap can be longer. Between editions, up-to-date information is available in our free, monthly email bulletin *Comet* (w www.lonelyplanet.com/newsletters). You can also check out the *Thorn Tree* bulletin board and *Postcards* section of our website, which carry unverified, but fascinating, reports from travellers.

Tell us about it! We genuinely value your feedback. A well-travelled team at Lonely Planet reads and acknowledges every email and letter we receive and ensures that every morsel of information finds its way to the relevant authors, editors and cartographers.

Everyone who writes to us will find their name listed in the next edition of the appropriate guidebook. The very best contributions will be rewarded with a free guidebook.

We may edit, reproduce and incorporate your comments in Lonely Planet products such as guidebooks, websites and digital products, so let us know if you don't want your comments reproduced or your name acknowledged.

How to contact Lonely Planet:
Online: e talk2us@lonelyplanet.com.au, w www.lonelyplanet.com
Australia: Locked Bag 1, Footscray, Victoria 3011
UK: 72-82 Rosebery Ave, London, EC1R 4RW
USA: 150 Linden St, Oakland, CA 94607

Introduction

Sri Lanka unfurls before the senses as soon you arrive: the heavy warm air, the endless array of rich green foliage, the luxuriant swirls of the Sinhalese alphabet, the multicoloured Buddhist flags, and the variety of saris, fruits, jewellery and spices on sale in the markets. Sri Lankan festivals announce themselves with multicoloured lights strung over town clock towers and bazaar alleys. The sky turns deepest thundercloud black before a replenishing downpour fills the hundreds of lakes and rivers. Marco Polo thought Sri Lanka was the finest island of its size in the entire world.

The island hangs like a pendant from the ear of India, physically and culturally. The main languages and religions were inherited from India, but Sri Lanka's culture and society have unique, distinct qualities. The island became a stronghold of Buddhism when that faith faded in its homeland 1000 years ago, and it was a bastion of Tamil Hindu culture when Muslim invaders threatened Tamils on the other side of the Palk Strait. The island has a longer history of Western rule than any other Asian country its size. Signs of Portuguese, Dutch and British influences linger in institutions such as churches, tea estates and forts, as well as in popular folk tunes, food and alcohol, and even the easy-listening classic rock played on the radio.

One of the country's sweetest surprises is the way that wildlife mixes into daily life here. Highways heading east from Kandy, the second-biggest city, are still closed at dusk because wild elephants are attracted to headlights. Cycling on an old rattler around Anuradhapura takes you not only into the romantically melancholy world of a vast ruined city, but into the realm of monkeys, mongooses, wild peacocks, flocks of butterflies and prehistoric monitor lizards. Across the island waterbirds perch on the muddy bunds between paddy fields, working elephants lumber by holding tasty *kitul* palm leaves with their trunks, and troupes of monkeys swing from telephone lines.

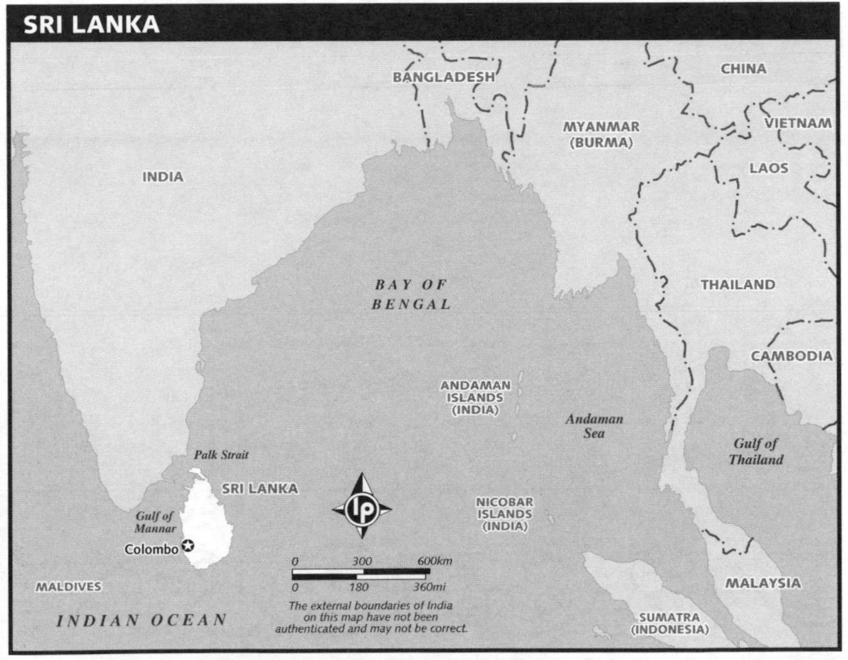

What takes your fancy? Beaches? The coastal stretch south of Colombo has palm-lined beach after palm-lined beach. Culture? Try the Kandyan dances, a procession of elephants or the masked devil dances. Ancient civilisations? Explore the man-made lakes, temples and 60m-high solid brick dagobas (Buddhist shrines) of the ancient capitals of Anuradhapura and Polonnaruwa. Scenery? Head for the hill country where the heat of the plains and the coast fades away to reveal gorgeous rolling hills often carpeted with tea plantations. Surfing? Many rave about the breaks at Arugam Bay, Kirinda and other beaches. Wildlife? There are a dozen major national parks inhabited by elephants, leopards, monkeys, crocodiles and deer. All this comes with welcoming, friendly people, good food, pleasant places to stay and reasonably low costs – all wrapped up in a compact, easy-to-navigate package.

To really immerse yourself in Sinhalese and Tamil culture, it's easy to get off the beaten track and venture into the rural hinterland of forests, tiny villages and overgrown ancient temples.

Since peace was brokered on the island in December 2001, Sri Lankans of all cultures have sighed with relief. The prospects of confining 20 years of brutality to the past have rarely looked better, though the ethnic conflict has confounded optimists before. In these more peaceful times, the beautiful long beaches of the east coast are being rediscovered. The adventurous can even head north to the Jaffna peninsula, an area with a history and culture of its own. It might not be long before the island's fabled tourism potential really takes off, so go there now.

Facts about Sri Lanka

HISTORY

Legend and history are deeply intertwined in the early accounts of Sri Lankan history. Did the Buddha leave his footprint on Adam's Peak (Sri Pada), visiting the island that lay halfway to paradise? Or was it Adam who took a last look at paradise from the top of Adam's Peak, leaving his footprint embedded in the rock? And isn't Adam's Bridge (the chain of islands linking Sri Lanka to India) the very series of stepping stones that Rama skipped across to rescue Sita from the clutches of the evil demon Rawana, King of Lanka, in the epic Ramayana?

It is probable that the story of the Ramayana actually does have some frail basis in reality, for Sri Lanka's history recounts many invasions from southern India. Perhaps some early invasion provided the backdrop for the story of Rama and his beautiful wife, a story that is recounted all around Asia.

Whatever the legends, the reality points towards the first Sinhalese people (who probably originated in North India) arriving in Sri Lanka around the 5th or 6th century BC, gradually replacing the prior inhabitants, the Veddahs or Wanniyala-aetto. The Veddahs were hunter-gatherers subsisting on the island's natural bounty who left few traces of their past.

The Rise & Fall of Anuradhapura

The Sinhalese kingdom of Anuradhapura developed on the dry northern plain in the 4th century BC. Later, the Sinhalese kingdom of Ruhuna appeared in the south and the west, but Anuradhapura remained the stronger. In the 3rd century BC Mahinda, the son of the great Buddhist emperor Ashoka (who reigned in India), came to the island to spread the Buddha's teachings. Mahinda soon converted the Anuradhapuran king and his followers to Buddhism, and his sister, Sangamitta, planted a cutting of the sacred Bodhi Tree under which the Buddha attained enlightenment. Sri Maha Bodhi (holy and resplendent Bodhi) still flourishes in Anuradhapura today, surrounded by a few of its thousands of descendants grown from cuttings. Buddhism went through a rejuvenation in Sri Lanka and it was here that the Theravada school of Buddhism developed, later spreading to Buddhist countries in Southeast Asia. Even today, Buddhists of the Theravada school in Myanmar (Burma), Thailand and other countries look to Sri Lanka for spiritual leadership and the original doctrines. Buddhism gave the Sinhalese people a sense of national purpose and identity, and also inspired the development of their culture and literature.

Anuradhapura was the centre of Sinhalese kingdoms for almost 1500 years, from around the 4th century BC to the 10th century AD. It suffered as a result of its proximity to South India, though, where Hinduism continued to flourish. There were repeated invasions and takeovers of Anuradhapura by South Indian kingdoms, and self-defeating entanglements in South Indian affairs by Anuradhapura's rulers. During this period a number of Sinhalese heroes arose to repel the

What's in a Name?

Changing the country's name from Ceylon to Sri Lanka in 1972 caused considerable confusion to foreigners, but it has always been known to the Sinhalese (who make up almost three-quarters of Sri Lankans) as Lanka, and to the minority Tamils as Ilankai. The 2000-year-old Hindu epic, the Ramayana, tells of Rama's beautiful wife being carried away by the evil king of Lanka. Later, the Romans knew it as Taprobane and Muslim traders talked of the island of Serendib. The name Serendib (which means island of jewels) became the root of the word serendipity – the art of making happy and unexpected discoveries by accident. The Portuguese somehow twisted Sinhala-dvipa (island of the Sinhalese) into Ceilão. In turn, the Dutch altered this name to Ceylan and the British to Ceylon. In 1972 the original Lanka was restored with the addition of Sri, which means 'auspicious' or 'resplendent' in the Sinhalese language. In the 1980s some pedants pushed the notion that the name should be spelled Shri Lanka but the name, Sri Lanka, now remains firmly entrenched.

invaders, two of the most famous being Dutugemunu (2nd century BC) and Vijayabahu I (11th century AD). It was Vijayabahu I who finally decided to abandon Anuradhapura and make Polonnaruwa, further southeast, his capital.

For centuries the kingdom was able to rebuild after its battles through *rajakariya*, the system of free labour every year for the king, organised on a grand scale to maintain the tanks (reservoirs) and irrigation systems. See the boxed text 'Tank-Building' for more details.

The Rise & Fall of Polonnaruwa

Polonnaruwa survived as a Sinhalese capital for more than two centuries and provided two other great kings. The nephew of Vijayabahu I, Parakramabahu I (r. 1153–86), not content with Vijayabahu's expulsion of South Indian Chola rulers from Sri Lanka, carried the fight to South India and even made a raid on Myanmar. Internally he indulged in an orgy of building at his capital, and constructed many new tanks around the country. But his warring and architectural extravagances wore the country out, and probably shortened Polonnaruwa's lifespan.

Tank-Building

The science of building tanks (or reservoirs), studying gradients and constructing channels is the key to early civilisation in Sri Lanka. The tanks, which dot the plains of the ancient dominions of Rajarata (in the northcentral part of the country) and Ruhuna (in the southeast), probably started as modest structures. But by the 5th century BC they reached such dimensions that local legends say they were built with supernatural help. It is claimed that Giant's Tank near Mannar Island was built by giants, while other tanks were said to have been constructed by a mixed workforce of humans and demons.

The irrigation system developed on ever-greater scales during the millennium before Christ ranks with the ancient *qanats* (underground channels) of Iran and the canals of Pharaonic Egypt in sophistication. These dry-zone reservoirs sustained and shaped Sri Lanka's civilisation for more than 2500 years, until war and discord overtook the island in the 12th to 14th centuries AD.

His successor, Nissanka Malla (r. 1187–96), was the last great king of Polonnaruwa. He was followed by a series of weak rulers; tanks were neglected and destroyed, malaria spread with the decay of the irrigation system and finally, like Anuradhapura before it, Polonnaruwa was abandoned. The jungle reclaimed it in a few decades.

Meanwhile the first Tamil kingdom established itself in Jaffna in the far north. Invasions and movements of people between India and Sri Lanka had been happening for millennia, but from the 5th and 6th centuries resurgent Hindu Tamil empires such as the Chola, Pallava and Pandya repeatedly threatened the Buddhist Sinhalese rulers. With the decline of the capitals of the north and the ensuing Sinhalese migration south, a wide buffer zone of jungle and forest separated the mostly coastal northern Tamil settlements and the Sinhalese in the southern interior. This jungle zone, called the Vanni, was sparsely inhabited by mixed Tamil-Sinhalese clans called the Vanniyars.

Early Muslim Links

From the 7th century onwards Arab traders sheltered for months at a stretch in the calm coastal rivers and lagoons during the southwest monsoon. They took back to the Middle East many accounts of a lush, hospitable country. Others were drawn to the rich gem fields of the southwest, and in Arabic the island was called Serendib, from *seren* (gem) and *dwip* (island).

Some Muslim towns on rivers just inland from the coast, such as Mutur on the east coast and Dargah Town between Galle and Colombo, grew from these early sea-trader camps. Other Muslim traders pushed inland with trains of bullock carts, the only animals strong enough to drag goods up into the hills.

The Portuguese Period

After Polonnaruwa, the centre of Sinhalese power shifted to the southwest of the island, and between 1253 and 1400 there were five Sinhalese capitals. During this period Sri Lanka also suffered attacks by Chinese and Malayans, as well as periodic incursions from South India. Finally, the Portuguese arrived in 1505.

At this time Sri Lanka had three main kingdoms: the Tamil kingdom of Jaffna in the far north, and the Sinhalese kingdoms of

Sinbad in Serendib

Tales of Sinbad the Sailor make up seven stories in *The Thousand and One Nights*. His last two journeys were to Sri Lanka, or Serendib as Arab mariners knew it. He first travelled to a coast of shipwrecks, where gems and jewels were washed up on the rocks. He later travelled inland and met the king, dwelling at length on the royal jewel collection.

'The island of Serendib being situated on the equinoctial line, the days and nights there are of equal length. The chief city is placed at the end of a beautiful valley, formed by the highest mountain in the world, which is in the middle of the island. I had the curiosity to ascend to its very summit, for this was the place to which Adam was banished out of Paradise. Here are found rubies and many precious things, and rare plants grow abundantly, with cedar trees and cocoa palms.'

After Sinbad's return from Serendib the Caliph, Haroun al-Rashid, sent him back for his seventh and last voyage. He was captured by pirates and sold as a slave. His new master sent him to another island to find the lost cemetery of elephants for the ivory – this is an old Sri Lankan legend. He was captured by an elephant while hiding in a tree, and was carried to a place full of their giant bones. He returned to find his master and took him to the ivory hill. Together they made a killing on the ivory trade, and Sinbad headed back to a prosperous retirement in Baghdad.

Kandy in the central highlands and Kotte, the more powerful of the two, in the southwest. When the Portuguese Lorenço de Almeida arrived in Colombo, he established friendly relations with the king of Kotte and gained a monopoly on the spice and cinnamon trade for Portugal, which soon became enormously important in Europe. Attempts by Kotte to capitalise on the strength and protection of the Portuguese, as well as pressure exerted by the Portuguese, resulted in Portugal taking over the entire coastal belt, but not the central highlands around Kandy.

With the Portuguese came religious orders such as the Dominicans and Jesuits. They found converts among the Karava fishing communities on the west coast. The Portuguese also brought soldiers and slaves from Mozambique. Barrack rebellions freed them and they became known as the Kaffirs, today almost totally assimilated. Perhaps their most obvious contribution to modern Sri Lankan culture are the folk tunes called *bailas*, love songs founded on Latin melodies and African rhythms.

The Dutch Period

The attempts by Kandy to enlist Dutch help in expelling the Portuguese only succeeded in substituting one European power for another. By 1658, 153 years after the first Portuguese contact, the Dutch had taken control over the coastal areas of the island. During their 140 years' rule the Dutch, like the Portuguese, made repeated unsuccessful attempts to bring Kandy under their control. The Dutch were much more interested in trade and profits than the Portuguese, and developed a canal system along the west coast to transport cinnamon and other crops. Roman-Dutch law, the legal system of the Dutch era, still forms part of Sri Lanka's legal canon.

The British Period

The French revolution resulted in a major shake-up among the European powers, and in 1796 the Dutch were easily supplanted by the British, who in 1815 also managed to win control of the kingdom of Kandy, thus becoming the first European power to rule the whole island. In 1802 Sri Lanka became a crown colony and in 1818 a unified administration for the island was set up.

In 1832 sweeping changes in property laws opened the doors to British settlers – at the expense of the Sinhalese, who in the eyes of the British did not have clear title to their land. Coffee was the main cash crop and the backbone of the colonial economy, but when a leaf blight virtually wiped it out in the 1870s, the plantations were quickly switched over to tea or rubber.

The British, unable to persuade the Sinhalese to labour on the plantations, imported large numbers of Tamil workers from South India. Today they form the biggest of the two main Tamil communities, with 850,000 people or 5% of the national population. About 700,000 of them still live and work on the estates.

The British imprint is still clear – the elite private schools with cricket grounds in Colombo, the army cantonments and train stations, the tea estate bungalows, not to mention the English language. English was demoted as a language after independence, but the requirements of a globalised economy have helped bring it back into vogue.

Independence

Following WWII, in the wake of Indian independence, it was evident that Sri Lanka would be granted independence very soon. In February 1948 Sri Lanka, or Ceylon as it was still known, became an independent member of the British Commonwealth. The first independent government was formed the United National Party (UNP), led by DS Senanayake. His main opponents were the Tamil parties from the North and the tea plantations, and communists.

At first everything went smoothly. The economy remained strong, and the government concentrated on strengthening social services and weakening the opposition. Having disenfranchised the hill-country Tamils by depriving them of citizenship, it certainly achieved the latter. Eventually deals in the 1960s and 1980s between Sri Lanka and India allowed some of the hill-country Tamils to be 'repatriated' to India while others were granted Sri Lankan citizenship.

DS Senanayake died in 1952 and was succeeded by his son, Dudley Senanayake. An attempt a year later to raise the price of rice led to mass riots and Dudley's resignation. Sir John Kotelawala, his uncle, replaced him, and the UNP earned the nickname 'Uncle Nephew Party'. Kotelawala was easily defeated in the 1956 general election by the Mahajana Eksath Peramuna coalition led by SWRD Bandaranaike.

The Bandaranaikes

The Bandaranaikes were a family of noble Kandyan descent who had converted to Anglicanism for a time in the 19th century, but had returned to the Buddhist fold. The 1956 election coincided with the 2500th anniversary of the Buddha's death and an upsurge in Sinhalese pride. SWRD Bandaranaike defeated the UNP primarily on nationalistic issues that harked back to the Dharmapala movement of the late 19th and early 20th centuries (see Religion later in this chapter).

Nearly 10 years after independence was granted, English remained the national language and the country continued to be ruled by an English-speaking, mainly Christian, elite. Many Sinhalese thought the elevation of their language to 'official' status, to be used in government and official work, would increase their power and job prospects.

Caught in the middle of this disagreement (English versus Sinhala, and Christian versus Buddhist) were the Tamils, whose mother tongue was Tamil. When Banaranaike enacted the 'Sinhala only' law, making Sinhalese the official language of the country, Tamil protests were followed by violence and deaths. The Tamils began pressing for a federal system of government with greater local autonomy in the main Tamil-populated areas, the North and the East.

The serious Sinhalese–Tamil difficulties really date from this time. From the mid-1950s, when the economy slowed, competition for wealth and work – intensified by the high expectations created by Sri Lanka's fine education system – exacerbated the Sinhalese–Tamil jealousies. The main political parties, particularly when in opposition, played on Sinhalese paranoia that their religion, language and culture could be swamped by Indians, who were thought to be the natural allies of the Tamils in Sri Lanka. The Tamils began to see themselves as a threatened minority.

Despite coming to power backed by Sinhalese chauvinism, Bandaranaike later began negotiating with Tamil leaders for a kind of federation, and for this he was assassinated by a Buddhist monk in 1959. To this day Bandaranaike is seen as a national hero who brought the government of Sri Lanka back to the common people.

In the 1960 general election, the Sri Lanka Freedom Party (SLFP), led by SWRD Bandaranaike's widow, Sirimavo, was swept to power. She was the first female prime minister in the world. Sirimavo pressed on with her husband's nationalisation policies and soured relations with the USA by taking over the Sri Lankan oil companies. Most of the remaining British tea planters left during this time. The economy became weakened, and in the 1965 election Dudley Senanayake scraped back into power, but his reluctance to turn back the clock on the SLFP's nationalisation program soon lost him much support. The UNP was massively defeated by the SLFP in the 1970 elections.

Soon after Sirimavo Bandaranaike took the reins for the second time, a wave of unrest and radical politics swept the Sinhalese heartland, feeding on a population boom and a generation of disaffected young men facing unemployment. In 1971 a Sinhalese Marxist insurrection broke out, led by a dropout from Moscow's Lumumba University, Rohana Wijeweera, under the banner of the Janatha Vimukthi Peramuna (JVP, People's Liberation Army). The rebellion broke prematurely, and after some early surprise successes it fell apart. Its members, mostly students and young men, were quickly and ruthlessly eradicated by the army. Around 25,000 people died, but the JVP eventually regrouped.

The revolt handed the government a mandate for sweeping changes, a new constitution, and a new Sinhalese name, Sri Lanka, for the country. The bureaucracy became politicised, and some date the entrenchment of corruption from this time. Meanwhile, the economy continued to deteriorate, and in the 1977 elections Sirimavo Bandaranaike and the SLFP (under its new guise as the United Left Front) went down in a stunning defeat at the hands of the UNP.

Tamil Unrest Meanwhile the Tamils were growing more alienated, with two pieces of legislation causing particular grievance. The first, passed in 1970, was designed to cut their numbers in universities – previously, Tamils had won a relatively high proportion of university places. The second was the new 1972 constitution's declaration that Buddhism had the 'foremost place' and that it was the state's duty to 'protect and foster' Buddhism.

When unrest grew among northern Tamils, a state of emergency was imposed on their areas for several years from 1971. As the police and army that enforced the state of emergency now included few Tamils (partly because of the 'Sinhala only' law) and were often undisciplined and heavy-handed, they came to be seen more and more as an enemy force by Tamils.

In the mid-1970s, some mostly left-wing young Tamils started to take to violence, fighting for an independent Tamil state called Eelam, which means precious land. They included a teenager named Velupillai Prabharakan, who stood out for his gun skills and dedication to military action. He went on to found the Liberation Tigers of Tamil Eelam (LTTE), often referred to as the Tamil Tigers. Many of the founders of the plethora of later Tamil guerrilla armies took up arms at this time.

Open Economy

The new UNP prime minister elected in 1977, Junius Richard (JR) Jayawardene, back-pedalled on socialism and made an all-out effort to lure back some of the foreign investment. Jayawardene's ideal of a successful 'open economy' was Singapore. His policies yielded some successes: unemployment was halved by 1983, Sri Lanka became self-sufficient in rice production in 1985, and tourism and the large numbers of Sri Lankans working in the Middle East began bringing in foreign currency.

Jayawardene fiddled with the constitution several times, which mostly resulted in handing himself more power. In 1978 he introduced a new constitution (Sri Lanka's third), which conferred greatest power on the new post of president, to which he himself was elected by parliament.

In 1982 he was re-elected president in national polls (after amending his own constitution to bring the voting forward two years) and then in the same year won a referendum to bypass the 1983 general election and leave the existing parliament in office until 1989. As usual there were allegations of electoral skullduggery.

Tamil Rebellion Jayawardene promoted Tamil to the status of a 'national language' to be used in official work in Tamil-majority areas, and also introduced greater local control in government. But these measures didn't stop the clashes between Tamil 'boys' and the security forces from growing into a pattern of killings, reprisals, reprisals for reprisals etc. All too often the victims were civilians. The powder keg finally exploded in 1983. The spark was the ambush and massacre of an army patrol by militant Tamil secessionists in the Jaffna region. For several days afterwards, mobs of enraged Sinhalese went on the rampage, killing Tamils and destroying their property. Between 400 and

2000 Tamils were killed and some areas with large Tamil populations – such as Colombo's Pettah district and the business districts of some hill-country towns – were virtually levelled.

The government, the police and the army were either unable or unwilling to stop the violence. There had been similar, smaller-scale, ethnic riots in 1958, 1977 and 1981, but this was the worst and for many it marked the point of no return. Tens of thousands of Tamils fled to safer, Tamil-majority areas while many others left the country altogether; Sinhalese started to move out of Jaffna and other areas dominated by Tamils.

Revenge attacks and counter-revenge attacks grew into all-out atrocities and there were several large-scale massacres. The government was widely condemned over acts of torture and disappearances, but it pointed to the intimidation and violence against civilians (including Tamils) by the Tamil fighters. The situation was hardly helped by the interference of the Research and Analysis Wing (RAW), the Indian equivalent of the CIA, which trained and armed half a dozen Tamil militant factions on Indian soil in the early 1980s. Nobody knows what the RAW expected to achieve, but most likely they wanted to split Sri Lanka as India had split Pakistan in 1971.

The area claimed by the Tamil militants for the independent state of Eelam was Sri Lanka's Northern and Eastern Provinces – roughly speaking, the region to the north of Vavuniya as well as a strip all the way down the east coast to Yala East National Park. This amounts to about one-third of Sri Lanka's land area, which the government was never going to concede. While Tamils made up the overwhelming majority in the Northern Province, in eastern Sri Lanka Muslims, Sinhalese and Tamils were nearly equal in numbers (although Tamils argued that the Sinhalese numbers had only been bumped up to this level due to newcomers settled on irrigation scheme lands).

By the end of 1985 fighting had spread not only throughout the North but also down most of the east coast, where the LTTE, the strongest and most hardline Tamil armed group, attacked Sinhalese villages, triggering reprisals on Tamil inhabitants. Clashes also began between Tamils and Muslims in the East.

The violence cost the economy dearly. Tourism slumped, the government had to spend crippling amounts on the defence forces, and foreign and local investment dried up.

Indian Intervention

In 1987 government forces pushed the LTTE back into Jaffna city, only to provoke increasingly serious threats of Indian intervention on the Tamil side. JR Jayawardene turned round and struck a deal with India by which an Indian Peace Keeping Force (IPKF) would disarm the Tamil rebels and keep the peace in northern and eastern Sri Lanka. A single provincial council would be elected to govern the region with substantial autonomy for a trial period.

Soon it became clear that the deal suited no-one. The LTTE complied initially under pressure from India, before the Indians tried to isolate the LTTE by promoting and arming other Tamil rebel groups. The LTTE leadership probably even surprised themselves when they took on the world's fourth-largest army. The Indians had ample experience of counter-insurgency warfare and matched the LTTE in the East, but were soon held down with guerrilla tactics in the North. Opposition to the Indians also came from the Sinhalese, including the SLFP, the reviving JVP and important sections of the Sangha (community of Buddhist monks), who feared Indian influence and considered the deal a sellout of non-Tamils in the East. This led to angry and sometimes violent demonstrations.

JR Jayawardene had been replaced as leader of the UNP by Ranasinghe Premadasa, the first leader from a common background. In the 1990 elections he promised the removal of the Indian peacekeepers from Sri Lanka. The LTTE, desperate to see the back of the peacekeepers, agreed to a cease-fire with the government to help speed up the Indian withdrawal. So the peacekeepers withdrew in March 1990, having lost more than 1000 lives in three years, and in June the war between the LTTE and the Sri Lankan government took up again. By the end of 1990, the LTTE held Jaffna and much of the North. The East was largely back under government control, though still subject to LTTE attacks on Sinhalese and Muslim villagers.

The Best of Sri Lanka

ANDERS BLOMQVIST

MARK DAFFEY

FROM TROPICAL BEACHES TO ROLLING HILLS

Top: Palm trees line a long stretch of beach, Mirissa

Left: Cyclist and palm trees at sunset, Midigama

Bottom: Coconuts for sale on the beach, Hikkaduwa

Title page: Traditional painted carving (Photograph by Chris Mellor)

DALLAS STRIBLEY

CHRIS MELLOR

Top: Pastel light over the lower plains as seen from World's End
Right: Vista from the top of Adam's Peak
Bottom: Women picking tea leaves near Nuwara Eliya

ANDERS BLOMQVIST

ANDERS BLOMQVIST

DALLAS STRIBLEY

GREG ELMS

HISTORY IN ART & ARCHITECTURE

Left: Fifth-century fresco of the Sigiriya damsels
Top right: Dutch-built Galle Fort at dusk
Bottom left: Dwarf carving on steps of the 4th-century Mahasen's Palace, Anuradhapura
Bottom right: Dambulla cave temple, thought to date back to the 1st century BC

ANDERS BLOMQVIST

ERIC L WHEATER

ANDERS BLOMQVIST

Top: Tank at the rock-top palace, Sigiriya
Right: Elephants carved in stone on the Ruvanvelisaya dagoba, Anuradhapura
Bottom: Standing and reclining Buddhas at Gal Vihara, Polonnaruwa

CHRIS MELLOR

ANDERS BLOMQVIST

DALLAS STRIBLEY

CHRIS MELLOR

EVERYDAY LIFE
Left: Mahout and his elephant
Top right: Young Buddhist monks outside the Malwatte monastery, Kandy
Bottom: Locals of Pettah, Colombo

DALLAS STRIBLEY

DALLAS STRIBLEY

ANDERS BLOMQVIST

Top: Fruit sellers, Pettah, Colombo
Right: An example of *kolam* (coloured-rice design) art at the entrance to a Tamil home
Bottom: Fishermen tend their nets, Hikkaduwa beach

CHRISTINE NIVEN

DALLAS STRIBLEY

MICHAEL AW

ANDREW BURKE

WATCHING WILDLIFE
Top: Elephant family, Uda Walawe National Park
Left: Young toque macaque in the hills above Kandy
Bottom left: Lizard
Bottom right: Leopard, Yala West (Ruhuna) National Park

MICHAEL AW

RAY TIPPER

Return of the JVP

The presence of the Indian peacekeeping force pushed the mood of the young and poor of the Sinhalese hinterland past boiling point. In 1987 the Marxist Janatha Vimukthi Peramuna (JVP) launched a revolution with political murders and strikes enforced on pain of death. With 16 years to study the failed 1971 revolt, and still led by Rohana Wijeweera, the JVP had prepared brilliantly. They were tightly organised and had recruited many students, monks, unemployed people, and even police and army personnel. They attempted a Khmer Rouge–style takeover of the country, aiming to capture the countryside and then isolate and pick off the cities. Rather like the Khmer Rouge, they envisioned a socialist utopia of no foreign ownership and a return to a society based on happy peasants working for the motherland. However, it catered to the interests of virtually no other groups, including the Tamils.

By late 1988 the centre and the south of the country were terrorised, the economy was crippled and the government was paralysed. The turning point came when the families of army officers were targeted by JVP death squads. The JVP politburo had made a fatal tactical error. The army officers regrouped and convinced the government to give them a free hand in exterminating the JVP. The army struck back with a ruthless counter-insurgency campaign that still scars the country. Shadowy secret militias and special army groups matched the JVP's underground warfare in brutality, and tracked down the JVP politburo one by one. The rebellion subsided soon after Rohana Wijeweera was captured and killed in November 1989. Up to 60,000 people died in the three-year insurrection.

Within a few years of Wijeweera's death, a new generation of leadership brought the JVP into the political mainstream, and it now has seats in parliament. But as one senior JVP leader put it, the crushing of the 1980s rebellion completely uprooted the party, while the 1971 uprising had merely pulled off a few branches. The modern JVP idolises its former leader, and there are many street posters of Rohana Wijeweera from his heyday, sporting a Che Guevara–style beret, beard, glasses and smile.

War in the 1990s

The new war reached a peak in mid-1991, soon after the assassination of India's prime minister, Rajiv Gandhi, by a female LTTE suicide bomber. The conflict centred on a series of battles around Jaffna, but then tailed off as the LTTE suffered some reverses. In mid-1992 the government army, after doubling in size in nine years to 75,000 and being better armed and trained than ever before, launched a big new assault in the North.

Although a high proportion of Tamils and Sinhalese longed for peace, and government troops were taking a more conciliatory attitude to the Tamil population, the extremists on either side pressed on with the war. President Premadasa was assassinated at a May Day rally in 1993; the LTTE was suspected, but never claimed responsibility. Prime Minister Dingiri Banda Wijetunge took his place. At the same time Chandrika Bandaranaike Kumaratunga, the daughter of SLFP leader Sirimavo Bandaranaike, made a successful challenge for the leadership of the opposition SLFP. She soon became head of the People's Alliance (PA), a coalition of the SLFP and several smaller parties. The PA narrowly won the parliamentary elections in August 1994, and Kumaratunga won the November 1994 presidential elections. She became Sri Lanka's first female president, and the first national leader whose parents were both former national leaders. She appointed her mother prime minister.

The PA had promised to end the civil war, but after yet another round of failed peace talks in 1995, the army invaded the Jaffna peninsula with Operation Riviresa. Jaffna city was taken in December, but not before a major exodus of its inhabitants. A major thrust to establish a land route from Vavuniya to Jaffna was begun in May 1997 (Operation Sure Victory). The LTTE, supplied by a highly developed naval and transport wing and with battle-hardened troops, counterattacked. By 1998 the ceasefire line between the army and the LTTE was fairly settled; the LTTE held the Vanni region, but not Jaffna, while the army were unable tocapture the A9 between Jaffna and Anuradhapura.

Kumaratunga was targeted by a suicide bomber just a few days before the December 1999 presidential election. She was injured and went on to win the election. Curiously enough, the economy was showing signs of life during this period. Garment exports grew, growth ticked along at 5% to 6% a year between 1995 and 2000, and the ongoing war partly solved unemployment in the rural south.

In the October 2000 parliamentary elections, President Kumaratunga's PA won a narrow victory. Sirimavo Bandaranaike, the president's mother and three-time prime minister of Sri Lanka, died shortly after casting her vote.

Peace at Last?

In late 2000, a Norwegian peace mission, led by Erik Solheim, was invited to bring the LTTE and the government to the negotiating table. A cease-fire had to wait until the UNP won fresh elections in December 2001, after the collapse of the short-lived PA government. Ranil Wickremasinghe became prime minister, and since then he and President Kumaratunga (who are from different parties) have circled each other warily – their relationship can best be described as prickly. The economy stalled in 2001, but is showing signs of recovery, and growth of around 5% is expected for 2002. The irony is that the end of the war led to a slowdown in the economy, once the government was no longer spending millions to keep the war effort going.

It could be said that the government and the LTTE finally began talking peace because they had exhausted all other options. The government was approaching bankruptcy, and corrupt deals among a clique of generals and politicians were making a farce of efforts to improve the army. On the LTTE's side, 20 years of war had brought them no closer to an independent Eelam. The LTTE had sunk to forcibly recruiting women and children to fill the places of 20,000 slain cadres. On the government side, morale plunged after a stunning LTTE attack on the country's international airport at Katunayake in July 2001 destroyed or crippled half of the SriLankan Airlines fleet and a fair proportion of the air force. Even if the government could recapture the Vanni region and defeat the LTTE on the battlefield, the chances of stopping LTTE attacks seemed slim, despite the hundreds of heavily guarded army checkpoints. Katunayake had been one of the most heavily guarded places in the country.

The events of 11 September 2001 in New York also changed the equation. Up until then the government was slowly succeeding in getting Western powers to declare the LTTE a terrorist movement. After 11 September, the LTTE faced having the USA giving substantial support to the government, while having their overseas funding cut. After a cease-fire in December 2001, peace talks started in February 2002, and have continued on a mostly positive note ever since. The most likely positive outcome will be some sort of federation – Sri Lanka remains one country but has a Tamil homeland in the North. This isn't so different from what Tamil leaders were proposing back in the 1950s.

GEOGRAPHY

Sri Lanka is shaped like a teardrop falling from the southern end of India. It stretches over 433km from north to south; it's only 244km at its widest point. Its area of about 66,000 sq km is about the same as that of Ireland or Tasmania.

The central hill country rises a little south of the centre of the island and is surrounded by a coastal plain. The flat northcentral and northern plain extends from the hill country all the way to the northern tip of the island – this region is much drier than the rest of the island. An archipelago of low, flat islands lies off Jaffna. The best beaches are on the southwest, south and east coasts.

The highest mountain is broad-backed Mt Pidurutalagala (2524m), rising above Nuwara Eliya. However, the pyramid profile of Adam's Peak, at 2243m, is better known and far more spectacular. The Mahaweli Ganga, Sri Lanka's longest river, has its source close to Adam's Peak and runs into the sea near Trincomalee.

CLIMATE

In a word, it's tropical, with distinct dry and wet seasons. The seasons are slightly complicated by having two monsoons. From May to August the Yala monsoon brings rain to the southwestern half of the country, while the dry season here lasts from December to March. The southwest has the highest rainfall – up to 4000mm a year. The Maha monsoon blows from October to January, bringing rain to the North and East, and the dry season is from May to September. The

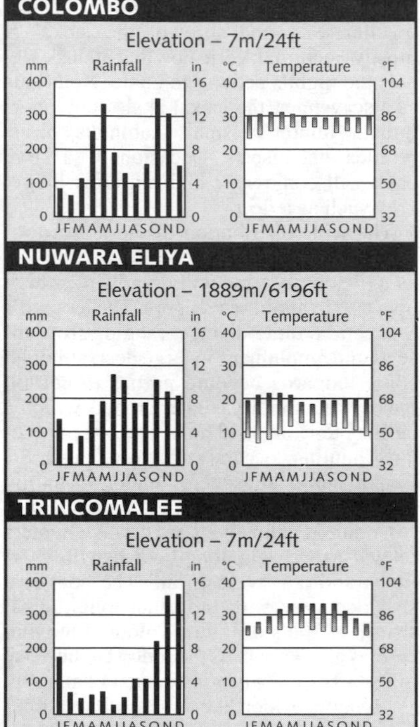

North and East are comparatively dry, with around 1000mm of rain annually. There is also an inter-monsoonal period in October and November when rain and thunderstorms can occur in many parts of the island.

Sri Lanka's climate means that it is always the 'right' beach season somewhere on the coast. The weather doesn't follow strict rules though – it often seems to be raining where it should be sunny, and sunny where it should be raining. Rainfall tends to be emphatic – streets can become flooded in what seems like only minutes.

Colombo and the low-lying coastal regions have an average temperature of 27°C. At Kandy (altitude 500m) the average temperature is 20°C while Nuwara Eliya (at 1889m) has a temperate 16°C average. The sea stays at around 27°C all year.

ECOLOGY & ENVIRONMENT

At the beginning of the 20th century about 70% of the island was covered by natural forest. By 1998 this had shrunk to about 24%. *Chena* (shifting cultivation) is blamed for a good part of this deforestation, but irrigation schemes and clearance for cultivation also contributed. In recent decades the biggest danger to the island's forests has been illegal logging.

Gem mining, sand mining and the destruction of coral reefs to feed lime kilns have also degraded the environment. On the west coast, between Chilaw and Puttalam, prawn farming has done major damage to the coastal ecology.

Some 82% of the land is controlled by the state in some form or other; the majority of natural forests are under state jurisdiction. There is a raft of legislation to combat destructive activity and to protect sensitive areas. Sri Lanka is a signatory to the Ramsar Convention on Wetlands and Bundala National Park has been recognised internationally under this convention. Sinharaja Forest Reserve is a World Heritage Site – saved after being logged during the early 1970s. Sri Lanka has two marine sanctuaries: the Bar Reef (west of Kalpitiya peninsula) and the Hikkaduwa Marine Sanctuary.

FLORA

The southwestern wet zone is tropical rainforest with characteristic dense undergrowth and a tall canopy of hardwood trees, including ebony, teak and silkwood. Here also are some of the most spectacular orchids and many of the plants used in traditional Ayurvedic medicine. The central hill zone has cloud forests and some rare highland areas populated by hardy grasslands and elfin (stunted) forests, and trees often draped in Spanish moss. The remainder of the island forms the arid dry zone, with a sparser cover of trees and shrubs, and grasslands that may erupt into bloom with the first rains.

The sacred bodhi tree *(Ficus religiosa)* was brought from India at the time Mahinda introduced the teachings of the Buddha to Sri Lanka. Saplings are planted in most Buddhist temples in Sri Lanka. The shape of a turned-over leaf is said to have inspired the shape of the dagoba (Buddhist temple). Also often found around Buddhist temples is the *sal,* also known as the cannonball tree. You'll understand how the tree got its name when you see the huge woody fruits clinging to the trunk. The frangipani is common throughout the island; its sweet-scented white, pink or yellow flowers are used as Buddhist temple offerings. You'll also see plenty of scarlet and magenta bougainvilleas in gardens. In the hill country there are many eucalyptus trees, which have often been planted to provide shade at tea estates.

Fruit trees such as mangoes, papayas and bananas grow in many private gardens in Sri Lanka, but two in particular will catch your eye, the jackfruit and the *del* or breadfruit. The jackfruit is a tall evergreen with the world's largest fruit. These green, knobbly skinned fruit, weighing up to 30kg, hang close to the trunk. The breadfruit is its smaller relative.

FAUNA

Mammals

Sri Lanka has 86 mammal species including leopards, monkeys and the famous elephant (see the boxed text 'The Royal Pachyderm' for details). Other interesting mammals include sloth bears, loris, porcupines, jackals, dugongs and flying foxes.

Primates The common langur, also known as the Hanuman or grey langur, is a slender, long-tailed monkey that bounds through the tree tops with remarkable agility. Troops of 15 to 20 forage mostly in the trees but will descend to the ground to collect fallen fruit. The endemic purple-faced langur has a black-brown body and limbs. Several subspecies have been proposed, including the shaggy bear monkeys of the montane forests. Open forest, dense jungle and temples are all prime habitats.

Noisy troops of toque macaques occupy most parts of the island. The top of the head has a distinctive thatch of hair parted down the middle.

The striking slender loris is a small, slow-moving, brown-grey primate. According to superstition, its large close-set eyes have the power to induce love! It snatches insects, amphibians, reptiles, birds and small mammals with a lightning quick lunge. Fruits and leaves supplement the diet. It is usually solitary, but is occasionally found in pairs.

Predatory Animals Sloth bears are typically black with a white v-shaped blaze across the chest. Powerful forearms end in great curved claws used for climbing and ripping apart termite mounds.

The golden jackal is a well-known fringe dweller. Shy and shrewd, the jackal is mostly nocturnal; eerie howling at dusk signals the night's activity to come. Notorious as a scavenger, the jackal is also an opportunistic hunter of small mammals, birds, reptiles and insects. Occasionally a large pack will congregate and run down larger prey such as a deer.

The wide distribution of the leopard attests to the adaptability of this predator. It is an agile climber and will drag its prey high up a tree to avoid scavengers. The leopard's diet can be quite diverse, ranging from insects and amphibians to large deer, although some leopards become partial to certain meats. This solitary creature roams within a defined territory, and most activity, particularly hunting, occurs at dawn or dusk. Sri Lanka has a subspecies endemic to the country, the *Panthera pardus kotika.*

Common palm civets are cat-like hunters related to weasels, long-bodied with short limbs and a very long tail. The coat is a speckled grey with indistinct longitudinal stripes or spots of lighter colour. The palm civet is also known as the toddy cat because of its taste for fermenting coconut palm sap.

Mongooses look like ferrets, with a speckled grey body colour. They prey on snakes, frogs, birds and small mammals and also eat birds' eggs and fruit. They actively hunt both day and night, usually alone but sometimes in pairs.

An armour plating of large, overlapping scales distinguishes the Indian pangolin. The grey scales, made from modified hair, cover the top of the head and the top and sides of the body. Shy and nocturnal, the pangolin ventures out at night to raid termite mounds and ant nests. When threatened, the pangolin curls itself into a ball, its tail tightly enveloping its vulnerable belly.

Ungulates The omnivorous wild boar is closely related to the slightly hairier wild boar of Europe. A strip of long black bristles, which rises when the animal is excited, runs down its spine. The elongated tusks of the upper and lower jaw, more pronounced in the male, are formidable weapons. Wild boars are common in open forests and near cultivation, where they can be pests.

The sambar is a big, brown and shaggy-coated deer with a mane. More active by

The Royal Pachyderm

Elephants occupy a special place in Sri Lankan culture. In ancient times elephants were crown property and killing one was a terrible offence. Legend has it that elephants stamped down the foundations of the great dagobas (Buddhist monuments) at Anuradhapura, and elephant iconography is common in Sri Lankan religious and secular art. Even today elephants are held in great affection and the Maligawa tusker, which carries the tooth relic on the final night of the Kandy Esala Perahera, is perhaps the most venerated of all.

There are some 2500 wild elephants in Sri Lanka (compared with 12,000 in 1900), plus about 300 domesticated elephants (of which most were born in the wild). There are two subspecies of the Asian elephant here: *Elephas maximus maximus* (Ceylon elephant) and *Elephas maximus vilaliya* (Ceylon marsh elephant). The Asian elephant is smaller than the African elephant; it also has a rounder back, smaller ears, one 'lip' rather than two on the tip of its trunk and four nails rather than three on its hind feet. In Sri Lanka, most females and many males are tuskless. Asian elephants congregate in family groups of up to 10 led by an adult female. Males, banished from the family group upon maturity, may form bachelor herds.

For farmers in elephant country, this means an ever-present threat from animals that may trample their crops, destroy their buildings and even take their lives. During the cultivation season farmers conduct around-the-clock vigils for up to three months to scare off the unwelcome raiders. It's understandable that for farmers on the breadline, elephants are a luxury they can't afford; swift and adequate compensation for elephant-inflicted damage is one solution to the problem. Arming farmers is occasionally mooted, but this would surely hasten the demise of elephants in Sri Lanka. Creating elephant corridors is another option, as has been done with the creation of Kaudulla National Park. Problem elephants are sometimes relocated, but seem to have a knack for finding their way back.

night than day, sambar can be observed at dawn and dusk, usually near water. A matriarch hind will lead a group of 10 to 20 deer. The mature male, or stag, leads a solitary life apart from the rutting season (November to December). Prior to the rut he develops antlers used in ritualistic combat against competing males.

Chital deer have reddish-brown backs and sides with rows of white spots. They graze in herds of 10 to 30, which may include two or three mature stags. Chital frequent open forest and places where forest meets grassland or cultivated land. Often they can be seen with langurs; the chital feed on fruit dropped by the monkeys, and both gain security from the extra eyes, ears and noses ready to sense danger.

Other Mammals The five-striped palm squirrel has a grey-brown body and a long, bushy grey tail. These squirrels are more commonly seen in gardens and town parks than native forest. They eat fruit, nuts, flowers, shoots, insects and birds' eggs. Their scurrying and bounding is accompanied by shrill, high-pitched chatter, and much flicking of the bushy tail.

The Indian flying fox is a fruit-eating bat with an impressive 1.2m wingspan. Camps (groups of roosting bats) can number up to several hundred bats. Very large trees are the favoured location, and soon after sunset the flying foxes decamp.

Reptiles & Fish

Sri Lanka has several species of large reptiles, including 83 species of snakes, five of them poisonous.

Mugger crocodiles can be seen on the banks of rivers, lakes and marshes. If a pond dries up, muggers will march great distances to reach water. They feed on fish, amphibians, birds, and mammals such as young deer. Muggers are social creatures, especially during mating season.

The water monitor is distinguished by its sheer size and colourful markings – black with yellow dappling on its back and a pale yellow belly. This scavenger is an expert swimmer, and it is particularly fond of crocodile eggs and bird eggs. It swallows its prey whole, mostly unchewed.

The Indian cobra is the famous hooded snake associated with the subcontinent's snake charmers. This highly venomous snake avoids confrontation and will usually retreat if threatened. Cobras are mostly nocturnal and feed on amphibians, reptiles and mammals, particularly mice and rats.

Some 54 species of fish are found in the waterways and marshlands, including prized aquarium varieties such as the red scissor-tail barb and the ornate paradise fish. The British introduced several kinds of fish, including trout, which are still common around Horton Plains. There are myriad colourful tropical marine fish.

Sri Lanka has five species of marine turtle, all endangered: the leathery, the olive ridley, the loggerhead, the hawksbill and the green. Though protected, they face significant threats from poachers, and environmental hazards caused by pollution and coastal development.

Birds

Sri Lanka is host to a rich abundance of birdlife. For more details, see the boxed text 'Birds of Sri Lanka' in The Hill Country chapter.

Endangered Species

The World Conservation Union (formerly the IUCN) *Red Databook* lists 43 animal species as threatened in Sri Lanka. They include Sri Lanka's two subspecies of Asian elephant, the sloth bear and the leopard. All five of Sri Lanka's turtle species are threatened, as is the estuarine crocodile (killed for its meat) and the mild-mannered dugong (a protected animal that is nevertheless killed for its meat). Also under threat are several species of birds, fish and insects.

NATIONAL PARKS & RESERVES

More than 2000 years ago royalty ensured certain areas were protected from any human activity by declaring them sanctuaries. Almost every province in the kingdom of Kandy had such *udawattakelle* (sanctuaries). All animals and plants in these sanctuaries were left undisturbed, the taking of life being anathema to Buddhist beliefs. Sri Lanka boasts the world's first wildlife sanctuary, Mihintale, which was created by King Devanampiya Tissa in the 3rd century BC.

Today's system of parks and reserves is mostly a synthesis of traditionally protected areas and those established by the British. There are 100 areas protected by the government, divided into three types: national parks, strict nature reserves (where no visitors are allowed) and nature reserves, in which human habitation is permitted. Parks in the northern and northeastern parts of Sri Lanka that are closed are currently unprotected; they have no onsite rangers and are being exploited by armed poachers and loggers. See the boxed text 'Major National Parks & Reserves' later, for specific details on Sri Lanka's national parks.

GOVERNMENT & POLITICS

The Democratic Socialist Republic of Sri Lanka, which gained independence from Britain in February 1948, adopted its first republican constitution in 1972 and its current constitution in August 1978. Sri Lanka's executive president is elected for a period of six years and has the power to appoint or dismiss members of the cabinet, including the prime minister, and to dissolve parliament. Members of the 225-seat unicameral parliament are elected by popular vote via a modified proportional representation system for a six-year term.

The country is divided into nine provinces: Central, North-Central, Northern, North-Eastern, North-Western, Western, Sabaragamuwa, Southern and Uva. There have been several changes to the status of the Northern and North-Eastern provinces over the past 20 years. The legal system is a complex mix of English common law and Roman-Dutch, Muslim, Sinhalese and customary law.

The main parties in parliament are United National Party (UNP), the People's Alliance (PA) and the Janatha Vimukthi Peramuna (JVP, People's Liberation Army). The UNP is vaguely right wing, or at least its senior leaders tend to come from Colombo's better schools. The PA used to be socialist in character, but in recent terms in government it has proved to be free market–oriented. Both the UNP and PA have been associated with corruption. The JVP runs on a left-wing populist platform, looking back in envy to the glorious Sinhalese past and forward to a radical Marxist future. It's notably anti-Tamil. A typical supporter would be a student or a young unemployed country person.

ECONOMY

Before independence Sri Lanka's economy centred on plantation crops (tea, rubber and coconut products) – a legacy of the colonial regime. In 1960 Sri Lankans had similar living standards to Singaporeans and were quite a bit richer than South Koreans. While plantation crops remain important, the economy today is considerably more diverse. The top earner is now the garment sector, which accounts for more than 50% of exports. Tea accounts for about 15% of exports, and gems 5%. The second-most important export crop after tea is coconuts. The fishing industry employs about 150,000 people, but the sector is yet to fully develop. Tourism has long been a promising earner, but the war stifled growth. The war also has stifled work of the Mahaweli scheme, which aims to substantially increase the amount of irrigated land in the north and east of the country.

A major source of income is repatriated money earned by Sri Lankans in the Middle East and elsewhere. Some claim that it is, after garments, the country's second-highest source of income. Muslims in particular might live for 20 years or more in the Middle East, visiting their families once every year or so.

Sri Lanka has a small population earning big money, but the majority earns little. A tea picker earns around Rs 125 per day, while a batik artist gets Rs 100 to Rs 150 per day, as does a worker in the garment manufacturing trade. A journalist can expect to start on around Rs 300 per day, while a bank manager should be pretty happy bringing home Rs 1500 to Rs 2000 per day. GDP per head is US$900, or US$3200 by the purchasing-power parity standard.

Consumer prices have risen by between 5% and 10% annually over the last five years. The economy is expected to tick along at a healthy 5% to 6% over the next couple of years, though with public debt rising to 100% of GDP the government is pretty strapped for spare cash to spend on social policies.

POPULATION & PEOPLE

Sri Lanka has a population of 19.8 million. In 1948 the population was only seven million, but after the ensuing baby boom that lasted until the 1980s the growth rate has slowed right down. The population is set to peak at about 25 million by 2020, then start to fall. Like many developed countries, Sri Lanka has a rapidly ageing population.

The social policies of most governments since independence have given Sri Lanka a creditable literacy and health record. Adult literacy (ie, people 10 years of age and over who can read and write) is a little over 86% (90.5% for men, 82.4% for women). The life expectancy for men is 70 years and for women 75.4 years. Sinhala, the first language of 80% of the total population, and Tamil (18%) are both national languages, with English commonly described as a link language. See the Language chapter for some useful words and phrases in Sinhala, Tamil and Sri Lankan English.

Ethnic Groups

Although the first Sinhalese settlers in Sri Lanka almost certainly came from North India, and the ancestors of most Tamils came from South India, their ranks have been mixed over the centuries, both with each other and with Sri Lanka's other ethnic groups. The president, Chandrika Kumaratunga, lists a Tamil and a European in her family tree.

From appearances you certainly can't do more than guess whether a person is Sinhalese or Tamil. The biggest differences are language and religion.

Sinhalese The Sinhalese constitute about 74% of the population. They speak Sinhala, are predominantly Buddhist and have a reputation for being easy-going. Their forebears probably came from somewhere around the northern Bay of Bengal. Their chronicles state that the first Sinhalese king, Vijaya, arrived in Sri Lanka with a small band of followers in the 6th century BC.

The Sinhalese have a caste system, although it is not seen as important as in India. Sinhalese see themselves as either 'low country' or 'Kandyan', and the Kandyan Sinhalese have a pride – some would say snobbishness – that stems from the time when the hill country was the last bastion of Sinhalese rulers against European colonists.

Tamils The Tamils are the second-largest group, constituting about 18% of the population. There are sometimes claims that the percentage is higher and that there is a Sinhalese plot to underestimate their numbers. Tamils are predominantly Hindu and speak Tamil. About 60 million more Tamils – far

Major National Parks & Reserves

Of the major Sri Lankan parks described here, in our opinion the best ones are Bundala, Horton Plains, Kaudulla, Minneriya, Uda Walawe, Yala East and Yala West (Ruhuna) National Parks, and Sinharaja Forest Reserve.

Many parks in the northern and northeastern parts of the country are closed. Kaudulla, Wilpattu, Maduru Oya and Wasgomuwa are open, although the latter two have attracted few visitors to date. When they reopen, parks in these two areas well worth visiting include Flood Plains and Somawathiya Chaitiya National Parks, and Chundikkulam and Kokkilai Lagoon Bird Sanctuaries. Contact the Ceylon Tourist Board (e tourinfo@sri.lanka.net) for the latest information.

Bundala National Park (6216 hectares)

Location: On the south coast between Hambantota and Tissamaharama

Bundala, which protects a brackish coastal lagoon, is the end of the line for migratory birds. It is one of the best places to watch birds, with flamingos a star attraction. Still referred to as the Bundala Bird Sanctuary, the park can also be good for viewing elephants. See The South chapter for more information.

Gal Oya National Park (62,936 hectares)

Location: Northwest of Arugam Bay, east Sri Lanka

This isolated park surrounds a large tank, the Senanayake Samudra, and provides an important sanctuary for elephants and a variety of other wildlife including sloth bears, leopards, deer and water buffaloes. The landscape of Gal Oya is rolling grasslands with a few substantial stands of evergreen forest. See The East chapter for details.

Horton Plains National Park (3160 hectares)

Location: In the southcentral hill country

The forests at this altitude (over 2000m) have unusual plant and animal life adapted to a cooler climate. The moss-covered, stunted forests are broken up with patches of marshy grassland. The spectacular World's End precipice is just one feature of this unusual landscape. See The Hill Country chapter for details.

Kaudulla National Park (6656 hectares)

Location: Northeast of Polonnaruwa

Established around the ancient Kaudulla Tank, this new park forms an elephant corridor between Somawathiya Chaitiya and Minneriya National Parks. There are also leopards, fishing cats, sambar deer, rusty spotted cats and sloth bears. The park is a mix of dry evergreen forest, scrub jungle and grassy plains. See The Ancient Cities chapter for details.

Minneriya National Park (8890 hectares)

Location: Northwest of Polonnaruwa

This park, which has a similar landscape to Kaudulla (which is just to the north), is dominated by the Minneriya Tank. Toque macaques, sambar deer and elephants (in numbers up to 150) are regularly

more than the entire population of Sri Lanka – live across the Palk Strait in India.

There are two distinct groups of Tamils in Sri Lanka. The origins of the so-called 'Sri Lanka' or 'Ceylon' Tamils go back to the South Indians who started coming to Sri Lanka during the centuries of conflict between Sinhalese and South Indian kingdoms 1000 or more years ago. These Tamils are concentrated in the North, where they now form nearly all the Tamil population, and down the east coast, where they are present in roughly equal numbers with the Sinhalese and Muslims.

The other group is the 'hill country' or 'plantation' Tamils whose ancestors were brought from India by the British colonialists to work on the tea plantations in the

Major National Parks & Reserves

seen. There is plenty of birdlife too including little cormorants and painted storks. See The Ancient Cities chapter for details.

Sinharaja Forest Reserve (18,899 hectares)
Location: In the southwest, just south of Pelmadulla near Ratnapura
This is Sri Lanka's last remaining patch of virgin rainforest and the richest in endemic flora and fauna. It has spectacular dense and hilly rainforest scenery and associated wildlife (the highest concentration of animals unique to Sri Lanka is found here). Sinharaja has been declared a World Heritage Site by Unesco. See The Hill Country chapter for details.

Uda Walawe National Park (30,821 hectares)
Location: About 200km southeast of Colombo, close to the southern end of the highlands
This park, which is mostly rolling grassland and thorn scrub with stands of valuable trees, contains the Uda Walawe Reservoir. Elephants are the highlight here; there are also spotted deer, water buffaloes and wild boars. See The Hill Country chapter for details.

Udawattakelle Sanctuary (105 hectares)
Location: Beside Kandy
This ancient hilly forest reserve offers pleasant walking as well as opportunities to see birds and other wildlife. You may not have to go far to see the monkeys (toque macaques) here, as they usually come to you. See The Hill Country chapter for more information.

Wilpattu National Park (131,693 hectares)
Location: 25km north of Puttalam, west Sri Lanka
This is Sri Lanka's largest park, most famous for its leopards, sloth bears, deer and birdlife. It was reopened in 2003 and facilities for visitors are being restored. The terrain is mostly dense jungle. See the West Coast chapter for details.

Yala East National Park (18,149 hectares)
Location: 25km south of Arugam Bay
This park contains the Kumana mangrove swamp and has a variety of water birds in spectacular numbers. It is divided from Yala West (Ruhuna) National Park by a strict nature reserve into which visitors aren't allowed. The terrain is mostly flat grassland with areas of scrub and jungle, interspersed with rocky outcrops. See The East chapter for details.

Yala West (Ruhuna) National Park (14,101 hectares)
Location: 305km southeast of Colombo
The open, undulating country of this park is studded with rocky formations and lagoons. Famous for elephants, the park is also home to sloth bears, leopards and water buffaloes. It is not possible to visit Yala East via this park. See The South chapter for details.

19th century. The hill-country Tamils and the Sri Lankan Tamils are separated by geography, history and caste (the hill-country Tamils come mainly from lower Indian castes and have largely kept out of the bloody conflict with the Sinhalese over the past 18 years). Caste distinctions among Tamils are seen as being more important than among Sinhalese.

Muslims About 9% of the population is Muslim. Most of these Muslims are so-called 'Sri Lanka Moors', whose presence goes back at least 1000 years and who are probably the descendants of Arab or Indian Muslim traders. They are scattered all over the island, perhaps more thinly in the South and North, and are still particularly active in trade and business. Muslim traders led teams of bullocks deep into the hilly interior, the only way of accessing the region at the time, and today many hill-town merchants are Muslims.

Muslims have largely steered clear of the Sinhalese–Tamil troubles, though there has been some conflict between Tamils and Muslims in the East. The Malays are a smaller group of Muslims; many of their ancestors came with the Dutch from Java. They still speak Malay and there's a concentration of them in Hambantota. The 'Indian Moors' form a second small group; they are more recent Muslim arrivals from India and Pakistan.

Veddahs The Veddahs, also called the Wanniyala-aetto (People of the Forest), are the original inhabitants of the country. The Sinhalese word *veddah* means 'hunter'. Their exact numbers are highly disputed. Some reports count as few as 200 Veddahs in Sri Lanka, while others suggest a collection of communities, including Sinhalese- and Tamil-speaking groups, numbering in the thousands. Others, though, believe that the Veddahs no longer exist as they are so intermarried and integrated into Sinhalese culture that they can no longer claim to be a distinct ethnic group. Only a small and diminishing number of people identifying themselves as Veddah have retained a semblance of their old culture, which stressed a hunting lifestyle and maintaining close relationships with nature and their ancestors. The preference, instead, for 'slash and burn' agriculture or a more modern lifestyle is witness to this departure. Most Veddahs (and the Sri Lankan government) appear apathetic about the future of the group. From time to time, Veddahs are arrested for hunting in national parks.

When the Dutch arrived in Sri Lanka there were Veddah communities as far north as Jaffna, but today they are limited to the area roughly between Badulla, Batticaloa and Polonnaruwa. The community is divided into two groups, the Kele Weddo or jungle Veddahs, and the Can Weddo or village-dwelling Veddahs.

While Sinhalese legends characterise the Veddahs as partly descended from evil spirits (which has certain political uses), the Veddahs are related to South Indian tribes such as the Vedas of Kerala. In the Sinhalese caste system, Veddahs are on a par with the landowning caste. One important difference is that the Veddahs have a matrilineal clan-based society.

Central to the whole issue are the traditional hunting grounds of the Veddah in what is now the national park of Maduru Oya. The park was created in 1983 to serve as a refuge for wildlife displaced by the gigantic Mahaweli irrigation scheme. Sri Lankan law specifically prohibits hunting and gathering in national parks. The area set aside for the park included five Veddah villages. All but one community eventually moved outside the park borders. Those who had made the move became unhappy with the situation. They could no longer hunt and gather on their ancestral lands, and wanted to go back. In 1990 an area was set aside inside the park for them, and they began to return, but discovered that the allocated area did not encompass all five villages, and neither did it provide sufficient area to sustain them. The Veddah continue to appeal for improved rights to the Maduru Oya National Park. For more information see the website **w** vedda.org.

Others The Burghers are Eurasians, primarily descendants of the Portuguese, Dutch and British. The term is also used to apply more specifically to 'white' Sri Lankans of European descent. For a time, even after independence, the Burghers had a disproportionate influence over the political and business life of Sri Lanka, but growing Sinhalese nationalism has reduced their advantage and many Burghers emigrated to Australia and Canada. Nevertheless, names such as Fernando, de Silva and Perera are still very common. There are also small Chinese and European communities and a small, downtrodden group of low-caste South Indians brought in to perform the most menial tasks.

EDUCATION

From about the 3rd century BC, formal learning primarily took place in monasteries. The present-day system, however, has been shaped by European, particularly British, influences. Free education from kindergarten to university was introduced shortly after WWII, and state education remains free to this day. There are also many private institutions catering for preschool and up. These private schools are often referred to as 'English-medium' schools.

A good education is greatly valued, and this is reflected in the high level of literacy in Sri Lanka. Schoolchildren heading to and from school, immaculately turned out in their pressed white uniforms (despite the fact that many children possess one uniform only), are a common sight all over the island.

The first university was established in 1942 at Peradeniya near Kandy. Today there are 12 universities, plus an open university. Many students from middle-class families aim to study overseas, especially in Australia, Canada and the USA.

ARTS

Dance & Theatre

Sri Lanka's famous Kandyan dance and *kolam* (masked dance-drama) have their origins in South India, but have developed a unique local character. The devil dancing of the low country almost certainly predates Buddhism in Sri Lanka. See the boxed text 'Sri Lanka's Dances & Masks' later in this chapter for more information.

Modern Theatre It wasn't until the 19th century that theatre started to move into the cities. The first inroads were made by a Parsi theatrical company from Bombay (present-day Mumbai) that introduced *nurti* (literally 'new theatre') to Colombo audiences. *Nurti* was a blend of European and Indian theatrical conventions: stage scenery, painted backdrops and wings; an enclosed theatre; costumes, music and song. It was to spawn a new profession – play writing. Until the arrival of *nurti*, writers had focused on prose and poetry, but now they drew on Sanskrit classical drama and other sources, including Shakespeare, for inspiration.

The arrival of cinema all but killed off theatre until after independence, with the biggest breakthrough coming in 1956 following the premiere of *Maname* (King's Name), a play written by university professor Ediriweera Sarachchandra. This used a *jataka* (a tale from the Buddha's life) as its theme, although the tale was altered somewhat, and was staged in the traditional style of *nadagam* (a form of Sinhalese drama that developed out of Catholic pageants and nativity plays). The combination of a familiar folk tale and popular staging made the play an instant hit and marked the beginning of a new era of experimentation and creativity. Sarachchandra is still recognised as a founder of Sri Lankan theatre.

Literature

Although inscriptions that predate Christ have been found, the earliest texts date from the 10th century AD. These are primarily aids for the study of the Pali (Sanskrit) texts on Buddhism. One striking aspect of Sinhalese literature is its early focus on the recording of history. The Mahavamsa (Great Chronicle) and the Culavamsa (Minor Chronicle), which detail the exploits of successive kings and nobles from the time of the arrival of Prince Vijaya from India (about 200 years before Buddhism spread throughout Sri Lanka), were compiled by monks. Together with such documents as the Thupavamsa (Chronicle of the Great Stupa) they record the history of all great Buddhist monuments in Sri Lanka.

Poetry was certainly an early literary form; the graffiti on the Sigiriya mirror wall attest to that. Tales from the Buddha's past lives were also expressed poetically in the Jataka tales. A genre that proved very popular in Sri Lanka was *samdesha* literature. This originated in Hindu India and centred on the theme of an exiled lover sending a message to his beloved on the monsoon clouds. Eulogies to the Buddha and secular figures and poems about war also existed.

Until the mid-19th century, literary endeavours were mostly religious in nature, but at this time there was a flurry of activity, aided by access to printing presses, including newspapers and periodicals in the vernacular. The first Sinhalese novel, *Meena*, appeared in 1905. Written by Aluthgamage Simon De Silva, its theme of young love didn't go down well in a conservative society. Other works appearing shortly thereafter, notably those by Buddhist writer and political activist Piyadasa Sirisena, as well as Martin Wickramasinghe and WA Silva, were more favourably received. Much of Sri Lanka's modern literature centres on the ramifications of the civil war. For more information about books, including fiction and nonfiction, see Books in the Facts for the Visitor chapter.

Architecture

Geoffrey Bawa (1919–2003) was Sri Lanka's most famous contemporary architect. His work is particularly accessible to visitors as it includes several well-known hotels, including the Lighthouse in Galle, the Kandalama Hotel in Dambulla, the YWCA National Headquarters at Rotunda Gardens in Colombo and the Bentota Beach Hotel.

At the other end of the scale, the *cadjan* (coconut frond) dwellings that one sees today were probably similar to the type of structures favoured in ancient times by ordinary people. *Cadjan* dwellings have a timber frame over which are placed woven coconut frond mats. This is a type of building particularly suited to Sri Lanka's climate. It's also inexpensive, although the *cadjan* needs replacing every three years or so.

Buddhist One of the most striking features of Sri Lanka's architectural landscape is the dagoba or stupa. Dagobas, sometimes located inside caves, are classified into six basic shapes resembling a heap of paddy (unhusked rice), a bell, a bubble and so on.

The smooth, lime-washed dagoba mounds protrude above the tree line along the coast, and dot the dry zone at Anuradhapura. In the intense tropical sun they give off an eerie glow. Above the mound is a square box-like structure called a *hataraes kotuwa*, which in the early days of dagoba building contained relics. Rising from this is the furled ceremonial parasol called the *chatta*. Because the staff left little room for relics in the *hataraes kotuwa*, they were eventually lodged inside an area of hollowed out brickwork just below the staff. A piece of granite (the mystic stone) with nine squares scooped out of its surface held the relics and offerings. These stones can be seen at museums in Anuradhapura, Mihintale and elsewhere. Dagobas are made of solid brick, then plastered and lime-washed. There is very often a *vahalakadas* (platform) surrounding the dagoba, used by devotees to make a clockwise circuit; stairways to the pathway pass through gates situated at the cardinal points.

Early dagobas were probably very simple structures, but became increasingly sophisticated during the time of the ancient kingdoms of the dry zone. Dagobas built in the 2nd century by King Dutugemunu – Ruvanvelisaya and Mirisavatiya in Anuradhapura – had their foundations established well below ground (stamped down by elephants, legend has it). The Jetavanarama Dagoba in Anuradhapura, dating from the 3rd century and the focus of a gigantic reconstruction project in recent times, is nearly as high as Egypt's Cheops pyramid.

A uniquely Sinhalese architectural concept is the *vatadage* or circular relic house. Today you can see *vatadages* in Anuradhapura and Polonnaruwa – perhaps the finest example is at Medirigiriya. They consist of a small central dagoba flanked by Buddha images and encircled by columns. Long ago these columns held up a wooden roof, but all traces of wooden architecture have long disappeared from the remains of the ancient cities, and you must get your imagination into top gear to picture how things really were. Only important buildings were constructed of stone – everything else was made of wood.

Another peculiarly Sinhalese style is the *gedige* – a hollow temple with extremely thick walls topped by a 'corbelled' (trussed) roof. Often the walls are so thick that stairways can be built right into them. There are a number of *gediges* in Anuradhapura and Polonnaruwa, and also restored one at Nalanda – with the exception of the latter almost all of their roofs collapsed long ago.

A distinction to bear in mind is that between the *vihara* and the *devale*. The former is generally a Buddhist complex that includes a shrine containing a statue of the Buddha, a congregational hall and a monks' house. See under Hindu following for details on *devales*.

Hindu In Sri Lanka Hindu temples are called *kovils* and are mostly dedicated to Shaivite (Shiva) worship. Essentially they consist of a prayer hall and shrine room. There is a covered space that allows worshippers to take a ritual walk clockwise around the hall and shrine room. Towering above all this is the *sikhara*, a central edifice, usually dome- or pyramid-shaped, that rises above the shrine room. Some temples also have *gopurams*, or ornate towering gateways. Both tend to be elaborately sculpted and brightly coloured.

A *devale* is a complex designed for worshipping either a Hindu deity or a local Sri Lankan one. At Polonnaruwa, *devales* are quite separate from Buddhist shrines, but in later centuries many Buddhist temples also had *devales*.

European The Europeans all made an impact on Sri Lanka's architectural styles. The Portuguese influence can be seen in certain conventions such as high-pitched roofs and covered verandas. Interestingly, the Portuguese style continued well after the Dutch defeated them because the Portuguese, barred from administrative duties, turned to the building trade to earn a living. Dutch influence is, however, far more apparent. The historic Fort in Galle has many wonderful examples of Dutch style. When the Dutch took over they changed the Portuguese forts, and the English continued the tradition, bringing their own ecclesiastic and secular architectural fashions with them as well. The buildings in hill stations such as Nuwara Eliya positively cry out 'England'.

Sculpture & Painting

Images of the Buddha dominate the work of Sri Lankan sculptors. Limestone, which is plentiful, was used for early works (which means they haven't weathered well), but a variety of other materials has been used over the centuries, including jade, rock crystal, marble, emerald, pink quartz, ivory, coral and sometimes wood or metal. The Buddha is represented in three poses – sitting, standing or lying – with his hands arranged in various *mudras,* or positions: *dhyana mudra* is a meditative pose where the hands are cupped and resting lightly in the lap (the right hand overlaps the left); in *abhaya mudra* the right hand is raised (conveying protection); in the *vitarka mudra* the index finger touches the thumb (a gesture symbolising teaching). Other notable examples of sculpture include the four solid panels of sculpture or *vahalkadas* at the Kantaka Chetiya at Mihintale (see The Ancient Cities chapter for details).

Staircases at Sri Lanka's ancient temples and palaces reveal a wealth of finely sculpted detail, with the elaborately carved moonstones being a notable feature. A moonstone comprises a series of rings, enclosed within flames of purifying fire, which contain various symbolic motifs, including the elephant (representing birth), the horse (old age), the lion (illness), the bull (death and decay), geese (purity) and serpents (lust and desire). In the centre sits the sacred lotus flower.

On either side of the foot of these staircases are guardstones (which have their origin in Indian art and depict the Naga king and his dwarf attendants) and, as you ascend, dwarfs that appear to hold up each stair. A mythical beast called a *makara* (a cross between a lion, a pig and an elephant) often decorates the balustrade.

Painting, like dance and music, was not approved of by orthodox Buddhists who saw no good in art for art's sake. Yet artists (influenced by Indian conventions) did paint; the best-known example of their efforts appears in the form of shapely nymphs on the walls of the Sigiriya fortress, although it's not known exactly who painted these. On the whole, painting centred on Buddhist themes, with the best examples to be seen in Dambulla and Polonnaruwa. By the 13th century, painting as an art form appears to have declined.

The rice-flour designs or *kolams* (also called *rangoli*) that adorn thresholds in Tamil areas are much more than mere decoration. Traditionally, *kolams* (meaning play, form or beauty in Tamil) are drawn by the women of the household at sunrise and are made of rice-flour paste, which may be eaten by small creatures – symbolising a reverence for all life, even the most apparently insignificant. This gesture is doubly blessed; giving as one's first act of the day is viewed as extremely auspicious.

Cinema

The first Sri Lankan–made film, *Kadavunu Poronduwa* (Broken Promise), was shown in Colombo in 1947, when audiences heard Sinhala spoken on screen for the first time. Movies continued to be produced mostly in Indian studios though, until the director Sirisena Wimalaweera opened a studio in Sri Lanka in 1951. Lester James Peries' first feature film, *Rekawa* (Line of Destiny), is known as the first truly Sinhalese film. It attempted to realistically portray Sri Lankan life and used its filming technique to express this – it was the first film in Sri Lanka shot outside a studio.

Contemporary Sri Lankan directors tend to explore themes directly relating to the war. *Death on a Full Moon Day,* made in 2000 by Prasanna Vithanage, is a recent production about a father who refuses to accept the death of his soldier son.

Today the local film industry is struggling to compete against Indian movies and against television. Some say the National Film Corporation (NFC) also stifled the industry – something which may change now that the NFC no longer has a monopoly on distribution.

Films shot on location in Sri Lanka include *Elephant Walk*, which starred Elizabeth Taylor and Peter Finch, and David Lean's *Bridge on the River Kwai*. More recently Sri Lanka has been used as a setting in *Indiana Jones and the Temple of Doom* and *Mountbatten: The Last Viceroy*.

SOCIETY & CONDUCT

If you are ever unsure about how to conduct yourself in an unfamiliar cultural situation (at a temple *puja*, for example), ask. Sri Lankans are invariably happy to explain. Overall, visitors are accorded great tolerance and your unwitting mistakes will usually be politely overlooked.

Traditional Society

Rites of Passage Sri Lanka is a very family-oriented society. The birth of a child is a great event, greeted by relatives near and far with joy. Everyone comes to visit the new baby, bearing gifts. The next important event is when the child takes its first solid food. *Kiri bath* (rice cooked in milk) is the traditional food given at this time, but it can be anything that's mild and chilli free. Another important milestone in the life of a child is when they first learn the alphabet. Birthdays were not traditionally celebrated but are now celebrated as a result of European influence.

In days gone by, traditional families would keep their daughter in the house for the duration of her first period, but this custom isn't really adhered to today. Coming-of-age parties are held to mark the occasion though, and the girl may receive gifts including jewellery from parents and other relatives.

Marriages in Sri Lanka are traditionally arranged. There are three main events in a Sri Lankan marriage: the engagement, the wedding reception (where gifts are given) and the homecoming. The celebrations can go on all night and generally involve a band of musicians.

Traditional Buddhist weddings take place on a *poruwa* (square platform) decorated with flowers. Buddhist priests do not officiate at weddings, so a special layperson chants religious stanzas in Sinhala and Pali. The master of ceremonies gives the groom betel leaves. The groom and bride pass some to their parents, and then rings and gifts are exchanged. Then comes the *kiri bath*; the bride and groom feed each other a small quantity. The bride's little finger on her right hand is tied with a gold thread to the little finger of the groom's left hand and the master of ceremonies pours water over their fingers. Young girls dressed in white sing a series of stanzas in Pali (the language of the original Buddhist scriptures) – these describe qualities of the Buddha that may bless the couple. As the couple leaves the *poruwa*, a coconut is sometimes broken behind it. The bride and groom then sign a register and sit at the wedding feast table. Toasts are made and the couple is congratulated. Leaving the romance aside for a moment, there is sometimes one more test – the production of a bloodied bed sheet offered as proof of the bride's chastity.

In old age, security comes from the family. The aged are accorded more respect than is often the case in the West, and remain an integral part of the extended family. Generally, an ageing parent will live with a son or daughter.

At funerals mourners invariably wear white, and white funeral flags are a fairly common sight at Hindu and Buddhist funerals in Sri Lanka; they are strung along fences and poles, providing a guided pathway to the place where the body is to be buried.

The Caste System Although Buddhism discourages distinctions between monks based on caste, a caste system does exist among Sri Lankan Buddhists, although it is not as marked as it once was. Unlike the orthodox Hindu system, there is no Brahmin or Kshatriya caste. Instead, the highest rung is occupied by the Govigama caste, who are descendants of landowners and cultivators. The Bandaras and Radalas are subgroups within this caste. Lower down come the Karava (fishing folk), the Hakurus (*jaggery* sweet makers), the Berawaya (drummers), the Paduvua (palanquin bearers), the Radhu (washer folk) and at the bottom, the Rodiya (beggars and itinerant entertainers). However, these distinctions are virtually irrelevant today. More commonly you'll hear people making a distinction between low-country Sinhalese and Kandyans.

Among Jaffna Tamils the Brahmin is the highest caste. Next come the Vellalas, who are cultivators and landlords. Beneath these two castes are various others with occupations involving varying degrees of ritual 'pollution' (eg, barbers, washer folk). At the very bottom are the Untouchable castes. The word 'pariah' comes from the Paraiyars, an Untouchable caste of itinerant workers and funeral drummers, traditionally forbidden from entering temples, owning land or drawing water from the same wells as other castes. The hill-country Tamils mainly come from these lower castes.

RELIGION

Buddhism is the dominant creed of the largest ethnic group, the Sinhalese, and is followed by 70% of the population. It plays an extremely important role in the country, both spiritually and culturally. Sri Lanka's literature, art and architecture are to a large extent a product of its Buddhist basis. About 15% of the population, mainly Tamils, is Hindu. Muslims account for about 9% and Christians about 7.5%. The Christians include both Sinhalese and Tamil converts.

However, there is much more mixing and melding among religious groups than these figures would suggest. A Catholic, for example, may well feel the need to pay his respects to the Hindu god Ganesh in order to ensure he has no obstacles or problems in his path in the course of a particular venture. Buddhist, Hindu, Muslim and Christian Sri Lankans all venture to some of the same pilgrimage sites, Adam's Peak and Kataragama in particular.

Buddhism

Strictly speaking, Buddhism is not a religion since it is not centred on a god but is rather a system of philosophy and a code of morality. It covers a wide range of interpretations of the basic beliefs that started with the enlightenment of the Buddha in North India around 2500 years ago. Siddhartha Gautama, born a prince, is said to be the most recent Buddha, or 'Enlightened One', and is not expected to be the last.

The most recent Buddha was born into the Sakya clan in Kushinagara, on the border of Nepal and India, around 563 BC. During his lifetime a political revolution was underway. Tribal clans with collective governments were replaced with monarchies. Legend tells that he was a prince, but the Buddhist scriptures also portray him as a displaced clan member unhappy with the loss of liberty under autocratic monarchs. He joined the ranks of homeless ascetic sages, who included followers of Mahavira, founder of the Jain monastic order, who believed that following austerities (eg, fasting, meditating) purified the soul.

In his lifetime the Buddha gained enlightenment, and gained many followers. He didn't write down his dharma (for Buddhists, this means 'teachings'), but organised a community of celibate monks, the Sangha, to memorise and spread his teachings as well as work towards their own enlightenment. While the Jains went for complete asceticism – isolation, rigorous self-denial, nakedness – the Buddha organised the Sangha along communal lines. The patronage of kings was vital to the dominance of Buddhism in India for more than 1000 years. Though the Sangha continued the traditions of the wandering hermit monks of the Buddha's age, it gave moral sanction to monarchies.

Ashoka, the great Indian emperor, was a devout Buddhist. He sent missions to all the known world, and according to legend his son Mahinda brought Buddhism to Sri Lanka. It took a stronghold almost immediately, and the relationship between Sri Lanka's kings and the Buddhist clergy made it a kind of Buddhist theocracy. Sri Lanka has since been looked upon as a centre for Buddhist culture and teaching.

Starting around the time of Ashoka, a schism developed in the Buddhist world, so that today there are two major schools of Buddhism, Theravada and Mahayana. The Theravada (*thera* means a learned elder) uses the Pali Canon of scriptures, written down around the time of Christ in Pali, a language related to the Buddha's native tongue. Mahayana (large vehicle) sees Theravada as too dry and academic, and attributes many miraculous powers to the Buddha. There are also differences in art and in the language of the scriptures – Mahayana scriptures are in Sanskrit, the ancient Indian language of philosophy and religion, not Pali. The Mahayana school has not rejected the Theravada teachings but claims that it has extended

Sri Lanka's Dances & Masks

Dances

Sri Lanka has a rich dance heritage comprising three main schools: Kandyan, *kolam* (masked dance-drama) and devil dancing. If you go to Kandy you'll certainly have the opportunity to witness Kandyan dance performances – a riot of movement, colour and sparkles fed by the arrhythmic pounding of drums. *Kolam* is a series of dance-theatre pieces exploring the themes of everyday life, while devil dancing is performed to exorcise evil spirits. You're most likely to see *kolam* and devil dancing at Ambalangoda (see the West Coast chapter for details).

Kandyan Dance This dance form flourished under the Kandyan kings and is today considered the national dance of Sri Lanka. There are four types: *pantheru, naiyaki, udekki* and *ves*. In addition there are 18 *vannamas* (representations in dance of animals and birds). These include the *gajaga vannama* (elephant) and the *mayura vannama* (peacock). The Ramayana has provided plenty of material for the dances, especially Rama's dash to Lanka to save Sita, aided by the loyal Hanuman. But over the centuries other stories have been absorbed, including those about kings and heroes. Under the Kandyan kings, the dance became so beautiful and refined that Buddhist monks admitted it to their temple courtyards and it became an integral part of the great Kandy Esala Perahera.

The best-known costume of male Kandyan dancers is a wide skirt-like garment. The dancer's bare chest is covered with necklaces of silver and ivory, and bangles of beaten silver are worn on the arms and ankles. These performances are extremely athletic, with great leaps and back flips. The dancers are accompanied by drummers who beat out complex rhythms on the *geta bera*, a Kandyan tapering double-ended drum – one end is covered with monkey hide and the other with cow hide in order to yield different tones.

Masked Drama There are four folk-drama forms: *kolam, sokari, nadagam* and *pasu*. Best known is the *kolam* (Tamil for costume or guise). *Kolam* has many characters – one estimate puts them at 53 – many of which are grotesque, with exaggerated deformities. These are the demons, who may have a cobra emerging from one nostril, bulging eyes or tusks.

Performances are traditionally held at the New Year, over a period of three to five nights. Included in the cast of performers are singers, two drummers and a master of ceremonies. The whole thing kicks off with songs in praise of the Buddha. The master of ceremonies then explains how the *kolam* began (an Indian king's wife had cravings while pregnant to see a masked dance-drama). The cast of characters is then introduced.

Of the many *kolam* plays, the two best-known are the *Sandakinduru Katava* and the *Gothayimbala Katava*. In the first, two creatures, half-bird half-human, live in the forest. A king out hunting kills the man-bird, who is later restored to life by the Buddha. In the second, a demon who falls in love with a beautiful woman is beheaded by the revenging husband. But the demon is able to regenerate itself over and over again, until the husband is rescued from his dilemma by the forest deity.

Devil Dance Traditionally, devil dancing is performed to free a person from demons, evil spirits or just plain bad luck caused by malignant spirits. The devil dancers themselves belong to a low-caste community and specialise in this art form.

them; the Theravada school, though, sees the Mahayana as a corruption of the Buddha's teachings.

Sri Lankan Buddhists saw that Mahayana Buddhism and its pantheon of new Buddhas and deities was coming to resemble Hinduism, which began a comeback in India from the 7th century, and so the Sri Lankan Buddhists stuck to Theravada. The last great Buddhist monasteries and universities in India were destroyed by Afghan Muslim raiders in the 10th century, and some of the holiest Buddhist sites such as Bodhgaya were taken over by Hindu priests. You could say the Sinhalese anxiety about being a lone stronghold of Buddhism dates back to here.

ERIC L WHEATER

Kandyan dancers in full regalia

CHRISTINE NIVEN

A carver paints a *kolam* (costume or guise)

ANDERS BLOMQVIST

Traditional *naga raksha* (cobra) dance mask

MICHAEL AW

Traditional dancers, Kandy

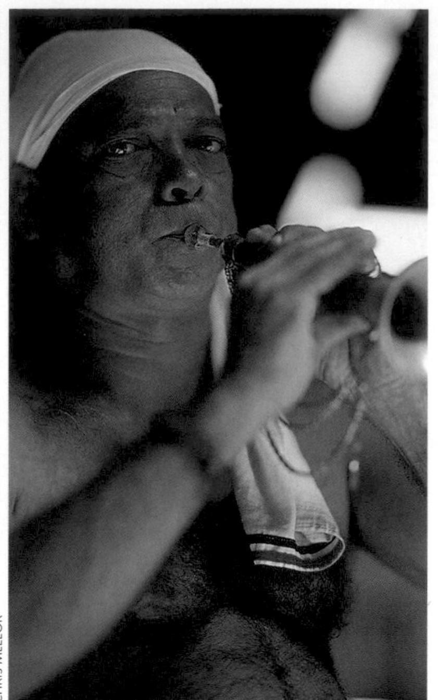
CHRIS MELLOR

Musician in the Temple of the Tooth, Kandy

ERIC L WHEATER

Dancer spins drums, Kandy

ERIC L WHEATER

Geta bera drummer, Kandy

ANDREW BURKE

Fire-eater, Kandy

Sri Lanka's Dances & Masks

There are many types of devil dance. One, the *sanni yakku*, is performed to exorcise the disease demon. The demon is represented by a range of characters including a pregnant woman and a mother. Other dances include the *kohomba kankariya*, which is performed to ensure prosperity, and the *bali*, which is performed for the benefit of heavenly beings.

Three beings must be propitiated in these ceremonies: demons, deities and semidemons. Before the dance begins, palm-leaf shrines dedicated to each of the beings are built outside the victim's house. The beings must be tempted out of these and into the arena. The dancers (all men) go through an extraordinarily athletic routine. Strips of palm leaves hang down from a red cloth tied around their heads; the white cloth wound tightly round their hips stays firm despite their gyrations. All the while bare-chested drummers beat out a frantic rhythm on the *yak bera* (a double-ended, cylindrical drum of the South). From time to time there is a break in the dancing while others perform mimes and magic. At the climax of their routine, the dancers put on masks representing the demons and explain who they are and why they've come. The demon that is considered to be causing the victim's distress or disease enters that person and the chief exorcist questions, exhorts and threatens the demon. He may even try to bribe it to make it leave.

Masks

There are three basic types of mask: *kolam*, *sanni* and *raksha*.

The *kolam* mask – literally a mask or form of disguise – is used in *kolam* masked drama in which all the characters wear masks. *Kolam* masks generally illustrate a set cast of characters, and although these masks are still made for dance performances, and some new characters are being introduced, they are not produced for tourist consumption.

The second type, *sanni*, is the devil-dancing mask that dancers wear in order to impersonate disease-causing demons and to thus exorcise them. The '18 disease' *sanni* mask depicts a demon figure, clutching one or more victims (often with another clenched in his teeth), flanked by 18 faces – each used to exorcise a different disease ranging from rheumatism, earache or boils to blindness or the 'morbid state of wind, bile and phlegm'. The whole grotesque ensemble is bordered by two cobras, with others sprouting from the demon's head.

Raksha masks are used in processions and festivals. There are about 25 varieties, including the common *naga raksha* (cobra) masks, in which a demonic face complete with protruding eyeballs, lolling tongue and pointed teeth is topped with a 'coiffure' of writhing cobras.

Legend has it that Sri Lanka was once ruled by a race called the Rakshasas, whose king was Rawana of the Ramayana story. The Rakshasas could assume the form of cobras to terrify and subjugate their enemies. Their victims, however, would sometimes plead for help from the *gurulu*, a bird that preys on snakes, and today the *gurulu raksha* is another frequently seen type of mask.

Most masks are made from a light balsa-type wood *(Strychnos nux-vomica)* called *kaduru*, which is smoke-dried before the mask is carved out of it. Yellow is applied as the base colour, with other colours being added as desired. The final stage of the process is the application of a mixture of resin powder and oil.

The best place to see *kolam* masks being made is Ambalangoda; there's even a museum here that explains how it all woks.

Mahayana Buddhism is followed in Japan, Korea, Vietnam and also among Chinese Buddhists. There are other, more culturally specific strains of Mahayana such as Tibetan Buddhism, which is also practised in Nepal. Sri Lankan monks later took Theravada Buddhism to Thailand, Myanmar (Burma), Laos, Cambodia and parts of south Vietnam. Over the centuries there has been a great deal of interaction between the various Buddhist schools. Senior Thai and Burmese *theras* have lived here to revive higher ordinations that have lapsed. The order of Buddhist nuns, the Bhikkuni, lapsed in Sri Lanka in the 11th century, and was re-established after a couple of false starts as recently as 1996.

The Buddha taught that suffering is an inescapable fact of life, tied up with the nature of consciousness, desire and attachment. Although there may be happiness in life this is mainly an illusion. Nothing – not even the human 'soul' – has an independent existence, and no-one escapes suffering as long as they are attached to the sensual aspects of life. Freedom from suffering comes from developing a higher consciousness (mostly through meditation and impeccably moral conduct). This is an evolutionary process through many states of spiritual development until the ultimate goal is reached – death, no further rebirths, and thus entry to nirvana.

The Buddha also taught that supreme enlightenment is the only reality in a world of unreality. All else is illusion and there is no unchanging soul that is reborn after life, but a consciousness that develops and evolves spiritually until it reaches the goal of nirvana or oneness with all. Central to the doctrine of rebirth is karma, the law of causation; each rebirth results from the actions one has committed in the previous life. Thus in Buddhism each person alone is responsible for his or her life. Gods such as those in the Hindu pantheon do exist, and in temples they're often shown listening to the Buddha's sermons, but the gods can't lead you to nirvana and they also grow old and, one day, die.

Modern Sri Lankan Buddhism Since the late 19th century an influential strand of 'militant' Buddhism has developed in Sri Lanka, centred on the belief that the Buddha – who visited Sri Lanka three times according to tradition – charged the Sinhalese people with the task of making the island a citadel of Buddhism in its purest form. This more campaigning, less tolerant style of Buddhism, perhaps taking its cue from the type of Christianity practised by the British colonial power, emerged under the inspiration of Anagarika Dharmapala. It sees threats to Sinhalese Buddhist culture in both European Christianity and Tamil Hinduism.

Sri Lankan Buddhism has become increasingly intertwined with politics, to the point where the clergy can exert great pressure on politicians by accusing them of failing to look after Buddhism. Some Buddhist monks are among the country's least tolerant people when it comes to compromise with the Tamils. Nor are all monks anything like as pure, virtuous and unworldly as you might imagine! On the other hand, many monks are genuinely dedicated to the personal and spiritual side of Buddhism and many of the people still practise the religion in a simple, gentle way. Besides the many festivals and the myriad ways that Buddhism permeates into people's daily lives, Buddhists still gather at temples on *poya* days to hear the ancient truths from the Sangha.

Books on Buddhism You've come to the right place – there's an almost endless supply of reading material on Buddhism available in Sri Lanka. Translating and interpreting the scriptures receives government support.

A Concise Encyclopaedia of Buddhism, by John Powers, attempts a nearly impossible comprehensiveness, and covers everything from Anuradhapura's Abhayagiri monastery to the Tibetan Lama Tupden Zopa.

The Footprint of the Buddha, by EFC Ludowyke, is a readable introduction to Buddhist practice and government in Sri Lanka.

Theravada Buddhism, by Richard Gombrich, has all the details on the context, history and practice of Buddhism in Sri Lanka. Other scholarly works written by Gombrich include *Buddhist Precept and Practice*, based on life in a village near Kandy, and *Buddhism Transformed*, which points out the links between Buddhism and Hinduism in Sri Lanka a little too comprehensively, so isn't sold in Sri Lanka.

What the Buddha Taught, by Rahula Walpola, spells out the basic doctrines clearly and precisely.

Hinduism

Tamil kings and their followers from South India brought Hinduism initially to northern Sri Lanka. Today there are significant Hindu communities in Colombo, Kandy and the tea plantation areas in the hill country, as well as in the North and the East.

Hinduism defies attempts to define it in any specific sense. Some argue that it's more an association of religions. It has no founder, central authority or hierarchy. The strictly orthodox maintain that only a person born in India of Hindu parents can truly claim to be Hindu, though converts are nearly always accepted at temples restricted to caste Hindus.

Hinduism often appears as a complex mix of beliefs and multiple gods. In theory it happily incorporates all forms of belief and worship. But for Hindus religious truth is ineffable; at its heart, Hinduism does not depend on the belief in the existence or otherwise of any individual or multiple gods. Essentially, all Hindus believe in Brahman, the One without a second, without attributes. Brahman is eternal, uncreated and infinite. The multitude of gods and goddesses are simply manifestations – knowable aspects of this formless phenomenon – and one may freely pick and choose among them.

Although beliefs and practices vary widely from region to region, there are several unifying factors. These include common beliefs in reincarnation, karma (conduct or action) and dharma (appropriate behaviour for one's station in life), and in the caste system.

Hindus believe earthly life is cyclical; you are born again and again (a process known as samsara), the quality of these rebirths being dependent upon your karma in previous lives. Living a dharmic life and fulfilling your duty enhances the chance of being born into a higher caste and better circumstances. Going the other way, rebirth may take animal form, but it's only as a human that you will gain sufficient self-knowledge to escape the cycle of reincarnation and achieve moksha (liberation).

For ordinary Hindus, fulfilling one's ritual and social duties is the main aim of worldly life. The Bhagavad Gita (a Hindu text, part of the Mahabharata) is clear about this; doing your duty is more important than asserting your individuality. That the householder and the renunciate may equally earn religious merit is a notion that was enshrined some 2000 years ago in the Brahmanic system. This kind of merit is only available to the upper three castes.

Hindu worship takes many forms, but have a particular connection to *darshan*, the act of being seen by the god present in a shrine. This simple act of seeing and being seen by it is enough; there's no set way to approach it, besides tipping the Brahmin to perform a *puja* or symbolic offering to the deity.

Gods & Goddesses The Hindu pantheon is prolific; some estimates put the number of deities at 330 million. Brahman is often described as having three facets, known as the Trimurti: Brahma, Vishnu and Shiva (also known as Mahesh). In many legends the male gods are powerful yet distant, and create or empower goddesses to use *shakti* or power to achieve their aims. Tamil Hindus usually revere Vishnu or Shiva (different castes often have a special relation with a particular god or one of his guises) but also pay respect to the many goddesses of the harvest, the arts, money and the home.

Brahma Regarded as an aloof figure, Brahma plays an active role only during the creation of the universe. The rest of the time he is in meditation, unlike the two other members of the Trimurti, Shiva and Vishnu. His consort is Sarasvati, goddess of learning, and his vehicle is a swan.

Vishnu The preserver or sustainer, Vishnu is associated with 'right action' and behaves as a lawful, devout Hindu. He is usually depicted with four arms, each respectively holding a lotus (whose petals are symbolic of the unfolding of the universe), a conch shell (as it can be blown like a trumpet it symbolises the cosmic vibration from which all existence emanates), a discus, and a mace (a reward for conquering Indra, the god of battle). His consort is Lakshmi, goddess of beauty and fortune. Vishnu has 22 incarnations, including Rama, Krishna and Narasimha. Krishna's dalliances with the *gopis* (milkmaids) and his love affair with Radha have inspired countless paintings and songs. He is depicted as blue in colour and usually carries a flute.

Shiva The destroyer, but without whom creation could not occur, Shiva is often symbolised by the lingam, a phallic symbol. With 1008 names, Shiva takes many forms, including Pashupati, champion of the animals, and Nataraja, lord of the *tandav* (dance), who paces out the creation and destruction of the cosmos.

Shiva is also depicted as lord of yoga; a third eye in his forehead symbolises wisdom. Sometimes he has snakes draped around his neck and is shown holding a trident (representative of the Trimurti) as a weapon while riding Nandi, his bull. Shiva's consort, Parvati, is capable of taking many forms.

Other Gods The elephant-headed Ganesh, chubby, wise and kind, is held in great affection. A son of Shiva, he is the lord of beginnings, remover of obstacles and patron of scribes (the broken tusk he holds is the very one he used to write down later sections of the Mahabharata).

Skanda (Kataragama), Ganesh's brother, has many aspects and names, including Murugan on occasion. He is associated with war (his colour is a brilliant red, and devotees offer crimson garlands when they visit his shrine) and disease. But he is also viewed as a protective deity by Buddhists, and Sinhalese generally associate him with the struggle in ancient times against South Indian Tamils. As the infant boy Ayyappan, this god is the focus of a reform movement active among Tamil men. Groups of men, mostly aged from 16 to 40, renounce alcohol, drugs and casual sex and make regular fasts for a year. They're recognisable by their black shirts and a black sarong trimmed with. Each looks out to see how his fellow devotees are behaving. Those who succeed can then make a pilgrimage to the holy mountain of Sabarimalai in Kerala, India. The movement is a growing force in Tamil Hinduism, often encouraged by wives and mothers who want the men in their lives to clean up their acts.

Hanuman, hero of the Ramayana and loyal ally of Rama, embodies bhakti, or devotion. Images of Rama and Sita are said to be emblazoned upon his heart. He is king of the monkeys, but is capable of taking on any form he chooses. It was Hanuman who discovered where the King of Lanka, Rawana, was hiding Sita. There is a cave at Ella that is claimed to be the site of her captivity.

Known as the 'black one', Kali is the most fearsome of the Hindu deities. She manifests Shiva's *shakti* (power) to destroy life. Kali is often depicted dancing on a corpse, garlanded with human heads. A particularly odd sect of ascetics known as Aghorins propitiate the goddess with mortifying acts of necromancy – it's supposed to be a short cut to ego death and a kind of enlightenment, but there's a high dropout rate into utter madness. You will occasionally come upon small Kali shrines in Sri Lanka's hill country.

Islam

Arab traders visiting Sri Lanka from the 8th century brought Islam to the island. Most of the 1.8 million Muslims here are Sunnis, although there are communities of Shiites who have more recently migrated from the Indian subcontinent. Sri Lankan Muslims see themselves as a community apart from the Sinhalese–Tamil conflict, though this kind of constructive neutrality hasn't always protected them. The community is divided by its origins; Indian Muslims see themselves as a separate community from Malay Muslims.

Islam was founded in present-day Saudi Arabia by the Prophet Mohammed in the 7th century. The Arabic term *islam* means to surrender: believers (Muslims) undertake to surrender to the will of God (Allah). The will of God is revealed in the poetic scriptures of the Quran (Arabic for reading or recitation), and it was to Mohammed that God revealed his will, through the angel Jibreel.

Islam is monotheistic – God is unique and has no equal or partner. Everything is believed to have been created by God and is deemed to have its own place and purpose in the universe. Only God is self-sufficient and unlimited. The purpose of all living things is submission to the divine will. Humankind's weakness is its pride and sense of independence. Although God never speaks to humanity directly, his word is conveyed through prophets (who are never themselves divine; Mohammed is the last prophet) who are charged with calling humanity back to God.

In the years after Mohammed's death a dispute over succession split the movement and the legacy today is the Sunnis and the Shiites. The Sunnis, the majority, emphasise the 'well-trodden' path or the orthodox way, interpreted by a number of different schools of Islamic law (eg, Hanifi, Sha'fi, Hambali). They look to tradition and the views of the majority of the community. Shiites believe that only imams (exemplary leaders) are able to reveal the hidden and true meaning of the Quran.

All Muslims share belief in the five pillars of Islam: the dual declaration of faith, 'there is no God but Allah; Mohammed is his prophet'; prayer (ideally five times a day and on one's own if one can't make it to a mosque); the zakat (tax), which today is usually a voluntary donation in the form of charity; fasting during the month of Ramadan; and the hajj (pilgrimage) to Mecca.

Christianity

Portuguese colonisers introduced Roman Catholicism to Sri Lanka in the 16th century, and the Catholic Church remains strong among the western coastal communities – imposing churches are prominent on the road north to Puttalam or south to Galle. The Dutch brought Protestantism and the Dutch Reformed Church, which has more of a presence in Colombo than elsewhere. Evidence of the British introduction of other denominations can be seen particularly in the hill country, where quaint stone churches dot the landscape. Protestant Christians form a small community of perhaps 400,000, but evangelist churches are very vigorous.

Facts for the Visitor

HIGHLIGHTS

Sri Lanka has so many highlights that it's almost unfair to single out a few options. For starters, Sri Lanka has seven World Heritage Sites: Galle, Kandy, Polonnaruwa, Sigiriya, Dambulla, Anuradhapura and Sinharaja Forest Reserve. If you're looking to sort out the best from the rest, consider checking out the following.

Beaches

For many visitors, there's one destination that looms large on any trip to Sri Lanka: the beach. Swaying coconut palms, glistening white sand, shimmering waters – it's the ultimate escape from bleak winters and drab cities. Hikkaduwa and Unawatuna have long, clean beaches lined with restaurants, and Mirissa is so laid-back and the water is so clear, you'll never want to leave. Or, if the security situation stays safe, you could head to the spotless sand of Nilaveli beach, a few kilometres north of Trincomalee. Others worth noting are Marawila and Bentota on the west coast, Tangalla and Kirinda in the South, and the up-and-coming (touch wood) Kalkudah on the east coast.

Hill Country

The hill country is a different world: tea plantations, colonial bungalows with fireplaces, crisp mountain air – all within hours of the tropical coast. There is plenty of potential in the hills for keen walkers, and there are tea factories to visit, while the must-do train rides will wind you through exquisite landscapes. Wander around for a full taste of its variety of cultures and landscapes: the deep valleys around Adam's Peak; the misty tea estates near Nuwara Eliya; the forested hills and brilliant green paddy fields of the Kandy area. For a highland retreat, choose the Knuckles Range or tiny Ella with stunning views to the plains.

Wildlife

Sri Lanka is blessed with an extraordinary wealth of fauna and flora. Visit Sinharaja

Safety in Sri Lanka

Many potential visitors have been scared away by the war in the North and East. Since negotiations began in February 2001, these areas have become accessible, but while you can travel by road, there are some very specific safety issues in this region – minefields and UXO (unexploded ordnance) being the most dangerous. Army camps in the North and East are heavily fortified (several old Dutch and Portuguese forts have been garrisoned by the army). High-security zones such as air bases are completely off limits. These are not places to wave around a camera. See the relevant chapters for more information.

So far, all reports are that in the North and East the army and the Liberation Tigers of Tamil Eelam (LTTE) cadres are treating foreigners with respect. Ethnic Sinhalese tourists have been almost universally welcomed on visits to Jaffna and other Tamil areas.

The war spawned other risks. Thousands of soldiers deserted during the long years of war, and some turned to armed banditry to survive. There have been some isolated but vicious attacks on foreigners by ex-soldiers. Illegal loggers have been stripping forests on the fringes of the conflict zone. Some of the national parks that appear on maps of these regions are potentially dangerous, should you stumble across an armed loggers camp. Before venturing into these areas, go armed with local knowledge and preferably with a local guide.

The government had tried to protect senior politicians from assassination by getting them to recruit dozens of private bodyguards. These armed henchmen soon became political tools, used to intimidate rivals. You're unlikely to meet them, but they're a scary bunch who consider themselves above the law. These goons, and the sons of politicians they're meant to protect, have been accused of several well-publicised bashings in posh Colombo nightclubs.

Over 400,000 tourists visit Sri Lanka each year, but as things can change quickly, you should check the latest situation with your embassy before you leave.

Forest Reserve to see a magnificent expanse of rainforest, or Yala West (Ruhuna) National Park to view elephants, sambar deer and, if you're lucky, leopards. Several parks in the North and East, such as Minneriya and Kaudulla, have become accessible, though facilities there are scarce. Lahugala National Park and Uda Walawe National Park attract large numbers of elephants, or you could take the easier (and cheaper) option and see them at the Pinnewala Elephant Orphanage. Birdwatchers won't need to step far from their hotel room to see birds, as the towns, reserves and tanks are home to dozens of species.

Festivals

Owing to the variety of religious faiths, Sri Lanka has frequent colourful and elaborate festivals. A highlight among these is the Kandy Esala Perahera, which is held in the full-moon month of Esala (July/August). This 10-day event builds up to a crescendo of dancing, drumming and parades of richly caparisoned elephants. At about the same time of year another elaborate festival is held at Kataragama in the South, where days of frenetic activity culminate in devotees walking across beds of glowing cinders. See Public Holidays & Special Events later in this chapter.

Ancient Cities

From a small temple hidden by lush vegetation to cities stretching for kilometres, the Cultural Triangle area, with its ancient cities, is rich with ruins waiting to be explored. Bicycle along the shady lanes of Polonnaruwa's ancient city – don't miss the reclining Buddha of Gal Vihara – or scramble up the Sigiriya rock fortress, past the saucy frescoes, to a superb view of the countryside. The cave temples of Dambulla are World Heritage–listed. Then there are the lesser known attractions such as Yapahuwa, Tantirimalai and the Buddha of Aukana.

Activities

Dust off your goggles and fins and save for a scuba diving course – you won't find the best coral in the world, but reefs and shipwrecks lie waiting for amateurs and the merely curious. Hikkaduwa and Tangalla are best for scuba diving, while at Unawatuna and Mirissa you can snorkel almost from your doorstep. Surfers will already know about famous Arugam Bay; when the surf bottoms out, head to Hikkaduwa. For hikers, there are plenty of walks in the pretty countryside around Ella. Most enjoy the superb views from World's End at Horton Plains. You shouldn't miss the sweaty slog up Adam's Peak – the dawn views alone make the venture worthwhile.

Shopping

Pad your wallet and get your elbows ready for a trolley-load of options: clothing, fabrics, painted masks, batik, tea, spices and gems, to name a few. You'll find fabrics, trash and flash clothing at Colombo's boutiques; Ratnapura is gem heaven (if you know your stuff); try Ambalangoda for masks; Jaffna specialises in products made from palmyra palm trees; and save your last rupees for handicrafts from the Kandy region.

SUGGESTED ITINERARIES

Time and money as well as your particular interests will obviously influence where you go and what you do. Because the country is not that big, it's easy to take in quite a wide variety of places and activities in a relatively short space of time, even if you're using public transport. You don't have to be on the move constantly to get the best from Sri Lanka; you can stay put just about anywhere and profitably explore the surrounding area, discovering little temples, villages and other delights that don't appear in any tourist literature or guidebook.

Sri Lanka can be divided into five zones: the west and south coasts; the hill country; the ancient cities; and the newly accessible regions of the North and East.

If you have just **one week** and you're travelling by public transport, it would be possible to take in a beach or two before jumping on the train to, say, Kandy in the hills (with maybe a day trip from there to Dambulla and Sigiriya). With a car you could head south and around the coast (taking in a few beaches) to Tissamaharama where you could visit Yala West (Ruhuna) National Park. Or you could head into the hills and the ancient city area.

In **two weeks** using public transport you could easily visit the hill country and the ancient cities or, alternatively, Kandy (with a day trip or two to the ancient cities), then down through Nuwara Eliya and Ella to, say,

Jewels of Lanka

This is our totally biased list of the places and experiences we most enjoyed, in order.

National Parks & Nature Reserves
Uda Walawe National Park, p 214-15
Sinharaja Forest Reserve, p 215-17
Yala West (Ruhuna) National Park, p 161-3
Kaudulla National Park, p 238

Beaches & Surfing
Mirissa, p 148-9
Tangalla, p 152-5
Arugam Bay, p 267-70
Kirinda, p 160-1
Nilaveli, p 262-4
Bentota, p 123-6

Hill Scenery
Ella, p 208-10
Adam's Peak, p 187-90
Horton Plains, p 200-3
Knuckles Range, p 187
Haputale, p 203-6

Cities & Towns
Kandy, p 168-80
Galle, p 135-41
Jaffna, p 272-9
Nuwara Eliya, p 194-200
Colombo, p 84-112

Places of Worship
Sri Dalada Maligawa, Kandy, p 171-2
Kelaniya Raja Maha Vihara, Colombo, p 94
Nallur Kandaswamy Kovil, Jaffna, p 275
Wolvendaal Church, Colombo, p 95
Wewurukannala Vihara, near Dikwella, p 151

Ancient Sites
Sigiriya, p 227-31
Polonnaruwa, p 231-7
Anuradhapura, p 241-9
Dambulla, p 225-7
Kataragama, p 163-5

Obscurities
Ritigala, p 239-40
British Garrison Cemetery, Kandy, p 173
Tantirimalai, p 249-50
Brief Garden, p 123-4
Jaffna's rural hinterland, p 279-83

Favourite Small Mercies
Fresh coconut milk on a hot day
The sound of drums at a temple ceremony
Buses with decent luggage racks
Eating *rotty* hot from the oven
The sight of water birds and blue-winged kingfishers in paddy fields

Tangalla or Mirissa on the coast, then back up the coast to Colombo. Two weeks with a car and driver will allow you to easily accomplish a circuit of the west and south coasts, the hill country and the ancient cities before heading back to Colombo.

If you have **three weeks** or more, you can afford to spend more time at the places already mentioned as well as taking in more on the way. Or you could head east to Arugam Bay and Kalkudah Bay or northeast to the beaches near Trincomalee. People with a special interest can travel to Jaffna by bus, car or plane from Colombo.

PLANNING

When to Go

Climatically, the driest and best seasons are from December to March on the west and south coasts and in the hill country, and from April to September for the ancient cities area and the east coast. December to March is the time when most foreign tourists come, the majority of them escaping the European winter. Out-of-season travel has its advantages – not only do the crowds go away but many air fares and accommodation prices drop right down. Nor does it rain *all* the time during the low season. July/August is the time of the Kandy Esala Perahera, the 10-day festival honouring the sacred tooth relic, and the Kataragama Festival in the south.

Maps

One of the best foreign-produced maps is the Nelles Verlag 1:450,000 (1cm = 4.5km) *Sri Lanka,* which also has maps of Colombo, Anuradhapura, Kandy and Galle. Berndston & Berndston *Sri Lanka Road Map* is excellent for detail on routes and sites. It seems more widely available in Europe than in Australia. Globetrotter's 1:600,000 (1cm = 6km) *Sri Lanka* has a decent colour country map and a handful of simplified town maps.

The Sri Lankan Survey Department's *Road Map of Sri Lanka* at 1:500,000 (1cm = 5km) is an excellent overall map and is clear to read; it also produces a *Road Atlas of Sri Lanka* at the same scale but with 17 town maps at the back. The Survey Department has 82 sheets at 1:50,000 covering the island in British ordnance survey style. In Colombo the **Survey Department Map Sales Centre** *(☎ 011-243 5328; 62 Chatham St, Fort)* has a useful selection, including the best Colombo street atlas, the *A to Z Colombo* (Rs 150), also available at major bookstores. For the full collection take your passport along with you to the map sales office at the **Surveyor General's Office** *(☎ 011-258 5111; Kirula Rd, Narahenpita)*. Both are open 9am to 4pm weekdays, not including government holidays.

What to Bring

If you are going to spend all your time on the beach, then obviously you can travel very lightly. Clothes (including popular brand names) can be readily bought in Colombo, Galle and Kandy, though tall people may struggle to find their size. In the main beach resorts there are many tailor shops and places selling Western-style beach wear. But, as one jaded shopper put it, you'd most likely wear your purchases again only on your next holiday.

It's not really necessary to bring a sleeping bag or sleeping sheet unless you think you'll be camping or really roughing it.

RESPONSIBLE TOURISM

You can minimise your impact on the environment by following a few pointers.

- Plastic bags are a real curse in Sri Lanka, so it helps a little if you decline plastic bags (which are used routinely) while shopping. You'll go through many plastic bottles of drinking water – try to dispose of them responsibly.
- If you're out diving or snorkelling, don't break coral or brush against it. Coral is basically a colony of living organisms and contact can kill them. All of Sri Lanka's five species of turtle are endangered. There's still a local trade in turtle shells and turtle eggs – spend your money elsewhere. For more on Sri Lanka's turtles, read the boxed text 'Turtle Watch' in The South chapter.
- If you are planning to hike in the hills, see the boxed text 'Responsible Hiking' in The Hill Country chapter for a few pointers on minimal-impact hiking.

Giving money, sweets, pens etc to children encourages begging. A donation to a recognised project – a health centre or school – is more constructive.

Unfortunately Sri Lanka has been attracting paedophiles for years. Local laws forbid relations with anyone aged under 18, punishable by a maximum of 20 years in jail. In recent years, Sri Lankan and foreign authorities have been keener to do something about it, and foreigners have been deported and in some cases prosecuted in Sri Lanka. Many countries have laws to prosecute paedophiles in their home country. If you're certain that child sex offences are being committed by a foreigner and you know their name and nationality, contact the police or their embassy. You can also contact an organisation such as **End Child Prostitution and Trafficking** *(ECPAT; w www.ecpat.org)*.

TOURIST OFFICES

Local Tourist Offices

The Colombo main office of the **Ceylon Tourist Board** *(☎ 01-437571; e tourinfo@sri.lanka.net; 80 Galle Rd, Kollupitiya, Colombo; open 9am-4.45pm Mon-Fri, 9am-12.30pm Sat)* is near the Lanka Oberoi Hotel. There is also an office in Kandy *(☎ 081-222 2661)* as well as a 24-hour **information office** *(☎ 011-225 2411; Katunayake)* at the airport. Staff can help with hotel bookings as well as answer queries and hand out booklets and leaflets. In Colombo the **JF Tours** office at Fort train station is very helpful.

The tourist board's main website is at w www.srilankatourism.org. Among their publications provided by offices within and outside Sri Lanka is an *Accommodation Guide*, updated every six months, with fairly thorough listings. *Explore Sri Lanka* has feature articles, and information on things to see and places to stay, shop and eat.

Tourist Offices Abroad

Ceylon Tourist Board offices located abroad include:

Australia (☎ 02-6230 6002, fax 6230 6066) 29 Lonsdale St, Braddon, Canberra, ACT 2612

Understanding Place Names

Sri Lanka's often fearsome-looking place names become much simpler with a little analysis. *Pura* or *puram* simply means town – as in Ratnapura (town of gems) or Anuradhapura. Similarly, *nuwara* means city and *gama* means village. Other common words that are incorporated in place names include *gala* or *giri* (rock or hill), *kanda* (mountain), *ganga* (river), *oya* (large stream), *ela* (stream), *tara* or *tota* (ford or port), *pitiya* (park), *watte* (garden), *kele* or *kelle* (jungle), *wela* (field), *deniya* (vegetable garden), *gaha* (tree), *arama* (park or monastery) and *duwa* (island).

Not surprisingly, many towns are named after the great tanks (artificial lakes developed for irrigation purposes in the dry regions) – *wewa* or *kulam*. The same word can appear in Sinhala, Sanskrit, Pali and Tamil! Finally *maha* means great. Put it all together and even a polysyllabic tongue-stretcher like Tissamaharama makes sense – it's simply '(King) Tissa's great park'.

France (☎ 01-42 60 49 99, ⓔ ctbparis@compuserve.com) 19 Rue du Quatre Septembre, 75002 Paris

Germany (☎ 069-287734, ⓔ ctbfra@t-online.de) Allerheiligentor 2-4, D-60311 Frankfurt am Main

Japan (☎ 03-3289 0771, ⓔ ctb-toky@zaf.att.ne.jp) Dowa Bldg, 7-2-22, Ginza, Chuo-ku, Tokyo

UK (☎ 020-7930 2627, ⓔ srilankatourism@aol.com) 26-27, Clareville House, Oxendon St, London SW1Y 4EL

USA (☎ 732-516 9800, ⓔ ctbusa@anlusa.com) 111 Wood Avenue South, Iselin, New Jersey 08830

VISAS & DOCUMENTS

Passport

You must have a passport with you all the time; it is the most basic travel document. Ensure that it will be valid for the entire period you intend to remain overseas.

Visas

Dozens of nationalities, including Australians, New Zealanders, North Americans and virtually all Europeans, receive a tourist visa upon entry valid for 30 days. It is sometimes possible to obtain a visa for longer than 30 days in your home country; this is more often the case at Sri Lanka's bigger overseas missions, in London and Washington for example. The latest regulations are given at ⓦ www.immigration.gov.lk.

Visa Extensions Extensions can be made at the **Department of Immigration** *(☎ 011-250 3629; 23 Station Rd; open 9am-4.30pm Mon-Fri)*, near Majestic City shopping centre in Bambalapitiya, Colombo. The last payments are received at 3.30pm. The department sets the cost in US dollars, but you pay in rupees. A visa extension gives you a full three months in the country and you can apply for your extension almost as soon as you arrive (your 30-day visa given upon entry is included in the three months, or 90 days). A further three-month extension is possible, but you must again pay the fee based on your nationality plus another Rs 10,000. Extensions beyond this are at the discretion of the department, and incur a Rs 15,000 fee plus whichever national fee applies.

The following fees apply for the first 90-day visa:

country of origin	cost US$
Australia	30
Canada	50
France	26
Germany	26.80
Italy	35
Netherlands	49
New Zealand	34.50
Switzerland	27.20
UK	54
USA	190

The whole process takes about an hour. First, go to the 1st-floor office and pick up a visa extension application form from the person sitting closest to the door. You then work your way along the counter, through six or seven stages of stamps and receipts, until you reach the end. Then you wait 30 minutes or so, while your passport works its way back down the counter and is returned to you.

You will need your passport, an onward ticket and either a credit card or foreign exchange receipts.

Visas for Onward Travel The cost of a six-month tourist visa to India depends on your nationality, and you'll need to supply two photographs. It takes at least five working days to process a tourist visa, but only one day if you are a foreign resident in Sri Lanka.

The **High Commission of India in Colombo** *(☎ 011-242 1605; Ⓦ www.indiahcsl.org; 36-38 Galle Rd, Kollupitiya; open Mon-Fri, not including Indian holidays)* is where tourist visa forms can be submitted between 9.30am and 12.30pm. Expect long queues.

The **Assistant High Commission of India** *(☎ 081-222 4563; Ⓔ ahciknd@mailandnews.com; Box 47, 31 Rajapihilla Mawatha, Kandy; visa applications 8.30am to 10.30am, Mon-Fri, not including Indian holidays)* is a good alternative to queuing in Colombo because it's not as busy.

Travel Insurance

A travel insurance policy to cover theft, loss and medical problems is a good idea. The policies with higher medical expense options are chiefly for countries such as the USA which have extremely high medical costs. There is a wide variety of policies available, so make sure you check the small print.

Some policies specifically exclude 'dangerous activities', which can include scuba diving, motorcycling and even trekking. A locally acquired motorcycle licence is not valid under some policies, so again check the fine print carefully.

You may prefer a policy that pays doctors or hospitals directly, rather than you having to pay on the spot and claim later. Check that the policy covers ambulances and an emergency flight home.

Driving Licence & Permits

An International Driving Permit can be used to roam Sri Lanka's roads, but it is valid for only three months. You need to get it endorsed by the **Automobile Association of Ceylon** *(☎ 011-242 1528-9; 40 Sir Macan Markar Mawatha, Galle Face, Kollupitiya)*, next to the Holiday Inn. If you hire a car the rental company may get the endorsement for you. After three months, turn up at the **Department of Motor Traffic** *(☎ 011-269 4331; Elvitigala Mawatha, Narahenpita)*. You need to bring your driving licence and two photos.

Travel Discounts

Bad news folks: an International Student ID Card won't get you much. You can't get a discount on the pricey Cultural Triangle round ticket but you can sometimes get half-price individual site tickets if you sweet talk the ticket seller. It's the same sad story for seniors, too.

Copies

All important documents (passport data page and visa page, credit cards, travel-insurance policy, air, bus and train tickets, driving licence etc) should be photocopied before you leave home. Leave one copy with someone at home and keep another with you, separate from the originals. You can store the digital images of documents at Ⓦ www.ekno.com.

EMBASSIES & CONSULATES

Sri Lankan Embassies & Consulates

There is a full list of Sri Lankan embassies and consulates at Ⓦ www.formin.gov.lk/ourmission/index.html

Australia (☎ 02-6239 7041, Ⓦ srilanka-highcommission.com) 35 Empire Circuit, Forrest, Canberra, ACT 2603
Belgium (☎ 2-344 5394, Ⓔ sri.lanka@euronet.be) 27 Rue Jules Lejeune, 1050, Brussels
Canada (☎ 613-233 8449, Ⓦ srilankahcottawa.org) Suite 1204, 333 Laurier Ave West, Ottawa, Ontario KIP 1C1
France (☎ 01 55 73 31 31, Ⓔ sl.france@wanadoo.fr) 16 Rue Spontine, 75016, Paris
Germany (☎ 030-80 90 97 49, Ⓦ www.srilanka-botschaft.de) Niklasstrasse 19, 14163 Berlin
Italy (☎ 06-855 4560, Ⓔ slembassy@tiscali.it) Via Adige No 2, 00198 Rome
Japan (☎ 03-3440 6911, Ⓔ lankaemb@mba.sphere.ne.jp) 2-1-54 Takanawa, Minato-ku, Tokyo 108 0074
Netherlands (☎ 070-365 5910, Ⓦ www.srilankanembassynl.org) Jacob de Graefflaan 2, 2517, JM, The Hague
South Africa (☎ 12-460 7702, Ⓦ www.srilanka.co.za) 410 Alexander St, Brooklyn, Pretoria 0181
UK (☎ 020-7262 1841, Ⓦ www.slhclondon.org) 13 Hyde Park Gardens, London W2 2LU
USA (☎ 202-483 4026, Ⓦ www.slembassyusa.org) 2148 Wyoming Ave NW, Washington DC 20008

Embassies & Consulates in Sri Lanka

It's important to realise the limits to what your embassy can do if you're in trouble. Generally speaking, their hands are tied if you've broken Sri Lankan law. In real emergencies you might get some assistance, but only if other channels have been exhausted. Embassies can recommend hospitals and dentists in a crisis, but expect you to have insurance to pay for it all.

If calling from outside Colombo, you will need to add the area code 011 to the following telephone numbers:

Australia (☎ 698767, W www.srilanka.embassy.gov.au) 3 Cambridge Place, Cinnamon Gardens, Colombo
Bangladesh (☎ 681310, fax 681309) 47/1 Sir Ernest de Silva Mawatha, Cinnamon Gardens, Colombo
Belgium (☎ 504351, e consul.belgium@unilink.lk) Police Park Terrace 3/1, Havelock Town, Colombo
Canada (☎ 695841, e clmbo@dfait-maeci.gc.ca) 6 Gregory's Rd, Cinnamon Gardens, Colombo
France (☎ 698815, W www.ambafrance.lk) 89 Rosmead Place, Cinnamon Gardens, Colombo
Germany (☎ 580431, W www.germanembassy.lk) 40 Alfred House Ave, Kollupitiya, Colombo
India (☎ 421605, W www.indiahcsl.org) 36-38 Galle Rd, Kollupitiya, Colombo
Italy (☎ 588388, W www.italianembassy.lk) 55 Jawatta Rd, Havelock Town, Colombo
Japan (☎ 693831, W www.lk.emb-japan.go.jp) 20 Gregory's Rd, Cinnamon Gardens, Colombo
Maldives (☎ 586762, e maldhc@eureka.lk) 23 Kaviratne Pl, Kirillapone, Colombo
Netherlands (☎ 596914, e nethemb@sri.lanka.net) 25 Torrington Ave, Cinnamon Gardens, Colombo
Sweden (☎ 795400, e ambassaden.colombo@sida.se) 49 Bullers Lane, Cinnamon Gardens, Colombo
UK (☎ 437336-43, W www.britishhighcommission.gov.uk/srilanka) 190 Galle Rd, Kollupitiya, Colombo
USA (☎ 448007) 210 Galle Rd, Kollupitiya, Colombo

CUSTOMS

You may bring 1.5L of spirits, two bottles of wine, 200 cigarettes or 250g of tobacco, small quantities of perfume and travel souvenirs (not exceeding US$250 in value) into the country. You may take out of the country anything you declared upon entering. Up to 3kg of tea may be exported duty free. For more details, check the customs department website at W www.customs.gov.lk.

To export an antique (any article older than 50 years) you need an exemption permit from the Commissioner of Archaeology. It is reported to be difficult dealing with all the red tape to get this permit. When expatriates pack up to leave, they've had trouble even for items they brought into the country but didn't keep the receipts for. If you're moving house, officials will come to do an inspection. Short-term visitors must go to the **Department of Archaeology** *(☎ 011-269 5255; e arch@diamondlanka.net; National Museum, Sir Marcus Fernando Mawatha, Colombo)*. Inspections and the issuing of permits are done on Wednesdays only!

MONEY

Currency

The Sri Lankan currency is the rupee (Rs), divided into 100 cents. There are coins in denominations of five, 10, 25 and 50 cents and one, two, five and 10 rupees. Notes come in denominations of 10, 20, 50, 100, 200, 500 and 1000 rupees. Break down larger notes (Rs 500 or Rs 1000) when you change money as most vendors never seem to have change. Exceptionally dirty or torn notes might not be accepted, except at a bank.

Exchange Rates

For up-to-the-minute exchange rates, check out W www.xe.com. Exchange rates at publication were:

country	unit		rupees
Australia	A$1	=	Rs 63.3
Canada	C$1	=	Rs 71.0
euro zone	€1	=	Rs 115.6
India	Rs10	=	Rs 20.7
Japan	¥100	=	Rs 82.4
Maldives	Rf1	=	Rs 7.7
New Zealand	NZ$1	=	Rs 56.2
UK	UK£1	=	Rs 160.7
USA	US$1	=	Rs 97.1

Exchanging Money

Cash Any bank or exchange bureau will change major currencies in cash, including US dollars, euros and pounds sterling. Moneychangers can be found in Colombo and the major cities, plus tourist centres such as Hikkaduwa, among other places. They generally don't charge commission and their rates are usually competitive. Change rupees back into hard currency before you leave the country for the best rates.

Travellers Cheques Fewer people use travellers cheques these days, but major banks still change them – Thomas Cook, Visa and American Express (AmEx) are the most widely accepted. Expect a smallish transaction fee of around Rs 150. Banks in major cities and tourist areas sometimes have special counters for foreign exchange.

ATMs Commercial Bank has a wide network of ATMs accepting international Visa, MasterCard and Cirrus/Maestro cards. Other options include Seylan Bank, Sampath Bank, Union Bank and HSBC. ATMs have spread to all of the cities and major regional centres, though you can't rely on the network paying up every single time.

Credit Cards MasterCard and Visa are the most commonly accepted cards. Other major cards such as AmEx and Diners Club are also accepted.

International Transfers Telegraphic transfer using a major bank or agency with branches worldwide such as Standard Chartered Grindlays or Thomas Cook is, all things being equal, efficient and fast. Western Union has offices nationwide. Ask ahead about all the identification required before turning up to collect.

Security

Sri Lanka is fairly safe but you still need to take some precautions. The best place for your travellers cheques, spare cash, air ticket and passport is next to your skin, in something like a moneybelt. Bum bags defeat their purpose by advertising where your money is kept. Having US$200 in cash stashed separately from your moneybelt or wallet covers most emergencies.

Costs

Sri Lanka is not the cheapest budget destination around, but costs are still reasonable – more comparable to Southeast Asia than India. Gourmands with a higher budget will appreciate that dinner at the country's best restaurants costs around US$20 per person. Budget double rooms with bathroom, mosquito net and fan cost about Rs 400 to 800; mid-range accommodation starts at Rs 1000 to 1500.

The cost of accommodation in the touristy beach areas drops considerably out of season. Expect to pay triple the usual accommodation price in Kandy during the *perahera* and in Nuwara Eliya during the April high season. Public transport is extremely cheap, averaging Rs 2.50 per kilometre by train or bus (trains are slightly cheaper than air-con intercity express buses but more expensive than CTB buses). Hiring a car (or van) and driver for a day costs about Rs 2500. Local food is reasonably priced, though about three times more expensive in guesthouses than in local restaurants: around Rs 150 to 350 at a guesthouse, or as little as Rs 70 at a local 'hotel'. Entry fees to national parks plus 4WD hire and a zillion little extras adds up to US$16 to US$50 a day; the major ancient city sites such as Anuradhapura, Sigiriya and Polonnaruwa cost US$12 to US$15 each a day.

Sri Lanka is no exception to the worldwide phenomenon of locals trying to overcharge tourists for anything from a bus fare to a gemstone necklace. There's also an *official* policy of charging foreigners much higher prices. Government departments continue to arbitrarily ramp up entry fees for foreigners, leading to disparities such as Rs 25 for locals versus Rs 575 for foreigners at Kandy's Udawattakelle Sanctuary. Of course most foreigners can easily afford these prices, but it seems a little unfair that budget travellers find they can't afford to visit more than one or two national parks, while affluent Sri Lankans pay a pittance.

Tipping & Bargaining

Although a 10% service charge is added to food and accommodation bills, this usually goes straight to the owner rather than the worker. So tipping is a customary way of showing your appreciation for services rendered. Drivers expect a tip, as do people who 'guide' you through a site. A rule of thumb is to tip 10% of the total amount due. If there's no money involved use your other thumb for this rule: Rs 10 for the person who minds your shoes at temples, and Rs 20 for a hotel porter.

Unless you are shopping at a fixed price store, you should bargain. Before you hit the open markets, peruse the prices in a fixed price store for an idea of what to pay. Generally, if someone quotes you a price, halve it. The seller will come down about halfway to your price, and the last price will be a little higher than halfway.

Taxes

A 10% service charge is applied to food and accommodation. Four- and five-star hotels and restaurants attract a further 10%. There is also a VAT (Value Added Tax) of 10% which generally applies only to top-end places and some upper-mid-range places. These taxes are included in the prices in this book; they are not refundable.

POST & COMMUNICATIONS

Post

It costs Rs 4.50 to post a letter locally and Rs 20.50 to send a parcel locally up to 1kg. Letters less than 10g sent by airmail to the UK, continental Europe or Australia cost Rs 26. The fee rises by Rs 10 for every additional 10g. Airmail letters up to 10g to North America cost Rs 28, plus Rs 15 for every additional 10g. Postcards to these destinations cost Rs 17. Private agencies as well as post offices sell stamps. To get up-to-date information on postal rates check out ⓦ www.lanka.net/slpost.

Ordinary airmail parcels sent from Sri Lanka can take longer than expected, eg, up to three weeks to Australia. If you have something valuable to send home, it may be wiser to use a courier service (see Post under Information in the Colombo chapter for details).

Post offices in larger centres have poste restante, and will generally keep your mail for two months. AmEx also has a mail holding service for its clients (see Post under Information in the Colombo chapter for contact details). Fewer people use poste restante these days; email has more or less replaced it.

Telephone

Local calls are timed, and cost about Rs 25 for two minutes, depending on the distance. To call Sri Lanka from abroad, dial the country code (☎ 94), and omit the 0 at the start of the local area code.

There are no national emergency phone numbers. Details of emergency numbers are presented under selected destinations throughout this book.

International calls can be made from thousands of communications bureaus and booths; many offices also have faxes and Internet access. The cheapest option is the card-operated International Direct Dialling (IDD) telephones, of which there are many in Colombo.

Many villages use what's called a wireless local loop network. This involves having a radio transmitter connected to a landline allowing a number of subscribers on a 'loop' to use telephones. Besides mobile phones and wireless local loop networks, Sri Lanka also has a dying breed of private pay phone operators. Cards are sold at small shops, usually displaying signs indicating which cards they sell. Each card is specific to that company phone booth.

Telephone Codes All regions have a three-digit area code. In addition, companies operating wireless loop systems also have three-digit prefixes. Calls to these phones cost about the same as to a standard telephone. Mobile phone companies also have separate prefix codes.

company	access code
Lanka Bell	☎ 075
Suntel	☎ 074
SLT (WLL)	☎ 070
Celltel	☎ 072
Mobitel	☎ 071
Dialog GSM	☎ 0777
Hutchison	☎ 078

Mobile Phones

There are four main network operators. Mobile (cell) phones are spreading like a virus and coverage is extending beyond the major cities and road corridors into regional areas. Phone rental costs around Rs 800 per month, and monthly bills might average Rs 2000. GSM phones from Europe, the Middle East and Australasia can be used in Sri Lanka.

Sri Lanka's main mobile-phone companies, roughly in order of size, are **Mobitel** (ⓦ *www.mobitellanka.com*), **Dialog GSM** (ⓦ *www.dialog.lk*), **Celltel** (ⓦ *www.celltelnet.lk*) and **Hutchison Telecom** (ⓦ *www.hutchison.lk*).

Email & Internet Access

You shouldn't have trouble finding Internet facilities in the major tourist towns – even most towns that are off the beaten track have access. Internet access in Colombo is cheap (Rs 4 per minute); elsewhere you can find places that charge Rs 4 per minute, but more often than not you'll have to fork out Rs 7 to 12.

Telephone Number Changes

Just before this book went to the printer, the **Telephone Regulatory Commission of Sri Lanka** *(TRCSL; W www.trc.gov.lk)* announced it planned to change every phone number in the country. Once we'd recovered from this blow and stopped crying, we did some research and found some details. The following tables list the structures of the old telephone numbers and the new numbers. An 'x' indicates each digit in the phone numbers.

Area code changes

location	old area code	new area code
Colombo	☎ 01	☎ 011
Galle	☎ 09	☎ 091
Kandy	☎ 08	☎ 081
SriLankan Airlines	☎ 073	☎ 019 73

Phone number changes

area code	old number	new number
☎ 011	☎ xx xxxx	☎ 2xx xxxx
☎ 042	☎ 83xxx	☎ 238 3xxx
☎ 043	☎ 84xxx	☎ 248 4xxx
☎ 060	☎ xx xxxx	☎ 2xx xxxx
☎ 081	☎ xx xxxx	☎ 2xx xxxx
all other codes	☎ xxxxx	☎ 22x xxxx

Note that the phone numbers provided in this book are based on the *new* numbers whenever these were brought to our attention. For mobile-phone numbers, it is expected that numbers with a 0777 prefix will remain unchanged, and those with either a 071 or 072 prefix will have a '2' added to the front of the phone number. It is not yet known how numbers with a 070, 074, 075 or 078 prefix will be affected.

For a variety of reasons, plans go astray (perhaps damage caused by the massive floods in southern and southwestern Sri Lanka during May 2003 for example), and should the proposed changes not be implemented by the time you use this book, take heart. Convert the new number (as provided in this book) to the old number using the table above (in reverse). If this doesn't work, every time you call an old number there will be a recording telling you the new number. You can also try directory assistance on ☎ 161, or operator-assisted calls on ☎ 101. Basically the changes expand all phone numbers to 10 digits, including a three-digit area code or a three-digit mobile-phone company prefix. All changes will hopefully be detailed on the TRCSL website.

Fungus-resistant floppy disks are needed in Sri Lanka's hot, damp climate.

INTERNET RESOURCES

Since the World Wide Web grew out of the old US military Arpanet, it has become a rich resource for travellers. You can research your trip, hunt down bargain air fares, book hotels, check weather conditions or chat with locals and other travellers about the best places to visit (or avoid!).

A good place to start your explorations is the Lonely Planet website (W www.lonelyplanet.com). Here you'll find everything from the Thorn Tree bulletin board, where you can ask questions before you go and dispense advice when you get back, to the subwwway section, which links you to the most useful travel resources elsewhere on the Web. Other good websites to surf include

Sri Lanka Web Server (W www.lanka.net) This has lots of links to newspaper and magazine websites.

Sri Lanka Tourist Board (W www.srilankatourism.org) The official tourism site, it has tons of information. It's a good starting point.

Daily News (W www.dailynews.lk) The English-language newspaper covers, no surprises here, the daily news, but it also has links to other sites (including sites dedicated to marriage proposals).

InfoLanka (W www.infolanka.com) InfoLanka has links to food, chat lines, news, organisations, nature, entertainment and more.

Art Sri Lanka (W www.artsrilanka.org) A gateway to Sri Lankan high culture, this site covers art history, contemporary art and religious art from various traditions.

Crazy Lanka (W www.crazylanka.com) It's a cheerfully silly website with lots of parodies of current news events. There are lots of in-jokes but some amusing gems nonetheless.

Official Website of the Government of Sri Lanka (W www.priu.gov.lk) Sober and clearly designed with bureaucratic 'flair', it has links to the major government departments and succinct feature articles.

TamilNet (W www.tamilnet.com) It describes itself as 'reporting to the world on Tamil affairs'. It has news on the North and East, feature articles and a good search engine.

Peace Process of Sri Lanka (W www.peaceinsrilanka.org) The official website of the government and the other parties involved, with details on the cease-fire and reconstruction efforts in the North and East.

BOOKS

Locally published books are cheap, but the range is generally limited to nonfiction – there seems no end to the list of tomes on Buddhism (see Religion in the Facts about Sri Lanka chapter for a selection). Imported books are relatively expensive, although they seem to disappear off the shelves quickly. Colombo has good bookshops; Kandy has a more limited range. In regional centres and beach resorts you might find a small selection of classics and tourist-targeted publications, and maybe second-hand bookshops with potboilers in half a dozen European languages.

Most books are published in different editions by different publishers in different countries. As a result, a book might be a hardcover rarity in one country but readily available in paperback in another. Your local bookshop or library can advise you on the availability of the following books.

Lonely Planet

Read This First: Asia & India is essential reading for those tackling Sri Lanka and Asia for the first time. *Travel with Children,* by Cathy Lanigan, contains a chapter on travelling in Sri Lanka as well as plenty of useful tips. Lonely Planet also has a *Sri Lanka phrasebook* as well as a guide to the *Maldives,* which many travellers include on their trip to this region. For those continuing on to India, Lonely Planet has a series of guides, including *Goa, South India, North India* and *India,* and city guides for *Mumbai* and *New Delhi*. Vijitha Yapa bookstores sell Lonely Planet titles.

Guidebooks

The Ministry of Cultural Affairs has put out a series of books on ancient cities and important sites, including *Anuradhapura, Kandy, Nalanda, Polonnaruwa* and *Sigiriya*. The following guides may also prove useful.

A Guide to the Waterfalls of Sri Lanka, by Eberhard Kautzsh, is the first and most comprehensive guide to the island's myriad tumbling cascades.

Trekkers' Guide to Sri Lanka, by Joanne Leestemaker et al, is for walkers.

Sri Lanka by Rail, by Royston Ellis, is a practical and interesting guide for train buffs, and will help to arrange a trip around Sri Lanka.

How to See Ceylon, by Bella Sidney Woolf, is a reprint edition of a 1922 guidebook by Virginia Woolf's sister-in-law. It's an absorbing read, with some odd travel tips ('A topee should always be worn until 4pm or 4.30pm' and 'Anuradhapura: ruins of an ancient city. Snipe and teal shooting').

Seeing Ceylon, by the Burgher writer RL Brohier, is a wonderfully detailed account of the author's travels as a surveyor around the 1930s. This book deals with the ancient cities and the rural south, while a companion book *Discovering Ceylon* covers nearly everywhere else.

History & Politics

There's plenty of material for sale on history and politics, though some of the locally published material falls on one or other side of the ethnic divide in its coverage of post-independence history.

An Historical Relation of Ceylon was written by Robert Knox, an Englishman captured near Trincomalee in 1659 and held captive by the king of Kandy for nearly 20 years. Despite his captive status he had considerable freedom to wander around the kingdom and observe its operation. After he escaped to a Dutch fort in 1679 and returned to England, his description of the kingdom of Kandy became a bestseller. It's equally readable today and is far and away the best book on this period of Sri Lankan history. It is usually sold in a two-volume hardback set.

A History of Sri Lanka, by Dr KM de Silva, is a monumental tome on Sri Lankan history up to modern times. Until its publication there had been something of a gap in books covering the country's post-independence history.

The Story of Ceylon and *The Modern History of Ceylon,* by EFC Ludowyke, provide good introductions to Sri Lankan history. Both were published in the 1960s.

The Prehistory of Sri Lanka Parts 1 & 2, by SU Deraniyagala, is the most authoritative work, though not exactly a light read.

Only Man Is Vile: The Tragedy of Sri Lanka, by William McGowan, is an excellent account of the modern ethnic troubles, mixing travelogue, history and reportage.

For a Sovereign State: A True Story of Sri Lanka's Separatist War, by Malinga H Gunaratne, is another attempt to make sense of the conflict.

Sri Lanka – A Lost Revolution? subtitled 'The inside story of the JVP' is by antiterrorism expert Rohan Gunaratna. The chronology of the two JVP (People's Liberation Army) uprisings can be hard to follow, but it delves deep into the hearts and strategies of these ultra-radicals.

The Will to Freedom, by Adele Balasingham, is the autobiography of the Australian wife of LTTE senior ideologue Anton Balasingham. It contains moving accounts of life and war with the LTTE, but in some ways is just as interesting for what it omits: the assassination of Rajiv Gandhi, for example. Nevertheless she has a remarkable perspective and story to tell.

Flora & Fauna

Sri Lanka's natural glories are well covered by locally and internationally published books. Many are glossy and pricey, but there's also plenty of high-quality, cheaper, locally produced material. For details of books on birds, see the boxed text 'Birds of Sri Lanka' in The Hill Country chapter.

A Field Guide to the Trees & Shrubs of Sri Lanka, by Mark S Ashton et al, is a detailed, well-illustrated hardback on Sri Lanka's flora.

Common Reef Fishes of Sri Lanka, by Dr Charles Anderson, is another well-illustrated guide that will be of interest to divers and snorkellers.

Field Guide to the Mammals of the Indian Subcontinent: Where to Watch Mammals in India, Nepal, Bhutan, Bangladesh, Sri Lanka and Pakistan, by KK Gurung & Raj Singh, has a small but useful section on Sri Lanka.

Fiction

There is a valuable and growing library by expat and local Sri Lankan writers.

Running in the Family, by Michael Ondaatje, is the Canadian writer's humorous account of returning to Sri Lanka in the 1970s after growing up there in the 1940s and '50s. It includes some superb sketches of upper-class life in Ceylon in the first half of this century, and captures precisely many of the little oddities that life in Sri Lanka often seems to be made up of.

Anil's Ghost, also by Michael Ondaatje, tells the story of a forensic anthropologist exploring the truth behind war murders, but it's also a story about love and identity.

A Village in the Jungle, by Leonard Woolf, first published in 1913, is a rather depressing account of local life set in Hambantota (southern Sri Lanka) around the early 20th century. Comparable in stature to George Orwell's *Burmese Days,* it's a classic. Woolf later became a leader of the literary Bloomsbury set between the world wars.

July, by Karen Roberts, tells an engaging, insightful story of two neighbours – one Sinhalese, one Tamil – growing up together.

Sam's Story, by Elmo Jayawardena, picked up literary prizes with the tale of an illiterate village boy working in Colombo. It's a simple, often lighthearted read with a deft touch dealing with the wider problems of society.

Monkfish Moon, by Romesh Gunesekera, contains nine short stories on the effects of the war on people's lives. His book *Reef,* which also examines lives changed irrevocably by war, was a 1994 Booker Prize nominee.

General

Sri Lanka is a photogenic country, and is the subject of many coffee-table books. Among the best are *Sri Lanka,* by Tim Page; *Sri Lanka: The Resplendent Isle,* by Dominic Sansoni & Richard Simon; *Sri Lanka: A Personal Odyssey,* by Nihal Fernando; and *Lunuganga* (the story of a garden near Bentota that was 40 years in the making), by Geoffrey Bawa, Christoph Bon & Dominic Sansoni. Other titles worth looking for are:

Architecture of an Island, by R Lewcock, B Sansoni & L Senanyake, is a wonderful hardback detailing Sri Lanka's architectural heritage. It's beautifully illustrated with Barbara Sansoni's pen-and-ink drawings. It's available through the Barefoot bookshop in Colombo.

Geoffrey Bawa, by Brian Brace Taylor, is a glossy tribute to Sri Lanka's most prominent architect.

The 43 Group: A Chronicle of Fifty Years in the Arts of Sri Lanka, by Neville Weereratne, is worthwhile for those interested in the evolution of modern art in Sri Lanka.

Fractured Paradise: Images of Sri Lanka, by UK journalist Paul Harris, covers the war zones of the 1990s, accompanied by some telling photography. The government refused Harris a new visa in 2001 and he was forced to leave the country.

NEWSPAPERS & MAGAZINES

English-language newspapers include the *Daily News,* which follows the government line, and the independently owned the *Island.* The *Daily Mirror* is a new arrival. There are several weekend papers including the *Sunday*

Leader and *Sunday Observer*. The *Sunday Times* is the best of the lot, and its defence correspondent Iqbal Athas regularly breaks new ground. All papers carry a mix of local news, such as 'Minister's son accused in nightclub attack', politics ('CBK stands by JVP over SLMC split'), and anniversaries of death notices. You'll read some odd choices of foreign news items ('Latvian cabinet reshuffle') plus a comprehensive round-up of local and world cricketing news. Cricket columnists swerve between paeans to victories ('HEROES crush Australia') and bitter ruminations on defeat ('Aussies cheat again').

Magazines with useful information for tourists and expats include *Explore Sri Lanka, LT,* the *Linc* and *Travel Lanka. Business Today* and *Lanka Monthly Digest* are both good magazines aimed at the business community. International and regional news magazines such as the *Economist, Time* and the *Far Eastern Economic Review* are available at hotel bookshops and at Lake House and Vijitha Yapa bookshops.

Buddhist Times (slogan: 'Do not stop. Go forward') is the English-language voice of the Sangha, the community of Buddhist monks. It offers interesting insights into the mindset of Sri Lanka's hugely influential Buddhist hierarchy. Demands to force the government to raise the status of Buddhism and stop Christian evangelists, and enraged rebuttals of claims for a Tamil homeland feature regularly beside sober discussions of philosophy and doctrine.

RADIO & TV

Programs in English, Sinhala and other languages are broadcast by the Sri Lanka Broadcasting Corporation's national radio network. You can pick up BBC radio broadcasts on 17790kHz, 15310kHz or 11955kHz. Private stations include the boppy English-language Yes FM, Gold FM and TNL.

There are seven TV channels, including the state-run SLRC (Sri Lanka Rupavahini Corporation), ITN (Independent Television Network) and privately owned ETV-1, ETV-2, MTV, Swarnawahini and TNL. BBC World Service can be picked up on ETV-1 and StarPlus on ETV-2. Soap operas, live concert broadcasts and the wonderfully tacky national lottery draw are viewer favourites.

PHOTOGRAPHY & VIDEO

Film & Equipment

You can buy transparency and print film in Sri Lanka. Cargills (in Colombo, Kandy, Bandarawela and Nuwara Eliya) generally has a good supply of both. It pays to check the use-by date before you buy, and ask for film that's been kept in a fridge. Millers in Fort is a reliable place to have your film developed.

Bring any equipment you'll need. There are a few camera sales places in Colombo, but they may not have what you want. For camera repairs, **Photoflex** *(☎ 011-258 7824; 1st floor, 451/2 Galle Rd, Kollupitiya, Colombo)* has been recommended, although many cameras are too advanced these days to be repaired there. The heat and humidity can gum up delicate machinery, so try to keep your camera or video in its case along with moisture-absorbing silica gel crystals except when you're shooting. Taking pictures of wildlife in national parks is usually done in a 4WD, so high-speed film is an advantage.

For invaluable photography tips see Lonely Planet's *Travel Photography: A Guide to Taking Better Pictures* by renowned photographer Richard I'Anson.

Restrictions

You aren't allowed to film or photograph dams, airports, road blocks or indeed anything associated with the military. In Colombo the port and the Fort district are especially sensitive. Take special care in the North and East, where there are many high security zones.

See the Social Graces section for tips on sensitivity when taking photos, especially regarding religious images.

Airport Security

Airport X-ray machines won't damage film carried in hand luggage. However, if you want to be on the safe side, put it in a lead-lined bag. Serious photographers won't put their film through any X-ray machine, preferring to put it in clear plastic containers and carry it through by hand. If you do this be prepared to have each and every canister inspected. Don't leave film in baggage that will go into aircraft holds, as it may be exposed to large doses of X-rays that can damage it.

TIME

Sri Lanka is six hours ahead of GMT, four hours behind Australian EST and 11 hours ahead of American EST.

ELECTRICITY

Blackouts and brownouts occur reasonably frequently. Drought in 2001 led to power cuts of up to eight hours a day in Colombo, as hydroelectric generators ceased functioning.

The electric current in Sri Lanka is 230V, 50 cycles, alternating current. If you are bringing sensitive electronic equipment into the country (eg, a laptop) buy a voltage stabiliser from an electrical goods store – they're quite common.

Plugs have three round pins, as in some parts of India. Adaptors are readily available at electrical stores for about Rs 100.

WEIGHTS & MEASURES

Sri Lanka now uses the metric system, but people commonly refer to the old imperial measures. There are still some roads with markers in miles rather than kilometres. Words you'll hear quite often are *lakh* (100,000 units of dollars or whatever) and *crore* (10 million units). Land is often measured in its crop potential: one *amuna* of paddy field (producing six bushels) is about one hectare near Colombo, but 0.8 hectares near Kandy. In the old Sinhalese civilisation, days were split into 60 hours *(paya)* of 24 minutes *(vinadi)* each – a perfectly accurate reversal of modern chronology.

LAUNDRY

All top-end and mid-range places to stay have laundry services, and guesthouses will make arrangements for you if you wish. Expect to pay around Rs 40 for a wash, dry and press for a T-shirt, Rs 75 for a dress. Laundry powder comes in boxes or in small packets for a few rupees and is on sale everywhere. Your guesthouse will happily supply you with a bucket, and you can launder away in the bathroom.

TOILETS

All top-end and mid-range places to stay have sit-down flush toilets, but if you're staying in budget accommodation you'll sometimes find squat toilets, though often there's a choice of commode. In budget digs you might not find toilet paper; it's sold in general stores. Public toilets are scarce, so you'll have to duck into restaurants and hotels.

HEALTH

Travel health depends on your predeparture preparations, your daily health care while travelling and how you handle any medical problem that does develop. The potential dangers can seem quite frightening, but in reality few travellers experience anything more than an upset stomach. The biggest risk is not having travel insurance – people do get into serious trouble without it.

Predeparture Planning

Immunisations Plan ahead for getting your vaccinations: some of them require more than one injection, while some vaccinations should not be given together. Note that some vaccinations should not be given to pregnant women or to people with allergies – discuss this with your doctor.

It is recommended you seek medical advice at least six weeks before travel. Be aware that there is often a greater risk of disease with children and during pregnancy.

Discuss your requirements with your doctor, but vaccinations you should consider for

Medical Kit Check List

Following is a list of items you should consider including in your medical kit – consult your pharmacist for brands available in your country.

- ☐ **Antibiotics** – consider including these if you're travelling well off the beaten track; see your doctor, as they must be prescribed, and carry the prescription with you
- ☐ **Loperamide or diphenoxylate** – 'blockers' for diarrhoea
- ☐ **Prochlorperazine or metaclopramide** – for nausea and vomiting
- ☐ **Rehydration mixture** – to prevent dehydration, which may occur with diarrhoea; particularly important when travelling with children
- ☐ **Insect repellent, sunscreen, lip balm and eye drops**
- ☐ **Calamine lotion, sting relief spray or aloe vera** – to ease irritation from sunburn and insect bites or stings

this trip include the following (see also the individual disease entries later in this section):

Standard Vaccinations Diphtheria; tetanus; hepatitis A; hepatitis B; polio; rabies

Suggested Vaccinations for Long-Term Visitors Japanese B encephalitis; tuberculosis; typhoid; yellow fever

If you've been travelling in Africa and parts of South America you may need to carry proof of yellow fever vaccination.

Malaria Medication Antimalarial drugs do not prevent you from being infected but do kill the malaria parasites during a stage in their development and significantly reduce the risk of becoming very ill or dying. Expert advice on medication should be sought, as there are many factors to consider, including the area to be visited, the risk of exposure to malaria-carrying mosquitoes, the side effects of medication, your medical history and whether you are a child or an adult or pregnant. Travellers to isolated, high-risk areas may like to carry a treatment dose of medication for use if symptoms occur. The only districts that are free of malaria are Colombo, Kalutara and Nuwara Eliya.

Travel Health Guides Lonely Planet's *Healthy Travel Asia & India* is a handy pocket size and is packed with useful information including pretrip planning, emergency first aid, immunisation and disease information and what to do if you get sick on the road. Lonely Planet's *Travel with Children* also includes advice on travel health for younger children.

There are a number of excellent travel health sites on the Internet. From the Lonely Planet home page there are links to the World Health Organization (WHO) and the US Centers for Disease Control & Prevention at w www.lonelyplanet.com/weblinks/wlheal.htm.

Basic Rules

Food Remember the old colonial adage that says: 'If you can cook it, boil it or peel it you can eat it...otherwise forget it'. Vegetables and fruit should be washed with purified water or peeled where possible. If a place looks clean and well run and the vendor also looks clean and healthy, then the food is probably safe. The food in busy restaurants is cooked and eaten quite quickly with little standing around and is probably not reheated. Ice cream which has melted and been refrozen is another possible hazard.

Water The number one rule is *be careful of the water* and especially of ice. If you don't know for certain that the water is safe, assume the worst. Reputable brands of bottled water or soft drinks are generally fine, although in some places bottles may be refilled with tap water. Use water only from containers with a serrated seal – not tops or corks. Take care with fruit juice, particularly if water may have been added. Milk should be treated with suspicion as it is often unpasteurised, though boiled milk is fine if it is kept hygienically.

Medical Problems & Treatment

An embassy, consulate or five-star hotel can usually recommend a local doctor or clinic. Although we do give drug dosages in this section, they are for emergency use only. Correct diagnosis is vital. In this section we have used the generic names for medications – check with a pharmacist for brands available locally.

Note that antibiotics should ideally be administered only under medical supervision. Take only the recommended dose at the prescribed intervals and use the whole course, even if the illness seems to be cured earlier. Stop immediately if there are any serious reactions and don't use the antibiotic at all if you are unsure that you have the correct one. Some people are allergic to commonly prescribed antibiotics such as penicillin; carry this information (eg, on a bracelet) when travelling.

There are good private hospitals in Colombo and quite a few decent clinics (often run by Christian groups) in the regions. Public hospitals vary in quality. Major towns have well-stocked pharmacies with qualified English-speaking pharmacists.

Environmental Hazards

Heat Exhaustion Dehydration and salt deficiency can cause heat exhaustion. Take time to acclimatise to high temperatures, drink sufficient liquids and do not do anything too physically demanding.

Salt deficiency is characterised by fatigue, lethargy, headaches, giddiness and muscle cramps; salt tablets may help, but adding extra salt to your food is better.

Anhidrotic heat exhaustion is a rare form of heat exhaustion caused by an inability to sweat. It tends to affect people who have been in a hot climate for some time. It can progress to heatstroke. Treatment involves removal to a cooler climate.

Heatstroke This serious, occasionally fatal, condition can occur if the body's heat-regulating mechanism breaks down and the body temperature rises to dangerous levels. Long, continuous periods of exposure to high temperatures and insufficient fluids can leave you vulnerable to heatstroke.

The symptoms are feeling unwell, not sweating very much (or at all) and a high body temperature (39°C to 41°C or 102°F to 106°F). Where sweating has ceased, the skin becomes flushed and red. Severe, throbbing headaches and lack of coordination will also occur, and the sufferer may be confused or aggressive. Eventually the victim will become delirious or convulse. Hospitalisation is essential, but in the interim get victims out of the sun, remove their clothing, cover them with a wet sheet or towel and then fan continually. Give fluids if they are conscious.

Prickly Heat Excessive perspiration trapped under the skin causes an itchy rash called prickly heat. It usually strikes people who have just arrived in a hot climate. Keeping cool, bathing often, drying the skin and using a mild talcum or prickly heat powder or resorting to air-conditioning may help.

Sunburn In tropical Sri Lanka you can get sunburnt surprisingly quickly, even through cloud. Use sunscreen, wear a hat and apply a barrier cream for your nose and lips. Calamine lotion or a commercial after-sun preparation is good for mild sunburn. Protect your eyes with good quality sunglasses, particularly if you will be near water or sand.

Infectious Diseases

Diarrhoea Simple things such as a change of water, food or climate can all cause a mild bout of diarrhoea, but a few rushed toilet trips with no other symptoms is not indicative of a major problem.

Dehydration is the main danger with any diarrhoea, particularly in children or the elderly as dehydration can occur quite quickly. Under all circumstances *fluid replacement* (at least equal to the volume being lost) is the most important thing to remember. Weak black tea with a little sugar, soda water or soft drinks allowed to go flat and diluted 50% with clean water are all good. With severe diarrhoea a rehydrating solution is preferable to replace minerals and salts lost. Commercially available oral rehydration salts (ORS) are very useful; add them to boiled or bottled water. In an emergency you can make up a solution of six teaspoons of sugar and a half teaspoon of salt to a litre of boiled or bottled water. You need to drink at least the same volume of fluid that you are losing in bowel movements and vomiting. Urine is the best guide to the adequacy of replacement – if you have small amounts of concentrated urine, you need to drink more. Keep drinking small amounts often. Stick to a bland diet as you recover.

Gut-paralysing drugs such as loperamide or diphenoxylate can be used to bring relief from the symptoms, although they do not actually cure the problem. Use these drugs only if you do not have access to toilets, eg, if you *must* travel. Note that these drugs are not recommended for children under 12 years.

In certain situations, antibiotics may be required, such as with diarrhoea with blood or mucus (dysentery), any diarrhoea with fever, profuse watery diarrhoea, persistent diarrhoea not improving after 48 hours, and severe diarrhoea. These suggest a more serious cause of diarrhoea; in these situations gut-paralysing drugs should be avoided.

In these situations, a stool test may be necessary to diagnose what bug is causing your diarrhoea, so you should seek medical help urgently. Where this is not possible the recommended drugs for bacterial diarrhoea (the most likely cause of severe diarrhoea in travellers) are norfloxacin (400mg twice daily for three days) or ciprofloxacin (500mg twice daily for five days). These are not recommended for children or pregnant women. The drug of choice for children would be co-trimoxazole with dosage dependent on weight. A five-day course is given. Ampicillin or amoxycillin may be given in pregnancy, but medical care is necessary.

Two other causes of persistent diarrhoea in travellers are giardiasis and amoebic dysentery.

Giardiasis is caused by a common parasite, *Giardia lamblia*. Symptoms include stomach cramps, nausea, a bloated stomach, watery foul-smelling diarrhoea and frequent gas. Giardiasis can appear several weeks after you have been exposed to the parasite. The symptoms may disappear for a few days and then return; this can go on for several weeks.

Amoebic dysentery, caused by the protozoan *Entamoeba histolytica*, is characterised by a gradual onset of low-grade diarrhoea, often with blood and mucus. Cramping abdominal pain and vomiting are less likely than in other types of diarrhoea, and fever may not be present. It will persist until treated and can recur and cause other health problems.

You should seek medical advice if you think you have giardiasis or amoebic dysentery, but where this is not possible, tinidazole or metronidazole are the recommended drugs. Treatment is a 2g single dose of tinidazole or 250mg of metronidazole three times daily for five to 10 days.

Fungal Infections These infections occur more commonly in hot weather and are usually found on the scalp, between the toes (athlete's foot) or fingers, in the groin and on the body (ringworm). You get ringworm (which is a fungal infection, not a worm) from infected animals or other people. Moisture encourages these infections.

To prevent fungal infections wear loose, comfortable clothes, avoid artificial fibres, wash frequently and dry yourself carefully. If you do get an infection, wash the infected area at least daily with a disinfectant or medicated soap and water, and rinse and dry well. Apply an antifungal cream or powder such as tolnaftate. Try to expose the infected area to air or sunlight as much as possible and wash all towels and underwear in hot water, change them often and let them dry in the sun.

Hepatitis A general term for inflammation of the liver, hepatitis is a fairly common disease worldwide. There are several viruses that cause hepatitis, which differ in the way that they are transmitted. The symptoms are similar in all forms of the illness, and include fever, chills, headache, fatigue, feelings of weakness, and aches and pains, followed by loss of appetite, nausea, vomiting, abdominal pain, dark urine, light-coloured faeces, jaundiced (yellow) skin and yellowing of the whites of the eyes. People who have had hepatitis should avoid alcohol for some time after the illness, as the liver needs time to recover.

Hepatitis A is transmitted by contaminated food and drinking water. You should seek medical advice, but there is not much you can do apart from resting, drinking lots of fluids, eating lightly and avoiding fatty foods. Hepatitis E is transmitted in the same way as hepatitis A; it can be particularly serious in pregnant women.

There are almost 300 million chronic carriers of **hepatitis B** in the world. It is spread through contact with infected blood, blood products or body fluids, for example, through sexual contact, unsterilised needles and blood transfusions, or contact with blood via small breaks in the skin. Other risk situations include having a shave, tattoo or body piercing with contaminated equipment. The symptoms of hepatitis B may be more severe than type A and the disease can lead to long-term problems such as chronic liver damage, liver cancer or a long term carrier state. Hepatitis C and D are spread in the same way as hepatitis B and can also lead to long-term complications.

There are vaccines against hepatitis A and B, but there are currently no vaccines against the other types of hepatitis. Following the basic rules about food and water (hepatitis A and E) and avoiding risk situations (hepatitis B, C and D) are important preventative measures.

HIV & AIDS Infection with the human immunodeficiency virus (HIV) may lead to acquired immune deficiency syndrome (AIDS), which is a fatal disease. Any exposure to blood, blood products or body fluids may put the individual at risk. The disease is often transmitted through sexual contact or dirty needles – vaccinations, acupuncture, tattooing and body piercing can be potentially as dangerous as intravenous drug use. HIV/AIDS can also be spread through infected blood transfusions. If you do need an injection, ask to see the syringe unwrapped in front of you, or take a needle and syringe pack with you. Fear of HIV infection should never preclude treatment for serious medical conditions.

The number of HIV cases in Sri Lanka in 2001 was estimated at 4800. That said, the social stigma of HIV infection and limited medical testing for the virus suggests that many cases are going unreported. The World Bank estimated the infection rate among Sri Lankan adults between the ages of 15 and 49 was 0.07% in 2001, compared to around 0.8% in neighbouring India. The 50,000-odd prostitutes and rent boys in Sri Lanka have high rates of STD infection, a reliable precursor to HIV infection. Awareness about the issues of HIV/AIDS is poor among Sri Lankans – surveys suggest only 10% to 25% of men use condoms in non-marital affairs.

Intestinal Worms These parasites are most common in rural, tropical areas. Different worms have different ways of infecting people. Some may be ingested on food such as undercooked meat (eg, tapeworms) and some enter through your skin (eg, hookworms). Infestations may not show up for some time, and although they are generally not serious, if left untreated some can cause severe health problems later. Consider having a stool test when you return home to check for these and determine the appropriate treatment.

Typhoid A dangerous gut infection, Typhoid fever is caused by contaminated water and food. Medical help must be sought.

In its early stages sufferers may feel they have a bad cold or flu on the way, as early symptoms include a headache, body aches and a fever that rises a little each day until it is around 40°C (104°F) or more. The victim's pulse is often slow relative to the degree of fever present – unlike a normal fever where the pulse increases. The victim may also suffer from vomiting, abdominal pain, diarrhoea or constipation.

In the second week the high fever and slow pulse continue and a few pink spots may appear on the body; trembling, delirium, weakness, weight loss and dehydration may occur. Complications such as pneumonia, perforated bowel or meningitis may occur.

Insect-Borne Diseases

Filariasis, leishmaniasis, Lyme disease and typhus are all insect-borne diseases, but they do not pose a great risk to travellers. For more information on them see Less Common Diseases at the end of this Health section.

Dengue Fever This viral disease is transmitted by mosquitoes and is fast becoming one of the top public health problems in the tropical world. Unlike the malaria mosquito, the *Aedes aegypti* mosquito, which transmits the dengue virus, is most active during the day, and is found mainly in urban areas, in and around human dwellings.

Signs and symptoms of dengue fever include a sudden onset of high fever, headache, intense joint and muscle pains, and nausea and vomiting. A rash of small red spots sometimes appears three to four days after the onset of fever. In the early phase of illness, dengue may be mistaken for other infectious diseases, including malaria and influenza. Minor bleeding such as nose bleeds may occur in the course of the illness, but this does not necessarily mean that you have progressed to the potentially fatal dengue haemorrhagic fever (DHF). This is a severe illness, characterised by heavy bleeding, which is thought to be a result of a second infection due to a different strain (there are four major strains), and it usually affects residents of the country rather than travellers. Recovery from even simple dengue fever may be prolonged, with tiredness often lasting for several weeks.

You should seek medical attention as soon as possible if you think you may be infected. A blood test can exclude malaria and indicate the possibility of dengue fever. There is no specific treatment for dengue. Aspirin should be avoided: it increases the risk of haemorrhaging. There is no vaccine against dengue fever. The best prevention is to avoid mosquito bites at all times by covering up and using insect repellents containing the compound DEET and mosquito nets – see Malaria later in this section for more advice on avoiding mosquito bites.

Japanese B Encephalitis This viral infection of the brain is transmitted by mosquitoes. Most cases occur in rural areas as the virus exists in pigs and wading birds. Symptoms include fever, headache and sensitivity to light, drowsiness, confusion and other signs of brain dysfunction. Hospitalisation is needed for correct diagnosis and treatment. There is a high mortality rate among those who have symptoms; of those who survive many are left intellectually disabled.

Malaria This serious and potentially fatal disease is spread by mosquito bites. If you are travelling in endemic areas it is extremely important to avoid mosquito bites and to take tablets to prevent this disease. Symptoms range from fever, chills and sweating, headache, diarrhoea and abdominal pains to a vague feeling of ill-health. Seek medical help immediately if malaria is suspected. Without treatment, malaria can rapidly become more serious.

If medical care is not available, malaria tablets can be used for treatment. You need to use a malaria tablet that is different from the one you were taking when you contracted malaria. The standard treatment dose of mefloquine is two 250mg tablets and a further two, six hours later. For Fansidar, it's a single dose of three tablets. If you were previously taking mefloquine and cannot obtain Fansidar, then other alternatives are Malarone (atovaquone-proguanil; four tablets once daily for three days), halofantrine (three doses of two 250mg tablets every six hours) or quinine sulphate (600mg every six hours). There is a greater risk of side effects with these dosages than in normal use if used with mefloquine, so medical advice is preferable. Be aware also that halofantrine is no longer recommended by the WHO as emergency stand-by treatment because of its side effects, and should only be used if no other drugs are available.

To minimise any contact with mosquitoes:

- Wear light-coloured clothing.
- Wear long trousers and long-sleeved shirts.
- Use mosquito repellents containing the compound DEET on exposed areas (prolonged overuse of DEET may be harmful).
- Use a mosquito net impregnated with mosquito repellent (permethrin) – it may be worth taking your own.
- Impregnate clothes with permethrin.

Cuts, Bites & Stings

See Less Common Diseases at the end of this section for details of rabies, which is passed through animal bites.

Bedbugs & Lice Bedbugs live in various places, but particularly in dirty mattresses and bedding, and are evidenced by spots of blood on bedclothes or on the wall. Bedbugs leave itchy bites in neat rows. Calamine lotion or a sting-relief spray may help.

All lice cause itching and discomfort. They make themselves at home in your hair (head lice), your clothing (body lice) or in your pubic hair (crabs). You catch lice through direct contact with infected people or by sharing combs, clothing and the like. Powder or shampoo treatment will kill the lice and infected clothing should then be washed in very hot, soapy water and left in the sun to dry.

Bites & Stings Bee and wasp stings are usually painful rather than dangerous. However, in people who are allergic to them severe breathing difficulties may occur and require urgent medical care. Calamine lotion or a sting-relief spray will give relief, and ice packs will reduce the pain and swelling. There are some spiders with dangerous bites but antivenins are usually available. Scorpion stings are notoriously painful and in some parts of Asia can be fatal. Scorpions often shelter in shoes or clothing.

There are various fish and other sea creatures that can sting or bite dangerously or which are dangerous to eat – seek local advice.

Jellyfish Avoid contact with these sea creatures, which have stinging tentacles – seek local advice. Dousing in vinegar will deactivate any stingers that have not 'fired'. Calamine lotion, antihistamines and analgesics may reduce the reaction and relieve the pain.

Leeches & Ticks Leeches may be present in damp rainforest conditions, particularly in the Sinharaja Forest Reserve; they attach themselves to your skin and suck your blood. Trekkers often get them on their legs or in their boots. Salt or a lighted cigarette end will make them fall off. Do not pull them off, as the bite is then more likely to become infected. Clean and apply pressure if the point of attachment is bleeding. An insect repellent may keep them away.

You should always check all over your body if you have been walking through a potentially tick-infested area, as ticks can cause skin infections and other more serious diseases. If a tick is found attached, press down around the tick's head with tweezers, grab the head and gently pull upwards. Avoid pulling the rear of the body as this may squeeze the tick's gut contents through the attached mouth parts into the skin, increasing the risk of infection and disease. Smearing chemicals on the tick will not make it let go and is not recommended.

Snakes There are five species of venomous snakes in Sri Lanka, and these are relatively commonly spotted, especially in the dry zone area around Anuradhapura and Polonnaruwa. Be careful when wandering around the ancient ruins. To minimise your chances of being bitten always wear boots, socks and long trousers when walking through undergrowth where snakes may be present. Don't put your hands into holes and crevices, and be careful when collecting firewood.

Snake bites do not cause instantaneous death and antivenins are usually available. Immediately wrap the bitten limb tightly, as you would for a sprained ankle, and then attach a splint to immobilise it. Keep the victim still and seek medical help, if possible with the dead snake for identification. Don't attempt to catch the snake if there is a possibility of being bitten again. Tourniquets and sucking out the poison are now comprehensively discredited.

Less Common Diseases

The following diseases pose a small risk to travellers, and so are mentioned only in passing. Seek medical advice if you think you may have any of these diseases.

Filariasis This is a mosquito-transmitted parasitic infection found in many parts of Asia. Possible symptoms include fever, pain and swelling of the lymph glands; inflammation of lymph drainage areas; swelling of a limb or the scrotum; skin rashes; and blindness. Treatment is available to eliminate the parasites from the body, but some of the damage already caused may not be reversible. Medical advice should be obtained if the infection is suspected.

Leishmaniasis This is a group of parasitic diseases transmitted by sandflies, which are found in Sri Lanka. Cutaneous leishmaniasis affects the skin tissue causing ulceration and disfigurement, and visceral leishmaniasis affects the internal organs. Seek medical advice, as laboratory testing is required for diagnosis and correct treatment. Avoiding sandfly bites is the best precaution. Bites are usually painless and itchy, and are yet another reason to cover up and apply repellent.

Lyme Disease This is a tick-transmitted infection that may be acquired throughout Asia. The illness usually begins with a spreading rash at the site of the tick bite and is accompanied by fever, headache, extreme fatigue, aching joints and muscles and mild neck stiffness. If untreated, these symptoms usually subside over several weeks, but over subsequent weeks or months disorders of the nervous system, heart and joints may develop. Treatment works best early in the illness. Medical help should be sought.

Rabies This fatal viral infection is found in many countries, including Sri Lanka. Many animals can be infected (such as dogs, cats, bats and monkeys) and it is their saliva which is infectious. Any bite, scratch or even lick from an animal should be cleaned immediately and thoroughly. Scrub with soap and running water, and then apply alcohol or iodine solution. Medical help should be sought promptly to receive a course of injections to prevent the onset of symptoms and death.

Tetanus This disease is caused by a germ which lives in soil and in the faeces of horses and other animals. It enters the body via breaks in the skin. The first symptom may be discomfort in swallowing, or stiffening of the jaw and neck; this is followed by painful convulsions of the jaw and whole body. The disease can be fatal. It can be prevented by vaccination.

Typhus This disease is spread by ticks, mites or lice. It begins with fever, chills, headache and muscle pains, followed a few days later by a body rash. There is often a large painful sore at the site of the bite, and nearby lymph nodes are swollen and painful. Typhus can be treated under medical supervision. Check your skin carefully for ticks after walking in tropical forests. An insect repellent can help, and walkers in tick-infested areas should consider having their boots and trousers impregnated with benzyl benzoate and dibutylphthalate.

SOCIAL GRACES

Temple Etiquette

When visiting a Buddhist temple you should remove your shoes and hat and if carrying an umbrella, furl it. Your legs and shoulders should be covered. You should walk around the stupa in a clockwise direction. Hindu temples also require you to remove your shoes and headwear. There is no circumambulation requirement, but you should be respectful and cover your legs and shoulders. Some Hindu temples require men to go shirtless to enter the inner sanctum.

In most temples you will be asked for a donation. The traditional practice is that you make a donation only if you wish to. If you decide to give money, the best place to put it is in the donation box.

Visiting Homes

If you're invited to someone's home, it's customary to bring a small gift. Flowers aren't used as gifts in Sri Lanka, and in particular don't offer frangipani flowers, which are associated with death. A packet of tea or quality sweetmeats will do. Don't be offended if the gift vanishes without comment; it's considered rude to inspect a gift in front of its giver. Expect to share in some slightly formal cups of tea and plenty of snacks when you visit. Remove your shoes before entering; some hosts waive this rule for foreigners, but it's polite to do it nevertheless.

The Right Hand Rule

Always give, receive and eat with your right hand. The left hand is used for and associated with unclean functions, so using it to eat has some rather unpleasant connotations.

Bathing

Nudity is a no-no everywhere, including the beach. You'll notice people bathing in streams and tanks all over the country, and how they artfully cover themselves with thin cloths and manage to soap and rinse themselves without removing the cloth. Wet sari scenes are a staple of Indian and Sri Lankan films, but you won't see nudity – that's the accepted social limit.

Treatment of Animals

Buddhism abhors the taking of life and traditionally animals have enjoyed respect and protection because of this. Many creatures are protected by law. Generally, animals are respected and left to go their own way. Despite the crowded roads, drivers are careful to let any living thing that crosses their paths pass safely. This courtesy is extended to all things, from poisonous snakes to stray dogs.

Photography

It's best to ask permission before taking pictures of either people or the inside of temples and other sacred places. Some places may allow photography but charge a fee. Payment for permission to film is usually higher than for still cameras. Using a flash on murals inside temples and other places can cause damage. Never pose beside or in front of a statue of the Buddha (ie, with your back to it). It is also forbidden to take photos of people inside the cave temple complex at Dambulla, but you can take photos of the shrines themselves. Tourists are sometimes asked for money for taking photos, for example, of working elephants – inquire before snapping away.

WOMEN TRAVELLERS

Covering your legs and shoulders helps you blend in more effectively, though you'll be stared at no matter what you wear. In Colombo you can relax the dress code a little and get away with wearing sleeveless shirts. Lone women travellers may be hassled walking around at night, or while exploring isolated places. Stray hands on crowded buses are something else to watch out for – keep an eye on who's around you, and let other passengers know what's happening if you're being bothered. However, don't imagine travelling in Sri Lanka is one long hassle. Such unpleasant incidents are the exception, not the rule. Women travellers are advantaged by the opportunity to enter the society of Sri Lankan women, something which is largely out-of-bounds for male travellers. On the other hand, there are many social environments which are almost exclusively male in character – local bars, for example. If you feel uncomfortable in local eateries or hotels, try to find one where women are working or staying.

Stock up on tampons, as they can be hard to find outside Colombo.

GAY & LESBIAN TRAVELLERS

Male homosexual activity is illegal in Sri Lanka (there is no law against female homosexuality) and the subject is not openly discussed. There have been some convictions in recent years so it would be prudent not to flaunt your sexuality.

According to a gay expat working in Colombo, Sri Lanka is particularly dull when it comes to a gay lifestyle. There are no clubs or pubs where expat or local gays congregate, and besides the 'beach boy' prostitution racket, local gay life is secretive to say the least. Many gays end up marrying and having children to escape family pressure. Probably the best way to tap into the local gay scene is via the Internet. Check out the **Sri Lankan Gay Friends' website** at w www.geocities.com/srilankangay. It provides information as well as a schedule of gay and lesbian activities.

Companions on a Journey (*e coj@sri.lanka.net; PO Box 48, Wattala*) is an organisation for the gay and lesbian community based in Colombo. It provides a drop-in centre, a library, film screenings, health-related advice and more. It also lobbies for legislative changes.

DISABLED TRAVELLERS

Though Sri Lanka is a challenge for disabled travellers, the ever-obliging Sri Lankans are always ready to assist. If you have restricted mobility you may find it difficult, if not impossible, to get around on public transport; for example, buses and trains don't have facilities for wheelchairs. Moving around towns and cities can also be difficult for those in a wheelchair or the visually impaired because of the continual roadworks and crummy roads (don't expect many footpaths). A car and driver is the best transport option, and if possible travel with a strong, able-bodied person.

Apart from top-end places, accommodation is generally not geared for wheelchairs. However, many places would be able to provide disabled travellers with rooms and bathrooms that are accessible without stairs. It might take a bit of time to find places with the right facilities, but it is possible. Medical facilities outside Colombo are limited.

Disabled travellers can get in touch with their national support organisation (preferably with the travel officer, if there is one). In the UK contact **Radar** (*☎ 020-7250 3222; 250 City Rd, London EC1V 8AS*) or the **Holiday Care Service** (*☎ 01293-774 535*).

SENIOR TRAVELLERS

Sri Lankans accord older people a great deal of respect. The country is rare among developing nations in that it has a rapidly growing proportion of elderly people, similar to the populations of many European countries. However, respect doesn't translate into concessions for senior citizens at museums and sites. If a car and driver is in reach of your budget, travel is fairly easy. Budget bus travel and extreme heat are strenuous for anybody, so don't plan to do too much too quickly. Older travellers will have company though. Some travellers have been coming to Sri Lanka for 40 years, and the kind of tourists who come to Sri Lanka tend to be from a wider age group than those that travel to other sun-and-sand destinations.

TRAVEL WITH CHILDREN

Sri Lankans adore children, and hotels and restaurants cater for children as a matter of course. Hotels and guesthouses invariably have triple rooms, and extra beds are routinely supplied on demand.

If you have a very young child, one dilemma is whether to bring a backpack carrier or a pram (buggy). Opinion seems divided on this – if you can, bring both. One reader who opted for a pram decided this was the best choice because a backpack would have been too sweaty in the tropical heat. However, prams have to contend with uneven footpaths and often no footpaths at all. Lonely Planet's *Travel with Children* has lots of road-tested advice for trips with kids in tow in the developing world.

Pharmaceutical supplies, as well as imported baby food and disposable nappies (diapers), are available at Keells and Cargills supermarkets, however, they can be relatively expensive. One mother reports that cloth nappies are easier to manage, and hotel staff will get them washed as a matter of course.

There aren't a great many attractions dedicated solely to children. One favourite for kids is the Pinnewala Elephant Orphanage. On the coast south of Colombo there are beaches where turtles lay eggs (a night-time trip). A safari in one of the national parks might also appeal. All top-end hotels have swimming pools and, of course, Sri Lanka is famous for its beaches. Car-rental companies usually have child car seats.

DANGERS & ANNOYANCES

Ethnic Tensions

You're most likely aware of the country's ethnic conflict. The situation on the ground is far more relaxed than old headlines suggest, though. See the boxed text 'Safety in Sri Lanka' earlier in this chapter for information on ethnic tensions.

Scams

Sri Lanka's tourism industry provides an income to many, from the owner of a fancy hotel to the driver of a three-wheeler who drops you at the door. At the top of the financial pyramid the money pours in seemingly endlessly; for the folks down the bottom, commissions are the name of the game. Touts, or as they like to call themselves 'friends' or 'guides', lurk around bus and train stations waiting to start chatting with you with the intention of taking you to a hotel or guesthouse of their choice. (The place you want to stay in, you see, is closed, full of giant bugs, overpriced etc.) If you stay at the hotel of their choice, the tout will gain a commission, sometimes up to 30% of your bill. This is sometimes subsidised by extra charges to you, but often the hotelier makes do with less money. Many travellers like going with a tout, as often you get better deals and you don't have the headache of tramping the streets. Saying you have a reservation, whether true or not, is a good ploy to fend off touts.

The airport is prime scam-breeding ground for tourists fresh off the plane. You may be approached with stories designed to make you sign up for a tour on the spot.

Restaurants also play the commission game: your guide gets a kickback for the lunch you ate. Relax. Most gem shops, handicraft stalls and spice gardens, basically any business connected to the tourist industry, have some kind of commission system set up. Just remember: this is how many make a living – you can help out, or you can spend your money elsewhere. Either way, don't get hung up on beating the commission racket.

Theft

With the usual precautions most people's visit to Sri Lanka proceeds without trouble. However, pickpockets can be active on crowded city buses, notably in Colombo along Galle Rd. They often work together – one to jostle you and the other to pick your pocket or slit your bag with a knife, often as you board the bus. All you can do is try to keep a little space around you and hold tight to what you're carrying. It's often unwise to sleep with your windows open – particularly if you're on the ground floor. Thieves sometimes use long poles with hooks to snaffle items of value. Monkeys are genetically gifted pilferers, and can slip through small gaps and steal food from your room.

One thieves' trick reported by a number of travellers is to take the bottom one or two of a block of travellers cheques, so that you don't notice anything missing until later.

If you do get robbed go to the police – you won't get your money back but passports and tickets are often jettisoned later. One Australian got her passport back from her embassy after the pickpockets dropped it in a mailbox!

Traffic

Sri Lankan driving – private bus drivers in particular – can be a real danger. It seems to be acceptable for a bus, car or truck to overtake in the face of oncoming smaller road-users – who sometimes simply have to get off the road or risk getting hit. To announce that they are overtaking, or want to overtake, drivers use a series of blasts on loud, shrill horns. If you're walking or cycling along any kind of main road make sure you keep all your senses on alert in every direction.

LEGAL MATTERS

Sri Lanka's legal system is a complex, almost arcane mix of British, Roman-Dutch and national law. The legal system tends to move fairly slowly, and even a visit to a police station to report a small theft can involve lots of time-consuming form-filling. The tourist police in major towns and tourist spots should be your first point of contact for minor matters such as theft.

Drug use, mainly marijuana but even heroin, is common in tourist centres such as Hikkaduwa, Negombo and Unawatuna. Dabbling is perilous; you can expect to end up in jail if you are caught dealing or using anything illegal. Besides the risks, one group of Aussie surfers asked us to warn visitors that 'the dope they sell here is shithouse, mate'.

BUSINESS HOURS

The working week in offices, including post offices, is usually from 8.30am to 4.30pm Monday to Friday. Some businesses also open until about 1pm on Saturday. Shops normally open from 10am to about 7pm weekdays, and until 3pm on Saturday. Businesses run by Muslims may take an extended lunch break on Friday so that staff can attend Friday prayers. Banks are generally open from 9am to 3pm on weekdays, although some banks are open on Saturday.

PUBLIC HOLIDAYS & SPECIAL EVENTS

Sri Lanka has many Buddhist, Hindu, Christian and Muslim festivals, and around 26 public holidays a year. A full working week is a rarity! Many of the holidays are based on the lunar calendar so the dates vary from year to year according to the Gregorian calendar: see Poya later in this section for the *poya* (full moon) holiday dates. The tourist board publishes an annual *Current Events Calendar* on its website at w www.srilankatourism.org. The main festivals are listed below.

The Muslim festivals Id-ul-Fitr (the end of Ramadan, 13 November 2004), Id-ul-Adha (the Hajj festival, 1 February 2004) and Milad-un-Nabi (the Prophet Mohammed's birthday, 1 May 2004) follow the lunar calendar and fall about 11 days earlier each year. The exact start of a festival depends on the sighting of the new moon by a local team of Muslim elders. If it's a smoggy night in Colombo but a clear night in Mutur where a sliver of the new moon is visible, local festivals will kick off on different days.

The dates of Hindu festivals often depend on fiendishly complicated astrological calculations, and the exact dates might not be known until a month or so in advance.

January

Duruthu Perahera Held on the *poya* day in January at the Kelaniya Raja Maha Vihara in Colombo and second in importance only to the huge Kandy *perahera*, this festival celebrates a visit by the Buddha to Sri Lanka.

Thai Pongal This is a Hindu harvest festival, held in mid-January, to honour the Sun God.

February

National Day This holiday (4 February) celebrates independence from Britain and features parades, dances and national games all over the country.

Navam Perahera First celebrated in 1979, Navam Perahera is one of Sri Lanka's biggest *peraheras*. Held on the February full moon around Viharamahadevi Park and Beira Lake in Colombo, it starts from the Gangaramaya Temple and includes elephants.

February/March

Maha Sivarathri In late February or early March the Hindu festival of Maha Sivarathri commemorates the marriage of Shiva to Parvati.

March/April

Easter The Christian Good Friday holiday usually falls in April, but can fall in late March. An Easter passion play is performed on the island of Duwa, off Negombo.

Aurudu (New Year) Both New Year's Eve on 13 April and New Year's Day on 14 April are holidays. This occasion for hospitality coincides with the end of the harvest season and the start of the southwest monsoon. See the boxed text 'Celebrating the New Year Sri Lankan Style'.

May

May Day As in other parts of the world, May Day (1 May) is a holiday.

Vesak This two-day holiday – full-moon day and the day after – commemorates the birth, enlightenment and death of Buddha. Puppet shows and open-air theatre performances take place and the temples are crowded with devotees bringing flowers and offerings. The high point is the lighting of countless paper lanterns and oil lamps. The Adam's Peak pilgrimage season ends at Vesak.

National Heroes' Day Although not a public holiday, 22 May is a day honouring soldiers who have died in the ethnic conflict.

June

Poson Poya The Poson full-moon day in June is a celebration of the bringing of Buddhism to Sri Lanka by Mahinda. Anuradhapura and Mihintale, where Mahinda met and converted the Sinhalese king, are the main sites for this celebration. On this day thousands of white-clad pilgrims climb the stairs to the summit of Mihintale.

July/August

Black Tiger Day This LTTE event on 5 July is relevant for Tamil areas of the North and East. It commemorates the first suicide bombing attack in 1987 by the Black Tigers, the LTTE suicide squad.

Kandy Esala Perahera The Kandy Esala Perahera, the most important and spectacular festival in Sri Lanka, is the climax of 10 days and nights during the month of Esala (July/August), ending on the Nikini full moon. This great procession honours the Sacred Tooth Relic of Kandy. Smaller *peraheras* are held at other locations around the island.

Vel This festival is held in Jaffna and Colombo. The gilded chariot of Skanda (or Murugan), the God of War, complete with his *vel* (trident), is ceremonially hauled from a temple in Sea St, Pettah, to another at Bambalapitiya. In Jaffna the Nallur Kandaswamy temple has a 25-day festival in honour of Skanda/Murugan.

Kataragama Another important Hindu festival is held at Kataragama, where devotees put themselves through the whole gamut of ritual masochism. A pilgrimage from Jaffna via Batticaloa to Kataragama takes place.

October/November

Deepavali The Hindu festival of lights takes place in late October or early November. Thousands of flickering oil lamps celebrate the triumph of good over evil and the return of Rama after his period of exile.

Heroes Day This day (27 November) is the big event in the LTTE calendar, held to commemorate the death of the first LTTE cadre at Velvettiturai near Jaffna on this day in 1982.

December

Adam's Peak The pilgrimage season, when pilgrims (and the odd tourist) climb Adam's Peak, starts in December.

Unduvap Poya This full-moon day commemorates Sangamitta who accompanied her brother Mahinda to Sri Lanka and brought a cutting from the sacred Bodhi Tree, which still stands in Anuradhapura today.

Christmas Day (25 December) The celebration of Christ's birth is a holiday.

Poya

Every *poya* or full-moon day is a holiday. *Poya* causes buses, trains and accommodation to fill up, especially if it falls on a Friday or Monday. No alcohol is supposed to be sold on *poya* days, and some establishments close. If you're likely to be thirsty, stock up in advance! Some hotels and guesthouses discreetly provide their needy guests with a bottle of beer 'under the table'.

The *poya* days in 2004 are 7 January, 6 February, 6 March, 5 April, 4 and 5 May, 3 June, 2 July, 31 July, 29 August, 28 September, 27 October, 26 November and 26 December. In 2005 *poya* days fall on 25 January, 23 February, 25 March, 24 April, 23 May, 22 June, 21 July, 19 August, 17 September, 17 October, 15 November and 15 December.

ACTIVITIES

Surfing

The best surf beach is at Arugam Bay on the east coast – surf's up from April to September. Guesthouses and surf shops here can give advice on other surf breaks along this coast. Kirinda near Tissamaharama is another option. On the west coast and south coast, the best time to surf is from November to April. Hikkaduwa is a long-time favourite for international surfers, and offers gentle breaks for novices (grommets in Australian parlance). Mirissa is becoming popular too. The point at Midigama further down the west coast is another good, if more isolated, spot.

You can hire surfboards, boogie boards, wetties and anything else you'll need from shops beside the beaches. You can also buy second-hand gear.

Diving & Snorkelling

The global bleaching event (where coral lost its cover of algae due to higher-than-average ocean temperatures and regional influences) in 1998 struck about half of the island's broken ring of coral reefs, but the affected reefs have started showing signs of recovery. Coral and interesting shipwrecks can be seen at several spots along the west coast such as Hikkaduwa and Tangalla. The reef at Kirinda is said to be in fine shape, but rough seas make it inaccessible for all but a couple of weeks in April and May. There are also reefs at the Basses in the southeast and along the east coast, but it will take a while for dive operators to refamiliarise themselves with these areas. Pigeon Island off Nilaveli (north of Trincomalee) is a fine place to go snorkelling. Diving shops can be found in Colombo and in the major west coast resorts. They hire and sell gear, including snorkelling equipment. PADI courses are available, as well as dives for beginners and experienced people. You can snorkel at Hikkaduwa, Unawatuna, Mirissa and at Polhena near Matara.

Celebrating the New Year Sri Lankan Style

When the sun moves from Pisces, the last zodiac sign in its cycle, to Aries, Buddhist and Hindu Sri Lankans celebrate their new year – Aurudu. Astrologically determined auspicious moments set the time for significant tasks, including the lighting of the hearth to cook *kiri bath* (milk rice), bathing and the anointing of oil, the first business transaction and the first meal of the new year. There are also auspicious colours to be worn and directions to face, all to help ensure good fortune for the year ahead.

Falling on April 14, this is the time when the harvest ends and the fruit trees produce bounteous crops. The festival brings the country to a standstill for almost a week after a hectic preparation. Public transport is packed on the eve of new year as everyone returns to their parental homes for the celebration. Bread supplies are scarce for a week – bakeries and businesses close down to allow staff to travel home for a few days.

The rituals begin with cleaning the house and lighting the oil lamp. The pounding of the *raban*, a large drum played by several women, sounds the dawning of the new year. The lighting of the hearth is the first ceremonial act for the new year, and even women who are not especially devoted to astrology ensure they light the fire to heat the new pot filled with milk. Families constantly watch the clock, assisted by countdowns on state television, until it is time to take the first meal for the new year. And just in case you missed it, a shrill chorus of firecrackers reminds everyone that the moment has arrived.

After the other rituals are performed, the family visits friends or joins the games being played in the village, and children ride high on swings hanging from a nearby mango or jackfruit tree.

Special Aurudu food is enjoyed during the following days. The ubiquitous plantains (bananas) are a staple, and special additions are *kaung* (a small oil cake) and *kokis* (a light, crisp sweetmeat of Dutch origin).

Family members exchange gifts after eating at the appointed time, usually clothes (a sari for mother, a shirt or sarong for father and clothing 'kits' for the children), and give sweetmeats or fruit to neighbours. Aurudu sales and markets give Sri Lankans the opportunity to shop for bargains of all sorts.

Aurudu has become deeply embedded in the culture of Sinhalese Buddhist and Tamil Hindu Sri Lankans. It is not celebrated by Buddhists or Hindus anywhere else in the world, evidence of the island's shared cultural heritage. Many expat Sri Lankans return to their homeland at this time of year to share the new year and holiday season with their family and friends. The wealthier expats often avoid the heat and humidity by escaping to the cooler hills around Nuwara Eliya. Accommodation prices here soar at this time of year – if you can find a room at all. The elite flock here for 'the season' and spend the days playing golf and tennis, horse riding or motor racing in the annual hill climb, and partying at night.

Along the west coast, the best time to dive and snorkel is generally from November to April. The seas are calmest from April to September along the east coast.

Windsurfing

Top-end hotels in the main west coast beach resorts are the only places that rent windsurfers. Bentota is the best spot to windsurf, and several outfits there hire out equipment and provide lessons.

White-Water Rafting, Canoeing & Boating

White-water rafting can be done at a few places, notably on the river near Kitulgala in the Hill Country (where *Bridge on the River Kwai* was filmed). **Adventure Sports Lanka** *(☎ 074 713334; W www.adventureslanka.com)* arranges trips here and in a few other places. Canoeing trips can also be arranged through this company.

Boat or catamaran trips for sightseeing, bird-watching or fishing are becoming very popular. You can organise excursions in Negombo, Bentota and Weligama. See the West Coast and The South chapters for details.

Cycling

Cycling is a great way to get around in Sri Lanka and mountain biking is also catching on. See Bicycle in the Getting Around chapter for more information.

Safe Swimming

Every year drownings occur off Sri Lanka's beaches. If you aren't an experienced swimmer or surfer it's easy to underestimate the dangers – or even be totally unaware of them. There are few full-time lifesaving patrols as there are in places such as Australia, so there's usually no-one to jump in and rescue you. A few common sense rules should be observed:

- Don't swim out of your depth. If you are a poor swimmer, always stay in the shallows.
- Don't stay in the water when you feel tired.
- Never go swimming under the influence of alcohol or drugs.
- Supervise children at *all* times.
- Watch out for currents. Water brought onto the beach by waves is sucked back to sea and this current can be strong enough to drag you out with it. This type of current is called a rip. The bigger the surf, the stronger the rip. Rips in rough surf can sometimes be seen as calm patches in the disturbed water. It's best to check with someone reliable before venturing into the water. If you do get caught in a rip, swim *across* the current if you can – *not* against it. If it's too strong for you to do this, keep afloat and raise a hand so someone onshore can see that you are in distress. A rip eventually weakens. The important thing is not to panic.
- Exercise caution when there is surf.
- Beware of coral; coming into contact with coral can be painful for the swimmer, and fatal for the coral. Always check with someone reliable if you suspect the area you're about to swim in may have coral.
- Never dive into the water. Hazards may be lurking under the surface or the water may not be as deep as it looks. It pays to be cautious.

Hiking

Hiking is gaining popularity in Sri Lanka. There isn't an organised hiking industry as there is in India, and it's usually a matter of striking out on your own. For details see The Hill Country chapter. Adam's Peak provides an opportunity for a good, stiff hike up Sri Lanka's most sacred mountain with stunning views as a reward.

Golf

There are three excellent golf courses in Sri Lanka. Green fees and other expenses including club hire comes to about US$50 a day. The most scenic course is definitely the Victoria Golf Club near Kandy, overlooking the Victoria Reservoir. There is also an excellent historic course (founded in 1889) at Nuwara Eliya. (See The Hill Country chapter for details on these two courses.) The Royal Colombo Golf Club also has a decent course. For more details, see Golf in the Colombo chapter.

COURSES

Kandy has meditation places that are open to foreigners (see Kandy in The Hill Country chapter for details). Several outfits run PADI courses for divers (see the Colombo, West Coast and The South chapters for details).

WORK

To become a resident in Sri Lanka with the right to work you need to make a substantial investment in a project approved by the Board of Investment. The other options are to go to Sri Lanka as an employee or contract worker for a company that can make the necessary arrangements, or as a volunteer. A few travellers work on an informal basis in diving schools and surfing-gear stores, but that old stand-by the English-teaching option doesn't really apply in Sri Lanka. French and German teachers might have more luck.

Volunteer Work

Sri Lanka is a base for many NGOs, and there are about half a dozen major volunteer agencies that operate in Sri Lanka. The best place to start searching for placements for volunteer workers is the Web. Check out W www.workingabroad.com and W www.vso.org.uk.

[Continued on page 70]

Cuisine of Sri Lanka

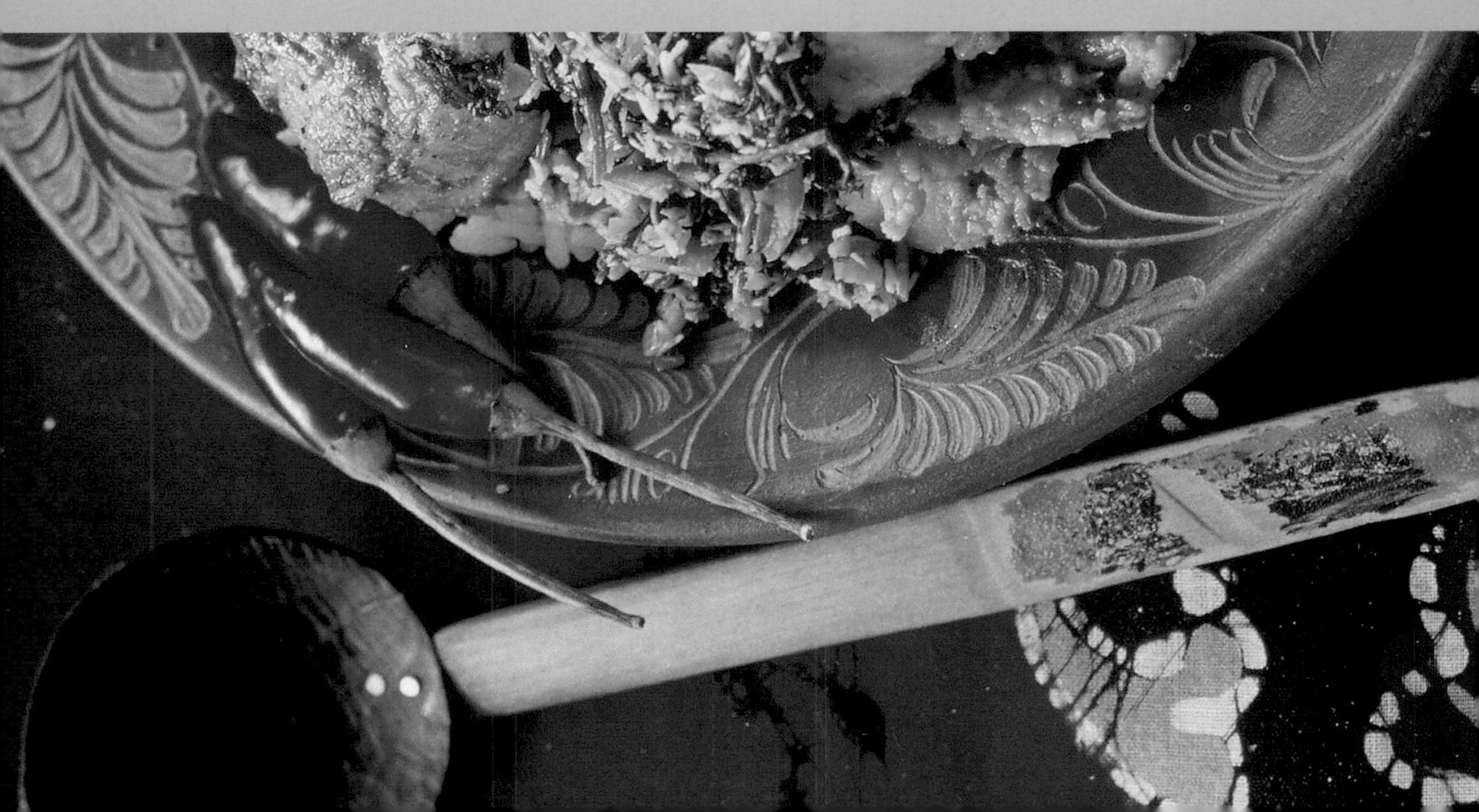

SIMON BRACKEN

RICHARD NEBESKY

CHRIS MELLOR

GREG ELMS

Title page: Typical lunch-time Sri Lankan fare, both colourful and spicy (Photograph by Richard Nebesky)

Top: Tropical mangosteens

Middle: A feast of rice and curry (clockwise from bottom left) dhal, green leafy vegetable, chicken, fried eggplant, pickled vegetables and the ubiquitous rice

Bottom left: Bananas

Bottom right: Fresh fruits

FOOD

Sri Lanka boasts a unique cuisine, shaped by the fruit and vegetables to be found in its abundant garden, and by recipes brought by traders and invaders – Indians, Arabs, Malays, Portuguese, Dutch and English have all left their mark on the Sri Lankan diet.

If you plan to eat at restaurants, remember that food takes a long time to prepare in Sri Lanka. Get into the habit of pre-ordering your meal.

Rice & Curry

Curries in Sri Lanka can be very hot indeed, but adjustments will often be made to suit sensitive Western palates. If you find you have taken a mouthful of something that is simply too hot, relief does not come from a gulp of cold water: that's like throwing fuel on a fire. Far better is a forkful of rice, or better still some cooling yogurt or curd (buffalo yogurt), or even cucumber. Alcohol also dissolves chilli oil, proving there's method in the madness of the British lager lout's vindaloo and beer extravaganza. Another surprisingly effective strategy is to sprinkle plain grated coconut over the curry – that's what those side dishes are for. Of course, if the curry is not hot enough the solution to that is there too – simply add some **pol sambol**, a red-hot side dish made with grated coconut, chilli and spices. Sambol is the general name used to describe any spicy-hot dish.

Sri Lankan rice and curry usually includes a variety of small curry dishes – vegetable, meat or fish. Chicken and fish or dried fish are popular, and beef and mutton are also available. Vegetarians won't have trouble finding tasty food – vegetable curries are made from banana (ash plantain), banana flower, breadfruit, jackfruit, mangoes, potatoes, beans and pumpkins, to name just a few. The **eggplant** (aubergine; also called brinjal) dishes are recommended. An accompaniment of **mallung** (shredded green leaves with spices, lightly stir-fried) is common, and the meal would not be complete without **parripu** (red lentil dhal) or another pulse curry.

The usual Indian curry varieties are also available, including South Indian vegetarian **thali** and the delicate North Indian **biryani**. From the northern Jaffna region comes **kool**, a boiled, fried and sun-dried vegetable combination.

The **spices** used to bring out the flavours of Sri Lankan curry are all made locally. It was spices, particularly cinnamon, that first brought Europeans to the island. The essential ingredients in most curries are chilli powder and fresh chillies, turmeric, cinnamon quills, curry powder, curry leaves, pandanus leaves, garlic, coconut milk and sometimes crushed 'Maldive fish' (dried sprats).

Disappointingly, and despite the huge amount of it eaten in Sri Lanka, the rice is often bland. There's even one variety that has a musty smell and tastes just like cardboard. Try the delicious partly hulled red rice instead.

Inset: Red-hot chillies (Photograph by Greg Elms)

Fish & Seafood

Coastal towns have excellent fish (often served with chips and salad). Prawns are also widespread, and in Hikkaduwa, Unawatuna and Tangalla, to name but a few places, you can find delicious crab and lobster. In the south of the island a popular dish is **ambul thiyal**, a pickle usually made from tuna, which is literally translated as 'sour fish curry'. Unfortunately, seafood is often spoiled by local attempts at catering to Western tastes.

Other Specialities

Unique Sri Lankan foods include **hoppers**, which are usually eaten for breakfast or as an evening snack. A regular hopper is rather like a small, bowl-shaped pancake, skilfully fried over a high flame and sometimes served with an egg fried into the middle or with honey and yogurt. String hoppers are tangled little circles of steamed noodles; used as a curry dip instead of rice, they make a tasty and filling meal at breakfast or lunch.

A popular breakfast among Sri Lankans is fresh bread dipped in dhal or a curry with a thin gravy called **hodhi**.

Another rice substitute is **pittu**, a mixture of flour and grated coconut steamed in a bamboo mould so that it comes out shaped like a cylinder.

Chilli lovers will thrive on 'devilled' dishes, such as devilled beef, where the meat is infused with chilli. It can rival Andhra chicken as the subcontinent's fieriest dish.

Lamprais, a popular dish of Dutch origin, is made of rice that's boiled in meat stock then added to vegetables and meat and slowly baked in a banana-leaf wrapping. It is much more appetising that the literal translation 'lump rice' suggests.

At lunch time you can dine lightly on a plate of **short eats**. This is the local term for a selection of 'Chinese' rolls (though they're not really like Chinese spring rolls), meat and vegetable patties (called cutlets), pastries, **vadai** (made with lentils or flour) and other snacks that are placed in the middle of the table. You eat as many as you feel like and the bill is added up according to how many are left.

A filling snack, which you can find mainly in streetside huts, is the **rotty**, a small parcel of anything you fancy wrapped up in a sort of elasticated,

ANDERS BLOMQVIST

Left: Small fry left out to dry

doughy pancake. Fillings can range from chilli and onion to bacon and egg. A rotty chopped up and mixed with vegetables (or meat or egg) is called a **kotthu rotty**. You'll soon become attuned to the chop-chop sounds of the *kotthu rotty* maker at the local hotel in the evening.

Lunch Packets

Office workers, and indeed anyone wanting a filling, tasty and quick meal at lunch, generally go for lunch packets. These are parcels of rice and curry sold at street corners and on footpaths all over the country between about 11am and 2pm. Inside a lunch packet you'll usually find a generous portion of steamed or boiled rice, a piece of curried chicken, fish or beef (if you're vegetarian you'll get an egg instead), a portion of curried vegetables and a *sambol*.

Desserts & Sweets

The Sri Lankans have lots of ideas for desserts, including **wattalappam**, an egg pudding of Malay origin that's vaguely caramel-like in taste. Curd and honey, or curd and treacle known as **kiri peni**, is good at any time of day. Curd is a rich and tasty yogurt made from buffalo milk. If you buy it to take away, it comes in a shallow clay pot complete with a handy carrying rope that is so attractive you'll hate to throw it away. The treacle, called **kitul**, is really syrup from the *kitul* palm. If it's boiled and set to form hard blocks you have **jaggery**, an all-purpose Sri Lankan candy or sweetener.

Kiri bath is a dessert of rice cooked in milk. It's served at weddings and is traditionally the first solid food fed to babies, but is also enjoyed as a tasty dish with a *sambol* or *jaggery*.

Like Indians, Sri Lankans waste no opportunity to indulge their sweet tooth – sweets are known as **rasakavili**. You could try **kavun**, spiced flour and treacle batter-cake fried in coconut oil, or **aluva**, a rice flour, treacle and cashew-nut fudge. Coconut milk, *jaggery* and cashew nuts give you the dark and delicious **kalu dodol**.

Fruit

Sri Lanka has a wide variety of delicious fruits: passion fruit, avocados and guavas (particularly the little pink variety which are like crispy pears) are just a few to be discovered and enjoyed. Try the sweet red bananas or a papaya (pawpaw) with a dash of lime for a delicious way to start the day.

Woodapples, a hard, wooden-shelled fruit, are used to make a delicious drink, a creamy dessert topping or a uniquely Sri Lankan jam. The infamous **durian**, in season from July to September, comes under its own category; this big, green, spiky-skinned fruit smells – but doesn't taste – like a blocked sewer. The **rambutan**, related to the lychee, is so sought after that growers must guard their trees keenly to prevent eager poachers. During rambutan season from July to September, stalls spring up along Kandy Rd at Nittambuwa and on Old Kandy Rd at Kaduwela.

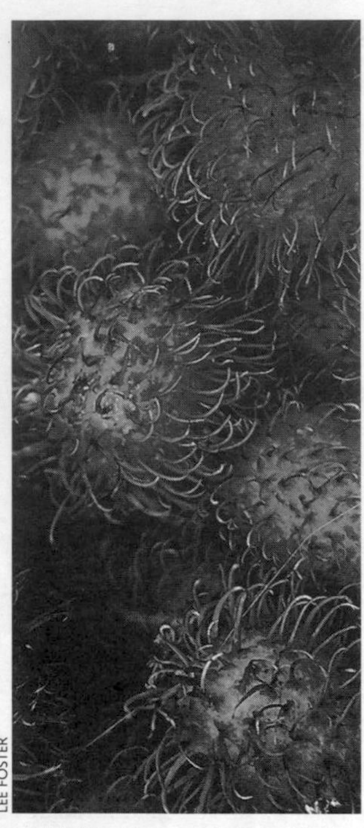
LEE FOSTER

The flavour of the **mangosteen** has been described as a combination of strawberries and grapes. Queen Victoria is said to have been so keen to sample one of these fruits that she offered a considerable prize to anyone who brought one back to her from the tropics. Mangosteens are in season from July to September, and if there are any to be found you'll see them for sale on the roadside at Kalutara, on the west coast, south of Colombo.

The ubiquitous **mango** comes in a variety of shapes and tastes, although generally in the green-skinned, peach-textured variety. The mangoes from Jaffna are considered by some to be the best.

The **jackfruit**, the world's biggest fruit, may be eaten fresh or cooked, and the seeds may also be cooked as a curry. The fruit breaks up into hundreds of bright orange-yellow segments that have a slightly rubbery texture.

Melons are widely available, but watermelons in particular can harbour bacteria in their pulp so they're best avoided.

Dining Etiquette

Sri Lankans say that it's only by eating with the fingers that you can fully enjoy the flavour combinations from the different curries – and it's true. To eat Sri Lankan–style, start by ladling a heap of rice onto your plate, followed by the desired quantities of the different curries. Then delve in with the ends of the fingers of your right hand – make sure you use the right hand – and mix things up a bit to mingle the flavours. With the aid of your thumb, mix a mouthful-sized wad of food. Lift the food with the same finger-ends, slightly cupped, and push it into your mouth with the thumb. Try not to let the food pass the middle knuckles on your fingers. A finger bowl will appear for you to wash your fingers when you have finished.

DRINKS

As in most parts of Asia, you're advised not to drink the water in Sri Lanka unless you're certain that it has been thoroughly boiled. Of course you've got no way of telling if this has really been done when in a restaurant, even when staff assure you that it has. You'll get awfully thirsty at times, so what are the safe substitutes available?

Above: Much-sought-after rambutans

Non-Alcoholic Drinks

MARTIN HUGHES

Although Sri Lanka is famous for its **tea**, the bulk of the best stuff is exported. Most Sri Lankans drink a concoction called 'milk tea' – tea, hot milk and sugar are mixed together before being poured into a cup.

Coffee is a lottery, and you will rarely win. The local version of coffee tastes nothing like what you're probably used to, but reasonable instant coffee is available. Unless you're staying in a top-end hotel, Colombo is the only place you can get a really good espresso.

Lime juice is excellent but unfortunately gets mixed with the highly questionable local water (unless you specifically ask for soda water). Coca-Cola and other multinational **soft drinks** are widely available. Elephant House is the most widespread of the Sri Lankan soft drinks; try the tart ginger beer (Rs 15), marketed as having healthy Ayurvedic qualities.

A refreshing, natural option is **thambili** (king coconut), the orange-coloured drinking coconut for sale at stalls and shops for about Rs 10.

Alcoholic Drinks

Beer, at around Rs 120 to 150 a bottle, is an expensive drink by Sri Lankan standards. Locally made Lion lager and Carlsberg are the most common beers; Three Coins is less common. You can buy all manner of imported grog too. The local **wines** are pretty dire – syrupy sweet and made with imported grape juice. Alcohol isn't sold on the monthly *poya* (full moon) holiday.

Popular local alcoholic beverages include **toddy**, a natural drink a bit like cider. There are three types of toddy in Sri Lanka: coconut toddy comes from the southern lowlands; hill-country toddy is made from the juice of the *kitul* palm, the source of *jaggery* as well as the favourite food of elephants; northern toddy is made from the spiky palmyra tree. Toddy dens are usually situated on the outskirts of villages and towns, where men can drink their fill without disturbing others.

Fermented and refined toddy becomes **arrack**. It's produced in a variety of grades and qualities, some of which are real firewater. Kalutara, 40km south of Colombo on the road to Hikkaduwa, is the toddy and arrack capital of Sri Lanka. Ginger ale, especially the Elephant House brand, is the best local mixer to drink with arrack.

Above: Limes make a delicious drink – but make sure the juice is not mixed with unboiled water

[Continued from page 64]

ACCOMMODATION

Sri Lanka has a good range of accommodation options, from five-star resorts to a room in a family home, but it doesn't cater well for shoestring travellers. Unlike India, for example, which is crawling with cheap-as-chips options, only a handful of places in the country have dormitory-style accommodation. The only other option for lone travellers is single rooms, and they're often doll-sized boxes or cost the same amount as double rooms. On the other hand, most places bigger than a family guesthouse have a 'family' room, usually 20% to 50% more than a double, with three or four beds. Still, Sri Lanka is perfectly set up for starry-eyed couples, groups and lone travellers with a bit of cash to splash. Most guesthouses and hotels can arrange transport or car hire for wherever you want to go, or tailor a tour for you.

Prices are very seasonal, particularly in beach resorts. The prices quoted in this guide are generally high-season rates, and you can often find spectacular bargains in the low season. The 'season', and its prices, has a more or less official starting date – 15 December on the west and south coasts, 1 April on the east – and the monsoon may have ended well before the season starts. High season ends around March in the South and West, and around September on the east coast. Of course, you can often bargain prices down at any time of the year.

Guesthouses and hotels are in big demand during April in Nuwara Eliya, and in Kandy

Volunteer Life Beats Travelling

There was no-one to meet me after midnight at the airport arrivals area – a bus stop was as close as nonauthorised visitors could get to the terminal. The next night, power workers started a four-day strike leaving homes without fans and water (if they had electric water pumps). Soon after, the government imposed power cuts of up to eight hours a day. Welcome to Sri Lanka!

During later months, a couple of bombs blasted Colombo targets killing dozens of people, a national parliamentarian was assassinated and a curfew was imposed to limit violence during local government elections. Tropical paradise? I think not.

At home in my bedsit flat, I handwashed clothes on the floor of the shower for 18 months. Outside, I travelled in crazily driven buses crammed full like sardine cans. But for every negative or confusing experience, there was an equally delightful interaction. The family at the general store who understood my charade-like request for candles during the power strike became friendly greeters whom I visited if I needed cheering up. My landlady-neighbour delivered the auspicious dish *kiri bath* (milk rice) on the first day of each month. When visiting friends without washrooms I enjoyed bathing in the garden at their private wells, and the excitement of the national cricket team winning an international tournament was never far away. Most touching were the invitations to witness the cycle of life events and the rituals attached to birth, adolescent rites of passage, marriage and death.

Working as a volunteer in another country is one of the best ways to experience life as it really is for citizens of the country. The opportunity provides unique challenges and rewards, and allows you to move beyond the sometimes superficial encounters and observations of a traveller. If visiting a place renders it part of your consciousness forever, then living in a country for a year or more means it is indelibly marked on your mind and heart. However, the longer-term experience often raises as many questions as it answers, and I doubt I will ever understand Sri Lanka's politics or the long and bloody ethnic conflict.

Living in the 'Third World' brings the inescapable realisation that although life is physically demanding and a struggle for most of the world's people, they generally meet the difficulties with resourcefulness and make the most of available opportunities. Like me, Sri Lankans also endured verbal and sometimes physical harassment, the frustration of working in a public sector bureaucracy, and the physical limitations and emotional trauma of living in a country at war with itself; but they generally don't have the freedom or opportunity to leave.

Brigitte Ellemor

The Accommodation Basics

To spare you tedious repetition in our Places to Stay listings, we've left out facilities common to most hotel/guesthouse rooms in Sri Lanka: attached bathrooms, mosquito repellent facilities (either a net or an electric 'mat') and fans. For example, most rooms in Sri Lanka have bathrooms – where rooms have shared bathrooms we've stated so. Similarly, most rooms have mosquito nets and fans. Again, if we don't mention them don't worry – if there are no mosquito repellent facilities or fans we'll say so.

In Sri Lanka the cost of accommodation is routinely quoted with and without meals. Prices quoted in this book are room only – ie, with no meals – unless otherwise stated. Generally you can get a range of prices from room only to bed and breakfast (B&B), half board (room plus breakfast and one main meal) and full board (breakfast, lunch and dinner). All places to stay listed in this book serve meals, unless otherwise stated.

Most room prices in this book are quoted in rupees, but some are in US dollars if a hotel quotes them that way. We've also included the service charge and VAT, where applicable, in hotel prices throughout the book.

Finally, all hill-country budget accommodation has hot water. Few budget places elsewhere in the country, ie, west coast, ancient cities, east coast, have hot water – if you don't read it, you won't have it. All top-end hotels and most mid-range hotels in Sri Lanka have hot water.

during the *perahera* (generally July/August). It would certainly pay to book well ahead if you plan to be in these places at these times.

Many places have a variety of rooms at different prices, and it's often worth asking, after staff have shown you their first room or quoted you their first price, if there are any cheaper rooms available.

National Parks

The **Department of Wildlife Conservation** *(☎ 011-269 4241; ⓔ wildlife@slt.lk; 18 Gregory's Rd, Cinnamon Gardens, Colombo)* has bungalows, each accommodating up to 10 adults and two children, in five national parks: Yala West (Ruhuna), Uda Walawe, Wasgomuwa, Gal Oya and Horton Plains. It costs US$27.60 per person per night in a bungalow, and a whopping US$30 'service charge' per stay. You must bring your own dry rations, kerosene and linen. Camp sites cost US$6 per site per day, plus US$5 'service charge' per trip. Students and children six to 12 years of age pay half price (kiddies under six stay for free). On top of these costs, there is a minimum park entry fee of US$14.40 for the most popular parks. You can book up to a month in advance.

The **Wildlife Trust** *(☎/fax 011-250 2271; 18 Gregory's Rd, Cinnamon Gardens, Colombo)* maintains bungalows in national parks, and offers some 'nature' tours; see the small shop at the Department of Wildlife Conservation for information. Companies such as Connaissance de Ceylan and Adventure Sports Lanka also arrange trips to parks (see Organised Tours in the Getting Around chapter for contact details).

Guesthouses

You'll find some very cheap places to stay in this category, plus some in the mid-range bracket and even the occasional top-end place. Sometimes a guesthouse will rent just a couple of rooms, like the English B&B establishments; other times guesthouses are like small hotels. It's a good idea to pin down exactly what you're getting for your money, or you might be surprised with a bill for every cup of tea.

Apart from the low cost, the 'meeting people' aspect is the big plus of guesthouse accommodation. If you're after privacy, stick to the guesthouses with a separate guest annexe; some guesthouses have separate entrances for guests, while others require you to tip-toe through the lounge after a night on the town.

If arriving late at night, consider a hotel room if you haven't organised yourself in time. Many guesthouses are family homes with only a few rooms to let; sometimes just one or two. Rather than simply turning up and hoping for the best, telephone first to see if a room is available. Most guesthouse owners are accommodating, but don't appreciate being woken up by unannounced arrivals.

Resthouses

Originally established by the Dutch for travelling government officials, then developed into a network of wayside inns by the British, resthouses now mostly function as small mid-range hotels. They're found all over the country, including in little out of the way towns (where they may be the only regular accommodation). Although they vary widely in standards and prices (those run by the Ceylon Hotels Corporation are usually the best maintained), the best resthouses are old fashioned, with big rooms, and are usually situated to enjoy the view from the highest hill or along the best stretch of beach. Prices in resthouses vary from the lower-middle price range to the bottom end of the upper price range. A double costs anywhere from US$12 up to US$36.

Hotels

The borderline between lower-price hotels and upper-range guesthouses is a blurred one, and not least in name since some 'hotels' are really guesthouses, while other small hotels may call themselves inns, lodges, villas and so on. You'll rarely find a double in a hotel for less than Rs 800. There are places going all the way up the price scale, as far as US$120 and above. For Rs 1500 you will usually get a spacious and clean double.

The larger hotels are of two basic types: modern resort hotels and older colonial-style places. The latter type definitely has the edge when it comes to atmosphere, and the facilities are often just as good. The newer places pride themselves on luxury facilities such as tennis courts, windsurfing instruction, nightclubs and prime beach, riverside or hill-top sites, and are mostly geared to package tourists. Resort-hotel doubles on the west coast go from around US$35 up to US$100 plus. People with residency visas get huge discounts on resort hotels, as much as 70% off the FIT (foreign individual tourist) rates.

FOOD & DRINKS

Sri Lankan cuisine shows clear links with India, yet has many of its own traditions. The staple meal is rice and curry, with all sorts of variations. In Colombo you have a wide array of cuisines from which to choose. In places such as Hikkaduwa you can get all the usual traveller stand-bys (pizza, french fries and so on). In many other places you'll find a curious kind of fusion cuisine – Sri Lankan meets whatever Western cuisine you dare to choose. Don't be surprised if pasta comes with curry leaves, for example. The fusions are sometimes quite good, but it has to be said that too many places, beach restaurants in particular, serve up dreadful mistakes and seem surprised that you aren't thrilled with oily fish, sweaty chips and a few vegetables well beyond exhaustion. On a more positive note, Sri Lanka rivals any country when it comes to tropical fruits.

Food preparation seems to take a long time in Sri Lanka: rice and curry can take up to 1½ hours to prepare. Get into the habit of pre-ordering your meal. Peruse the menu during the day, order, turn up at the allocated time, and everyone should be happy.

See the special section 'Cuisine of Sri Lanka' for some of the local specialities to savour.

ENTERTAINMENT

Cinemas

Hollywood blockbusters are screened in English in Colombo, though they're likely to be has-beens by the time they hit Sri Lanka's shores. See Entertainment in the Colombo chapter for details of venues. Art-house films (in English and European languages) are shown at cultural centres such as the British Council and the Alliance Française in Colombo and Kandy. See Cultural Centres in the Colombo chapter and in the Kandy section of The Hill Country chapter for details. Ubiquitous billboards confront you with Sri Lankan–made and Indian-made films that show in cinemas everywhere.

Discos & Nightclubs

Possibly because of the long years of war, late-night partying and clubbing is rare in Sri Lanka. Outside Colombo you will find a few clubs in resort areas such as Negombo, Bentota and Hikkaduwa. Kandy has a couple of pubs, a nightclub and a casino called the Lake Club. Most of the action is found at top-end hotels, and will fleece your wallet. Colombo's nightlife is starting to stir, and some interesting new venues have opened. See Entertainment in the Colombo chapter for details.

Theatre, Classical Music & Galleries

Theatre of European heritage, for example, Shakespeare, is performed at cultural centres such as the British Council and Alliance Française, both found in Colombo and Kandy, and the Goethe Institut in Colombo. Colombo is where most things happen. Theatre written and directed by Sri Lankans is often performed at the Lionel Wendt Gallery & Theatre and the Elphinstone Theatre – ring ahead to find out if it's in English or Sinhala. The Lumbini Theatre shows Sinhala theatre. These theatres and the cultural centres are the main venues for classical music (Western and Eastern), though top-end hotels have occasional performances. If you're into art, there are often exhibitions at the Lionel Wendt, the National Art Gallery or at the 'in' cafes in Colombo.

Apart from the British Council and Alliance Française in Kandy, there is little happening outside Colombo.

Traditional Music & Dance

Traditional music and dance is an important, though fading, part of Sri Lankan culture. The dances for tourists are usually sanitised snapshots of various types blended into one performance. Still, it's worth seeing. The Lionel Wendt Gallery & Theatre in Colombo holds occasional performances, as do top-end hotels in major resorts and in Colombo. The School of Dance at Ambalangoda (see the West Coast chapter for details) has irregular performances that are worth catching. Dancing and drumming are also performed nightly at several venues in Kandy (see that section in The Hill Country chapter for details).

Pubs & Bars

Sri Lankans who drink alcohol tend to do it at home or in seedy venues. The few pubs and bars that do exist tend to be congregated around tourist haunts. Many are attached to top-end hotels, with top-end prices, and often have a cheesy 'British' or 'German' theme and imported ales. Women travellers seeking a bar will feel most comfortable in these places. The resort towns such as Hikkaduwa and Negombo have a handful of bopping drinking holes. In other places you're more likely to find yourself drinking at a restaurant or, perish the thought, in your hotel room. Some of the colonial mansions-cum-hotels have lovely wide verandas, perfect for a sunset beer.

SPECTATOR SPORTS

Although Sri Lankans play volleyball, netball, soccer, tennis and a few other sports, the most popular is cricket. Radio commentaries of big games are broadcast down streets, boys play the game on the roadside or in forest clearings, and Sri Lankans whose knowledge of English is otherwise limited can tell you 'First innings, two hundred and twelve, eight wickets, declared'. See the boxed text 'The Cricket-Crazy Nation' for an insight into Sri Lanka's obsession with cricket.

It's usually easy to see a big match – the main international stadium is the Premadasa Stadium at Kettarama, with other venues including the Sinhalese Sports Club (SSC) in Cinnamon Gardens, Colombo, and ovals at Moratuwa, Borella (Sara Stadium), Kandy, Dambulla and Galle. You can buy tickets for matches at the office of the **Board of Control for Cricket in Sri Lanka** *(BCCSL; ☎ 011-268 1601; e toc@itmin.com; 35 Maitland Place, Colombo)* next to the SSC. You can catch a club match or international game at almost any time of year. Check the local newspapers to find out what's coming up.

One entirely sedentary sport enjoyed by large numbers of Sri Lankans is betting – on British horse and dog racing! With racing in Sri Lanka frowned upon by the Buddhist establishment, you'll see people in hole-in-the-wall betting shops throughout the land avidly studying the day's runners and riders from Aintree, Ascot and Hackney. Commentaries on the races are beamed over from Britain starting at about 6pm. This passion is one reason for the mushrooming of satellite dishes in Sri Lankan towns.

SHOPPING

Sri Lanka has a wide variety of attractive handicrafts on sale. Laksala, a government-run store, is found in most cities and tourist towns. Each store has a good collection of items from all over the country and its stock is generally of reasonable quality, moderately priced, and with fixed price tags. There are other handicraft outlets in Colombo; see that chapter for details. Street stalls can be found in touristy areas, but you'll need to bargain – expect the vendor to start the bidding at two to three times the value of the article.

The Cricket-Crazy Nation

The nation stops when Sri Lanka's First Eleven play cricket. Workers take leave from their workplaces for the day or afternoon, transistor radios reveal the score in the corner of the office, crowds gather around television screens in the Singer stores, radios blare on buses with coverage in Sinhala, Tamil and English. Almost everyone follows the game, men and women. And if Sri Lanka wins, fire crackers sound around the neighbourhood.

Ever since their 1996 World Cup victory in Lahore, Pakistan, Sri Lanka's cricketers have become national heroes, shopping centre stars, advertising icons, the idols of would-be cricketers and the pin-ups of teenage girls. Cricket largely transcends Sri Lanka's ethnic conflict. One of a couple of Tamil players in the squad, the brilliant off-spinner Muttiah Muralitharan, is equally applauded by Sinhalese and Tamil fans.

Cricket is a curious game, like baseball designed by Freemasons. It has a welter of strange, almost comical terms for the uninitiated. A maiden over is a spell of six balls by the same bowler in which no runs are scored by the batsmen. Silly mid-off is a fielding position perilously close to the batsman – hence 'silly'. Arcane terms abound for different types of bowling deliveries, such as flippers, googlies, off-cutters and yorkers. There are two forms of matches; one is held over three or five days and widely regarded by noncricket fans as the world's most boring sporting contest, but it's revered by fans as a sublime mix of strategy, persistence and luck. International contests are held over five days and are called test matches. The other format is the much faster and more flamboyant one-day contest. Even so, watching a poor-quality one-day match is a bit like hearing someone count down from 1000 to one, and getting excited when they reach 10.

In the international contest there are 10 test-playing teams, all former parts of the British Empire. The game's biggest support base by some margin is in South Asia. Cricket completely eclipses all other sports in India, Pakistan, Sri Lanka and Bangladesh.

You'll see people playing some sort of match everywhere – adults on Sunday at certain known gathering places and children anywhere, any day, with almost any objects sufficing for a bat and ball. However, at the youth level the game is dominated by a wealthy handful of schools. Cricket gear is expensive – it costs at least Rs 14,000 to fit out a batsman.

If you come from a noncricket playing nation, you might find all the fuss rather confusing. If you come from a cricket-playing country but don't know much about the game or your national team, you may well be regarded as mad.

Masks

Sri Lankan masks are a popular collector's item for visitors. They're carved at a number of places, principally along the southwest coast, and are sold all over the island, but Ambalangoda, near Hikkaduwa, is the mask-carving centre. You can visit several of the showroom-workshops here.

Touristy or not, the masks are remarkably well made, good value and look very nice on the wall back home. They're available from key-ring size for a few rupees up to big, high-quality masks for over Rs 2000. See the boxed text 'Sri Lanka's Dances & Masks' in the Facts about Sri Lanka chapter for more information.

Batik

The Indonesian art of batik making is a relatively new development in Sri Lanka but one that has been taken to with alacrity. You'll see a wide variety of batiks made and sold around the island. Some of the best and most original are made in the west coast towns of Marawila, Mahawewa and Ambalangoda. Batik pictures start from about Rs 200, and go up to well over Rs 1000. Batik is also used for a variety of clothing items.

Leather

You can find some very low-priced and good-quality leatherwork – particularly bags and cases. Look in the leatherwork and shoe shops around Fort in Colombo. The bazaar on Olcott Mawatha, beside Fort Station, is cheaper than Laksala for similar-quality goods. The Leather Collection in Colombo is a more upmarket place to shop. Hikkaduwa is also a good place for leather bags.

Gems

There are countless showrooms and private gem dealers all over the country. In Ratnapura, the centre of the gem trade, everybody and their brother is a part-time gem dealer! At the government **Gem Testing Laboratory** in Colombo tourists can get any stone tested free. The only snag with the testing service is that it's not always easy, or practical, to 'borrow' a stone to take it in for testing before you buy it. However, one reader wrote that a reputable dealer, at least in Colombo, would accompany you to the Gem Testing Laboratory for a testing. See the shopping section of the Colombo chapter for details on the laboratory.

There have been letters from readers who have had Sri Lankans try to sell them large amounts of gems with the promise that they can be resold for a big profit in other countries. It's a scam, and unless you happen to be a world-class gem expert you're sure to lose money. Guidebooks from 100 years ago make exactly the same warning. For more information see the boxed text 'Gems' under Ratnapura in The Hill Country chapter.

Other Souvenirs

If you like to spend, there are countless other purchases waiting to tempt your rupees out of your moneybelt. The ubiquitous coconut shell is carved into all manner of souvenirs and useful items. Like the Thais and Burmese, Sri Lankans also make lacquerware items such as bowls and ashtrays – layers of lacquer are built up on a light framework, usually of bamboo strips. Kandy is a centre for jewellery and brassware, both antique and modern. There are some nice chunky silver bracelets, as well as some rather dull stuff. The brass suns and moons are attractive, or you could try a hefty brass elephant-head door-knocker for size.

Coir (rope fibre made from coconut husks) is made into baskets, bags, mats and other items. Weligama on the south coast turns out some attractive lacework.

Spices are integral to Sri Lanka's cuisine and Ayurvedic traditions. A visit to a spice garden is an excellent way to discover the alternative uses of spices you've probably been using for years, although the prices you come across are often extortionate. You'll see cinnamon, cloves, nutmeg, vanilla beans, cardamom and black pepper, to name just a few. You can buy the pure products, oils or Ayurvedic potions. Watch the prices, and check in local markets beforehand to get an idea of costs.

Getting There & Away

AIR

Airports

The only international airport in Sri Lanka is Bandaranaike International Airport at Katunayake, 30km north of Colombo. There are 24-hour money-changing facilities in the arrivals and departures halls. The travel desks in arrivals often have discounts for mid-range and top-end hotels in Negombo and Colombo. You may well be offered a full 10- or 20-day package with hotel, van and driver on the spot. There are also bank counters, a few duty-free shops and a cafeteria in the departures lounge, but prices are high.

Tickets

The plane ticket will probably be the most expensive item in your budget. Some of the cheapest tickets have to be bought months in advance and some popular flights sell out quickly. You may discover that impossibly cheap flights advertised in newspapers are 'fully booked, but we have another one that costs a bit more...' or that the flight leaves you waiting in the world's dullest airport mid-journey for 14 hours. The other thing you can do is surf the Internet. Although some travel sites are quite laborious to navigate, and it often seems easier to call a travel agent, the Web is ideal for research.

Colombo is not as good as some other Asian centres for cheap flights and you may be better off booking your onward tickets before you leave home. For details on travel agencies in Colombo see Organised Tours in the Getting Around chapter.

The departure tax is Rs 1000, to be paid at the airport. It's unlikely you'll forget; there are plenty of signs there to remind you!

Airlines

Sri Lanka isn't quite on the A-list of destinations for major airlines. The big European carriers – KLM, British Airways, Lufthansa – no longer fly here. Most of the airlines flying between Europe and Sri Lanka are from the Arab world – Kuwait Airways, Emirates, Royal Jordanian and Qatar Airways. A generally better range of airlines fly between Sri Lanka and Asia (with connections elsewhere), including Singapore Airlines, Cathay Pacific, Thai Airways, Malaysia Airlines and SriLankan Airlines.

It's worth reconfirming flights 72 hours in advance in Sri Lanka, as the country is a turning point for flights. Sometimes if a 200-seater plane is scheduled to fly to Sri Lanka but only 80 seats are full, an airline will send a 120-seater plane instead. If there are 200 or so passengers waiting to leave Sri Lanka on that plane, difficulties arise. The passengers who bothered to reconfirm stand a better chance of leaving as planned. If you're flying with **SriLankan Airlines** *(☎ 011-242 1161, reconfirmation ☎ 019 733 5500)* absolutely, definitely reconfirm – you'll need the flight number plus a contact address – as they're notorious for bumping passengers who fail to do so. For contact details of other airlines serving Sri Lanka, see Air under Getting There & Away in the Colombo chapter.

> **Warning**
>
> The information in this chapter is particularly vulnerable to change: Prices for international travel are volatile, routes are introduced and cancelled, schedules change, special deals come and go, and rules and visa requirements are amended. You should check directly with the airline or a travel agent to make sure you understand how a fare (and ticket you may buy) works and be aware of the security requirements for international travel.
>
> The upshot of this is that you should get opinions, quotes and advice from as many airlines and travel agents as possible before you part with your hard-earned cash. The details given in this chapter should be regarded as pointers and are not a substitute for your own careful, up-to-date research.

UK Discount air travel is big business in London. Advertisements for many travel agencies appear in the travel pages of the weekend broadsheet newspapers, in *Time Out*, the *Evening Standard* and in the free magazine *TNT*.

Major travel agencies in the UK include:

Bridge the World (☎ 0870-444 7474, **W** www.b-t-w.co.uk)
Flightbookers (☎ 0870-010 7000, **W** www.ebookers.com)
Flight Centre (☎ 0870-890 8099, **W** www.flightcentre.com)
North-South Travel (☎ 01245-608 291, **W** www.northsouthtravel.co.uk)
Quest Travel (☎ 0870-442 3542, **W** www.questtravel.com)
STA Travel (☎ 0870-160 0599, **W** www.statravel.co.uk)
Trailfinders (long-haul line ☎ 020-7938 3939, **W** www.trailfinders.co.uk)
Travel Bag (☎ 0870-890 1456, **W** www.travelbag.co.uk)

Fares from London to Sri Lanka start at UK£360/490 one way/return. CSA (Czech Airlines) and Royal Jordanian have consistently cheap fares. The return fares to London with Emirates start at UK£530.

Continental Europe SriLankan Airlines has two weekly flights between Stockholm and Colombo (via Dubai). It also has three weekly direct flights from Rome and Milan. The main European carriers with flights to Sri Lanka are CSA (three times a week from Prague) and Austrian Airlines (a seasonal schedule, peaking with two or three flights a week around New Year).

Germany SriLankan Airlines has one weekly flight between Frankfurt and Colombo. Return flights from Frankfurt to Colombo with Qatar Airways, CSA and SriLankan Airlines cost from €600 to €750. German charter companies with seasonal flights include Condor and LTU.

Recommended agencies (websites are in German only) include:

Expedia (☎ 0180-500 6025; **W** www.expedia.de)
Just Travel (☎ 089-747 3330; **W** www.justtravel.de)
Lastminute (☎ 01805-284 366; **W** www.lastminute.de)
STA Travel (☎ 01805-456 422; **W** www.statravel.de)

France SriLankan Airlines has two flights a week between Paris and Colombo. Return flights with Saudi Arabian Airlines, CSA and SriLankan Airlines range in price from €730 to €840.

France has a network of travel agencies that can supply discount tickets to travellers of all ages. Recommended agencies (the websites are in French only) include:

Anyway (☎ 0892-893 892; **W** www.anyway.fr)
Lastminute (☎ 0892-230 101; **W** www.lastminute.fr)
Nouvelles Frontières (☎ 0825-000 747; **W** www.nouvelles-frontieres.fr)
OTU Voyages (☎ 0820-817 817; **W** www.otu.fr)
Student and young person specialist agency
Voyageurs du Monde (☎ 01 42 86 16 00; **W** www.vdm.com)

Australia Singapore Airlines, Cathay Pacific and Malaysia Airlines have similar return fares starting at around A$1400 from the east coast. Return fares from Perth are a little cheaper at around A$1320 with Malaysia Airlines and Singapore Airlines.

Flight Centre *(☎ 131 600; **W** www.flight centre.com.au)* and **STA Travel** *(**W** www.sta travel.com.au)* have offices throughout Australia. For addresses of STA Travel branches call ☎ 1300 360 960. For online bookings, try **W** www.travel.com.au. Check for other travel agency ads in the *Yellow Pages* and major newspapers.

New Zealand Both **Flight Centre** *(☎ 0800 243 544; **W** www.flightcentre.co.nz)* and **STA Travel** *(☎ 0800 874 773; **W** www.statravel.co .nz)* have branches throughout the country. A website recommended for online bookings is **W** www.travel.co.nz.

An Auckland–Colombo return flight with Singapore Airlines should cost you around NZ$1600.

Asia & The Middle East With Singapore Airlines, you'll pay around US$205 for a Singapore–Colombo flight. With Emirates and SriLankan Airlines, one-way/return fares are US$195/305 for a Dubai–Colombo flight. For Thai Airways or SriLankan Airlines, expect to pay US$170/290 for a Bangkok–Colombo flight.

India New routes keep opening between India and Sri Lanka, and soon there could be 10 or more cities with direct flights to Colombo. Currently, the choice is either SriLankan Airlines or Indian Airlines. SriLankan Airlines flies daily between Thiruvananthapuram (Trivandrum) in Kerala and Colombo. One-way/return fares start at US$49/110. Tiruchirappalli (Trichy) in Tamil Nadu is only slightly more; there are three weekly flights, with fares starting at US$56/116. Other destinations include Bodhgaya in the northern state of Bihar, and Bangalore in Karnataka. Indian Airlines and SriLankan Airlines have flights between Colombo and Chennai (Madras) for $75/155.

For Indian travel agencies, **STIC Travels** *(in Delhi ☎ 011-2332 0239, in Mumbai ☎ 022-2218 1431; W www.stictravel.com)* is recommended. Also in Mumbai (Bombay) is **Transway International** *(☎ 022-2262 6066; W www.transwayinternational.com)*.

When buying a ticket to the Maldives, you can also buy a flight on to Thiruvananthapuram. One-way fares in either direction on SriLankan Airlines start at around US$179.

USA The *New York Times*, the *LA Times*, the *Chicago Tribune* and the *San Francisco Examiner* all have weekly travel sections in which you'll find any number of travel agency ads. San Francisco is the discount ticket capital of America, although some good deals can be found in Los Angeles, New York and other big cities.

Recommendations for online bookings include:

American Express Interactive Travel (☎ 1 800 346 3607; W www.itn.net)
Atevo Travel (☎ 650-652 1000; W www.atevo.com)
Cheap Tickets (☎ 1 888 922 8849, outside the US 719-799 8609; W www.cheaptickets.com)
Expedia (☎ 1 800 397 3342; W www.expedia.com
Lowestfare.com (W www.lowestfare.com)

A return New York–Colombo flight with Continental and Cathay Pacific costs around US$2700. From Los Angeles, you'll pay US$1580 for a Cathay Pacific/Thai Airways return flight via Hong Kong and Bangkok, or US$1650 for a Cathay Pacific/SriLankan Airlines return flight with one stop in Hong Kong.

Canada The *Globe & Mail*, the *Toronto Star*, the *Montreal Gazette* and the *Vancouver Sun* carry travel agency ads and are good places to look for cheap fares. **Travel CUTS** *(☎ 800 667 2887; W www.travelcuts.com)* is Canada's national student travel agency. For online bookings try W www.expedia.ca and W www.travelocity.ca.

The cheapest return fares from Vancouver to Colombo (via Hong Kong) start at C$2830 with Air Canada, Thai Airways and SriLankan Airlines. Eastern Canada is about as far you can get from Sri Lanka – fares start from C$4430 with British Airways/Gulf Air, via London and Abu Dhabi.

Africa The cheapest connections between Sri Lanka and Africa are via the Middle East – alas, there are no direct flights. **Rennies Travel** *(W www.renniestravel.com)* and **STA Travel** *(W www.statravel.co.za)* have offices throughout Southern Africa. Check their websites for branch locations. Emirates flies from Colombo to Johannesburg via Dubai for US$730 return. Saudi Arabian Airlines flies to Johannesburg via Jeddah for US$640 return.

SEA

Plans to resume ferry services across the Gulf of Mannar to India come and go with the tide. A venture to run a service between Colombo and Tuticorin came unstuck in 2001. Any plans to relaunch the previous route between Talaimannar and Rameswaram must wait until the port terminals are repaired. Check with the **Sri Lanka Ports Authority** *(W www.slpa.lk)* for the latest information.

A handful of cruise liners that voyage around India and the Maldives, or on longer cruises across the Indian Ocean, dock in Colombo. The cruising season is from October to May and cruises last about 12 to 16 days. Two cruise-related websites worth a look are W www.value-cruise.com and W www.planacruise.com.

ORGANISED TOURS

Most visitors to Sri Lanka come on package tours (mainly from Europe). See Organised Tours in the Getting Around chapter for a list of companies that specialise in package trips and tours around Sri Lanka.

Getting Around

The only domestic flights in Sri Lanka are the regular flights between Jaffna and Colombo. Public transport is therefore a choice between buses and trains. Both are cheap. Trains can be crowded, but its nothing compared with the seemingly endless numbers of passengers that squash into ordinary buses. Trains are a bit slower than buses, but a seat on a train is preferable to standing on a bus. Even standing on a train is better than standing on a bus.

On the main roads out of Colombo to Kandy, Negombo and Galle, buses can cover about 40km to 50km per hour. On highways across the southern and northern plains, it might be as much as 60km or 70km each hour. In the hill country, it can slow to just 20km an hour.

All public transport gets particularly crowded around *poya* (full moon) holidays and their nearest weekends, so try to avoid travelling then if you can.

AIR

The only domestic flights are between Colombo's Ratmalana airport (near Mount Lavinia) and Palali airport near Jaffna. The three domestic airlines are keen to fly to other cities such as Trincomalee, but the decision rests with the Sri Lankan air force, which controls all major airfields.

Meanwhile, there are three domestic airlines on the one route. UN agency staff fly solely with **Lionair** *(☎ 074 515715, ⓔ lionairsales@sierra.lk)*, the only carrier to fulfil their safety criteria. Lionair usually charges Rs 4000/6950 one way/return. Unfortunately Lionair runs a dual-pricing policy between Sri Lankans *living* in Sri Lanka, and expat Sri Lankans and foreigners.

The two smaller airlines, **Serendib Express** *(☎ 011-250 5632, ⓔ serendibexpress@sltnet.lk)* and also **Expo Aviation** *(☎ 074 512666, ⓔ info@expolanka.com)* both charge Rs 2425/4550 one way/return. These airlines have been using old Soviet-era Antonov 24 aircraft, so you better not be too fussy about travelling in comfort. All three airlines were engaged in a price war at the time of research, and one airline manager predicted fares will rise to around Rs 4000/7000 one way/return.

For addresses of airline offices in Colombo and Jaffna, see the relevant chapters. Checking in takes at least 2½ hours due to security measures.

BUS

There are two kinds of bus in Sri Lanka – Central Transport Board (CTB) buses and private buses. Just to confuse things, the government has been moving hesitantly to break up and privatise the CTB. Meanwhile, yellow CTB buses ply most long-distance and local routes. Private bus companies have vehicles ranging from late-model Japanese coaches used on intercity express runs to decrepit old minibuses that sputter and limp along some city streets or on short runs between towns and villages. Private air-con intercity buses cover all the major routes; for long-distance travel they are by far the most comfortable.

Bus travel in Sri Lanka can be interesting. Vendors board to sell all sorts of snack foods, and even books, on long-distance routes. Blind singers sometimes get on and work their way down the aisle, warbling away and collecting coins. Beggars may approach passengers with a litany of misfortunes – and they may also be singing them. Buses sometimes stop at temples so the driver and passengers can donate a few coins and earn merit.

The first two seats on CTB buses are reserved for 'clergy' (Buddhist monks) and this is never ignored. If you want to guarantee a seat, you'll need to board the bus at the beginning of its journey. Sri Lankans seem to know when to sprint after the right bus as it pulls in, and throw a bag or a handkerchief through the window to reserve a seat.

For bus travel to Jaffna, see the boxed text 'Up & Down the A9' in the Jaffna & the North chapter.

Costs

In most cases private bus companies run services parallel to CTB services. Intercity express buses charge about twice as much as CTB buses, but are more than twice as comfortable, and are usually faster. Fares for CTB buses and ordinary private buses are very cheap. The journey between Kandy and Colombo costs Rs 44 on a CTB bus and Rs 95 on an air-con intercity express, while the trip from Colombo to Trincomalee costs Rs 90 on an ordinary private bus and Rs 180 by intercity express.

Most buses have unbelievably small luggage compartments and they rarely have storage on the roof. For your own sake, travel light. If you have a large pack, you can buy an extra ticket for your bag.

TRAIN

Sri Lanka's rickety railways are a great way to cross the country. Although they are slow, distances are short so there are few overnight or all-day ordeals to contend with. A train ride is almost always more relaxed than a bus ride.

There are three main lines. The Coast Line runs south from Colombo, past Aluthgama and Hikkaduwa to Galle and Matara. The Main Line pushes east from Colombo into the hill country, through Kandy, Nanu Oya (for Nuwara Eliya) and Ella to Badulla. The Northern Line launches from Colombo through Anuradhapura to Vavuniya – it once ran beyond Jaffna to the northern tip of Sri Lanka. One branch line off the Northern Line reaches Trincomalee on the east coast, while another branch heads south to Polonnaruwa and, recently, on to Batticaloa.

The Puttalam Line runs along the coast north from Colombo. However, rail buses run between Chilaw and Puttalam. The Kelani Valley Line winds 60km from Colombo to Avissawella.

Trains are often late. For long-distance trains, Sri Lankans sometimes measure the lateness in periods of the day: quarter of a day late, half a day late etc.

There's a helpful information desk (No 10) at Fort station in Colombo, and also an **Information Office** *(☎ 011-244 0048; open 9am-5pm Mon-Fri, 9am-1pm Sat)*, to the right of the main entrance, run by JF Tours. The staff are helpful and can provide information on timetables and routes.

Classes

There are three classes on Sri Lankan trains. Third class is dirt-cheap but invariably crowded, so with luck you sit on benches. Second class has padded seats and fans that sometimes work, and it's generally less crowded. There are no 2nd-class sleeping berths, only sleepers (fold-down beds in a compartment shared with others). First class comes in three varieties (all with air-con): coaches, sleeping berths and observation saloons (with large windows).

Reservations

You can reserve places on 1st-class coaches and on intercity expresses. On weekends and public holidays it pays to make a booking for observation saloons, which are only found on the Main Line (the booking fee is Rs 50), as these carriages often fill up. The best seats to book are Nos 11, 12, 23 and 24, which have full window views. The observation saloon is at the end of the train and jolts around quite a lot. Reservations cost Rs 75 for 1st-class sleeping berths, Rs 25 for 2nd-class seats and Rs 18 for 3rd-class seats.

Reservations can be made at stations up to 10 days before departure. You may book a return ticket up to 14 days before departure (these tickets are not open-dated).

If travelling more than 80km you can break your journey at any intermediate station for 24 hours without penalty. However, you must make fresh reservations for seats on the next leg.

Costs

The intercity express from Kandy to Colombo costs Rs 172 in the 1st class observation saloon or Rs 72 in 2nd class. A return 1st-class ticket from Kandy to Colombo costs Rs 208. From Colombo to Anuradhapura costs Rs 277 in 1st class or Rs 116 in 2nd class.

CAR & MOTORCYCLE

Self-drive car hire is possible in Sri Lanka, though it is far more common to hire a car and driver for a day or several days. If you're on a relatively short visit to Sri Lanka on a mid-range budget, the costs of hiring a car and driver can be quite reasonable.

Motorcycling is an alternative for intrepid travellers. Distances are relatively short and some of the roads are simply a motorcyclist's delight. The quieter hill country roads offer some glorious views and secondary roads along the coast and the plains are reasonably quick. The trick is to stay off the main highways. There are motorcycle-rental agencies in Hikkaduwa and Kandy. In addition to a cash deposit you must provide your passport number and leave your airline ticket as security. The official size limit on imported motorbikes is 350cc.

Road Rules & Conditions

The speed limit for vehicles is 56km/h in built-up areas and 72km/h in rural areas. Driving is on the left-hand side of the road as in the UK and Australia. The **Automobile Association of Ceylon** *(☎ 011-242 1528, 40 Sir Mohamed Macan Markar Mawatha, Kollupitiya; open 9.30am-4.30pm Mon-Fri)* sells a booklet called *The Highway Code*.

Although you may see a number of accidents during your time on the road, driving seems fairly safe provided you take care – watch out for other road users. Country roads are often narrow and potholed, with the constant surprise of pedestrian, bicycle and animal traffic to navigate. If travelling by three-wheeler, you may think that the driver is not obeying any road rules; you are probably right.

Punctures are a part of life here, so every little village seems to have a repair expert doing an excellent, although rather time-consuming, job.

Rental

Car & Driver You can find taxi drivers who will happily become your chauffeur for a day or more in all the main tourist centres. Guesthouse owners will probably be able to put you in touch with a driver, or you can ask at travel agencies or big hotels.

Various formulas exist for setting costs – rates per kilometre plus lunch and dinner allowance etc. The simplest way is to agree on a flat fee with no extras. Expect to pay about Rs 2500 per day, or more for a newer, air-con vehicle. Most drivers will expect a tip of around 10%, though of course it's up to you. You may have to pay for fuel – deduct it from the total when you settle accounts at the end of the journey. It also pays to meet the driver before you set off, as there may be a difference between what the travel agent has led you to expect and who turns up. Some travellers find themselves being almost bullied by their drivers – the driver chooses where they go, where they stay and what time they leave. Hiring a driver for only two or three days at first can avoid these problems. The drivers seem to prefer spending only three or four days away from home as well.

Road Distances (km)

	Anuradhapura	Colombo	Galle	Jaffna	Kandy	Nuwara Eliya	Polonnaruwa	Trincomalee
Anuradhapura	---							
Colombo	206	---						
Galle	322	116	---					
Jaffna	195	396	512	---				
Kandy	138	116	232	320	---			
Nuwara Eliya	216	180	290	398	77	---		
Polonnaruwa	101	216	332	283	140	217	---	
Trincomalee	106	257	373	238	182	259	129	---

Some travel agencies may suggest you take a guide along as well. Unless you speak absolutely no English or Sinhala, this is unnecessary.

Be aware that drivers make a fair part of their income from commissions. Most hotels and many guesthouses pay drivers a flat fee or a percentage, while others refuse to. This can lead to disputes between you and the driver over where you're staying the night – they'd prefer to go where the money is. Another problem is that some hotels have appalling accommodation for drivers – a dirty mattress under the stairs. Some of the worst conditions are in the big hotels. Drivers share a dormitory and prison-style meals, drivers come and go all night and no-one gets a good night's rest. The smarter hotels and guesthouses know that keeping drivers happy is good for their business, and provide decent food and lodgings and sometimes money.

Self-Drive Mackinnons Travels and Quickshaws Tours are the two main companies offering self-drive cars (see Organised Tours later in this chapter for contact details). Mackinnons is the agent for Avis. Quickshaws has self-drive air-con Toyota Corollas from Rs 2088 per day (including insurance, tax and the first 100km) or Rs 13,810 per week; there is a Rs 14 charge for each kilometre in excess of 100km. Avis has air-con cars from Rs 3700 per day (including insurance) for unlimited mileage. Generally you're not allowed to take the car into national parks, wildlife sanctuaries or jungle, or along other unsealed roads. For information on driving licences and other documentation, see the Facts for the Visitor chapter.

BICYCLE

Keen cyclists will probably find Sri Lanka a joy, apart from the uphill sections of the hill country and the major arteries out of Colombo. If you're heading out of Colombo in any direction, take a train out beyond the urban corridors and start cycling.

It's a good idea to start early each day to avoid the heat, and remember to bring lots of water and sunblock. The distances you cover will be limited by the state of the roads – be prepared for a large amount of 'eyes down' cycling.

Hired bicycles with gears are an exception and you'll find that that most range from merely adequate to desperately uncomfortable with dodgy brakes. Chinese-made mountain bikes are just starting to flood onto the market. Nevertheless, you should seriously consider bringing your own gear, and be prepared to be self-sufficient. Contact Adventure Sports Lanka, Connaissance de Ceylan and Walkers Tours to arrange mountain-biking excursions (see Organised Tours, later, for contact details). Adventure Sports Lanka also sells parts and can help you plan your trip.

If you decide to bring your own bicycle, be sure to also bring a supply of spare tyres and tubes as these can suffer from the poor road surfaces. The normal size bicycle tyre in Sri Lanka is 28 by 1½ inches. Some imported 27-inch tyres for 10-speed bikes are available but only in a few shops in Colombo and at high prices. Keep an eye on your bicycle at all times and use a good lock.

When taking a bicycle on a train, every part has to be described on the travel documents, so you should deliver the bicycle at least half an hour before departure. At Colombo's Fort station you may want to allow even more time (up to two hours). It costs about twice the 2nd-class fare to take a bicycle on a train.

HITCHING

Hitchhiking is never entirely safe in any country in the world, and we don't recommend it. Travellers who decide to hitch should understand that they are taking a small but potentially serious risk. People who do choose to hitch will be safer if they travel in pairs and let someone know where they are planning to go. Sri Lanka's cheap fares make hitching an unnecessary option.

LOCAL TRANSPORT

Many Sri Lankan towns are small enough to walk around. In larger towns, you can get around by bus, taxi or three-wheeler.

Bus

Buses go to most places, including villages outside main towns. Their signboards are usually in Sinhala or Tamil, so you'll have to ask which is the right bus. The fares are low, though.

Taxi

Sri Lankan taxis are often reconditioned Japanese vans. They're common in all the sizable towns and even some villages will be able to dig up a taxi from somewhere. Only a few are metered, but over longer distances they compare on price with three-wheelers and provide more comfort and security. Radio cabs are available in Kandy and Colombo.

Three-Wheeler

These vehicles – known in other parts of Asia as *tuk-tuks, bajajs* or autorickshaws – are everywhere: turn a corner and you'll find one. Agree (or haggle your heart out) on the fare before you get in. Some keen drivers will offer to take you to the moon, but believe us, it's no fun being in a three-wheeler for more an hour – this comes from hard experience. As a rule of thumb, a three-wheeler should cost about Rs 30 per kilometre, but twice as much in central Colombo. Three-wheelers and taxis waiting outside tourist hotels and similar places expect higher-than-usual fares.

ORGANISED TOURS

Competition is fierce between the travel agents and tour companies in Sri Lanka. Most would like to take care of everything, some do specialised tours (eg, steam-train trips and wildlife safaris) and others can't organise anything. Word of mouth is the best way to find out which operators are good; ask fellow travellers about their experiences. You can organise everything before you leave home, or once you hit the island. There are comprehensive lists of tour operators at **w** www.srilankatourism.org, **w** www.atsrilanka.com and **w** www.visitsrilanka.org (the website of the Travel Agents Association of Sri Lanka).

You can organise a tour to Yala West (Ruhuna) National Park from Colombo or Hikkaduwa, or you do it at Tissamaharama, where every second guesthouse can put together a half-day tour or more for you.

Listed below are some of the biggest operators plus some recommended niche-market companies.

Adventure Sports Lanka (☎ 074 713334, e adventure@sri.lanka.net) 12A Simon Hewavitharana Rd, Kollupitiya, Colombo. This company arranges outdoor activities including white-water rafting, diving, mountain biking and walks.

Aitken Spence Travels (☎ 011-230 8308, W www.aitkenspencetravels.com) Vauxhall Building, 305 Vauxhall St, Slave Island, Colombo. One of the biggest tour operators, Aitken Spence organises tour packages, hires cars and drivers, and books hotels.

Alpine Adventurers (☎ 052-222 3500) Alpine Hotel, 4 Haddon Hill Rd, Nuwara Eliya. It specialises in trekking, camping, mountaineering and rafting tours.

A Baur & Co (Travel) Ltd (☎ 011-244 8087, W www.baurs.com) Baur's Building, 5 Upper Chatham St, Fort, Colombo. This company specialises in bird-watching tours.

Connaissance de Ceylan (☎ 011-268 5601, W www.connaissanceceylan.com) 58 Dudley Senanayake Mawatha, Borella, Colombo. Another big player, Connaissance runs upmarket hotels and a range of tours.

George Steuarts Travel (☎ 011-234 2411, e gstours@celltelnet.lk) Steuart House, 45 Janadhipathi Mawatha, Fort, Colombo. This established company specialises in cricket, golf and adventure tours.

George Travels (☎ 078 663433, e skashok77@hotmail.com) 2nd floor, Ex-Servicemen's Bldg, Bristol St, Fort, Colombo. It's a reliable, highly experienced budget-flight specialist.

Jetwing Travels (☎ 074 714830, W www.jetwing.net) Jetwing House, 46/26 Nawam Mawatha, Slave Island, Colombo. Another big operator, Jetwing has a large chain of upmarket hotels and organises tours within Sri Lanka and to the Maldives.

JF Tours & Travels (☎ 011-258 7996, W www.jftours.com) 189 Bauddhaloka Mawatha, Bambalapitiya, Colombo. This company specialises in steam-train tours, which can be tailored to suit groups.

Mackinnons Travels (☎ 011-244 8065, W www.mackinnonstravels.com) 4 Leyden Bastian Rd, Fort, Colombo. Mackinnons organises tours, accommodation, flights and car hire (and is the agent for Avis).

Mambo Surf Tours (☎ 075 458131, W www.mambo.nu) Chill Space Surf Café, 434/3 Galle Road, Wewala, Hikkaduwa. Mambo runs surf tours along the southern coast.

Quickshaws Tours (☎ 011-258 3133, W www.quickshaws.com) 3 Kalinga Place, Havelock Town, Colombo. This company organises standard tours but specialises in personalised tours with a car and driver.

Walkers Tours (☎ 011-242 1101, W www.walkerstours.com) 130 Glennie St, Slave Island, Colombo. Walkers offers a range of activities, from golfing and weddings to mountain biking.

Colombo

☎ 011 • pop 1.2 million

Sri Lanka's capital, biggest city and major port has its supporters and detractors. Some people appreciate its colonial heritage, fine dining and shopping opportunities, and dash of urban buzz in an overwhelmingly rural country. Others quickly tire of the diesel fumes and the indifferent modern building styles seen on Galle Rd, the city's main artery. If you're only on a short trip to Sri Lanka, you may wish to pass Colombo by, but if you have a bit of extra time – at least two days – there are plenty of cultural and historical attractions in areas such as Fort (the centre), Cinnamon Gardens and Pettah.

Colombo is the political, economic and cultural centre of Sri Lanka, so if you need to extend your visa, or perhaps buy a plane ticket, you'll find yourself here. The city was the scene of quite a few bombings during the war years, but security has been relaxed since a cease-fire was declared and peace talks began.

If staying in the hustle and bustle of central Colombo doesn't appeal, a short train ride will drop you along the restaurant-lined beachfront of Mt Lavinia; from here you can take day trips to the city centre.

Highlights

- Chewing, sipping and slurping your way through the huge variety of food on offer
- Elbowing your way through the street stall 'boutiques' at Pettah; squeezing into this and buying that at the city's plentiful shopping malls
- Relishing peaceful Viharamahadevi Park after navigating the darting three-wheelers and the jungle of streets
- Taking a sunset promenade along the beach at Mt Lavinia or on Galle Face Green
- Visiting Hindu *kovils* (temples) during the Thai Pongal festival or watching elephants and dancers parade during the Gangaramaya Temple Navam Perahera

HISTORY

Colombo's history can be traced back to at least the 5th century, when it was a way station for sea trade between Asia and the West. Colombo was a small port with the bustling market area of Pettah beside it, and Kotte, on the southeast fringe of Colombo, was the capital of a major Sinhalese kingdom (until the 1870s Galle had been the largest port in the country). During the 8th century Arab traders settled near the port and, in 1505, the Portuguese arrived. By the mid-17th century the Dutch had taken over, growing cinnamon in the area now known as 'Cinnamon Gardens', but it wasn't until the British arrived that the town became a city and, in 1815, was proclaimed the capital of Ceylon.

In the 1870s the breakwaters were built and 'Fort' was created by flooding surrounding wetlands. Colombo remained the capital under British rule and after Sri Lanka achieved independence. A new parliament (designed by Geoffrey Bawa) was built in Kotte in 1982. Today, Kotte goes under the name Sri Jayawardenepura–Kotte, and is really just an outer suburb of Colombo. The numerous bomb attacks in the Fort district before the cease-fire brought about the dispersal of the city's major businesses and institutions across the city.

Colombo continues to spread north and south along the coast as people move to the city to work. But there hasn't been the kind of massive rural influx here as witnessed in many other Asian countries, perhaps because the gap between city and rural wages isn't as vast as in other countries. So while Colombo is growing it still has a fairly modest population of 1.2 million in the inner city and another million living in the urbanising city fringes.

Colombo was never Sri Lanka's tourism trophy, even before the ethnic problems, but it was at least a stopover point for the many leisure cruises passing by, and tourists would spend a day or two in the city, using it as a base for day trips. There is a story that sailors would dab cinnamon oil on the decks before arriving in Colombo, so that when passengers emerged to view the approaching city they inhaled spice-scented breezes.

ORIENTATION

Colombo is split into 15 suburban postal code areas (see the boxed text 'Colombo's Suburb

Codes' for a listing). These areas are also sometimes used to identify specific areas, eg, Pettah is also often referred to as Colombo 11 (or just Col 11) and Slave Island is referred to as Col 2. Once you've got a few directions down, it is relatively easy to find your way around the city. From the visitor's point of view, it's virtually a long coastal strip extending about 12km south from the central area, Fort (Col 1). The spine of this strip is Galle Rd – which eventually leaves Colombo far behind and ends up in Galle. If you head straight inland from Fort you arrive in Pettah (Col 11). Colombo's main train station, Fort, is actually in Pettah, as are the main bus stations – all 10 or 15 minutes' walk from Fort itself.

Travelling south down Galle Rd from Fort you come to a large lawn area called Galle Face Green. Inland from here is Slave Island (Col 2), which isn't really an island at all as only two of its three sides are surrounded by water (though it really was used for keeping slaves in the Dutch colonial era). Many multinational companies have offices in the smallish business district on Slave Island's Nawam Mawatha. The Galle Face Green area and neighbouring Kollupitiya are Col 3. Further south are Bambalapitiya (Col 4) and Wellawatta (Col 6), followed by Dehiwala and the old beach resort of Mt Lavinia, which aren't officially part of Colombo but are definitely within its urban sprawl.

Finding addresses along Galle Rd is slightly complicated by the street numbers starting again each time you move into a new district. Thus there will be a 100 Galle Rd in Kollupitiya, in Bambalapitiya, in Wellawatta, in Dehiwala and in Mt Lavinia.

If you turn inland (east) from Kollupitiya along Dharmapala Mawatha or Ananda Coomaraswamy Mawatha, you'll soon find yourself in Cinnamon Gardens (Col 7) – home of the national art gallery, museum, university, Viharamahadevi Park (the city's biggest), some of the most exclusive residential quarters and many embassies.

Some Colombo streets have both an old name and a new name; we've adopted the name most commonly used. The road running through Viharamahadevi Park, for example, is called both Ananda Coomaraswamy Mawatha and Green Path; and RA de Mel Mawatha, which runs parallel to Galle Rd for a few kilometres, is also still known as Duplication Rd. Some alternative names are given in brackets in this chapter.

Colombo's Suburb Codes

zone (Colombo)	suburb
1	Fort
2	Slave Island
3	Kollupitiya
4	Bambalapitiya
5	Havelock Town
6	Wellawatta
7	Cinnamon Gardens
8	Borella
9	Dematagoda
10	Maradana
11	Pettah
12	Hulftsdorp
13	Kotahena
14	Grandpass
15	Mutwal

Maps

If you're going to be spending some time in Colombo, the 90-page *A-Z Street Guide* (Rs 375) extends as far south as Dehiwala and Mt Lavinia and inland as far as Kelaniya, as well as covering Galle, Kandy, Nuwara Eliya, Anuradhapura and Polonnaruwa. It includes information on Colombo's suburban and inner-city buses. Its main competitor, *A to Z Colombo* (Rs 145), has only 45 pages and doesn't cover Mt Lavinia, but for central Colombo it is more detailed and more accurate.

Both publications are available from bookshops, and you can also pick up the *A to Z Colombo* at the Survey Department Map Sales Centre on Chatham St in Fort.

INFORMATION

The nearest thing to a *Time Out*–style magazine and listings guide is *LT*, distributed free through luxury hotels, Cargills Food City outlets, the Odel Unlimited store in Cinnamon Gardens, and bars and restaurants aiming for the expat market (many of which are listed later in this chapter). It carries reviews and listings of bars, clubs, restaurants, galleries and cultural events. The *Linc* is a comparatively inferior free magazine with a smattering of information tucked between advertisements and advertorials. *Travel Lanka* has information about

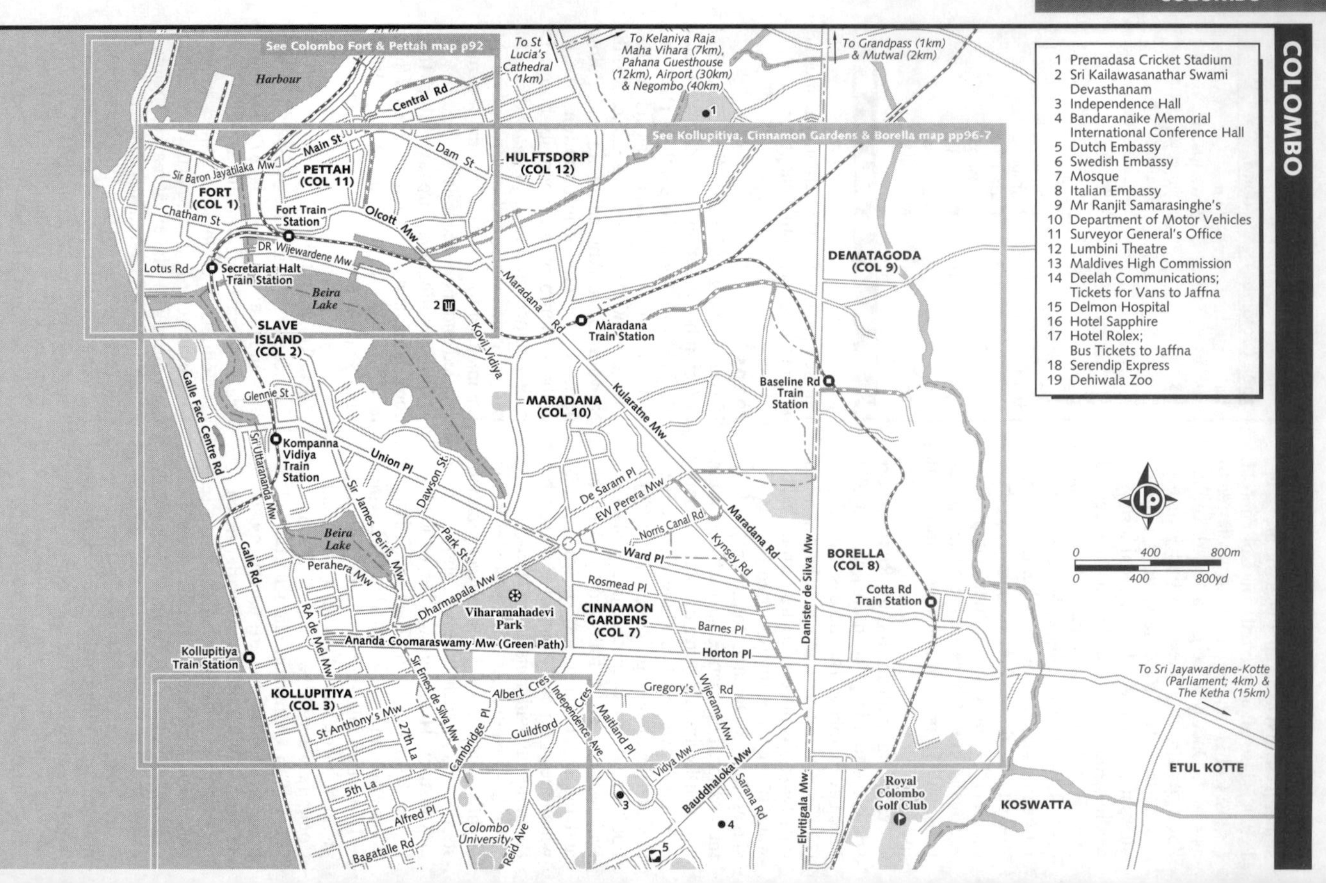
COLOMBO
1 Premadasa Cricket Stadium
2 Sri Kailawasanathar Swami Devasthanam
3 Independence Hall
4 Bandaranaike Memorial International Conference Hall
5 Dutch Embassy
6 Swedish Embassy
7 Mosque
8 Italian Embassy
9 Mr Ranjit Samarasinghe's
10 Department of Motor Vehicles
11 Surveyor General's Office
12 Lumbini Theatre
13 Maldives High Commission
14 Deelah Communications; Tickets for Vans to Jaffna
15 Delmon Hospital
16 Hotel Sapphire
17 Hotel Rolex; Bus Tickets to Jaffna
18 Serendip Express
19 Dehiwala Zoo
0 400 800m
0 400 800yd
See Colombo Fort & Pettah map p92
See Kollupitiya, Cinnamon Gardens & Borella map pp96-7
To St Lucia's Cathedral (1km)
To Kelaniya Raja Maha Vihara (7km), Pahana Guesthouse (12km), Airport (30km) & Negombo (40km)
To Grandpass (1km) & Mutwal (2km)
To Sri Jayawardene-Kotte (Parliament; 4km) & The Ketha (15km)
Harbour
Central Rd
Main St
Dam St
HULFTSDORP (COL 12)
Sir Baron Jayatilaka Mw
PETTAH (COL 11)
FORT (COL 1)
Chatham St
Fort Train Station
Olcott Mw
DR Wijewardene Mw
Lotus Rd
Secretariat Halt Train Station
Beira Lake
SLAVE ISLAND (COL 2)
Kovil Vidiya
Maradana Rd
Maradana Train Station
DEMATAGODA (COL 9)
Baseline Rd Train Station
MARADANA (COL 10)
Kularatne Mw
Glennie St
Galle Face Centre Rd
Kompanna Vidiya Train Station
Sri Uttarananda Mw
Union Pl
Dawson St
Sir James Peiris Mw
De Saram Pl
EW Perera Mw
Norris Canal Rd
Maradana Rd
Kynsey Rd
Danister de Silva Mw
BORELLA (COL 8)
Cotta Rd Train Station
Park St
Ward Pl
Galle Rd
Perahera Mw
Dharmapala Mw
Rosmead Pl
Viharamahadevi Park
CINNAMON GARDENS (COL 7)
RA de Mel Mw
Barnes Pl
Ananda Coomaraswamy Mw (Green Path)
Horton Pl
Kollupitiya Train Station
Sir Ernest de Silva Mw
Albert Cres
Independence Ave
Gregory's Rd
Wijerama Mw
KOLLUPITIYA (COL 3)
St Anthony's Mw
27th La
Cambridge Pl
Guildford Cres
Maitland Pl
Vidya Mw
Baudhaloka Mw
Sarana Rd
Elvitigala Mw
Royal Colombo Golf Club
KOSWATTA
ETUL KOTTE
5th La
Alfred Pl
Colombo University
Reid Ave
Bagatalle Rd

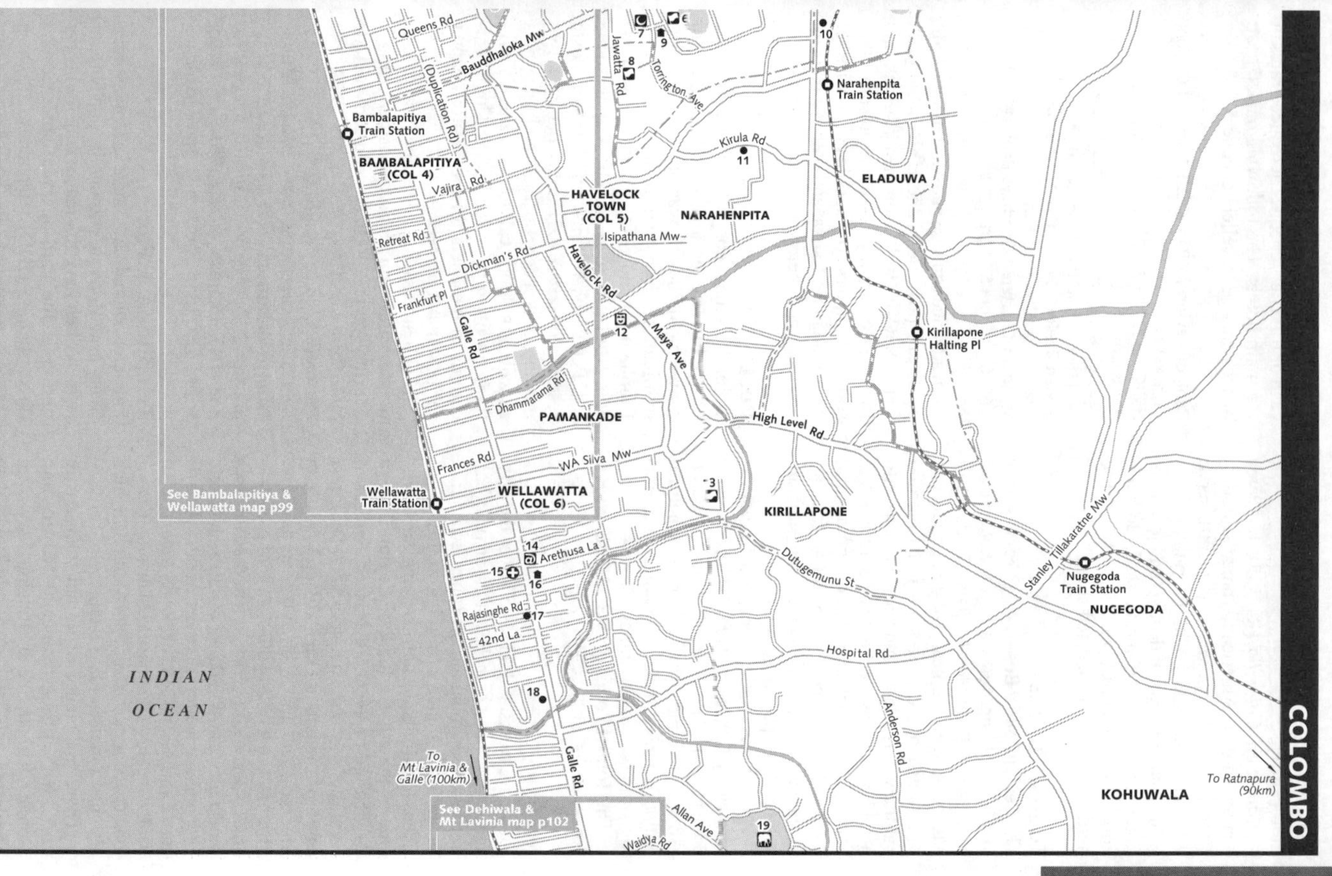
COLOMBO
Queens Rd
Baudhaloka Mw
(Duplication Rd)
Jawatta Rd
Torrington Ave
7
8
9
10
Narahenpita Train Station
Bambalapitiya Train Station
BAMBALAPITIYA (COL 4)
Vajira Rd
Kirula Rd
11
ELADUWA
HAVELOCK TOWN (COL 5)
NARAHENPITA
Isipathana Mw
Retreat Rd
Dickman's Rd
Havelock Rd
Frankfurt Pl
Galle Rd
12
Maya Ave
Kirillapone Halting Pl
Dhammarama Rd
PAMANKADE
High Level Rd
Frances Rd
WA Silva Mw
3
See Bambalapitiya & Wellawatta map p99
Wellawatta Train Station
WELLAWATTA (COL 6)
KIRILLAPONE
14
Arethusa La
15
16
Dutugemunu St
Stanley Tillakaratne Mw
Nugegoda Train Station
NUGEGODA
Rajasinghe Rd
17
42nd La
Hospital Rd
INDIAN OCEAN
18
Anderson Rd
To Mt Lavinia & Galle (100km)
Galle Rd
To Ratnapura (90km)
KOHUWALA
See Dehiwala & Mt Lavinia map p102
Allan Ave
19
Waidya Rd

concerts, plays, and lectures held by cultural centres.

Hands on Colombo (Rs 555), by Peter Kamps, and the American Women's Association's *Colombo Handbook* (Rs 300), serve the expat community with everything from listings and reviews of dentists and jewellers to advice on hiring domestic staff. Both are good, though *Hands on Colombo* is the heftier tome and is updated annually.

Tourist Offices

The **Ceylon Tourist Board** *(☎ 243 7571; e tourinfo@sri.lanka.net; 80 Galle Rd, Kollupitiya; open 9am-4.45pm Mon-Fri, 9am-12.30pm Sat)* has its head office near The Lanka Oberoi. The tourist office covers not just Colombo but the whole island, and staff can help with hotel bookings as well as answer queries and hand out the accommodation guide and leaflets. It has the coolly superior air familiar to the rest of the bureaucracy, but staff are helpful with specific questions.

At Fort train station, there is a **Tourist Information Office** *(☎ 244 0048; open 9am-5pm Mon-Fri, 9am-1pm Sat)*, in fact a branch office of JF Tours. The staff are very helpful with timetables, making bookings and finding addresses in Colombo.

The **Tourist Police** *(☎ 243 3342; Lotus Rd)* are at the Fort police station.

Money

There are banks and ATMs all over the city, and several bank branches in the arrivals hall at the international airport (open 24 hours). There are a couple of foreign-exchange offices open outside normal banking hours. One of these is the **Bank of Ceylon Bureau de Change** *(☎ 242 2730; York St, Fort; open 9am-6pm Mon-Fri, 9am-4pm Sat & Sun)*, just south of the Grand Oriental Hotel. You can get cash advances on Visa cards here. **Thomas Cook** *(☎ 244 5971; 15 Sir Baron Jayatilaka Mawatha, Fort; open 8.30am-5pm Mon-Fri, 10am-12.30pm Sat)* also sells and exchanges travellers cheques, as does **American Express** *(☎ 268 2787; e amextrs@sri.lanka.net; 104 Dharmapala Mawatha, Cinnamon Gardens; open 9am-5pm Mon-Fri)*, which also has a mail-holding facility.

There are plenty of moneychangers in Fort, with offices concentrated in and around Chatham St and Mudalige Mawatha. Their cash-only rates are a little higher than you would get in a bank. You can change cash or travellers cheques at reduced rates in the main hotels. The following banks' head offices change travellers cheques:

Bank of Ceylon (☎ 244 6790) 4 Bank of Ceylon Mawatha, Fort
HSBC (☎ 232 5435) 24 Sir Baron Jayatilaka Mawatha, Fort
People's Bank (☎ 232 7841) 74 Chittampalam Gardiner Mawatha, Slave Island
Seylan Bank (☎ 243 7901) 33 Sir Baron Jayatilaka Mawatha, Fort
Standard Chartered Grindlays Bank (☎ 244 6150) 37 York St, Fort

Cash advances on Visa and MasterCard credit cards are possible at the HSBC, Sampath Bank, Seylan Bank, Commercial Bank and Bank of Ceylon. If you are carrying any other sort of credit card you should check whether it's viable in Sri Lanka, and with which bank you can use it, before you leave home.

Post

Colombo's main post office was kicked out of its historic premises on Janadhipathi Mawatha in 2000. It was once such a communications hub that it was called the Clapham Junction of the East. It now operates from premises on DR Wijewardene Rd, Pettah *(open 7am-6pm Mon-Sat)*. Poste restante *(☎ 232 6203)* holds mail for two months, and accepts parcels and telegrams as well as letters – call to ask if there's anything awaiting you. See Post & Communications in the Facts for the Visitor chapter for postal and parcel rates.

If you are sending home anything of particular value you should consider using a courier service. Reliable couriers include **IML** *(local agent for UPS; ☎ 233 7733, 140 Vauxhall St, Slave Island)*, **DHL** *(☎ 254 1285; Keells, 130 Glennie St, Slave Island)*, **Mountain Hawk Express** *(local agent for Federal Express; ☎ 257 7055; 300 Galle Rd, Kollupitiya)* and **TNT Express** *(also called Ace Cargo; ☎ 244 5331; 315 Vauxhall St, Slave Island)*.

Telephone & Fax

For international calls there are many relatively pricey private communication bureaus (which often have fax machines). A cheaper option is the card-operated international direct dialling (IDD) telephones, of which there are many in Colombo. The main post

Colombo's Phone Numbers

Colombo's telephone area code is scheduled to change from ☎ 01 to ☎ 011 during October 2003. See the boxed text 'Telephone Number Changes' in the Facts for the Visitor chapter for details of this and other changes to Sri Lanka's telephone numbers.

office sells Sri Lanka Telecom phonecards – calls from these card phones are slighter cheaper than those from the private card-phone booths. The only drawback is that these phones are located only in some post offices. You'll probably find it more convenient to use one of the yellow Lanka Pay or Tritel card-phone booths. All five-star hotels have business centres that offer a range of communication services, from email and fax to telephone. However, they are fairly expensive. Mobile (cell) phones are becoming increasingly common. See Post & Communications in the Facts for the Visitor chapter for general information on phone services.

Email & Internet Access

Places offering Internet services are popping up all over the city. On Galle Rd you're rarely more than walking distance from one. There are two or three Internet cafés on the top floor of the Majestic City shopping centre in Bambalapitiya. Nearby, there's **Cafe@internet** *(491 Galle Rd)*. In Kollupitiya try **Lanka Internet** *(Walukarama Rd)* or **Enternet** *(157 Galle Rd)*; in Wellawatta head to **Infotech Internet** *(46 Galle Rd)*. Closer towards Fort, you'll find **Berty's Cyber Cafe** *(380 Galle Rd, Kollupitiya)*. In Fort try the **Nisalka Agency Post Office** *(126 York St)* near the World Trade Centre. **Rainbow Travels** *(113 Chatham St, Fort)* also has Internet facilities.

Travel Agencies

Colombo's many travel agencies can help organise a tour, car hire or whatever you're after. See Organised Tours in the Getting Around chapter for contact details.

Photographic Supplies & Repairs

Stores at luxury hotels and at the main shopping centres such as Majestic City in Bambalapitiya and Crescat Boulevard and Liberty Plaza in Kollupitiya sell film. In Fort, head to **Millers** *(☎ 257 5399, York St)* for purchasing print and slide film. A reader reports that **Hayley's Photoprint** *(☎ 267 8915; 501 Union Place, Slave Island)* is reliable and fast, prints on high-quality paper and can handle APS films. **Senkada** *(☎ 074 793100; 466 Union Place, Slave Island)* is open 24 hours.

Orient Electronics *(☎ 293 0257; 360 Hendala Rd, Wattala)* sells tripods, flashes and other photographic arcana; the store is near the corner of Negombo and Hendala Rds, about 10km north of the city.

The latest digital cameras are beyond the ability of most repair shops to fix, and this doesn't apply just to Sri Lanka. **Photoflex** *(☎ 258 7824; 451/2 1st floor, Galle Rd, Kollupitiya)* has been recommended for repairs to nondigital cameras, as has **Photo Technica** *(☎ 257 6271; 288 Galle Rd, Kollupitiya)*, which also has branches in the Majestic City and Liberty Plaza shopping centres.

Bookshops

Colombo has some excellent bookstores. Two of the largest stockists are Vijitha Yapa and Lake House, but there are many smaller places. Top-end hotels also have bookshops where you'll find up-to-date foreign magazines and newspapers, though prices are generally higher than you would pay elsewhere.

Barefoot (☎ 258 9305) 704 Galle Rd, Kollupitiya. Better known for its textiles, the bookshop downstairs is excellent. There's a broad range of quality books on local and foreign art, culture, architecture travel and literature.

Bibliomania (☎ 243 2881) 32 Hospital St, Fort. It's jam-packed with a random selection of second-hand fiction and a mixed bag of periodicals, educational books and more. Most are in English.

Bookland (☎ 256 5248) 430-432 Galle Rd, Kollupitiya. It offers the usual range of books about Sri Lanka plus English titles and magazines.

Lake House Bookshop (☎ 257 4418) Liberty Plaza shopping centre, RA de Mel Mawatha, Kollupitiya. Lake House has an extensive range of books on Sri Lanka and on other subjects. Foreign and local periodicals and newspapers are also stocked.

MD Gunasena Bookshop (☎ 255 3379) 27 Galle Rd, Bambalapitiya. It has handsome new premises opposite Majestic City but the selection of titles seemed fairly weak when we visited.

Vijitha Yapa Bookshop (☎ 259 6960) Unity Plaza shopping centre, Galle Rd, Bambalapitiya. It has a comprehensive collection of foreign and local novels, classics, magazines and pictorial tomes on Sri Lanka. There's a smaller branch in the Crescat Boulevard shopping centre.

Cultural Centres

Events organised by cultural centres, such as concerts, plays, and lectures, are listed in *LT*, the *Linc* and *Travel Lanka* and are often posted at cafés and hotels frequented by foreigners. International performers will often do gigs at their national cultural centres.

Alliance Française (☎ *269 4162*) 11 Barnes Place, Cinnamon Gardens, just east of Viharamahadevi Park. Hosts seminars and shows films at 3pm on Tuesday and 6pm on Wednesday. It has a library.

American Information Resource Center (☎ *233 2725*) 44 Galle Rd, Kollupitiya. Also puts on films, seminars and so on, and has a library.

British Council (☎ *258 1171*) 49 Alfred House Gardens, Kollupitiya, just inland off RA de Mel Mawatha. Puts on regular free cultural events including films (usually Friday and Saturday), exhibitions, concerts and lectures. There is a library as well.

Goethe Institut (☎ *269 4562*) 39 Gregory's Rd, Cinnamon Gardens. Offers German language courses, screens German films and puts on music concerts, seminars and more.

Russian Centre (☎ *268 5440*) 10 Independence Ave, Cinnamon Gardens. Has one of the city's best auditoriums and is often used for performances such as piano recitals. Tickets cost from Rs 250 to 2000.

Left Luggage

There is a left-luggage facility *(open 4.30am-11.30pm daily)* at Fort train station. As you approach the station from the main road, it's on the extreme left of the building, labelled 'cloakroom'. It charges Rs 17 a bag per day.

Medical Services

If you have to go to hospital, the private hospitals are superior. **Nawaloka Hospital** *(☎ 254 4444; 23 Sri Saugathodaya Mawatha, Slave Island)*, off Union Place, has emergency care and an English-speaking doctor available 24 hours. As an outpatient, except for the initial (and free) consultation, you must pay to see a specialist so bring cash with you.

The main public hospital here, **Colombo General** *(☎ 269 1111; EW Perera Mawatha, Borella)*, has few inpatient facilities and suffers from overcrowding. Its accident ward is on Ward Place off De Soysa (Lipton) Circus, Cinnamon Gardens. **Osu Sala** *(☎ 269 4716; 255 Union Place, Slave Island; open 24 hrs)* is a state-run pharmacy. Other hospitals, clinics and pharmacies are listed in *Travel Lanka*.

Emergency

Here are a few phone numbers you hopefully won't need:

Accident Service	☎ 269 1111
Fire	☎ 242 2222
Police	☎ 243 3333
Police (Tourist)	☎ 250 3629
Red Cross Ambulance	☎ 269 5434, 269 1095
Medi-Calls Ambulance	☎ 257 5475

Dangers & Annoyances

Thankfully the bombing atrocities seem to have come to an end, but should hostilities flare up again, the Fort and Pettah areas are the traditional targets.

Bus Travel Women may find riding the buses extremely trying at times; ordinary buses are so packed that sometimes it's impossible to avoid bodily contact with other passengers. If a sleazebag is making a concerted effort to invade your space, such as it is, you have a few options: put your bag up as a shield; move to another part of the bus if you can; or if things are unbearable, get off and catch another bus. In Colombo buses are so frequent that you generally don't have to wait long for one that's less crowded.

If you are touched or groped, shout *'epaa!'* ('don't!'), grab the perpetrator's arm and draw attention to them; humiliation seems to be effective and fellow passengers may step in to deal with the miscreant (thus offering sweet, satisfying revenge).

Crime While violence towards foreigners is uncommon, it helps to tell someone reliable where you are going and when to expect you back.

Women in particular are urged to take care at night. Even couples should be very wary about walking along lonely beach areas, such as those near Mt Lavinia, after dark. Solo male travellers can confidently expect that every second three-wheeler driver you meet after dark will be keen to introduce you to prostitutes. Solo women should be cautious taking taxis and three-wheelers at night; if, as occasionally happens, your taxi turns up with two men inside, call another. Travellers should avoid taking three-wheelers between the airport and Colombo at night; robberies are not unknown.

Kasippu Dens

Like any city, Colombo has its seamy side – prostitution, drugs, pimps and speakeasy drinking dens. There's a concentration of all of these in Grandpass, northeast of the city centre, in particular in a notorious neighbourhood called Thotalanga, located between the two bridges over the Kelani Ganga. Thotalanga's speciality is *kasippu* – moonshine liquor, the tipple of choice for working-class alcoholics. *Kasippu* is booze at its most basic – sugar, yeast and water fermented in steel drums. In country areas you might see stacks of confiscated *kasippu* drums in the grounds of police stations.

Kasippu has a fearsome reputation, but it is cheap and it gives more of a kick than arrack. The drums are left to ferment in wetlands and other hidden places, and rumour has it that lizards, snakes and birds come to drink the sweet juice, die, fall in and add their special flavour to the brew. Extra additives such as cement, oil and even battery acid aren't unknown. Fortunately perhaps, the high alcohol content means unadulterated *kasippu* usually sterilises itself. The drinking dens are usually a room in a house with a secret back exit in case of police raids, a doorkeeper and perhaps a few lads posted in the neighbourhood to raise the alarm in case of a raid. *Kasippu* dens stay open 24 hours, even on *poya* (full moon) days. A foreigner at a *kasippu* den would be an oddity, to say the least.

Pickpockets Watch out for pickpockets when on public transport. Never get on a bus or train with your shoulder bag unzipped – in fact, don't even walk down the road with it in that state. If you are carrying valuables such as a passport, travellers cheques or reasonably large amounts of cash, keep them out of sight and out of reach in a moneybelt or a pouch under your clothes. Bum bags, besides being a fashion error, are far too conspicuous.

Touts Colombo has its share of touts and con artists. Fort train station is a favourite hang-out and touts here are particularly skilful and persuasive. You will likely be approached at some stage by someone who, after striking up a conversation, asks for a donation for a school for the blind or some such cause – these people are invariably con artists. Galle Face Green is another of their favourite hunting grounds.

Traffic Colombo's drivers are star graduates of the Parisian school of motoring. Bus drivers delight in weaving in and out of the traffic, three-wheelers zip through every narrowing space between vehicles, taxis rush from one job to the next and private vehicles jockey and toot for road space. Never assume, as a mere pedestrian, that you have right of way, even on the yellow crossings. If you do manage to get part of the way across the yellow stripes, don't assume that all traffic will stop; some seem to use the opportunity of a stationary vehicle to overtake, crossing or no crossing. Be alert until you reach the other side. When alighting from a bus, always check that the way is clear between the bus and the footpath.

FORT

During the European era 'Fort' was indeed a fort, surrounded by the sea on two sides and a moat on the landward sides. Today it's a curious mix of brash modern structures such as the World Trade Centre, venerable institutions such as Cargills and Millers, with their wood panelling, brass fittings and display cases, and buildings of all eras shattered by repeated terrorist bombings (some are being repaired). The security presence is heavy here, which has curtailed vehicle access to most of it and pedestrian access to some of it. Fort can be eerily quiet in spots, though vendors still line the Cargills side of York St, selling everything from fluorescent alarm clocks to padded bras. The lack of traffic at least makes it easy to take a walk around.

A good landmark in Fort is the **clock tower** at the junction of Chatham St and Janadhipathi Mawatha (once Queen St), which was originally a lighthouse. There's also the busy **port** (off limits) and the large white dagoba (Buddhist temple) of **Sambodhi Chaitiya** perched about 20m off the ground on stilts – a landmark for sea travellers.

PETTAH

Adjacent to Fort, and immediately inland from it, the bustling bazaar of Pettah is one of the oldest districts in Colombo. It is traditionally one of the most ethnically mixed

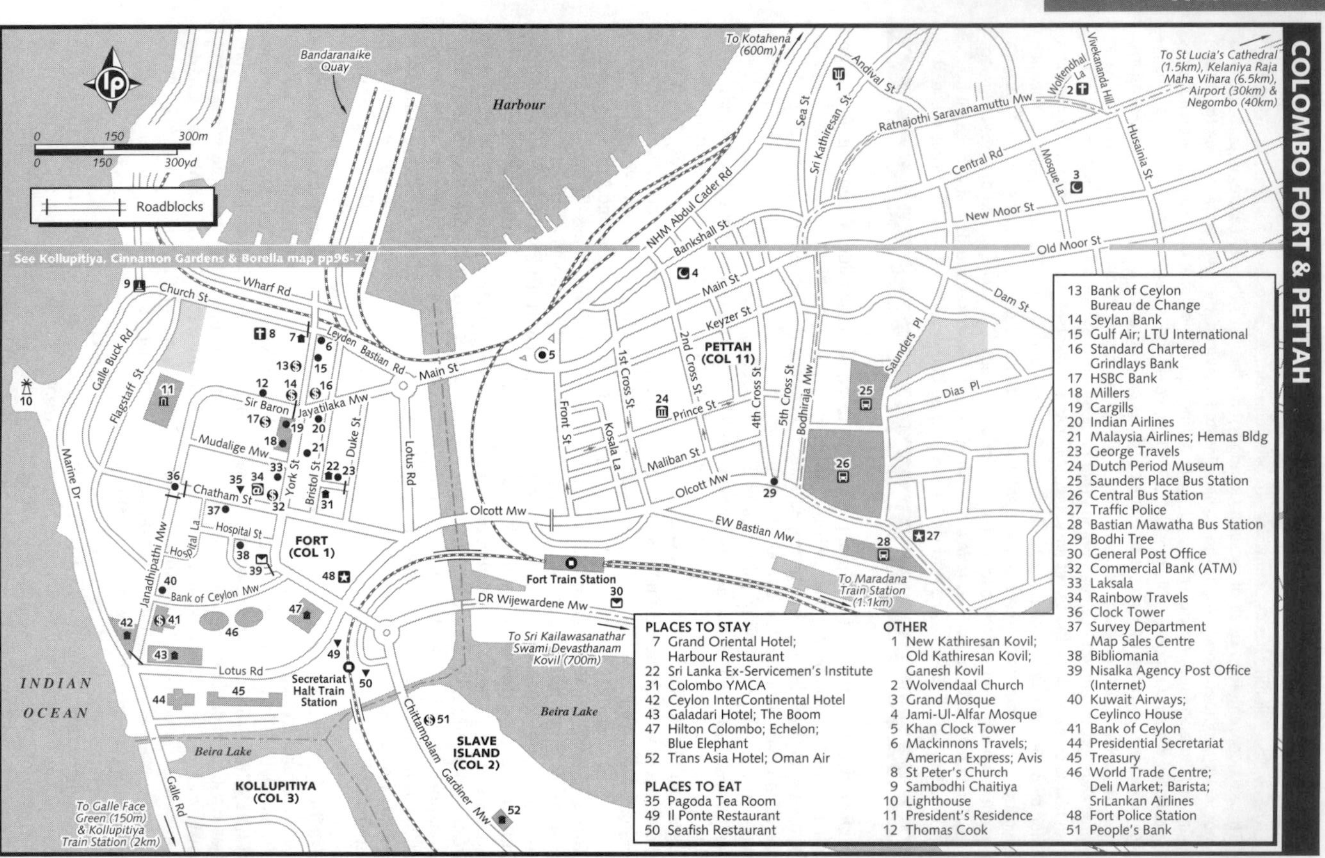
COLOMBO FORT & PETTAH
PLACES TO STAY
7 Grand Oriental Hotel; Harbour Restaurant
22 Sri Lanka Ex-Servicemen's Institute
31 Colombo YMCA
42 Ceylon InterContinental Hotel
43 Galadari Hotel; The Boom
47 Hilton Colombo; Echelon; Blue Elephant
52 Trans Asia Hotel; Oman Air
PLACES TO EAT
35 Pagoda Tea Room
49 Il Ponte Restaurant
50 Seafish Restaurant
OTHER
1 New Kathiresan Kovil; Old Kathiresan Kovil; Ganesh Kovil
2 Wolvendaal Church
3 Grand Mosque
4 Jami-Ul-Alfar Mosque
5 Khan Clock Tower
6 Mackinnons Travels; American Express; Avis
8 St Peter's Church
9 Sambodhi Chaitiya
10 Lighthouse
11 President's Residence
12 Thomas Cook
13 Bank of Ceylon Bureau de Change
14 Seylan Bank
15 Gulf Air; LTU International
16 Standard Chartered Grindlays Bank
17 HSBC Bank
18 Millers
19 Cargills
20 Indian Airlines
21 Malaysia Airlines; Hemas Bldg
23 George Travels
24 Dutch Period Museum
25 Saunders Place Bus Station
26 Central Bus Station
27 Traffic Police
28 Bastian Mawatha Bus Station
29 Bodhi Tree
30 General Post Office
32 Commercial Bank (ATM)
33 Laksala
34 Rainbow Travels
36 Clock Tower
37 Survey Department Map Sales Centre
38 Bibliomania
39 Nisalka Agency Post Office (Internet)
40 Kuwait Airways; Ceylinco House
41 Bank of Ceylon
44 Presidential Secretariat
45 Treasury
46 World Trade Centre; Deli Market; Barista; SriLankan Airlines
48 Fort Police Station
51 People's Bank
Roadblocks
0 150 300m
0 150 300yd
Bandaranaike Quay
Harbour
To Kotahena (600m)
To St Lucia's Cathedral (1.5km), Kelaniya Raja Maha Vihara (6.5km), Airport (30km) & Negombo (40km)
See Kollupitiya, Cinnamon Gardens & Borella map pp96-7
PETTAH (COL 11)
FORT (COL 1)
SLAVE ISLAND (COL 2)
KOLLUPITIYA (COL 3)
INDIAN OCEAN
Beira Lake
Fort Train Station
Secretariat Halt Train Station
To Maradana Train Station (1.1km)
To Sri Kailawasanathar Swami Devasthanam Kovil (700m)
To Galle Face Green (150m) & Kollupitiya Train Station (2km)
Andival St
Sea St
Sri Kathiresan St
Wolfendhal La
Vivekananda Hill
Husainia St
Ratnajothi Saravanamuttu Mw
Central Rd
Mosque La
New Moor St
Old Moor St
Dam St
NHM Abdul Cader Rd
Bankshall St
Main St
Keyzer St
2nd Cross St
1st Cross St
4th Cross St
5th Cross St
Bodhiraja Mw
Saunders Pl
Dias Pl
Front St
Kosala La
Prince St
Maliban St
Olcott Mw
EW Bastian Mw
DR Wijewardene Mw
Chittampalam Gardiner Mw
Lotus Rd
Galle Rd
Marine Dr
Galle Buck Rd
Flagstaff St
Church St
Wharf Rd
Leyden Bastian Rd
Sir Baron Jayatilaka Mw
Mudalige Mw
York St
Bristol St
Duke St
Chatham St
Hospital St
Hospital La
Janadhipathi Mw
Bank of Ceylon Mw

places in the country. You name it, and some shop or 'boutique' (street stall) will be selling it in Pettah – each thoroughfare seems to have its own speciality. Gabo's Lane and 5th Cross St specialise in the raw materials of Ayurvedic medicine while jewellery stores line 2nd Cross St. Leading up to major holidays such as Christmas, the Pettah crowds reach Biblical proportions. If crowds leave you cold, *poya* (full moon) days are a good time to have a look around. Pettah also harbours many religious buildings – see Places of Worship later in this chapter. Colombo's bus and train stations are on the east and south fringes of Pettah, respectively.

The **Dutch Period Museum** *(☎ 244 8466; 95 Prince St; adult/child Rs 65/35; open 9am-5pm Sat-Thur)* has been used as the Dutch town hall, a residence, an orphanage, a hospital, a police station and a post office. The building, dating from 1780, has been restored to its former glory, with a pleasant garden courtyard.

GALLE FACE GREEN

Immediately south of Fort is Galle Face Green, a long stretch of lawn facing the sea. It was originally cleared by the Dutch to give the cannons of Fort a clear line of fire. Today it's a popular rendezvous spot, recently upgraded with fresh lawns; on weekdays it's dotted with joggers, kite flyers and strollers, and on weekends (especially Sunday evenings) food vendors gather to feed the hordes. Lovers meet here and hide their sweet nothings under umbrellas – it's a shame the police harass them. The remaining structures of the 19th-century **Colombo Club** face the green from the grounds of the Taj Samudra hotel – the clubrooms are still used for functions. At opposite ends of the green are the delightful old Galle Face Hotel and the Ceylon Continental skyscraper.

GALLE ROAD

Galle Rd – the 'backbone' of Colombo – is noisy, choked with pollution and lined with some of the city's worst architecture. Badly ageing modern buildings feature prominently. Hold your breath and launch in – you'll find some yummy restaurants, shopping centres brimming with goodies and, near the northern end, the Indian and British high commissions, the US embassy and the prime minister's fortified official residence, **Temple Trees**.

CINNAMON GARDENS

Cinnamon Gardens, about 5km south of Fort and about 2km inland, is Colombo's ritziest address, full of overgrown residences and embassies. A century ago it was covered in cinnamon plantations. Today, as well as elegant tree-lined streets and the posh mansions of the wealthy and powerful, it contains the city's biggest park, several sports grounds and a cluster of museums and galleries.

Viharamahadevi Park

This is Colombo's biggest park, originally called Victoria Park but renamed in the 1950s after the mother of King Dutugemunu (see the boxed text 'Viharamahadevi' for details). It's notable for its superb flowering trees in March, April and early May. Cutting across the middle of the park is the broad Ananda Coomaraswamy Mawatha (Green Path). Colombo's white-domed old **Town Hall** or 'white house' overlooks the park from the northeast. Working elephants sometimes spend the night in the park, happily chomping on palm branches.

Viharamahadevi

In the 3rd century BC, King Devanampiya Tissa ruled the western part of Sri Lanka. He suspected that a monk was involved in an intrigue between the queen and his brother. Spitting the dummy quite spectacularly, he ordered the errant monk to be boiled alive in a cauldron of oil. His courtiers were horrified, his subjects terrified, and even the gods were so disgusted that they drowned the coastal fringe of his kingdom beneath the sea.

To make amends, the King set his gorgeous daughter, Viharamahadevi, adrift on the open sea in a golden boat, with enough food and water to last a month. Alone, she drifted around the south coast of Sri Lanka, until the boat ran aground at Kirinda, near Tissamaharama. The king of the region, Kavantissa, felt that a princess arriving in a golden boat had to be a positive sign, so he married her. Viharamahadevi and Kavantissa later became the proud parents of the first king to unite Sri Lanka, Dutugemunu. The image of the beautiful princess and her precious vessel adrift on the sea is a favourite subject of painters.

Independence Hall

Critics lambast this modern recreation of a Kandyan audience hall as a concrete non-entity, but it's a rather impressive structure nonetheless, and makes a good photo opportunity. As the name suggests, it was built to commemorate Sri Lanka's independence in 1948. The parkland surrounding it is painstakingly well kept.

NATIONAL MUSEUM

Housed in a fine colonial-era building in Viharamahadevi Park, the museum *(Albert Crescent; adult/child Rs 65/35; open 9am-5pm Sat-Thur)* has a good collection of ancient royal regalia, Sinhalese artwork (sculptures, carvings and so on), antique furniture and china, and *ola* (palm leaf) manuscripts. There are fascinating 19th-century reproductions of English paintings of Sri Lanka, and an excellent collection of antique demon masks.

Behind the National Museum you'll find a drab but extensive collection of dusty stuffed creatures at the **Natural History Museum** *(adult/child Rs 35/20; open 9am-5pm Sat-Thur)*.

ART GALLERIES

The **National Art Gallery** *(106 Ananda Coomaraswamy Mawatha, Cinnamon Gardens; open 9am-5pm daily, closed poya days)* is in Viharamahadevi Park. The permanent collection is mostly portraits, but there are also some temporary exhibitions of Sri Lankan artists.

The stylish **Lionel Wendt Centre** *(18 Guildford Crescent, Cinnamon Gardens; open 9am-1pm & 2pm-4pm Mon-Fri)* has contemporary art and craft exhibitions. It stages musical performances and the occasional sale of antiques and other items.

The **Sapumal Foundation** *(32-34 Barnes Place, Cinnamon Gardens; open 10am-1pm Thur-Sat)* was the home of artist Harry Pieris. Today this rambling bungalow is packed with some of the best examples of Sri Lankan art from the 1920s onwards. Pieris' studio still has his easel and a few tubes of paint, as he left them.

Art galleries are sometimes attached to upmarket cafés, for example Paradise Road's **The Gallery** *(2 Alfred House Gardens, Kollupitiya)* and **The Commons** *(74A Dharmapala Mawatha, Cinnamon Gardens)*. Barefoot *(704 Galle Rd, Kollupitiya)*, the popular textiles sales outlet, has exhibitions in **Gallery 706**, downstairs next to the Garden 706 Cafe.

DEHIWALA ZOO

By the standards of the developing world, the zoo *(☎ 271 2751; Dehiwala; adult/child Rs 200/100; open 8.30am-6pm daily)*, 10km south of Fort, treats its animals well – though the big cats and monkeys are still rather squalidly housed. It has its detractors, however: 'a disgrace to mankind' is how one visitor described it. You wonder what they'd have to say about the zoo in Dhaka. The major attraction is the elephant show at 5.15pm, when elephants troop on stage in true trunk-to-tail fashion and perform a series of feats of elephantine agility.

The zoo has a wide collection of other creatures, including a fine range of birds and an aquarium. There is a charge for bringing in a camera. You can get there on a No 118 bus from Dehiwala train station.

PLACES OF WORSHIP

Buddhist Temples

Most of Colombo's Buddhist temples date from the late 19th-century Buddhist Revival. The most important Buddhist centre is the **Kelaniya Raja Maha Vihara**, 7km east of Fort, just off the Kandy road. Even if the thought of seeing yet another temple sends you reaching for the arrack, this one is worth the effort. The Buddha is reputed to have preached here over 2000 years ago. The temple later constructed on the spot was destroyed by Indian invaders, restored, destroyed again by the Portuguese, and restored again in the 18th and 19th centuries. The dagoba, which is unusual in being hollow, is the focus of a festival, the Duruthu Perahera, in January each year. There is a very fine reclining Buddha image here. To reach the temple take bus No 235 from in front of the traffic police station just north-east of the Bastian Mawatha bus station.

Other important Buddhist centres in Colombo include the rather bizarre **Gangaramaya Temple** *(Sri Jinaratana Rd, Slave Island; compulsory 'donation' around Rs 80)*, near Beira Lake. Controlled by one of Sri Lanka's more politically adept monks, the ever-expanding temple complex has a library, a 'museum' and an extraordinarily eclectic array of bejewelled and gilt gifts presented by devotees and well-wishers over the years. Gangaramaya is the focus of the Navam Perahera on the *poya* day in February each year (for more information see Public Holidays & Special Events in the Facts for the Visitor chapter). Close by on Beira Lake is the **Seema Malakaya** temple complex, two island pavilions designed by Geoffrey Bawa and run by the Gangaramaya Temple. The pavilions are especially striking when illuminated at night.

The **Vajiraramaya Temple** *(Vajira Rd, Bambalapitiya)* is a centre of Buddhist learning from where monks have taken the Buddha's message to countries in the West. The modern **Gotami Vihara**, 6km southeast of Fort near Cotta Rd train station in Borella, has some impressive murals of the life of the Buddha. The **Isipathanaramaya Temple** *(Isipathana Mawatha, Havelock Town)* has particularly beautiful frescoes.

Hindu Temples

Known as *kovils* in Sri Lanka, Hindu temples are numerous. On Sea St, the goldsmiths' street in Pettah, the **New Kathiresan Kovil** and the **Old Kathiresan Kovil**, both dedicated to the war god Skanda, are the starting point for the annual Hindu Vel Festival (see Public Holidays & Special Events in the Facts for the Visitor chapter), when the huge *vel* (trident) chariot is dragged to *kovils* on Galle Rd in Bambalapitiya. There is also a temple to Ganesh on Sea St.

In Kotahena, 600m northeast of Fort, you'll find the **Sri Ponnambalam Vanesar Kovil**, which is built of South Indian granite. Many other *kovils* are blessed with some equally unpronounceable names. The **Sri Kailawasanathar Swami Devasthanam**, reportedly the oldest Hindu temple in Colombo, has shrines to Shiva and Ganesh and is at Captain's Gardens, off DR Wijewardena Mawatha, 600m west of Maradana station. There is also the huge **Sri Shiva Subramania Swami Kovil** *(Kew Rd, Slave Island)* and the **Sri Muthumariamman Kovil** *(Kotahena St, Kotahena)*.

During the harvest festival of Thai Pongal (held in January) devotees flock to these temples, which become even more colourful and lively.

Mosques

The **Grand Mosque** *(New Moor St, Pettah)* is the most important of Colombo's many mosques. In Pettah you'll also find the decorative 1909 **Jami-Ul-Alfar Mosque** *(cnr 2nd Cross & Bankshall Sts)* with its candy-striped red-and-white brickwork. There are many mosques in Slave Island, dating from the British days when it was the site for a Malay regiment.

Churches

The 1749 **Wolvendaal Church** *(Wolfendhal Lane, Pettah)* is the most important Dutch building in Sri Lanka. When the church was founded, this crowded inner-city district was a wilderness beyond the city walls. The Europeans mistook the packs of roaming jackals for wolves, and the area became known as wolf's dale, or Wolvendaal in Dutch. The church is in the form of a Greek cross, with walls 1.5m thick, but the real treasure is its Dutch furniture. The Dutch governors had a special pew made with elegant carved ebony chairs, and the workmanship on the wooden pulpit, baptismal font and lectern are just as beautiful. The stone floor includes the elaborate tombstones of five Dutch governors, moved here from an older Dutch church in Fort in 1813. The congregation dwindled as the Burgher community emigrated, but it still holds services – in Sinhala, English and Tamil – on Sunday mornings.

St Peter's Church, near the Grand Oriental Hotel in Fort, was converted from the Dutch governor's banquet hall and first used as a church in 1804.

The enormous **St Lucia's Cathedral** *(St Lucia's St, Kotahena)* lies in the Catholic heart of the Kotahena district. The biggest church in Sri Lanka, it can hold up to 5000 worshippers. The interior is rather plain but the immense domed mass of the church is quite impressive.

One of the Colombo's most interesting shrines is **St Anthony's Church** *(St Anthony's Mawatha, Kotahena)*. Outside it looks like a typical Portuguese Catholic church, but inside the atmosphere is distinctly subcontinental. The queues of devotees offering *puja* (prayers or offerings) to a dozen ornate statues behind glass cases recall a Hindu temple. A statue of St Anthony endowed with miraculous qualities is the centre of devotions. Mothers often bring pubescent daughters here to pray for protection from malevolent spirits that might take advantage

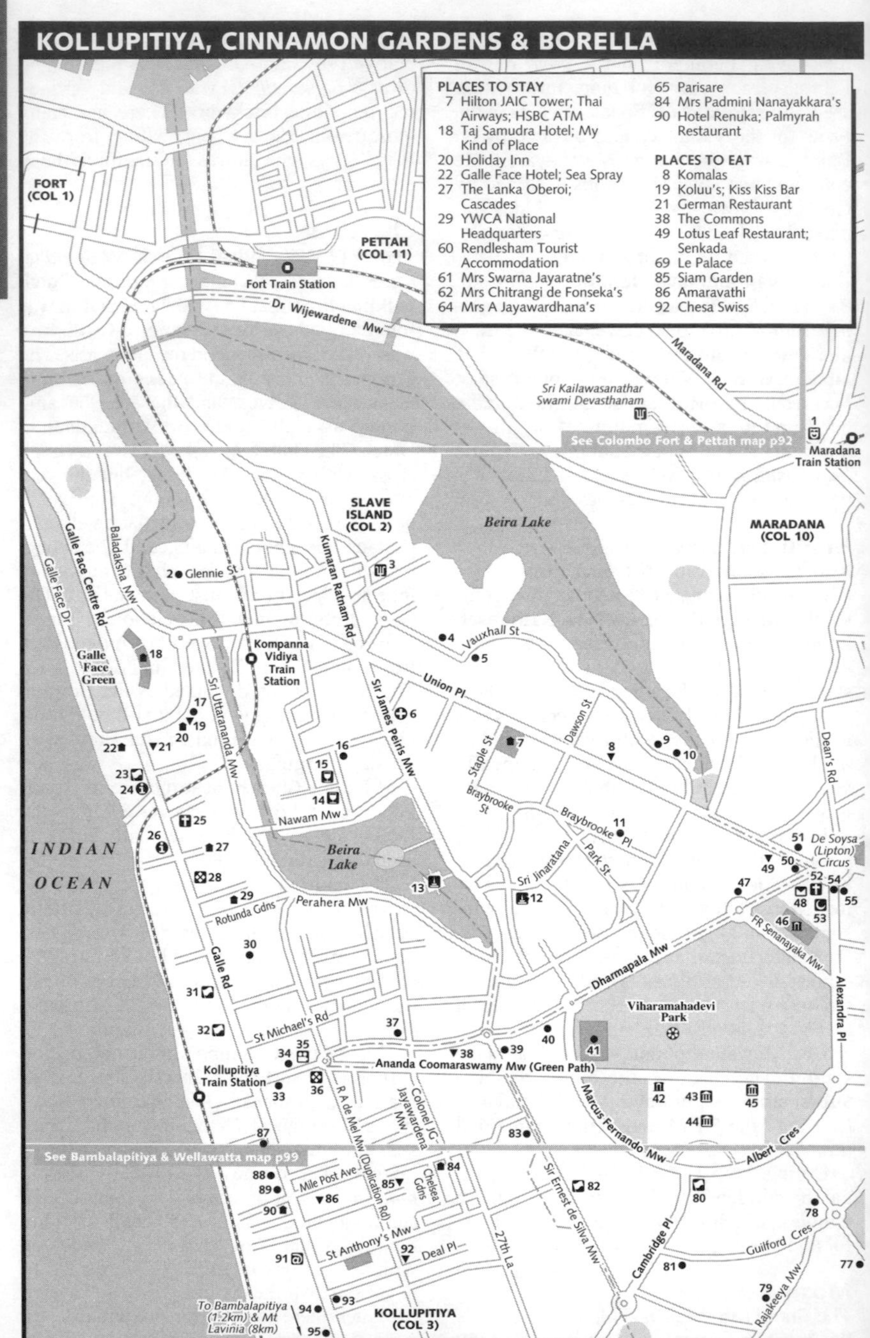

KOLLUPITIYA, CINNAMON GARDENS & BORELLA
PLACES TO STAY
7 Hilton JAIC Tower; Thai Airways; HSBC ATM
18 Taj Samudra Hotel; My Kind of Place
20 Holiday Inn
22 Galle Face Hotel; Sea Spray
27 The Lanka Oberoi; Cascades
29 YWCA National Headquarters
60 Rendlesham Tourist Accommodation
61 Mrs Swarna Jayaratne's
62 Mrs Chitrangi de Fonseka's
64 Mrs A Jayawardhana's
65 Parisare
84 Mrs Padmini Nanayakkara's
90 Hotel Renuka; Palmyrah Restaurant
PLACES TO EAT
8 Komalas
19 Koluu's; Kiss Kiss Bar
21 German Restaurant
38 The Commons
49 Lotus Leaf Restaurant; Senkada
69 Le Palace
85 Siam Garden
86 Amaravathi
92 Chesa Swiss
FORT (COL 1)
PETTAH (COL 11)
Fort Train Station
Dr Wijewardene Mw
Maradana Rd
Sri Kailawasanathar Swami Devasthanam
See Colombo Fort & Pettah map p92
Maradana Train Station
SLAVE ISLAND (COL 2)
Beira Lake
MARADANA (COL 10)
Galle Face Centre Rd
Galle Face Dr
Baladaksha Mw
Glennie St
Kumaran Ratnam Rd
Vauxhall St
Kompanna Vidiya Train Station
Galle Face Green
Sri Uttarananda Mw
Sir James Peiris Mw
Union Pl
Dawson St
Staple St
Braybrooke St
Braybrooke Pl
Dean's Rd
Nawam Mw
INDIAN OCEAN
Beira Lake
Park St
Sri Jinaratana
De Soysa (Lipton) Circus
Rotunda Gdns
Perahera Mw
FR Senanayaka Mw
Galle Rd
Dharmapala Mw
Viharamahadevi Park
Alexandra Pl
St Michael's Rd
Ananda Coomaraswamy Mw (Green Path)
Kollupitiya Train Station
R A de Mel Mw (Duplication Rd)
Colonel JG Jayawardena Mw
Marcus Fernando Mw
Albert Cres
See Bambalapitiya & Wellawatta map p99
Mile Post Ave
Chelsea Gdns
Sir Ernest de Silva Mw
27th La
Cambridge Pl
Guilford Cres
St Anthony's Mw
Deal Pl
Rajakeeya Mw
To Bambalapitiya (1.2km) & Mt Lavinia (8km)
KOLLUPITIYA (COL 3)

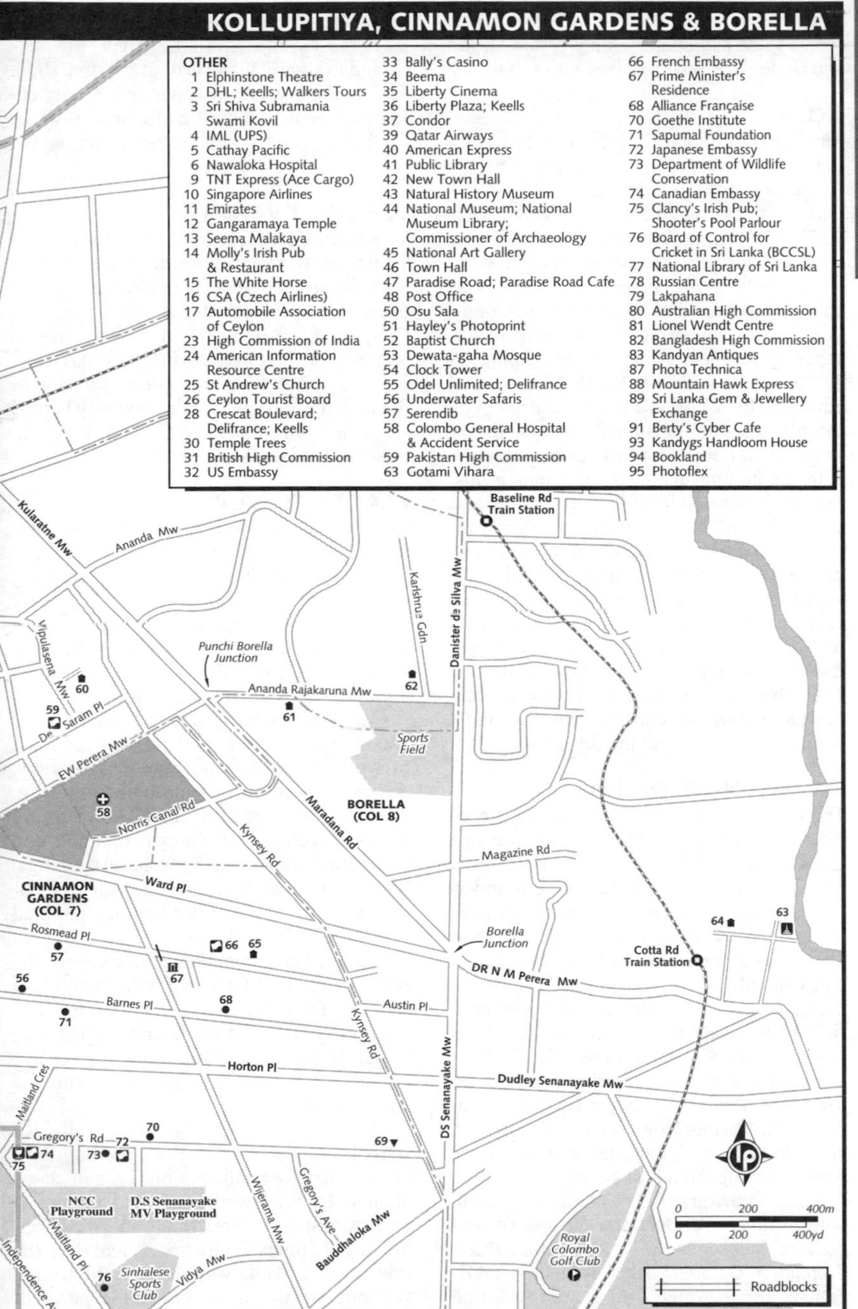
KOLLUPITIYA, CINNAMON GARDENS & BORELLA
OTHER
1 Elphinstone Theatre
2 DHL; Keells; Walkers Tours
3 Sri Shiva Subramania Swami Kovil
4 IML (UPS)
5 Cathay Pacific
6 Nawaloka Hospital
9 TNT Express (Ace Cargo)
10 Singapore Airlines
11 Emirates
12 Gangaramaya Temple
13 Seema Malakaya
14 Molly's Irish Pub & Restaurant
15 The White Horse
16 CSA (Czech Airlines)
17 Automobile Association of Ceylon
23 High Commission of India
24 American Information Resource Centre
25 St Andrew's Church
26 Ceylon Tourist Board
28 Crescat Boulevard; Delifrance; Keells
30 Temple Trees
31 British High Commission
32 US Embassy
33 Bally's Casino
34 Beema
35 Liberty Cinema
36 Liberty Plaza; Keells
37 Condor
39 Qatar Airways
40 American Express
41 Public Library
42 New Town Hall
43 Natural History Museum
44 National Museum; National Museum Library; Commissioner of Archaeology
45 National Art Gallery
46 Town Hall
47 Paradise Road; Paradise Road Cafe
48 Post Office
50 Osu Sala
51 Hayley's Photoprint
52 Baptist Church
53 Dewata-gaha Mosque
54 Clock Tower
55 Odel Unlimited; Delifrance
56 Underwater Safaris
57 Serendib
58 Colombo General Hospital & Accident Service
59 Pakistan High Commission
63 Gotami Vihara
66 French Embassy
67 Prime Minister's Residence
68 Alliance Française
70 Goethe Institute
71 Sapumal Foundation
72 Japanese Embassy
73 Department of Wildlife Conservation
74 Canadian Embassy
75 Clancy's Irish Pub; Shooter's Pool Parlour
76 Board of Control for Cricket in Sri Lanka (BCCSL)
77 National Library of Sri Lanka
78 Russian Centre
79 Lakpahana
80 Australian High Commission
81 Lionel Wendt Centre
82 Bangladesh High Commission
83 Kandyan Antiques
87 Photo Technica
88 Mountain Hawk Express
89 Sri Lanka Gem & Jewellery Exchange
91 Berty's Cyber Cafe
93 Kandygs Handloom House
94 Bookland
95 Photoflex
Baseline Rd Train Station
Kularatne Mw
Ananda Mw
Karlshrue Gdn
Danister de Silva Mw
Vipulasena Mw
Punchi Borella Junction
Ananda Rajakaruna Mw
De Saram Pl
EW Perera Mw
Sports Field
Norris Canal Rd
Maradana Rd
BORELLA (COL 8)
Kynsey Rd
Magazine Rd
CINNAMON GARDENS (COL 7)
Ward Pl
Rosmead Pl
Borella Junction
Cotta Rd Train Station
DR N M Perera Mw
Barnes Pl
Austin Pl
Horton Pl
DS Senanayake Mw
Dudley Senanayake Mw
Maitland Cres
Gregory's Rd
Wijerama Mw
Gregory's Ave
Baudhaloka Mw
NCC Playground
D.S Senanayake MV Playground
Maitland Pl
Independence Ave
Sinhalese Sports Club
Vidya Mw
Royal Colombo Golf Club
0 200 400m
0 200 400yd
Roadblocks

of the girl's nascent sexuality. The church seems to be as popular with worried Hindu and Buddhist mothers as it is with Catholics.

GOLF

The **Royal Colombo Golf Club** *(☎ 269 5431; Borella)* has an 18-hole golf course at the Ridgeway Golf Links dating to 1879 – it was only the third club to earn the 'royal' appellation. It's quite an institution, with 300-odd staff (including 100 ground staff and an equal number of caddies). The clubhouse and the links are both in immaculate condition. Visitors are welcome but ring in advance to let them know you're coming. A day on the course costs Rs 1800 on normal days and Rs 2400 on public holidays. You can hire a set of clubs for Rs 1000 and golf shoes for Rs 300. Caddies are compulsory, with a minimum fee of Rs 175 plus a customary tip (around Rs 100 to 200). The dress code here is stricter than at other golf courses, requiring collars, decent shorts or trousers with zippers for men, while for women there's a one-word dress code: decency. The elegant clubhouse has a bar, a restaurant and a broad veranda. Golfers say the course is quite good but showing its age. They also comment that balls can sink without trace during the monsoon, but skip madly across the grass during the dry season.

SWIMMING & DIVING

The only Colombo beach where you'd consider swimming is at Mt Lavinia, a somewhat faded resort area 11km south of Fort – and even that's borderline, with a severe undertow at times and some foul waterways issuing into the ocean just to the north.

Visitors can use the pools at several top-end Colombo hotels for a fee. One of the nicest spots is the **outdoor saltwater pool** right by the seafront at the Galle Face Hotel *(2 Kollupitiya Rd)*, which costs Rs 200 for nonguests (you must bring your own towel). A dip in the magnificently positioned Mt Lavinia Hotel pool *(100 Hotel Rd)* costs Rs 300 and includes access to the hotel's private stretch of beach.

Many **shipwrecks** near Colombo are available to divers. **Underwater Safaris** *(☎ 269 4012; e scuba@eureka.lk; 25C Barnes Place, Cinnamon Gardens)* runs four-day PADI courses (open water with a group of four costs US$385 per person) and organises sea dives and snorkelling trips. You can buy fins, masks and snorkels (divers are expected to supply their own) at the dive shop. The company is part-owned by science-fiction legend and diving aficionado Arthur C Clarke, who lives in the house behind the office.

SPECIAL EVENTS

The Duruthu Perahera is held on *poya* in January at the Kelaniya Raja Maha Vihara. The Navam Perahera on the February *poya* is led by 50 elephants; it starts from the Gangaramaya Temple and is held around Viharamahadevi Park and Beira Lake. During the Hindu Vel, the gilded chariot of Skanda, the war god, is ceremonially hauled from the Kathiresan *kovils* in Sea St, Pettah, to a *kovil* at Bambalapitiya.

PLACES TO STAY

Colombo has a variable range of accommodation options: some cheapies are forlorn and overpriced; there's a small but growing collection of mid-range places; and there are so many top-end options you won't know where to start. Some of the budget and mid-range places not in this book but promoted by touts are fronts for prostitution.

Colombo doesn't have a backpacker ghetto as in some Asian cities, so you need to work out what kind of area (eg, ritzy, commercial, colourful) you'd like to stay in.

If you head to Fort you'll find the big hotels as well as their fancy restaurants and nightclubs, plus some Spartan budget digs. Slave Island has hectic streets, a heavy police presence and small dwellings jammed in between office blocks.

Kollupitiya covers Galle Face Green, the ritziest stretch of Galle Rd with the highest security. The other chunk of Kollupitiya follows noisy Galle Rd south, and is lined with larger shops, restaurants and businesses; inland, expensive dwellings mix with the commercial.

Moving into Bambalapitiya, Galle Rd starts losing some of its gloss, the buildings are smaller, footpaths are busier, and shops abound. By Wellawatta, Galle Rd has lost all pretentiousness. Here, small shops and elbowing shoppers vie for space, and even the odd cow wends its way through the traffic. It's one of the most colourful parts of Colombo.

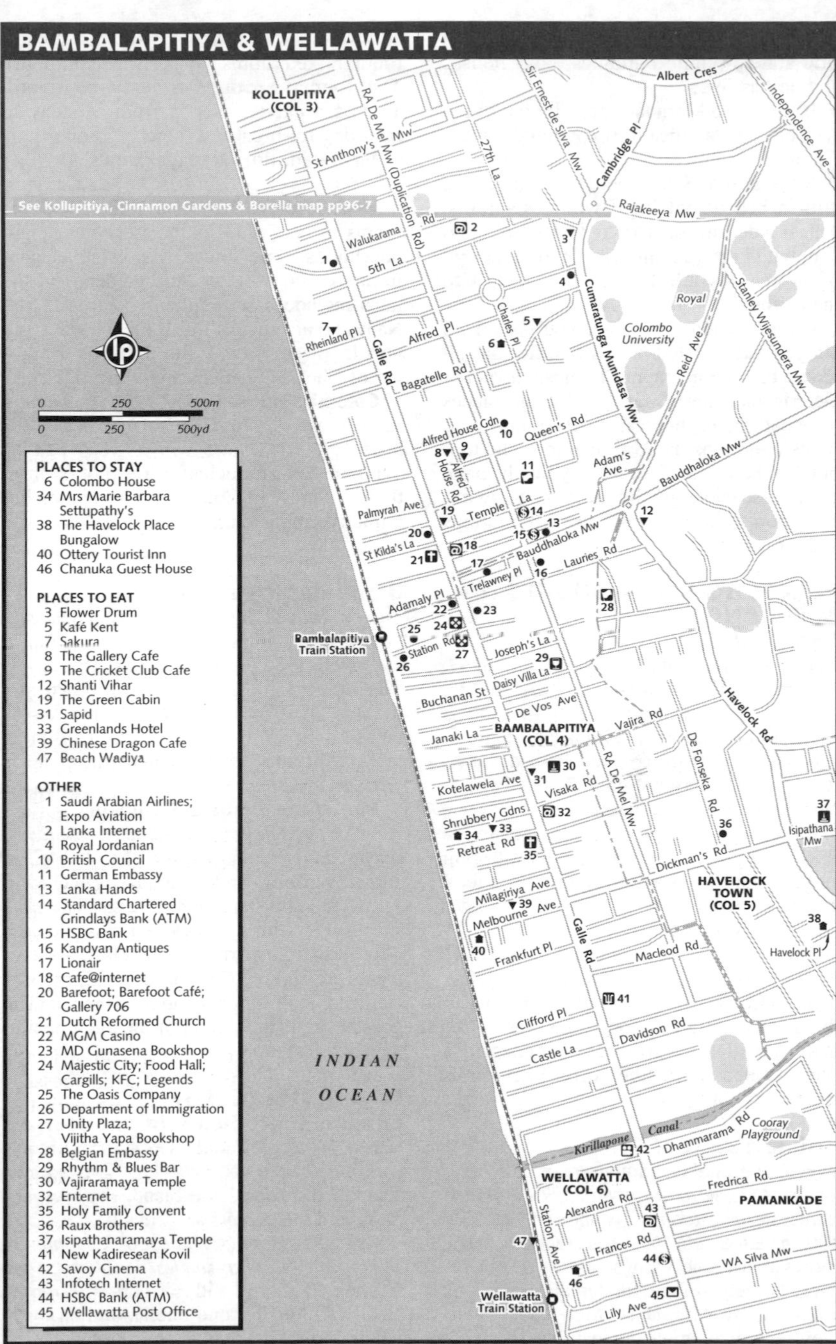
BAMBALAPITIYA & WELLAWATTA
See Kollupitiya, Cinnamon Gardens & Borella map pp96-7
KOLLUPITIYA (COL 3)
BAMBALAPITIYA (COL 4)
HAVELOCK TOWN (COL 5)
WELLAWATTA (COL 6)
PAMANKADE
INDIAN OCEAN
Bambalapitiya Train Station
Wellawatta Train Station
Royal Colombo University
Cooray Playground
Kirillapone Canal
Albert Cres
Independence Ave
Sir Ernest de Silva Mw
Cambridge Pl
Rajakeeya Mw
RA De Mel Mw (Duplication Rd)
St Anthony's Mw
27th La
Walukarama Rd
5th La
Rheinland Pl
Alfred Pl
Charles Pl
Galle Rd
Bagatelle Rd
Cumaratunga Munidasa Mw
Reid Ave
Stanley Wijesundera Mw
Alfred House Gdn
Queen's Rd
Alfred House Rd
Adam's Ave
Bauddhaloka Mw
Palmyrah Ave
Temple La
St Kilda's La
Lauries Rd
Trelawney Pl
Adamaly Pl
Station Rd
Joseph's La
Daisy Villa La
Buchanan St
De Vos Ave
Janaki La
Vajira Rd
Havelock Rd
De Fonseka Rd
Kotelawela Ave
Visaka Rd
RA De Mel Mw
Shrubbery Gdns
Retreat Rd
Isipathana Mw
Dickman's Rd
Milagiriya Ave
Melbourne Ave
Havelock Pl
Frankfurt Pl
Macleod Rd
Clifford Pl
Davidson Rd
Castle La
Dhammarama Rd
Fredrica Rd
Alexandra Rd
Station Ave
Frances Rd
WA Silva Mw
Lily Ave
0 250 500m
0 250 500yd
PLACES TO STAY
6 Colombo House
34 Mrs Marie Barbara Settupathy's
38 The Havelock Place Bungalow
40 Ottery Tourist Inn
46 Chanuka Guest House
PLACES TO EAT
3 Flower Drum
5 Kafé Kent
7 Sakura
8 The Gallery Cafe
9 The Cricket Club Cafe
12 Shanti Vihar
19 The Green Cabin
31 Sapid
33 Greenlands Hotel
39 Chinese Dragon Cafe
47 Beach Wadiya
OTHER
1 Saudi Arabian Airlines; Expo Aviation
2 Lanka Internet
4 Royal Jordanian
10 British Council
11 German Embassy
13 Lanka Hands
14 Standard Chartered Grindlays Bank (ATM)
15 HSBC Bank
16 Kandyan Antiques
17 Lionair
18 Cafe@internet
20 Barefoot; Barefoot Café; Gallery 706
21 Dutch Reformed Church
22 MGM Casino
23 MD Gunasena Bookshop
24 Majestic City; Food Hall; Cargills; KFC; Legends
25 The Oasis Company
26 Department of Immigration
27 Unity Plaza; Vijitha Yapa Bookshop
28 Belgian Embassy
29 Rhythm & Blues Bar
30 Vajiraramaya Temple
32 Enternet
35 Holy Family Convent
36 Raux Brothers
37 Isipathanaramaya Temple
41 New Kadiresean Kovil
42 Savoy Cinema
43 Infotech Internet
44 HSBC Bank (ATM)
45 Wellawatta Post Office

Within leafy Cinnamon Gardens you'll find stately public buildings, posh houses and embassies.

Borella and Maradana are a bit out of the way but give an idea of life in middle-class Colombo.

Mt Lavinia is an ageing beach resort, with a beachfront lined with restaurants. This is a decent spot to avoid busy Colombo and, with Fort's skyline visible from the end of the beach, you'll feel like you're close to the action.

Unless stated otherwise, you'll find no budget places listed have hot water but all have a bathroom, fan, meals, mosquito net or electric mosquito 'mat'. Mid-range places have bathrooms, hot water, nets or mosquito 'mats', and most have air-con too. The top-bracket hotels in Colombo typically have elegant, spacious public areas, large swimming pools, shops, gyms, several restaurants and air-con.

PLACES TO STAY – BUDGET & MID-RANGE

Fort (Col 1)

Colombo YMCA *(☎ 232 5252, fax 243 6263; 39 Bristol St; dorm bed Rs 125, singles Rs 175, singles/doubles with fan Rs 300/400, rooms with fan & bathroom Rs 650)* is a basic institutional place with cramped 16-bed dorms (men only). There are no lockers so you'll have to chain up your gear or risk it. There's a Rs 5 daily membership charge and a Rs 100 key deposit. Billiard tables, a gym and other facilities are available (for a fee). The busy cafeteria will feed you for under Rs 100; it's open only for lunch.

The **Sri Lanka Ex-Servicemen's Institute** *(☎ 242 2650; dorm bed Rs 200, singles/doubles Rs 400/1000)*, virtually next door to the YMCA, is an option of last resort for male travellers. It has rickety bunks in a grim 10-bed dorm; the coffin-like rooms are exorbitant.

Kollupitiya (Col 3)

YWCA National Headquarters *(☎ 232 3498, fax 243 4575; ⓔ natywca@sltnet.lk; 7 Rotunda Gardens; singles/doubles women only Rs 300/600, mixed Rs 900/1500)* has eight tidy, basic rooms that come with breakfast. It's a secure, homely refuge for female travellers, ably run by Mrs Dias. Men can stay if they're with a female companion. There are also women-only rooms with shared bathroom (mixed rooms have private bathroom). The rooms surround a leafy courtyard. There's a cafeteria open from Monday to Saturday for breakfast, lunch and dinner.

Mrs Padmini Nanayakkara's *(☎ 071 278758, fax 573095; 20 Chelsea Gardens; singles/doubles Rs 940/1400)* offers three cute rooms in one of Colombo's classier neighbourhoods. The house has some elegant furniture and a pretty little garden, and the rates include a scrumptious breakfast. Mrs Nanayakkara speaks fluent French. This is a popular place so book ahead. It's on the corner of Chelsea Gardens and Flower Terrace.

Colombo House *(☎ 257 4900; ⓔ colombohse@eureka.lk; 26 Charles Place; singles/doubles Rs 1045/1375, with air-con Rs 1430/1760)* lies on a quiet leafy street not far from the University of Colombo. This ageing but attractive mansion has four large but basic guestrooms.

Bambalapitiya (Col 4)

Ottery Tourist Inn *(☎ 258 3727; 29 Melbourne Ave; singles/doubles Rs 330/600)* is a 1920s-era lodging house with eight rooms. The modern incarnation is run-down and the staff are diffident, but the rooms are spacious, if Spartan. The inn has a billiards table, with ripped felt roughly stitched up as an extra challenge.

Mrs Marie Barbara Settupathy *(☎ 258 7964; ⓔ jbs@slt.lk; 23/2 Shrubbery Gardens; singles/doubles Rs 850/1000)* has five clean and tidy rooms and breakfast is included. The Settupathys are helpful hosts. There's a sitting area with a TV and a minuscule pebble courtyard. Apart from breakfast, no other meals are served. Coming down Shrubbery Gardens, look for the church on the left. The guesthouse is at the end of the alley next to the church.

Wellawatta (Col 6)

Chanuka Guest House *(☎ 258 5883; 29 Frances Rd; singles/doubles Rs 440/550, rooms with hot water Rs 770)* has five rooms. Though the rooms are bland, they're very clean and the owners are friendly.

Hotel Sapphire *(☎ 238 3306; ⓔ sapphire@slt.lk; 371 Galle Rd; singles/doubles US$44/53)* has 40 rooms with air-con. The rooms have a fridge, TV and phone, and an overwhelming 1970s feel.

Cinnamon Gardens (Col 7)

If you're heading to the guesthouses along Rosmead Place, ask the driver to take you via the Kynsey Rd entrance; the approach from the other end of the street is blocked as the prime minister's residence is at that end.

Parisare *(☎ 269 4749; e sunsep@visualnet.lk; 97/1 Rosmead Place; singles/doubles upstairs Rs 600/1200, deluxe Rs 750/1500)* is a fine example of modern architecture. There are two rooms upstairs. The deluxe room downstairs has a four-poster bed, en suite and private garden. All rooms have hot water. Parisare is very popular – book ahead.

Ranjit Samarasinghe's guesthouse *(☎ 250 2403; e ranjitksam@hotmail.com; 53/19 Torrington Ave; singles/doubles Rs 1540/1980, with air-con Rs 2040/2480)* has three homely rooms (two with bathroom). The house is modern and airy with a small leafy courtyard and a wealth of books on Buddhism. Finding it is a bit tricky. Coming down Torrington Ave from Bauddhaloka Mawatha, look for the mosque on the right, then take the first left at a small playground, and then the first right. It's the second house on the left.

Borella (Col 8) & Maradana (Col 10)

Mrs A Jayawardhana's *(☎ 269 3820; e samera@sri.lanka.net; 42 Kuruppu Rd; singles/doubles Rs 500/600)* is an unpretentious family home with three tidy rooms, a large garden and an excellent library of books on Buddhism. Two rooms share a bathroom. This place is a bit out of the way: you can get here by train or bus to Cotta Rd train station. For the bus, catch a bus from Fort (bus No 168, 174 or 177, Rs 5). A three-wheeler from Fort will cost about Rs 150 – ask the driver to head to the Gateway International School. If you ring, the family may be able to arrange to pick you up from the bus or train stations in Fort/Pettah.

Mrs Swarna Jayaratne's guesthouse *(☎ 269 5665; e indcom@sltnet.lk; 70 Ananda Rajakaruna Mawatha; singles/doubles Rs 650/850, hot water Rs 100 extra)* has two clean rooms with a shared bathroom. There's a guest sitting area (with satellite TV), a balcony and a small patch of lawn. To get here catch bus No 103 or 171 (Rs 4 from Fort train station) and get off at Punchi Borella Junction.

Rendlesham Tourist Accommodation *(☎ 268 4985; e suriyadelivera@yahoo.com; 165 Vipulasena Mawatha; singles/doubles including breakfast Rs 1500/2100)* is a fine old villa packed with antiques. The handsome guest rooms have air-con, and the garden is crammed with parrots and potplants. The glamorous owner, Mrs Suriya De Livera, is a fashion designer. Rendlesham is situated on a little alley that runs off Vipulasena, close to the corner of Hedges Court.

Mrs Chitrangi de Fonseka's guesthouse *(☎/fax 269 7919; 7 Karlshrue Garden; rooms US$40)* is a modern home bubbling with eccentricity, including chintzy decor, lots of porcelain and an indoor fountain. The three spacious rooms have TV, hot water, air-con, and laptop and phone connections, and there's a fully equipped guest kitchen. Bus No 103 or 171 from Fort will take you nearby (see the directions to Mrs Swarna Jayaratne's place earlier).

Mt Lavinia

Blue Seas Guest House *(☎ 271 6298; 9/6 De Saram Rd; singles/doubles Rs 750/850)* has 12 clean, simple and spacious rooms (some with balconies); breakfast is included. There's a large sitting room decked out with colonial furniture, and a garden. Guests praise the staff for their helpful attitude.

Mr Lyn Mendis' *(☎ 273 2446; e ranmal@bigfoot.com; 11 College Ave; singles/doubles Rs 1000/1350, doubles with air-con Rs 1750)*, opposite Tropic Inn, is a clean, peaceful and friendly guesthouse with rates that include breakfast. There's a light-filled guest sitting area and a kitchen complete with a stove and fridge.

Ivory Inn *(☎ 271 5006; 21 Barnes Ave; singles/doubles Rs 1100/1340)* is a motel-like place which has 21 bare, cell-like rooms with balconies. Rooms include breakfast; some have a view to the sea. There's a garden but, overall, this place lacks character.

Tropic Inn *(☎ 273 8653; e abdeen@mail.lgo.lk; 6 College Ave; singles/doubles Rs 1100/1540, with air-con Rs 1430/1925)* has 15 spotless rooms in a simple, stylish building. There's an internal courtyard and many of the rooms have a balcony – all rooms have hot water. Rates are a little high, but they include breakfast.

Cottage Gardens *(☎ 271 9692; e aquila@eureka.lk; 42-48 College Ave; bungalows*

US$21) offers five charming self-contained bungalows each equipped with fan, cooking facilities and fridge, set in a small garden.

Haus Chandra *(☎ 273 2755, fax 273 3173; 37 Beach Rd; singles/doubles US$27/37, suites US$60)* has rooms with air-con, TV, telephone and fridge; some can be cramped so check them out before you book in. The two-person suites have antique furnishings, carpets and a fully equipped kitchen; breakfast is included.

Colombo's Hinterland

Pahana Guesthouse *(☎ 074 810428; 600/4 Sanghabo Mawatha, Makola North; singles/doubles Rs 600/800)* is the closest thing to a typical village house in the vicinity of Colombo. The friendly owners have two simple guest rooms. You wouldn't have a hope in hell of finding this guesthouse on your own, so call in advance and they'll send someone to pick you up from Colombo (for Rs 400) or the airport (Rs 600). The guesthouse is 15km from Fort, off the Kandy road.

The Ketha *(☎ 250 2403; ⓔ ranjitksam@hotmail.com; Kotalawala; singles/doubles Rs 1250/1540, with air-con Rs 1750/2040)* is a handsome large bungalow with a garden set in a cinnamon plantation on the fringe of wetlands. You can take walks in the area, and there is lots of birdlife. The whole bungalow can be rented out for Rs 5000. Arrange transport through the owner, Ranjit Samarasinghe. Kotalawala is about 18km due east of Colombo.

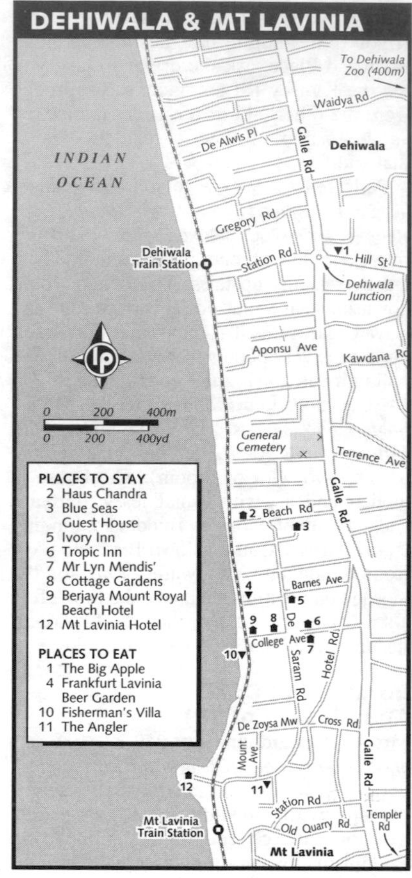

PLACES TO STAY – TOP END

Fort (Col 1)

Grand Oriental Hotel *(☎ 232 0391-2; ⓔ goh@sltnet.lk; 2 York St; singles/doubles US$50/60, suites US$100)*, opposite the harbour, was Colombo's finest 100 years ago, when Bella Sidney Woolf wrote 'it is said that if you waited long enough in the hall…you would meet everyone worth knowing'. It's a real shame the rooms have been stripped of original features and renovated like a Spanish motel. The suites are pleasant but the standard rooms are boxy. There are superb views from its 4th-floor Harbour Restaurant, but it lacks the open spaces that make some other top hotels appealing.

Galadari Hotel *(☎ 254 4544; ⓔ galadari@sri.lanka.net; 64 Lotus Rd; singles/doubles US$75/80)* is an unexceptional top-end joint with tacky decor and rooms of standard quality for the price. On the other hand, it does have good views.

Ceylon Continental Hotel *(☎ 242 1221; ⓔ hotel@ceyloncontinental.com; 48 Janadhipathi Mawatha; singles/doubles US$84/90, suites US$105)* is beautifully located facing the sea on one side and the north end of Galle Face Green on another. Rooms are very comfortable but disappointingly small for the money.

Hilton Colombo *(☎ 254 4644; ⓔ hilton@sri.lanka.net; Lotus Rd; standard singles/doubles US$180/200, executive US$215/225)* has everything a Hilton should have. With seven restaurants, four bars, a disco, a 24-hour business centre, a gym and even a masseur at hand, you needn't step outside.

Slave Island (Col 2)

Hilton JAIC Tower *(☎ 230 0613; e towers@itmin.com; 200 Union Place; 2-/3-bedroom apartments per month from US$2520/2990)*, with 175 fully furnished apartments in a 34-storey tower, is a top-end apartment complex. Amenities include parking for guests, a tennis court, pool, squash court, gym and private restaurant and bar. There is a shopping arcade on the ground floor.

Trans Asia Hotel *(☎ 249 1000; e tah_asia@sri.lanka.net; 115 Chittampalam Gardiner Mawatha; standard singles/doubles US$72/84, suites US$174)* offers comfortable rooms, tennis courts, a fitness centre and swimming pool. The lobby is particularly grandiose.

Kollupitiya (Col 3)

Galle Face Hotel *(☎ 254 1010-6; e gfh@diamond.lanka.net; 2 Kollupitiya Rd; standard rooms US$55, rooms with air-con from US$67, suites US$91-195)*, at the south end of Galle Face Green, is an 1864 hotel with an authentic air of post-colonial neglect. It was the superior establishment during the British colonial era and still has charm. The suites are wonderful, but the cheaper rooms are reached on frayed jute hall runners and are looking deeply tired. Have an evening drink on the terrace overlooking the ocean or try the oceanside restaurant Sea Spray. Nonguests can use the helpful travel desk on the veranda to the left of the main entrance.

Hotel Renuka *(☎ 257 3598; e renukaht@panlanka.net; 328 Galle Rd; singles/doubles with air-con US$55/60)* is a good-quality place with 80 spotless rooms that are a little dated but in good shape. The hotel's restaurant, Palmyrah, is renowned for superb Sri Lankan food (see Places to Eat, later).

Holiday Inn *(☎ 242 2001-9; e holiday@sri.lanka.net; 30 Sir Mohamed Macan Markar Mawatha; singles/doubles US$108/120)* has 94 rooms. A step down from most other top-end hotels, this hotel has all the mod cons, but is smaller and less grandiose. Discounts are fairly easy to come by with an advance booking, lowering the cost of doubles to around US$95.

Taj Samudra Hotel *(☎ 244 6622; e taj@sri.lanka.net; 25 Galle Face Centre Rd; singles/doubles with pool views US$132/144, with sea views US$142/154)* is a vast edifice with some particularly elegant public areas and a large, well-tended garden. The remaining buildings of the Colombo Club stand near the entrance.

The Lanka Oberoi *(☎ 243 7437; e lkoberoi.bc@netgate.mega.lk; 77 Steuart Place; singles/doubles US$168/186)* is, despite its address, actually on Galle Rd a short distance from Galle Face Green. Externally it's a bland tower block, but the atrium features gigantic batik banners.

Havelock Town (Col 5)

The Havelock Place Bungalow *(☎ 258 5191; e havelock.bungalow@mega.lk; 6-8 Havelock Place; singles/doubles US$60/72)* is one of the brightest new entries on the accommodation scene. This handsome boutique hotel has six rooms, refined decor, comfy lounge areas, a garden and a small bathing pool. The little café here is worth a visit as well; gnocchi costs Rs 460, grilled swordfish Rs 500 and a calamari and avocado salad Rs 330.

Mt Lavinia

Berjaya Mount Royal Beach Hotel *(☎ 273 9610-5; e berjaya@slt.lk; 36 College Ave; singles/doubles US$45/55)* is a fading 1970s resort hotel with dated but reasonably comfortable rooms. It does have a prime beach position.

Mt Lavinia Hotel *(☎ 271 5221-7; e lavinia@sri.lanka.net; 100 Hotel Rd; singles/doubles governor's wing US$48/60, bay wing US$120/132)*, once the flashy residence of the British governor, is a magnificently marbled hotel on the waterfront and is very close to Mt Lavinia train station. There's a private sandy beach and a beautifully positioned pool and terrace.

PLACES TO EAT

Colombo has the best selection of restaurants in Sri Lanka. In addition to good Sri Lankan food you will find German, Swiss, French, Italian, Lebanese, Indian, Japanese, Chinese and Korean cuisine. Some of the best restaurants can be found in the five-star hotels, but the real innovation is coming from independent cafés and restaurants bringing a mix of cuisines to Colombo's wealthier classes.

For cheap, tasty food, it's hard to beat **lunch packets**. Sold between about 11am and 2pm on street corners and footpaths all over the city, they generally cost between

Rs 45 and Rs 65. A lunch packet consists of rice and curry – usually boiled rice with vegetables, with fish or chicken as optional extras. Restaurants will also prepare your meal for you to take away if that's what you want; ask for a parcel.

Vegetarian fare can be found at The Green Cabin in Bambalapitiya and Shanti Vihar in Havelock Town. Some other establishments listed offer vegetarian options.

Fort (Col 1)

For self-caterers, **Cargills** has a food city in its Fort store. There are a couple of relatively pricey air-con cafés in the World Trade Centre, including **Barista** and **Deli Market**.

Central YMCA *(39 Bristol St; meals about Rs 60)* has a cafeteria serving cheap, tasty food; it's open for lunch only.

Pagoda Tea Room *(105 Chatham St; meals Rs 65-130)* Hungry like the wolf? Duran Duran filmed their classic '80s video for that very song in this venerable establishment. It's one of the oldest eating establishments in Fort and the service is graciously old-fashioned. There's a variety of Asian and Western food. Basic rice and curry is Rs 65, and there are different daily lunch specials for Rs 130.

Harbour Restaurant *(lunch/dinner buffet Rs 250/500)* at the Grand Oriental Hotel is worth visiting for its superb harbour views. The lunch buffet is served only on weekdays; the dinner buffet is available daily.

Seafish *(☎ 232 6915; 15 Chittampalam Gardiner Mawatha; mains Rs 300-400)*, at the southern edge of Fort, has excellent seafood. Try the sweet-and-sour prawns for Rs 380.

Il Ponte *(Lotus Rd, Fort; mains Rs 600-800)* is light and airy with a range of Italian and continental dishes, imported wines and beers, and a good salad bar.

More upmarket dining can be had at any of the Hilton's restaurants *(Lotus Rd, Fort)*. **Curry Leaf** *(buffet Rs 750; open dinner only)* has excellent Sri Lankan food. It has a garden setting aimed at recreating the atmosphere of a traditional village. In addition to all sorts of local specialities, there is an arrack bar. **Moghul Ghar** *(mains Rs 500-750)* specialises in Pakistani halal cuisine. **Ginza Hohsen** *(mains Rs 900-1100)* serves sushi and other Japanese fare (with all-imported ingredients). For good Chinese food try the **Emperor's Wok**.

Slave Island (Col 2)

Lotus Leaf *(466 Union Place; mains around Rs 100)* is a popular air-con brasserie-style Sri Lankan eatery, popular with students. The food is fresh and cheap, and it serves alcohol.

Komalas *(323 Union Place; meals Rs 250-350)* is a modern, efficiently run franchise doing the best of Indian cuisine, next door to Pizza Hut. It does great lassis for Rs 60.

Kollupitiya (Col 3)

Self-Catering & Cafés Self-caterers can head to **Beema** near Liberty Plaza on the 2nd floor of the big market building. It's an indoor place with fruit, vegetables and a good range of imported foods at very competitive prices. A supermarket popular with expats is **Keells** at Liberty Plaza.

Barefoot Garden Cafe *(704 Galle Rd; sandwiches around Rs 200)*, located on the lower level of the well-known Barefoot shop, is set in a pretty courtyard next to the gallery and bookshop. The menu is mostly sandwiches, cakes and snacks such as falafel in pita bread (Rs 250), and there's a wine list as well.

Kafé Kent *(35 Bagatalle Rd; mains Rs 200-400)* has a cosy atmosphere, comfortable for women travellers. There are several sitting areas for a drink, and multiple dining rooms upstairs for a quiet dinner. Unfortunately, the food's not quite as good as the ambience.

The Gallery Cafe *(☎ 258 2162; 2 Alfred House Rd; mains Rs 420-1100)* contains what used to be an office belonging to Sri Lanka's most famous architect, Geoffrey Bawa. Entry is through a series of colonnaded courtyards featuring ornamental pools; from the outer latticed gate you can gaze right through to the inner courtyard via a series of similarly latticed gates that frame, right at the end, a large terracotta storage jar. Exhibitions of paintings and photography are hung in these courtyards as well as further inside. The lounge bar is where Bawa's old office used to be and his desk is still there. The open-air café area looks over a pebbled courtyard. As a cheaper option, come for an afternoon coffee. It's definitely one of the places to be seen in Colombo, but more importantly it's a stunning spot and a terrific retreat from the bustle of Colombo. Dress up a little, in case you stumble in and gatecrash a swish scene at the opening of an exhibition while you're wearing…oh never mind.

Restaurants YWCA National Headquarters (see Places to Stay, earlier) has a busy **cafeteria** *(open Mon-Sat)* offering a wide variety of dirt-cheap eats.

Amaravathi *(2 Mile Post Ave; meals around Rs 150)*, near Hotel Renuka, has air-con, attentive service and scrumptious South Indian food for very reasonable prices. Thalis (South Indian meal consisting of rice with vegetable curries and pappadams, from Rs 110) are served at lunch (from 11am to 3pm), but there is a wide selection of other dishes: chicken biryani (Rs 150), vegetable korma (Rs 100), or for a special treat, brain *masala* (Rs 120).

Crescat Boulevard *(Galle Rd)*, a couple of minutes from the Lanka Oberoi Hotel, has a good **food hall** downstairs (there is also a Keells supermarket here). You have a choice of Sri Lankan, Chinese, Indian and international food. Service is efficient, the surroundings are clean (with clean toilets nearby), it's got air-con and the prices are moderate (Rs 170 for rice and curry).

Siam House *(55 Abdul Caffour Mawatha; mains Rs 200-300)* is in a villa on a side street off RA de Mel Mawatha. The decor is simple but the Thai food is excellent. Chicken *massaman* curry costs Rs 220 and prawn curry Rs 275, and the service is attentive.

Flower Drum *(29 Cumaratunga Munidasa Mawatha; mains around Rs 250)* is a spotless, dark air-con eatery that is well known for good Chinese food. The soups cost around Rs 200.

Palmyrah Restaurant *(328 Galle Rd; mains around Rs 300)* is in the basement of Hotel Renuka. Lurking in a nondescript kitchen a chef is whipping up some of the finest Sri Lankan curries in Colombo. Rice-and-chicken curry costs Rs 240, and the chef's good with other cuisines as well.

Chesa Swiss *(☎ 257 3433; 3 Deal Place; mains from Rs 300; open 7pm-11pm Tues-Sun)* serves good Swiss food. It's simple and spotless, and the service is attentive. Soup (for example, carrot and ginger) starts at Rs 180, and sliced venison in Cognac-pepper sauce costs Rs 1000. A good selection of imported wines and beers is available.

Sakura *(☎ 257 3877; 15 Rheinland Place; mains around Rs 300)* is Colombo's oldest Japanese restaurant. The food is simple and the menu fairly straightforward, but it's quite good quality. If you sit at the bar you can scan between the sushi chef and delightfully weird Japanese game shows on the TV. It also has a private dining room with *tatami* mats.

The Cricket Club Cafe *(34 Queens Rd; meals Rs 350-600)* is one of the most popular places to meet, drink and eat. In an older-style bungalow with a garden, veranda and air-con, the setting is very pleasant. It is packed with cricket memorabilia, making it the ideal place to discuss whether Muttiah Muralitharan is a chucker or if Shane Warne is stupid. There are menus for both snacks and meals, and a special children's menu. Options range from pasta dishes for Rs 170 to 250, to a meat pie for Rs 345, plus seafood and burgers with salad and chips. There's a good bar and an excellent selection of beers and wines.

Koluu's *(☎ 244 6589; 32B Sir Mohamed Macan Markar Mawatha; mains from Rs 400)* is a fashionable place with striking decor, a few doors from the Holiday Inn. The menu of French, Italian and Indonesian cuisine changes regularly – some succeed more than others but at least you won't get bored. The rather fun in-house Kiss Kiss Bar has some mind-blowing cocktails.

German Restaurant *(11 Galle Face Court; meals Rs 400-600)*, opposite the Galle Face Hotel, does all things German. Main meat dishes are around Rs 450. You may wish to make your visit coincide with the happy hour (7pm to 8pm) to sample the draught German beer and wines.

Sea Spray *(☎ 254 1010; lunch/dinner buffet Rs 490/700)* is a quaint oceanside restaurant in the Galle Face Hotel that serves Sri Lankan and Western-style food. The veranda is a great place for a sunset drink, though with Lion lager at Rs 200, you're paying for the privilege.

Bambalapitiya (Col 4)

A good spot for a cheap but reasonable-quality lunch is the **food hall** in the basement of Majestic City. And there's plenty of choice, including Malay, Chinese, Sri Lankan, Western-style fast food (including pizza and fried chicken) and Indian. There's air-con, so it's pleasantly cool, and there's a play area for young children next to the eating area. Majestic City also has a **KFC** and a good **Cargills** on the ground floor.

Greenlands Hotel *(3A Shrubbery Gardens; meals Rs 60-120)*, despite its ward-like interior, whips up mean, fresh South Indian food. There's an air-con section and a busy, clean canteen area. The prices are so low you won't mind that you may have to beg to be served: Superb rice and curry costs Rs 55, *masala dosa* (curried vegetables inside a lentil and rice-flour pancake) Rs 40 and *idli* (South Indian rice dumpling) Rs 13.

The Green Cabin *(453 Galle Rd; mains Rs 100-150)* is a bit of an institution in the restaurant trade and still serves good food at very reasonable prices. The lunch-time buffet (Rs 130 for vegetarian) is excellent value – the mango curry, if it's on, is very good. For a snack, try the vegetable pastries or the fish-and-egg pies.

Sapid *(2A Vajira Rd; mains Rs 100-300)* has good Sri Lankan food. It's got air-con and has some pleasantly breezy upstairs rooms.

Chinese Dragon Cafe *(11 Milagiriya Ave; mains around Rs 200)* is an old mansion serving inexpensive rice and noodle dishes. Heed the sign 'Complaints Welcome at Reception' but save your breath if you want to complain that the restaurant doesn't serve or allow alcohol on the premises.

Havelock Town (Col 5) & Wellawatta (Col 6)

Shanti Vihar *(3 Havelock Rd, Havelock Town; meals Rs 80-125)* is popular with locals and foreigners because of its deliciously spicy vegetarian food for very reasonable prices. It's a basic, well-worn eatery, though there is a fancier air-con section. The menu's South Indian offerings are especially good: *masala dosa* for Rs 45, *curd vadai* (a deep-fried lentil or flour patty with yogurt), Madras thalis for Rs 90 and special thalis for Rs 125. Shanti Vihar also has a home-delivery service.

Beach Wadiya *(☎ 258 8568; 2 Station Ave, Wellawatta; mains around Rs 400)* is a beach hut at the bottom of Station Rd, near the Wellawatta train station. It's a popular spot for seafood, but the main drawcard is the photoboards of people – many famous (ie, cricketers), others drunk, some both – who have visited the restaurant. The last order is at 10.15pm. It might pay to book, as this place gets busy.

Cinnamon Gardens (Col 7)

The **Paradise Road Cafe** *(213 Dharmapala Mawatha; light meals Rs 100-150)*, part of the shop of the same name, serves great coffee for Rs 100, milkshakes for Rs 150, cakes and light meals such as quiche and spaghetti, in an airy veranda-style atmosphere upstairs. It's just southwest of De Soysa (Lipton) Circus.

Delifrance *(5 Alexandra Place, De Soysa/Lipton Circus; coffee & lunch Rs 300)*, a busy café on the ground floor of the very popular Odel Unlimited store, is delighted to siphon off your shopping change. Sweet and sticky pastries go for Rs 75; real coffees cost Rs 100. There's also an outlet at Crescat Boulevard on Galle Rd.

The Commons *(74A Dharmapala Mawatha; light meals Rs 200-300, coffee Rs 140; open daily)*, which is part garden, part gallery and part open-lounge café (with large, soft sofas), is a safe retreat for women and tired visitors generally. It's a perfect spot to take a break or settle in to read the Sunday papers. There's a good selection for the sweet-toothed, with fudge brownies, and a delicious 'brunch' that features pancakes, bacon and syrup for Rs 300. Sandwiches cost from Rs 200.

Le Palace *(☎ 269 5920; 79 Gregory's Rd; mains from Rs 500)*, in a beautiful old mansion in one of Colombo's most exclusive streets, is run by a French chef, and the pastries and bakery products are first class. If your budget's tight you can always come during the day and enjoy a pastry for Rs 75. If you are coming here by taxi or three-wheeler ask the driver to take you via the Kynsey Rd entrance; there are many schools in this street, which means much of it is closed to traffic.

Dehiwala & Mt Lavinia

There are many places to eat and drink along Mt Lavinia's beachfront; it's a great place to watch the sun set and to 'people watch'. Note that some restaurants have limited menus on weekdays, as most local tourists come on the weekend.

The Big Apple *(21 Hill St, Dehiwala)* is an air-con complex of Chinese, Sri Lankan and Indian restaurants as well as a rooftop beer garden; all are open from 7.30pm to 11.30pm.

The Angler *(71 Hotel Rd, Mt Lavinia; mains around Rs 250)* received several plaudits from readers for its Sri Lankan and Western-style cooking (with an emphasis on seafood, as you might have guessed).

Frankfurt Lavinia Beer Garden *(34/8A De Saram Rd, Mt Lavinia; mains around Rs 400)* serves German speciality food in a leafy garden setting. Home-made sausages cost Rs 370 – most mains are around this price. Food orders are taken until 10.30pm.

Fisherman's Villa *(☎ 074 202821; 43/19 College Ave, Mt Lavinia; mains Rs 250-800)* is a posh, beachfront place with great food and service. With seafood dishes you have to order a minimum of 300g, so the prices can be high (jumbo prawns with herbs and mustard costs Rs 920), but there are cheaper meals, eg, fish satay with fries for Rs 250.

Mt Lavinia Hotel (see Places to Stay, earlier) has excellent food, as it should for US$15 per dinner, but some have complained about sloppy service and a lack of attention to detail.

ENTERTAINMENT

The long years of war put a dampener on Colombo's nightlife – after dark, people preferred to stay at home. This is starting to change, and a small but vigorous series of pubs and clubs are loosening up the city's young and wealthy. Colombo even has a couple of Irish pubs. A big night out might start at a restaurant or pub, segue into revelry at a dance club, and finally collapse in a heap at a casino.

Pubs & Bars

Single women should feel more or less comfortable at any of the places listed below, barring the first one. Shooter's Pool Parlour has a beer-and-cigs male atmosphere, so it might be better to bring a companion.

Sri Lanka Ex-Servicemen's Institute *(29 Bristol St, Fort)* has a bar that serves local Lion lager for Rs 80 a bottle, which is about the cheapest you'll buy it anywhere – but you're not paying for atmosphere.

Colombo has two Irish pubs, neither of them very Irish, which is not necessarily a bad thing. **Clancy's Irish Pub** *(29 Maitland Crescent, Cinnamon Gardens)* has pub meals and a loungey feel but no Guinness on tap. A pint of draught costs Rs 150. Drinks are served to your table and there are quiz nights, live music (light rock, blues or jazz) on weekends and a few couches to sink into. Upstairs, **Shooter's Pool Parlour** has four billiards tables, a bar and hard rock over the PA.

Molly's Irish Pub & Restaurant *(46/38 Nawam Mawatha, Slave Island)* is tucked away in the little office district on Nawam Mawatha. Like Clancy's, it has regular quiz nights, acoustic duos, pub meals and retro dance nights.

The White Horse *(2 Nawam Mawatha, Slave Island)* is close enough to Molly's that you could almost lead a conga line between them. Inside it's a sparse, modern space with stainless steel decor and low couches and tables. The sound system was working just fine when we visited and, with enough people, dancing may break out. A mixed crowd of Sri Lankan and expats often spill out onto the street at the end of working weeks.

Rhythm & Blues Bar *(19/1 Daisy Villa Ave, Bambalapitiya)*, near the Atlantic Club, has live music on Friday and Saturday nights, and billiard tables.

All of the top-end hotels have bars. Spruce up and head to the colonial-style **Echelon** at the Hilton Colombo in Fort. It has a billiard table, darts and occasionally bingo. The Hilton also has a **karaoke bar** open from 8pm if you like embarrassing yourself. The **bar** at the Galle Face Hotel is very pleasant.

Some good places to drink are also listed under Places to Eat, earlier. Try The Cricket Club Cafe, or for something more glamorous the Kiss Kiss Bar at Koluu's, next to the Holiday Inn. For German booze head to the German Restaurant or Frankfurt Lavinia Beer Garden in Mt Lavinia. In Dehiwala, The Big Apple has a rooftop beer garden.

Nightclubs

Most of Colombo's nightlife centres on the top hotels. All clubs have a cover charge of about Rs 500 and are open nightly. The dress code is fashion-conscious but casual. Things only really get going at about 10pm and continue through to 6am. These clubs are the haunts of the sons and nephews of politicians, who have the advantage of bodyguards if a fight breaks out. Entry is usually restricted to mixed couples and single women.

Some choices include the **Blue Elephant** at the Hilton and **The Boom** in the Galadari Hotel (both in Fort), **Cascades** at The Lanka Oberoi and **My Kind of Place** at the Taj Samudra (both in Kollupitiya). Another possibility is **Legends**, on the 5th floor at Majestic City in Bambalapitiya.

Casinos

Most casinos are along Galle Rd and RA de Mel Mawatha in Bambalapitiya and Kollupitiya. One of their main functions may be to launder money for Indian business 'identities', while creaming off their cut – the signs outside say 'foreigners only'. The casinos have all sorts of incentives to lure punters, including free meals and drinks, free transport to and from the casino and so on. Most are open 24 hours. They include **Bally's Casino** *(14 Dharmapala Mawatha, Kollupitiya)*, near Liberty Plaza, and the **MGM Casino** *(772 Galle Rd, Bambalapitiya)*, near Majestic City. These casinos are run by the same management.

Cinemas

TV and video have largely killed off the cinema scene – many old movie houses are hanging on by catering to the raincoat brigade with lurid skin flicks such as *Amazon Women* and *Bedroom Eyes*. Some are foreign productions, others are B-grade Indian flicks, often the story of a busty victim of an outrage seeking vengeance with heavy weaponry, with expensive scenes (explosions, etc) spliced in from other films.

There are three nonsleazy cinemas that show Hollywood blockbusters, often quite a while after they've been released elsewhere in the world. The volume and aircon systems tend to be turned up high. The most modern cinemas are the **Savoy** *(Galle Rd, Wellawatta)* and the **Majestic Cinema** *(level 4, Majestic City, Bambalapitiya)*. Tickets cost Rs 150 for adults and Rs 100 for children under 12. Another older cinema, **Liberty Cinema**, is opposite Liberty Plaza. Shows run in the morning and evening (usually starting at 6.30pm or 7pm). Most of the other cinemas attract male thrillseekers with films advertised as 'strictly for adults'.

The foreign cultural centres show arthouse films; for what's on see *LT*, *Travel Lanka* and the *Linc*.

Theatre

Lionel Wendt Centre *(☎ 269 5794; 18 Guilford Crescent, Cinnamon Gardens)* sometimes puts on theatre. The foreign cultural centres such as the British Council also host shows. These are advertised in newspapers and magazines such as *LT*, and at cafés and hotels frequented by expats.

The finely restored **Elphinstone Theatre** *(☎ 243 3635; Maradana Rd, Maradana)* is an 80-year-old theatre with a busy programme of music, drama and films.

Lumbini Theatre *(Havelock Rd, Havelock Town)* hosts Sinhala theatre.

SPECTATOR SPORTS

The top spectator sport in Sri Lanka is, without a doubt, cricket. You can buy tickets for major games from the **Board of Control for Cricket in Sri Lanka** *(BCCSL; ☎ 268 1601; e toc@itmin.com; 35 Maitland Place, Cinnamon Gardens)*, next to the Sinhalese Sports Club. See Spectator Sports in the Facts for the Visitor chapter for more details.

SHOPPING

Handicrafts

Colombo is a good place to shop for handicrafts. The longest-established place is the government-run **Laksala** *(60 York St, Fort)*. Here you'll find two floors showcasing all manner of traditional Sri Lankan crafts, batik and wood carving. The decent prices are clearly marked so there's no need to bargain.

Lanka Hands *(135 Bauddhaloka Mawatha, Bambalapitiya)* has a good variety of local crafts, including jewellery, brightly painted wooden toys and puzzles, cane and basketry, drums, brasswork and more. The prices are reasonable.

Lakpahana *(21 Rajakeeya Mawatha, Cinnamon Gardens)* has items mostly created along traditional lines, including lacework, jewellery, batik, tea and masks.

Hand-loomed Fabrics

Barefoot *(704 Galle Rd, Kollupitiya)* is very popular, especially among expats, for its bright hand-loomed textiles fashioned into bedspreads, cushions and serviettes (or you can buy material by the metre). You'll also find irresistible soft toys, textile-covered notebooks, lampshades and albums, and a large selection of stylish, simple clothing downstairs. The items are quite pricey but of uniformly good quality.

The Oasis Company *(18 Station Rd, Bambalapitiya)* is another place for fabrics. Here you'll find similar fare to Barefoot but some of the textiles are blockprinted; there are carpets too.

Kandygs Handloom House *(333 Galle Rd, Kollupitiya)* has a selection of hand-painted cotton and jute bed spreads, wall hangings, rugs and more.

Clothing

Sri Lanka is a major garment manufacturer and all manner of clothing, from beach wear to warm padded jackets, is easy to find in Colombo. Many of the items are Western-style clothes – you'd be able to find them in department stores all over the world – while others, fortunately, you'll only find here. You'll find many clothing stores along RA de Mel Mawatha.

Odel Unlimited *(5 Alexandra Place, Cinnamon Gardens)* is the place to shop with the glamorous. You'll find everything here from homewares, designer-label clothing and sportswear to banana soap.

Collectibles

Serendib *(36 1/1 Rosmead Place, Cinnamon Gardens)* sells sculpture, paintings, rare Sri Lankan maps, prints, books, antique furniture and porcelain. You will find similar wares at **Paradise Road** *(213 Dharmapala Mawatha, Cinnamon Gardens)*.

Paradise Road's other outlets (Gallery Cafe in Kollupitiya, Hilton JAIC Tower shopping mall in Slave Island, Trans Asia shopping gallery at the Trans Asia Hotel in Slave Island) sell selected delectable collectibles; they are good places to look for small gifts to take home.

Kandyan Antiques *(36 Sir Ernest de Silva Mawatha, Cinnamon Gardens • 106 Bauddhaloka Mawatha, Bambalapitiya)* has heaps of items – some junky, others funky – though they're not prepared to bargain much.

Raux Brothers *(7 De Fonseka Rd, Havelock Town)* is a big colonial house with a range of furniture, and artworks crafted from wood. It sells genuine antiques as well as handcrafted new pieces.

Gems & Jewellery

There are many gem dealers and jewellers along Galle Rd and RA de Mel Mawatha, and in Sea St, Pettah, where the shops can be on a tiny scale. The biggest outlets employ the best silver-tongued sales people in the business. The **Sri Lanka Gem & Jewellery Exchange** *(310 Galle Rd, Kollupitiya)* has about 30 shops. On the 2nd floor the **Gem Testing Laboratory** has a free testing centre. Obviously you can't just borrow a huge sapphire from a store to get it assessed, but you could ask the store to send someone with you.

GETTING THERE & AWAY

Colombo is the gateway to Sri Lanka from abroad, and is also the centre of the island's bus and rail networks. See the Getting Around chapter for general information on bus and train travel.

You may find leaving Colombo by train is easier than by bus, though trains are usually less frequent and a little more expensive than buses. There's more order at the train stations than at the bus stations, and often less overcrowding on board.

Air

Domestic Colombo's domestic airport is at Ratmalana, south of Mt Lavinia. There is no public transport to or from this airport. It's still used as an airforce base, so the security presence is heavy and you need to check in two hours before takeoff. On the positive side, the airport terminal is a wood-panelled colonial classic with a baggage conveyor that simply spits luggage onto the floor – here's hoping they never renovate it.

There are three airlines on the only domestic route, between Colombo and Jaffna. At the time of research a price war had broken out between the airlines, and fares were Rs 2450/4550 one-way/return. This situation probably won't last long, and one airline manager suggested fares will rise to about Rs 4000/7000. The domestic airline offices are

Expo Aviation (☎ 074 512666, ⓔ info@expolanka.com) 464 Galle Rd, Kollupitiya
Lionair (☎ 074 515715, ⓔ lionairsales@sierra.lk) 14 Trelawney Place (cnr Galle Rd & Bauddhaloka Mawatha), Bambalapitiya
Serendip Express (☎ 250 5632, ⓔ serendibexpress@sltnet.lk) 500 Galle Rd, Wellawatta

International Bandaranaike International Airport is at Katunayake, 30km north of the city and about 2km east of the Colombo–Negombo road.

For arrivals, departures and other airport information, call the **hotlines** *(☎ 019 733 5555, 019 733 2677)*. Don't forget the departure tax (Rs 1000).

For information about transport to/from the airport (including to/from Negombo and further afield), see Getting Around following.

Offices for international airlines flying to Sri Lanka are listed following.

Cathay Pacific Airways (☎ 233 4145) 186 Vauxhall St, Slave Island
Condor (☎ 244 8167) 57A Dharmapala Mawatha, Kollupitiya
CSA (Czech Airlines) (☎ 238 1200) Jetwing House, 26/46 Nawam Mawatha, Slave Island
Emirates (☎ 230 0200) 9th floor, Hemas Bldg, 75 Braybrooke Place, Slave Island
Gulf Air (☎ 243 4662) 11 York St, Fort
Indian Airlines (☎ 232 3136) 4 Bristol St, Fort
Kuwait Airways (☎ 244 5531) Ceylinco House, 69 Janadhipathi Mawatha, Fort
LTU International (☎ 242 4483) 11A York St, Fort
Malaysia Airlines (☎ 234 2291) Hemas Bldg, 81 York St, Fort
Oman Air (☎ 234 8495) Trans Asia Hotel, 115 Chittampalam Gardiner Mawatha, Slave Island
Qatar Airways (☎ 074 525700) 201 Sir James Peiris Mawatha, Cinnamon Gardens
Royal Jordanian (☎ 230 1621) 40A Cumaratunga Munidasa Mawatha, Kollupitiya
Saudi Arabian Airlines (☎ 074 717747) 466 Galle Rd, Kollupitiya
Singapore Airlines (☎ 230 0757) 315 Vauxhall St, Slave Island
SriLankan Airlines (☎ 242 1161, reconfirmation ☎ 019 733 5500) Level 19-22, East Tower, World Trade Centre, Echelon Square, Fort
Thai Airways (☎ 243 8050) Ground floor, JAIC Hilton, 200 Union Place, Slave Island

Bus

Colombo has three main bus stations, or rather yards, all on the south edge of Pettah, just east of Fort train station. The most important, and the most chaotic, is the **Bastian Mawatha station**, where you catch buses to, among other places, Kandy, Nuwara Eliya, Trincomalee, Ambalangoda, Hikkaduwa, Galle, Matara, Tangalla, Kataragama and the airport (No 187). Buses to the airport are easy to find, as there are men screaming out 'Airport! Airport!' whenever one is filling up. The buses to Negombo, Ratnapura, Kurunegala, Haputale, Badulla, Anuradhapura and Polonnaruwa leave from the **Saunders Place station**. The **Central Bus Station** on Olcott Mawatha is where many suburban buses start and stop, and it is quite orderly. For details on fares see Getting There & Away under the individual destinations.

Private air-con coaches to Jaffna (Rs 1000) start from and can be booked through **Hotel Rolex** *(360 Galle Rd, Wellawatta)*, in the block south of Rajasinghe Rd on the sea side. There's a service on Monday, Wednesday and Friday nights. Also, there are many businesses in Wellawatta selling tickets on nightly vans to Jaffna. These tickets cost the same as the private buses, are not as comfortable, but you're likely not to have to wait as long for them to fill up as with the buses. Try at **Deelah Communications** *(☎ 075 514274-5; 285 Galle Rd, Wellawatta)*, which is opposite the Delmon Hospital.

Train

The main train station, Colombo Fort, is within walking distance of the city centre. Trains in transit often stop only for two or three minutes. See the boxed text 'Main Trains from Fort' for details of services.

There's an **information office** *(☎ 244 0048; open 9am-5pm Mon-Fri, 9am-1pm Sat)*, actually a branch office of JF Tours, at the front of the station. The helpful staff know everything about transport in and out of Colombo. Or you could try the information desk (No 10) at the station. There's a left-luggage facility at the station (Rs 17 per bag per day, open 4.30am to 11.30pm daily). Fort station is crawling with touts waiting to hook you up with their 'uncle's' hotel in Kandy or down the coast.

GETTING AROUND

To/From the Airport

Taxis and buses are the most convenient forms of transport to and from the international airport. Only taxis, though, go to the domestic airport at Ratmalana.

If you're arriving in the dead of the night it's best to book a room and let the hotel or guesthouse know what time you'll be arriving. They *should* be able to organise a driver to pick you up from the airport, though it's easy enough to jump in a taxi. Buses to the airport (No 187) depart from the Bastian Mawatha station in Pettah from 6am until 9pm (Rs 25). From the airport, they leave every 30 minutes between 4.30am and 11pm. Taxi drivers will tell you there is no public transport. There is no bus directly to Negombo from the airport but you can catch the air-con bus to Katunayake junction (Rs 8) from where you can catch a bus for Negombo (Rs 15 for an intercity express). Buses from Negombo head to the airport every 15 to 20 minutes from about 5am to 9pm – again, change at the junction. The trip takes about 45 minutes.

It's possible, although not particularly convenient, to catch a commuter train to

Main Trains from Fort

destination	departure time	fare (Rs) 3rd	2nd	1st class	duration (hrs)
Anuradhapura	5.45am & 2.05pm, 5.45pm	42	116	277	8
Anuradhapura *(Intercity Express)*	3.55pm	-	115	250	4½
Batticaloa	6.15am, 8pm	na	na	na	9 to 10
Badulla via Kandy *(Podi Menike)*	5.55am	60	165.50	339*	9
Badulla via Peradeniya Junction, not Kandy *(Udarata Menike)*	9.45am	60	165.50	339*	9
Badulla *(Night Mail)*	7.40pm, 10pm	60	165.50	289	9
Kandy via Peradeniya *(Intercity Express)*	7am, 3.35pm	-	72	172*	2½
Kandy via Rambukkana for elephant orphanage	5.56am, 10.30am & 12.40pm, 4.55pm, 5.50pm, 7.40pm	25	68.50	-	3
Matara via Bentota, Hikkaduwa, Galle	7.10am, 9am, 10.30am & 2.05pm**, 4pm, 5pm, 5.52pm	33	89	-	4
Negombo	4.30am, 5.20am, 6am, 8.40am, 9.25am & 1pm, 1.45pm, 2.50pm, 4.55pm, 5.20pm, 5.35pm, 5.40pm, 6.20pm, 6.55pm, 8.20pm	11	26	-	2
Polonnaruwa	6.15am, 8pm, 10.30pm	53.50	147	331	6 to 9
Trincomalee	6.15am, 8pm, 10.30pm	61	168	-	8

* First-class observation saloon fare includes a booking fee of Rs 50.
** On Saturday only 3rd class is available.

Colombo. The station is near the turn-off from the main road, but is a bit of a hike (500m) from the terminal.

If you want a taxi, head to the **Ceylon Tourist Board's information desk** *(open 24 hrs)*, in the first arrivals hall after you exit through customs, and find out the latest fixed rates. At the time of writing a one-way fare was Rs 900 (40 minutes to 1½ hours) to Colombo; Rs 500 (20 minutes) to Negombo; and Rs 2700 (two to three hours) to Kandy. Armed with this information, after you've exited the second arrivals hall full of hotel and hire-car agencies (see the boxed text 'Airport Tout Scam'), you'll be pounced on by an army of taxi drivers – take your pick, as you know what to pay. Taxis *to* the airport cost Rs 1200 from Colombo (Rs 1500 from

Mt Lavinia), Rs 600 from Negombo and Rs 3000 from Kandy.

Avoid taking a three-wheeler between the airport and Colombo; it's a long, miserable journey and you'll be sucking in exhaust fumes all the way. Three-wheelers get really uncomfortable after about 20 minutes – as veterans of a three-wheeler ride from Colombo to Negombo we can swear by this. Three-wheeler fares between the airport and Negombo should be around Rs 350 (30 minutes). Three-wheelers may not pick up passengers from the terminal but you can pick one up on the road outside the airport.

Bus

The *A-Z Street Guide* has the low-down on bus routes, as does *Travel Lanka*. The Central Transport Board (CTB) and private buses operate parallel services. A timetable is not necessary – the buses can hardly be described as running to one. Buses going down Galle Rd from Fort or Pettah, include Nos 100, 101 and 400 and can be picked up at the Central Bus Station. While there are supposedly fixed fares on buses, you may come across minor variations in price. From Fort to Dehiwala down Galle Rd should be about Rs 6.

Private semiluxury and luxury buses are a recent addition to the Galle Rd service, though they are far fewer in number than the regular buses. Sometimes they have a destination sign in English in the front window. Generally they have curtains and soft seats. The fare is about twice that for ordinary buses, but still a bargain, really.

Train

You can use the train for reaching the suburbs dotted along Galle Rd – Kollupitiya, Bambalapitiya, Wellawatta, Dehiwala and Mt Lavinia – and avoid the smog, noise and hassle of bus travel. The Kelani Valley Line could be used to get to outlying suburbs such as Narahenpita (via Cotta Rd station) from Fort. Timetables are clearly marked at the stations, though if you just turn up you shouldn't have to wait long. If you board the train at Fort train station, double check it stops at all stations or you may end up speeding to Galle before you'd planned to. Train fares are fixed and usually marginally lower than bus fares.

Airport Tout Scam

Touts (sometimes disguised as officials) gather inside the second arrivals hall waiting for jet-lagged visitors to emerge. You may be approached with claims that for some reason or another (eg, a bomb's just gone off somewhere) it's dangerous to travel any further unaccompanied. The pitch is that the tourists should, for their own safety, sign up for a tour on the spot. This can end up being a convenient scam if you do want to take a tour, but if you want to travel independently double-check the current security situation with the Ceylon Tourist Board's information desk in the first arrivals hall.

Taxi

Some taxis are metered but often the driver won't use the meter and you must agree on the fare before setting off. A taxi from Fort train station to the Galle Face Hotel (a little over 2km) should be about Rs 100, and getting to Mt Lavinia should cost around Rs 500.

A less fraught alternative is using one of Colombo's radio cab companies; they usually take 15 to 20 minutes to arrive. All have air-con cars with meters and average about Rs 30 per kilometre. Companies include **Ace Cabs** *(☎ 250 1502)*, **GNTC** *(☎ 268 8688)* and **Quick Radio Cabs** *(☎ 250 2888)*.

Three-Wheeler

Darting through traffic in a three-wheeler might be called exhilarating by some and downright reckless by others.

Everywhere you look you'll see a three-wheeler. As a rule of thumb, you should pay about Rs 30 per kilometre, but agree on a fare before getting in. At times three-wheeler drivers will try their luck by asking for a ridiculous initial fare, in the hope that you haven't got a clue. Try rolling your eyes and heading for another three-wheeler for the best discounts. From Fort, expect to pay Rs 100 to 150 to get to Cinnamon Gardens, Rs 200 to Bambalapitiya, and Rs 400 to Mt Lavinia.

You'll often get a better price hailing a three-wheeler on the street rather than using one that's waiting outside a hotel or sitting at a three-wheeler stand.

JOHN BORTHWICK

West coast sunset

DALLAS STRIBLEY

Waiter at the colonial-era Galle Face Hotel, Colombo

DALLAS STRIBLEY

Washing up, Pettah, Colombo

MARK DAFFEY

Palm trees at sunset, south of Colombo

DALLAS STRIBLEY

Bustling bazaar, Pettah, Colombo

CHRIS MELLOR

Statues of deities on a Hindu temple, Colombo

West Coast

For 450 years the west coast was the European colonial heartland, a fertile belt of cinnamon and spice plantations, walled warehouses and ports linked by canals. Other seafarers landed here over the centuries, with Arab sailors and Indian fisherfolk settling along the beaches at river inlets. Proximity to Colombo and the international airport meant that tourism discovered the west coast earlier than other regions, and by the 1980s the miles of beaches and the short, spectacular sunsets had spawned a string of seaside resorts and hotels.

This area is at its best from November/December to March. From May to August the southwest monsoon makes it less palatable than eastern Sri Lanka. Most accommodation is concentrated in a few touristy towns along the coast, but there are also many small guesthouses and hotels scattered in secluded spots between the larger centres.

All along this coast you have to watch out for dangerous currents, undertows and rip tides, particularly with the bigger seas during the wet season from April/May to October/November. Watch where other people are swimming or ask reliable locals about when or where to go for a dip. In some places sea pollution is another deterrent – the further you are from town centres, and from Colombo, the better.

This chapter covers Puttalam and Chilaw, two towns of minimal interest but often used as stopovers between Anuradhapura and Colombo; Negombo (about 36km north of Colombo, close to Bandaranaike International Airport); and the southwest coast between Colombo and Galle, including Kalutara, Beruwela, Bentota, Aluthgama, Induruwa, Ahungala, Ambalangoda and Hikkaduwa.

Highlights

- Cycling along Negombo's Dutch canals and breaking for lunch at a beachside restaurant
- Lolling on the beach, lapping up the sun, living it up at Bentota
- Surfing the surf or busting the boogie board at Hikkaduwa
- Watching the *kolam* (masked drama) dancers strut their stuff and buying a grotesque devil dancer's mask at Ambalangoda

PUTTALAM & AROUND

☎ 032 • pop 41,000

The ancient trading, pearling and fishing town of Puttalam is a scruffy, neglected market town in its modern incarnation, but you may pass through if you're travelling from Anuradhapura to Colombo, or vice versa.

A Portuguese regiment of soldiers from Mozambique originally settled the village of **Sellankandal** about 10km inland from Puttalam. As late as the 1930s, Sellankandal villagers still spoke a form of Portuguese and sang Afro-Portuguese *bailas* (songs). Here and in Puttalam you might see some people of mixed African descent.

The turn-off to the peninsula towns of Kalpitiya and Talawila is south of Puttalam, and leads past saltpans and a salt factory. **Kalpitiya** was recently home to many refugees from the north, who are now being resettled. A small number have jobs locally and have settled in Kalpitiya. The well-preserved Dutch fort dating from 1670 is still manned by the Sri Lankan army. To the north a string of barrier islands guards Dutch Bay and Portugal Bay. The saltpans and thin coconut plantations on the peninsula are home to a herd of wild donkeys.

At **Talawila** there's a Catholic shrine to St Anne. The church features satinwood pillars and is pleasantly situated on the seafront. Thousands of pilgrims come here in March and July when the major festivals honouring St Anne are held. The festivals include huge processions, healing services and a fair.

In Puttalam, the following places have bathrooms.

Senatilake Guest Inn *(☎ 226 5403, fax 226 5299; 81A Kurunegala Rd; rooms Rs 660-1650)* is a solid old place with eight reasonable rooms, some with air-con. Tasty rice and curry dishes cost Rs 180 for dinner or lunch.

Dammika Holiday Resort *(☎ 226 5192; 51 Good Shed Rd; rooms Rs 1000, with air-con Rs 1500)* is about 1km south of the town centre, signposted on the Colombo road. It's quite a

substantial guesthouse, sometimes used by nongovernmental organisation (NGO) staff. There are two rooms with air-con, and rice and curry in the pleasant dining rooms costs Rs 300.

The **Rest House** *(☎/fax 226 5299; Beach Rd; rooms Rs 1100, with air-con Rs 1650)* near the council park is a last resort. It's quite basic but it's expensive, and most of the customers come for the bar and restaurant.

The road south to Chilaw is a good strip of bitumen, but the road inland to Anuradhapura is not as smooth. There are frequent buses to Chilaw and Colombo, but for Anuradhapura you may have to change at Kala Oya, on the boundary between Western Province and North-Central Province.

Wilpattu National Park

Wilpattu, 26km to the north of Puttalam and covering 1085 sq km, is Sri Lanka's largest park, and used to be the most visited until ethnic violence forced it to close in 1985. The park partly reopened in 2003. A few tracks are open, including a 35km route from the main gate to a tank. It's about a five-hour return trip.

The reserve's flora is mostly dense pockets of jungle scrub interspersed with small clearings and tanks that shrink in the dry season and swell in the monsoon. There have been a few sighting of leopards, but visitors note that the wildlife, including deer and wild boar, seems very disturbed and wary of humans. Poaching was common while the park was closed.

The park's main gate is at Hunuwilagama, signposted on the A12 between Puttalam and Anuradhapura, about 37km from Puttalam or 5km past the town of Kala Oya. The easiest way to arrange a visit is through hotels and guesthouses in Anuradhapura, about 45km from the park.

CHILAW

☎ 032

Chilaw has little going for it except a lively market, its strong Roman Catholic flavour and **Munneswaram**, which is a rather interesting Hindu temple 5km to the east of the town. The temple is an important centre of pilgrimage. There are three shrines at this complex, the central one dedicated to Shiva. A major festival occurs in August, when devotees test their faith by walking on red-hot coals. About 12km to the north of Chilaw is another important temple, **Udappuwa**. This seaside structure also features a complex of three shrines. A colourful festival featuring fire-walking is held here in August.

There's very little accommodation in Chilaw. The shabby **resthouse** *(☎/fax 222 2299; rooms Rs 900, with air-con Rs 1330)* has 16 overpriced rooms (singles and doubles with bathrooms cost the same). Rice and curry costs Rs 220.

Chilaw is easily visited on a day trip from Negombo (expect to pay around Rs 2500 for a taxi). Buses also run frequently along this route. You may find that the pretty scenery along this coastal road – fishing villages, toddy tappers and coconut palms – is the best part of the trip. Alternatively, there are frequent buses from Puttalam, and also between Kurunegala and Chilaw.

NEGOMBO

☎ 031 • pop 122,000

Negombo was Sri Lanka's first beach resort, and it no longer compares to rivals further south and those opening up in the east. The beach north of town is long, but often narrow and grubby. The big hotels keep the beach directly in front of their premises clean, but apparently couldn't care less about the rest of it. One of the better stretches of this beach is in the Browns Beach Hotel area – and with the sea rarely clean enough for a swim, outsiders can use the pool at this hotel for a fee. There are plenty of beachside restaurants, shops and bars, and a good range of accommodation.

101 Uses for a Coconut

The scrape-scraping sound of an *ekel* broom on bare earth is one that becomes very familiar very quickly in Sri Lanka. *Ekel* brooms, made from the tough mid-rib of the coconut frond, are plied on gardens and driveways all over the country every day. It's just one application of the extraordinarily versatile coconut palm tree, every part of which seems to have one use or another.

Sri Lankan cuisine wouldn't be what it is without the rich, white flesh of the coconut kernel. Grated coconut is made into *pol sambol* (*pol* means coconut in Sinhala), a fiery condiment laced with chilli. But minus the chilli it can be sprinkled over a curry to reduce it to something less explosive. Dried, the scrapings are known as *copra*, which is exported and used to make confectionery. Coconut oil is extracted from *copra* locally, and *poonac* (the desiccated residue) is used as fodder for animals.

The flesh of a newly opened coconut can be squeezed to produce a creamy white milk that adds a silky richness to curries; *pol hodda*, for example, is a spicy gravy made from coconut milk. Delicious *kiri bath* (rice cooked in coconut milk) is traditionally the first solid food fed to a baby and is essential at weddings and other social events.

The bud on top of the stem, called the *bada*, can be pickled and eaten.

Piles of *thambili* (king coconuts) are a familiar sight along roadsides. The liquid they contain is sweet and refreshing, and cheaper than soft drinks. *Kurumba* (green coconuts), actually younger versions of those used for cooking, are also good for drinking, but are slightly less sweet.

To extract coconut-palm sap to make the drink known as toddy, agile toddy tappers move from tree to tree like tightrope artists. Toddy trees are not permitted to bear fruit; the opened flowers are bound and bent over, and their sap is drawn off after about three weeks. Every morning and evening the toddy tappers go from flower to flower, changing the pots. One palm yields an average of 270 litres of toddy annually and a good tapper can get about a month's sap from one flower. Toddy can be boiled down to form a type of brown sugar called *jaggery*. Fermented and distilled, toddy becomes *arrack*, a popular honey-coloured alcoholic drink that's especially nice mixed with ginger ale. Vinegar is a by-product of distillation.

As for the rest of the tree, it seems to have 101 uses. In rural areas you can still see *cadjan* (coconut frond) roofing, fencing made from dried coconut branches, and roof supports of coconut wood. Bowls made from polished coconut shells are widely available. The fibrous husk that clings to the nut is stripped off, soaked in pits and then beaten to separate the fibres. These are woven into surprisingly strong coir ropes, or are used to make matting and upholstery, brushes and brooms. The shells are sculpted into tacky souvenirs such as monkeys and elephants. The versatile coconut shell also fulfils a spiritual role – it's often smashed at temples to bring good fortune.

Bustling Negombo town is a historically interesting place strongly influenced by the Catholic Church. The narrow strip of land between the lagoon and the sea and the many canals make for good exploring.

The Dutch captured the town from the Portuguese in 1640, lost it again the same year, then captured it again in 1644. The British then took it from them in 1796 without a struggle. Negombo was one of the most important sources of cinnamon during the Dutch era, and there are still reminders of the European days.

Many people make Negombo their last stop in Sri Lanka before flying out, as it's conveniently close to Bandaranaike International Airport at Katunayake.

Negombo has a reputation for seediness, including drugs and prostitution. This is perhaps unfair – these things exist all over the country – but single male travellers can expect lots of depressing sales pitches after dark, and some hotels and guesthouses not listed below rely on short-term customers.

Orientation & Information

The busy centre of Negombo lies to the west of the bus and train stations. In the centre of town you'll find the post office, a Bank of Ceylon and a Vijitha Yapa Bookshop with English-language novels and magazines. Most places to stay in Negombo line the main road that heads north from the town centre, running almost parallel to the beach. Closer to town the road is called Lewis Place; in the centre of town it becomes Sea St. Here you'll find laid-back, cheap accommodation. Continue 1km north and the name changes to Porutota Rd; the prices increase, the hotels have multiplied (as have the room rates) and the streets are alive with tourist-oriented shops by day and bars by night. Most top-end places are up this end of the beach strip and in Waikkal (see Around Negombo later in this chapter). There are a dozen or more Internet and telephone offices scattered along Lewis Place and Porutota Rd, among the gem stores and souvenir shops.

Things to See

Close to the seafront near the lagoon mouth are the ruins of the old **Dutch fort** with its fine gateway inscribed with the date 1678. Also here is a green where cricket matches are a big attraction.

Several old Dutch buildings are still in use, including the **lagoon resthouse** *(Custom House Rd)*. The Dutch also revealed their love of **canals** here as nowhere else in Sri Lanka. Canals extend from Negombo all the way south to Colombo and north to Puttalam, a total of over 120km. You can hire a bicycle in Negombo from various

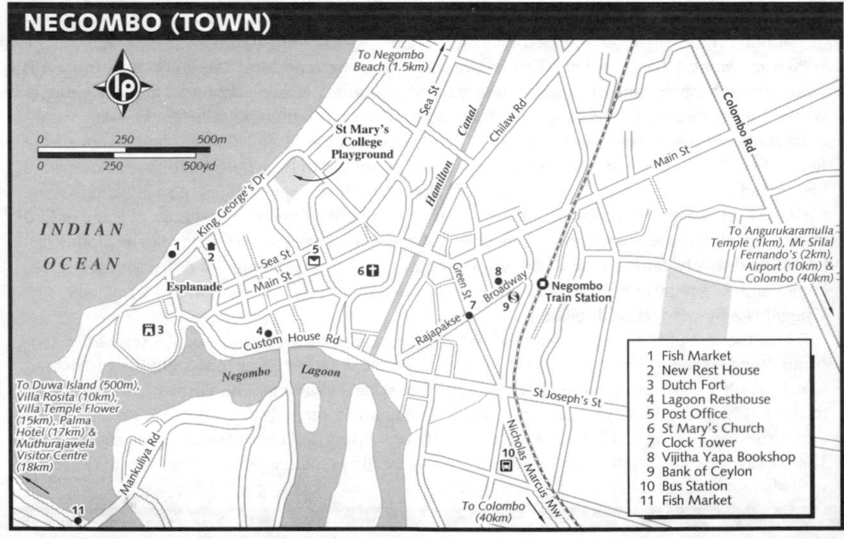

hotels and ride the canal-side paths for some distance.

Each day, fishermen take their *oruvas* (outrigger canoes) and go out in search of the fish for which Negombo is well known. They're a fine sight as they sweep home into the lagoon after a fishing trip. Fish auctions on the beach and fish sales in the market near the fort are common – the shark catch is brought in to the beach in the early afternoon. The catch is not all from the open sea: Negombo is at the northern end of a lagoon that is well known for its lobsters, crabs and prawns. If you're hanging around the markets you won't have to wait long before you're invited to go out on an *oruva* or another kind of vessel. Expect to pay around Rs 500 per boat per hour. A **Fishers' Festival** is held here in late July.

Negombo is dotted with churches – so successfully were the locals converted to Catholicism that today the town is often known as 'little Rome'. **St Mary's Church** in the town centre has very good ceiling paintings by a local artist. East of town, the **Angurukaramulla Temple**, with its 6m-long reclining Buddha, is also worth seeing. A three-wheeler from Lewis Place should cost Rs 250 for the return trip. The island of **Duwa**, joined to Negombo by the lagoon bridge, is famed for its Easter passion play.

Small villages dot the coast to the north and south, and these can be reached by bicycle. Across the lagoon bridge there's a second fish market. If you can stagger out of bed at 6am, it's a good place to watch the fishing boats returning with their catches. The road over the lagoon bridge continues as a small coastal road between lagoon and ocean almost all the way to Colombo.

Places to Stay – Budget & Mid-Range

Town & Airport Towards the airport is **Mr Srilal Fernando's** *(☎ 222 2481; 67 Parakrama Rd, Kurana; singles/doubles with bathroom Rs 450/585)*. There are six clean rooms in a handsome family home with a garden. The family will pick you up or drop you off at the airport or Kurana bus stop. Ring to find out how much (if anything) they charge for this service. You can also take a Colombo–Negombo bus (No 240; get off at the RAC Motors Kurana bus stop and walk east 1km from the main road). Dinners cost Rs 250.

New Rest House *(☎ 222 2299; 14 Circular Rd; singles/doubles with bathroom Rs 950/1050)*, in town, is for you if you want air-con but are lacking cash. It has lots of history and colonial charm (Queen Elizabeth II stayed here in 1958). The rooms are bare and simple, but some rooms have balconies looking over the sea – and a distinctly odoured fish market.

Lewis Place Area The five clean rooms at **Jeero's Guest House** *(☎ 223 4210; 239 Lewis Place; rooms Rs 500-600)* are enlivened by wooden ceilings. The cheaper rooms face away from the sea.

Star Beach *(☎ 222 2606, fax 223 8266; 83/3 Lewis Place; singles/doubles Rs 500/700)* is a decent family-run guesthouse on the beach. Three of the 14 clean rooms face the sea.

Beach Villa Guest House *(☎ 222 2833; ⓔ nissajet@sltnet.lk; 3/2 Senavirathna Mawatha; rooms Rs 500-800, with air-con Rs 1000)* is right on the beach, with cheerfully gaudy decor and a bar and restaurant downstairs. The 16 rooms are clean, but it's a shame they don't have balconies.

Oceanview *(☎/fax 223 8689; 104 Lewis Place; rooms Rs 500-1000)* has 12 neat and clean rooms – the more expensive ones are in a new wing and each has a balcony. There are views from the rooftop, and the family that runs the place is superfriendly.

Dephani Guest House *(☎ 223 4359; ⓔ dephanie@slt.lk; 189/15 Lewis Place; rooms downstairs/upstairs Rs 605/715)* has clean, spacious rooms, some with colonial-style furnishings. Upstairs rooms have a balcony. There's a pretty garden opening onto the beach, a restaurant, and helpful, pleasant hosts.

Hotel Silver Sands *(☎ 222 2880; ⓔ silversands@wow.lk; 229 Lewis Place; rooms Rs 650-850)* has a Moorish touch to its arched walkways and central courtyard garden. The rooms have their own balcony or patio. Some were a bit musty when we visited, so maybe check a few before choosing.

Ice Bear Guest House *(☎ 223 3862; 103/2 Lewis Place; rooms Rs 1500, with air-con Rs 1700)* is a gorgeous traditional villa, but the quaint rooms needed a good airing when we visited. The leafy garden opens onto the beach.

Sunflower Beach Hotel *(☎ 223 8154; ⓔ sunflo@eureka.net; 289 Lewis Place; singles/doubles Rs 1800/2000)* is a curved building

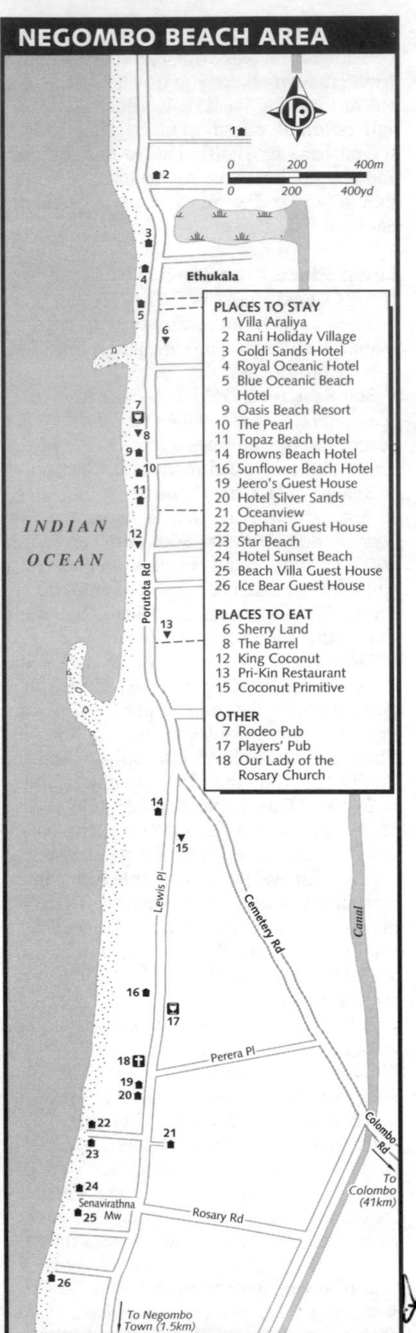

with wedge-shaped rooms. The rooms are looking tired for the price, but there's a swimming pool (Rs 150 for nonguests).

Hotel Sunset Beach *(☎ 222 2350; ✉ jethot@sri.lanka.net; 5 Senavirathna Mawatha; singles/doubles US$40/43.50)*, run by Jetwing, has a scrap of lawn and a beachfront pool. All rooms have sea views. It's a sparkling white, busy place but it's lacking in character.

Porutota Rd Area Stunningly ugly, the **Oasis Beach Resort** *(☎ 227 9526, fax 227 9022; 31 Porutota Rd; singles/doubles Rs 900/1000, with air-con Rs 1100/1200)* is redeemed by its cheap rooms with air-con and the added bonus of a swimming pool. The guests seem satisfied with it.

Topaz Beach Hotel *(☎ 227 9265; ✉ topaz@sltnet.lk; 21 Porutota Rd; singles/doubles Rs 1250/1500, with air-con Rs 1500/1950)* has a plain exterior that belies its clean if ageing rooms.

Villa Araliya *(☎ 071 728504; ✉ stephanieselhorst@hotmail.com; 154/10 Porutota Rd; rooms Rs 1950, with air-con Rs 2200)* lies inland, on a lane just past the Rani Holiday Village. Run by a Dutch–Sri Lankan couple, this charming guesthouse has been recommended by several readers. It also has a new wing with studio apartments. Villa Araliya offers a swimming pool, tastefully decorated rooms and Italian food – the owner once lived in Italy.

Rani Holiday Village *(☎ 074 870718; ✉ ranihv@slt.lk; 154/9 Porutota Rd; singles/doubles US$26/28, 2-bedroom apartments US$46)* has modern studio apartments in a garden setting. There are double-room villas with hot water and a kitchen (with fridge), and a villa with two bedrooms. Discounts are available for long stayers.

The Pearl *(☎ 074 872824, ✉ info@pearl-negombo.com; 13 Porutota Rd; singles/doubles US$34/43)* is a great little beach hotel which belies its concrete exterior. The six spacious rooms are excellent, with probably the best bathrooms in town! All come with a CD player and air-con, and TV if need be. The restaurant is terrific too – proper fish and chips for Rs 290, grilled tiger prawns for Rs 390, and rice and curry for Rs 250.

Places to Stay – Top End

Goldi Sands Hotel *(☎ 227 9021; ✉ goldi@eureka.lk; singles/doubles US$34/43)* is an ageing no-frills hotel with friendly staff and rooms with air-con. The clean rooms have a balcony and garden or beach views, and there's a swimming pool.

Browns Beach Hotel *(☎ 222 2031; ⓔ ashmres@lanka.ccom.lk; 175 Lewis Place; singles/doubles US$52/69)* is a 30-year-old place with pleasant if unexceptional rooms with air-con, sea views, great showers and a balcony. There's a private beach area, heaps of facilities, a lunch buffet (Rs 470) and live music on Sunday.

Royal Oceanic Hotel *(☎ 227 9000; ⓔ jethot@sri.lanka.net; rooms from US$90)*, run by Jetwing, has spacious rooms with polished floorboards and a balcony, but it's overpriced. There's a pool and a beach disco on Friday and Saturday nights.

Blue Oceanic Beach Hotel *(☎ 227 9000; ⓔ jethot@sri.lanka.net; singles or doubles US$105)* is a standard resort hotel of early '80s vintage.

Places to Eat & Drink

Maybe we just hit a bad patch, but we had some awful meals in Negombo. On more than one occasion a tender piece of uncooked tuna steak came back from the kitchen smothered in a mix of tomato sauce and sweet-and-sour sauce, and accompanied by limp sweaty fries. Perhaps the lesson is to ask around first, and don't push your luck with unfamiliar Western dishes. We did enjoy eating at **The Pearl** and **Villa Araliya** (see Places to Stay, earlier).

The Barrel *(33 Porutota Rd, mains Rs 150-200)* is one place where you'll enjoy delicious food such as devilled fish or fried rice, all in a beachfront setting. If you indulge in a very long lunch you can join the busy bar crowd for a sunset beer.

Sherry Land *(74 Porutota Rd, mains Rs 180-300)* lacks a beachfront spot, but it makes up for it by having a pretty garden setting (bring insect repellent), attentive service and tasty food.

King Coconut *(11 Porutota Rd, mains Rs 200-300)* is a lively, popular spot beside the beach. You can either have just a drink here (Carlsberg Rs 130, Lion lager Rs 110), a snack (eg, french fries) or a meal. There's a proper pizza oven (pizzas from Rs 190), as well as a good range of seafood (baked crab Rs 260) and the ubiquitous rice and curry (Rs 250).

Coconut Primitive *(108 Lewis Pl; mains Rs 250-350)* has a laid-back, undercover restaurant beside the beach. You can wash your meal down with a beer (around Rs 120), and there's usually music in the evening. It does better-than-usual Western food and the service is particularly friendly.

Pri-Kin Restaurant *(10 Porutota Rd; mains Rs 270-380)* has cooks trained under a chef from Beijing who concoct good Chinese, Sri Lankan and Western-style dishes. The service can be slow, but the sweet-and-sour dishes are delicious and there's an undercover eating area.

Rodeo Pub on Porutota Rd and **Players' Pub** on Lewis Place kick on to the small hours. Players' is a new place with a snooker table; Rodeo is small and a bit rough around the edges, but convivial. Be warned that bully boys from Colombo sometimes turn up on weekends, get blitzed and start fights.

The major hotels are good places for stuff-your-face buffets: the **Browns Beach Hotel's** lunch buffet has been recommended. Prices are around Rs 500.

Getting There & Away

Bus & Train Private, CTB and intercity express buses run between Colombo (Saunders Place, Pettah) and Negombo every 20 minutes (Rs 13/30 for CTB/express, about one hour by express). Long queues form at Negombo bus station on weekend evenings as day-trippers return to the capital. There are also trains (Rs 10, 3rd class only, 1½ hours), but they're slower and rarer than the buses.

Buses to Kandy start at 5.30am and run on the half hour until 7.30am, with three or four buses in the afternoon until 4pm. CTB buses cost Rs 44 (four hours); express buses charge Rs 95 (three hours). You could take a bus to Veyangoda (Rs 10) and then a train to Kandy.

Taxi You can get a taxi between Negombo and Colombo for about Rs 1800. Any hotel, guesthouse or travel agent will arrange a taxi for you.

Getting Around

The Airport One of Negombo's strongest points is being a transit point for the Bandaranaike International Airport at Katunayake, and airport transport is cheaper from Negombo than from Colombo. Private and CTB buses (Rs 8, both are bus No 270) run every 15 minutes from about 5am to 9pm. The trip takes about 45 minutes. A taxi costs about Rs 500 from the bus station (southeast of town) and Rs 600 from Lewis Place; the trip takes about 20 minutes. A three-wheeler is about half those prices.

Bus & Three-Wheeler To get from the bus station to Lewis Place or Porutota Rd, catch a Kochchikade-bound bus. A three-wheeler will cost about Rs 100 to the middle of Lewis Place from either the bus or train station.

Bicycle A rented bicycle is good for a leisurely look around Negombo, along the canals or over the lagoon bridge to the peninsula between the lagoon and the sea. Many guesthouses rent bicycles for around Rs 150 per day.

AROUND NEGOMBO

Waikkal & Marawila

☎ 031

North of Negombo, houses are dotted among jungle, palm trees and farmland. The trees thin out and paddy fields dominate the closer you get to Chilaw.

The town of Marawila lies about 3km inland on the Negombo–Chilaw road, and features some tile factories and batik workshops. The coast here is quiet, with seemingly endless aisles of coconut trees that stretch inland to Kurunegala. There are several mostly upmarket hotels between Marawila and Kochchikade. The hotels are all self-sufficient (so there's no effort made to share the wealth with the local people) and most guests don't stray beyond the walls. Whether you stay put in a hotel or explore, it's ideal for a quiet holiday away from the jewellery shops, sunscreen sellers and tourist touts. It's a very different scene from the bars and tourist shops at Negombo.

About 15km to the north of Negombo, at Wilagedera, Gonawilla, is the **Netherlands Welcome Village** *(☎ 229 9785; admission free, donations welcome; open 8am-4.30pm daily)*. Some 100 traditional Dutch houses were built here in 1996 with funding initiated by a Dutch expat. The inhabitants are elderly homeless people from all over Sri Lanka. From Negombo, a three-wheeler should cost Rs 1000 for the return trip.

Thirty kilometres north along the coast from Negombo is **Mahawewa**, a village renowned for its batiks.

Places to Stay The first two places are on the coast near Waikkal.

Ranweli Holiday Village *(☎ 222 2136; ⓔ ranweli@slt.lk; singles or doubles US$60)* is a spacious beach resort reached by a short ferry punt. The hotel arranges canoeing and bird-watching tours. Most of the rooms are in separate bungalows with a small lounge, balcony and lagoon or sea views.

Club Hotel Dolphin *(☎ 227 8565; ⓔ dolphin@slt.lk; singles/doubles US$72/78)* has 73 rooms and 50 cottages with air-con. There's a gigantic pool and a palm-studded lawn, but the hotel looks a little weather-beaten.

Sanmeli Beach Hotel *(☎ 225 4766, fax 225 4768; singles/doubles US$20/32, with air-con US$25/37)* is an older-style resort hotel with a swimming pool and 20 rooms facing the sea. It is reached from Marawila junction.

Aquarius Sport Hotel *(☎ 225 4890; ⓔ aquarius@sri.lanka.net; singles/doubles US$27/30)* has 31 cabanas with fans fronting a lovely stretch of beach, as well as sports facilities. It is about 2.5km from Marawila junction.

The hotel furthest north is the massive **Club Palm Bay** *(☎ 225 4956; ⓔ palmbay@lankacom.net; Talwilawella; singles/doubles US$100/127)*, about 3.5km off the main road (from Talwila junction). The resort has 104 rooms spread across 22 acres of land surrounded by lagoons. The mostly German clientele seem to pass the day in the enormous swimming pool.

South of Negombo

The narrow belt of land between the gulf and lagoon south of Negombo is sometimes called **Pamunugama** after its biggest settlement. It's a lovely strip of coconut palms, old Portuguese-style churches, cross-studded cemeteries on dunes, and so many pockets of houses that in parts it almost feels suburban. There are some cute little hotels along here. The beach is steep and swimming could be perilous – consult with the locals before wading in.

Muthurajawela Marsh (which evocatively translates as 'supreme field of pearls') is a little-known gem of a wetland at the southern end of Negombo lagoon. The area had been a rich rice-growing basin before the

Portuguese constructed a canal that ruined the fields with sea water. Over the centuries mother nature turned Muthurajawela into Sri Lanka's biggest saline wetland, home to purple herons, cormorants and kingfishers. However, the marsh is part of a large Export Processing Zone (see the boxed text 'The Garment Makers Behind the Bargains') and is under pressure from encroaching industrial development. The old visitor centre had to be abandoned on the pretext of being levelled for a highway; however, it wasn't bulldozed and is now in the possession of a political family. The new **Muthurajawela Visitor Centre** *(074 830150; Indigaslanda, Bopitiya, Pamunugama; open 7am-6.30pm Tues-Sun)* is at the southern end of the road along Pamunugama, next to the Hamilton Canal. It has displays and a 20-minute video show on the wetland's amazing variety of fauna. A two-hour guided boat ride (Rs 600 per person) is highly recommended.

Places to Stay On the ocean side of the road 15km to the south of Negombo, **Villa Temple Flower** *(☎ 011-223 6755; e eipper-rottenburg@t-online.de; Pamunugama; singles/doubles US$12/15, with air-con US$16/19)* has lush gardens, a swimming pool and an ebullient owner. The simple and comfy rooms each have a small veranda.

Villa Rosita *(☎ 075 349682; e irosita@zeynet.com; 144/6 Seththappaduwa, Pamunugama; singles/doubles US$16/18, with air-con US$18/20)*, on the fringe of the lagoon 10km from Negombo, is a comfortable family home with two rooms. It's a quiet, green, rural hideaway, and the owners garner praise for their hospitality and cooking. The 15-minute taxi trip from Negombo will cost Rs 300, or Rs 800 from the airport.

Palma Hotel *(☎ 011-223 6619; e vilpal@eureka.lk; Beach Rd, Pamunugama; rooms US$15-29)*, 18km from Negombo, is a mid-sized hotel located right next to the sea. The

WEST COAST

The Garment Makers Behind the Bargains

When you're breezing around Colombo's fashionable stores, amazed at the low prices and reasonable quality, the bargains seem too good to be true. Garments account for more than 40% of Sri Lanka's export income, mostly from sales to the USA (60%) and EU (35%), and the off-loading of seconds and excess stock from the powerful garment export industry lets local stores set prices well below those overseas. Along with Sri Lankan women working in Europe and the Middle East as domestic help, the army of women employed by the garment industry produces much of the country's hard currency earnings without much reward. Working 12-hour days, seven days a week for Rs 3650 to 5850 a month, they certainly can't afford anything off the rack from Odel in Colombo.

There are 280,000 workers employed in almost 900 export-oriented factories across the country, and one million people employed indirectly. About half of these factories are located in Export Processing Zones (EPZs, also called Free Trade Zones), set up in the late 1970s by JR Jayewardene. The largest is the Katunayake EPZ on the Negombo–Colombo road, close to the country's main port and airport. EPZs offer foreign investors a cheap and highly productive 80% female workforce with little union interference, plus tax breaks and other incentives.

But this drive for productivity means something different for the workers, both inside and outside the factory. Transnationals Information Exchange Asia (TIE-Asia), an advocate for regional labour issues, has investigated the garment workers' situation, especially in EPZs. They have found there are weekly time limits for toilet breaks, forced overtime (up to 60 hours per month, not usually paid at the correct rate), unrealistically high production targets and sexual harassment. Workers are actively discouraged from joining unions.

Most of the workforce has migrated from rural areas, living in cramped conditions in private boarding houses. Up to 12 women might share a room measuring 3.3m by 4m. Often there is no electricity, not enough fresh water and poor ventilation and sanitation. Outside the zones, wages and work conditions are also poor, but living conditions are better because workers stay in their home community, and there's more freedom to form unions.

According to TIE-Asia, the workers don't want people to boycott the bargains, they just want the rights that are recognised in national labour laws and International Labour Organisation conventions. For more information, visit TIE-Asia's website W www.tieasia.org.

rooms are quite swish, and there's a very nice secluded area around the swimming pool.

KALUTARA & WADDUWA

☎ 034

Kalutara, 42km south of Colombo, was once an important spice-trading centre controlled at various times by the Portuguese, Dutch and British. Today it has a reputation for fine **basketware** and also for the best mangosteens on the island.

Immediately south of the Kalu Ganga bridge on the main road is the impressive **Gangatilaka Vihara**, which has a hollow dagoba (Buddhist shrine) with an interesting painted interior. By the roadside there's a small shrine and bodhi tree where drivers often stop to make offerings to ensure a safe journey. Wadduwa is 8km to the north of Kalutara.

Places to Stay

Kalutara and Wadduwa have beaches and a number of mid-range and top-end places to stay. But there's little to halt the individual traveller en route to more laid-back beach spots further south.

Tangerine Beach Hotel (*☎ 222 2982; e tanbch@sltnet.lk; De Abrew Rd, Waskaduwa, Kalutara North; singles/doubles US$72/76*) is a busy and friendly place with homely rooms with air-con. Ducks enjoy the hospitality of the pools in the garden.

Siddhalepa Ayurveda Health Resort (*☎ 229 6967-0; e siddalep@slt.lk; Samanthara Rd, Wadduwa; singles/doubles US$75/98*), north of Kalutara, is run by Siddhalepa, the respected Ayurvedic hospital at Mt Lavinia. It offers everything from stress relief to detoxification. Seven-day packages including treatment are available; prices include all meals and accommodation.

Royal Palms Hotel (*☎ 222 8113-7; e tangerinetours@eureka.lk; De Abrew Rd, Kalutara North; singles/doubles US$80/98*) has immaculate rooms with air-con, two executive suites and two royal suites. It has a simply stunning garden and an even more stunning swimming pool.

The Blue Water (*☎ 038-223 5067; e blwater@sltnet.lk; Thalpitiya, Wadduwa; rooms from US$120*) is quite elegant. The chic rooms come with air-con. Facilities include squash, tennis and a health club.

BERUWELA & MORAGALLE

☎ 034

Beruwela, 58km to the south of Colombo, together with Bentota further south, has been developed into Sri Lanka's chief package-tour resort zone. It has a long string of mid-range and top-end hotels along its fine beach, where locals address foreigners initially in German. There's little to attract independent travellers here. Moragalle is technically slightly north of Beruwela, but it has practically merged with it.

The first recorded Muslim settlement on the island took place at Beruwela in 1024. The **Kechimalai Mosque**, on a headland north of the hotel strip, is said to be built on the site of the landing and is the focus for a major Id-ul-Fitr festival at the end of Ramadan.

Places to Stay

The tourist hotels are all very much aimed at the package groups that come to Sri Lanka to escape from the European winter. All the hotels have various facilities including tennis and water sports. Some have Ayurvedic health centres.

Blue Lagoon Hotel (*☎/fax 227 6062; Galle Rd, Moragalle; singles/doubles Rs 1320/1650*) is good value given the location just 50m from the beach. It's not a new building but it's been well maintained. The turn-off to the hotel is opposite the Mendis arrack distillery. The beachfront restaurant is worth a try.

Ypsylon Guest House (*☎ 227 6132; e ypsylon@slt.lk; Moragalle; singles/doubles Rs 1800/2010*) is the pick of the cheapies. It has clean rooms, a pool, a restaurant and a prime beachfront position. Rooms come with hot water.

Hotel Sumadai (*☎ 227 6404; e info@sumadai.com; 61 Maradana Rd, Beruwela; singles/doubles US$18/24.50*) is in a lagoonside spot, with 16 decent rooms and hot water. Half of the rooms have a balcony overlooking the lagoon.

Barberyn Beach Ayurveda Resort (*☎ 227 6036; e barberyn@slt.lk; Moragalle; singles/doubles US$55/75*) has more character than most of the other 'top enders'. The Barberyn's room rates include all meals (no room-only rates), plus an optional Ayurvedic cure supplement for a staggering US$230. There's no pool but it's on the waterfront.

Tropical Villas Hotel (*☎ 227 6780; e tropvilla@eureka.lk; Galle Rd, Moragalle;*

singles/doubles US$91/97) has no direct access to the beach but it has a swimming pool and the rooms are stylish; each has a separate lounge, and they are set around a quiet, leafy garden.

Getting There & Away

Beruwela is on the main Colombo to Matara railway line. See Getting There & Away under Bentota, Aluthgama & Induruwa for details on getting to Beruwela and Moragalle.

BENTOTA, ALUTHGAMA & INDURUWA

☎ 034

Bentota's beach is one of the best on the west coast, protected from Galle Rd by the broad sweep of the Bentota Ganga. While it is dominated by big package hotels, it also has a number of smaller places catering to independent travellers. There are more such places in Aluthgama, a small town on the main road between Beruwela and Bentota.

Aluthgama has a raucous fish market, local shops and the main train station that services the area. Induruwa doesn't really have a centre – it's spread out along the coast.

Orientation & Information

Just south of the town centre of Aluthgama, the main road crosses the Bentota Ganga into Bentota where, on its seaward side, there's the Bentota resort centre with a post office, a Bank of Ceylon, a tourist office, tourist shops and a few restaurants. From the bridge, the river turns to flow north, parallel to the coast, for a few hundred metres, divided from the sea only by a narrow spit of land on which are built some of Bentota's top hotels (they're reachable only from the beach or by boat across the river). Induruwa is 5km south of Bentota.

There are Internet facilities in the big hotels and others are sprinkled throughout the towns.

Things to See

In addition to **beaches** that are as fine as Beruwela's, Bentota, like Aluthgama, enjoys the beautiful calm waters of the **Bentota Ganga**, good for water sports.

Aluthgama has a bustling **market** every Monday, over the train line towards Dharga Town. A few kilometres inland, on the south bank of the river, is the **Galapota Temple**, said to date from the 12th century. To reach it, take the side road to your left, 500m after crossing the bridge. It's signposted.

Fine beaches continue several kilometres south from Bentota. Induruwa has a small cluster of places to stay on a lovely, quiet length of beach, at the north end of which is one of the **turtle hatcheries** that you can visit in this area (see Kosgoda later in this chapter for more information).

Ten kilometres inland from Bentota is the pretty **Brief Garden** *(☎ 227 0462; admission Rs 125; open 8am-5pm daily)*. It used to be the home of Bevis Bawa, older brother of renowned Sri Lankan architect Geoffrey

I Do...Want to Marry in Sri Lanka

Tying the knot, getting hitched – whatever you call it, Sri Lanka is a hot destination for starry-eyed couples on their way to the altar. The palm-lined beaches and sunsets on balmy evenings seem conducive to matrimonial bliss, while also helping to kick start that saucy first wedding night!

Never slow to spot opportunity when it knocks, travel agents are clamouring to send you down the aisle in this pretty isle. There is a plethora of options ranging from simple design-your-own-weddings to lavish, quasi-traditional Sri Lankan events complete with traditional wedding attire, dancers and drummers. You can arrive at your wedding on caparisoned elephants, with girls in white sprinkling frangipani flowers along the path, or you can choose to have a sandy beachside wedding, a Kandyan-style function, or one with touches of ancient tradition. The options are endless. A typical package includes airfares, accommodation, transfers, licence and legal fees, foreign-language translation, Foreign Ministry documentation, a wedding cake and outfits for the couple. Optional extras include video coverage of the event and firecrackers – the only limit is your imagination (and your budget). Connaissance de Ceylan and Walkers Tours organise weddings (for contact details see Organised Tours in the Getting Around chapter), but you'll also find many travel agencies in your own country that are ready and willing to help.

Bawa. Bawa's house is the highlight and the artwork on display is eclectic, ranging from homoerotic sculpture to a wonderful mural of Sri Lankan life in the style of Marc Chagall. The mural was created by the Australian artist Donald Friend, who originally came for six days but stayed for six years. Other, more short-term guests included Vivien Leigh and Laurence Olivier during the filming of *Elephant Walk* in 1953. The beautiful garden covers two hectares. To get there, follow the road south from Aluthgama to Matagama Rd and turn inland from there to the Muslim village of Dharga Town. From here you will see periodic yellow signs saying 'Brief', but as everyone knows this place, it's easy enough to ask directions. You do need your own transport though – a three-wheeler from Aluthgama should cost about Rs 500 and a taxi about Rs 700 return.

Activities

The attraction of this part of the coast is the huge variety of fish (including large specimens such as barracuda), which seem unperturbed by the presence of divers. Major hotels at Bentota and Aluthgama can provide details of diving outfits in the vicinity.

The area has plenty of opportunities for other water sports. If you'd like to try windsurfing, water-skiing, deep-sea fishing or virtually anything else watery, try the **Fun Surf Centre** *(☎ 071 765029; River Ave, Aluthgama)*.

Boat trips along the Bentota Ganga are quite popular. Most trips go for three hours and charge Rs 400 to 600 per person with a minimum of five people per boat. There are also five-hour dinner cruises for around US$20 per person. The further you go upstream the better it gets; you're likely to see water monitors and some bird species.

Places to Stay – Budget & Mid-Range

Bentota The **Hotel Susantha** *(☎ 227 5324; ⓔ susanthas@sltnet.lk; Holiday Resort Rd; singles/doubles US$15/17.50)* has clean, moderately sized rooms (some of which are bungalows) in a leafy garden setting. There's a restaurant that serves reasonably priced Western and Eastern food. It's only a short walk over the train tracks to the beach.

Southern Palm Villa *(☎ 227 0752; ⓔ malrajm@sltnet.lk; singles/doubles Rs 1540/1760)*, behind the Taj Exotica (and across the train tracks), has 14 clean rooms with breakfast included. It's not the newest building around but it's kept tidy and the grounds are spacious. Some rooms have balcony views over the garden. It's a short walk to the beach.

Ayubowan *(☎ 227 5913; ⓦ www.ayubowan.ch; 171 Galle Rd, Bentota South; singles/doubles B&B Rs 1500/1800)* isn't right beside the beach but the four large spotless bungalows are set in pretty gardens. It's a good place for dinner, and has an interesting Swiss-German/Asian menu with nasi goreng (fried rice) for Rs 180 and fillet steak for Rs 300. There's a resident masseur as well.

Aluthgama The riverside **Hotel Sunil Lanka** *(☎ 074 582535; 45 River Ave; singles/doubles Rs 1100/1400)* has sparkling white rooms, each with a double waterbed and a porch.

Terrena Lodge *(☎/fax 074 289015; River Ave; singles/doubles B&B Rs 1495/1595)* is handsomely furnished and has a pretty garden leading down to a riverside seating area. It has five colourful, clean rooms. Reservations are recommended.

Hotel Hemadan *(☎ 227 5320; ⓔ hemadan@sltnet.lk; 25 River Ave; singles/doubles Rs 1700/2000)* has 10 large, clean rooms in an ageing building. It's pricey for the standard of the rooms (no air-con) but there's a leafy courtyard and prime river viewing.

Induruwa About 200m north of Induruwa train station, **Long Beach Cottage** *(☎ 227 5773; ⓔ hanjayas@sltnet.lk; 550 Galle Rd; rooms Rs 770)* has five slightly faded rooms (three upstairs with shared balcony, and two downstairs). There's a pretty, sandy garden fronting on to the beach, and welcoming hosts who will arrange free transport from the Bentota or Aluthgama train stations if you phone ahead.

Ikrams Holiday Bungalow *(☎ 227 6775; ⓔ ikrams@dynanet.lk; 622 Galle Rd; 2-bedroom bungalows Rs 2500, with air-con Rs 3000)* has two little holiday homes with kitchen, fridge and plenty of space, right next to the beach. Breakfast is included. It's next to the 66km marker on Galle Rd.

Places to Stay – Top End

Bentota Right on the beach, **Lihiniya Surf Hotel** *(☎ 227 5126; ⓔ lihiniya@sti.lk; singles/doubles US$75/80)* has rooms with air-con.

It's a middle-of-the-range package tour resort, and is clean though bland. It's popular with British tour groups.

Hotel Serendib *(☎ 227 5248; e serendib@slt.lk; singles/doubles US$80/100)*, also right on the beach, has 90 rooms with air-con. The rooms are a bit small, but each has a balcony or terrace.

Bentota Beach Hotel *(☎ 227 5176; e bbh@keells.com; singles/doubles US$145/164)* has 133 spotless rooms. It's right on the beach and every room has beach views from a balcony or terrace. Nonguests can use the swimming pool here for Rs 275.

For a touch of style there are two beautiful old villas near the main hotel area. The railway line is nearby, so it may help if you love trains.

Club Villa *(☎ 227 5312; e clubvilla@itmin.com; 138/15 Galle Rd; singles/doubles US$70/77, with air-con US$83/90)* has its turn-off about 1.5km south of town down the main road. It's a spacious, elegant, 19th-century Dutch-style villa with a big coconut-grove garden and a swimming pool, all within a two-minute walk of the beach.

Taruvillas Taprobana *(☎ 0777 748064; e taprobana@taruvillas.com; 146/4 Galle Rd, Robolgoda, Bentota; singles/doubles from US$110/133)* is one of the best boutique hotels in Sri Lanka. We're talking glossy magazine subject material here. There are nine elegant rooms with amazing furniture, classic Lionel Wendt photographs set on shining whitewashed walls, and a tranquil garden. You could live it up here with dinner one night (salads Rs 400, mains up to Rs 1500 for the seafood platter) and sweat over the bill later.

Taj Exotica *(☎ 227 5650; e exotica@sri.lanka.net; singles/doubles from US$155/170)*, near the Bentota Beach Hotel, is the most luxurious big hotel here, with lots of marble, fountains, and rooms with extra bells and whistles. There's also a nightclub here, open to all except perhaps groups of hungry-eyed men.

The Villa Mohotti Walauwa *(☎ 227 5311; e reservation@thevilla.eureka.net; 138/18 Galle Rd; singles/doubles US$175/195, 4-bed family suites US$280)*, next door to Club Villa, is a stunning 19th-century villa done up in traditional style, but with discreet modern touches. The 14 rooms are large, elegantly furnished and attentively cared for. It's another contender for best boutique hotel. There's also a tiny swimming pool. If you want just a taste of what it might be like to stay, you can pop by for dinner, which costs around Rs 1500 per person.

Aluthgama Beruwela is so close to this area that some of the top-end hotels listed under that heading could equally suffice for Aluthgama.

Hotel Ceysands *(☎ 227 5073, fax 227 5395; singles/doubles US$72/85)* has a prime position, with the river on one side and the beach on the other – you arrive and leave by boat. It's a large resort hotel, which could use some kind of refurbishment to justify the prices.

Induruwa If you don't mind the beige colour theme, **Induruwa Beach Resort** *(☎ 227 5445; e inbeachr@sltnet.lk; Kaikawala; singles/doubles US$35/40)* has large rooms with air-con that come with breakfast. There's a pool (Rs 125 for nonguests), a billiard table and more. The rooms have all the mod cons to enjoy.

Saman Villas *(☎ 227 5435, fax 227 5433; e samanvil@sri.lanka.net; Aturuwella; suites from US$200)* is outrageously expensive and absolutely divine. There are luxury suites though rates vary greatly depending on when you want to visit. There's a Japanese-style garden, great views and a superbly sited pool. The plush chalets have a private garden, open-roofed bathroom, CD player and satellite television – need we say more?

Places to Eat

There are a number of eating places near the main hotel complex at Bentota. Restaurants tend to come and go and the best strategy is to ask other travellers for their recommendations. Prices are relatively uniform and generally mid-range. If you want all-you-can-eat buffets, head to the top-end hotels.

The restaurant at the **Hotel Susantha** serves reasonable Eastern and Western food including fried fish, roast chicken with vegetables, and rice and curry for moderate prices, as well as a variety of snacks.

Golden Grill *(meals Rs 250-350)* has a pleasant spot beside the river, near the Bank of Ceylon, with pasta (Rs 200), sweet-and-sour prawns (Rs 260) and more.

Aida Restaurant & Bar *(meals around Rs 300)*, with river views, is on the main road opposite the resort complex. Choose from grilled prawns with garlic butter, steaks, and rice and curry at prices similar to the Golden Grill.

Getting There & Away

Bentota and Beruwela are both on the main Colombo to Matara railway line, but Aluthgama, the town sandwiched between them, is the station to go to as many trains do not make stops at the smaller stations at Bentota and Beruwela. Aluthgama has five or six express trains daily to/from Colombo (Rs 12.50/34 in 3rd/2nd class, 1½ to two hours), and a similar number to/from Hikkaduwa, Galle and Matara. Avoid the other, slower trains.

When you get off the train you'll hear the usual boring tales from the touts that the hotel of your choice is 'closed', 'fried' and/or 'putrid'. Just ignore them. A three-wheeler to Bentota should cost Rs 200, and to Induruwa or Beruwela should cost around Rs 300.

Aluthgama is also the best place to pick up a bus when you're leaving, although there's no trouble getting off a bus at Bentota or Beruwela when you arrive.

KOSGODA

There are five turtle hatcheries along this stretch of coast, testament both to the five species of turtle that nest here and to the curious effect of the lure of the tourist dollar. The **Kosgoda Turtle Hatchery** *(1hr tour Rs 100; open 7am-6pm daily)* was originally a nonprofit NGO project, but the idea took off and commercial rivals sprang up. We're not sure of the ecological value of all of this, but arguably if more eggs turn into turtles than omelettes, as still sometimes happens, it's got to be a good thing.

The Kosgoda Turtle Hatchery has prepared, protected beds of sand for eggs and a dozen large tanks where the hatchlings are kept for three days. Apparently the turtles (or one species at least) are less vulnerable to having parasites after this period. Depending on the time of the year there are loggerhead, leatherback, olive ridley, green and hawksbill babies paddling in the tanks. Their clumsy early efforts at swimming are very cute. A couple of mature albino turtles are kept here – this seems more like a budget zoo exhibit than a fair deal between conservation and local jobs.

AMBALANGODA & AROUND

☎ 091

South of Bentota the road and railway run close to the continuously beautiful coast. Ambalangoda, 86km from Colombo, is a fair-sized town, but its touristy near neighbour, Hikkaduwa, overshadows it as a destination. It does, however, have a beautiful sweep of sandy beach to its north, some famous mask carvers, whom you will find concentrated on the northern edge of town, and a bustling fish market. Other crafts include handwoven cotton and finely carved wooden doors, screens and lintels. If you want to see a traditional dance performance, Ambalangoda is the place to ask. Genuine devil dances – performed to drive out spirits causing illness – still occur irregularly in the hinterland villages. Visitors are welcome, though you do have to expect more curiosity and less English from the villagers, so it pays to make a good impression by dressing well and being polite.

Commercial Bank has an ATM on Galle Rd heading towards Hikkaduwa, and the **Bank of Ceylon** is on Main St.

Things to See & Do

About 800m north of the train and bus stations, towards Colombo, there are two mask shops (with museums) on either side of an intersection. Each is owned by a son of the famous mask carver Ariyapala. The **Ariyapala Mask Museum** *(admission free; 8.30am-5.30pm daily)* is the better museum, with dioramas and explanations in English. It also sells the booklet *The Ambalangoda Mask Museum* if you want to delve into the mysterious world of dance, legend, exorcism and psychology behind the masks. The **Mask and Puppet Museum** is in the other shop. The pieces on sale at both are rather expensive, and there are smaller workshops in town worth investigating if you have the time. **MH Mettananda**, on the Colombo road about 500m north of the train and bus stations, is among the good mask carvers here.

Dudley Silva *(53 Elpitiya Rd)* is a good place to visit for batik – there's a signpost a little past MH Mettananda's shop as you are heading towards the centre of town.

The School of Dance *(☎ 225 8948; ⓔ bandu@sri.lanka.net)* teaches the southern forms of dance such as *kolam* (masked dance-drama) as well as South Indian dance traditions. It's across the road from two major carving studios. The school is run by Bandu Wijesuriya, himself a descendant of a long line of famous mask carvers. Anyone can join the classes: there's a fee of Rs 200 per class for foreigners. Bandu Wijesuriya will also teach anyone interested how to carve and paint masks, as well as traditional drumming and singing. He's planning to open a hostel so foreign students can stay on site.

Sailatalarama Vihara lies 7km inland from Ambalangoda. This temple sits on a domed hill with broad views from the coast, over the plantations and lakes towards the ranges of the Province of Sabaragamuwa. The temple has a 35m-long sleeping Buddha statue, built by donations. Pilgrims approach the stupas and *devales* (complexes) via 208 steps, but there's also a road to the summit. The statue is new and not the most outstanding example of its type, but it's worth coming for the rural scenery and the views. A taxi from Ambalangoda should cost about Rs 500 return, plus waiting time of an hour or so.

Balapitiya, north of Ambalangoda, is a town on the Madu Ganga. The **Madu Boat Service** *(☎ 075 451317)* runs two-hour boat trips through the intricate coves and islands on the lower stretches of the river. The Madu Ganga is home to more than 100 bird species, plus a wide variety of amphibian and reptile species. There are 64 islands in the river, including one for the **Koduwa Vihara**, a 150-year-old meditation retreat temple that's home to five monks.

Places to Stay & Eat

Most places are north of the centre – keep in mind that Main St is one block west of the main road.

Sumudu Tourist Guest House *(☎ 225 8832; 418 Main St, Patabendimulla; singles Rs 375, doubles Rs 500-800)*, about 500m north of the Bank of Ceylon, past the post office, is a large, cool, old-style house run by a friendly family. There are six pleasant, clean rooms. Meals are available, but they're a bit expensive. It's a 10-minute walk to the beach; a three-wheeler to/from the bus station should cost Rs 50.

Piya Nivasa *(☎ 225 8146; singles/doubles Rs 400/450)*, about halfway between Ambalangoda and Hikkaduwa, is on the main road, opposite the beach, at Akurala. If you like old-style houses, you'll love this white mansion. The six clean rooms are great value, and you can eat your meals in the family's sitting room. From Ambalangoda bus or train station a three-wheeler should cost around Rs 150. Otherwise you can catch a Hikkaduwa-bound bus and ask the driver to let you off at the doorstep (there's no sign so look carefully for the name plaque on the house).

Inoka Rest & Restaurant *(☎ 225 8119; 501 Galle Rd; singles/doubles Rs 800/1000)* has six double rooms right by the sea (breakfast included). It's a fairly modern building, and the rooms are simple but well-kept. Grilled prawns with salad costs Rs 250; mixed fried rice is Rs 150.

Shangrela *(☎ 225 8342, fax 225 9421; 38 Sea Beach Rd; singles/doubles Rs 1000/1200)* is a modern, spotless place with 25 rooms, sometimes used for wedding receptions and parties. It's right opposite the beach and meals are available. The manager is happy to arrange local tours to waterfalls and gem mines, as well as boat trips.

Dream Beach Resort *(☎ 225 8873; ⓔ dbra@sltnet.lk; 509 Galle Rd; singles/doubles Rs 2400/3400)* is close to a photogenic stretch of beach and has a wide garden under coconut palms. It has plain, spacious rooms with balconies in a multistorey building, and a swimming pool.

Several readers recommended **Rasika Guesthouse & Restaurant** *(☎ 075 450301; Akurala)*, a family-run guesthouse about 50m from Piya Nivasa. 'Lovely beach, great food' was one comment.

Ahungala is 9km north of Ambalangoda. The only place to stay is the top-end **Triton Hotel** *(☎ 226 4041; ⓔ ashmres@aitkenspence.lk; singles/doubles US$102/132)*. There are plush air-con rooms, but it's much cheaper as part of a package.

Getting There & Away

Ambalangoda is on the main transport route from Colombo to Hikkaduwa, Galle and the South. From Colombo, take a CTB bus (Rs 20) or train (Rs 17.50/47.50 in 3rd/2nd class). Frequent buses come through en route to and from Hikkaduwa (Rs 10).

HIKKADUWA & AROUND

☎ 091

Hikkaduwa, 98km south of Colombo, has long been among the most popular of Sri Lanka's beach spots. It's the variety that attracts people – accommodation ranges from a handful of top-end hotels to heaps of laid-back guesthouses for backpackers. Add to this an equally varied selection of restaurants, bars and cafés and you've got a busy, fun town. Hikkaduwa has swallowed the villages south of it and it's three or four kilometres long – spread out on either side of the road and along the beach.

There's a varied choice of beach and sea – coral for snorkellers, waves for board and body surfers, and good wide strips of sand, backed by cafés, if you just want to sit back and relax.

During the May to October monsoon season, many places close and the water can get quite rough.

Orientation

Services such as the train and bus stations, banks, post office and non-tourist-oriented shops congregate in the northern end of Hikkaduwa proper, which was the original settlement. Further south is where the first tourist hotels, guesthouses and restaurants opened up, but this area now seems overdeveloped and a bit shabby compared with Wewala and Narigama, further south again (around 2km from the stations), where most independent travellers stay. These areas are more relaxed and spread out, and have better beaches than Hikkaduwa proper. South of Narigama the waters tend to be rougher and less safe for bathing – but there are even more guesthouses scattered along the beach and on the road through Thiranagama and Patuwata, even as far as Dodanduwa, only 14km from Galle.

Information

Commercial Bank has an ATM, and you can change money or travellers cheques at the **Bank of Ceylon**. There are various moneychangers along Galle Rd that are open daily, but it may pay to check the exchange rate in a newspaper beforehand, and count your money.

The **main post office** *(Baddegama Rd)* is a five-minute walk inland from the bus station. There are numerous IDD telephone bureaus on Hikkaduwa's main street, many of them with Internet facilities.

You can borrow books in numerous European languages from **tourist libraries** along Galle Rd. There's usually a small fee (Rs 75) per read, plus a deposit (say Rs 200), which is refunded on the safe return of the book.

Coral Sanctuary

Hikkaduwa's dismally overexploited 'coral sanctuary' stretches out from the string of 'Coral' hotels (see under Places to Stay, later) to a group of rocks a couple of hundred metres offshore. You can swim out to the rocks from the Coral Gardens Hotel, where the reef runs straight out from the shore. The water over the reef is never more than three or four metres deep. Many visitors have been disappointed with the coral and the lack of fish. In many places the coral has died, due directly to being disturbed or broken. The reef was struck by bleaching caused by oceanic and atmospheric conditions in 1998, affecting about half the coral, but there are signs of a recovery taking place. At least in the sanctuary the coral isn't being torn up and burnt to make lime for building, as is happening elsewhere at Hikkaduwa – with the consequence that the beach is being eroded in places.

If you really want to see it anyway, you can rent a mask, snorkel and fins from the dive centres listed under Scuba Diving later. Most places hire out a set for around Rs 50 an hour or Rs 200 a day. Stay alert in the water – we heard from one unhappy pair of snorkellers who were nearly run over by a glass-bottomed boat.

There are two or three enterprises that will take you out in a glass-bottomed boat – don't bother. These boats have caused damage to the reef, especially at low tide, and we've also had complaints about the behaviour of some of the crews. The best way to see the reef is by going snorkelling. Check out the boxed text 'Responsible Diving & Snorkelling'.

Scuba Diving

The season runs from November to April. All the companies listed below offer Professional Association of Diving Instructors (PADI) courses for similar prices (open-water for US$320, advanced for US$220), plus a selection of dives such as wreck

Buddhist prayer flags

Fresh-fruit stand, Kalutara

Fishermen return with their last catch of the day, Hikkaduwa

ALL PHOTOGRAPHS BY DALLAS STRIBLEY

GREG ELMS

Palm trees at Tangalla beach

DALLAS STRIBLEY

Stilt fisherman

ANDREW BURKE

Taking in the sunrise from the beach at Uppuveli, near Trincomalee

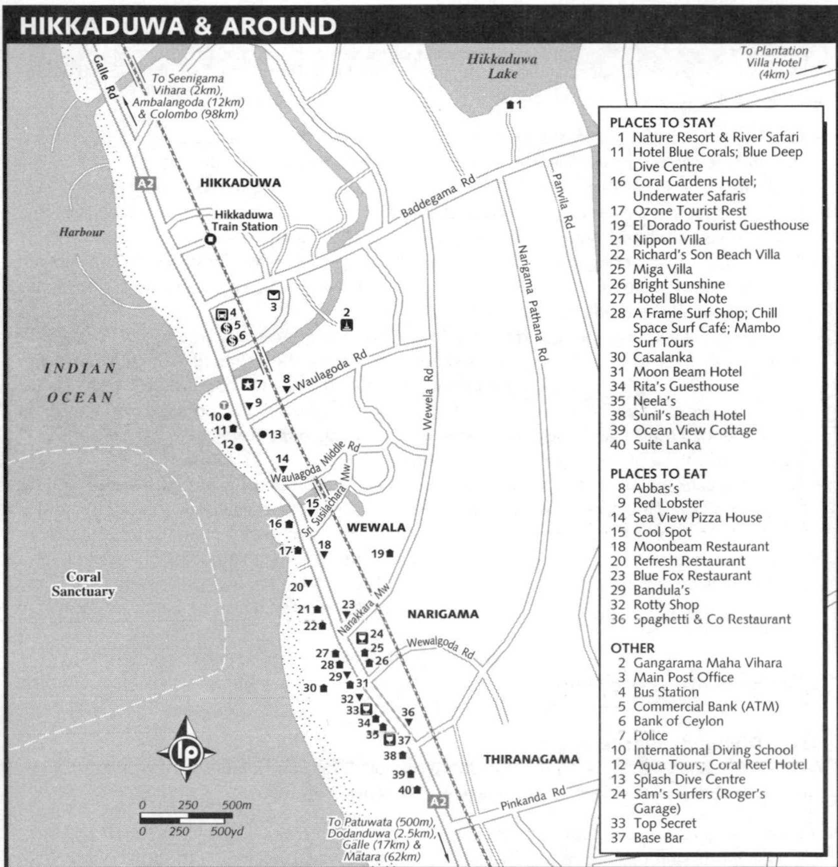

dives, night dives and dives for those who just want to try out diving.

Blue Deep (☎ 074 383190, ⓔ bluedeepdive@yahoo.co.uk) 332 Galle Rd. This centre, at the Hotel Blue Corals, runs PADI courses, Confédération Mondiale des Activités Subaquatique (CMAS) courses and two-day discovery courses (US$60, equipment included). It works with a lecturer on marine biology at Colombo University.

The International Diving School (☎ 072 231683, ⓔ internationaldivingschool@hotmail.com) 330 Galle Rd. This school runs PADI courses and two-day discovery courses (US$60). It rents snorkelling equipment for Rs 100 an hour. There are also deep-sea fishing trips for US$100.

Aqua Tours (☎ 227 7197, ⓔ aquatour@sri.lanka.net) This outfit, based at the Coral Reef Hotel, has two-day discovery courses for US$60, and four-day PADI courses for US$325.

Splash Dive Centre (☎ 0777 654478, ⓔ wewala@sltnet.lk) 279 Galle Rd. This one has similar prices – US$60 for a two-day course, PADI course for US$320.

Underwater Safaris (☎ 011-269 4012, ⓔ scuba@eureka.lk) Operating as Scuba Safari from the Coral Gardens Hotel, this outfit has a range of PADI courses (from US$245), discovery dives (US$35) and specialist programmes including a dive-photography session. Fins, snorkels and masks can be hired for US$14 a day.

Surf & Beach

A short distance south of the coral reef, at Wewala, there's good surf for board riders; international surfers flock here. The best time to surf is from November to April.

Responsible Diving & Snorkelling

Sri Lanka is a wonderful place for diving and snorkelling, but it is important to observe a few simple rules to minimise your impact, and help preserve the ecology and beauty of marine areas:

- Don't use anchors on a reef, and take care not to ground boats on coral. Encourage dive operators and regulatory bodies to establish permanent moorings at popular dive sites.
- Avoid touching living marine organisms with your body or dragging equipment across reefs. Polyps are damaged even by gentle contact. Never stand on corals, even if they look solid and robust. If you must hold onto the reef, only touch exposed rock or dead coral.
- Be conscious of your fins. Even without contact the surge from heavy fin strokes near a reef can damage delicate organisms. When treading water in shallow reef areas, avoid kicking up clouds of sand. Settling sand can easily smother delicate organisms.
- Practise and maintain proper buoyancy control. Major damage can be done by divers descending too fast and colliding with the reef. Make sure you're correctly weighted and that your weight belt is positioned so that you stay horizontal in the water. If you have not dived for a while, have a practice dive in a pool before heading out. Be aware that buoyancy can change over the period of an extended trip; initially you may breathe harder and need more weight, but a few days later you may breathe more easily and need less weight.
- Take great care in underwater caves. Spend as little time within them as possible as your air bubbles may be caught beneath the roof and leave previously submerged organisms high and dry. Take turns to inspect the interior of a small cave to lessen the chances of damaging contact.
- Ensure that you take home all your rubbish and any litter you may find. Plastic in particular is a serious menace to marine life – turtles can mistake it for jellyfish and eat it.
- Resist the temptation to feed the fish. You may disturb their normal eating habits or encourage aggressive behaviour.
- Minimise your disturbance of marine animals. In particular, do not ride on the backs of turtles as this causes them great anxiety. Similarly, discourage your boat driver from circling around turtles, which also puts them under stress.

Safer Diving & Snorkelling

Before embarking on a scuba-diving, skin-diving or snorkelling trip, careful consideration should be given to having a safe, as well as an enjoyable, experience. You should:

- Possess a current diving certification card from a recognised scuba diving instructional agency.
- Obtain reliable information about physical and environmental conditions at the dive site (eg, from a reputable local dive operator).
- Dive only at sites within your realm of experience; if available, engage the services of a competent, professionally trained dive instructor or dive master.
- Be aware that underwater conditions vary significantly from one region, or even site, to another. Seasonal changes can significantly alter any site and dive conditions. These differences influence the way divers dress for a dive and what diving techniques they use.

At Narigama the beach widens out into a fine strip for sunbathing, with, in places, good waves for body surfing. Some of the guesthouses and beach cafés rent out surfboards and boogie boards. The **A Frame Surf Shop**, next to Hotel Blue Note, rents out surfboards and boogie boards for Rs 150 per hour or Rs 400 per day.

While surfing, beware of the sharp coral in places. Ask around about which spots to avoid. As with anywhere on the west coast, take care in the water at Hikkaduwa – the currents can be tricky and there are no life-saving facilities. There have been drownings.

Inland Attractions

Life at Hikkaduwa isn't only sea and sand, although it may often feel that way. There are countless **shops** along the road selling Sri Lankan goodies: masks, gems, jewellery, batik and antiques. There are also clothes shops making all the usual travellers' gear: skirts, light cotton trousers and so on. Unfortunately a lot of traffic – notably, of course, private buses – screams through Hikkaduwa far too fast, which makes walking or cycling along the road an unpleasant, sometimes dangerous, activity.

To leave the beach scene, just walk or cycle along any of the minor roads heading inland. They lead to a calmer, completely different, rural world. Just off Baddegama Rd from the bus station is **Gangarama Maha Vihara**. This is an interesting Buddhist temple that has lots of popular educational paintings (the work of one man over nearly a decade). The monks are happy to show you around. A further 2km along Baddegama Rd you come to **Hikkaduwa Lake**, home to monitor lizards and a lot of birdlife. Boat tours can be organised on the lake (see Nature Resort & River Safari in Places to Stay).

About 2km north of Hikkaduwa, towards Colombo, is the **Seenigama Vihara**, perched on its own island. It's one of only two temples in the country where victims of theft can seek retribution. People who have been robbed visit the temple and buy a specially prepared oil made with chilli and pepper. With the oil they light a lamp in their homes and recite a mantra. Sooner or later, maybe within weeks, the thief will be identified when they're struck down with misfortune, such as having a bicycle accident or being hit on the head by a falling coconut.

Places to Stay – Budget & Mid-Range

Virtually all of Hikkaduwa's places to stay are strung out along the main road. The best way to find something to suit is simply to wander down the road and look at a variety of rooms. All bottom-end prices can be bargained over. Those given here are what you'd expect to pay in the high season; out of season the same room may go for half the quoted price. For lower prices, ask for rooms with shared bathroom – or look on the 'jungle side' of the road. Prices also vary according to which stretch of the strip you're on – down the Narigama end, where the sands are wider, room rates tend to get higher. In high season, the best-value, smaller places fill up quickly; you may need to make a booking a few days ahead.

The places that follow are just a cross-section of the wide choice along the strip, starting in Hikkaduwa proper and moving south. If mosquitoes are in season you'll probably find fewer of them on the beach side of the road.

Hikkaduwa Generally the beach is narrower and less attractive and the buildings are closer together up in this northern end, though there are some good-value places to be found.

Ozone Tourist Rest *(☎ 074 383008; 374 Galle Rd; rooms Rs 500)* has no-frills basic rooms, and it's right on the beach.

Plantation Villa Hotel *(☎/fax 011-258 7454; rooms US$22)* is about 8.5km from Hikkaduwa, at Halpatota, Baddegama. This is a comfortable house not unlike a suburban villa but set in lovely, peaceful grounds (it's right in the St Mary's tea estate). Dinners cost about US$9 per person.

Nature Resort & River Safari *(☎ 074 383006; e tyronew@panlanka.net; Pathana, Hikkaduwa; cabins Rs 1500)* is on Hikkaduwa Lake about 2.5km from the beach. The cute wooden cabins are reached by duckboards, set among mangrove trees on the edge of the lake. The beds and bathrooms are new, and the cabins each have a balcony and air-con. The owner can arrange boat trips for Rs 2000 (up to five people) and bird-watching. The restaurant here is rather nice too, and on Saturdays there's live music.

Wewala The beach is steep and thin but this area has the best surf spots.

El Dorado Tourist Guesthouse *(☎ 227 7091; Nanakkara Mawatha; rooms Rs 400)* offers breakfast for Rs 100 but no dinners. It's a clean, friendly family home in a quiet location down a side road off Galle Rd and across the train tracks.

Richard's Son Beach Villa *(☎ 227 7184; Galle Rd; rooms Rs 500)* has a huge garden planted with coconut palms, a remnant of what Hikkaduwa once must have been before development took off here. The rooms are small but clean singles or doubles. There's no food available.

Miga Villa *(☎/fax 075 451559; Galle Rd; rooms around Rs 500)* is an attractive older house set in pretty gardens. The rooms are clean, but as it's mainly geared towards wedding receptions it may be noisy; ask for

Budget Beaches

Every tropical tourist destination has a scene like Hikkaduwa. Hotel and restaurant names are spun from a combination of words like sun, beach, garden, moon, happy, coral and surf. Beachside restaurants, whether roofed with palm leaves or trying a modern take on traditional architecture, serve up beer, seafood, Western snacks and fruit juices under coloured lights. Shops on the main road sell batteries, water, postcards, rolling papers, lubricants, gaudy beachwear (tie-dye anyone?) and also handicrafts. As sure as the brief but spectacular sunset draws a crowd of chilled-out young travellers in various stages of scruffiness, people will then drift into bars playing Bob Marley bootlegs, decorated in Rastafarian colours. After a few days or weeks of torpor, some people wonder if they shouldn't hit the hard roads again, but others never seem to even brush the sand from their toes.

the rooms near the pond. There's no food available.

Bright Sunshine *(☎ 074 383113; 501 Galle Rd; singles/doubles Rs 600/800)* has six clean and airy rooms. Although there's no garden and it's not beside the beach, the owners are delightful and very keen to please.

Casalanka *(☎/fax 074 383002; Galle Rd; downstairs/upstairs rooms Rs 500/1200)* has 11 rooms. The downstairs rooms are nothing flash but they look onto a bare garden. The upstairs rooms have hot water – a luxury for Hikkaduwa!

A Frame Surf Shop *(☎ 075 458131; Galle Rd; rooms Rs 880-1100)* has eight clean rooms, right next to the main surf break. The upstairs rooms have great views, but you pay a little extra for them.

Hotel Blue Note *(☎ 227 7016; ⓔ bluenote@eureka.lk; 424 Galle Rd; rooms Rs 1440)*, next to A Frame Surf Shop, has bungalows set around a sandy garden. The rooms are clean, though nothing special. One drawcard might be the hotel's sitting room, complete with satellite television.

Moon Beam Hotel *(☎ 075 450657; ⓔ hotelmoonbeam@hotmail.com; 548/1 Galle Rd; singles/doubles Rs 1210/1760)* has 12 sparkling clean rooms with hot water (rates include breakfast). Don't bother paying the Rs 100 extra for an upstairs room – they're the same as the rooms downstairs.

Nippon Villa *(☎/fax 227 7103; 412 Galle Rd; singles/doubles B&B Rs 1500/1800, with air-con Rs 2700/3000)* has rooms with hot water. There's a small courtyard in a colourful, quite handsome building. The rooms are airy and clean but slightly overpriced.

Narigama & Thiranagama This end of the beach is wider and better for swimming and sunbathing. It's crowded with hotels and restaurants, but it's still pleasant.

Neela's *(☎/fax 074 383166; 634 Galle Rd; cabanas Rs 150, rooms Rs 750)* has eight rooms and also two dirt-cheap cabanas. The family-run rooms are clean, but nothing special; the cabanas are a little dark, but comfortable. The food is delicious.

Rita's Guesthouse *(☎ 227 7496; Galle Rd; downstairs/upstairs rooms Rs 700/1000)* has nine basic rooms and a sandy, palm-treed garden. Doubles or singles are available.

Ocean View Cottage *(☎ 227 7237; Galle Rd; rooms Rs 1800-2400)*, with its three mini-apartments, is the place to head if you like plenty of space. Each has a large bedroom, lounge, fridge and veranda. There's a huge garden leading down to the beach.

Sunil's Beach Hotel *(☎ 227 7186, fax 227 7187; Galle Rd; rooms US$23.40/31.20)* is a standard-issue package tour complex with a fenced garden surrounding a small pool (nonguests can swim in the pool for Rs 140). The rooms are large and have a balcony.

Places to Stay – Top End

There are a few top-end places overlooking the coral sanctuary – and just to ensure that you get them nicely confused, they nearly all have 'coral' in their name.

Hotel Blue Corals *(☎ 227 7679; ⓔ bluecorals@itmin.com; 332 Galle Rd; singles/doubles US$24/31)* is a busy, leafy hotel with a pool and 42 rooms with air-con. Breakfast is included in the room rate. The rooms with balconies are good value; the ones without aren't.

Suite Lanka *(☎ 227 7136; ⓔ suitelan@panlanka.net; Galle Rd, Narigama; singles/doubles US$35/40, with air-con US$55/60)* is a small, friendly hotel with a choice of fan-only or air-con rooms; rates include breakfast. There's a small pool, a garish restaurant and a shaded garden lining the beachfront.

Coral Gardens Hotel *(☎ 227 7023; e coral@keells.com; singles/doubles from US$64/78)* has groovy '80s decor, but while it's the poshest in town it's not all that special. The rooms with air-con have views, but no balcony. There's an Ayurvedic centre, a pool and most other facilities you'd expect for this price.

Places to Eat

Hikkaduwa's restaurants mostly have very similar menus: the ubiquitous banana pancakes, rotty and all manner of things homesick foreigners crave (french fries, pizza, good coffee, cake etc). The regional speciality is, naturally, seafood. Baked crab, served with salad, french fries or ginger sauce, is a must. There are a few stores selling imported foods that you can stock up on before heading further afield.

Rotty Shop *(Narigama; meals under Rs 40)* is the stand-by for travellers with late-night hunger pangs as it offers supercheap stomach fillers (such as chocolate-banana-honey *rotty*) till the wee hours of the morning. For another cheapie, **Bandula's** *(Narigama; meals around Rs 100)* all-you-can-eat rice, veggie and fish curry for Rs 80 will fill you up (you must order by 3pm).

Sea View Pizza House *(Wewala; mains around Rs 200)* has superb pizzas, and decent pastas and seafood.

Moonbeam Restaurant *(Wewala; mains Rs 80-200)* has cheap, tasty meals (most of the dishes on the menu are Chinese) and friendly service.

Cool Spot *(Wewala; mains Rs 150-250)* has been here since the 1970s (and it looks it). The food is still very good and inexpensive, and the menu surprisingly varied. The veranda is the best place to sit.

Abbas's *(Waulagoda Rd)* serves good Western food with many German items on the menu, as well as Sri Lankan fare. The restaurant is upstairs; it's pleasantly cool and removed from the noise of the main road. There's an indoor pub (Kings) with music downstairs until late.

Red Lobster *(273 Galle Rd)* is a friendly place set back from the road. Tasty dishes include devilled fish and baked crab.

Blue Fox Restaurant *(397 Galle Rd)* has a great 1st-floor spot perfect for people-watching on the street below. It's a vibrant, busy place with decent prices but the food is only average and it's understaffed. Fried prawns cost Rs 230; rice and curry Rs 90 (ask for Sri Lankan–style curry if you like it hot; otherwise they'll assume that you, like most tourists, don't want chilli and other hot spices added).

Spaghetti & Co *(644 Galle Rd, mains about Rs 300)* is run by an Italian couple and gets our vote for the best food in town. The vibe is relaxed, the garden is lush and the Italian cuisine is fresh and filling. Lasagne costs Rs 370, pasta with shrimp is Rs 320, and they do excellent pizzas and a few vegetarian options. It also has some basic rooms set around a courtyard in an old house, for Rs 400/600 for a single/double.

Refresh Restaurant *(384 Galle Rd, mains from Rs 300)* is good if you feel like splurging. With its simple, modern decor it's a pleasant spot, especially in the evening. Prices are rather higher here than at some other places (devilled prawns for Rs 320, baked crab for Rs 750), but it's reliably good.

Entertainment

Hikkaduwa's nightlife is clustered around Narigama. Down here you'll find a stack of choices including the buzzing **Base Bar** and **Top Secret**. Top Secret is usually a bar but on Saturday nights you can kick your feet in the sand to live music.

Sam's Surfers *(Roger's Garage; 403 Galle Rd)* is a laid-back place with showings of recent movies every night at 7.30pm, or you may prefer to shoot some pool, or swill a beer with a cheap bite to eat.

Chill Space Surf Café in front of the A Frame Surf Shop looks like a surf clothing label advertisement, with nodding DJs spinning post-reggae beats, beers, and a table tennis table if you need to shake off the lethargy. The service is laid-back too.

Getting There & Away

Bus There are frequent buses from Colombo, both private (from the Bastian Mawatha bus station) and CTB. The express buses are best (Rs 60, two to 2½ hours). Buses to Galle or beyond will take you through Hikkaduwa and drop you somewhere south of the bus station if you know where you're headed. Buses also operate frequently to nearby Ambalangoda (Rs 10) and Galle (Rs 15). When leaving Hikkaduwa, you stand more chance of a seat if you start at the bus station.

Train This route can get very crowded, and can also attract a number of touts who try to latch on to you at Colombo Fort station or on the train. Avoid the really slow trains that stop everywhere. The rail schedules seem fairly flexible on the Coast Line, so it's best to check at the station.

Express trains to Colombo leave at 7.08am, 8.07am, 9.35am, 11.05am, 2.33pm, 3.05pm and 6.35pm (Rs 20/55 in 3rd/2nd class).

Trains to Matara via Galle leave at 9.33am, 11.07am, 12.41pm, 4.27pm, 6pm, 6.53pm and 8.21pm (Rs 4/11 in 3rd/2nd class to Galle).

The Kandy direct express leaves Hikkaduwa at 3.05pm (Rs 44.50/122.50 in 3rd/2nd class, six hours). The express train to Vavuniya (for Anuradhapura) leaves at 11.05am (Rs 62/170 in 3rd/2nd class to Anuradhapura, eight hours).

Taxi Most of the Hikkaduwa taxis are small minibuses able to hold about eight passengers, so they can be relatively cheap if there's a group of you. Most gather in front of the top-end hotels. Some example fares are: Galle Rs 800, Unawatuna Rs 1000, Colombo or Tangalla Rs 1800 to 2000, and Bandaranaike International Airport Rs 2500.

Motorcycle Motorcycles are readily available for rent in Hikkaduwa, for both local use and travelling further afield. A traveller has recommended **Sri Lanka Travels & Tours** *(☎ 227 7354; e slttours@mail.ewisl.net; 371 Galle Rd)*. A 125cc machine costs around Rs 500 a day. You can negotiate a discount for several days or a week, though it pays to rent one for a day and see how it runs, rather than pay up for a whole week first. Some of the operators offer insurance (costing 10% of the hire rate).

Getting Around

A three-wheeler costs about Rs 70 from the train or bus station to Wewala or Narigama. Once you're settled in, a bicycle is a nice way to get around and it's easy to hire a bike here for Rs 100 to 150 a day.

The South

The South differs from the west coast: the towns are less touristy, there are still beautiful beaches ringed with palm trees, and the resorts have petered out. There are plenty of nature spots too, so your visit could include a wildlife park safari or a night watch for turtles. Then there's the pretty fort of Galle – a World Heritage–listed historic colonial town. But mostly this area offers calm respite, with lazy afternoons on a beach and snorkelling dips in the clear water. The coast is at its best from November to April.

The South starts at the provincial capital Galle, then heads around the coast to lovely Unawatuna, less-visited Weligama, sleepy Mirissa and bustling Matara. The coast road continues to Tangalla, where you might see sea turtles, and on to Hambantota, a base for visits to Bundala National Park. The road then tucks inland to Tissamaharama, a busy town close to the coastal village of Kirinda and Yala West (Ruhuna) National Park. Continuing north, you'll find Kataragama, an important pilgrimage site.

While swimming anywhere on this coast, watch out for dangerous currents, undertows and rip tides. Watch where other people are swimming and if in any doubt keep asking around. Pollution is another deterrent to swimming in some places – the further you are from towns the better.

Highlights

- Taking a stroll with the locals at sunset around Galle Fort's historic ramparts
- Boozing into the night at a beach bar in Unawatuna after a day of diving or snorkelling and pigging out at beach restaurants
- Reading a favourite book, brushing sand from your toes – whiling away time at sleepy Mirissa
- Waiting, hoping, wishing for the turtles to come in at Rekawa
- Spotting the elusive leopard on a safari in Yala West (Ruhuna) National Park
- Witnessing the rituals and remarkable acts of penance at the Kataragama Festival

GALLE

☎ 091 • pop 91,000

The port of Galle (pronounced 'gawl' in English, and 'gaar-le' in Sinhala), Sri Lanka's fourth-biggest town, is 116km south of Colombo. Galle is Sri Lanka's most historically interesting living city. Although Anuradhapura and Polonnaruwa are much older, they are effectively abandoned cities – the modern towns are quite divorced from the ancient ruins. Until the construction of breakwaters at Colombo harbour in the late 19th century, Galle was the major port in Sri Lanka and still handles shipping – and cruising yachts.

Historians believe Galle may be the Tarshish of Biblical times – where King Solomon obtained gems, spices and peacocks – but it became prominent only with the arrival of the Europeans. In 1505 a Portuguese fleet bound for the Maldives was blown off course and took shelter in the harbour at dusk. It is said that, on hearing a cock (*galo* in Portuguese) crowing, they gave the town its name. Another story is that the name is derived from the Sinhala *gala* (rock). In 1589, during one of their periodic squabbles with the kingdom of Kandy, the Portuguese built a small fort, which they named Santa Cruz. Later they extended it with a series of bastions and walls, but the Dutch, who took Galle in 1640, destroyed most traces of the Portuguese presence.

In 1663 the Dutch built the 36-hectare fort (which is now a World Heritage Site), occupying most of the promontory that forms the older part of Galle. By the time Galle passed into British hands in 1796, commercial interest was turning to Colombo, and old Galle has scarcely altered since. It's delightfully quiet and easy-going.

Unfortunately the town has a guild of con artists. Be prepared to fend off all sorts of fabricated stories, such as the Fort is closed, or there are no buses to Unawatuna, or there are tours to see crocodiles (actually water monitors by the canal on Havelock Place). The usual aim is to set you up for the centuries-old gem scam, where you pay absurdly high prices for gemstones, or buy

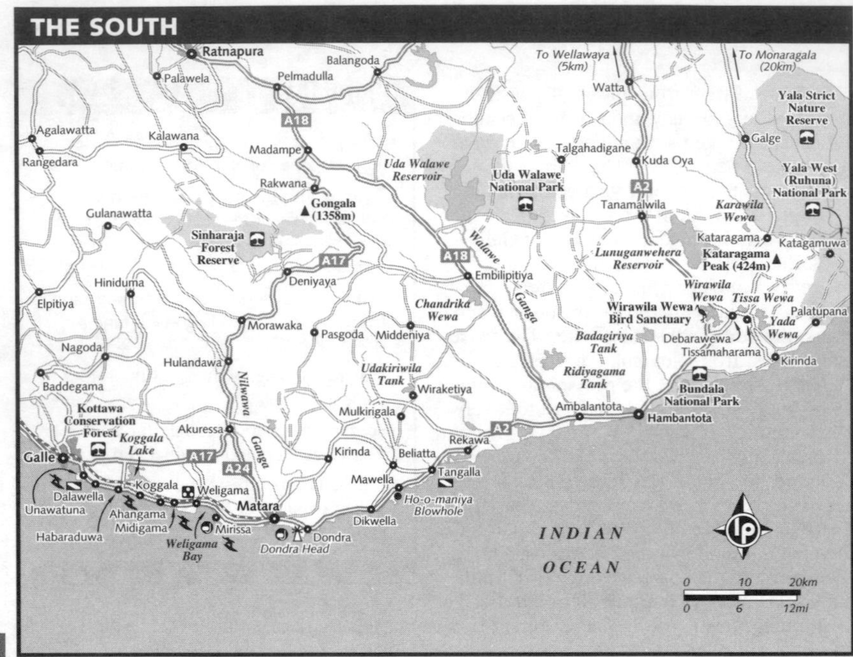

a fake, or are asked to buy gems and resell them for a profit in other countries.

Galle is an easy day trip from Hikkaduwa or Unawatuna, but there is a variety of places to stay if you want to soak up more of the atmosphere.

Orientation & Information

The old town, or Fort, occupies most of a south-pointing promontory. Where the promontory meets the 'mainland' is the centre of the new town, with the bus and train stations, shops and banks. Galle has a busy market area in the new town, on Main Rd.

The **tourist information centre** *(☎ 224 7676; open 9am-4.45pm Mon-Fri)*, near the train station, can organise customised tours with accredited Ceylon Tourist Board guides (in fact they're planning to train some touts as guides). The **main post office** *(Main St)* is near the market and has a poste restante counter and an air-con Internet centre (Rs 4 per minute). **Gold Sea Communications** *(2 Main St)* and **TG Communications** *(Pedlar St)* have fax, International Direct Dialling (IDD) and Internet facilities (Rs 8 per minute).

There's no shortage of banks with ATMs, both in the Fort and the new town. **Vijitha Yapa Bookshop** *(2F Selaka Bldg, Gamini Mawatha)* has a branch near the train station. You can book or reconfirm flights with **SriLankan Airlines** *(☎ 224 6942; Level 3, 16 Gamini Mawatha)*. The nearest thing Galle has to a supermarket is the self-service grocery **Paranagama** *(168 Main St)*.

The Fort Walls

One of the most pleasant strolls you can take in town is the circuit of the Fort walls at dusk. As the daytime heat fades away, in an easy hour or two you can walk almost the complete circuit of the Fort along the top of the wall. Only once – between Aurora Bastion and the Old Gate – is it necessary to leave the wall (part of the area between the Star and Aeolus Bastions is an off-limits military compound).

The **Main Gate** in the northern stretch of the wall is a comparatively recent addition – it was built by the British in 1873 to handle the heavier flow of traffic into the old city. This part of the wall, the most heavily fortified because it faced the land, was originally

Galle's Phone Numbers

Galle's telephone area code is scheduled to change from ☎ 09 to ☎ 091 during October 2003. See the boxed text 'Telephone Number Changes' in the Facts for the Visitor chapter for details of this and other changes to Sri Lanka's telephone numbers.

built by the Portuguese with a moat, and was then substantially enlarged by the Dutch, who in 1667 split it into separate Star, Moon and Sun Bastions.

Following the Fort wall clockwise you soon come to the **Old Gate**. On its outer side the British coat of arms tops the entrance. Inside, the letters VOC, standing for Verenigde Oostindische Compagnie (Dutch East India Company), are inscribed in the stone, flanked by two lions and topped by a cock, with the date 1669. The National Maritime Museum (see Inside the Fort, following) is housed in the walls, and is entered via the Old Gate. Just beyond the gate is the **Zwart Bastion**, or Black Fort, thought to be Portuguese-built and the oldest of the Fort bastions.

The eastern section of the wall ends at the **Point Utrecht Bastion**, close to the powder magazine and topped by the 18m-high lighthouse, which was built in 1938.

Flag Rock, at the end of the next stretch of wall, was once a Portuguese bastion. From there the Dutch signalled approaching ships to warn them of dangerous rocks – hence its name. Musket shots were fired from Pigeon Island, close to the rock, to further alert ships to the danger. On the **Triton Bastion** there used to be a windmill that drew up sea water, which was sprayed from carts to keep the dust down on the city streets. This part of the wall is a great place to be at sunset. There's a series of other bastions, as well as the tomb of a Muslim saint outside the wall, before you arrive back at your starting point.

Inside the Fort

Most of the older buildings within the Fort date from the Dutch era. Many of the streets still bear their Dutch names, or are direct translations. The Dutch also built an intricate sewer system that was flushed out daily by the tide. With true colonial efficiency, they then bred musk rats in the sewers, which were exported for their musk oil. There's a large Muslim community living and working inside the Fort, particularly at the southern end of the walled town. Many shops close for a couple of hours around noon on Friday for prayer time.

The **Historical Mansion** *(31-39 Leyn Baan St; admission free; open 9am-5.30pm Mon-Thur, Sat & Sun, 10am-noon & 2.30-5.30pm Fri)*, in a well-restored Dutch house, is not really a museum as many of the exhibits have price tags and there's also a gem shop. It's a junkyard of colonial artefacts, including collections of antique typewriters, VOC china, spectacles and jewellery.

The **National Maritime Museum** *(admission Rs 65; open 9am-5pm Sat-Wed)* is inside the thick, solid walls of former storehouses. The dusty exhibits are poorly displayed, but have a certain kitsch appeal: fibreglass whales, pickled sea creatures, models of catamarans. Fishermen from this area once made pilgrimages to Kataragama hoping that they could increase their catches. There's a small exhibit on this subject.

The **National Museum** *(Church St; admission Rs 45; open 9am-5pm Wed-Sun)* is housed in a Dutch building near the main gate. It has a poorly displayed collection of traditional masks, the lace-making process and religious items, including a relic casket.

The **New Oriental Hotel** was built in 1684 to house the Dutch governor and officers. It became a hotel in 1863. At the time of research the hotel was closed, awaiting refurbishment.

The **Dutch Reformed Church** (Groote Kerk, or Great Church), near the New Oriental Hotel, was originally built in 1640, but the present building dates from 1752–55. Its floor is paved with gravestones from the old Dutch cemetery, and the friendly caretaker will tell you where the remains are held in the walls and under the floor of the building. The 1760 organ still sits in the building and the impressive pulpit, made from calamander wood from Malaysia, is an interesting piece. Services are held each Sunday. The Dutch government has funded repairs to the roof and ceiling.

Near the church are a 1701 **bell tower** and the old **Dutch Government House**, now the Royal Dutch House Hotel. Over the doorway a slab bears the date 1683 and Galle's ubiquitous cock symbol.

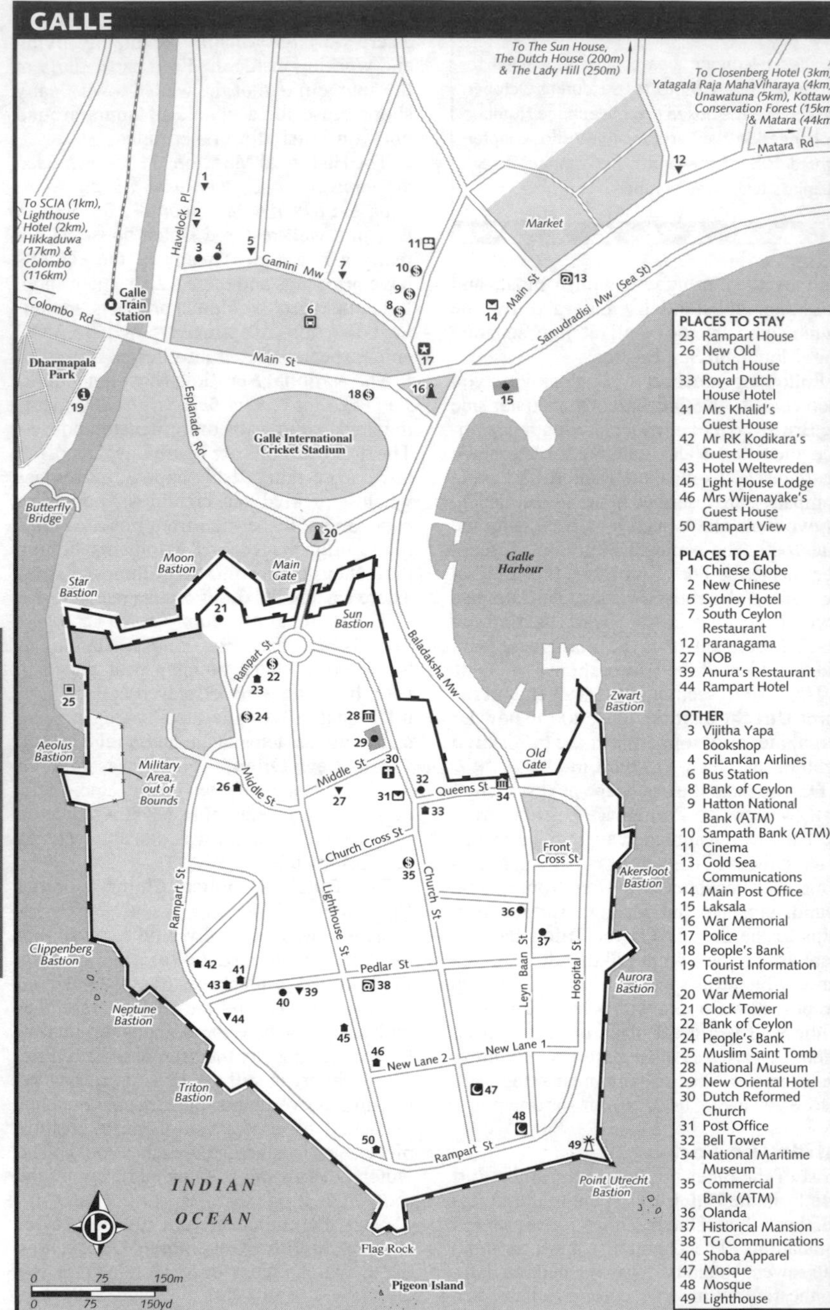
GALLE
To The Sun House, The Dutch House (200m) & The Lady Hill (250m)
To Closenberg Hotel (3km), Yatagala Raja MahaViharaya (4km), Unawatuna (5km), Kottawa Conservation Forest (15km) & Matara (44km)
Matara Rd
To SCIA (1km), Lighthouse Hotel (2km), Hikkaduwa (17km) & Colombo (116km)
Havelock Pl
Gamini Mw
Market
Main St
Samudradisi Mw (Sea St)
Galle Train Station
Colombo Rd
Main St
Dharmapala Park
Esplanade Rd
Galle International Cricket Stadium
Butterfly Bridge
Moon Bastion
Main Gate
Star Bastion
Sun Bastion
Galle Harbour
Baladaksha Mw
Rampart St
Zwart Bastion
Aeolus Bastion
Military Area, out of Bounds
Middle St
Old Gate
Queens St
Church Cross St
Front Cross St
Church St
Lighthouse St
Akersloot Bastion
Rampart St
Leyn Baan St
Hospital St
Clippenberg Bastion
Pedlar St
Aurora Bastion
Neptune Bastion
New Lane 2
New Lane 1
Triton Bastion
Rampart St
Point Utrecht Bastion
INDIAN OCEAN
Flag Rock
Pigeon Island
0 75 150m
0 75 150yd
PLACES TO STAY
23 Rampart House
26 New Old Dutch House
33 Royal Dutch House Hotel
41 Mrs Khalid's Guest House
42 Mr RK Kodikara's Guest House
43 Hotel Weltevreden
45 Light House Lodge
46 Mrs Wijenayake's Guest House
50 Rampart View
PLACES TO EAT
1 Chinese Globe
2 New Chinese
5 Sydney Hotel
7 South Ceylon Restaurant
12 Paranagama
27 NOB
39 Anura's Restaurant
44 Rampart Hotel
OTHER
3 Vijitha Yapa Bookshop
4 SriLankan Airlines
6 Bus Station
8 Bank of Ceylon
9 Hatton National Bank (ATM)
10 Sampath Bank (ATM)
11 Cinema
13 Gold Sea Communications
14 Main Post Office
15 Laksala
16 War Memorial
17 Police
18 People's Bank
19 Tourist Information Centre
20 War Memorial
21 Clock Tower
22 Bank of Ceylon
24 People's Bank
25 Muslim Saint Tomb
28 National Museum
29 New Oriental Hotel
30 Dutch Reformed Church
31 Post Office
32 Bell Tower
34 National Maritime Museum
35 Commercial Bank (ATM)
36 Olanda
37 Historical Mansion
38 TG Communications
40 Shoba Apparel
47 Mosque
48 Mosque
49 Lighthouse

Places to Stay – Budget

Mrs Wijenayake's Guest House *(☎ 223 4663; e thalith@sri.lanka.net; 65 Lighthouse St; rooms Rs 300-800)*, also called Beach Haven, is a modern home with tidy guestrooms. The cheaper rooms are in the family home, and the larger and more expensive ones are upstairs at the back, with sitting areas on the balcony. There's ample living space and the family is very welcoming.

Light House Lodge *(☎ 075 450514; e umayangaya@yahoo.com; 62B Lighthouse St; singles/doubles Rs 375/475)* has friendly owners, but shoebox-like rooms. The small sunny balcony and Internet access are redeeming features.

Hotel Weltevreden *(☎ 222 2650; e piya sen2@sltnet.lk; 104 Pedlar St; singles/doubles Rs 500/600)*, a protected Dutch building, has characterful rooms surrounding a leafy courtyard, and a pretty garden. The welcoming host will be happy to make your meals.

Mr RK Kodikara's Guest House *(☎ 222 2351; e kodi.galle@lanka.com.lk; 29 Rampart St; rooms downstairs Rs 500, upstairs Rs 900 1000)* is a charming ramshackle mansion overlooking the ramparts. There are four clean, simple rooms downstairs, and a larger suite upstairs as well as two value-for-money rooms with views over the ramparts. If you're tall, Mr Kodikara has made 2m-long beds with timber from the old roof.

Mrs Khalid's Guest House *(Huize Bruisen de Zee; ☎ 223 4907; e khalid@dialogsl.net; 102 Pedlar St; rooms Rs 500-1000)* has moved into a tastefully restored Dutch house. It's still a homely place and has two rooms with hot water, balconies and sea views (Rs 800/1000 for a single/double) and other rooms without the view. Mrs Khalid's meals get good reviews and she'll cook Persian or Moroccan food as well as rice and curry.

Rampart House *(☎ 223 4448; 3 Rampart St; rooms Rs 450-650)* is a large, 1970s home whose triple rooms have a view of the ramparts. One room has a small study, another has a small balcony, bathtub and hot water, and there's also a single downstairs. There isn't a sign outside; look for the street number on the fencepost.

Rampart View *(☎ 074 380566; 37 Rampart St; singles/doubles Rs 600/800)* has some of the best views of the ramparts in Galle. The rooms are bare and basic (no mosquito nets), but the views are unforgettable.

Places to Stay – Mid-Range & Top End

New Old Dutch House *(☎ 074 385032, fax 074 384920; 21 Middle St; singles with shared bathroom & breakfast Rs 750, rooms with breakfast Rs 1500, with air-con & breakfast Rs 2500)* is a sparkling new place close to the sea. If you fancy eating breakfast under the pawpaw trees and listening to the waves break on the rocks below the ramparts, this is the spot.

Royal Dutch House Hotel *(☎ 224 7160; 15 Queens St; singles/doubles Rs 1200/1500)*, in the former Dutch Government House, has enormous rooms under colonial timber ceilings, and a recommended restaurant. There are loads of period features, including a grand staircase and high ceilings.

The upmarket places to stay are all out of Galle, away from the hustle and bustle of the town and fort.

Closenberg Hotel *(☎/fax 222 4313; 11 Closenberg Rd; singles/doubles US$30/42, with air-con US$35/47)*, built as a 19th-century P&O captain's residence in the heyday of British mercantile supremacy, sits out on a promontory with views over Galle beach and the Fort. The 21 rooms have colonial wooden furniture, 16 of them in a modern wing with balconies overlooking the beach. The older rooms are a bit gloomy with their dark timber fittings and lack of windows and mod cons.

The Lady Hill *(☎ 224 4322; e ladyhill@slt net.lk; 29 Upper Dickson Rd; rooms US$48)* has spotless, modern rooms with balconies that let you enjoy one of the highest views in Galle. It's a cool, shaded and airy place where rooms come with all the mod cons. There's a rooftop bar/restaurant and a small pool.

The Sun House *(☎/fax 222 2624; e sun house@sri.lanka.net; 18 Upper Dickson Rd; standard rooms US$99, garden rooms US$161, cinnamon suite US$245)* is a gracious old villa built in the 1860s by a Scottish spice merchant and renovated with superb taste and attention to detail. As the villa is on a hilltop, you have wonderful views towards the Fort on one side and the port on the other. There's a large, well-kept garden and a small pool. The food is excellent, as is the hospitality. The owners also manage the house on Taprobane island (see under Weligama, later in this chapter), The Dutch House and several other villas.

Lighthouse Hotel *(☎ 222 3744; ⓔ lighthousehotel@lanka.com.lk; rooms US$240)* occupies a prime position on the seafront, 2km from town on the Colombo side. It beautifully blends Dutch colonial style with modern design. Check out the staircase sculpture *The Portuguese Arriving in Ceylon under a Cloud* for some macabre metalwork.

The Dutch House *(Doornberg; ⓔ sunhouse@sri.lanka.net; 23 Upper Dickson Rd; suites US$309)*, a former residence of a Dutch East Indies admiral, was built in 1712 and has been beautifully restored with Dutch colonial furniture. The four spacious suites have a private garden, views to the fort, a bathtub and romantic net-covered four-poster bed. There's a pool, croquet green, garden dining and plenty of little extras to keep you entertained.

Places to Eat

Two guesthouses in the Fort, **Mrs Khalid's Guest House** *(meals from Rs 250)* and **Mrs Wijenayake's Guest House** *(meals from Rs 250)*, welcome nonguests for meals, but you should book in advance. For fine dining, you'll need to head to one of the good hotels.

The Lady Hill *(lunch/dinner Rs 500/600)* has set and à la carte menus. The food is as good as the 270-degree views from the rooftop restaurant.

Closenberg Hotel *(breakfast/lunch/dinner US$3/5/7)* has a pretty, grassed terrace with views over Galle beach, and a heavily timbered dining room – it's a great spot for breakfast or lunch.

The Sun House *(set menu Rs 2400)* accepts bookings from nonguests for its three-course dinners. Call to check availability and to make a booking. This is a great way to experience the hospitality if you're not staying.

Lighthouse Hotel *(breakfast/lunch/dinner US$7.20/10.80/14.40)* often puts on buffets. Telephone to make a reservation.

Rampart Hotel *(☎ 074 380103, fax 091-224 2794; 31 Rampart St; mains from Rs 300)* has delicious food. Seating is on a wide, wooden balcony that overlooks the ramparts. It has a fixed lunch menu (Rs 360) and à la carte options such as roast beef (Rs 300).

Anura's Restaurant *(65 Pedlar St; mains Rs 150-230)* is one of the few travellers' places to eat in Galle, let alone the Fort. The pizzas (from Rs 180) are reasonably authentic.

NOB *(3 Middle St; mains Rs 125-185)*, also in the Fort, is an established old-fashioned place and does decent rice and curry at lunch time and snacks at other times.

Sydney Hotel *(Gamini Mawatha; mains Rs 40-80)*, near the South Ceylon Restaurant, is a friendly and popular local lunch-time eatery. You can enjoy three delicious courses for Rs 80: ginger beer, rice and curry, and ice cream!

South Ceylon Restaurant *(6 Gamini Mawatha; mains Rs 70-230)*, opposite the bus station above the South Ceylon Bakery, serves tasty food in a friendly atmosphere. Lion lager costs Rs 95. The bakery serves good short eats and minipizzas (Rs 27.50).

Around the corner are **Chinese Globe** *(38 Havelock Place)* and the **New Chinese** *(14 Havelock Place)*. New Chinese is the better of the two; it's brighter and is Chinese-run. The food – Western, Chinese and Sri Lankan – is very reasonable (mains cost from around Rs 120 to 220) and filling.

Shopping

Galle's history makes it an interesting place to fossick for colonial pieces and antiques. Jewellery, ceramics and bric-a-brac are common. **Olanda** *(30 Leyn Baan St)* has Dutch period furniture and reproductions, including carved wooden window and door lintels from Rs 4500 (or reproductions for a lower price). Brass door hinges, Buddhist and Hindu statues, and ceramic door knobs (from Rs 150) will be easier to take home.

For more standard Sri Lankan handicrafts, there's a **Laksala** *(Sumudradisi Mawatha)* in the new town and a small enterprise, **Shoba Apparel** *(Pedlar St)*, in the Fort.

South Ceylon Industrial Agency & Handicraft Factories *(SCIA; 73A Kandewatta Rd)* employs traditional craftspeople from specialising villages. You can watch jewellery, leatherwork, batik, lace and machine embroidery being created. Galle is famous for its lace making (a Dutch legacy). Prices are negotiable. A three-wheeler from the station costs about Rs 50.

Getting There & Away

Bus There are plenty of buses running up and down this busy coastal strip. The bus fare to Colombo is Rs 43 for a CTB bus and Rs 85 for an intercity express (every 15 minutes or so between 4.30am and 10pm; three hours);

to Hikkaduwa it costs Rs 15 (Rs 20 on an intercity express); Unawatuna Rs 5; and Matara Rs 17.50. There are buses to Tangalla (Rs 28.50, 2½ hours), Tissamaharama (Rs 50, five hours), Kataragama (Rs 67, 5½ hours), Ampara (Rs 125, seven hours) and Ella (via Deniyaya on the Nuwara Eliya bus).

Train Fast passenger trains to Colombo's Maradana station leave at 6.45am, 7.40am, 9.05am, 10.40am (continuing to Vavuniya), 2.10pm, 2.45pm and 6.05pm. The fare to Colombo is Rs 23/64.50 3rd/2nd class; to Hikkaduwa it's Rs 4/11 3rd/2nd class. The direct train to Kandy leaves at 2.45pm (Rs 48/133 in 3rd/2nd class) and arrives at 9pm. There is no 1st class on this service and there are no sleepers. The 6.05pm train continues to Polonnaruwa (Rs 76/211.50 in 3rd/2nd class).

Trains to Matara leave regularly: the expresses run at 10.15am, 11.45am, 1.25pm, 5.15pm and 6.35pm (Rs 9/24.50 in 3rd/2nd class).

Three-Wheeler A three-wheeler between Galleand Unawatuna costs about Rs 100.

AROUND GALLE

You could spend half a day taking an interesting scenic route to Unawatuna, or just do the route as an outing from Galle.

The road heading north out of Galle passes the **Kottawa Conservation Forest**, a 14-hectare wet evergreen forest about 15km northeast of Galle. There are walking tracks in the forest, but first get permission from the forest department office near the gate. Wear good walking shoes and trousers: the leeches are ferocious. Trees are identified with their botanical names, making this a good opportunity to get to know your Sri Lankan flora. On the other side of the road, near the forest entrance, is a swimming spot fed by a waterfall.

There are a couple of **tea factories** tucked away in this area. Tallangaha and Kottawa are open to visitors and sell tea.

About 10km east of Kottawa, the 10m-high seated Buddha at **Kaduruduwa Temple** *(admission by donation)* rises above the surrounding paddy fields. Just 4km from Unawatuna, the **Yatagala Raja Maha Viharaya** is a quiet rock temple with a 9m-long reclining Buddha. The mural-covered walls are painted in the style t[illegible] Kandyan period. There are[illegible] meditation spots among t[illegible]

UNAWATUNA

☎ 091

About five kilometres southeast of Galle is Unawatuna, a wide, curving bay with a picturesque sweep of golden beach. Swimming is safe thanks to the reef that protects the beach, and, unlike Hikkaduwa, Unawatuna does not have a dangerously busy road running right through it. These factors have made Unawatuna popular with travellers, including package-tour groups, and locals. Unfortunately, Unawatuna isn't immune to the problems associated with popularity. On public holidays and weekends in particular, Unawatuna can get very crowded. Petty crime and drugs have become issues in recent years. Take care with your possessions, especially on the beach. Overall, though, Unawatuna is less hectic than Hikkaduwa.

Information

The post office is out of town, but there's an informal **postal agency** *(Wella Dewala Rd)*. There are Internet facilities all around the bay. The biggest places arc **Internet Cafe@E-world**, near Yaddehimulla Rd, and **Surfcity Internet Cafe**. There are no banks, but The Villa Hotel changes travellers cheques.

Water Sports

Unawatuna has a local surf scene and is a good place to learn to surf. King Fisher's Restaurant rents surfboards for Rs 200 per hour or Rs 400 per day. King Fisher's and some other places organise surfing tours to other good surf spots.

You can hire **snorkelling** equipment from some of the beachfront places (or borrow it from guesthouses) to explore the reef a short distance out from the west end of the beach. See the boxed text 'Responsible Diving & Snorkelling' under Hikkaduwa in the West Coast chapter for advice.

There are several interesting **wreck dives** around Galle, as well as reef and cave diving. The wreck dives include the *Lord Nelson*, a cargo ship wrecked about 10 years ago, which has a 15m-long cabin to explore. The 33m-long *Rangoon* is one hour south of Galle. There are three diving outfits in Unawatuna:

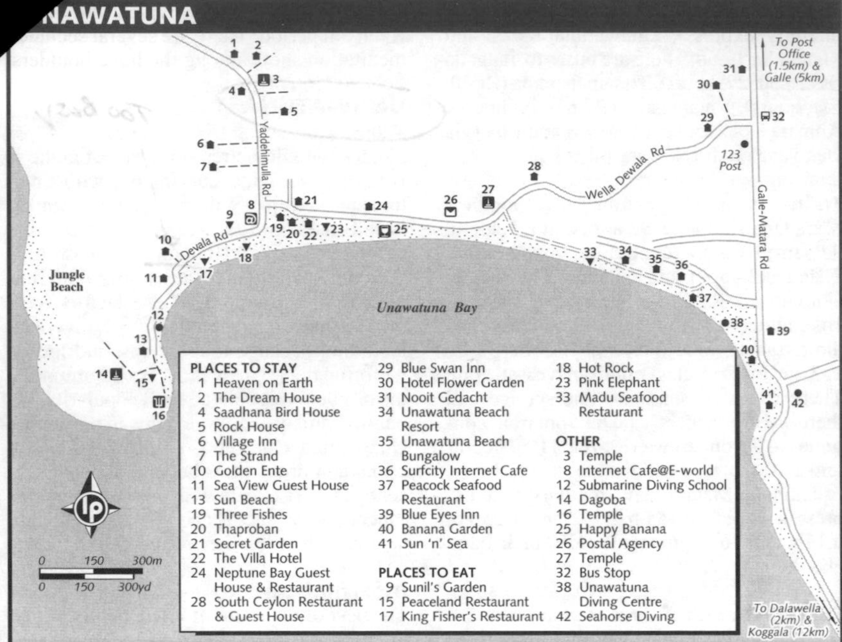

Seahorse Diving (☎/fax 228 3733, ⓔ krohana@hotmail.com) charges US$30 for one dive and US$125 for five dives (including equipment). A snorkelling boat trip costs Rs 1700 per hour and snorkel hire costs Rs 165 per hour.

Submarine Diving School (☎ 074 380358) rents snorkelling gear for Rs 150 per hour or Rs 700 per day. Its PADI open water course costs US$350. One dive costs US$25 and a five-dive package is US$100.

Unawatuna Diving Centre (☎ *224 4693;* Ⓦ una watunadiving.com) runs both PADI and CMAS courses for €325.

Walks

You can take some interesting walks over the rocks rising from the west end of the beach or along the tracks back past the guesthouses on Yaddehimulla Rd and up the hill to catch views to the other side of the promontory. The rocky outcrop on the west end of the beach, **Rumassala**, is known for its protected medicinal herbs. Legend has it that Hanuman dropped herbs carried from the Himalaya here. The temple right on the promontory is fenced off, but you can stroll up to the **dagoba** (Buddhist temple) on top of the hill and to **Jungle Beach** on the other side.

Places to Stay

Unawatuna is packed with places to stay for all budgets. There are only a couple of top-end places, and these are on a relatively modest scale compared with other beach resorts. If you're on a tight budget, you can save a lot of money by staying a few minutes' walk from the beach.

Places to Stay – Budget

South Ceylon Restaurant & Guest House *(☎ 224 5863; Wella Dewala Rd; rooms with shared bathroom Rs 250)* has four rough and bare, but cheap, rooms. There's a wide range of vegetarian food on offer (see Places to Eat), as well as meditation courses.

Sun Beach *(☎ 224 2284; Devala Rd; rooms Rs 250-400)* is probably the cheapest place on the beach with sea views. This wooden shack is laid-back, rough and ready (no fans), but what a location.

Golden Ente *(☎ 074 381228; Devala Rd; singles Rs 350-500, doubles Rs 500-750)* is a three-storey block with a palm-tree-studded lawn. The nine neat and tidy rooms each have their own balcony or veranda. It's good value. There's no food served, though.

Heaven on Earth *(☎ 224 7775; Yaddehimulla Rd; rooms Rs 350, with bathroom Rs 500)* has four straightforward rooms. The host is friendly and there's a pretty, leafy garden.

Village Inn *(☎/fax 222 5375; rooms Rs 350-900)* has an assortment of rooms spread over three buildings, and an individual bungalow. The pick of the bunch are the rooms with balconies facing the back yard. It's run by a hospitable family and the service is good.

Peacock Seafood Restaurant *(☎ 075 384998; rooms Rs 600)*, right on the beach, has stunning views, making these otherwise plain rooms good value. You can rent a motorcycle here for Rs 500 per day.

Surfcity Internet Cafe *(☎/fax 224 6305-6; ⓔ surfcity@itmin.com; singles/doubles with breakfast Rs 800/950)* is a one-stop Dutch-run place: it has good rooms, an interesting café menu, an art gallery of local works and Internet access. Can't they bring the beach inside too? Some rooms have hot water.

Saadhana Bird House *(☎ 222 4953; ⓔ strand_u@sltnet.lk; Yaddehimulla Rd; rooms Rs 1000)* is a welcoming family home with three rooms and a rooftop garden for bird-watching. There's a check list to tick off the birds you've spotted, and you can hire a motorcycle (Rs 500 per day) or bicycle (Rs 200 per day), or have some clothes tailored.

Blue Eyes Inn *(☎ 074 380445; Galle-Matara Rd; singles/doubles including breakfast from Rs 750/1000, with hot water & breakfast Rs 900/ 1200)* is neat and well-run with six rooms. There is also a villa with two bedrooms, a living area and an indoor garden that costs Rs 1250. The food is recommended (see Places to Eat).

Places to Stay – Mid-Range

Neptune Bay Guest House & Restaurant *(☎/fax 223 4014; ⓔ neptunbay@eureka.lk; rooms Rs 700-1500)* was rebuilding its old wing at the time of writing, with plans for rooms with air-con, fridge, television, hot water and a swimming pool in the grounds. There's a tour office (with Internet facilities) here.

Unawatuna Beach Bungalow *(☎ 222 4327; ⓔ unawatunabeachbungalow@yahoo.com; singles/doubles with breakfast Rs 1000/1350)* has a garden and well-kept rooms with beach-facing balconies: you could lie in bed and look out to sea.

Nooit Gedacht *(☎/fax 074 381476; ⓔ nooitgedacht@hotmail.com; Galle-Matara Rd; rooms Rs 1000, rooms with bathroom from Rs 1500)*, just before you get to the turn-off to Unawatuna from Galle, on Galle–Matara Rd, is a 1735 Dutch colonial mansion with a small pool and a large garden. A four-bed family apartment for Rs 3500 is large and airy. There's lots of antique furniture, heavy timber panelling and loads of character.

Sea View Guest House *(☎ 222 4376, fax 23649; Devala Rd; singles half board Rs 1000, doubles half board 1800-2200)* is one of Unawatuna's longest-running guesthouses, with 24 comfortable rooms spread over four buildings. There's a large garden, but the service is a bit impersonal. Some rooms have hot water. There is only one single but there are also triples and family rooms.

Hotel Flower Garden *(☎ 222 5286; ⓔ flowerga@pan.lk; singles/doubles including breakfast Rs 1250/1450)* has nine comfortable and spotless cabanas, each with its own cutesy flower garden. Rooms inside the main, modern house have hot water and air-con, and four of the cabanas have air-con. Bicycles are supplied free to guests.

Blue Swan Inn *(☎/fax 222 4691; Wella Dewala Rd; singles/doubles from Rs 1200/1800)* is a huge, modern and spacious family home with equally impressive rooms. It offers a little bit of luxury. The one room that has air-con costs Rs 2000.

Banana Garden *(☎/fax 074 381089; rooms Rs 1300-1700)* has nine rooms including quirky wooden shacks on the beach – go for these first. There are cheaper rooms on the other side of the road for Rs 800.

Sun 'n' Sea *(☎ 228 3200; ⓔ muharam@sltnet.lk; rooms including breakfast Rs 1925, with air-con, hot water & breakfast Rs 2425)* is on a clean and uncrowded spot of beach – it's so close you'll hear the waves crashing on the rocks – with great views of the bay. It has an established leafy garden, and a restaurant.

Three Fishes *(☎ 224 1857; rooms Rs 600/1200)* is a low-key guesthouse with a colonial ambience. There are five rooms – two singles and three doubles, and a jungle-like garden beside the beach and shaded verandas.

The Strand *(☎/fax 222 4358; ⓔ strand_u@sltnet.lk; family bungalow with breakfast per night Rs 2500, singles per week US$30, apartment with breakfast per week US$185, suite* *with breakfast per week US$140)* is an attractive early-20th-century house set in large gardens. There are five charming rooms as well as an apartment ideal for families (four beds). The rooms are starting to show their age, but the colonial-style furniture adds the right atmosphere.

Places to Stay – Top End

Thaproban *(☎/fax 074 381722; w www.thaproban.com; rooms Rs 2500-4000)*, a three-storey place right on the beach, has nicely furnished rooms with hot water and some with air-con. Some rooms have good sea views and there's a restaurant. Thaproban recently opened a new place, **Thambapanni Retreat**, set in lush gardens nearby.

Secret Garden *(☎/fax 074 721007; e secretgardenvilla@msn.com; single/double bungalows US$30/35, rooms US$60, house US$180)*, near Three Fishes, is very secret indeed; entry is through a discreet door in the garden wall. There are four big bedrooms and four cute bungalows in this pleasant, old-style place. You can hire the entire house (including a kitchen) or you can rent the bedrooms and bungalows. There's also a meditation pagoda.

Unawatuna Beach Resort *(☎ 074 384545; e ubr@sri.lanka.net; singles half board US$36-45, doubles half board US$54-65)* has ageing, spacious rooms with balconies. The more expensive rooms have sea views, bathtub, air-con and more mod cons. There's also a pool (nonguests pay Rs 200). There are no room-only rates.

The Dream House *(☎ 074 381541, fax 074 381212; rooms with breakfast US$40)* is a delightful Italian-run guesthouse that has four spacious rooms with colonial ambience, four-poster beds, private balconies and hot water. The spiral staircase upstairs takes some negotiating.

The Villa Hotel *(☎ 224 7253; e thevilla@slt.lk; rooms with breakfast from US$50)* is a two-storey treat on the beach. All rooms have air-con, hot water, TV, minibar and the little touches you expect.

Places to Eat

Almost all places to stay provide meals, and the home-cooked food can be very good indeed. Restaurants along the beachfront are numerous, all offer seafood and often there isn't much to distinguish them. Even the prices at the simple huts and the upmarket hotels don't vary much. As staff and chefs tend to come and go, the best strategy is to ask around for recommendations.

Hot Rock, near Three Fishes, has consistently good food and a great central location on the bay. There's a good selection of seafood (around Rs 250) and the mixed fried noodles (Rs 150) are extremely tasty.

Sunil's Garden is back from the beach, but it's ringed by a leafy garden and the service is friendly and attentive. Spaghetti and salad costs Rs 200, and fish dishes cost from Rs 190. There's always music playing and it's a good chill-out spot for a beer.

King Fisher's Restaurant gets good reviews and is a good spot to watch the surfers catch the breaks. Fish dishes start at Rs 210, and 500g of lobster costs Rs 950.

Madu Seafood Restaurant *(mains Rs 100-250)* is a popular place with excellent seafood and other standards. Try the baked crab (Rs 925), full fish (Rs 350) or the recommended grilled lobster (Rs 850 for 500g).

Peaceland Restaurant *(rice & curry Rs 150)*, close to the temple on the point, is still developing its menu, but hey maan, it is *the* chill-out place in Una.

Pink Elephant, in a beach hut close to the sea, has tasty food at reasonable prices. Seafood dishes cost from Rs 170. There is one unique item on the menu: ice cream and arrack (Rs 70).

South Ceylon Restaurant *(☎ 224 5863)* has vegetarian and vegan food, which makes a refreshing change from the standard menu. The choice includes Mexican, Thai and Italian food (order early). There's Internet access here as well.

Thaproban *(mains Rs 120-250)* serves great seafood pizza from Rs 220, pasta from Rs 200, pilau for Rs 175 and a Saturday night barbecue buffet for Rs 385. Lion lager costs Rs 120 and imported wine is available.

The Villa Hotel *(mains Rs 150-600)* has a great location with a sea-facing restaurant offering a reasonably standard menu (pizza, pasta, rice and curry, seafood) and a small wine list. A seafood basket special is Rs 600.

Blue Eyes Inn *(☎ 074 380445; Galle-Matara Rd)*, near the Banana Garden, produces good food in its spotless and efficient restaurant. It does pasta from Rs 190, garlic prawns for Rs 250, and the intriguingly named Buddhist's pasta food for Rs 150.

The Dream House *(mains Rs 200-950)* is a good place for Italian coffee and food. The cappuccinos cost Rs 100. There's a pleasant veranda where you can sit and relax.

Entertainment

Unawatuna has something approaching a nightlife. There's a DJ and disco at **Happy Banana** on Friday nights and **King Fisher's Restaurant** on Saturday nights.

Getting There & Away

You'll hardly notice Unawatuna from the main coastal road, so make sure you don't miss the stop if you're coming by bus. The town is only 10 or 15 minutes east from Galle – take any bus heading that way (Rs 5). From Colombo, a Matara-bound bus is the best bet. Leaving Unawatuna, the easiest place to get a bus to stop is near the few shops along Galle-Matara Rd, north of the Wella Dewala Rd junction. A taxi from Unawatuna to Bandaranaike International Airport costs Rs 2800 to 3000 and a three-wheeler to Galle costs about Rs 100 (happy negotiating!).

UNAWATUNA TO WELIGAMA

☎ 091

Beyond Unawatuna the road runs close to the coast for most of the 23km to Weligama and beyond. There are numerous beautiful stretches of beach and picturesque coves in this area, as well as a number of attractive, secluded places to stay.

Along this part of the coast you will see stilt fishermen if the tides are running right (often around 6am to 8.30am and 4pm to 6pm). Each fisherman has a pole firmly embedded in the sea bottom, close to the shore. When the sea and fish are flowing in the right direction, the fishermen perch on their poles and cast their lines. Stilt positions are passed down from father to son and are highly coveted. The fishermen expect payment if you photograph them.

Things to See & Do

Just before Koggala there's a **WWII airstrip**. Beside the airstrip a small road turns inland, past the **Free Trade Zone**. The large **Koggala Lake**, next to the road, is alive with birdlife and dotted with islands. It also provides many prawns (you've probably just eaten some). You can take a **catamaran** ride on the lake for Rs 300 per person per hour. One island features a cinnamon plantation and another has a Buddhist temple, which attracts many visitors on *poya* (full moon) days.

A visit to **Ananda spice garden** *(☎ 228 3805; e spicegarden@sltnet.lk; open 7am-7pm daily)* will help you cure your bad breath or sunburn, or perhaps you'd like to taste the herbal wine. All items have marked prices. Both the catamaran and spice garden are managed by the same people. The return trip (including waiting time) by three-wheeler from Unawatuna to the spice garden should cost Rs 400.

Near Hotel Horizon, a little inland from the road and railway line (a sign will direct you), the **Martin Wickramasinghe Folk Art Museum** *(admission Rs 15; open 9am-5pm daily)* is in beautiful gardens. It includes the house where this respected Sinhalese author was born. The exhibits are interesting and well displayed, with information in English and Sinhala. Among them is a good section on dance (costumes and instruments), puppets, *kolam* masks, kitchen utensils and carriages (including one to be pulled by an elephant). All the other houses in this area were demolished in WWII to make way for an airbase, but this important house was left alone.

Just east of Koggala, the **Kataluwa Purwarama temple**, which dates from the 13th century, has some recently restored murals and the feeling of a once-significant temple that time has forgotten. The turn-off is in Kataluwa – you'll see the signs on the inland side of the road. Continue a couple of kilometres inland and ask for directions. A friendly monk will open the building and explain the murals if you ask. The statues are encased in glass and there are glass arches over the doorways leading into a central hall. Some of the Jataka tales (episodes from the Buddha's lives) scenes painted here are said to be 200 years old. Look for the cameo-style paintings of Queen Victoria and the Queen Mother, apparently included because of Queen Victoria's role in ensuring the free practice of Buddhism outlined in the Kandyan agreement.

Along this stretch of coast, **Ahangama** and **Midigama** are popular surfing and swimming spots, and **Dalawella**, which has a thin, clean beach with a naturally protected swimming area nearby, is within a short three-wheeler ride of Unawatuna's action.

Places to Stay & Eat

Dalawella Just east of the 124km post, **Shanthi Guest House** *(☎/fax 074 380031; ⓔ mohan1@itmin.com; rooms Rs 500-900)* has six cabanas and six rooms close to the sea. Some are spotless, others are less so, but there's a garden and stilt fishermen on your doorstep, and Internet access.

Sri Gemunu Guest House *(☎ 074 385022; ⓔ susi@sltnet.lk; rooms Rs 1050-1320, with air-con & hot water 1650)*, two doors east of the Shanthi, has 21 rooms in new and old buildings, a pleasant garden and sea frontage. A family apartment (Rs 1760) has a kitchen and two rooms.

Wijaya Beach Cottage *(☎ 228 3610; ⓔ lizinsrilanka@yahoo.co.uk; doubles with breakfast Rs 1400-1600)*, a few hundred metres on from the Sri Gemunu, has pleasant rooms and cabanas. There's a sandy palm-treed garden, a terrace to chill out on, and friendly hosts.

Ahangama Just after the 137km post, **Villa Gaetano** *(☎ 228 3968; ⓔ vgaetano@sltnet.lk; per person with breakfast US$10)* is right on the beach. The rooms are large and the four rooms upstairs at the front have balconies and views. Internet access is available.

Surfers Dream *(singles/doubles Rs 275/450)* is a good budget option run by the owners of Villa Gaetano. The small house is signposted off the road before Midigama.

Hotel Club Lanka *(☎ 228 3296, fax 228 3361; singles/doubles with breakfast Rs 998/1651)*, on the beach, has clean, comfy rooms with hot water; rooms with air-con are being planned. The rooms have simple but stylish furnishings and most have sea views. There's a pool and grassy gardens, and stilt fishermen in front.

Ahangama Easy Beach *(☎ 228 2028; ⓔ easyb@sltnet.lk; singles/doubles with breakfast Rs 1300/1500)* is a Norwegian-run place close to a couple of surfing points. It has bright and beachy bathrooms, direct sea views, Italian coffee and a menu with a difference (croissants, tortilla, lasagne). You can rent snorkelling gear for Rs 50 per day, a boogie board for Rs 75 per day, or a surfboard for Rs 200 per day.

Midigama Right beside the train tracks near Midigama train station, **Subodanee** *(☎/fax 228 3383; rooms with shared bathroom Rs 200-450)* has 13 rooms, all with shared bathroom, in a big ramshackle house. There are 10 new rooms with private bathrooms on the way. It's a messy, colourful, family-run hang-out – it'll frighten some and charm others. Surfboard rental costs Rs 150 to 250 per day.

Hot Tuna *(☎ 228 3411; rooms Rs 300, with bathroom Rs 350)* is a friendly family home with slightly dark but reasonable rooms. There's a pleasant front sitting area.

Hiltens Beach Resort *(☎ 041-225 0156; ⓔ surfcity@itmin.com; singles Rs 300, with bathroom Rs 650)*, at the 139km post on the seaward side of the main road, is neither a 'resort' nor a 'Hilten', but it is near the beach. The rooms are small, but it has a plum position overlooking the point.

At the 140km post, **Villa Samsara** *(☎/fax 225 1144; singles/doubles half board €53/77)* is a country house built in colonial style. Austrian-owned, it has four spotless rooms with hot water, all furnished in English/Dutch colonial style. There's a large tranquil sitting area, and a palm-studded lawn that fronts onto the beach.

Getting There & Away

There are frequent buses along the southern coastal road connecting Koggala, Dalawella, Ahangama and Midigama with other places along the coast between Galle and Matara and other points. The bus from Galle costs Rs 10 to Midigama. The main train stations are at Talpe and Ahangama, where some trains from Colombo stop. Only a few local trains stop at smaller stations such as Midigama.

WELIGAMA

☎ 041

About 30km east of Galle, the town of Weligama (which means 'sandy village') has a fine sandy sweep of bay – just as its name might suggest. It's a busy fishing town, and as there are not many things to do, it's not a popular haunt for travellers.

Very close to the shore, so close in fact that you could walk out to it at low tide, is a tiny island known as **Taprobane**. It looks like an ideal artist's or writer's retreat, which indeed it once was: novelist Paul Bowles wrote *The Spider's House* here in the 1950s. Even better, it was once owned by the French Count de Maunay. It's possible to rent the whole house (e eden@sri.lanka.net) but it doesn't come cheap.

Orientation & Information

The main road divides to go through Weligama, with one branch running along the coast, and the other running parallel through the town centre, a short distance inland. The **bus station** and **Bank of Ceylon** are in the middle of town. To reach the centre from the coast road, turn inland 500m east of Taprobane.

Things to See & Do

Scenic though the bay is, Weligama beach is close to the main road and none too clean near the town centre. It's primarily a fishing village and **catamarans** line the west end of the bay. You can organise an hour-long ride in one – expect to pay Rs 1500 per catamaran – by approaching a fisherman along the beach. Fishermen will also take you out in a 3.3m motorised boat to the deep sea to see sharks and dolphins. This will cost Rs 4000 per person for the four-hour trip.

Snorkelling at Weligama is good, or you can scuba dive. **Bavarian Divers** *(☎ 225 2708; w www.cbg.de/bavariandivers)*, near Bay Beach Hotel, runs PADI courses as well as excursions such as wreck dives. A PADI open-water course costs US$295 and a single dive costs US$30.

Turning inland off the inland road west of the centre takes you over the railway line to **Kustaraja**, a large rock-carved figure in a peaceful, small park. The statue, said to date from the 8th century, has been described as a king who was mysteriously cured of leprosy, or as Avalokitesvara. Further along the road, turning right at the small shop, there's a temple with a large modern standing Buddha.

Weligama is famous for its **lacework** and stalls are located on the main road along the coast. You can spend anything from Rs 100 for a small lace doily and Rs 500 for a cotton nightdress, to Rs 5000 for a large, finely worked tablecloth.

Places to Stay & Eat

The following places are listed from the western end of town.

Bay Beach Hotel *(☎/fax 225 0201; e has hani@sltnet.lk; singles/doubles US$15/25)*, on the Galle end of the bay, has rooms with air-con, an attractive swimming pool and extensive gardens. The standard rooms are plain, but you could always share the company of government ministers and opt for the penthouse – lots of brass, batik, a bathtub, balcony and 180-degree views for US$100.

Weligama Bay Inn *(☎ 225 0299; e chc@sltnet.lk; 247 New Matara Rd; rooms with breakfast US$25)* is an attractive place near Taprobane island. It has a wide veranda and pleasant green gardens, and rooms have a private balcony with views across the beach.

Samaru Beach House *(☎ 225 1417; 544 New Matara Rd; rooms Rs 550-750)*, at about the middle of the bay, is a neat place close to the beach. The rooms inside the house are cheaper, and the Rs 750 rooms have a veranda. There are exercise bars in the sandy front garden so you can work on your pecs.

Crystal Villa *(☎ 225 0635; e crystal@lanka.ccom.lk; Matara Rd; rooms/bungalows half board US$45/50)* is a modern airy place facing the sea. It has four rooms (three with air-con) and two bungalows (without air-con) and boasts a swimming pool as well.

Raja's Guesthouse *(☎ 0777 960656; Matara Rd; singles/doubles Rs 350/450)* has four rooms, each with a small terrace, right on the beach towards the Mirissa end of town. The rooms are basic, but you can't beat the location.

Jaga Bay Resort *(☎/fax 225 0033; Matara Rd; singles/doubles Rs 550/650, with hot water Rs 750/850)*, some 2.5km on the main road before Mirissa, is a very pleasant spot on the seaward side of the road. The open restaurant has excellent views, as do some of the rooms.

Keerthi's Seafood Restaurant *(☎ 225 1172)* is on a side road near Bay Beach Hotel. It's a small, simple hut beside the owner's house. Keerthi is a seafood supplier, so you know the catch will be fresh – the food is also tasty and reasonably priced at Rs 210 for rice and fish, Rs 220 for calamari and Rs 160 for 100g of lobster.

Getting There & Away

Weligama is on the Colombo–Matara train line. The journey from Colombo takes three to 3½ hours. There are also frequent buses in both directions along the coast. Fares include: to Galle Rs 14, Mirissa Rs 6 and Matara Rs 10.50.

MIRISSA

☎ 041

Sleepy Mirissa, 4km southeast of Weligama on the Matara road, has a headland dividing its small fishing harbour from its beautiful curve of sandy beach with calm, clear waters. It's a low-key, peaceful spot that was once the preserve of budget travellers, but now has a couple of more upmarket places to stay. Mirissa is becoming very popular as travellers seek out quieter alternatives to Unawatuna and Hikkaduwa.

Orientation & Information

Most of the places to stay are on the beach. You'll need to go to Matara to change money or use a post office. You can make phone calls from some guesthouses, and some have Internet access.

Things to See & Do

The water is utterly clear and perfect for **snorkelling**. The best stretch is at the Galle (western) end of the bay along the rocky coastline. Ask your guesthouse if they have gear to lend. The rocky outcrop to the east of the bay, Parrot Rock, is the perfect place to watch the sunset, and it's also a popular fishing spot. Snorkellers also see plenty of fish on the west side, and flat-bottom coral and sometimes sea turtles on the south side. **Surfing** is good in the western end of the bay. Water Creatures Beach Restaurant hires surf boards.

There are pleasant **walks** around Mirissa. One heads up a steep series of steps from the main road to the small **Kandavahari temple**. The headland is a good spot to view Weligama Bay. About 6km inland, there's a **snake farm** with an Ayurvedic practitioner. Ask your guesthouse how to get there.

Some guesthouses organise **boat trips** on the lake about 2km inland.

Places to Stay & Eat

Places to stay are listed in order from west (the end closest to Weligama) to east. Meals are available at all of these places.

Calm Rest *(☎/fax 225 2546; Suranda Rd; rooms Rs 500, cabanas Rs 1200)* is exactly what it's named. Four good-quality cabanas (no fan) and three rooms are set in a peaceful leafy garden about 300m from the beach.

Paradise Beach Club *(☎/fax 225 0380; e mirissa@sltnet.lk; singles/doubles half board Rs 1705/2200, with air-con Rs 2035/2530)* is Mirissa's most upmarket hotel. It's a resort-style place with 40 bungalows in landscaped gardens. There's a pool (nonguests pay Rs 100) and a busy beachfront restaurant (mains cost around Rs 330 and the Rs 140 breakfast buffet is good value). Apartment-style family rooms are available.

Sun Shine Beach Inn *(☎ 225 2282; rooms Rs 400)* is a superclean, neat and sunny place run by a friendly family and their three smiling sisters. The rooms stretch down to the beach and there's a garden restaurant.

Ocean Moon *(☎ 225 2328; rooms Rs 440, cabanas Rs 990)* has cabanas with verandas set on a lawn fronting onto the beach. The rooms are inside the family home.

Mirissa Beach Inn *(☎ 225 0410; e beachinn@sltnet.lk; bungalows Rs 450-650, rooms Rs 750-850)* has bungalows close to the beach, and a three-storey building – you can just about pick the coconuts from the balcony. The newer upstairs rooms are fresher.

Amarasinghe's *(☎ 225 1204; e chana7@sltnet.lk; rooms Rs 250, singles/doubles with bathroom Rs 300/500)* is not on the beach, but is in a pleasant, lush spot away from the guesthouse hub. It's signposted from the main road. Amarasinghe will be a familiar name to those who have enjoyed the hospitality of the manager's brother in Haputale. There are six basic rooms: two with bathroom and four with shared bathroom. A three-wheeler from the main road costs Rs 30 to 40. Internet access is available, and there's bird-watching on the reservoir, a couple of kilometres away.

Mount Garden *(☎ 225 1079; standard singles/doubles Rs 250/400, guestrooms Rs 500/ 600)* is signposted on an inland road near the eastern end of Mirissa. It's a super-friendly family home, set back from the beach. If it's full, the family has another place nearby with four rooms at the same price.

Giragala Village *(☎ 225 0496; e nissanka.g@lycosmail.com; rooms Rs 450-880)*, almost opposite the road heading to Mount Garden, is an unpretentious place on a stunning spot that fronts onto Parrot Rock. There's a huge, palm-treed lawn with hammocks, good food and, to top it all off, well-priced rooms. If you're staying you can use the free snorkelling gear. The guesthouse has excellent information about where to swim and snorkel.

Getting There & Away

The bus fare from Weligama is Rs 6; a three-wheeler costs Rs 150. The fare to Matara is Rs 30 in an air-con bus or Rs 8 in a CTB bus; a three-wheeler costs Rs 300. If you're heading to Colombo, it's better to catch a bus to Matara and change as many buses will be full by the time they pass through Mirissa.

MATARA

☎ 041 • pop 42,800

Matara, 160km from Colombo, is at the end of the southern railway line. It's a busy, sprawling mass set beside a grubby, long beach. The main attractions are the ramparts and well-preserved Dutch fort, and the beachside suburb of Polhena, 3km towards Colombo. Polhena has a good coral reef that you can snorkel to, and there's a surfing point. However, it's not really the place for a long beach holiday.

The **post office** is in the old part of town, to the south of the Nilwala Ganga. There is a clutch of banks with ATMs just north of Uyanwatta Stadium. **Mighty Vision Computer Systems** *(171 Anagarika Dharmapala Mawatha)* and **Trans Technologies** *(Kumarathunga Mawatha)* have Internet facilities. There's a **Vijitha Yapa bookshop** at the eastern end of Anagarika Dharmapala Mawatha. At the time of research, the Deshanee Shopping Complex was going up on New Tangalla Rd. This will host a supermarket, cinema, restaurants and shops.

Swimming in the Nilwala Ganga is not recommended; crocodiles have taken children here.

If you're interested in batik, drop into **Jez Look Batiks** *(12 St Yehiya Mawatha)*, where you could even take some lessons, or **Art Batiks** *(58/6 Udyana Rd)*.

Star Fort & Dutch Rampart

The **Dutch rampart** occupies the promontory separating the Nilwala Ganga from the sea. Built in the 18th century to protect the Dutch East India Company's administrative buildings, the area inside the rampart is a quiet and picturesque part of old Matara. Its structure is a little peculiar, as it was to be a fort but cost cutting at the time dictated otherwise.

The **Star Fort** *(open 8am-5pm daily)*, about 350m from the main rampart gate, across the river, was built by the Dutch to compensate for deficiencies in the fortification built on the other side of the river. The date of construction (1765) is embossed over the main gate along with the VOC company insignia and the coat of arms of the governor of the day. If you look carefully, you can see the slots that once secured the drawbridge beams.

The fort, built for 12 large cannons, is surrounded by a mosquito-infested moat. Inside there's a model replica of the site, a well, and what remains of the original quarters. There are also two eerie prisoners' quarters. A guide will show you around the fort, for a tip. The Star Fort fulfilled its purpose as an administrative building, and was never attacked. It was the last major defensive construction by the VOC in Sri Lanka.

Places to Stay

Matara Matara has quite a few places to stay, but just a minority are passable.

Blue Ripples *(☎ 222 2058; 38 Wilfred Gunasekera Mawatha; singles/doubles Rs 355/450)* is a peaceful place in a shady, riverside garden. Two rooms with cute balconies are set right by the river; another two are a little way back.

River Inn *(☎ 222 2215; 96/1 Wilfred Gunasekera Mawatha; singles/doubles from Rs 440/605)* has neat rooms in its three-storey building on the river. Rooms upstairs have river views.

Browns Beach Resort *(☎ 222 6298; Sea Beach Rd; single Rs 600, singles/doubles with air-con Rs 720/1440)* is on a bleak stretch of Sea Beach Rd and an uninviting stretch of beach, but it's one of the few places with air-con and the rooms are OK.

The **Rest House** *(☎/fax 222 2299; singles/doubles in old wing US$13.20/16.50, in new wing US$16.50/19.80)*, about 200m from the bus station, is beautifully situated right by the beach. It's said to be built on a site where captured elephants were corralled. The older rooms are a bit worn, but there's a large garden and a decent restaurant.

Polhena Many travellers stay in Polhena, about 3km southwest of the centre. Meals are available at these places to stay.

Sabine *(☎ 222 7951; Beach Rd; rooms Rs 300)*, in a prime spot on the beach, is a small house with four rooms. It's rough around the edges, but is friendly and cheap. There's a small garden, hammocks and

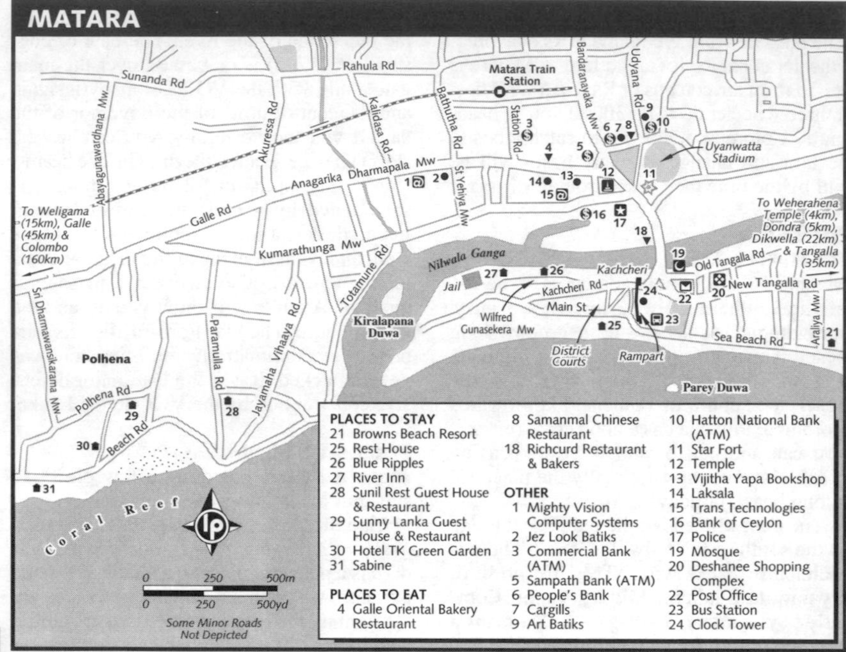

cheap eats. This is a good place to organise low-budget camping and other tours.

Hotel TK Green Garden *(☎ 222 2603; 116/1 Beach Rd; singles/doubles from 350/400)* has neat and tidy rooms and a large grassed garden. There are rooms upstairs (with balconies) and downstairs; the prices vary slightly.

Sunny Lanka Guest House & Restaurant *(☎ 222 3504; 93 Polhena Rd; singles/doubles Rs 350/440)* has five rooms. This is a friendly, relaxed and clean place, and it has good food too. You can rent scuba and snorkelling gear, as well as bicycles (Rs 100 per day).

Sunil Rest Guest House & Restaurant *(☎ 222 1983; 16/3A 2nd Cross Rd; singles Rs 250, doubles Rs 300-600)* has three basic rooms in one house and four newer rooms in another house nearby. There's a kitchen, and Sunil hires out motorbikes (Rs 500 per day) and snorkelling gear (Rs 250 per day). Guests can use his bicycles for free. If you're travelling by three-wheeler, make sure you're taken to Sunil's; many drivers like to take you where they get a tip from the guesthouse.

Places to Eat

The **Rest House** *(meals Rs 250)* has a pleasant setting and serves a range of decent meals. The rice-and-curry buffet lunch with dessert costs Rs 250.

Richcurd Restaurant & Bakers *(1 Anagarika Dharmapala Mawatha; mains Rs 30-50)*, just north of the bridge, is worth a try for cheap rice-and-fish curry (Rs 35) at lunch time. Some well-stocked **fruit stalls** can be found nearby.

Galle Oriental Bakery Restaurant *(41 Anagarika Dharmapala Mawatha; mains from Rs 65)* does rice-and-vegie curry for Rs 65 (lunch time only) as well as cakes and tasty short eats. It's a popular place to eat.

Samanmal Chinese Restaurant *(64 Udyana Rd; mains Rs 135-250)*, next to Cargills supermarket, is a dark den but serves good food that is accompanied with boppy music. Try the sweet-and-sour fish (Rs 140) or fried prawns with salad (Rs 225), or just sip a beer (Rs 85).

Getting There & Away

Buses travel to/from Colombo and intermediate coastal points about every 15 minutes from 4.30am to 8pm. Colombo is a 3½- to four-hour trip (Rs 57) and there's also an air-con intercity bus (Rs 120) every 45 minutes, 24 hours. The 1½-hour trip east to Tangalla costs Rs 15, and it's Rs 17.50 to Galle. There are direct buses to Ratnapura (Rs 75, 4½ hours) and an air-con bus to Badulla (Rs 140, 5½ hours). If you miss the direct ones you can get to Wellawaya and take a connection if you don't leave it too late in the afternoon. Heading east, there is an unreliable service to Pottuvil (for Arugam Bay), and three buses daily to Ampara (Rs 120, eight hours).

Trains from Matara head to Colombo at 5.40am, 7.25am, 9.10am, 1.15pm and 4.50pm (Rs 33/89/155 in 3rd/2nd/1st class). The express train to Vavuniya (for Anuradhapura) leaves at 9.10am. The 1.15pm train to Kandy costs Rs 57/157 in 3rd/2nd class and takes seven hours.

Getting Around

Polhena is a short ride by bus from Matara bus station (check that it will drop you off), but no buses go right to the beach. Get off at the junction of Galle and Sri Dharmawansikarama Rds and walk a kilometre or so to the beach. To reach the beach with the reef, turn left at the T-junction 500m south of the main road, then right at the next junction.

A three-wheeler from the Matara train or bus station to Polhena costs about Rs 100.

MATARA TO TANGALLA

At Meddawatte, on the main road a few kilometres east of Matara, is the impressive Ruhuna University campus. There are several other places of interest just off the 35km of road from Matara to Tangalla, including two superb examples of what one visitor labelled 'neo-Buddhist kitsch'.

Weherahena Temple

Just as you leave the outskirts of Matara, a turn inland will take you to the gaudy Weherahena Temple *(admission by donation)*, where an artificial cave is decorated with about 200 comic-book-like scenes from the Buddha's life. There's also a huge Buddha statue. You can get here from Matara on bus No 349, or a three-wheeler will charge Rs 200 from Matara's bus station.

At the time of the late November/early December *poya*, a *perahera* (procession) is held at the temple to celebrate the anniversary of its founding. During the evening there's a big procession of dancers and elephants. Foreigners at the 2002 *perahera* were charged Rs 1000 for tickets.

Dondra

About 5km southeast of Matara you come to the town of Dondra. Travel south from here for 1.2km and you'll reach the lighthouse at the southernmost point of Sri Lanka. The nearby **Lighthouse View Resort** *(Hammana Rd; mains Rs 100-300)* is exquisitely sited (it's signposted about 250m from the lighthouse itself). At the time of research there were plans to build a luxury resort with a water-sports and entertainment centre and a floating restaurant on this site, and to open the lighthouse to the public.

A CTB bus from Matara will drop you in the centre of Dondra. From there you can three-wheel it or walk to the lighthouse.

Wewurukannala Vihara

If the Weherahena Temple is 'Marvel Comics meets Lord Buddha', then here it's Walt Disney who runs into him. At the town of Dikwella, 22km from Matara, a road turns inland towards Beliatta. About 1.5km along you come to a 50m-high seated Buddha figure – the largest in Sri Lanka.

The temple *(admission Rs 25, camera/video Rs 50/100)* has three parts. The oldest is about 250 years old but is of no particular interest. The next part, a real hall of horrors, has life-size models of demons and sinners shown in graphic, gory detail. Punishments for those who've strayed from the path include being dunked in boiling cauldrons, sawn in half, disembowelled and so on. Finally there's the gigantic seated figure that was constructed in the 1960s. As if to prove that it really is as high as an eight-storey building, what should be right behind it but an eight-storey building? You can climb up inside and peer right into the Buddha's head. The walls of the backing building have been painted with hundreds of scenes of events in the Buddha's lives. There's one other thing to see: an interesting clock in the adjoining building, made by a prisoner about 70 years ago.

Pujas (offerings or prayers) are held every morning and evening.

Mawella

About 6km northeast of Dikwella, near the 186km post, a road heads off for 1km to the (sometimes) spectacular **Ho-o-maniya blowhole**. During the southwest monsoon (June is the best time) high seas can force water 23m up through a natural chimney in the rocks and then spout out up to 18m in the air. At other times the blowhole is disappointing.

Places to Stay & Eat

Manahara Beach Cottage & Cabanas *(☎/fax 047-224 0585; singles/doubles half-board Rs 1500/2200)*, near the 189km post and about 6km west of Tangalla, has six clean, comfortable and roomy cabanas, and three good rooms. There's a large leafy garden, a pool and beach frontage. It's a quiet spot.

Dickwella Village Resort *(☎ 041-225 5271-2; ⓔ dickwella@mail.ewisl.net; singles/doubles half board €40/55)* is a spectacularly sited Italian-built place on a headland on the Matara side of Dikwella. The comfortable rooms with air-con have terraces and stunning sea views, and there is a host of sporting activities available.

Claughton *(☎ 041-225 5087; singles/doubles half board US$99/110, house full board US$390)*, 11km west of Tangalla off the main road (look for the Nilwella sign), is for those who are looking for something special. This beautiful villa has a distinctly Mediterranean flavour. The garden runs down to a secluded beach and there's a fine swimming pool. The house can be rented by the room (one double and two twin-bed rooms, all with their own bathrooms) or in its entirety (up to six people, full board).

Eva Lanka *(☎/fax 047-224 0940-1; ⓔ eva.lanka@mail.ewisl.net; single/double chalets half board US$80/100)*, on the Matara side of Tangalla, is the closest really upmarket resort to Tangalla. The Italian-owned hotel has stylish rooms and chalets in a beautiful setting on the beach. There are three swimming pools throughout the lush garden, a water slide, sports, games and a restaurant, including a pizzeria. Each room has a shell mosaic made by the owner's grandmother. The entire hotel is wheelchair-friendly.

TANGALLA

☎ 047

Situated 195km from Colombo, Tangalla (also spelt Tangalle but usually pronounced ten-gol) is one of the nicest spots along the coast, particularly if you just want somewhere to laze and soak up the sun. The town itself is an easy-going place with some reminders of Dutch days, including the Rest House, which was once home for the Dutch administrators. It's one of the oldest resthouses in the country, originally built, as a plate on the front steps indicates, by the Dutch in 1774.

From the Rest House the long white sands of Medaketiya Beach shimmer away into the distance, while to the west is a whole series of smaller bays. But beware: some of the beaches, including Medaketiya, shelve off very steeply, and the resulting waves make them dangerous for swimmers if there's any sort of wind or tidal current.

The bay, just on the town side of the Tangalla Bay Hotel, is probably the most sheltered spot, although right beside the Rest House is a tiny bay with a roped-off swimming area that is shallow and generally calm. There are some basic changing rooms on the grassed area, and it's popular with snorkellers. By the Palm Paradise Cabanas, near the village of Goyambokka, is a picturesque and fairly secluded bay. A natural swimming pool past Nature Resort, northeast of Tangalla, is safe most of the time.

Information

The **Hatton National Bank** *(Main Rd)* and **Bank of Ceylon** *(9 Hambantota Rd)* have ATMs. There is an agency **post office** opposite the main bus station. The **main post office** is west of the Rest House. You can use the Internet at **Sawsiri Communications** *(138 Main Rd)* and **Samagi Communication** *(6 Medaketiya Rd)*.

Things to See & Do

Scuba diving can be arranged at **Let's Dive** *(☎ 0777 902073, fax 047-224 0401)*, 1.5km along the beach road, northeast of the centre of town. Trips include two dives (US$50). PADI courses cost US$325 for open-water beginner and US$210 for advanced. The dive sites are at reefs inhabited by coral fish, angel fish, puffer fish, stingrays and reef sharks. There is a 150-year-old steamer wreck and a 40m-long cargo ship that's been lying here for 20 years.

Turtle-watching at Rekawa (see the boxed text 'Turtle Watch' later in this chapter) is a

THE SOUTH

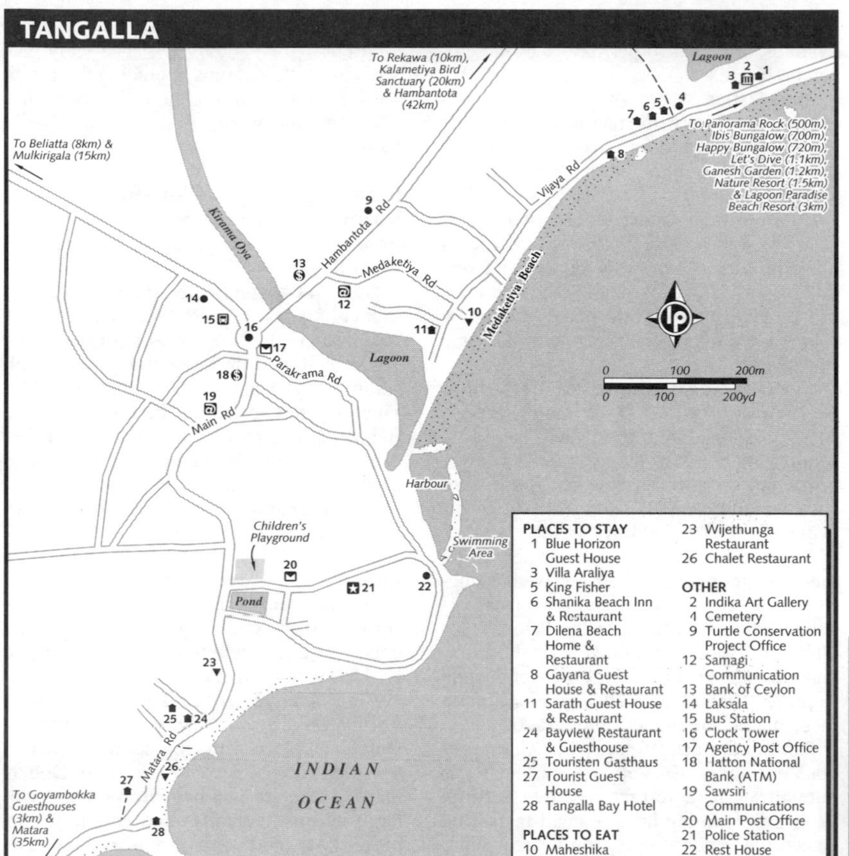

highlight of many travellers' visit to Tangalla. It's possible to go **bird-watching** at Kalamatiya Bird Sanctuary, but there's no structured programme at this stage.

Places to Stay

Most accommodation is in small, relaxed guesthouses with just a few simple rooms, typically with bathroom, fan and mosquito net, but no hot water. These are mostly concentrated around the area northeast of the centre, close to the town. The area further on has some laid-back, more mid-range accommodation.

Places to Stay – Budget

Northeast of the Centre If you head northeast from the bus station over the bridge, then take the first road on the right, you'll find yourself travelling towards Medaketiya, the long beach stretching about 3km northeast of Tangalla's town centre. Several guesthouses dot the beachfront track. Unless stated otherwise, these places have shared bathrooms.

Shanika Beach Inn & Restaurant *(☎ 224 2079; singles/doubles Rs 200/350)* has six straightforward rooms. They're OK value for money.

Sarath Guest House & Restaurant *(☎ 224 2630; singles/doubles Rs 250/500)* is a lively family home with clean and neat rooms, and Italian espresso.

Dilena Beach Home & Restaurant *(☎ 224 2240; rooms Rs 350, cabana Rs 900)* is a family home with a light and airy sitting area as well as good rooms. Snorkelling gear is available for Rs 150 per day, and bicycles can be hired.

King Fisher *(☎ 224 2472; rooms Rs 500)* is a colourful German-run place close to the beach. Its four rooms are neat and the indoor/outdoor dining room has beautiful sea vistas.

Blue Horizon Guest House *(☎/fax 224 0721; rooms Rs 500-1000)* has two rooms upstairs with sea-view balconies and one downstairs. If you like views and value for money, you'll love this place. Two new rooms were under construction at the time of research.

Gayana Guest House & Restaurant *(☎ 224 0659, fax 224 0477; rooms Rs 550-1100)*, set back from the beach, has some rooms with beach frontage as well as newer upstairs rooms with a balcony. Rooms are spotless and simple. Guests can hire bicycles for Rs 250 per day.

If you follow the beach further along there are more places; all are wedged between the beach and the lagoon (you can organise catamaran trips on the lagoon). An alternative route to this area is via the Hambantota road – places to stay are signposted. A three-wheeler from the bus station to these places should cost about Rs 60.

Panorama Rock *(☎/fax 224 0458; singles/doubles from Rs 500/750)*, on the beach, has bungalows in a terraced garden setting. With a welcoming host, a small restaurant beside the beach, the lagoon nearby and a library, you won't want to leave.

Happy Bungalow *(☎ 0777 905480, fax 047-224 0401; rooms Rs 600)* has bungalows (no fan) on the beach.

Ibis Bungalow *(☎ 0777 905480, fax 047-224 0401; rooms Rs 800)*, next to Happy Bungalow, has three roomy, spotless cabanas spread throughout a large garden. There's a small pond and the hosts are very welcoming.

South of the Centre With excellent views over the bay, **Bayview Restaurant & Guesthouse** *(☎ 224 2431; 230 Matara Rd; singles/ doubles Rs 350/700)* has two new rooms and a cabana (Rs 400). The young Sri Lankan owner has worked in Germany and this could become a happening place.

Further along, **Touristen Gasthaus** *(☎/fax 224 0370; ⓔ tourist@sltnet.lk; 19 Pallikkudawa Rd; singles/doubles Rs 500/550, doubles/triples upstairs Rs 650/750)* has a leafy garden and spotless rooms, including three with sea-facing balconies. One of the rooms has a kitchen and would make a good family room.

Places to Stay – Mid-Range

Northeast of the Centre A three-wheeler from town to this group of places costs about Rs 60.

Ganesh Garden *(☎ 224 2529; ⓔ magnet@mail.evisl.net; rooms Rs 800, bungalows Rs 1000)* has eight bungalows with their own verandas dotted throughout a garden (with hammocks). A family room costs Rs 1440. There's a hut restaurant beside the beach. Board games, regular barbecues, and free snorkelling and surfing gear for guests will keep you entertained.

Lagoon Paradise Beach Resort *(☎ 224 2509, fax 224 0401; singles/doubles Rs 800/1200)*, 3km from town on the lagoon, has spacious resort-style rooms with verandas front and back. The hotel ferries guests across to a swimming spot. There's an open-air disco from 9pm on Saturdays (men Rs 250, women free).

Villa Araliya *(☎/fax 224 2163; rooms Rs 990, bungalows Rs 1500)* is a gorgeous, Dutch-run place with colonial furniture and a garden (complete with a friendly Doberman). There are two bungalows, each with large inviting verandas and enticing four-poster beds, and some rooms in the house. The food is delicious, but is only for guests. Book ahead.

Nature Resort *(☎/fax 224 0844; doubles/triples US$40/46)* has smart and spotless bungalows, a billiards table and a pool (nonguests pay Rs 150). It's a relaxed place with a garden and a quiet location on the, beachfront.

South of the Centre Opposite the big Tangalla Bay Hotel, **Tourist Guest House** *(☎ 224 0389, 224 2269; Matara Rd; rooms from Rs 440, singles/doubles with air-con & hot water Rs 1430/1650)* has stylish, modern and clean rooms, hot water and some sea-facing balconies. You can hire bicycles for Rs 150 a day. The owners will pick you up for free from the bus station if you telephone, or you can catch a three-wheeler (Rs 50).

Tangalla Bay Hotel *(☎ 224 0683, fax 224 0346; singles/doubles US$26/28, with air-con US$31/33)* is a 1970s monstrosity built to look like a boat. It's kitsch and dated in an endearing kind of way (look for the loo flusher in the porthole). It certainly has a great location right on a promontory, the service is attentive and there is a swimming pool (nonguests Rs 100). The beach on the Matara side of the hotel has very dangerous currents; stick to the other side.

If you continue for 3km along the Matara road, you'll come to a signposted turn-off at Goyambokka, and a road lined with a few guesthouses, most with cabanas. This is a quiet, leafy area with a clean secluded beach. You can catch any Matara-bound bus to drop you at the turn-off. A three-wheeler from Tangalla bus station costs Rs 100.

Calm Garden Cabanas *(☎ 224 0523; singles/doubles with breakfast Rs 700/1000)* is about 200m up the track from the turn-off. It's a family-run affair, back from the beach, and there's a large lawn garden.

Palm Paradise Cabanas *(☎/fax 224 0338; ⓔ ppcabana@sltnet.lk; singles/doubles half board US$26/34)*, near Calm Garden Cabanas, has large, homely wooden cabanas (no fan or net) scattered around a secluded beachside palm grove. All have their own sitting area and breezy veranda. The beach here is safe for swimming. There's an open-air bar selling imported wines, and a good restaurant. Bicycles can be rented here for Rs 200 per day.

Goyambokka Guest House *(☎/fax 224 0838; singles/doubles with breakfast Rs 1000/1200)*, further on from Palm Paradise Cabanas, has four small, spotless rooms (with no mosquito nets). It's away from the beach, but there's a pretty garden and a small shared veranda.

Rocky Point Beach Bungalows *(☎ 224 0834; ⓔ rockypointbeach@yahoo.com; singles/doubles Rs 1400/1800, bungalows Rs 1700/2250/2500)* is a popular, relaxed spot with great views. The light rooms and bungalows are in a large garden. There's a restaurant (with board games) overlooking a small beach.

Places to Eat

Maheshika *(mains Rs 175-300)*, a low-key beach hut lit by kerosene lamps, is one of the best seafood places in town. The kitchen is a hut at the back with clay pots on a wood fire. Breakfast starts at Rs 130, a prawn cocktail is Rs 175 and 1kg of lobster is Rs 950. Maheshika's garlic sauce deserves a special mention. It's a small, friendly, family-run place.

Wijethunga Restaurant *(rice & curry Rs 50)* is a local place with good food just near the popular lookout spot on Matara Rd.

Chalet Restaurant *(Matara Rd; mains Rs 175-320)* is a popular tour-group stop with an extensive seafood menu and great views across to the Tangalla Bay Hotel. A lobster cocktail is Rs 275, fish of the day is Rs 320, and there are lots of 'market prices' as well. Check before you order.

Of the places to stay, the restaurants at Panorama Rock and Ganesh Garden, at the far end of the beach, are recommended for their food. The Gayana Guest House & Restaurant does standard dishes for the usual prices.

Shopping

If you want to take home something unique, drawings and paintings by Indika Pathmananda are for sale at **Indika Art Gallery** *(☎ 0777 903253)*. The artist paints in a range of media and styles, from realist landscapes, birds and wildlife, to cubist works. Ink drawings start at Rs 200. There's a **Laksala** *(35 Beliatta Rd)* in town.

Getting There & Away

To get to Galle (Rs 70), catch the intercity express bus bound for Colombo. The express all the way to Colombo costs Rs 140 and leaves about every 30 minutes, between 2.30am and 5.30pm. There are regular buses to Wellawaya (on their way to Bandarawela, Monaragala and Ampara) for Rs 54; an intercity express costs Rs 110. There are regular buses to Matara (Rs 15), Hambantota (Rs 20) and Tissamaharama (Rs 28).

MULKIRIGALA

The rock temple at Mulkirigala *(admission Rs 100)*, about 16km northwest of Tangalla, has a little of Dambulla and Sigiriya about it. Steps lead up to a series of cleft-like caves in the huge rock. As with Dambulla, the caves shelter large reclining Buddhas, together with wall paintings and other smaller sitting and standing figures. You can then continue on your barefoot way to a dagoba perched on

Turtle Watch

It's close to 9.30pm at Rekawa, a small fishing village some 10km east of Tangalla. A few tourists stand on the darkened beach, scanning the ocean. They've come to see five species of marine turtles, familiar but endangered visitors to this part of the coast. Between February and July, the peak nesting season, you have a good chance of seeing turtles making their slow, deliberate journey up the beach. The eggs are later reburied by Department of Wildlife Conservation staff in a different part of the beach where they can hatch safely. As soon as they hatch, the turtles are released to act on their instincts, scuttle to the sea and swim for their lives.

The nightly ritual goes on year-round without interference from poachers or predators, thanks to a local organisation, the **Turtle Conservation Project** *(TCP; ☎ 0777 902915, fax 047-224 0581, e tcpsl@sltnet.lk; 73 Hambantota Rd)*. Turtle watches start at the TCP's Rekawa signposted beach hut at 8pm nightly. Tickets cost Rs 350, children and students pay Rs 250, and Sri Lankans Rs 50. If you don't see a turtle, you don't pay, but donations are welcome.

Set up in 1996, the programme protects marine turtles and provides a source of income to local people (17 people in 2002) who used to gather eggs illegally and sell them as food. TCP trains local people as tourist guides, and runs community education programmes about turtle conservation, mangrove rehabilitation and other environmental issues.

If you have experience in this sort of work, you may apply to volunteer with the TCP. A commitment of at least three months is required.

There are a few guidelines to follow on turtle watch:

- Wear dark clothing. Light-coloured clothing can be seen by turtles and may disturb them.
- As a courtesy to the local people and as protection from chilly evening weather, you should wear long skirts/dresses or trousers – at least something that covers your legs – and tops that cover the shoulders.
- Still or video cameras are not allowed as the bright light disturbs the turtles. If you bring a torch (flashlight), don't use it on the beach.
- Don't go onto the beach without a TCP research officer.

The olive ridley turtle is one of five species of marine turtle found in the seas surrounding Sri Lanka

Rekawa Beach is a 20-minute drive from Tangalla. Take the turn-off at the Netolpitiya Junction (from Hambantota Rd). A return trip from town in a three-wheeler costs Rs 600.

THE SOUTH

top of the rock, where there are fine views over the surrounding country. There is a Buddhist school for young monks nearby.

Pali manuscripts found in the monastic library by a British official in 1826 were used for the first translation of the Mahavamsa, which unlocked Sri Lanka's early history for Europeans.

Mulkirigala can be reached by bus from Tangalla via either Beliatta or Wiraketiya (depending on the departures, it might be quicker to go via Wiraketiya rather than wait for the Beliatta bus). A three-wheeler from Tangalla costs about Rs 400 for a return trip.

HAMBANTOTA

☎ 047 • pop 11,200

Between Tangalla and Hambantota, 237km from Colombo, you move from a wet zone into a dry zone, which continues right across Yala West (Ruhuna) National Park. Hambantota is a bustling town with little going for it, although there are some magnificent sweeps of beach both east and west of the small promontory in the town, and this is the closest major town to Bundala National Park. A large collection of outrigger fishing boats is often beached on the sands.

Hambantota's main claim to fame is as home to Leonard Woolf, the husband of

Virginia Woolf, when he served as government agent in 1908–11. He documented some of his experiences in *A Village in the Jungle*.

Hambantota has a large Malay Muslim community, many of whom speak Malay as well as Tamil and Sinhala. A major industry in Hambantota is the production of salt by the age-old method of evaporating sea water from shallow salt pans. You will see these pans alongside the road on the east side of Hambantota as you turn inland from the coast.

There is a **Bank of Ceylon** almost opposite Hambantota Rest House. The **Hatton National Bank** *(47 Wilmot St)*, about 200m up from the clock tower, has an ATM. **Singhe Communication** *(7 MR Thassim Mawatha)* has Internet access.

Hambantota has a number of touts angling to take travellers to Bundala or Yala West (Ruhuna) National Park, but the most reliable places to organise a trip are places to stay (see the boxed text 'Snagging the Perfect Safari Tout' later in this chapter). However, there's no advantage in going to Yala from Hambantota rather than from Tissamaharama.

Between Hambantota and Tissamaharama there are a number of **roadside stalls** selling delicious curd and honey or treacle.

Places to Stay & Eat

Sunshine Tourist Rest *(☎ 222 0129; 47 Main St; rooms with shared bathroom Rs 400, rooms with bathroom Rs 600-650)*, a five-minute walk from the bus station in the Tissamaharama direction, has two rooms with shared bathroom and six rooms with bathroom. Mrs Nihar, the manager, is an excellent cook. The traffic noise quietens down after about 8pm.

Lake View *(☎ 222 1013; 12 Well Rd; rooms Rs 650)* is more of a long-term lodge for locals, but the rooms (no nets) are OK. It has lake views and verandas. Follow Wilmot St up from the clock tower and veer left onto Well Rd at the mosque.

Hambantota Rest House *(☎/fax 222 0299; rooms from US$24)* is nicely situated on top of the promontory overlooking the town and beach, about 300m south of the bus station. The rooms in the old wing are almost palatial and are definitely the pick of the bunch. Most rooms have pleasant views, and the food is good (rice and curry costs Rs 210).

Oasis Hotel *(☎/fax 222 0650-1; e theoasish@eureka.lk; Sisilasagama; doubles/triples US$48/54)*, about 7km along the main road before you reach Hambantota from Tangalla, is a modern place with a swimming pool, sloping gardens and rooms with air-con. The restaurant serves set breakfast/lunch/dinner menus for Rs 350/500/600.

Peacock Beach Hotel *(☎ 222 0377; e peacock@sltnet.lk; doubles/triples US$50/60)* is on the Tissamaharama side of town, about 600m out of Hambantota. It has rooms with air-con, lush gardens, an open-air bar and terrace, plus a fine swimming pool that nonguests can use for Rs 100 (and where you'll probably see a peacock). Breakfast/lunch/dinner costs Rs 305/480/600.

Getting There & Away

Hambantota is about six hours from Colombo by intercity express bus (Rs 150). To get to Tissamaharama costs Rs 15 (one hour); the 1¼-hour trip to Tangalla costs Rs 20. There are a few buses between Hambantota and Ratnapura via Embilipitiya (about Rs 57, four hours), as well as others heading north to Wellawaya (Rs 23, two hours) and the hill country.

BUNDALA NATIONAL PARK

Bundala *(adult/child US$8.40/4.20, Rs 72 per vehicle, Rs 144 service charge)* is an important wetland sanctuary that's been declared a Ramsar site. It shelters at least 149 species of bird and a small population of elephants (between 25 and 60 depending on the season) within its 62-sq-km area. It's a winter home to the greater flamingo and up to 2000 have been recorded here at any one time. Many other birds journey from Siberia and the Rann of Kutch in India to winter here, arriving between August and April. See the boxed text 'Birds of Sri Lanka' in the Hill Country chapter for more details.

As well as elephants, Bundala provides sanctuary to civets, giant squirrels and crocodiles. Between October and January four of Sri Lanka's five species of marine turtle (olive ridley, green, leatherback and loggerhead) lay their eggs on the coast. Marsh and estuarine crocodiles are also found in Bundala.

Bundala's lagoons, beaches, sand dunes and scrubby jungle stretch nearly 20km along a coastal strip starting just east of

Hambantota. The main road east of Hambantota passes along Bundala's northern boundary. The park is less visited than Yala West (Ruhuna). A four-hour, five-person 4WD trip to Bundala from Hambantota costs Rs 1500 Rs 2000, plus entry fees.

There are two camp sites in the park. For information contact the **Wildlife Department** *(☎ 011-269 4241, fax 269 8556; 18 Gregory's Rd, Cinnamon Gardens, Colombo)*.

TISSAMAHARAMA

☎ 047

Often called Tissa, Tissamaharama is a busy town surrounded by rice paddies that are dotted with ancient temples. Yala West (Ruhuna) National Park is the main reason most visitors come to Tissa, so it's something of a cowboy town with 'safari' touts lurking at guesthouses and bus stops, and everybody else trying to get their cut of the safari business. For some advice on arranging a safari see the boxed text 'Snagging the Perfect Safari Tout' later in this chapter.

Orientation & Information

If you're coming via Hambantota or Wellawaya you'll pass the village of Deberawewa (look for the clock tower), about 2km from Tissa. Ignore the signs announcing 'Tissamaharama' as you enter it and the accommodation touts who board buses and advise travellers to get off because 'this is Tissa'. Tissa itself is the best place to organise a Yala trip. At the time of research, the Tissa bus station had moved to a temporary spot further east on Main Rd while the new bus station was being redeveloped.

Nearly all facilities are on Main Rd. Here there are **banks** with ATMs and an agency **post office**. If you want to make IDD calls or use the Internet try **Sakura Communication** or **Dhammika Printers**.

Tissa Wewa & Dagobas

The tank in Tissa, the Tissa Wewa, is thought to date from the 3rd century BC. The large white restored dagoba between Tissa town centre and the tank is credited to Kavantissa, a king of the ancient southern kingdom of Ruhunu, which was centred on Tissamaharama. Next to the dagoba is a statue of Queen Viharamahadevi. The dagoba has a circumference of 165m and stands 55.8m high. It is thought to have held a sacred tooth relic and forehead bone relic. A small bookshop inside the grounds sells books on Buddhism.

According to legend, Viharamahadevi landed at Kirinda, about 10km south of Tissa, after being sent to sea by her father King Devanampiya Tissa as a penance for his killing of a monk. The daughter landed unharmed and subsequently married Kavantissa. Their son, Dutugemunu, was the Sinhalese hero who, starting from Ruhunu, liberated Anuradhapura from Indian invaders in the 2nd century BC. See the boxed text 'Viharamahadevi' in the Colombo chapter for more details.

The Sandagiri Wehera, a dagoba yet to be restored, behind the Tissa dagoba, is also credited to Kavantissa. A walk around the dagoba will give you an insight into the construction of the great dagobas.

By the Tissa–Deberawewa road is Yatala Wehera, built 2300 years ago by King Yatala Tissa, who fled Anuradhapura after a palace plot and founded the Ruhunu kingdom. There's a small museum next to the dagoba, but the exhibits are not labelled. The attendant will expect a tip for his one-word descriptions.

Places to Stay

Tissamaharama Town Centre Unless stated otherwise these places come with shared bathrooms.

Surrounded by rice paddies, **Traveller's Home** *(☎ 223 7958; e supuncj@sltnet.lk; singles/doubles with shared bathroom Rs 250/300, with bathroom Rs 400/600, with air-con & breakfast US$17)* is just off the main road about halfway between Tissa and Deberawewa. It's superfriendly, neat and basic. There are free bicycles for guests and a safari display. Ebert, **the owner,** has his own safari 4WDs.

Hotel Tissa *(☎ 223 7104; Main Rd; singles/doubles Rs 440/770, with air-con Rs 990/1650)* has nine rooms that are a mixed bag: some rooms are dark; others have a bit more character. There are elephant skulls to greet you.

New Queen's Resthouse *(☎ 223 7264; singles/doubles Rs 400/550, with air-con Rs 750)*, off Main Rd, is an eclectic building with lots of living space and basic rooms. There's also a restaurant and a bar.

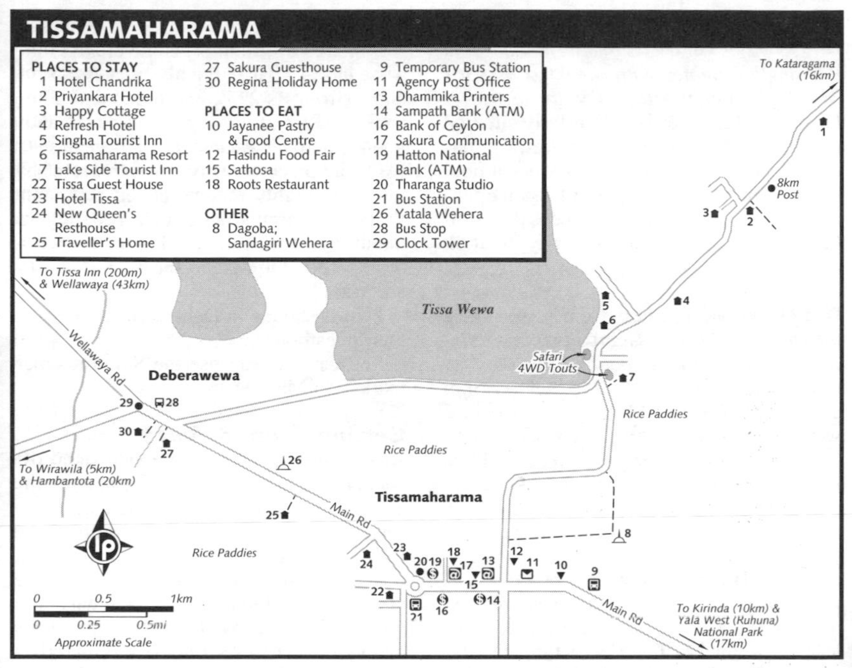

Tissa Guest House (☎ *223 7057; Molawatte Rd; rooms Rs 850)*, near the new bus station, is a large, pleasant family home, with four clean guest rooms and a colourful garden. The owners run the photography shop and studio, Tharanga Studio, on Main Rd, opposite the bus station.

Around Tissa Wewa Most of Tissa's accommodation is near the Tissa Wewa, about 1.5km from the centre of Tissa, and on or near the road to Kataragama. It's easy enough to get into town by bus (Rs 5) or by three-wheeler (Rs 60) from this area.

Singha Tourist Inn (☎ *223 7090; singles/doubles Rs 500/600)* is a no-frills place with a palm-studded lawn reaching down to the lake's edge. It has 10 basic rooms (some are a bit dark). Ask for a net.

Happy Cottage (☎ *223 7085; rooms from Rs 1000, cottages Rs 3000)* has cottages, each with three bedrooms, a sitting area and kitchen. You can rent an entire cottage or a room. At the time of research, Happy Cottage was building eight new rooms, which will cost Rs 1375 a double, or Rs 2750 with air-con. New family rooms will also be available.

Lake Side Tourist Inn (☎ *223 7216; singles/doubles Rs 850/950, with air-con Rs 1250/1350, Rs 100 extra for hot water)* has views to the lake from some of its 24 rooms. The rooms vary in quality, so look at a couple before you choose. There is a bar and restaurant. This place is quite popular with groups.

Refresh Hotel (☎ *223 7357; Kataragama Rd; singles/doubles Rs 1150/1390, with air-con Rs 1550/1790)* has four colourful, stylish rooms facing a small courtyard. The restaurant's food is delicious (see Places to Eat).

Hotel Chandrika (☎*/fax 223 7143;* ⓔ *chandrikahotel@yahoo.com; Kataragama Rd; singles/doubles Rs 1200/1400, with air-con Rs 1650/1850)*, about 2km further towards Kataragama, is a quiet place with rooms facing onto a colonnaded veranda and a courtyard-style garden.

Priyankara Hotel (☎ *223 7206;* ⓔ *prihotel@sltnet.lk; Kataragama Rd; singles/doubles Rs 1750/2000, with air-con Rs 2250/2500)*, about 500m further on, is a modern place with rooms with hot water. Each room has a small balcony with views over rice paddies. The restaurant has a touch of class.

The old resthouse, **Tissamaharama Resort** (*☎ 223 7299; e chc@sltnet.lk; Kataragama Rd; singles/doubles with breakfast US$30/35, singles/doubles/triples with air-con & breakfast US$32/38*) is delightfully situated right on the banks of the Tissa Wewa. It has comfortable rooms (with hot water), a pool (Rs 125 for nonguests) and a pleasant open-air restaurant and bar. This place is the number one choice for groups, so it pays to book ahead.

Deberawewa Furthest from town, **Tissa Inn** (*☎ 223 7233; e tissainn@sltnet.lk; Wellawaya Rd; older singles/doubles Rs 605/715, newer singles/doubles Rs 715/825*), 1.5km along the northern road from the Deberawewa clock tower, has a touch of class for a reasonable price. The newer rooms have French windows and a balcony, while the older rooms downstairs at the back have a veranda. There's a restaurant and bar, and Internet facilities.

Regina Holiday Home (*☎ 223 7159; singles/doubles from Rs 250/300, newer singles/doubles Rs 450/900*), heading towards Tissa, leads off a small road. It is a friendly, family-run hotel with six neat and fresh-feeling rooms with verandas. Bicycles are available for hire (Rs 100 per day), and the hosts will pay for your three-wheeler from the Tissa bus station.

Sakura Guesthouse (*☎ 223 7198; singles/doubles from Rs 275/440, cottages Rs 770*), on the opposite side of the creek to Regina Holiday Home, is a friendly, traditional family home set in spacious, quiet grounds. There are three rooms plus two 'cottages' that sleep three. If you're having trouble with 'guides' ring ahead, and the family will pick you up (for free) from the bus station in Tissa or Deberawewa. A three-wheeler from the Tissa bus station will cost Rs 60.

Places to Eat

Jayanee Pastry & Food Centre (*Main St; mains Rs 60-90*), run by a friendly young family, has a Rs 60 lunch buffet and very good rice and curry for dinner from Rs 90, as well as short eats and juices.

Hasindu Food Fair (*12 Vihara Mawatha; mains Rs 50-100*), a lunch spot in the centre of town, has cheap and tasty rice and curry (Rs 50). Fried rice is Rs 100.

Roots Restaurant (*mains Rs 60-250*), set a few metres off Main St, is the closest thing Tissa has to a bar, and it also serves rice and curry (from Rs 225), and lunch and dinner packets (Rs 60). It's a relaxed place, and a good spot to have a chat and a beer (Rs 90).

Of the places to stay, **Refresh Hotel** has the most highly recommended restaurant. Pasta costs around Rs 380, vegetable fried noodles go for Rs 180 and there's espresso for Rs 180. Lion lager and imported wine are available.

People staying in Deberawewa can eat at their guesthouse.

Self-caterers can use the Sathosa supermarket on Main St.

Getting There & Away

An ordinary bus from Colombo to Tissa costs about Rs 90 and takes about nine hours, while an air-con bus costs Rs 200 and takes about seven hours. The trip to Hambantota costs Rs 15 (one hour). Only a few buses go directly to the hill country, and if you can't get one you'll need to change at Wirawila junction (Rs 7) and/or Wellawaya (Rs 26). From Tissa you can reach Kirinda (Rs 7.50) by bus, but not Yala West (Ruhuna) National Park.

AROUND TISSAMAHARAMA

Wirawila Wewa Bird Sanctuary

Between the northern and southern turn-offs to Tissamaharama, the Hambantota–Wellawaya road runs on a causeway across the large Wirawila Wewa. This extensive sheet of water forms the Wirawila Wewa Bird Sanctuary. The best time for birdwatching is early morning. From Hambantota or Tissa you can get a bus to Wirawila junction on the south side of the tank and walk north; from Tissa you can go to Pandegamu on the north side and walk south. See the boxed text 'Birds of Sri Lanka' in the Hill Country chapter for more details.

Kirinda

On the coast, about 10km south of Tissa, the village of Kirinda has a fine beach and a Buddhist shrine on the huge round rocks. Kirinda was used as a land base by Arthur C Clarke's party when diving for the Great Basses wreck (see Clarke's *The Treasure of the Reef*). The Great and Little Basses reefs, southeast of Kirinda, have some of the most spectacular scuba diving around Sri Lanka, but only on rare occasions are conditions suitable for diving. For much of the year fierce currents sweep across the reefs. A lighthouse was erected on the Great Basses in 1860.

Suduweli *(☎ 072 631059; rooms Rs 250, with bathroom from Rs 350, cabanas Rs 600)* is on a peaceful family farm with a shady garden. The cabanas' verandas look towards the rice paddy and lake. The friendly Sri Lankan–German couple will share their home with you, and cook meals made with rice from their own paddy fields, or prepare German food. There's a motorbike and bicycle available for guests, and a 4WD for safaris into Yala.

Kirinda Beach Resort *(☎ 047-222 3405, fax 222 3402)* was planning a three-storey hotel with pool at the time of research.

There is a bus from Tissa to Kirinda every half-hour or so (Rs 7.50). A three-wheeler from Tissa costs about Rs 500.

YALA WEST (RUHUNA) NATIONAL PARK

Yala West (Ruhuna) National Park *(adult/child US$16.80/8.40, vehicle Rs 144, service charge US$7.20; open 6.30am-6.30pm daily 16 Oct-31 Aug)* combines a strict nature reserve and a national park that brings the total protected area to 126,786 hectares of scrub, plains, brackish lagoons and rocky outcrops. It is divided into five blocks with the most visited being Block 1 (14,101 hectares). Also known as Yala West, this block was originally a reserve for hunters, and was given over to conservation in 1938.

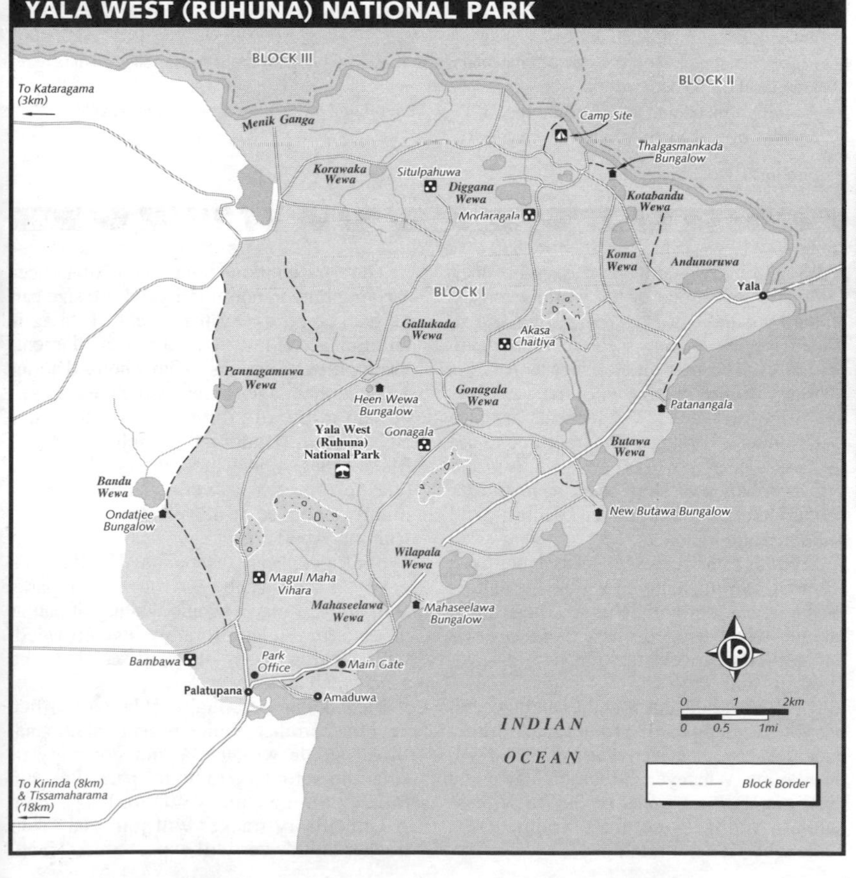

Snagging the Perfect Safari Tout

If you decide to go on a safari you're not going to have to go far to find someone willing to take you – for a price. Guides generally also drive the 4WD, (hopefully) offering titbits of wildlife information. You may be told you need a driver *and* a guide, but this is not the case – you'll always have to hire a 'tracker' when you enter the park anyway.

Choosing a good guide from a dud is a challenge, though, and in this game it's (unfortunately) often true that you get what you pay for. Guides who know their stuff (and charge accordingly) know where the animals are and when/how to find them. Other guides splutter fumes into the air as they zoom around the park hoping, wishing and praying to find wildlife.

Here are some tips to help you spend your money wisely:

- Chat to other travellers for recommendations. If you don't like chatting, many travellers write about the safari they did in guestbooks. Bear in mind that people often write to compliment, but rarely to complain.
- Ask the guide how regularly his tours see elephants or leopards, for example. If beads of sweat appear on his forehead when he says 'every tour' you'll know it's time to walk on.
- Check the vehicle and ask the driver to turn it on; some are potentially lethal rust buckets that sound like lawn mowers – not conducive to wildlife spotting.
- Once you're inside the park, if your driver is speeding around chasing wildlife and scaring it away, ask him to slow down.
- Make sure the driver has a pair of binoculars. You may also want to see if he supplies wildlife identification books.
- A good outfit should let you share the 4WD you have hired with other, new-found travelling companions, allowing you to reduce your costs.

Good luck!

With 35 individual leopards seen in Block I, Yala West has one of the world's densest leopard populations. *Panthera pardus kotiya*, the subspecies you may well see, is unique to Sri Lanka. The best time to spot leopards is February to June or July, when the water levels in the park are low. Elephants are also well-known inhabitants (the best time to see them is also from February to July), and you'll probably see sloth bears, sambar deer, spotted deer, wild boar, crocodiles, wild buffaloes and monkeys.

Around 130 species of birds have been recorded at Yala, many of which are visitors escaping the northern winter. These birds include white-winged black terns, curlews and pintails. Locals include jungle fowl, hornbills and orioles.

If you visit between October and December you're guaranteed to see a lot of birdlife, deer and crocodiles – anything else then will be a bonus. Whatever the season, dawn and dusk are the best times of day to witness animals. You'll also see more wildlife if you come when it's not raining.

The park contains the remains of a once-thriving human community, whose size can be gauged partly by the extent of its agricultural activities. A monastic settlement, **Situlpahuwa**, appears to have housed about 12,000 inhabitants. Now restored, it's an important centre of pilgrimage. A 1st-century BC *vihara* (Buddhist complex), Magul Maha Vihara, and a 2nd-century BC *chetiya* (shrine) point to a well-established community believed to have been part of the Ruhunu kingdom.

Some people are disappointed by Yala. It's not in the same league as Africa's safari parks and, with so many people visiting, it can at times seem uncomfortably overcrowded, with a dozen or so 4WDs all searching the same small area.

Tickets can be bought at the park office near the entrance, which is near Palatupana. Most people will use a tour company or safari operator to get into the park (Rs 1500 to 2200 for the entire 4WD for half a day). A compulsory tracker will join you. Your tracker and driver will expect a tip. Trackers are poorly paid and work long hours; Rs 150 to 200 per tracker per group will generate goodwill and go a long way in his pocket.

There are six **bungalows** and two **camp sites** in the park, which must be booked in Colombo through the **Department of Wildlife Conservation** *(☎ 011-269 4241, fax 698556; 18 Gregory's Rd, Cinnamon Gardens)*. You have to supply all your own provisions.

There are two hotels close to the park entrance on a rather desolate stretch of coast at Amaduwa. Both organise safaris.

Browns Safari Beach Motel *(☎ 070 473216, fax 011-267 4377; singles/doubles full board Rs 2200/3000)* has it all: sea views, visiting wildlife, and simple, comfortable rooms in an idyllic setting on the edge of the park. Triple and interconnecting rooms are available, as are half-board rates.

Yala Safari Beach Hotel *(☎/fax 047-223 8015; e yalasafari@eureka.lk; doubles/triples US$85/95, with air-con US$105/115)* is so close to the beach you can hear the waves from your room. There's a pool, treed gardens, restaurant and bar, and safari-suited staff.

KATARAGAMA

☎ 047

Fifteen kilometres northeast of Tissa is Kataragama. Along with Adam's Peak, this is the most important religious pilgrimage site in Sri Lanka. It is a holy place for Buddhists, Muslims and Hindus, and across the Menik Ganga from the small residential part of town is a sprawling religious complex containing buildings of all three religions. It is difficult to sort fact from legend at Kataragama. Many believe that King Dutugemunu built a shrine to the Kataragama Deviyo (the resident god) here in the 2nd century BC, and the Buddhist Kirivehera dagoba dates back to the 1st century BC, but the site has been significant for longer than this.

The most important shrine is the **Maha Devale**, which supposedly contains the lance of the six-faced, 12-armed Hindu war god, Skanda, who is seen here as being identical to the Kataragama Deviyo. Followers make offerings at the daily *pujas* at 4.30am, 10.30am and 6.30pm (no 4.30am offering on Saturday). Neighbouring shrines are dedicated to Buddha and Ganesh (remover of obstacles and champion of intellectual pursuits).

THE SOUTH

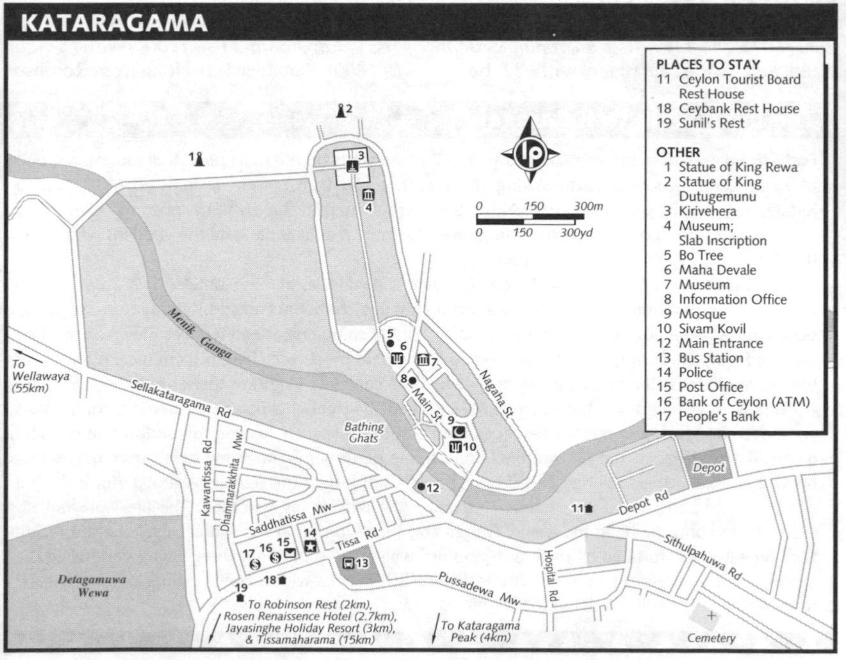

The Muslim area, close to the main entrance, features a beautiful small **mosque** with coloured tilework and wooden lintels, and tombs of two holy men.

Apart from the shrines, there are some other points of interest inside the temple complex. An **archaeological museum** *(admission by donation)* has a collection of Hindu and Buddhist religious items, as well as huge fibreglass models of statues from around Sri Lanka. A small **museum** has a display of Buddhist statues. Don't expect much help from the information office.

In July and August the predominantly Hindu Kataragama Festival draws thousands of devotees who make the pilgrimage over a two-week period (see the boxed text 'The Long Walk to Kataragama').

Apart from festival time, the town is busiest at weekends and on *poya* days. At these times it may be difficult to find accommodation, and the places to stay will be buzzing with Sri Lankans. At other times it can feel like a ghost town. If you're staying in Tissamaharama you may just want to visit on a day trip.

Places to Stay & Eat

Ceybank Rest House *(☎ 223 5229, reservations ☎ 011-254 4315; Tissa Rd; rooms Rs 540)* is an airy, well-run place with 22 basic rooms. Some rooms have views across to Kataragama mountain and others overlook the town. You're supposed to reserve your room from Colombo but there are often on-the-spot vacancies. You'll need to book in for the vegetarian food (no alcohol, meat, fish or eggs allowed). Rice and curry costs Rs 90.

Ceylon Tourist Board Rest House *(☎ 223 5227, reservations ☎ 011-243 7571; Depot Rd; singles/doubles/family Rs 605/800/1210)*, near the junction of Situlpahuwa road, has basic rooms, including some with air-con. Guests are entitled to one free dinner (vegetarian only) each. The food is tasty, cheap and spicy.

Sunil's Rest *(☎ 223 5300; 61 Tissa Rd; rooms Rs 660)*, a clean, family-run place, has three rooms, a pleasant garden and a kitsch waterfall feature.

Robinson Rest *(☎ 223 5175; e anjulaj@sltnet.lk; Tissa Rd; rooms Rs 935, with air-con Rs 1375)*, about 2km south of town on the road to Tissamaharama, has basic rooms with balconies and verandas. If you don't like sharing a hotel with caged animals, be warned: there's a rabbit, squirrel and guinea pig in a small cage.

Jayasinghe Holiday Resort *(☎ 223 5146; Tissa Rd; rooms Rs 1100, with air-con Rs 1600)* is another 1km along from Robinson

The Long Walk to Kataragama

Forty-five days before the annual Kataragama Festival starts on the Esala *poya* (full moon), a group of Kataragama devotees start walking the length of Sri Lanka, from Jaffna and Mullaitivu to Kataragama, for the pilgrimage, Pada Yatra. Seeking spiritual development, the pilgrims believe they are walking in the steps of the god Kataragama (also known as Skanda), and the Veddahs who made the first group pilgrimage on this route.

The route follows the east coast from the Jaffna peninsula, via Trincomalee and Batticaloa to Okanda, then through Yala East and Yala West (Ruhuna) National Parks to Kataragama. It's an arduous trip, and the pilgrims rely on the hospitality of the communities and temples they pass for their food and lodging. During the war, the risks to them were great, and though there were attempts at the walk, 2002 was the first time pilgrims walked the complete length of the route since 1983.

Pilgrims arrive in time for the festival's feverish activity. Elephants parade, drummers drum. Vows are made and favours sought by devotees who demonstrate their sincerity by performing extraordinary acts of penance and self-mortification on one particular night: some swing from hooks that pierce their skin; others roll half naked over the hot sands near the temple. A few perform the act of walking on beds of red-hot cinders – treading the flowers, as it's called. The fire-walkers fast, meditate and pray, bathe in the Menik Ganga and then worship at the Maha Devale before facing their ordeal. Then, fortified by their faith, the fire-walkers step out onto the glowing path while the audience cries out encouragement. The festival officially ends with a water-cutting ceremony (said to evoke rain for the harvests) in the Menik Ganga.

Rest. It has a swimming pool (which can be used by nonguests for Rs 100) and 25 clean, characterless rooms. Some rooms have hot water and a TV, and ordinary meals are available.

Rosen Renaissance Hotel *(☎/fax 223 6030-3; ⓔ rosenr@sltnet.lk; Tissa Rd; singles/doubles US$40/50)* is a plush new hotel that attracts a lot of tour groups. Rooms have air-con, satellite TV and all the usual features, plus there's a pool with underwater music.

Getting There & Away

Buses to Tissamaharama (ordinary/air-con Rs 10.50/30) are fairly frequent. The air-con bus goes through to Colombo. There are some direct buses to Colombo and places on the south coast. The intercity express to Colombo costs Rs 200 (you can pick up the same bus in Tissa; 7½ hours). There are direct buses to Ella (Rs 43), Nuwara Eliya (Rs 75), Kandy (Rs 102) and Wellawaya (Rs 30). For Pottuvil (for Arugam Bay), take the bus to Monaragala (Rs 29.50).

The Hill Country

The hill country lives in a cool, perpetual spring, away from the often enervating heat and heavy air of the coastal regions or the hot dry air of the central and northern plains. Everything here is green and lush, and much of the region is carpeted with the glowing green of the tea plantations, with montane forest hugging the higher slopes.

The kingdom of Kandy resisted European takeover for more than 300 years after the coastal regions had succumbed, and the city of Kandy remains the Sinhalese cultural and spiritual centre. Since the 19th century there has been a large population of Tamils in the hill country, brought from India by the British to labour on the tea estates.

The hill country is a relaxed area, where it's very easy to find the days just drifting by. Higher up into the hills are many towns that are worth a visit, and an abundance of walks and climbs, refreshing waterfalls and historic sites.

Highlights

- Watching the throbbing throng of elephants, drummers and dancers at the Kandy Perahera
- Meandering around Lake Kandy in the evening
- Slogging up Adam's Peak (Sri Pada) to be rewarded by a perfect sunrise
- Rattling through the high tea plantations in a hill-country train
- Hiking through the countryside around Ella while enjoying the views to the plains
- Exploring the pristine Sinharaja Forest Reserve with an expert guide
- Digging up the perfect gem in one of Ratnapura's gem shops
- Rising early to walk through Horton Plains and peer over stunning World's End

COLOMBO TO KANDY

The **Henerathgoda Botanic Gardens** near Gampaha, off the Colombo–Kandy road about 30km northwest of Colombo, are overshadowed by the better-known Peradeniya Botanic Gardens near Kandy. However, it was at Henerathgoda that the first rubber trees planted in Asia were carefully grown and their potential proved – some of those original rubber trees are still in the gardens today. It's worth a stop if you have the time and an interest in botany.

Some 47km from Colombo is the village of Pasyala, where there's a turn-off leading to the **Pasgama tourism village** *(☎ 033-228 5183; tourist admission US$11)* about 1.5km from the main road. This privately owned venture is an attempt to bring to life a pre-1940 settlement showcasing craftspeople and other features of traditional village life. Some enjoy this place, while others may see it as corny, crafty (excuse the pun) commercialism – few will be delighted by the entry fee. There's a shop selling handicrafts. Hire a three-wheeler from Pasyala to get there.

About 3km further towards Kandy from Pasyala is **Cadjugama**, a village famous for its cashew nuts. Stalls line the road and brightly clad cashew-nut sellers beckon passing motorists. More villages specialising in various products can be found along this road. At the 48km post is **Radawaduwa**, where all sorts of cane items are woven and displayed for sale at roadside stalls.

Kegalle, 77km from Colombo, is the nearest town to the Pinnewala Elephant Orphanage (see later). A little further towards Kandy you can see **Utuwankandu**, a prominent rocky hill from which the 19th-century Robin Hood–style highwayman, Saradiel, preyed on travellers until he was caught and executed by the British.

Around 2.5km down the access road to Pinnewala (by the 3km post), towards Kandy, is another elephant sanctuary and bathing spot, **The Millennium Elephant Foundation** *(admission Rs 300; open 8am-5pm daily)*. This place is far less crowded than the elephant orphanage. There are eight elephants including Lakshmi and her calf, Puja, and a small 'museum' with information on the life cycle and habits of elephants. The river is just inside the entrance and the elephants are often bathing here. Entry includes an elephant ride (if you wish).

At Kadugannawa, just after the road and railway make their most scenic climbs –

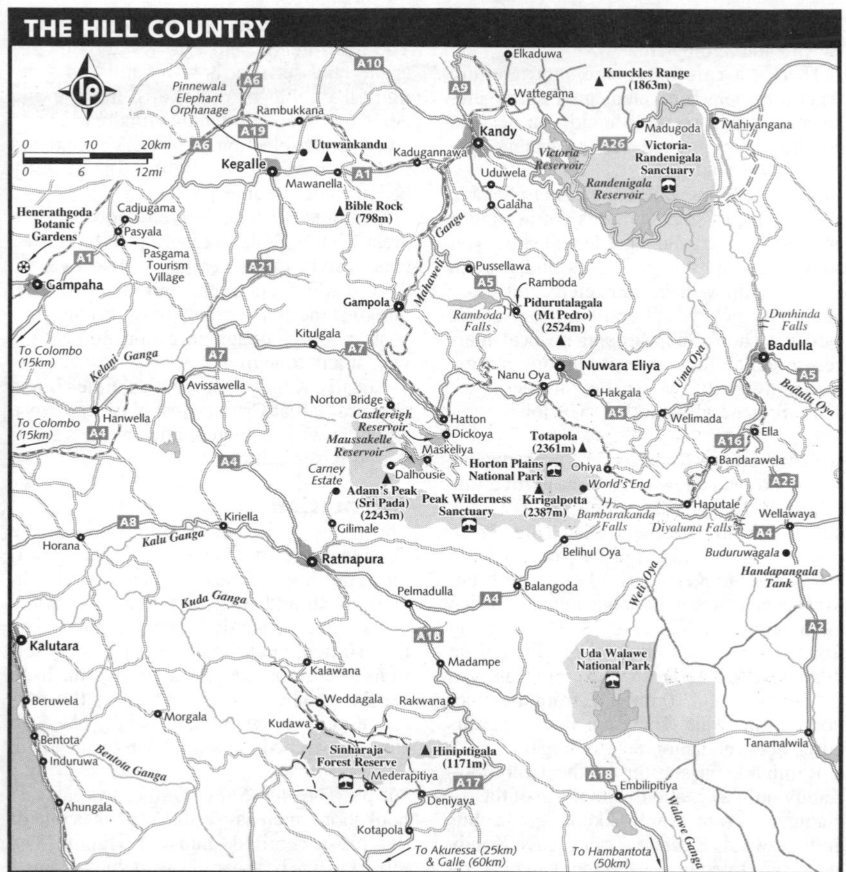

with views southwest to the large **Bible Rock** – is a tall pillar erected in memory of Captain Dawson, the English engineer who built the Colombo–Kandy road in 1826.

Getting There & Away Pasyala, Cadjugama, Kegalle and Kadugannawa are on the A1, and are all accessible by buses travelling between Colombo and Kandy. The train is useful for getting to the Henerathgoda Botanic Gardens at Gampaha, and Kadugannawa.

Pinnewala Elephant Orphanage

The government-run Pinnewala Elephant Orphanage *(adult/child under 12 Rs 200/100, video Rs 500; open 8.30am-5.30pm daily)*, near Kegalle, was set up to save abandoned or orphaned wild elephants. It has now grown into the most popular jumbo attraction in Sri Lanka, and with good reason, for nowhere else except at *peraheras* (processions) are you likely to see so many elephants at close quarters. The elephants are controlled by their mahouts (keepers), who ensure they feed at the right times and don't endanger anyone, but otherwise the elephants roam freely around the sanctuary area.

There are 60 or so young elephants and some are surprisingly small; this must be one of the few places where an elephant can step on your foot and you might walk away with a smile! Bathing times for the babies are from 10am to noon and from 2pm to 4pm, with meal times at 9.15am, 1.15pm and 5pm. Most of the elephants become working elephants once they grow up. Occasionally, one of the older female elephants produces a baby to add to the herd.

There's a **café** and some shops selling snacks, camera film, elephant T-shirts, elephant toys and so on. Should you need to change money, outside the orphanage is a **Hatton National Bank**.

Near the Pinnewala Elephant Orphanage are a couple of **spice gardens**. You can turn up unannounced and a guide will show you around, explaining their uses and growth habits. A tip will be expected, and more often than not, you'll end your tour at the garden's shop. Shop around in local markets to get an idea of prices before you get carried away; the salespeople in these gardens are generally good at their jobs.

Getting There & Away The orphanage is on a good road a few kilometres north of the Colombo–Kandy road. The turn-off is just out of Kegalle on the Kandy side. From Kandy you can take a private bus or CTB bus No 662 to Kegalle (Rs 18) – get off before Kegalle at Karandupona junction. From the junction catch bus No 681 (Rs 8) going from Kegalle to Rambukkana and get off at Pinnewala. It's about an hour from Kandy to the junction, and 10 minutes from the junction to Pinnewala. There are also numerous buses between Colombo and Kegalle.

Rambukkana station on the Colombo–Kandy railway is about 3km north of the orphanage. From Rambukkana get a bus going towards Kegalle. Trains leave Kandy at 6.45am (arriving at Rambukkana station at 8am), 10.30am (arriving at noon) and 3.40pm (arriving at 4.40pm). Trains for Kandy leave from Rambukkana at 12.45pm and 2.45pm.

KANDY

☎ 081 • 120,000

Some say Kandy is the only other real 'city' in Sri Lanka, other than Colombo. The easy-going capital of the hill country has a lot to offer – history, culture, forested hills and a touch of urban buzz. Only 115km inland from the capital, climatically it is a world away due to its 500m altitude. Kandy was also the capital of the last Sinhalese kingdom, which fell to the British in 1815 after defying the Portuguese and Dutch for three centuries.

The town, and the countryside around it, is lush and green and there are many pleasant walks both from the town or further afield. The town centre, close to Kandy's picturesque lake set in a bowl of hills, is a delightful jumble of old shops, antique and gemstone specialists, a bustling market and a very good selection of hotels, guesthouses and restaurants. As night falls the city becomes eerily quiet.

Kandy is particularly well known for the great Kandy Esala Perahera (see the boxed text 'Kandy Esala Perahera') held over 10 days leading up to the Nikini *poya* (full moon) at the end of month of Esala (July/August), but has enough attractions to justify a visit at any time of year.

Locally Kandy is known as either Maha Nuwara (Great City) or just Nuwara (City), which is what some conductors on Kandy-bound buses call out.

Orientation

The focus of Kandy is its lake, with the Temple of the Tooth (Sri Dalada Maligawa) on its north side. The city centre is immediately north and west of the lake, with the clock tower a handy reference point. The train station, market and the various bus stations and stops are just a short walk from the lake. The city spreads into the surrounding hills, where many of the places to stay are perched, looking down on the town.

Maps The *A-Z Street Guide*, available at bookshops such as Vijitha Yapa, has one of the most detailed maps of Kandy. The tourist office has maps as well, but the quality tends to be a bit dodgy. Nelles Verlag produces a reasonable map of Kandy.

Information

Tourist Office Housed beside the Olde Empire Hotel, the **Tourist Information Centre** *(☎ 222 2661; Palace Sq; open 9am-1pm & 1.30-4.45pm Mon-Fri)* is helpful for information on transport and things to do in the Kandy area, and also has some information on places to stay. There are plans for the tourist office to move to new premises across the road.

Cultural Triangle Office This office *(open 9am-12.30pm & 1.30-4pm daily)*, where you can buy Cultural Triangle round-trip tickets that cover many of the sites of the ancient cities, is located in a white building across the road from the tourist office. Books are available for sale (see Bookshops later) though they're often out of stock.

Within Kandy the round-trip ticket covers the four Hindu *devales* or shrines (Kataragama, Natha, Pattini and Vishnu), two monasteries (Asgiriya and Malwatte), the National Museum and the Archaeological Museum. It is customary to make a donation (usually Rs 30 and upwards) at the *devales* and monasteries, though you are unlikely to be asked to produce a Cultural Triangle ticket. The National Museum costs Rs 65 to enter without a triangle ticket, although the Archaeological Museum insists on one. See later in this section for more details on these places. See the boxed text 'Cultural Triangle Tickets' in the Ancient Cities chapter for more details on these tickets.

Money There are quite a few banks in town. On Dalada Vidiya there's the **Hatton National Bank**, which has an ATM, and the **Bank of Ceylon**, which offers cash withdrawals on Visa (but not MasterCard) and changes travellers cheques. There are also ATMs at the **Commercial Bank** and **HSBC**, both on Kotugodelle Vidiya.

Post & Communications The **main post office** is over the road from the train station. There are a few smaller, more central post offices, including one next door to the Olde Empire Hotel. There are numerous private communications bureaus in town.

There are five or so Internet cafés in the town centre, plus a few poky telephone offices with one dusty computer jammed into the corner underneath a fax machine and photocopier. **Koffeepot** *(36 Dalada Vidiya)* is on the ground floor of The Pub and has air-con; it charges Rs 110 per hour. There are heaps of computers, attentive service and also cappuccino (Rs 90). **The Café@Internet** *(77 Kotugodelle Vidiya)* also has air-con, and charges Rs 120 per hour. **Cyber Cottage** *(1st floor, 154 Kotugodelle Vidiya)* charges only Rs 66 per hour, but it was a little slow when we visited.

Bookshops The good **Vijitha Yapa** *(5 Kotugodelle Vidiya)* bookshop sells periodicals, newspapers (including foreign papers) and assorted fiction and nonfiction.

Kandy's Phone Numbers

Kandy's telephone area code is scheduled to change from ☎ 08 to ☎ 081 during October 2003. See the boxed text 'Telephone Number Changes' in the Facts for the Visitor chapter for details of this and other changes to Sri Lanka's telephone numbers.

Mark Bookshop *(15 1/1 Dalada Vidiya)* has a good selection of books about Sri Lanka, as well as fiction and nonfiction. It's pokey, but the staff are very helpful.

The **Cultural Triangle Office**, opposite the tourist office, has a selection of books for sale on the ancient cities. *Kandy*, by Dr Anuradha Seneviratna, is an informative guide to the city's heritage. Also available here is *The Cultural Triangle*, published by Unesco and the Central Cultural Fund, which provides good background on the ancient sites and monuments.

If you're interested in books on Buddhism, visit the friendly folks at the **Buddhist Publication Society** towards the east end of the lake. Local scholars, such as the American monk Bhikku Bodhi, sometimes give lectures here. It also has a comprehensive library.

Libraries & Cultural Centres The **British Council** *(☎ 223 4634; ⓔ bckandy@britcoun.lk; 178 DS Senanayake Vidiya; open 9.30am-5pm Tues-Sat)*, on what was formerly Trincomalee St, has a library with back copies of British newspapers, cassettes and videos. It sometimes holds film nights, exhibitions and plays. Nonmembers may read newspapers (but only on presentation of a passport).

Alliance Française *(☎ 222 4432; 412 Peradeniya Rd; open 8.30am-6pm Mon-Sat)*, to the southwest of town, has film nights (the films are in French but often have English subtitles), as well as books and periodicals. Good coffee is available. Nonmembers are welcome to browse in the library (membership, and therefore borrowing rights, costs Rs 500).

Medical Services If you need a doctor in Kandy, the **Lakeside Adventist Hospital** *(☎ 222 3466; 40 Sangaraja Mawatha)* offers good, efficient service.

KANDY

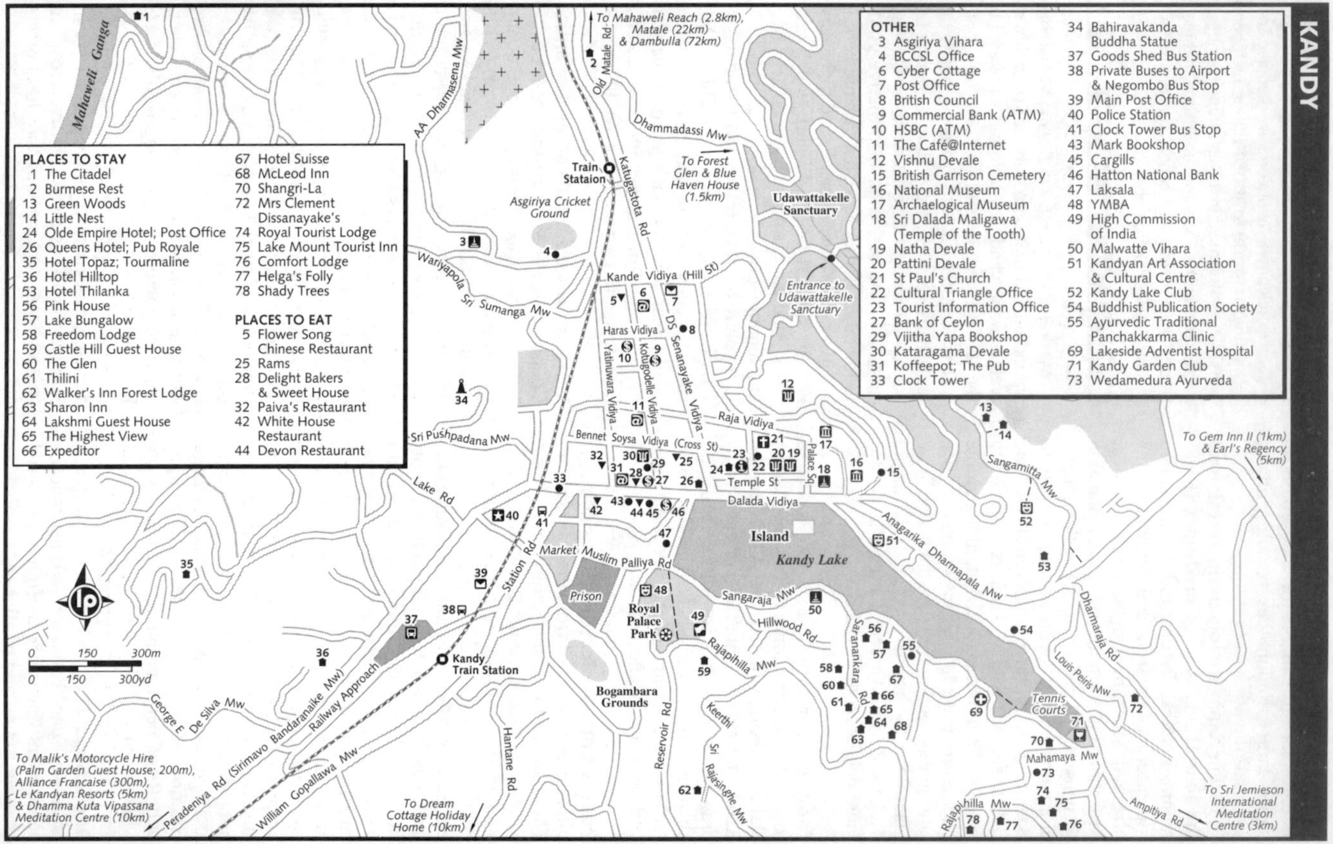

PLACES TO STAY
1 The Citadel
2 Burmese Rest
13 Green Woods
14 Little Nest
24 Olde Empire Hotel; Post Office
26 Queens Hotel; Pub Royale
35 Hotel Topaz; Tourmaline
36 Hotel Hilltop
53 Hotel Thilanka
56 Pink House
57 Lake Bungalow
58 Freedom Lodge
59 Castle Hill Guest House
60 The Glen
61 Thilini
62 Walker's Inn Forest Lodge
63 Sharon Inn
64 Lakshmi Guest House
65 The Highest View
66 Expeditor
67 Hotel Suisse
68 McLeod Inn
70 Shangri-La
72 Mrs Clement Dissanayake's
74 Royal Tourist Lodge
75 Lake Mount Tourist Inn
76 Comfort Lodge
77 Helga's Folly
78 Shady Trees

PLACES TO EAT
5 Flower Song Chinese Restaurant
25 Rams
28 Delight Bakers & Sweet House
32 Paiva's Restaurant
42 White House Restaurant
44 Devon Restaurant

OTHER
3 Asgiriya Vihara
4 BCCSL Office
6 Cyber Cottage
7 Post Office
8 British Council
9 Commercial Bank (ATM)
10 HSBC (ATM)
11 The Café@Internet
12 Vishnu Devale
15 British Garrison Cemetery
16 National Museum
17 Archaelogical Museum
18 Sri Dalada Maligawa (Temple of the Tooth)
19 Natha Devale
20 Pattini Devale
21 St Paul's Church
22 Cultural Triangle Office
23 Tourist Information Office
27 Bank of Ceylon
29 Vijitha Yapa Bookshop
30 Kataragama Devale
31 Koffeepot; The Pub
33 Clock Tower
34 Bahiravakanda Buddha Statue
37 Goods Shed Bus Station
38 Private Buses to Airport & Negombo Bus Stop
39 Main Post Office
40 Police Station
41 Clock Tower Bus Stop
43 Mark Bookshop
45 Cargills
46 Hatton National Bank
47 Laksala
48 YMBA
49 High Commission of India
50 Malwatte Vihara
51 Kandyan Art Association & Cultural Centre
52 Kandy Lake Club
54 Buddhist Publication Society
55 Ayurvedic Traditional Panchakkarma Clinic
69 Lakeside Adventist Hospital
71 Kandy Garden Club
73 Wedamedura Ayurveda

To Mahaweli Reach (2.8km), Matale (22km) & Dambulla (72km)
To Forest Glen & Blue Haven House (1.5km)
To Gem Inn II (1km) & Earl's Regency (5km)
To Sri Jemieson International Meditation Centre (3km)
To Dream Cottage Holiday Home (10km)
To Malik's Motorcycle Hire (Palm Garden Guest House; 200m), Alliance Francaise (300m), Le Kandyan Resorts (5km) & Dhamma Kuta Vipassana Meditation Centre (10km)

0 150 300m
0 150 300yd

Dangers & Annoyances The back alleys of the town centre are worth avoiding after dark – they're home to sour bars, gambling dens and the homeless.

Touts are particularly numerous around the train station and the lake. They'll hound you with Kandyan dance tickets, ghastly necklaces and wobbly headed elephant figurines. Another neat trick is the man who says he works at your hotel, who's off shopping for tonight's dinner. Of course he doesn't work at your hotel, and any money you give him for a special meal disappears.

The touts will also generally have a well-rehearsed stock of stories about guesthouses they don't want you to patronise (presumably because those guesthouses won't pay them commission).

Kandy Lake

A lovely centrepiece to the town, Kandy Lake was created in 1807 by Sri Wickrama Rajasinha, the last ruler of the kingdom of Kandy. Several small-scale local chiefs, who protested because their people objected to labouring on the project, were put to death at stakes in the lake bed. The island in the centre was used as Sri Wickrama Rajasinha's personal harem, to which he crossed on a barge. Later the British used it as an ammunition store and added the fortress-style parapet around the perimeter of the lake. On the south shore, in front of the Malwatte Vihara, there's a circular enclosure which is the monks' bathhouse.

Sri Dalada Maligawa (Temple of the Tooth)

Just north of the lake, the Temple of the Tooth *(admission Rs 200, camera/video Rs 100/300; open 6am-5pm daily)* houses Sri Lanka's most important Buddhist relic – a sacred tooth of the Buddha. The temple sustained damage when a bomb was detonated near the main entrance in early 1998, but the scars have been repaired.

The tooth is said to have been snatched from the flames of the Buddha's funeral pyre in 543 BC, and was smuggled into Sri Lanka during the 4th century AD, hidden in the hair of a princess. At first it was taken to Anuradhapura, but with the ups and downs of Sri Lankan history it moved from place to place before eventually ending up at Kandy. In 1283 it was carried back to India by an invading army, but was soon brought back again by King Parakramabahu III.

Gradually, the tooth came to assume more and more importance. In the 16th century the Portuguese, in one of their worst spoilsport moods, seized what they claimed was the tooth, took it away and burnt it with Catholic fervour in Goa. 'Not so' is the Sinhalese rejoinder; they were fobbed off with a replica tooth and the real incisor remained safe.

The present Temple of the Tooth was constructed mainly under Kandyan kings from 1687 to 1707 and 1747 to 1782. It is an imposing pink-painted structure, surrounded by a deep moat. The octagonal tower in the moat was built by Sri Wickrama Rajasinha and used to house an important collection of *ola* (palm-leaf) manuscripts. However, this section of the temple was heavily damaged in the 1998 bomb blast. The eye-catching gilded roof over the relic chamber was added by President Premadasa.

The temple has a constant flow of worshippers and flocks of tourists. *Pujas* (offerings or prayers) are held at 6am, 10am and 6pm. Wear clothes that cover your legs and your shoulders and remove your shoes (which are kept by shoe minders near the entrance). The security at the temple's entry points, which has been fairly rigorous for some time, was tightened following the bomb attack in early 1998. You have to pass through two bag and body searches before the place where you leave your shoes. There is another bag and body search once you're in the temple.

Drums beat throughout the *pujas* while the heavily guarded room housing the tooth is open to devotees and tourists. Of course you don't actually see the tooth – just a gold casket said to contain a series of smaller and smaller caskets and eventually the tooth itself. Or perhaps a replica – nobody seems too sure. There are rumours that the real tooth is hidden somewhere secure, as it has been so many times in its past. The casket is behind a window and two decidedly mean-looking monks stand heavily on either side.

Behind the shrine in the main building there is a **museum** *(admission Rs 100; open 9am-5pm)* with a stunning array of gilded and bejewelled reliquaries and gifts to the temple. It also has a sobering display of photographs of the damage caused by a truck bomb in 1988.

To see the stuffed remains of the Maligawa Tusker who died in 1988 (see the boxed text 'Kandy Esala Perahera'), take a left after ascending the first steps up to the temple, after passing security.

National Museum

The National Museum *(adult/child under 12 Rs 55/30, camera Rs 135; open 9am-5pm Sun-Thur)*, beside the Temple of the Tooth, was once the quarters for Kandyan royal concubines and now houses royal regalia and reminders of pre-European Sinhalese life. It has a copy of the 1815 agreement that handed over the Kandyan provinces to British rule. This document announces a major reason for the event.

> ...the cruelties and oppressions of the Malabar ruler, in the arbitrary and unjust infliction of bodily tortures and pains of death without trial, and sometimes without accusation or the possibility of a crime, and in the general contempt and contravention of all civil rights, have become flagrant, enormous and intolerable.

Sri Wickrama Rajasinha was therefore declared, 'by the habitual violation of the chief and most sacred duties of a sovereign', to be 'fallen and deposed from office of king' and 'the dominion of the Kandyan provinces' was 'vested in the sovereign of the British Empire'.

The audience hall, notable for the tall pillars supporting its roof, was the site for the convention of Kandyan chiefs that ceded the kingdom to Britain in 1815.

Kandy Esala Perahera

This *perahera* (a parade or procession) is held in Kandy to honour the sacred tooth enshrined in the Sri Dalada Maligawa (Temple of the Tooth). It runs for 10 days in the full-moon month of Esala (July to August), ending on the Nikini *poya* (full moon). The big night of the year in Kandy comes at the culmination of these 10 days of increasingly frenetic activity.

The first six nights are relatively low-key; on the seventh things start to take off as the route lengthens, the procession becomes more and more splendid and accommodation prices go right through the roof.

The procession is actually a combination of five separate *peraheras*. Four come from the four Kandy *devales* (shrines to deities who protect the island and are also devotees and servants of the Buddha): Natha, Vishnu, Kataragama and Pattini. The fifth and most splendid *perahera* is that of the Sri Dalada Maligawa itself.

The procession is led by thousands of Kandyan dancers and drummers beating thousands of drums, cracking whips and waving colourful banners. Then come long processions of elephants – 50 or more of them. The brilliantly caparisoned Maligawa Tusker is the most splendid of them all – decorated from trunk to toe, he carries a huge canopy that shelters, on the final night, a replica of the sacred relic cask. A carpet-way of white linen is laid in front of the elephant so that he does not step in the dirt.

The Kandy Esala Perahera is the most magnificent annual spectacle in Sri Lanka, and one of the most famous in Asia. It has been an annual event for many centuries and is described by Robert Knox in his 1681 book *An Historical Relation of Ceylon*. There is also a smaller procession on the *poya* day in June, and special *peraheras* may be put on for important occasions. It's essential to arrive early for roadside seats for the *perahera* – by 2pm for the final night. Earlier in the week you can get seats about halfway back in the stands quite cheaply.

There's a daylight procession on the first day of the Nikini full-moon month, which marks the end of the Kandy Esala Perahera.

ANDERS BLOMQVIST

The Temple of the Tooth houses the sacred tooth of the Buddha

The National Museum, along with the less-interesting Archaeological Museum behind the temple, four *devales* and two monasteries – but not Sri Dalada Maligawa itself – together make up one of Sri Lanka's Cultural Triangle sites. You can buy a Cultural Triangle round ticket at the office across the road from the tourist office.

British Garrison Cemetery

The British Garrison Cemetery *(donations appreciated; open Mon-Sat 8am-5pm)* is a short walk uphill behind the National Museum. There are 163 graves and probably 500 burials in total here, lovingly cared for by the friends of the cemetery. The friendly and amusing caretaker is more than happy to show people around and provide information about many of the graves. Some of the demises were due to sudden sunstroke, or elephants, or jungle fever. The Cargills of supermarket fame lie here. James McGlashan survived the battle of Waterloo but disregarded instructions given on mosquitoes, which ultimately proved deadlier.

The office, once the chapel of rest, has pamphlets and the old cemetery records.

Devales

There are four *devales* (shrines) to the gods who are followers of Buddha and who protect Sri Lanka. Three of the four *devales* stand close to the Temple of the Tooth. The 14th-century **Natha Devale** is the oldest. It perches on a stone terrace with a fine *vahalkada* gateway. Bodhi trees and stupas stand in the *devale* grounds, and there's a fine icon in the main shrine. Natha is a future Buddha with a special connection to Kandy. Next to the Natha Devale is the small, simple **Pattini Devale**, dedicated to the goddess of chastity. The **Vishnu Devale** on the other side of Raja Vidiya is reached by carved steps and features a drumming hall. Vishnu is the guardian of Sri Lanka and an indicator of the intermingling of Hindu and Buddhist beliefs since he is also one of the three great Hindu gods.

The **Kataragama Devale** is a little way from the others – a brightly painted tower gateway fights for attention with the bustle on Kotugodelle Vidiya. Skanda, the god of war (also called Saman), here appears with six heads and 12 hands wielding weapons, riding a peacock.

Monasteries

Kandy's principal Buddhist *viharas* (monasteries) have considerable importance – the high priests of the two best known, Malwatte and Asgiriya, are the most important in Sri Lanka. These temples are the headquarters of two of the main Nikayas, or orders of monks. The priests also play an important role in the administration and operation of the Temple of the Tooth. The **Malwatte Vihara** is directly across the lake from the Temple of the Tooth, while the **Asgiriya Vihara** is on the hill off Wariyapola Sri Sumanga Mawatha to the northwest of the town centre, and has a large reclining Buddha image.

Elephants

In and around Kandy elephants can be seen frequently. Working elephants might be spotted anywhere, and you may catch the Temple of the Tooth elephant chained up along the lakeside near the temple. There are elephants in the River Side Elephant Park as well (see Around Kandy later in this chapter).

From Kandy it's a fairly easy trip to the Pinnewala Elephant Orphanage (see Colombo to Kandy earlier in this chapter).

Udawattakelle Sanctuary

North of the lake is this cool and pleasant forest *(admission adult/child under 12 Rs 575/250; open 7am-5pm)*. There are lots of huge trees, much bird and insect life and many monkeys, but visitors are advised to be careful in this woodland if they're alone. Muggers are rare in Sri Lanka but not unknown, and single women especially should take care. The odd leech is likely to accompany you after rain. Entry to the sanctuary is seriously overpriced. You enter through the gate, which you reach by turning right after the post office on DS Senanayake Vidiya (there's a sign at the junction). There are clear paths, but it's worth paying attention to the map at the entrance.

Activities

Walks There are many walks around the centre of Kandy, such as up to the **Royal Palace Park** *(admission Rs 25; open 8.30am-4.30pm)*, also constructed by Sri Wickrama Raja-sinha, overlooking the lake. Further up the hill on Rajapihilla Mawatha there are even better views over the lake, the town and the surrounding hills, which disappear in a series of gentle ranges stretching far into the distance. If you're in the mood for a longer walk, there are also a couple of paths, along from Rajapihilla Mawatha, that head up into the hills.

Looming over Kandy, the huge concrete **Bohiravokanda Buddha statue** *(admission Rs 100)* can be reached by walking 20 minutes uphill from near the police station on Peradeniya Rd. Save your sweat and money – there are no views from the top and the statue is unremarkable.

Ayurveda Located next to Hotel Suisse, the **Ayurvedic Traditional Panchakkarma Clinic** *(☎ 222 3101; 32/4 Sangaraja Rd)* has qualified male and female masseurs. A full massage and steam bath will set you back Rs 1200, and what they almost menacingly call the 'full treatment', lasting two hours, costs Rs 2000. Actually the staff here are friendly and are happy to answer questions.

Wedamedura Ayurveda *(☎ 074 479484; 7 Mahamaya Mawatha)*, southeast of the lake also has male and female masseurs. A one hour massage costs Rs 800, or a full 2½-hour treatment costs Rs 3800.

You could also splurge at the Ayurvedic treatment centre at **Le Kandyan Resorts** *(☎ 223 3521-2)* (see Places to Stay under Around Kandy). A body oil massage and steam bath (1½ hours) costs Rs 2250. The steam bath is *very* hot. A 30-minute facial treatment (oil massage, sandalwood mask, steam) costs Rs 750. Although Le Kandyan Resorts is a bit far from town, you can relax around the pool after the treatment with a drink, and make an afternoon (or morning) of it. A three-wheeler from Kandy should cost Rs 650 return.

Swimming South of the lake, **Hotel Suisse** charges Rs 150 (including a towel) for nonguests to use the pool, in a garden setting. In the centre of town, **Queens Hotel** also has a good pool (Rs 150) and a pretty garden. There are some stunningly positioned pools around Kandy, including those at: **Hotel Thilanka** (Rs 122), on a terrace along Sangamitta Mawatha looking down

Ayurveda

Ayurveda (pronounced *eye-yer-veda*) – or the science of life – is an ancient system of medicine that uses herbs, oils, metals and animal products to heal and rejuvenate. It's a common misconception that Ayurveda uses only herbs and other organic materials – it simply isn't true. Heavily influenced by the system of the same name in India, Ayurveda is widely used in Sri Lanka for a range of ailments. Essentially, Ayurveda postulates that the five elements (earth, air, ether, water and light) are linked to the five senses and these in turn shape the nature of an individual's constitution – their *dosha* or life force. These *doshas* are referred to in Sanskrit as *vata, pitta* and *kapha*. Each has a cluster of qualities that distinguish it from the others. Disease and illness occurs when they are out of balance. The purpose of Ayurvedic treatment is to restore the balance and thus good health.

Therapeutic treatments generally take some time; the patient must be prepared to make a commitment of weeks or months. More commonly tourists avail themselves of one of the large number of Ayurvedic massage centres attached to major hotels. The full treatment involves a head massage with oil, an oil body massage and a steam bath followed by a herbal bath (leaves and all). But this sort of regimen is really mostly only for relaxation. Standards at some Ayurvedic centres are low; the massage oils may be simple coconut oil and the practitioners may be unqualified, except in some cases as sex workers. The University of Colombo and the University of Gampaha offer degrees in Ayurvedic medicine. In this book we've included only clinics where the staff are qualified with degrees.

Ayurvedic herbs, many of which are collected from the wild, are available from Ayurvedic pharmacies. Popular treatments include *paspanguwa*, a collection of plant seeds, leaves and twigs boiled in water and reduced to an acrid-tasting brew to treat colds. Packets of a more pleasant instant *peyava* (cold treatment) are available at *kades* (corner shops). In cases of severe illness, products with mercury are sometimes prescribed. Several poisoning cases have resulted from mercury products being misdiagnosed or misused, so it pays to inquire precisely what the medicine contains and then consult with a conventional physician.

on the lake; **Hotel Hilltop** (Rs 100); and **Le Kandyan Resorts** (Rs 100), southwest of Kandy, from whose terrace you get great views over the countryside.

Snooker **Hotel Suisse** has a large, well-kept snooker table where you can play billiards or snooker for Rs 150 per half hour.

Golf The **Victoria Golf Club** *(☎ 237 5570; ⓔ info@victoriagolfclub)*, is 20km east of Kandy. Surrounded on three sides by the Victoria Reservoir and with the Knuckles Range as a backdrop, it's worth coming out here for lunch at the clubhouse just to savour the views. It's a fairly challenging 18-hole course; green fees are Rs 2000 on weekdays or Rs 2500 on weekends. Golf-club rental is Rs 600 a day and a caddie charges Rs 150 a day.

Meditation Visitors can learn or practise meditation and study Buddhism at several places in the Kandy area. Ask at the **Buddhist Publication Society** *(☎/fax 223 7283)*, by the lake, for details about courses. Many centres offer free courses, but they'd obviously appreciate a donation. Give what you'd normally be paying per day for food and accommodation in Sri Lanka. See Meditation under Around Kandy for details of some of the centres that offer courses.

Places to Stay

Kandy has heaps of good guesthouses. In the middle and top brackets there are some lovely, luxurious houses and an increasing number of good hotels. Many places are set on the hills surrounding the town – in some cases 3km or more from the centre – but they are worth the effort of reaching because of their outstanding locations and views.

At the time of the Kandy Esala Perahera, room prices in Kandy can treble or quadruple; even worse, you may not be able to find a room at all. If you're intent on coming to see the *perahera*, booking far ahead may secure you a more reasonable price.

Take the stories that Kandy's touts tell you about guesthouses with several large grains of salt.

It's impossible to list all the places to stay in Kandy. The Tourist Information Centre in Kandy can help you find places as well.

Places to Stay – Budget

North & West of the Lake Formerly a guesthouse for pilgrims, **Burmese Rest** *(Katugastota Rd; singles/doubles Rs 100/200)* has six large rooms (no fans). It's very basic – no showers, just a water tank and small plastic buckets – and the shared bathrooms probably haven't been repainted since it was built (the building recently acquired heritage status). You are welcome to drink as much tea as you want, but there are no meals. If you ask permission, you may use the kitchen to prepare your own food. The monks living here are friendly, and the crumbling courtyard has its charms.

Olde Empire Hotel *(☎ 222 4284; ⓔ fernandovja@eureka.lk; 21 Temple St; rooms Rs 290-440)* has been run by the same family for 100 years. The building has oodles of character as well as affable owners. The rooms are simple, with shared bathrooms that have cold water only. Some of the rooms at the back are a little dingy, but there's a great balcony with old chairs and tables at the front, overlooking the lake. There's a good, dirt-cheap restaurant here.

Anagarika Dharmapala Mawatha, which goes up the hill past the Temple of the Tooth, leads to a number of popular guesthouses on the edge of the town. Bus Nos 654, 655 and 698 (or just ask for 'Sangamitta Mawatha' at the clock tower bus stop) will get you to this area and beyond. There's a handful of small places on Sangamitta Mawatha, the road up to the left off Anagarika Dharmapala Mawatha at the top of the hill. There are also places to the right on Dharmaraja Rd and Louis Pieris Mawatha.

Little Nest *(34 Samgamitta Mawatha; rooms hald board Rs 350)* is run by a family that is quite poor and the house reflects this side of rural life in Sri Lanka. The rooms are dingy, there are no fans, and the bathroom isn't for the faint-hearted. But don't despair! The food's delicious, the hosts are welcoming and the price is right.

Mrs Clement Dissanayake's *(☎ 222 5468; 18 First Lane; singles Rs 350, doubles Rs 500-660)* on Dharmaraja Rd is a friendly place. There are four double rooms and the most expensive has hot water. The food is very good: breakfast costs Rs 175; rice and curry with dessert is Rs 275. Phone from the main post office when you arrive in Kandy and they'll come and pick you up for free.

Green Woods (*☎ 223 2970; 34A Sangamitta Mawatha; singles Rs 500, doubles Rs 600-700*), next to Little Nest, is a quiet village house with guestrooms, on the green verge of Udawattakelle Sanctuary. The owner keeps a log of wildlife spotted from the balcony. Basic, pleasant rooms are available, one with hot water. The food is excellent: breakfast is Rs 200; rice and curry Rs 300.

South of the Lake Saranankara Rd is jam-packed with decent-value (and extremely competitive) guesthouses. The places up towards the top of the road have views.

Pink House (*☎ 0777 809173; 15 Saranankara Rd; singles/doubles Rs 250/350, with bathroom Rs 450*) has seven rooms with shared bathroom and one with private bathroom. It's a quaint old rambling house, but the facilities are pretty basic: imagine living in an unrenovated 180-year-old house. The owners are very friendly and helpful.

Thilini (*☎ 222 4975; 60 Saranankara Rd; rooms Rs 350-400*) has two simple rooms in a cute old cottage. It's a friendly place with good food (the owner used to cook for Peace Corps workers). Some people make a booking to have dinner here.

Lakshmi Guest House (*☎ 222 2154; 57 Saranankara Rd; rooms Rs 350-450*) is old-fashioned and fairly basic. There are clean rooms. No food is served.

Shady Trees (*66/65 Rajapihilla Mawatha; singles/doubles Rs 350/450*) is a simple, friendly little guesthouse on the edge of a forested area. The house has only cold water, but the mother's cooking gets warm reports. Take the steep lane heading up from the junction of Rajapihilla and Mahamaya Mawathas; it's about 120m up on the left.

The Glen (*☎ 223 5342; 58 Saranankara Rd; rooms Rs 400, with bathroom Rs 450*) has clean, homely rooms, two with shared bathroom and one with private bathroom. The couple here are friendly and there's also a pretty garden. Guests rave about the food.

Lake Mount Tourist Inn (*☎ 223 3204, fax 223 5522; ⓔ hirokow@sltnet.lk; 195A Rajapihilla Mawatha; rooms Rs 440-1100*) is clinical and tidy, and run by a Sri Lankan–Japanese husband and wife. There are a variety of rooms, with and without bathroom, and some quiet, tidy lounge areas. The more expensive rooms have hot water. It offers a free pick-up if you call when you arrive in Kandy.

Shangri-La (*☎ 222 2218; ⓔ shang@slt.lk; 2 Mahamaya Mawatha; singles/doubles Rs 500/600*), near the southeast end of the lake, has four basic rooms with hot water and a nice garden. The sitting area and usable kitchen add to the communal feel.

Expeditor (*☎ 223 8316; ⓔ expeditorkandy@hotmail.com; 58A Saranankara Rd; rooms Rs 550-1200*) has eight rooms in a new building, each with hot water and balconies. This place gets consistently good reports. It also has Internet facilities and friendly hosts who can arrange off-the-beaten-track tours.

Lake Bungalow (*☎ 222 2075; ⓔ shiyan_d@ispkandyan.lk; 22/2B Sangaraja Mawatha; rooms Rs 550-880, apartments Rs 2500*) has six clean, cheerful rooms with hot water, decorated with floral prints, in a multistorey building that looks like a school. In fact there's a preschool on the ground floor – here's hoping you like kids. The living rooms have kitchenettes. You can rent a floor with three bedrooms as an apartment. The rooms look out over the villa of the head abbot of the Malwatte Vihara. It's on a lane off Sangaraja Mawatha, just one street along from Saranankara Rd.

McLeod Inn (*☎ 222 2832; 65A Rajapihilla Mawatha; singles/doubles from Rs 650/750*) has six clean rooms with hot water, some with stunning views (these cost Rs 100 extra). It's a modern place with pleasant lounge areas, and we've had a few positive reports from people who've stayed here.

Walker's Inn Forest Lodge (*☎ 223 5407; ⓔ walker_in@hotmail.com; 32/3 Keerthi Sri Rajasinghe Mawatha; singles/doubles Rs 650/800*) is a steep walk uphill from Rajapihilla Mawatha. The friendly family here has four rooms with hot water, all scrupulously clean, a sitting room and good food. If you ring they'll pick you up from town.

Freedom Lodge (*☎ 222 3506; ⓔ freedom@sltnet.lk; 30 Saranankara Rd; rooms Rs 725-825*), further up on the other side of the road, has three spotless, bright rooms, all with hot water. The double upstairs has a balcony. There's a small garden and the hosts are very welcoming.

Places to Stay – Mid-Range

The Highest View (*☎/fax 223 3778; 129/3 Saranankara Rd; rooms Rs 600-1200*) has spotless, slightly sterile rooms with hot water and a balcony with good views.

Rooms without a balcony are cheaper; the only complaint is they're a bit small.

Sharon Inn *(☎ 222 2416; ⓔ sharon@sltnet.lk; 59 Saranankara Rd; rooms Rs 1000-1400)*, at the top of the road, is a terrific guesthouse. The Sri Lankan–German owners keep everything scrupulously clean, are helpful and serve up good nosh. The newer rooms upstairs have better views, but the older rooms on the 1st floor are a little more spacious. There's a rooftop balcony with great views, Internet facilities, hot water in every room and some have a TV as well.

There are several good mid-range guesthouses along Rajapihilla Mawatha, high above the south side of the lake. All have good views.

Royal Tourist Lodge *(☎ 222 2534; ⓔ royalxx@slt.lk; 201 Rajapihilla Mawatha; rooms Rs 1400-1700)* has Internet facilities in a comfortable modern middle-class home with three guestrooms. The more expensive room has a balcony, and all have hot water. Meals are available if you order in advance.

Comfort Lodge *(☎ 074 473707; ⓔ comfort@sri.lanka.net; 197 Rajapihilla Mawatha; singles/doubles Rs 1430/1650)* has six modern but smallish rooms with all mod cons, including hot water, TV and telephone. There's a large sitting area, a roof garden and cooking facilities.

Castle Hill Guest House *(☎ 222 4376; ⓔ ayoni@sltnet.lk; 22 Rajapihilla Mawatha; rooms Rs 2200)*, overlooking the lake, is a lovely Art Deco guesthouse with four rooms, all with bathroom. It's good for a luxury stop and the view from the lovely garden is stunning. The rooms are immense, and the lounge room has a piano and French doors to the gardens.

Places to Stay – Top End

Kandy has a couple of hotels that hark back to colonial-era style, as well as several modern luxury places.

Queens Hotel *(☎ 223 3290; ⓔ queens@kandy.ccom.lk; Dalada Vidiya; singles/doubles US$20, with air-con US$25)*, right in the centre of town and minutes from the Temple of the Tooth, is an 1840s-vintage Raj classic, complete with the 'Royal Ballroom'. If you consider the pretty garden and its clean pool, it's good value. The large rooms have polished floorboards, old-style furniture (bedspreads your grandmother would probably love) and modern bathrooms.

Hotel Hilltop *(☎ 222 4162; ⓔ hilltop@ispkandyan.lk; 200/21 Bahirawakanda; singles/doubles US$36/48, air-con US$42/54)* is a five-minute walk up off Peradeniya Rd. It has colourful rooms, great views over the town and surrounding hills, and a peaceful garden with a good-sized, clean swimming pool.

Hotel Thilanka *(☎ 223 2429, fax 222 5497; ⓔ thilanka@ids.lk; 3 Sangamitta Mawatha; singles/doubles US$40/45)* is a pleasant place amid trees and overlooking the lake. The older rooms near the front are dark and a bit neglected, but the new wing is very nice indeed, with great views and light, airy rooms. The oldest part of the hotel (near the reception) still has some original features including elegant tiles and furniture. Its pool has a a great view over the town and lake.

Hotel Suisse *(☎ 223 3024; ⓔ suisse@kandy.ccom.lk; 30 Sangaraja Mawatha; singles/doubles US$48/60)*, south of the lake, was once a British governor's house before sprouting extra ballrooms and billiards rooms and turning into a rambling hotel. Parts date back to the 1840s. The rooms have been updated with satellite TV, minibar and comfy chairs, but six rooms have antique or reproduction furniture for the full colonial attack. It's secluded and quiet, but not too far to stroll around the lake to the town centre. There are spacious public areas, including a snooker room, and a fine garden and swimming pool.

Helga's Folly *(☎ 223 4571; ⓔ chalet@sltnet.lk; 32 Frederick E de Silva Mawatha; rooms/suites US$60/110)*, off Rajapihilla Mawatha, is a deeply eccentric place crammed with palatial furnishings, puffed with comfy cushions and partially lit by wax-dripping candelabras. You'll either love it or find it slightly disconcerting. It's possibly the only hotel in the world that discourages having too many guests, and package tourists are banned. The plush rooms and the suites don't have air-con. There's a pool surrounded by fairies (we kid you not), and a restaurant where merely curious nonguests can eat. Lunch or dinner costs US$14 – book ahead.

Hotel Topaz *(☎ 223 2326; ⓔ topaz@eureka.lk; Anniewatte; rooms US$73, singles/doubles with air-con US$83/100)*, way up on top of a hill overlooking the town from the west about 2km up from Peradeniya Rd, has 77 rooms (36 with air-con). It's rather bland but the superb views and swimming pool help justify the prices. Owned by the same company, the **Tourmaline** on the hill below is similar but pricier. The Topaz is better value for money.

Places to Eat

Many people eat in their guesthouses, where some of Kandy's tastiest food is to be had and where you can also enjoy some of the local specialities, particularly at *poya*. (Hotel Suisse's food has been recommended.) There are a number of popular cheap places in central Kandy but they all seem to yo-yo between acceptable and absolutely awful. Most of them are along Dalada Vidiya, or in the back streets to the north.

Delight Bakers & Sweet House *(Dalada Vidiya)* has reasonable bread, pastries, cakes and short eats, and dozens of sweets waiting to march out the door.

Olde Empire *(mains around Rs 60)*, at the Olde Empire Hotel, is a characterful old place still serving up a delicious spicy rice and curry for Rs 75 and lunch packets for Rs 45.

Devon Restaurant *(Dalada Vidiya; mains Rs 50-300)* has a food court on the 1st floor and is stylish on the outside, ugly on the inside. The food is cheap, edible and filling: fried rice, beef curry and so on.

White House Restaurant *(mains Rs 100-150)*, down the street from the Devon, is tacky but cheap. It has snacks, drinks and ice cream, or you can fill up on meals such as mixed fried rice, chicken fried noodles and sweet-and-sour chicken.

Paiva's Restaurant *(37 Yatinuwara Vidiya; mains Rs 60-300)* has a North Indian menu, a Chinese menu and a bakery. You can sit in the airy, busy section downstairs, or you can go upstairs to the office-like surrounds. The food is good and ranges from *dosas* to Chinese mains (from Rs 130 to 300). There's also lunchtime rice and curry, from Rs 55 to 85.

Rams *(87 Bennet Soysa Vidiya; open 7.30am-about 10pm; mains Rs 150-250)*, on the street also known as Cross St, serves excellent South Indian food in a wonderfully colourful setting. A vegetarian thali (a South Indian meal consisting of rice with vegetable curries and pappadams) costs Rs 175, *masala dosas* (curried vegetables inside a lentil and rice-flour pancake) Rs 145 and smaller *dosas* Rs 40 to 50. Plain rice costs a ridiculous Rs 110, as does a large bottle of water.

The Pub *(☎ 232 4868; Dalada Vidiya)* has decent food and friendly bar staff. The balcony is a great place to unwind and meet other travellers, while indoors has air-con. It's something of a Western enclave but it makes a nice change from rice and curry after a couple of weeks. Spaghetti carbonara costs Rs 260 and a nicoise salad is Rs 160. A pint of draft beer costs Rs 150, and there is a decent selection of imported wines. It's open until 10pm Sunday to Thursday, later on Friday and Saturday nights. You'll find it above the Koffeepot Internet café, west of the Bank of Ceylon.

Flower Song Chinese Restaurant *(☎ 222 3628; 137 Kotugodella Vidiya; mains Rs 330-470)* is a surprise with old-fashioned service and clean, air-con surrounds, and it even has a wine list. It's a very family-friendly place, and a good retreat from the bustle of town. The small serves are enough for one.

Self-caterers can check out **Cargills** *(Dalada Vidaya)* or dive into the market.

Entertainment

Pubs/Bars Thankfully this quiet town has been injected with a new night-time venue, the originally named **The Pub** (see Places to Eat earlier). It's a busy, comfy place with music, an overgrown TV screen and a balcony packed with cane chairs.

Kandy Garden Club *(☎ 222 2675; Sangaraja Mawatha)*, at the far end of the lake, is a venerable gentlemen's club that has opened its doors to visitors. For a temporary membership fee of Rs 100 you can relax in the bar or on the veranda with a Lion lager (Rs 85) and fried devilled cashews. The bar is open 5pm till late daily. The billiards room is still something of a male bastion, but you can rack up on the old tables for Rs 100 for 30 minutes. There's also a couple of tennis courts (Rs 100 per hour plus rackets and balls).

Pub Royale, beside the Queens Hotel, is a large, airy bar with an old-fashioned flavour. It's a place for a quiet drink, and a cheap one too at Rs 100 for a Lion.

Le Garage, at the Le Kandyan Resorts, 20 minutes southwest of town by three-wheeler (Rs 250), is Kandy's only nightclub. It's open Saturday nights only, from 9pm till 2am or 3am. Entry for women is free, and it's Rs 450 for mixed couples, but there's no entry allowed for men from outside the hotel. The dress code specifies no shorts, sandals or baseball caps, which is particularly discriminatory to balding men.

The top hotels all have **bars**, but be careful of the cost of the drinks. You can buy beer to take away at **Cargills**.

Kandyan Dancers & Drummers The famed Kandyan dancers are not principally a theatrical performance, but you can see them go through their athletic routines each night at three locales around Kandy.

Kandy Lake Club *(admission Rs 300)*, 300m up Sangamitta Mawatha, starts its show at 7pm. It's very popular; the finale is a display of fire-walking. The front seats are usually reserved for groups and if you want to get good seats, turn up at least 20 minutes early. The Kandy Lake Club is also a casino. Beware of the price of drinks. There are also shows in the **Kandyan Art Association & Cultural Centre** *(admission Rs 300)* at 6pm, which culminate in fire-walking. The auditorium here makes it easier to take photographs than at Kandy Lake Club. It's on the northern lakeshore. There are also dance shows at the **YMBA** *(Young Men's Buddhist Association)*, southwest of the lake, at 6.30pm (admission Rs 300).

You can also hear Kandyan drummers every day at the Temple of the Tooth and the other temples surrounding it – their drumming signals the start and finish of the daily *pujas*.

Spectator Sports

The modest **Asgiriya Cricket Ground**, north of the town centre, hosts crowds of up to 15,000 cheering fans at international one-day and test matches. Ticket prices depend on the popularity of the two teams. India versus Sri Lanka matches are the most valued; seats in the grandstand can cost up to Rs 1750, while standing room in the public areas will cost Rs 100. Tickets are also sold on the day, or you can book grandstand seats up to a month in advance through the **BCCSL office** *(☎ 223 8533, fax 222 8540)* here.

If you're a rugby fan and you're in Kandy between May and September, you can take in a game or two at the **Nittawella rugby grounds**. Check with the tourist office for details on who's playing when.

Shopping

Kandyan Art Association & Cultural Centre, beside the lake, has a good selection of local lacquerwork, brassware and other craft items in a colonial-era showroom covered in a patina of age. There are some craftspeople working on the spot.

There's a government-run **Laksala** arts and crafts shop to the west of the lake with cheaper prices than the Art Association & Cultural Centre, but it has nothing on the big Laksala in Colombo.

Central Kandy has a number of shops selling antique jewellery, silver belts and other items. You can also buy crafts in and around the colourful **main market** on Station Rd. Kandy has a number of batik manufacturers; some of the best and most original are the batik pictures made by **Upali Jayakody** and by **Fresco Batiks** on Peradeniya Rd outside Kandy.

Getting There & Away

Bus Kandy has one main bus station (the manic Goods Shed) and a series of bus stops near the clock tower. It can be hard to work out which one to head to. A rule of thumb worth following is that the Goods Shed bus station has long-distance buses, ie, to Colombo, Polonnaruwa and Nuwara Eliya, while local buses, ie, Peradeniya, Ampitiya, Matale and Kegalle, leave from near the clock tower. However, just to complicate things further some private intercity express buses (to the airport, Negombo and Colombo, for example) leave from Station Rd between the clock tower and the train station. If you're still confused, ask a passer-by.

Colombo CTB buses run from the Goods Shed bus station every 30 minutes till 8.30pm (Rs 44, 3½ hours). There are also ordinary private buses (Rs 60 to 75, three hours), and air-con intercity express buses (Rs 95, 2½ to three hours); both services start at about 5am and leave when full throughout the day. The express and ordinary buses leave from stand No 1.

International Airport & Negombo Private intercity express buses to Bandaranaike International Airport and Negombo leave from the Station Rd bus stop. CTB buses leave from the Goods Shed. The first intercity bus departs at about 6.30am and the last at about

5.30pm. They tend to leave when full, every 20 to 30 minutes. The fare for the three- to 3½-hour journey is Rs 52 for the CTB bus and Rs 85 for the air-con express bus.

Nuwara Eliya & Hatton Private air-con buses go to Nuwara Eliya, and some go on to Hatton (or you can change in Nuwara Eliya for Hatton). They leave from the Goods Shed bus station. The fare is Rs 90.

Haputale & Ella For these destinations, change at Nuwara Eliya.

Anuradhapura & Dambulla Buses to Anuradhapura also leave from the Goods Shed bus station. Air-con intercity express buses start running at about 5.30am and depart approximately every hour until 6.30pm. The trip takes three hours and costs Rs 105. Ordinary buses take about 30 minutes longer and cost Rs 57. You can also catch an air-con Anuradhapura-bound bus to Dambulla, but you must pay the full amount regardless. The trip to Dambulla on an ordinary private bus costs Rs 30.

Polonnaruwa Air-con buses to Polonnaruwa leave the Goods Shed bus station from about 5.30am and go approximately every hour until 6.30pm. Tickets are Rs 105 and the journey takes three hours. The ordinary bus takes about 30 minutes longer and costs Rs 48.

Sigiriya There's a CTB bus to Sigiriya from the Goods Shed bus station at 8am, which returns at 3pm (Rs 35). There are a couple of ordinary private buses a day for Rs 40.

Other Destinations Bus No 594 to Matale (intercity express Rs 25, CTB Rs 13) leaves from beside the central clock tower. Buses to Kegalle via Kurunegala (intercity express Rs 45, CTB Rs 18) stop at clock tower stops.

Train For details of the train services from Kandy to the main destinations, see the boxed text, 'Main Trains from Kandy'.

Taxi It's easy to get long-distance taxis to or from Kandy (see Getting Around, following). To Bandaranaike International Airport costs about Rs 3000 and to Colombo about Rs 2600.

Many taxi drivers hang around outside the entrance to the Temple of the Tooth waiting for work. Your guesthouse or hotel can organise taxi tours but you'll probably get a cheaper deal if you organise it through these chaps. You could do a day trip to Sigiriya (via Dambulla) for example, or even just visit the three temples and the botanic gardens (see Around Kandy later in this chapter). For a whole van, expect to pay about Rs 2500 a day, which includes driver and fuel.

Getting Around

Bus Buses to outlying parts of Kandy and nearby towns such as Peradeniya, Ampitiya, Matale and Kegalle leave from near the clock tower.

Car, Motorcycle & Bicycle Rental You can hire motorbikes from **Malik** *(☎ 223 3903; e maliktsl@yahoo.com; Palm Garden Guest House, William Gopallawa Mawatha)*. It costs Rs 800 per day for a Honda 125, or Rs 650 per day for a week. The price includes a helmet and insurance – but double check. You can hire bicycles for Rs 150 per day, and Malik takes tours around the island (he's fluent in French). He also hires out cars; a Nissan Charade or Toyota Corolla costs Rs 2000 per day with unlimited kilometres.

Taxi With metered air-con taxis, **Radio Cabs** *(☎ 223 3322)* are a comfortable alternative to three-wheelers. However, be aware that you may have to wait some time for your cab, especially if it's raining and demand is heavy. Settle on a price before you start your journey with taxis (vans) that are not metered.

Three-Wheeler It costs about Rs 80 to take a three-wheeler from the train station to places towards the southeast end of the lake, and Rs 120 or so to places a bit further out such as the Little Nest or Green Woods.

AROUND KANDY

☎ 081

There are a few things worth seeing around Kandy that can be done in a morning or afternoon trip or, if you're not in a rush, you could take the day.

Main Trains from Kandy

Tickets can be bought and reserved (up to 10 days in advance) at Kandy's train station from counter No 1, which is open from 5.30am to 5.30pm daily.

Four seats in the 1st-class observation saloon are available from Kandy. The other seats are reserved for passengers making day trips from Colombo. If you want to break your journey between Kandy and Ella or beyond you can, but you must use your ticket within 24 hours.

destination	departure time	fare (Rs) 3rd	2nd	1st class	duration (hrs)
Badulla (*Podi Menike*)	8.55am	38	104	231.50*	7½
Bandarawela (*Podi Menike*)	8.55am	31	85.50	199*	6
Colombo (*Intercity Express*)	6.25am, 3pm	-	68	172*	2½
Colombo via Rambukkana (for Pinnewala Elephant Orphanage)	6.45am, 10.30am, 3.40pm, 4.50 pm	25	68.50	-	3
Ella (*Podi Menike*)	8.55am	33.50	97	211*	6½
Haputale (*Podi Menike*)	8.55am	28.50	79	187*	5½
Hatton (*Podi Menike*)	8.55am	13.50	37.50	135*	2½
Matale	5.45am, 7.15am, 10.05am, 2.35am, 5.20am, 6.55pm	6	-	-	1½
Matara via Bentota, Galle	5.25am	57	157	-	6
Nanu Oya (for Nuwara Eliya) (*Podi Menike*)	8.55am	20.50	56.50	147.50*	4

* The 1st-class observation saloon includes a booking fee of Rs 50.

Peradeniya Botanic Gardens

The gardens *(adult/student & child under 12 Rs 300/200; open 7.30am-4.30pm daily)* are 6km out of Kandy towards Colombo. Before the British came these were royal pleasure gardens: today they're the largest botanic gardens in Sri Lanka, covering 60 hectares and bounded on three sides by a loop of the Mahaweli Ganga. They're beautiful and well worth a visit.

There's a fine collection of orchids and a stately avenue of royal palms that was planted in 1950. A major attraction is the giant Javan fig tree on the great lawn – it covers 1600 square metres. There's an avenue of cannon ball trees and another of cabbage palms. Don't miss the avenue of double coconut palms or coco de mer – each coconut weights from 10kg to 20kg. The spice garden, near the entrance, allows you to see nutmeg, cinnamon, cloves and more without the hassle of a salesperson breathing down your neck. The snake creeper close by is also well worth seeing. Then there are the giant bamboo and Assam rubber trees, and who could resist hunting down the sausage tree? You can easily spend a whole day wandering around the gardens.

The **Royal Botanical Garden Cafeteria** *(mains Rs 250-400)*, about 500m north of the entrance, has a good buffet lunch or you can choose à la carte. Prices are on the high

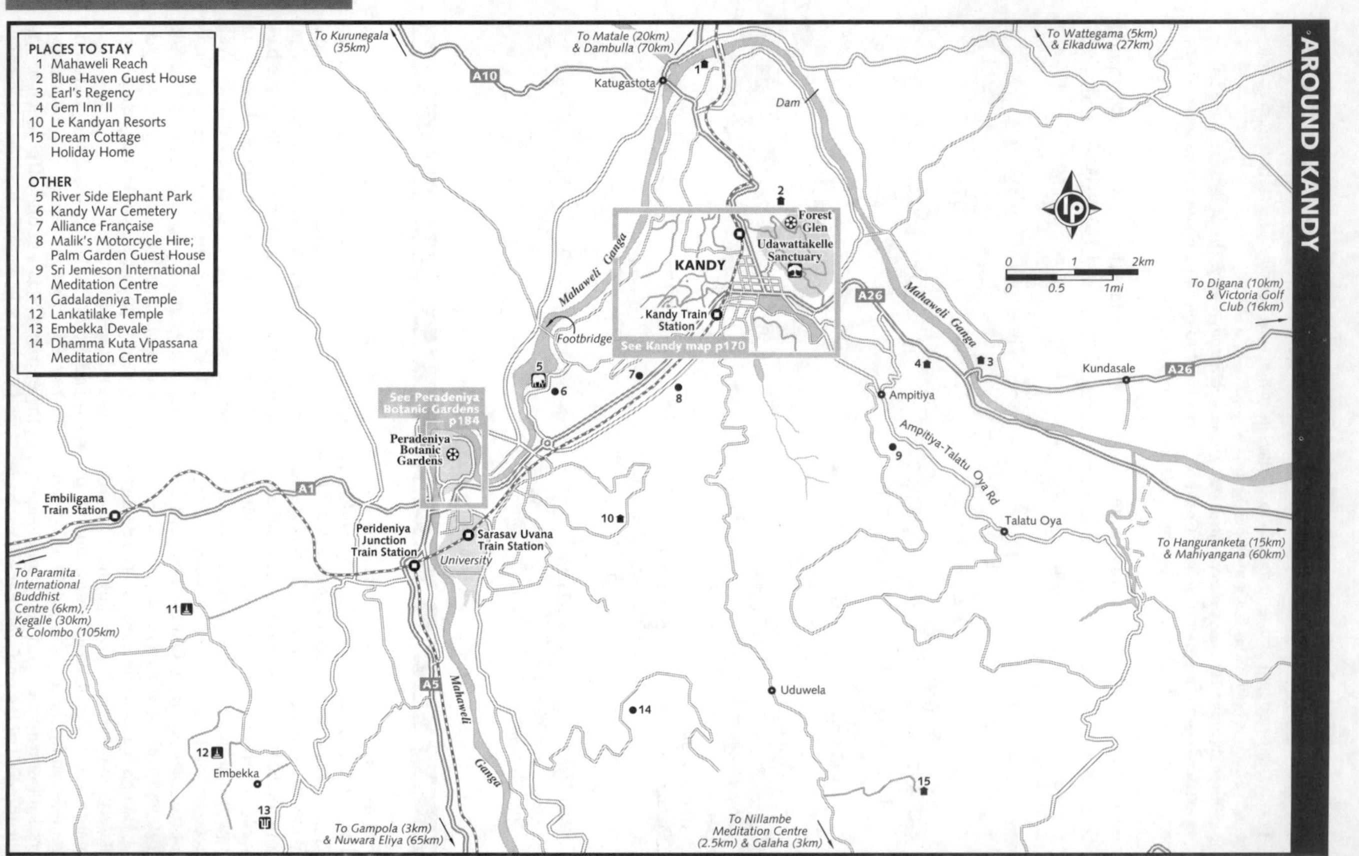
AROUND KANDY
PLACES TO STAY
1 Mahaweli Reach
2 Blue Haven Guest House
3 Earl's Regency
4 Gem Inn II
10 Le Kandyan Resorts
15 Dream Cottage Holiday Home
OTHER
5 River Side Elephant Park
6 Kandy War Cemetery
7 Alliance Française
8 Malik's Motorcycle Hire; Palm Garden Guest House
9 Sri Jemieson International Meditation Centre
11 Gadaladeniya Temple
12 Lankatilake Temple
13 Embekka Devale
14 Dhamma Kuta Vipassana Meditation Centre
To Kurunegala (35km)
To Matale (20km) & Dambulla (70km)
To Wattegama (5km) & Elkaduwa (27km)
To Digana (10km) & Victoria Golf Club (16km)
To Hanguranketa (15km) & Mahiyangana (60km)
To Paramita International Buddhist Centre (6km), Kegalle (30km) & Colombo (105km)
To Gampola (3km) & Nuwara Eliya (65km)
To Nillambe Meditation Centre (2.5km) & Galaha (3km)
Katugastota
Dam
Mahaweli Ganga
Forest Glen
Udawattakelle Sanctuary
KANDY
Kandy Train Station
See Kandy map p170
Footbridge
See Peradeniya Botanic Gardens p184
Peradeniya Botanic Gardens
Embiligama Train Station
Perideniya Junction Train Station
Sarasav Uvana Train Station
University
Ampitiya
Ampitiya-Talatu Oya Rd
Talatu Oya
Kundasale
Uduwela
Embekka
A10
A26
A1
A5
0 1 2km
0 0.5 1mi

side. A club sandwich costs Rs 275, and a mere lime and soda Rs 100 (compared to outside – Rs 12). Those on a budget can always take a picnic.

At the entrance you can buy a copy of the *Illustrated Guide, Royal Botanic Gardens,* which has a map and suggested walks through the gardens. There are other books available too – all decently priced.

Bus No 654 from the clock tower bus stop in Kandy will take you to the gardens for Rs 4.50. A three-wheeler from the centre of Kandy to the gardens will set you back about Rs 400 (return trip) and a van will cost Rs 500.

Kandy War Cemetery

This beautifully kept garden cemetery *(open 7.30am-4pm daily)* is managed by the Commonwealth War Graves Commission. Most of the 203 graves date from WWII, half of them British and the rest mostly Indian, Sri Lankan and East African. This peaceful, rather sad place is close to the River Side Elephant Park on Deveni Rajasinghe Mawatha, 2km southwest of Kandy.

River Side Elephant Park

The park *(admission Rs 400; open 7.30am-4.30pm daily)* usually has four elephants. The Rs 400 admission price includes a short ride, while Rs 1000 buys a longer ride, very popular with Sri Lankan visitors in particular. The elephants knock off work at around noon and bathe in the Mahaweli Ganga.

Meditation

Nillambe Meditation Centre *(☎ 0777 804555; ⓔ upulnilambe@yahoo.com)*, near Nillambe Bungalow Junction about 13km south of Kandy, can be reached by bus (catch a Delthota bus via Galaha and get off at Office Junction; the trip takes about an hour). It's a pretty spot, with great views. There's a daily set schedule of meditation classes, and basic accommodation for about 40 people. You can stay for Rs 300 a day (including food), and although blankets are supplied you may wish to bring a sleeping bag. There's no electricity, so bring a torch (flashlight). There's a large modern library here. To reach Nillambe from Office Junction you have a steep 3km walk through tea plantations (or a three-wheeler may be at the junction to take you for Rs 150). A taxi to/from Kandy costs Rs 650. The road up to the centre is a narrow, partially sealed track, so you might want to summon a van rather than a sedan.

At Ampitiya, southeast of Kandy, the **Sri Jemieson International Meditation Centre** *(☎ 222 5057)* on Ampitiya Samadhi Mawatha runs free five- and 10-day courses. Phone to find out when the next course starts. There are eight rooms for male students only – this is a monastery and temple. Women must stay off-campus. To get there, catch a Talatu Oya bus from the clock tower bus stop in Kandy (Rs 5). Look for the sign on the right-hand side about 3km along the Ampitiya–Talatu Oya road. There's a 1.2km walk up a winding track to the centre.

The **Dhamma Kuta Vipassana Meditation Centre** *(☎ 070 800057; ⓔ dhamma@slt net.lk; Mowbray, Hindagala)* is in the hills and has superb views. It offers free 10-day courses following the SN Goenka system; you must book into one of the courses – you can't just turn up. There's dorm accommodation for about 90 students, with separate male and female quarters. Take a Mahakanda-bound bus from the clock tower bus stop in Kandy and get off at the last stop. There's a small sign at the bottom of the track to the centre. It's a very steep 2km walk, or you can catch a three-wheeler for Rs 150. A taxi to/from Kandy should cost Rs 350.

The **Paramita International Buddhist Centre** *(☎ 257 0732)* at the top of the Bolana Pass, 1km past Kadugannawa on the Colombo road, is a new meditation centre. It runs two free fortnight-long meditation programs per month, starting every second Saturday. It has clean accommodation for 15 people (men and women), lush gardens and a library. A typical day kicks off at 4am. Several teachers including a Dutch monk lead courses in SN Goenka's Vipassana. A three-wheeler from here to Kadugannawa's train or bus stations will cost Rs 30.

A Temple Loop from Kandy

Visiting some of the many temples around Kandy gives you a chance to see a little rural life as well as observe Sri Lankan culture. This particularly pleasant loop will take you to three temples and back via the botanic gardens. There's quite a bit of walking involved so if you're not in the mood you could narrow down your visit to one or

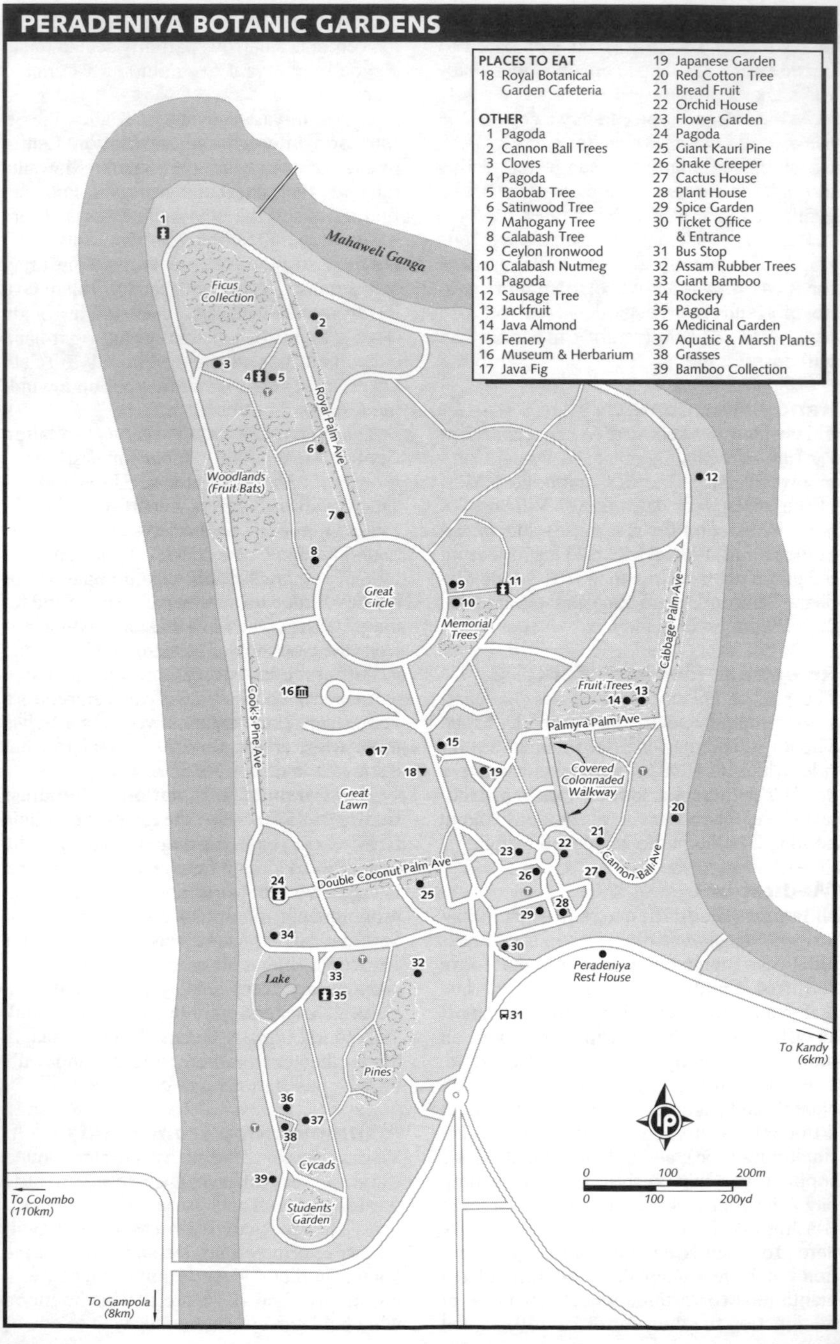

PERADENIYA BOTANIC GARDENS

PLACES TO EAT
18 Royal Botanical Garden Cafeteria

OTHER
1 Pagoda
2 Cannon Ball Trees
3 Cloves
4 Pagoda
5 Baobab Tree
6 Satinwood Tree
7 Mahogany Tree
8 Calabash Tree
9 Ceylon Ironwood
10 Calabash Nutmeg
11 Pagoda
12 Sausage Tree
13 Jackfruit
14 Java Almond
15 Fernery
16 Museum & Herbarium
17 Java Fig
19 Japanese Garden
20 Red Cotton Tree
21 Bread Fruit
22 Orchid House
23 Flower Garden
24 Pagoda
25 Giant Kauri Pine
26 Snake Creeper
27 Cactus House
28 Plant House
29 Spice Garden
30 Ticket Office & Entrance
31 Bus Stop
32 Assam Rubber Trees
33 Giant Bamboo
34 Rockery
35 Pagoda
36 Medicinal Garden
37 Aquatic & Marsh Plants
38 Grasses
39 Bamboo Collection

Mahaweli Ganga
Ficus Collection
Royal Palm Ave
Woodlands (Fruit Bats)
Great Circle
Memorial Trees
Cabbage Palm Ave
Fruit Trees
Cook's Pine Ave
Palmyra Palm Ave
Covered Colonnaded Walkway
Great Lawn
Cannon Ball Ave
Double Coconut Palm Ave
Peradeniya Rest House
Lake
Pines
To Kandy (6km)
Cycads
Students' Garden
To Colombo (110km)
To Gampola (8km)
0 100 200m
0 100 200yd

two of the temples listed or take a taxi trip to all three; expect to pay about Rs 1400 from Kandy.

The first stop is the **Embekka Devale** *(admission Rs 100)*, for which you need catch bus No 643 (to Vatadeniya via Embekka) from near the clock tower in Kandy. The buses run only about once an hour and the village of Embekka is about seven twisting and turning kilometres beyond the botanic gardens. From the village you've got a pleasant countryside stroll of about 1km to the temple, built in the 14th century. Its carved wooden pillars, thought to have come from a royal audience hall in the city, are said to be the finest in the Kandy area. The carvings include swans, double-headed eagles, wrestling men and dancing women. A miniature version of the Kandy Esala Perahera is held here in September.

From here to the **Lankatilake Temple** *(admission Rs 100)* is a 1.5km stroll along a path through the rice paddies until you see the blue temple loom up on the left. From Kandy you can go directly to the Lankatilake Temple on bus No 666 or take a Kiribathkumbara or Pilimatalawa bus from the same stop as the Embekka buses. It's a Buddhist and Hindu temple with fine views of the countryside, featuring a Buddha image, Kandy-period paintings, rock-face inscriptions and stone elephant figures. It's likely that an ungracious *paan*-spitting monk will unlock the shrine and demand a donation. A festival is held here in August.

It's a further 3km walk from here to the **Gadaladeniya Temple** *(admission Rs 100)*, or you can catch a bus from Kandy (No 644, among others, will take you there). Built on a rocky outcrop and covered with small rock pools, the temple is reached by a series of steps cut directly into the rock. This Buddhist temple with a Hindu annexe dates from a similar period to the Lankatilake Temple and the Embekka Devale. A moonstone marks the entrance to the main shrine. The shrine's murals and some of the statues have been erased or damaged by water seepage – but repairs are now (somewhat fitfully) underway. A resident artist will be happy to show you around.

From Gadaladeniya Temple the main Colombo–Kandy road is less than 2km away – you can reach it close to the 105km post. It's a pleasant stroll, and from the main road almost any bus will take you to the Peradeniya Botanic Gardens or on into Kandy.

Places to Stay

If you want quiet days spent wandering along shaded tracks, with views of rolling hills, then stay just out of Kandy. It's always easy to get into town should you want to – a taxi or three-wheeler is never far away.

Places to Stay – Budget & Mid-Range

Gem Inn II *(☎ 222 4239; 102/90 Hewaheta Rd, Talwatta; rooms Rs 440-1100)* is about 2.5km southeast of Kandy's town centre, perched on a hillside with wonderful views over the Mahaweli Ganga and the Knuckles Range. There are seven rooms, all looking a bit tired; most have their own balcony. There's a large garden and good food.

Blue Haven Guest House *(☎ 222 9617; ⓔ bluehaven@kandyan.net; 30/2 Poorna Lane; singles Rs 500-600, doubles Rs 600-800)* is on the north side of the Udawattakelle Sanctuary in Kandy. Each of the five rooms has florid decor, hot water and a large, airy balcony overlooking the jungle setting. It also has Internet facilities and the owner can arrange road trips and walks around Kandy and into the Knuckles Range.

Forest Glen *(☎ 222 2239; ⓔ forestglen@ids.lk; 150/6 Lady Gordon's Dr, Sri Dalada Thapowana Mawatha; rooms Rs 750-1200)* is tucked away on a winding road on the edge of Udawattakelle Sanctuary. The eight rooms have spotless bathrooms and views over a leafy little valley. The double rooms with a balcony cost the most.

Dream Cottage Holiday Home *(☎ 071 283626; ⓔ siribas@sltnet.lk; Uduwela; singles/doubles Rs 1100/1500)* is 10km south of Kandy, set in the countryside at the foot of the Uragala Range. The road here leads through tea estates. This modern villa has intriguing architecture, incorporating two huge boulders. It has three rooms, or you can rent out the whole place for Rs 4000 – it has room for eight. Minibuses from the clock tower to Uduwela cost Rs 20; from there a three-wheeler should cost Rs 300. It's on the site of the former Metiyagulla Tea Estate, in case no-one in Uduwela has heard of the place.

Painting the Buddha's Eyes

In making a Buddha image, craftsmen leave the *netra pinkama* (eye ritual) until last, and then only paint them in at an auspicious moment, painstakingly charted out by astrologers. Creating a new temple shrine is a long and highly elaborate ritual carried out by specialist craftsmen.

The act of creating the eyes consecrates the Buddha statue. For the *netra pinkama*, the painter, from the Sittaru subcaste of temple craftsmen and artists, is locked into the shrine with an assistant. Rather than looking directly at the face of the image, the painter adds the eyes using a mirror. When the eyes are finished, the painter is blindfolded and led outside to a place where his first gaze can be upon something that can be symbolically destroyed, such as a pool of water, which can be hit with a stick. Unusually in Sri Lankan Buddhist rituals, there is quite a fear of dire consequences if there's a slip-up in the *netra pinkama*. In the 16th century Robert Knox explained the ritual this way: 'Before the eyes are made, it is not accounted a God, but a lump of ordinary metal…the eyes being formed, it is thenceforward a God.'

Mirrors are also used in the *nanumura mangalya* ritual, on the same day that Buddhists bathe for New Year. A mirror is set up to reflect the face of the Buddha, and a monk bathes in the reflection of the mirror, using special oils made of turmeric, coconut and other ingredients, and finally with water.

Places to Stay – Top End

The Citadel *(☎ 223 4365/6; e htlres@keells.com; 124 Srimath Kuda Ratwatte Mawatha; singles/doubles with air-con US$66/72)*, 5km west of the town centre, is a pretentiously named package-tour resort beside the Mahaweli Ganga. All rooms have balconies overlooking the river. The swimming pool is worth a visit. A taxi from Kandy will cost Rs 350.

Le Kandyan Resorts *(☎ 223 3521/2; e lekandy@sltnet.lk; Bowalawatta, Heerassagala; rooms US$95, suites US$184)* sits on a grassy slope high in the hills 20 minutes' drive southwest of Kandy. The air-con rooms are decorated with Kandyan craftwork, and there's an inviting pool with superb views and a well-equipped Ayurvedic centre, which is also open to nonguests.

Earl's Regency *(☎ 242 2122; e erhotel@sltnet.lk; singles/doubles US$96/120)* at Kundasale is a substantial hotel with all mod cons, great views and immaculate rooms – all stylishly packaged. The rooms have air-con, a slick black bathroom and polished floorboards, and most have a balcony.

Mahaweli Reach *(☎ 074 472727; e mareach@slt.lk; singles/doubles US$108/120)* vies to be Kandy's best hotel. The palatial white building sits on the banks of the Mahaweli Ganga north of town. The 115 rooms have all mod cons, and there are elegant restaurants and a particularly nice swimming pool. International cricket teams stay here, and the hotel sometimes hosts concerts (jazz or classical music typically) sponsored by foreign cultural centres in Colombo. Car buffs will get a thrill from the vintage car fleet in the basement.

EAST OF KANDY

Most travellers from Kandy go west to Colombo, north to the ancient cities or south to the rest of the hill country. It's also possible to go east to Mahiyangana, beyond which you will find Badulla on the southeast edge of the hill country and Monaragala on the way to Arugam Bay, the Gal Oya National Park and, further north, Batticaloa on the east coast.

The Buddha is said to have preached at Mahiyangana and there's a dagoba (Buddhist temple) here to mark the spot. There are two roads to Mahiyangana, on either side of the Mahaweli Ganga and the Victoria and Randenigala Reservoirs. The A26 north road goes past the Victoria Golf Club and the Victoria Reservoir to Madugoda, before twisting through no less than 18 hairpin bends, a dramatic exit from the hill country to the Mahaweli lowlands and the dry-zone plains. From the top you have a magnificent view of the Mahaweli Development Project. It makes for one of the country's hairiest bus rides – on the way up you worry about overheating, on the way down you try not to think about the brakes. You usually pass at least one 4WD or truck that didn't make it and lies in the jungle beneath.

Drivers prefer the road along the southern shores of the Victoria and Randenigala Reservoirs, which is much faster and in better condition. This road closes at dusk, however, because wild elephants from the nature reserve are attracted to headlights. To get from Kandy to the hills of Uva Province (Ella, Haputale), it's quicker taking this road and then the route south to Badulla than via Nuwara Eliya.

Mahiyangana

☎ 055

The town was laid out to serve the new irrigation districts, so it is sprawling and not densely settled. Besides the **Mahiyangana dagoba**, where according to legend Buddha on his first visit to Lanka preached to the primitive people who then inhabited these parts, there are a couple of passable hotels.

The Venjinn Guest House *(☎ 225 7151; 42 Rest House Rd; singles/doubles Rs 350/400, with air-con Rs 700/750)* has 10 fairly ordinary rooms, plus an outdoor restaurant (rice and curry Rs 150) and a bar. It's a short three-wheeler ride from the bus station.

Tharuka Inn *(☎ 225 7631; 89/1 Padiyathalawa Rd; singles/doubles Rs 650/750)* is about 1km from the bus station on the Ampara road. It's a multistorey new building with slow country service. The clean, bland rooms (cold water only) will do for a night.

Mahiyangana UDA Rest House *(☎/fax 225 7304; singles/doubles US$15/18, with air-con US$22/25)*, on the banks of the Mahaweli Ganga, is a lowrise building in reasonably clean condition. The rooms with air-con are spacious.

Mahiyangana is something of a transport hub, and there are regular buses to Badulla (CTB Rs 32), Polonnaruwa (private bus Rs 52), Ampara (CTB and private Rs 54), Monaragala (CTB Rs 37) and Kandy (private bus Rs 35, three hours). Travellers from Mahiyangana to Monaragala may need to change buses at Bibile.

Knuckles Range

So named because the range's peaks look like a closed fist, this 1500m-high massif is home to pockets of rare montane forest. The area, which offers some pleasant walks, has been declared a conservation area. There are a couple of hotels at Elkaduwa, and several more developments are planned in the area.

Green View *(☎ 0777 811881; ⓔ bluehaven@kandyan.net; Elkaduwa Rd, Elkaduwa; singles/doubles Rs 800/1000)* is a hillside lodge with seven rooms, all with hot water. It's a good spot for walks.

Hunas Falls Hotel *(☎ 081-234 5700, fax 071 735134; ⓔ hunasfalls@eureka.lk; rooms US$112, suites from US$120)* is a luxury hotel with one of the most spectacular settings in the country. It's 27km out of Kandy, high up in a tea estate at Elkaduwa. Rooms come with air-con; there are all the mod cons including a swimming pool, tennis court, a well-stocked fish pool above the Hunas waterfalls and plenty of walks in the surrounding hills. There's a US$10 supplement in July, when people flee here from the heat of the plains.

A taxi from Kandy to Elkaduwa should cost Rs 600. Alternatively, take a bus to Wattegama (from near the clock tower in Kandy) and catch another to Elkaduwa from there.

ADAM'S PEAK (SRI PADA)

A beautiful and fascinating place, this lofty peak has sparked the imagination for centuries. It is variously known as Adam's Peak (the place where Adam first set foot on earth after being cast out of heaven), Sri Pada ('Sacred Footprint', left by Buddha as he headed towards paradise) or Samanalakande (Butterfly Mountain, where butterflies go to die). Some believe the huge 'footprint' on the top of the 2243m peak to be that of St Thomas, the early apostle of India, or even of Lord Shiva.

Whichever legend you care to believe, the fact remains that it has been a pilgrimage centre for over 1000 years. King Parakramabahu and King Nissanka Malla of Polonnaruwa provided *ambalamas* (resting places) up the mountain to shelter the weary pilgrims.

These days the pilgrimage season begins on *poya* day in December and runs until the Vesak festival in May. The busiest time is January and February. At other times the temple on the summit is unused, and between May and October the peak is obscured by cloud for much of the time. During the pilgrimage season a steady stream of pilgrims (and the odd tourist) makes the climb up the countless steps to the top from the small settlement of Dalhousie, 33km by road southwest of the tea town of Hatton, which is on the Colombo–Kandy–Nuwara Eliya railway and road. The route is illuminated in season by a string of lights, which look very pretty as they snake up the mountainside. Out of season you can still do the walk, you'll just need a torch (flashlight). Many pilgrims prefer to make the longer, much more tiring – but equally well-marked and lit – seven-hour climb from Ratnapura via the Carney Estate, because of the greater merit thus gained.

It's not only the sacred footprint that pilgrims seek. As the first rays of dawn light up the holy mountain you're treated to an extremely fine view – the hill country rises to the east, while to the west the land slopes away to the sea. Colombo, 65km away, is easily visible on a clear day. It's little wonder that English author John Stills described the peak as 'one of the vastest and most reverenced cathedrals of the human race'.

Interesting as the ascent is, and beautiful as the dawn is, Adam's Peak saves its *pièce de résistance* for a few minutes after dawn. The sun casts a perfect shadow of the peak onto the misty clouds down towards the coast. As the sun rises higher this eerie triangular shadow races back towards the peak, eventually disappearing into its base. As you scramble back down to the bottom you can reflect on how much more straightforward the ascent is today than it was in the 19th century – as described in a Victorian-era guidebook:

> ...others struggle upwards unaided, until, fainting by the way, they are considerately carried with all haste in their swooning condition to the summit and forced into an attitude of worship at the shrine to secure the full benefits of their pilgrimage before death should supervene; others never reach the top at all, but perish from cold and fatigue; and there have been many instances of pilgrims losing their lives by being blown over precipices or falling from giddiness induced by a thoughtless retrospect when surmounting especially dangerous cliffs.

The Climb

You can start the 7km climb from Dalhousie (del-**house**) soon after dark – in which case you'll need at least a good sleeping bag to keep you warm overnight at the top – or you can wait till about 2am to start. The climb is up steps most of the way (about 5200 of them), and with plenty of rest stops you'll get to the top in 2½ to four hours. A 2.30am start will easily get you there before dawn, which is around 6.30am. Start on a *poya* day, though, and the throng of pilgrims might add hours to your climb.

From the car park the slope is gradual for the first half hour or so. You pass under an entrance arch, then by the Japan–Sri Lanka Friendship Dagoba, the construction of which started in 1976. From here the path gets steeper and steeper until it becomes a continuous flight of stairs. There are tea houses for rest and refreshments all the way to the top, some of which are open through the night. A handful are open out of season. The authorities have banned litter, alcohol, cigarettes, meat and recorded music (!) so that the atmosphere remains suitably reverent.

Since it can get pretty cold and windy on top, there's little sense in getting to the top too long before the dawn and then having to sit around shivering. Bring warm clothes in any case, including something extra to put on when you get to the summit, and bring plenty of water with you. Some pilgrims wait for the priests to make a morning offering before they descend, but the sun quickly rises and the heat does too, so it pays not to linger too long.

Many people find the hardest part is coming down again. The endless steps can shake the strongest knees, and if your shoes don't fit well toe-jam starts to hurt too. It's a good idea to take a hat – the morning sun gets strong quite fast. Try to remember to stretch your leg muscles before and after the climb, or you'll be limping for the next few days.

Between June and November, when the pathway isn't illuminated and there are few people around, travellers are urged to go up in pairs, at least. If you are travelling alone, try to organise for someone to climb with you through your guesthouse. Expect to pay around Rs 500 for a guide.

Leeches may be about. A popular method of deterring these unpleasant little beasties is an Ayurvedic balm produced by Siddhalepa Hospital. From the way climbers enthusiastically smear it on one would think it does for leeches what garlic does for vampires. It costs only a few rupees and is available in Dalhousie and indeed throughout Sri Lanka.

Places to Stay & Eat

The area surrounding Adam's Peak has a handful of places to stay. Dalhousie is the best place to start the climb, and it also has the best budget accommodation in the area. Head to Dickoya if you're seeking mid-range choices. Neither Maskeliya or Hatton, though, have much to offer and hold little interest.

Dalhousie Out of pilgrimage season you may be dumped by the bus in the bare main square, but during the season the buses stop near the beginning of the walk.

In the season there are a few **tea shops**, some of which stay open all night, where you can get something to eat, buy provisions for the climb, or get a place to sleep (before you start the climb).

About 1.5km before you get to the place where the buses stop are a handful of guesthouses (on your left as you approach Adam's Peak).

The **River View Wathsala Inn** *(☎ 052-227 7427; rooms Rs 450-1500)* is a rather ugly modern place with 14 large, plain rooms with hot water. The cheapest rooms have shared bathrooms. There's a restaurant here. You can arrange rafting and canoeing on rivers feeding into the Maskeliya Reservoir.

Sri Pale *(☎ 011-270 1345; singles/doubles Rs 400/600)* has four very rustic rooms but a nice location by a small river. The hosts are a congenial local farming family.

Yellow House *(☎/fax 051-222 3958; singles/doubles Rs 330/440)* is a new structure next to Sri Pale. There are 12 rooms, and the owner plans to put in hot water. Breakfast costs Rs 170, and dinner around Rs 200.

Further up the road, closer to the bus stop is **Punsisi Rest** *(☎ 070 521101; rooms Rs 400)*, above a shop. It has nine small rooms with hot water. The rooms on the top floor are the best, but the stairs are steep and narrow.

Green House *(☎ 051-222 3956; rooms Rs 300-400)* is across the bridge at the start of the walking path. Yes, it's painted green. There are simple, clean rooms in a characterful little house. A huge breakfast, dinner or a snack before the walk will cost Rs 400 per person. There's a pretty garden and the host can prepare a herbal bath (Rs 100) for an après-pilgrimage soak.

Dickoya About 7km from Hatton towards Maskeliya are two old plantation homes converted into hotels.

Upper Glencairn *(☎ 051-222 2348, fax 011-244 7845; singles/doubles Rs 960/1200)* is a grand old place, built in 1906, surrounded by pretty gardens. It has a bar and leather couches to sink into in the lounge, and food is available. The area around it is still a working tea estate. If you have your own transport it is possible to do Adam's Peak from Dickoya without needing to stay overnight at Dalhousie.

Lower Glencairn *(☎ 051-222 2342; singles/doubles Rs 990/1320)* is below the main road. It's rather jaded and shabby, yet costly, but the garden is nice, as are the views. No meals are served.

Further along the road to Hatton look for the sign for **Castlereigh Family Cottages** *(☎ 051-222 3607; e castle@sltnet.lk; Norton Bridge Rd; cottages Rs 2500-5000)* just after a bridge. The cottages are in a lovely spot under eucalyptus trees on the edge of the Castlereigh Reservoir. The smaller cottage has a double bed and a room with two bunks. The bigger one has three double rooms, plus a kid's room that could fit six to 10. Both have kitchens and hot water, and are nicely decorated.

About 1.5km from Maskeliya, **Madusha Rest** *(☎ 052-227 7406; Upcot Rd; singles/doubles Rs 500/750)* is surrounded by tea gardens, though the trees block any views. The 10 rooms have hot water. The family doesn't speak much English but the food is good – rice, curry and chicken costs Rs 175. A three-wheeler from Maskeliya bus station will cost about Rs 40.

Hatton Should you ever find yourself in this ramshackle market town and need a bed for the night, you can try **Ajantha Guest House** *(☎ 051-222 2337; 83 Nursing Home Rd; singles/doubles Rs 400/800)*. It's a seven-minute walk from the train station (signposted on Main St) in the Ratnapura direction. It has simple rooms with hot water, and there's a restaurant here.

Getting There & Away

Reaching the base of Adam's Peak is quite simple, and if you're making a night ascent you've got all day to arrive. Buses run to Dalhousie from Kandy (from the Goods

Shed bus station), Nuwara Eliya and Colombo in the pilgrimage season. Otherwise, you need to get first to Hatton or to Maskeliya (which is about 20km along the road from Hatton to Dalhousie).

Year-round there are buses to Hatton from Colombo, Kandy (three hours) or Nuwara Eliya. There are also some direct buses from Nuwara Eliya and Colombo to Maskeliya, which enables you to avoid stopping in Hatton if you wish.

There are buses from Hatton to Dalhousie via Maskeliya every 30 minutes in the pilgrimage season (private bus Rs 30, CTB Rs 22; two hours). Otherwise you have to take a bus from Hatton to Maskeliya (Rs 10.50, last departure about 7.30pm), then another to Dalhousie (Rs 10, last departure about 8.30pm). There are usually hotel touts on, in, above and beside the bus when it terminates at Dalhousie.

The *Podi Menike* train from Colombo and Kandy and the *Udarata Menike* from Colombo (not via Kandy) reach Hatton at 11.28am and 2.14pm, respectively. These trains continue to Nanu Oya (for Nuwara Eliya) as do local trains that leave Hatton at 7.26am and 4.20pm. In the other direction (to Kandy and Colombo) the *Podi Menike* passes through Haputale and Nanu Oya and reaches Hatton about 2.12pm; the *Udarata Menike* leaves Hatton at 10.55am. The No 46 mail train leaves at 10.48pm.

A taxi from Hatton to Dalhousie should cost Rs 600. If you're really running late, taxis from Nuwara Eliya will take you to Hatton or Dalhousie.

KITULGALA

☎ 036

Southwest of Kandy and north of Adam's Peak, Kitulgala's main claim to fame is that it was here that David Lean filmed his 1957 Oscar-winning epic *Bridge on the River Kwai*. You can walk down a paved pathway to the site where the filming took place along the banks of the Kelaniya Ganga. The pathway is signposted on the main road, about 1km from the Plantation Hotel in the direction of Adam's Peak. It is virtually impossible to head down the path without attracting an entourage of 'guides', who expect a consideration for their troubles. If you know the film you can recognise some of the places.

Kitulgala's second claim to fame is **white-water rafting**. You can organise this through the Plantation Hotel (see later) or in advance (see Organised Tours in the Getting Around chapter for companies offering rafting). The Kelaniya Ganga has good **swimming** spots – a popular hole is beside the Plantation Hotel.

Rest House *(☎/fax 228 7528; rooms US$33)* has a dining room that is a veritable shrine to the David Lean epic; black-and-white photos of the stars grace the walls. Each of the large rooms has a veranda facing the river.

Plantation Hotel *(☎ 228 7575, fax 228 7574; Kalukohutenna; singles/doubles US$33/42)*, further towards Adam's Peak than Rest House, is a great place to stay. Stylish rooms come with all mod cons and there's a restaurant beside the river. It also advertises 'relaxation, bird-watching and rafting'.

It's easy enough to have a quick stop at Kitulgala even if you are travelling by bus. If you're coming from Ratnapura, you'll have to change at Avissawella; catch the bus to Hatton and get off at Kitulgala (Rs 26). When you're over Kitulgala, flag a bus to Hatton from the main road (Rs 30).

KANDY TO NUWARA ELIYA

The 80km of road from Kandy to Nuwara Eliya is an ascent of nearly 1400m but you start to climb seriously only after about halfway.

At Pussellawa, 45km from Kandy, there's a 120-year-old **Rest House** *(☎ 081-247 8397; rooms Rs 1750-2905)* with three rooms and fine views. It's in a reasonable state but foreigners are seriously overcharged.

Kothmale Reservoir can be looked down on from a little further up the road. It's a large place created as part of the Mahaweli Development Project, and partly blamed by some locals for unusual climatic conditions in recent years.

Ramboda Falls Hotel *(☎ 052-225 9582; e rambodafalls@quicklanka.com; rooms from US$17)*, about 58km from Kandy, by Ramboda Falls and near the Kothmale Reservoir, is down a very steep driveway to your right. The view you get of the falls from here is quite marvellous and there's a restaurant with a pleasant veranda to view them from. There's a narrow path to the falls. The food has been recommended: rice and curry costs

Rs 280. There are 16 rooms, some a bit musty but others airy and bright with balconies. Indian movie superstar Amitabh Bachchan once stayed here, and there are photos of him looking inscrutably cool.

About 15km before Nuwara Eliya, the **Labookellie Tea Factory** *(open 8am-6.30pm daily)* is a convenient factory to visit as it's right on the roadside and they'll willingly show you around. You can buy boxes of good tea cheaply here – Rs 100 for 200g – and enjoy a cup of tea with a slice of their good chocolate cake (Rs 20 for the cake, the tea is free).

Closer to Nuwara Eliya there are roadside stalls overflowing with all manner of vegetables, a legacy of Samuel Baker who first came to the area in 1846 and decided it would make a pleasant summer retreat. He introduced vegetables here, and they're still grown in abundance today. Also grown in abundance are flowers, which are transported to Colombo and abroad. Along the steep roadside approach to Nuwara Eliya you'll come across children selling flowers. If you don't buy their wares, they hurtle down a path to meet you at each hairpin turn until (hopefully) you'll fork out some cash.

The Tea Hills

Tea remains a cornerstone of the Sri Lankan economy and a major export. Tea came to Sri Lanka as an emergency substitute for coffee when the extensive coffee plantations were all but destroyed by a devastating disease in the 19th century. The first Sri Lankan tea was grown in 1867 at the Loolecondera Estate, a little southeast of Kandy, by one James Taylor. Today the hill country is virtually one big tea plantation, for tea needs a warm climate, altitude and sloping terrain. This is a perfect description of the Sri Lankan hill country.

Tea grows on a bush; if it isn't cut it can grow up to 10m high. Tea bushes are pruned back to about one metre in height and squads of Tamil tea pluckers (all women) move through the rows of bushes picking the leaves and buds. These are then 'withered' (demoisturised by blowing air at a fixed temperature through them) either in the old-fashioned multistorey tea factories, where the leaves are spread out on hessian mats, or in modern mechanised troughs. The partly dried leaves are then crushed, which starts a fermentation process. The art in tea production comes in knowing when to stop the fermentation, by 'firing' the tea to produce the final, brown-black leaf. Tours of tea plantations and factories are readily available all over Sri Lanka.

There is a large number of types and varieties of teas, which are graded both by size (from cheap 'dust' through fannings and broken grades to 'leaf' tea) and by quality (with names such as flowery, pekoe or souchong). Tea is further categorised into low-grown, mid-grown or high-grown. The low-grown teas (under 600m) grow strongly and are high in 'body' but low in 'flavour'. The high-grown teas (over 1200m) grow more slowly and are renowned for their subtle flavour. Mid-grown tea is something between the two. Regular commercial teas are usually made by blending various types – a bit of this for flavour, a bit of that for body.

Sri Lanka may grow some very fine tea but most of the best is exported. Only in a small number of hotels, guesthouses and restaurants will you get a quality cup. But you can buy fine teas from plantations or shops to take home with you.

ANDERS BLOMQVIST

Picking tea in the hill country

Birds of Sri Lanka

A tropical climate, long isolation from the Asian mainland and a diversity of habitats have helped endow Sri Lanka with an astonishing abundance of birdlife. There are more than 400 bird species, of which 26 are unique to Sri Lanka, while others are found only in Sri Lanka and adjacent South India. Of the estimated 198 migrant species, most of which stay here from August to April, the waders (sandpipers, plovers etc) are the long-distance champions, making an annual journey from their breeding grounds in the Arctic tundra.

Reference books on Sri Lanka's birds include *A Selection of the Birds of Sri Lanka,* by John & Judy Banks, a slim, well-illustrated book that's perfect for amateur bird-watchers. *A Photographic Guide to Birds of Sri Lanka,* by Gehan de Silva Wijeyeratne, Deepal Warakagoda & TSU de Zylva, is a notch above. It's pocket-sized and jam-packed with colour photos. *A Field Guide to the Birds of Sri Lanka,* by John Harrison, is a hardback with colour illustrations; it's pricey but one of the best field guides available.

Cities, Towns & Villages

Food scraps and flower gardens around dwellings attract insects, which in turn attract many birds. The call of the black house crow *(Corvus splendens)* is one of the first bird sounds you'll hear. Like the common myna and house sparrow, this species is ubiquitous around settlements. The common swallow *(Hirundo rustica)* can be seen chasing insects over virtually any open space, while Loten's sunbirds *(Nectarinia lotenia)*, little with iridescent plumage and a sharp down-curved bill, are often seen flitting in flower gardens. The black-headed oriole *(Oriolus xanthornus)* has a bright-yellow back and belly, a black head, orange beak and yellow-and-black wings. It usually hides in the treetops; its frequent singing is a giveaway. Some species are so accustomed to human settlement that they are rarely found far away, eg, house swifts *(Apus affinis)*, which nest under eaves.

Best Bird-Watching Spots You'll see many species at Viharamahadevi Park in central Colombo. Try the beautiful Peradeniya Botanic Gardens near Kandy. Sigiriya village is also home to dozens of species.

The Countryside

A surprising variety of birds can be seen on rice paddies, in open wooded areas and by the roadside. These birds are often lured by the insects that crops and livestock attract. The shiny black drongos *(Dicrurus macrocercus)* have forked tails; noisy and ostentatious, they're often seen swooping after flying insects. Tiny black palm swifts *(Cypsiurus balasiensis)* sweep low over the fields chasing prey, while white cattle egrets *(Bubulcus ibis)*, whose breeding plumage is actually fawn-coloured, pluck lice from water buffalo. Egrets also flock around farmers as they plough. Brahminy kites *(Haliastur indus)* may be spotted flying overhead. Adults of this species have a white head and chest and chestnut-brown wings and belly. Green bee-eaters *(Merops orientalis)* are often seen in pairs, perched low to the ground or flitting around catching flying insects. You can identify this bird by the black stripe on each side of its head, its aqua-coloured throat and chin, the orange on the back of its head, and its green wings. The Ceylon junglefowl *(Gallus lafayettii)*, an endemic relative of the domestic chicken, is widespread in remote areas but rarely found near settlements.

Best Bird-Watching Spots Most of these species are easily spotted from the comfort of a bus seat.

Wetlands, Waterways & Tanks

In the dry regions, bodies of water and their fringe vegetation provide an important habitat for many birds. You can't miss the clumsy-looking painted stork *(Mycteria leucocephala)*, with its distinctive orange face and pink rump feathers. Great egrets *(Casmerodius albus)*, huge white birds with yellow beaks, pick off fish with deadly precision. Spoonbills *(Platalea leucorodia)* swish their peculiar flattened bills from side to side, snapping up small creatures.

ANDERS BLOMQVIST

Cattle egret

DAVID TIPLING

Brahminy kite

MICHAEL AW

Green bee-eater

RAY TIPPER

Kingfisher

RAY TIPPER
Great white egret

RAY TIPPER
Spoonbill

MICHAEL AW
Little cormorant

RAY TIPPER
Pheasant-tailed jacana

MICHAEL AW
Painted stork

Birds of Sri Lanka

Little cormorants *(Phalacrocorax niger)* are regularly seen in large flocks. The little cormorant is smaller and less heavily built than the Indian cormorant *(Phalacrocorax fuscicollis)*, and it has a shorter neck and beak. Both birds are dark brown to black and are often seen with wings outstretched to dry. Keep an eye out for the Indian darter *(Anhinga melanogaster)*, which has a lanky brown neck and spears fish underwater with its dagger-like bill. It is also known as the snake bird because of its peculiar habit of swimming like a snake.

The common kingfisher *(Alcedo atthis)*, with striking blue plumage and a tan belly and flank, is often seen skimming the water or watching for fish from a vantage point.

The dark-brown-and-white pheasant-tailed jacana *(Hydrophasianus chirurgus)* trots across lily pads on incredibly long, slender toes. Its long tail feathers are shed after the breeding season.

The famous greater flamingos *(Phoenicopterus ruber)* have short bent beaks, spindly legs and white-and-pink plumage. They are mostly found in Bundala National Park.

Best Bird-Watching Spots Virtually any tank or large body of water is host to a selection of water birds. Try the tanks at Anuradhapura and Polonnaruwa. Bundala and Yala West (Ruhuna) National Parks are also particularly good spots.

Best Bird-Watching Times Water birds are active for most of the day. Although morning is always the best time to go bird-watching, you will see noisy flocks of birds preparing to roost in the evening.

Rainforests & Jungle

Most of Sri Lanka's endemic birds are found in the rainforests of the hill zone. A walk in the forest can be eerily quiet until you encounter a feeding party, and then all hell breaks loose! Birds of many species travel in flocks, foraging for bark and leaves in the forest canopy and among the leaf litter of the forest floor. You'll probably see noisy orange-billed babblers *(Turdoides rufescens)*, which have brown plumage and orange beaks (hence their name). Then there's the Ceylon paradise flycatcher *(Terpsiphone paradisi ceylonensis)*, which has a distinctive chestnut-coloured back and tail, white chest and black-crested head. The male of this species has a long, showy tail. You may also see the black Ceylon crested drongo *(Dicrurus paradiseus ceylonicus)* with its deeply forked tail and noisy chattering, or if you are lucky, the beautiful blue-and-chestnut Ceylon blue magpie *(Urocissa ornata)*. Noisy flocks of blossom-headed parakeets *(Psittacula cyanocephala)* are often seen flying between patches of forest in the lower hills.

Best Bird-Watching Spots Sinharaja Forest Reserve contains many endemic species, while others are found at Horton Plains National Park. Udawattakelle Sanctuary in Kandy is also rewarding while being easy to reach as well.

Best Bird-Watching Times Get there early – at first light, if possible – because birds that are active at dawn may be quiet for the rest of the day.

Tips for Bird-Watchers

Visit a variety of habitats – rainforest, water bodies of the dry zone, and urban parks – to see the full diversity of birdlife in Sri Lanka.

February to March is the best time for bird-watching – you miss the monsoons and the migrant birds are still visiting.

A pair of binoculars is an invaluable tool to help with identification. Small models can be bought cheaply duty-free and don't weigh much.

Consider taking a tour with a specialist if you're keen to see the endemic species and achieve a healthy bird-watching tally, particularly if time is short. See Organised Tours in the Getting Around chapter for details.

NUWARA ELIYA

☎ 052 • pop 25,100

The summer resort of Nuwara Eliya (pronounced nu-**rel**-iya, meaning 'City of Light') stands at 1889m, and keeps its hill station atmosphere more completely than any place in the subcontinent. The town centre is a concrete tangle but the outskirts still keep the atmosphere of a misplaced British village, with hedges, rose gardens and red-roofed bungalows sporting twee names. It was a favoured stomping ground for the tea planters – the 'wild men of the hills' as one British governor called them. The old pink-brick post office, the racecourse, the English-country-house-styled Hill Club with its hunting pictures, mounted fish and hunting trophies, and the 18-hole golf course all somehow seem more British than Britain. Nuwara Eliya had been suffering from inadequate rubbish collection, however the new town council has introduced recycling schemes and improved the town's appearance no end.

Nuwara Eliya has a fair assortment of country-style houses with large gardens – many now turned over to vegetables to make this one of Sri Lanka's main market-gardening centres.

Come prepared for the evening cool – Nuwara Eliya is much higher than Kandy. In January and February you may find yourself needing to sleep with two blankets and all your clothes on. The town can be grey and grim in a peculiarly Scottish way on rainy days. Nuwara Eliya is the 'in place' for Sri Lankan socialites to be during April, around the Sinhalese and Tamil New Year. At that time of year the cost of accommodation – if you can find any – goes through the roof. Horse races are held on the picturesque semi-derelict racecourse then too.

Nuwara Eliya is in the middle of the tea-growing country and there are occasional outbreaks of tension between the local Sinhalese and Tamils. The town was damaged in the 1983 riots, but this is now invisible to anyone unaware of what the place looked like previously.

The town has an abundance of touts angling to get a commission for a guesthouse or hotel. You'll very likely be approached by at least some of them when you step off the train at Nanu Oya (the train station for Nuwara Eliya) or at the bus stations.

Orientation

A renovated bus station was sort of under construction (the money keeps running out), so at the time of writing CTB buses were leaving from Railway Station Rd and from the private bus station on New Bazaar St. Over the road is Victoria Park. Further north along New Bazaar St is the central market and a collection of cheap eateries. At the top of the street is the Windsor Hotel and nearby is the Bank of Ceylon. If you veer left into Kandy Rd, you will come to Cargills (you can see the golf course on your left). If you head south from the bus station along New Bazaar St, you will enter Queen Elizabeth Rd (also known as Badulla Rd) – many of the cheaper guesthouses are clustered nearby.

Information

The **Commercial Bank** (with ATM) and **Seylan Bank** are on Park Rd, while the **Bank of Ceylon** is on Lawson Rd. On weekends you can change travellers cheques at the Grand Hotel.

The **post office** *(open 7am-8pm Mon-Sat, closed public holidays)* sells stamps and lets you make telephone calls. International calls can be made from **Salika Communications**, further north.

For Internet facilities head over to **Vijitha Graphics** *(28 Daily Fair Trade Complex, Kandy Rd; open 9am-5.30pm daily)*, a tiny office in a crowded, ramshackle bazaar.

Things to See

The splendid **Victoria Park** *(admission Rs 10, open 8am-5pm daily)* at the centre of town comes alive with flowers around March to May and August to September.

If you're keen to see where a good, strong cuppa comes from, head to the **Pedro Tea Estate** factory about 3.5km east of Nuwara Eliya on the way to Kandapola. Factory tours, at Rs 50 per person, run for 30 minutes from 8.30am to 12.30pm and again from 2pm to 5pm. There's a pleasant tea house overlooking the plantations where you can have a tea break. A three-wheeler from Nuwara Eliya should cost Rs 400 return, including waiting time. On the way out you'll pass Hawa Eliya, the site of the Lion brewery is (alas, no tours). A side road takes you up to what's locally known as **Lovers Leap** (there are various stories as to who the

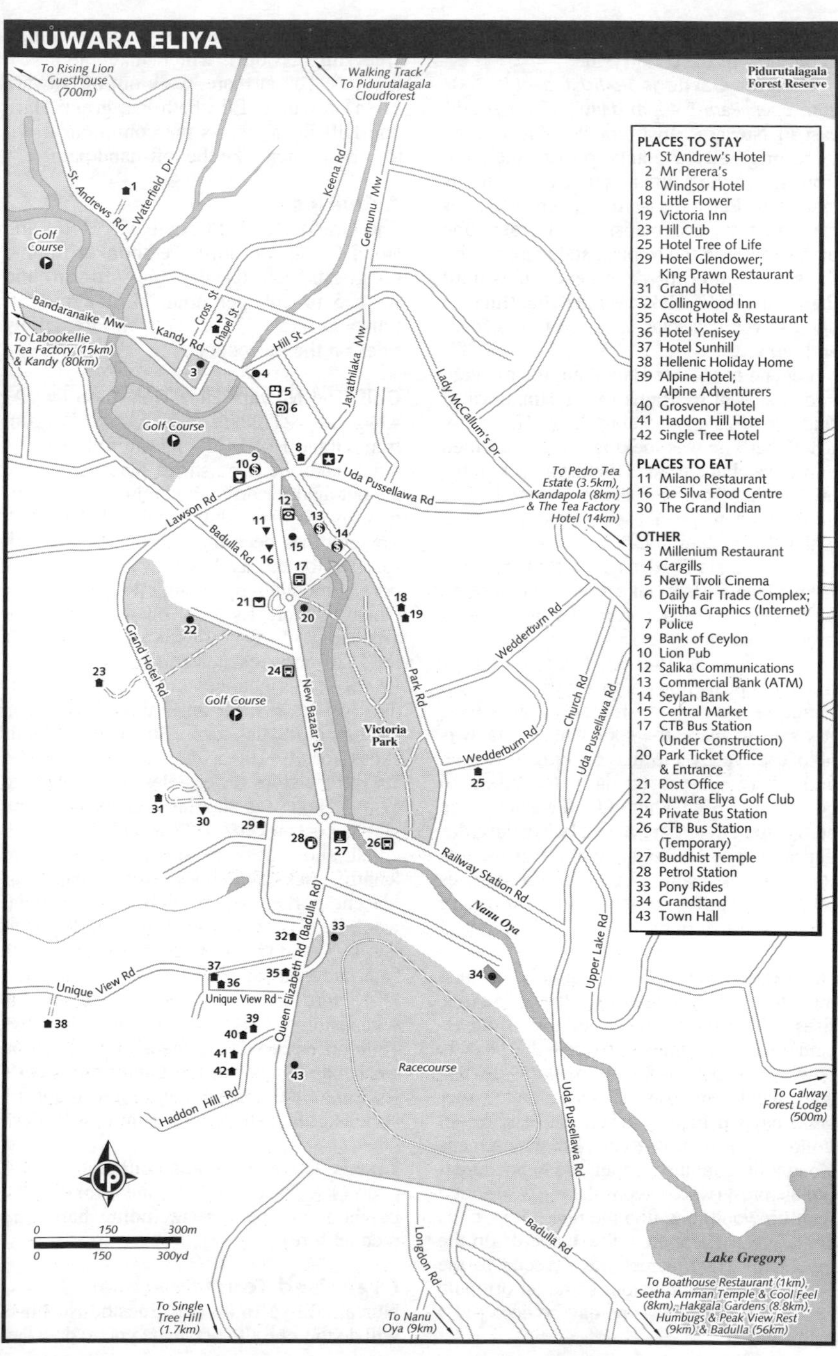
NUWARA ELIYA
To Rising Lion Guesthouse (700m)
Walking Track To Pidurutalagala Cloudforest
Pidurutalagala Forest Reserve
PLACES TO STAY
1 St Andrew's Hotel
2 Mr Perera's
8 Windsor Hotel
18 Little Flower
19 Victoria Inn
23 Hill Club
25 Hotel Tree of Life
29 Hotel Glendower; King Prawn Restaurant
31 Grand Hotel
32 Collingwood Inn
35 Ascot Hotel & Restaurant
36 Hotel Yenisey
37 Hotel Sunhill
38 Hellenic Holiday Home
39 Alpine Hotel; Alpine Adventurers
40 Grosvenor Hotel
41 Haddon Hill Hotel
42 Single Tree Hotel
PLACES TO EAT
11 Milano Restaurant
16 De Silva Food Centre
30 The Grand Indian
OTHER
3 Millenium Restaurant
4 Cargills
5 New Tivoli Cinema
6 Daily Fair Trade Complex; Vijitha Graphics (Internet)
7 Police
9 Bank of Ceylon
10 Lion Pub
12 Salika Communications
13 Commercial Bank (ATM)
14 Seylan Bank
15 Central Market
17 CTB Bus Station (Under Construction)
20 Park Ticket Office & Entrance
21 Post Office
22 Nuwara Eliya Golf Club
24 Private Bus Station
26 CTB Bus Station (Temporary)
27 Buddhist Temple
28 Petrol Station
33 Pony Rides
34 Grandstand
43 Town Hall
St Andrews Rd
Waterfield Dr
Keena Rd
Gemunu Mw
Golf Course
Bandaranaike Mw
Kandy Rd
Cross St
Chapel St
Hill St
Jayathilaka Mw
Lady McCallum's Dr
To Labookellie Tea Factory (15km) & Kandy (80km)
Uda Pussellawa Rd
To Pedro Tea Estate (3.5km), Kandapola (8km) & The Tea Factory Hotel (14km)
Lawson Rd
Badulla Rd
Wedderburn Rd
Grand Hotel Rd
New Bazaar St
Park Rd
Victoria Park
Church Rd
Railway Station Rd
Nanu Oya
Upper Lake Rd
Queen Elizabeth Rd (Badulla Rd)
Unique View Rd
Racecourse
Haddon Hill Rd
To Galway Forest Lodge (500m)
London Rd
Lake Gregory
To Boathouse Restaurant (1km), Seetha Amman Temple & Cool Feel (8km), Hakgala Gardens (8.8km), Humbugs & Peak View Rest (9km) & Badulla (56km)
To Single Tree Hill (1.7km)
To Nanu Oya (9km)
0 150 300m
0 150 300yd

lovers actually were). From here you get a good view of the countryside.

Hakgala Gardens *(adult/student Rs 300/200; open 8am-5.45pm daily)*, 10km southeast of Nuwara Eliya (about 200m lower), were originally a plantation of cinchona, from which the antimalarial drug quinine is extracted. Later the gardens were used for experiments in acclimatising temperate-zone plants to life in the tropics, and were run by the same family for three generations until the 1940s. Today Hakgala is a delightful garden of over 27 hectares, famed for its roses and ferns.

Legend has it that Hanuman, the monkey god, was sent by Rama to the Himalaya to find a particular medicinal herb. He forgot which herb he was looking for and decided to bring a chunk of the Himalaya back in his jaw, hoping the herb was growing on it. The gardens grow on a rock called Hakgala, which means 'jaw-rock'.

The Hakgala Gardens are a Rs 8 bus ride from Nuwara Eliya (take a Welimada-bound bus). There are accommodation options nearby (see Places to Stay, later).

On the way out to Hakgala Gardens, near the 83km post, stop off to see the colourful Hindu **Seetha Amman Temple** at Sita Eliya. It's said to mark the spot where Sita was held captive by the demon king Rawana, and where she prayed daily for Rama to come and rescue her. On the rock face across the stream are a number of circular depressions said to be the footprints of Rawana's elephant. Tamil wedding parties make it a point to stop here for *pujas* (prayers or offerings).

Mountain Walks Sri Lanka's highest mountain, Pidurutalagala (Mt Pedro, 2524m), rises behind the town. On its top is the island's main TV transmitter and the peak is now out of bounds to the public. You can walk about 4km up as far as a concrete water tank; beyond here is a high security zone. Follow the path from Keena Rd, which leads along a little ravine through the exotic eucalyptus forest (which keeps the town supplied with firewood) and into the rare, indigenous cloudforest. There are a few leopards on the mountain, which sometimes descend to the edges of town and devour some unfortunate pooch. The area may one day be declared a national park.

An alternative walk is to go to **Single Tree Hill** (2100m), which takes about 90 minutes. To get there, walk out of Nuwara Eliya on Queen Elizabeth Rd, go up Haddon Hill Rd as far as the communications tower and then take the left-hand path.

Activities

The Grand Hotel, St Andrew's Hotel and Hotel Glendower all have **snooker rooms**; nonguests can usually play for around Rs 125 to 200 per hour. Holidaying Sri Lankans like to give their children **pony rides** on the racecourse.

Golf The **Nuwara Eliya Golf Club** *(☎ 223 4360, fax 222 2835)*, which spreads north from Grand Hotel Rd, is beautifully kept. It didn't take the Scottish tea planters long to lay out land for drives and putts in their holiday town, and the club was founded in 1889. The club has been through tough times but survives to this day. You may become a temporary member by paying Rs 100 a day. Green fees are Rs 1400 on weekdays (but after 3pm it's Rs 600 for six holes) and Rs 1520 on weekends and public holidays. Practice tees (including clubs, balls and caddie) cost Rs 690 for up to three hours. You can hire golf clubs for Rs 300 a day and golf shoes for Rs 100 a day. Caddie fees are Rs 150 for 10 or fewer holes and Rs 175 for 11 to 18 holes (caddies are compulsory). The club expects a certain dress code: shirt with collar and slacks or shorts (of a decent length), socks and shoes. Women can wear 'decent' golf attire. The club has a convivial wood-lined bar that almost encourages you to talk in a fake Oxbridge accent. It also has a badminton hall and billiard room, in addition to 11 spruce, comfortable twin-bed rooms with bathroom (Rs 1100 on weekdays, Rs 1500 on weekends). It tends to get busy on weekends. Dinner in the dining room costs Rs 300 to 400; classic bland English cuisine such as grilled chops with mint cost Rs 220.

Tennis There are **tennis courts** at the Hill Club (see Places to Stay, later) for Rs 250 per hour per person (including balls and racquet hire).

Organised Tours

Nuwara Eliya touts and guesthouse hosts will do their best to persuade you to do a day trip by car or 4WD to Horton Plains and World's End. The standard price for up to five passengers is Rs 1500. The road is better than it used to be and the trip takes about 1½ hours one way. It costs about the same from Haputale. For more information on this destination see Horton Plains National Park & World's End later in this chapter.

Places to Stay

Nuwara Eliya is not great for cheap accommodation, although prices come down during the quieter times of the year. During the 'season', around Sinhalese and Tamil New Year in April, rooms are three to five times their normal price. Prices also increase during long-weekend holidays and in August when package tours descend from abroad.

You'll need blankets to keep warm at night at almost any time of year, owing to the altitude. All places to stay *claim* to have hot water, but in many you have to wait for it to heat up; only a handful have a 24-hour hot water service. It's worth double checking before booking in. Another way of keeping warm is to get a fire lit in your room, for which you'll be asked to pay Rs 100 or more. Make sure the room has ventilation or an open window, or you may get carbon monoxide poisoning (which can be fatal), especially if coal heaters are used.

Places to Stay – Budget & Mid-Range

South End of Town A large number of good-value guesthouses are along or tucked in behind Queen Elizabeth Rd.

Haddon Hill Hotel *(☎ 222 3500; 8B Haddon Hill Rd; singles Rs 400, doubles Rs 600-1250)* won't win prizes for architecture but the rooms are nice and clean and guests can use the kitchen. Some of the rooms have a small balcony.

Ascot Hotel & Restaurant *(☎ 222 2708; 120 Queen Elizabeth Rd; singles/doubles Rs 500/700; hot water Rs 200 extra)* is a soulless place with an uninviting dirt front yard. Masochists can stick to cold showers and save money. The owners are very friendly.

Single Tree Hotel *(☎ 222 3009; 1/8 Haddon Hill Rd; singles/doubles Rs 700/800)* has 10 rooms, with renovations underway, and a helpful owner. The rooms upstairs are best.

Hotel Sunhill *(☎ 222 2878, fax 222 3770; 18 Unique View Rd; rooms Rs 750-880, deluxe rooms Rs 1300)* has box-like standard rooms but better-value deluxe rooms. Joy of joys, the bar has a karaoke machine.

Collingwood Inn *(☎ 222 3550, fax 223 4500; 112 Queen Elizabeth Rd; singles Rs 500-900, doubles Rs 700-1200)* is a colonial-era home with antique furniture. The rooms at the front are the best.

Hotel Yenisey *(☎ 223 4000; 16B Unique View Rd; singles/doubles US$10/12)* has 12 very clean rooms (some a bit dark) with sparkling bathrooms, and friendly staff.

Grosvenor Hotel *(☎ 222 2307; 6 Haddon Hill Rd; singles/doubles Rs 1100/1320)* is more than 100 years old and once belonged to a governor. It has 10 spacious, simple rooms and a comfortable lounge room, but the food is only average.

Hellenic Holiday Home *(☎/fax 223 4437; 49/1 Unique View Rd; singles/doubles Rs 1100/1340)* has superb views and 10 modern, carpeted rooms of reasonable quality. A three-wheeler here from the bus station should cost Rs 100.

Hotel Glendower *(☎ 222 2501; e hotel_glendower@hotmail.com; 5 Grand Hotel Rd; rooms Rs 1550, suites Rs 2250)* is a renovated colonial house with sizeable, squeaky-clean rooms. It's a cut above its rivals, with helpful, friendly managers, a pretty garden with a croquet set, a large lounge with soft couches, a bar and a snooker table. The hotel has Internet facilities. This place gets rave reviews.

Alpine Hotel *(☎ 222 3500; e alpine_hotel@hotmail.com; 4 Haddon Hill Rd; singles/doubles Rs 1500/1950)* is a new, comfortable hotel with 25 rooms, each with satellite TV, carpet and a decent bathroom. It also has a large restaurant. Mountain bikes can be hired for Rs 550 a day, and there are Internet facilities as well. The front desk can arrange hiking, trekking and bird-watching tours for guests.

East End of Town In a quiet spot opposite Victoria Park, **Victoria Inn** *(☎ 222 2321; 15/4 Park Rd; rooms Rs 500-600)* has basic rooms, but the new manager was planning to renovate the place when we visited. The cheaper rooms have a shared bathroom.

Little Flower *(☎ 223 4897; 22 Park Rd; singles/doubles Rs 770/1100)* is a fallback option, with characterless, overpriced rooms in a bland modern building.

The **Hotel Tree of Life** *(☎ 222 3684, fax 222 3127; 2 Wedderburn Rd; singles/doubles US$32/45)* is an old-style bungalow with a lovely garden, but the rooms weren't in a condition to justify the price when we visited.

North End of Town Friendly **Mr Perera's** *(9 Chapel St; rooms Rs 150-400)* has three no-frills rooms. Breakfast costs Rs 80 and Mrs Perera will do dinners on request. You can relax with a book in the living room or chat with the family. It's one of the few homestay-style places in town. The house is unsigned – look for the Millennium Restaurant on Kandy Rd; Chapel St is opposite.

Rising Lion Guesthouse *(☎ 222 2083, fax 223 4042; 3 Sri Piyatissapura; rooms Rs 700-1500)*, perched above the town, has cheerfully odd taste in furnishings and art. The hosts are very personable and have lots of advice on interesting side trips in the area. The 13 clean, homely rooms all have fireplaces ready, and the more expensive ones have spiffing views. If you ring ahead, the guys will pick you up from the bus station for free, or from Nanu Oya for Rs 150.

Sita Eliya & Hakgala Close to the Seetha Amman Temple, **Cool Feel** *(☎ 223 4715; rooms Rs 1200)* is a smart new place about 8km from Nuwara Eliya. It's close to the road and lacking a garden, but the rooms are spacious and clean and it has a restaurant and a bakery for snacks. The mixed menu has sweet-and-sour chicken for Rs 175 and grilled chicken for Rs 150.

Humbugs *(☎/fax 222 2709; ⓔ sj99@sltnet.lk; rooms Rs 750-900)*, just beyond the Hakgala Botanic Gardens entrance, has some slightly frayed rooms with hot water and floor-to-ceiling windows that look out on a stunning view. If you like you can take your shower in a waterfall at the bottom of the garden. The roadside café has rice and curry (Rs 70), strawberry pancakes (Rs 100) and strawberries and cream (Rs 77). It also rents out a five-bedroom bungalow surrounded by a garden just downhill for Rs 3500 (for up to 12 people).

Peak View Rest *(☎ 011-286 5850; rooms Rs 1100-1650)* is 200m downhill from Humbugs, on a road dipping down on the left. It's the modern house painted blueish-green. It has three comfortable, modern rooms and a sitting room with soft leather chairs, a stereo and a TV – all very young urban professional in style.

Places to Stay – Top End

Windsor Hotel *(☎ 222 2554, fax 222 2889; 2 Kandy Rd; singles/doubles US$37/43)* looks jaded from the outside but the interior is more tasteful. The rooms are clean, it's right in the heart of town and the staff are friendly.

Grand Hotel *(☎ 222 2881-7; ⓔ tangerinetours@eureka.lk; singles/doubles in old wing US$40/42, in new wing US$58/60)*, right by the golf course, is a vast mock-Tudor pile with immaculate lawns, a reading lounge and a wood-panelled billiards room. However, the rooms have lost most of their original features. Some say the service could be better.

Galway Forest Lodge *(☎ 222 3728; ⓔ info@galway.lk; 89 Upper Lake Rd, Havelock Dr; singles/doubles US$42/48)*, about 2km east of town, is a dull package-tour place with decent rooms.

Hill Club *(☎ 222 2653; ⓔ hillclub@eureka.lk; rooms US$55-60, suites US$90-110)* positively revels in its colonial heritage. A preserve of the British male until 1970, the Hill Club now admits both Sri Lankans and women, but remains very much in the colonial tradition. There is a ladies lounge (next to the dining room) and the nearby restroom has a full-length mirror, dressing tables and lamps. Temporary members (Rs 60 a day) are welcome to help keep the tills ringing. In the reading room you can sink back into old-fashioned leather armchairs while a waiter brings you a drink. Mounted trophies still glare down from the walls, and the library mostly covers hunting, fishing and team sports. It's like a living museum of British colonial male privilege – and in fact the current members have reciprocal rights with upper-class London clubs. Tennis courts are available to guests and nonguests. The lawns and gardens are immaculate.

The rooms don't have as much charm as the rest of the place, but they're clean and the bathrooms are modern and spotless. Some of the rooms are a bit small, so pay a little extra for a larger one. In the evening someone will carefully turn down your bed and, if you wish, place a hot water bottle between the sheets. Dinner is an experience in itself (see Places to Eat & Drink later).

St Andrew's Hotel *(☎ 222 2445; ⓔ standrew@eureka.lk; 10 St Andrew's Dr; rooms US$84-108)*, north of the town on a beautifully groomed rise overlooking the golf course, was once a planter's club. There are terraced lawns with white cast-iron garden furniture. It has a small wine cellar and serves five-course European dinners in the dining room for Rs 720, beneath a pressed-copper roof. The rooms are immaculate. The hotel conducts nature walks in the Pidurutalagala cloudforest directly behind the hotel and keeps detailed records of rare bird species seen flitting through the gardens.

The Tea Factory Hotel *(☎ 222 3600, fax 070 522105; ⓔ ashmres@aitkenspence.lk; Kandapola; singles/doubles US$96/120)*, 14km east of Nuwara Eliya, is a beautifully renovated tea factory overlooking a tea estate. Bits and pieces of factory machinery are on display. The views from the hotel and the walks around it are very pleasant and there's plenty of information available from the front desk on what to see and do. The rooms are luxurious.

Places to Eat & Drink

Guesthouses and hotels are probably your best bet when it comes to eating and drinking in Nuwara Eliya, as most places in the town centre aren't particularly inspiring.

The Grand Indian *(Grand Hotel Rd; dosas Rs 85-170, mains Rs 150-220)*, out the front of the Grand Hotel, is an Indian restaurant which resembles a slick fast-food franchise. The food, however, is excellent. Try a cone-shaped *kheema dosa* (rice pancake with fillings) for Rs 170, or a vegetarian thali for Rs 200. Warming chicken and lamb curries cost around Rs 220.

Boathouse Restaurant *(Badulla Rd, Lake Gregory; mains around Rs 100)* is a popular local bar and restaurant with a nautical theme taken a step too far by shaping the building like a boat. There are *carrom* boards to pass the time. (*Carrom* is like a cross between tiddlywinks and snooker – you flick disks into corner pockets.) A three-wheeler from town will cost Rs 100.

De Silva Food Centre *(90 New Bazaar St; mains Rs 75-200)* is a reasonable mid-range eatery on the busy main street. Vegetarian rice and curry costs Rs 75; Chinese dishes cost around Rs 200.

Milano Restaurant *(94 New Bazaar St; mains from Rs 150)* is in a modern place and offers friendly service and a reliable if unimaginative menu – Western, Chinese, rice and curry.

King Prawn Restaurant *(Hotel Glendower; mains Rs 220-350)* has good Chinese food. Try the sweet-and-sour pork (Rs 275) or the vegetable fried rice (Rs 220). There are also buffet lunches (Rs 500).

The Tea Factory Hotel *(mains around Rs 300)* has a restaurant and bar; the food is good. You can work up an appetite by going for a walk in the surrounding tea estate. A taxi there and back will cost Rs 750. (See Places to Stay – Top End for contact details.)

Dinner at the **Hill Club** *(set course dinner US$14.40)* is quite special. The delicious five-course set menu is served promptly at 8pm. You can also order off the à la carte menu and spend considerably less, but you still have to eat at 8pm. The whole thing is carried off with delightful panache: white-gloved waiters, candles, flowers on every table, and linen tablecloths and serviettes. Men must wear a tie and jacket (they'll lend you one from their heritage collection – the grey velvet smoking jacket goes well with anything). Women seem to get away with fairly casual attire, but some turn up in evening wear. There is also a bar and billiards table. It sounds stuffy but it's actually laid-back and great fun, with excellent service. If you're not staying the night here, you'll have to pay a Rs 60 temporary joining fee.

Self-caterers should heard for the local **market** for fresh produce and to **Cargills** for canned goods.

Lion Pub *(Lawson St)* is a local beer joint with draught Lion lager for Rs 40.

Getting There & Away

Bus The trip from Kandy takes about four hours and costs Rs 90 in a private intercity express bus. It's a spectacular climb. Buses leave every 30 minutes to an hour. There are also buses to/from Colombo (six hours; Rs 152 by intercity express). For Haputale you usually have to change at Welimada. To get to Bandarawela you will also have to change at Welimada. To get to Matara on the south coast, an intercity express bus (Rs 200) is scheduled to leave at 7.30am and takes seven to eight hours.

Train Nuwara Eliya does not have its own train station, but is served by Nanu Oya, about 9km along the road towards Hatton and Colombo. Buses (Rs 10 to Nuwara Eliya) meet the main trains, so don't get sucked in by touts. You can always take a taxi (Rs 250) from the station, and there are many of these.

The 5.55am *Podi Menike* from Colombo (via Kandy) reaches Nanu Oya at 1pm. The 9.45am *Udarata Menike* from Colombo (not via Kandy) reaches Nanu Oya at about 3.40pm. Fares onwards to Badulla cost Rs 18/49/85 in 3rd/2nd/1st class. Going west, the *Udarata Menike* to Colombo (but not Kandy) leaves Nanu Oya at 9.35am; the *Podi Menike* leaves at 12.55pm, reaching Kandy at about 5pm before continuing on to Colombo. Fares to Kandy cost Rs 20.50/56.50/147.50 in 3rd/2nd/1st class. The 1st-class fare includes a booking fee of Rs 50 for the observation carriage.

HORTON PLAINS NATIONAL PARK & WORLD'S END

The Horton Plains form an undulating plateau more than 2000m high, about 20km south of Nuwara Eliya and 20km west of Haputale. They consist mainly of grasslands interspersed with patches of forest with some unusual high-altitude vegetation. Sri Lanka's second- and third-highest mountains – Kirigalpotta (2395m) and Totapola (2359m) – rear up from the edges of the plateau, but the most famous and stunning feature is World's End, where the plateau comes to a sudden end and drops almost straight down for 880m.

The plains are a beautiful, silent, strange world with some excellent walks. Unfortunately the view from World's End is often obscured by mist, particularly during the rainy season from April to September. The early morning (between 6am and 10am) is the best time to visit, before the clouds roll in. In the evening and early morning you'll need long trousers and a sweater, but the plains quickly warm up, so take a hat as well.

Farr Inn, a local landmark, and the nearby national park office are reachable by road from Ohiya or Nuwara Eliya (vans and 4WDs can make it up, but smaller cars might not), or by a stiff three-hour walk uphill from Ohiya train station. There are plans to turn Farr Inn into a visitors centre. The **national park office** *(☎ 070 522042; adult/child US$16.60/8.30; open 6am-4pm)* is at the start of the track to World's End.

Flora & Fauna

Vegetation includes a type of tufty grass called *Crosypogon*, and bog moss (sphagnum), which grows in the marshy areas. Flowering plants include *Aristea ekloni*, which has tiny blue flowers, and *Exacum*

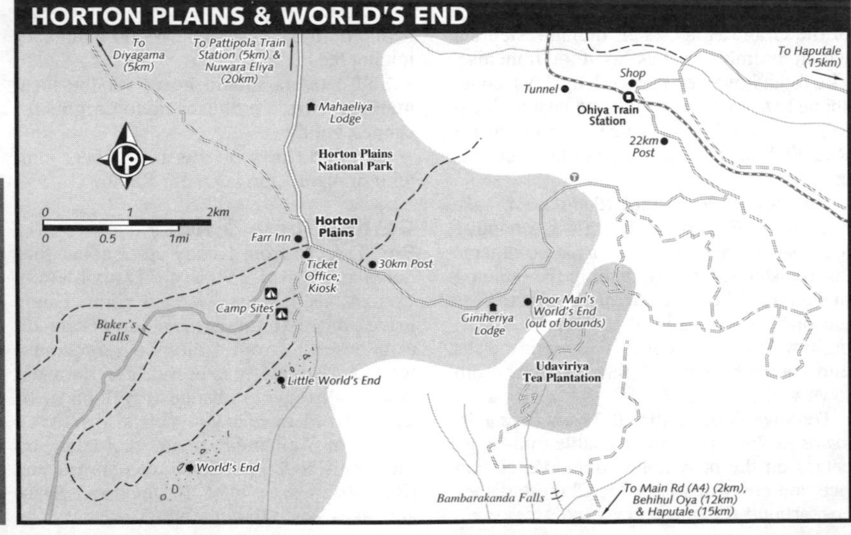

macranthum, which is similar. The main canopy tree of the montane forest is the umbrella-shaped, gnarled, white-blossomed *keena (Callophylum)*. The stunted trees and shrubs are draped in lichen and mosses, giving them a strange, Tolkienesque appearance. Another notable species is *Rhododendron zelanicum*, which has blood-red blossoms. The purple-leafed *Strobilanthes* blossoms once after five years, and then dies.

The last few elephants departed the area in the first half of the 20th century. But there are still a few leopards, and any droppings you see containing animal fur are likely to be leopard droppings. The shaggy bear-monkey (or purple-faced langur) is sometimes seen in the forest on the Ohiya road, and occasionally in the woods around World's End (its call is a wheezy grunt). Sambar might also be present.

The plains are very popular with birdwatchers. Endemics include the yellow eared bulbul, the fantailed warbler, the ashy headed babbler, the Ceylon hill white eye, the Ceylon blackbird, the Ceylon white-eyed arrenga, the dusky blue flycatcher and the Ceylon blue magpie. Birds of prey include the mountain hawk eagle.

Walks

The walk to World's End is about 4km, but the trail loops back to Baker's Falls (2km) from where you can walk to the entrance (another 3.5km); the round trip is 9.5km and usually takes around three hours. Be aware that after about 10am the mist usually comes down – and it's thick. All you can expect to see from World's End after this time is a swirling white wall. Although the ticket gate is open from 6am you can actually start walking earlier and pay on the way out. Try to avoid doing this walk on Sunday and public holidays, when it can get crowded. Guides at the national park office expect about Rs 300 to accompany you on the walk – they say there's no fee for the volunteer guides, but expect to donate a similar amount. Some guides are well informed on the area's flora and fauna, and hiring one might be a consideration for solo women travellers.

Wear strong and comfortable walking shoes, a hat and sunglasses. Bring sunscreen (you can get really burnt up here) and lots of water, as well as something to eat. The shop at the park office makes a killing from people who forget to bring supplies. The weather can change very quickly on the plains – one minute it can be sunny and clear, the next chilly and misty. Bring warm clothing just in case. The authorities have cracked down on litter, and it is forbidden to leave the paths. There are no toilets en route to World's End though there are toilets on the road coming up to Farr Inn from Ohiya train station.

There used to be a free alternative to World's End, dubbed Poor Man's World's End, but it has been fenced off and anyone caught in the area will get a Rs 10,000 fine. Travellers' haunts in Haputale are good sources for innovative ways to see the plains without being slugged with the entry fees, although of course you follow the advice at your own risk.

Places to Stay & Eat

There are two basic Wildlife Conservation Department bungalows where you can stay: **Giniheriya Lodge**, which used to be known as Anderson Lodge, and **Mahaeliya Lodge**. There are 10 beds in each. It costs US$16.60 a day for park entry, US$24 per person per night in a bungalow, US$2 per person for linen hire and a whopping US$30 'service charge' per stay. You must bring all of your own dry rations and kerosene. The lodges open up only when people are staying, and you must book ahead through the **Department of Wildlife Conservation** *(☎ 011-269 4241, fax 269 8556; 18 Gregory's Rd, Cinnamon Gardens, Colombo)*.

There are two **camp sites** (signposted near the start of the World's End track). These can also be booked through the Department of Wildlife Conservation. There is water at the sites but nothing else; you must bring everything you need. As you are inside the World's End park, you are obliged to pay a US$16.60 daily park entry fee plus the site fee (US$6 per day, plus US$5 service charge per stay).

Opposite the Ohiya train station, the first small **shop** *(☎ 0777 404658)* you come to has two rooms for Rs 500 if you're desperate. It also sells food at half the price of the **kiosk** near Farr Inn.

Getting There & Away

Train & Foot Given that the mist comes down at World's End at around 10am, you'll want to get there by at least 9.30am. It is

Responsible Hiking

Sri Lanka offers plenty of scope for great hiking. The hill country especially has popular trails such as World's End as well as relatively little-known ones that are rewarding to explore. Please consider the following tips when hiking.

Rubbish

- Carry out all your rubbish. Don't overlook those easily forgotten items, such as silver paper, orange peel, cigarette butts and plastic wrappers. Make an effort to carry out rubbish left by others.
- Never bury your rubbish: digging disturbs soil and ground cover and encourages erosion. Buried rubbish will more than likely be dug up by animals, who may be injured or poisoned by it. It may also take years to decompose.
- Minimise the waste you must carry out by taking minimal packaging and taking no more food than you will need. If you can't buy in bulk, unpack small-portion packages and combine their contents in one container before your trip. Take reusable containers or stuff sacks.
- On longer walks, don't rely on plastic water bottles, as their disposal is a major problem. Use iodine drops or purification tablets instead.

Human Waste Disposal

- Contamination of water sources by human faeces can lead to the transmission of hepatitis, typhoid and intestinal parasites such as *Giardia*, amoebas and roundworms.
- Where there is no toilet, bury your waste. Dig a small hole 15cm (six inches) deep and at least 100m (320 feet) from any watercourse. Consider carrying a lightweight trowel for this purpose. Cover the waste with soil and a rock. Use toilet paper sparingly and bury it with the waste.

Washing

- Don't use detergents or toothpaste in or near watercourses, even if they are biodegradable.
- For personal washing, use biodegradable soap and a water container (or even a lightweight, portable basin) at least 50m (160 feet) away from the watercourse. Disperse the waste water widely to allow the soil to filter it fully before it finally makes it back to the watercourse.
- Wash cooking utensils 50m (160 feet) from watercourses, using a scourer or sand instead of detergent.

Erosion

- Hillsides and mountain slopes, especially at high altitudes, are prone to erosion. It is important to stick to existing tracks and avoid short cuts that bypass a switchback.
- If a well-used track passes through a mud patch, walk through the mud: walking around the edge will increase the size of the patch.
- Avoid removing the plant life that keeps topsoils in place.

possible to walk to World's End, but it's a 30km round trip from Ohiya with some steep ascents – it's for serious hikers only. Theoretically it would be possible to catch a night train to Ohiya and start the walk in the early hours, but as the trains are often delayed you risk walking 15km up to World's End only to find the clouds have rolled in. It would be better to arrive the day before in Ohiya if you really want to do the walk. The walk from Ohiya to Farr Inn is 11.2km, or 2½ to 3½ hours, along the road – you'll need a torch (flashlight) if you do it at night. Then you've got another 1½ hours to World's End. It's a slog but it is doable. You'll need about two hours for the walk back down towards Ohiya. You'll sleep well after.

You could also catch a taxi from Ohiya train station to Farr Inn (see under Taxi following).

There used to be a shortcut from the railway tunnel (near Ohiya train station) to Farr Inn, which is now closed. The trip up the main road is a pretty walk with great views and you can be sure you won't get lost. Near the 27km post you'll find a toilet block.

Keen walkers can also strike out for Farr Inn from Pattipola, the next train station north of Ohiya (a walk of about 10km along a 4WD track), or from Bambarakanda Falls, about four hours downhill from the plains (see Belihul Oya later in this chapter).

Taxi If you don't feel like walking up the road to Farr Inn, there is often a taxi waiting at the Ohiya train station. From there getting to Farr Inn (40 minutes one way) should cost about Rs 1000 return, including waiting time.

It takes about 1½ hours to get from Haputale to Farr Inn by road (Rs 1500 return). From Ohiya, the road rises in twists and turns through forest before emerging on the open plains. It's a pleasant journey (the road's in good condition) and on the way through the forest you may catch sight of monkeys.

You can also get to Farr Inn from Nuwara Eliya. The road has been much improved in recent times and the trip takes about 1½ hours one way. A taxi costs about Rs 1500 return.

There is a 4WD road that goes past the Bambarakanda Falls (the road signposted on the main road between Haputale and Belihul Oya) and emerges near Ohiya train station. It's pretty rough and would probably be impassable in wet weather.

Organised Tours Guesthouses in Nuwara Eliya and Haputale operate trips to Horton's Plains and World's End. See those entries for details.

BELIHUL OYA

☎ 045

Belihul Oya isn't a town as such, but a pretty hillside region worth passing through on your way to/from the hill country – it's 35km from Haputale and 57km from Ratnapura. From here you can walk up to Horton Plains, a seriously strenuous undertaking.

About 11km from Belihul Oya towards Haputale, near the village of Kalupahana, are the **Bambarakanda Falls**. (Ask the bus driver to let you off at Kalupahana.) At 240m, they're the highest in Sri Lanka. March and April are the best months for viewing the falls; at other times the water flow may be reduced to a disappointing trickle. There's a four-hour trail from here to Horton Plains – it's a fair challenge.

Places to Stay & Eat

Belihuloya Rest House *(☎ 228 0156, 228 0199; singles/doubles US$25/33)* is exquisitely situated, perched beside a stream that rushes down from Horton Plains, but it is overpriced. There's a restaurant here and a lounge packed with comfy chairs near a natural rock pool – feel like a dip? The clean but ageing rooms lack mosquito nets.

River Garden *(☎ 228 0222; e reachme@srilankaecotourism.com; singles/doubles half board US$17.50/19.50)* has three cottages with spotless rooms set in a shady terraced garden above a stream. There's a restaurant beside the road.

HAPUTALE

☎ 057

The largely Tamil and Muslim village of Haputale is perched at the southern edge of the hill country. It lies along a ridge with the land falling away steeply on both sides. The railway hugs one side of the ridge. On a clear day you can see all the way to the south coast from this ridge, and at night the Hambantota lighthouse may be visible. The town centre is a squall of traffic and small shops, but a short walk out of town quickly repays the effort with extraordinary views.

As in many places in the hill country, the legacies of the British planters live on. There are tea estates, which cling to the hillsides, and the old plantation bungalows, some of which have lovely gardens. There's also a pretty little Anglican church (St Andrew's) on the Bandarawela road. The headstones in its well-kept cemetery make for interesting reading.

Haputale is a pleasant place with some good cheap accommodation, and makes a good base for visiting Horton Plains, exploring other places in the area, or just taking pleasant walks in cool mountain air. Guesthouses arrange vans and 4WDs to Horton Plains for Rs 1500.

Information

The town isn't too small to have a branch of the **Bank of Ceylon** *(Station Rd)*, where you can change money and travellers cheques, and get cash advances on Visa cards.

The **post office** is in the centre of town. Amarasinghe Guest House and Cues-Ta Inn have Internet facilities (see Places to Stay & Eat, later).

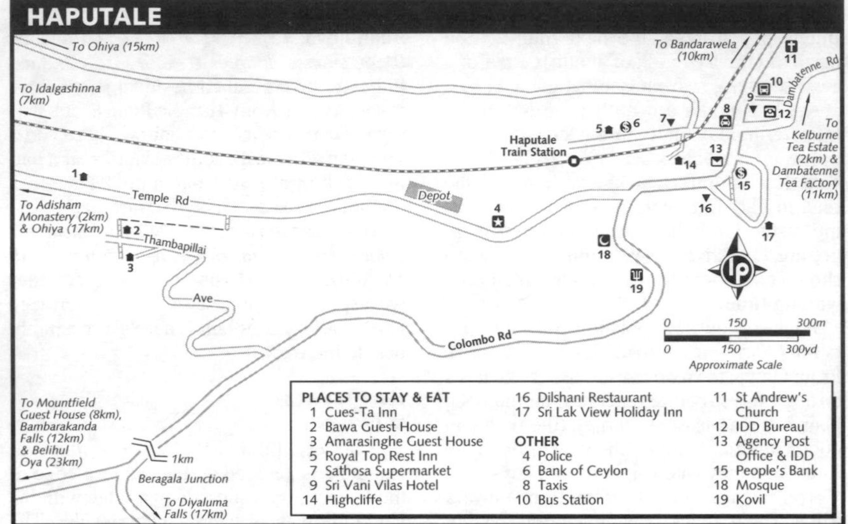

Dambatenne Tea Factory

A few tea factories in this area are happy to have visitors. This factory *(admission Rs 180)* built in 1890 by Sir Thomas Lipton, 11km from Haputale, is popular and easily accessible. For your entry fee you get a tour around the whole works. On an average day a tea picker can bring in around 15kg of tea leaves (and earn around Rs 150); in the high season up to 20,000kg comes into the factory from the fields each day. The leaves then go through a process of drying, rolling, chopping and sieving before being graded. For more details about tea production, see the boxed text 'The Tea Hills' earlier in this chapter.

A bus (for the estate workers) goes from the town bus station to the factory and back again about every 25 minutes (Rs 7). Alternatively, a taxi there and back will cost about Rs 300. If you are fit and energetic this is a great walk, with wonderful views.

Diyaluma Falls

Heading towards Wellawaya, you'll pass the 170m-high Diyaluma Falls, one of Sri Lanka's highest waterfalls, just 5km beyond the town of Koslanda. The stream is fairly small, though it quickly builds up after a downpour. By bus, take a Wellawaya service from Haputale and get off at Diyaluma (1¼ hours). The falls leap over a cliff face and fall in one clear drop to a pool below – very picturesque and clearly visible from the road.

If you're energetic you can climb up to the beautiful rock pools and a series of minifalls at the top of the main fall. Walk about 500m down the road from the bottom of the falls and take the estate track that turns sharply back up to the left. From there it's about 20 minutes' walk to a small rubber factory, where you strike off left uphill. The track is very indistinct, although there are some white arrows on the rocks – if you're lucky, people in the rubber factory will shout if they see you taking the wrong turn! At the top the path forks: the right branch (more distinct) leads to the pools above the main falls, the left fork down to the top of the main falls. The pools above the second set of falls are good for a cool swim.

Adisham Monastery

Adisham *(admission Rs 50; open 9am-12.30pm & 1.30-5pm Sat & Sun, poya days & school holidays)* is a Benedictine monastery about an hour's walk from Haputale. Follow Temple Rd until you reach the sign at the Adisham turn-off. The monastery is an old British planter's house. There's a small shop selling produce from the monastery's lovely gardens and orchards. The industrious monks have added lots of stonework, including garden walls, steps and terracing. Inside, visitors are allowed to see the living room and library, and occasionally a couple more rooms. There's a sign at the main gate that reads 'Silence is Golden'. A taxi should cost Rs 200 return, including waiting time.

Before you reach Adisham you pass by **Tangamalai**, a bird sanctuary and nature reserve (admission is free).

Other Attractions

If you can't get enough of the views, take the train to **Idalgashinna** train station, 8km along the railway west of Haputale. You can walk back beside the train tracks enjoying a spectacular view since the land falls away steeply for a great distance on both sides.

Near the Dambatenne Tea Factory the **Lipton's Seat** lookout has some exclaiming that it rivals the views from World's End (and it's free). Take the signed narrow paved road from the tea factory, and climb about 7km through tea plantations to the lookout. From the tea factory, the ascent should take about 2½ hours.

Places to Stay & Eat

Bawa Guest House *(☎ 226 8260; 32 Thambapillai Ave; singles Rs 250-350, doubles Rs 250-400)*, run by a friendly Muslim family, is a basic house nestled on the hillside. There are five cosy rooms with tolerable shared bathrooms in the original building, and two rooms with bathroom in the newer building next door. Breakfast is Rs 100 and rice and curry is Rs 150. There's lots of good information in their guestbooks.

Amarasinghe Guest House *(☎ 226 8175; e agh777@sltnet.lk; Thambapillai Ave; rooms Rs 400, rooms in main house Rs 600)* is a terrific guesthouse in a neat, white house. There are two rooms in a separate block and four modern spotless rooms (with balconies) in the house. There's also a family room. The food here is very good. Mr Amarasinghe will pick you up from the train station if you ring, and he keeps a guestbook with some interesting comments and advice.

If you're arriving by foot to the Bawa Guest House or Amarasinghe Guest House follow Temple Rd until you see a yellow Amarasinghe Guest House sign to the south, just off the side of the road. Go down the first flight of stairs and head along the path (past the mangy truck) for about 250m. You'll come to Bawa first; a further flight of steps will take you in the back way to Amarasinghe Guest House.

Cues-Ta Inn *(☎ 226 8110; e kacp@sltnet.lk; 118 Temple Rd; singles/doubles Rs 330/440)* has five basic rooms, each with a small balcony, and the large sitting room has superb views over tea plantations. The hosts are welcoming and will happily arrange excursions around the area. There are also Internet facilities.

Royal Top Rest Inn *(☎ 226 8178; 22 Station Rd; singles/doubles Rs 385/440, with bathroom Rs 440/550)* is a friendly place with pleasant views and a cheerfully gaudy living room. There's a restaurant, a small outdoor area and a little sunny shared balcony. The rooms are simple and clean.

Highcliffe *(☎ 226 8096; 15 Station Rd; singles/doubles Rs 450/650)* mostly pays its way as a local bar. It was one of the first budget-traveller stops in town, and the original rooms sure look like it. Some new rooms were being built upstairs when we visited.

Sri Lak View Holiday Inn *(☎ 226 8125; Sherwood Rd; rooms Rs 650-850)* is a modern, squeaky-clean spot with 11 rooms. The more expensive rooms have a skinny balcony with unimpeded views down the mountain. The tiles shine and the host smiles. If you call you'll get picked up from the train station for free.

Mountfield Guest House *(☎ 226 8463; Haldumulla; rooms Rs 750, whole lodge Rs 2000)* is 9km from Haputale on the Belihul Oya road. It's a new stone lodge close to the road in a little plantation, and has two rooms, both with kitchenettes.

Kelburne Tea Estate *(☎ 011-257 3382; e kelburne@eureka.lk; bungalows Rs 4000-5000)*, about 2km east of Haputale train station, is an absolute gem and would be a fine place to unwind for a few days. Three estate bungalows have been made available to visitors, complete with staff (including a cook) and all the trimmings. There's one bungalow with two bedrooms and two bungalows with three bedrooms with bathroom. Each bungalow comes with huge baths, overstuffed couches and lots of magazines. Meals cost Rs 325 to 450. You must book ahead. A taxi from the train station will cost about Rs 150.

Dilshani Restaurant *(27 Colombo Rd)* is a small lunch-time spot with superb views.

Rice and curry costs Rs 80; short eats sell for around Rs 20.

There are a few basic local eateries, including **Sri Vani Vilas Hotel** *(meals around Rs 50)* next to the bus station, where you can get short eats, *dosas*, rice and curry etc cheaper than in the guesthouses. There's also a **Sathosa** supermarket, tucked away near the abandoned Old Resthouse, if you want to buy your own supplies.

Getting There & Away

Bus There are direct buses to Nuwara Eliya at 7am and 2pm (Rs 35), but if you miss these buses you'll have to go to Welimada (Rs 22 by private bus) and get an onward service. To/from Bandarawela there are frequent buses (Rs 15) that run into the early evening. There are also express buses to Colombo (Rs 200, six hours).

For the south coast you usually have to change at Wellawaya (Rs 21), 1½ hours down the hill from Haputale. The last bus from Haputale to Wellawaya is at about 5pm.

Train Haputale is on the Colombo–Badulla line, so you can travel directly by train to/from Kandy or Nanu Oya (the station for Nuwara Eliya). It's 8½ to nine hours from Colombo, 5½ hours from Kandy, 1½ hours from Nanu Oya, 40 minutes from Ohiya, 30 minutes from Bandarawela and two hours from Badulla.

The daily departures in the Badulla direction are at 4.28am, 6.48am, 11.25am, 1pm, 2.33pm *(Podi Menike)* and 5.14pm *(Udarata Menike)*. In the Colombo direction they depart at 7.56am *(Udarata Menike)*, 11.13am *(Podi Menike)*, 3.11pm, 7.57pm (night mail) and 9.24pm. The *Udarata Menike* doesn't go to Kandy.

BANDARAWELA

☎ 057

Bandarawela, 10km north of Haputale but noticeably warmer at only 1230m, is a busy market town that is a good base for exploring the surrounding area. It's a popular area to retire to, due to the agreeable climate. Each Sunday morning the town has a lively market.

The focal point of the town is the busy junction just north of the train station. From here Haputale Rd goes southwest; Welimada Rd heads northwest then turns sharply left by a mosque; and Badulla Rd, with the main bus and taxi stops, heads downhill to the east.

Information

Woodlands Network A good source of information on walks and things to see and do in and around Bandarawela is **Woodlands Network** *(☎ 223 2668; e info@woodlandsnetwork.org; 38/1C Esplanade Rd)*. Headed by Sarojinie Ellawela, Woodlands Network is a nonprofit ecotourism venture. It offers less conventional activities, including local and jungle walks, cooking lessons, visits to temples, tea plantations, farms and waterfalls, and can arrange meditation classes. It can also arrange homestays for groups and individuals. The staff at Woodlands Network are well informed on what's new and interesting. Through this organisation, you can see places not normally accessible to visitors, such as forest hermitages. It's also worth popping by their offices to use their Internet facilities.

Money The **Hatton National Bank** *(Badulla Rd)* gives cash advances on MasterCard and Visa. There's a **Bank of Ceylon** and a **Commercial Bank** ATM nearby.

Post & Communications The **main post office** is near the Bandarawela Hotel, and there are plenty of telephone offices on the main streets. You can send emails from **Micro Services**, off Welimada Rd, or at Woodlands Network (see earlier).

Dowa Temple

About 6km east of Bandarawela on the road to Badulla, the little Dowa Temple is pleasantly situated close to a stream on the right-hand side of the road, with a beautiful 4m-high standing Buddha cut in low relief into the rock face below the road. The temple is easy to miss so ask the bus conductor to tell you when to get off.

Ayurveda

About 3.5km from Bandarawela is an Ayurvedic treatment centre called **Suwa Madhu** *(☎/fax 222 2504; Badulla Rd; open 8am-8pm daily)*. It's a large, plush place catering to tourists. The 1½-hour programme includes a 45-minute oil massage, steam and herbal sauna for Rs 2000.

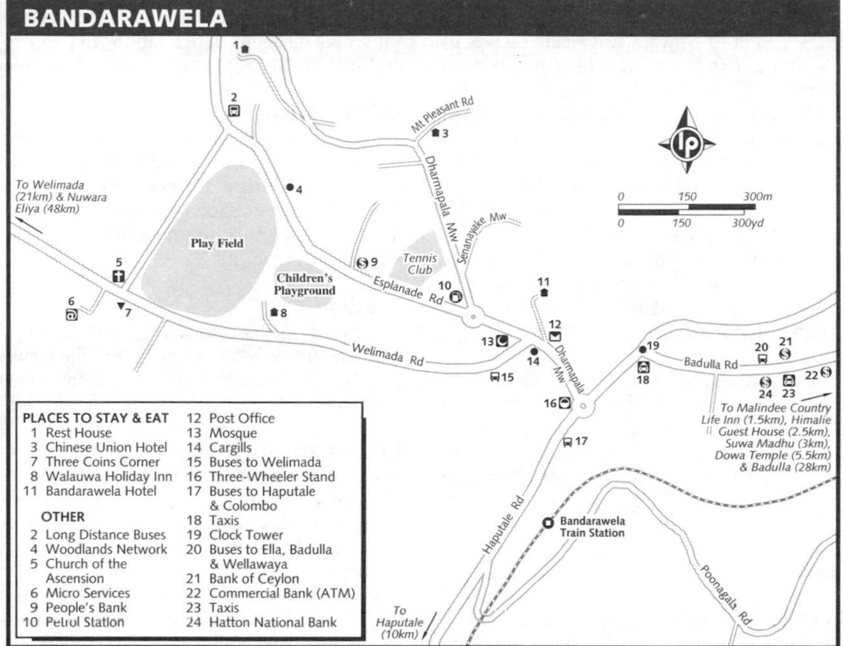

Places to Stay & Eat

Chinese Union Hotel *(☎ 222 2502; 8 Mt Pleasant Rd; singles/doubles Rs 385/550)* is an old-fashioned place with four clean rooms and one cheaper room with a shared bathroom, run by an interesting Sri Lankan–Chinese couple. There's a curio shop in the foyer, for some unusual browsing. The restaurant does Chinese food, such as noodle dishes for Rs 110 and sweet-and-sour chicken for Rs 180.

Walauwa Holiday Inn *(☎ 222 2212; singles/doubles Rs 550/650)*, just off Welimada Rd, doesn't see many tourists, but this characterful 60-year-old villa has clean, spacious rooms with some fine wood carvings.

Himalie Guest House *(☎ 222 2362; singles/doubles including breakfast Rs 650/1300)* is an old-fashioned place set on a hill surrounded by an attractive garden and a tea plantation. It's about 3km out of town towards Badulla; a three-wheeler will cost about Rs 70.

Malindee Country Life Inn *(☎ 222 3124; Badulla Rd, Bindunuwela; singles/doubles Rs 750/950)* is 2km east of town, rather close to the road. It's a family-run inn with some quirky taste on display (lots of marble and brass). The staff are nice and the foyer/living room is an intriguing place to relax. A three-wheeler from town should cost Rs 50.

Rest House *(☎ 222 2299, fax 222 2718; singles/doubles Rs 1000/1500)* is a quiet spot with nine rooms. The five clean but bland rooms in the newer wing have a balcony with a view over the town. There are two decent family rooms in the older wing for Rs 1850. There's a pretty garden here and friendly service.

Bandarawela Hotel *(☎ 222 2501; e bwhotel@sltnet.lk; 14 Welimada Rd; singles/doubles US$30/43)* used to be the tea planters' club. This large chalet-style building stopped updating its furnishings in the 1930s. There are vast easy chairs to sink into in the lounge, and bathrooms with lots of hot water in spacious rooms. There is a little courtyard garden with tortoises, and a restaurant and bar.

Three Coins Corner *(Welimada Rd)* is a shack with tasty lunch-time rice and curry from Rs 50. Other eateries are near the bus stops, but none of them are too flash, so you may want to eat in your guesthouse.

Getting There & Away

Bus To get to Nuwara Eliya catch a bus to Welimada (Rs 12) and another from there to Nuwara Eliya (Rs 18) – buses leave for Nuwara Eliya from Welimada every 10 to 15 minutes. There are regular buses between Bandarawela and Haputale (Rs 15), Ella (Rs 10) and Badulla (Rs 17). Long-distance services include runs to Colombo (Rs 150, six hours), Tissamaharama, Tangalla and Galle. Change at Wellawaya for buses to Tissa or the south coast. Buses to Tissa, Tangalla and Galle leave from the long-distance station on Esplanade Rd.

Train Bandarawela is on the Colombo–Badulla railway. Main trains to Colombo (via Haputale) leave at 7.26am *(Udarata Menike)* and 10.42am (*Podi Menike*, via Kandy), 2.20pm, 7.21pm and 8.50pm. Main trains to Badulla (via Ella) leave at 5am, 7.28am, 12.10pm, 2.15pm, 3pm, 5.40pm and 6.12pm.

ELLA

☎ 057

Sri Lanka is liberally endowed with beautiful views, and Ella has one of the best. The sleepy village is nestled in a valley peering straight through Ella Gap to the coastal plain nearly 1000m below, and over to the coast where, on a clear night, you can see the Kirinda lighthouse. As if views weren't enough, Ella is surrounded by hills perfect for walks through tea plantations to temples and waterfalls.

Information

There's a **post office** in the centre of town but for banking you'll need to head to Bandarawela. **Rodrigo Communications** and **RMS Communications** on the main road have Internet and international direct dialling (IDD) facilities.

Walks

Ella is a great base for keen walkers to explore the surrounding countryside – the views can be spectacular. For more details see Walks under Around Ella later in this chapter.

Places to Stay

Touts might approach you on the train with tales that the hotel of your choice is too expensive, closed down, or rat-infested.

Garden View Inn *(☎ 222 8792; singles/doubles Rs 200/250)* has three simple rooms with bright, clean bathrooms in a family home. The owner has lots of info on walks in the area. Rice and curry costs Rs 125, so all together it's very good value.

Beauty Mount Tourist Inn *(☎ 222 8799; rooms Rs 200-450, cottage Rs 750)* is an unpretentious little place with five rooms. Up the hill is a cute little cottage with a kitchen,

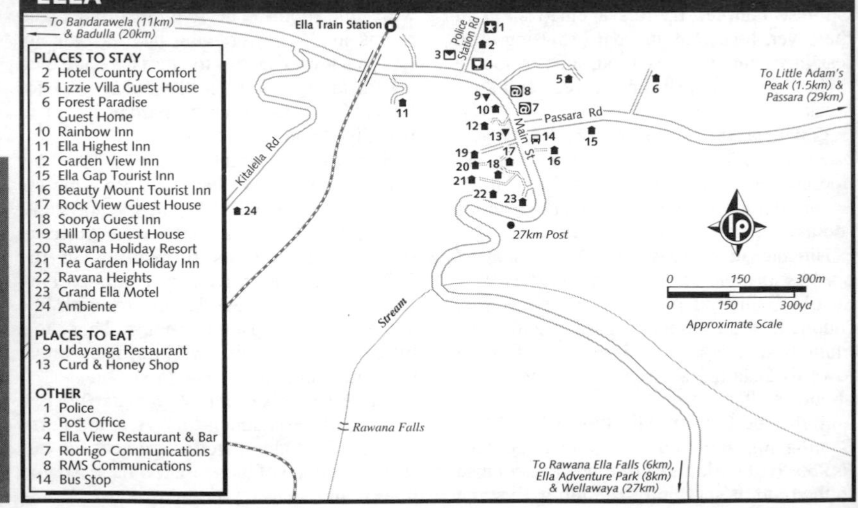

fridge, one large bedroom and lots of privacy. The owner is a particularly good-natured fellow who likes to serve up home-grown coffee. The rooms are clean enough and the food is cheap.

Lizzie Villa Guest House *(☎ 222 8643; rooms Rs 200-600)* is signposted on the main road; the track to this place is about 150m long. Lizzie's is one of the longest-running establishments in Ella. This quiet location has a spice garden (source of much of the home cooking), simple rooms with hot water and a shady veranda.

Rainbow Inn *(☎ 222 8788; singles/doubles Rs 350/450, hot water Rs 50 extra)* has been heartily recommended by several readers. The friendly family rents out five clean rooms, and the food gets praise – rice and curry costs Rs 80.

Ella Highest Inn *(☎ 222 8608; singles/doubles Rs 400/550)* is set in a tea plantation. It's a hike up the track from the main road, but it's worth it – you'll get great views of the hilly countryside. The rooms are basic, with small bathrooms.

Soorya Guest Inn *(☎ 222 8906; singles/doubles Rs 400/600)* is a new, clean little place with three rooms, with a common balcony and a kitchen for guests to use.

Rock View Guest House *(☎ 222 8761; rooms Rs 400-600)* is a large old house with views over the main road to Ella Gap. The clean but worn rooms are set around a large living area.

Hill Top Guest House *(☎ 222 8780; singles Rs 450-600, doubles Rs 650-800)* has rooms downstairs with verandas surrounded by a garden, as well as upstairs rooms that share a balcony with superb views of Ella Gap.

Rawana Holiday Resort *(☎ 222 8794; rooms Rs 500-600)* has clean, basic rooms that line a veranda with OK views. The hosts are friendly, and their home-cooked speciality is rice and curry with garlic. The rooms lack mosquito nets.

Hotel Country Comfort *(☎ 222 8500; ⓔ info@hotelcountrycomfort.com; Police Station Rd; older rooms Rs 600-850, new rooms Rs 1500-2000)* is an older building with a new annexe. The original building is a beautifully maintained 60-year-old villa, but the rooms here are smaller. The new wing positively gleams, and the rooms have lots of space, bay windows and modern bathrooms. It's an excellent choice if you want a little more comfort. It also has a restaurant.

Forest Paradise Guest House *(☎ 222 8797; ⓔ forestparadise@123india.com; singles/doubles Rs 660/770)* has four rooms in a handsome bungalow, with clean bathrooms. It backs onto a pine forest. The owner arranges trips into the Namunugala Hills 16km away for Rs 800 per person, including a BBQ lunch (minimum three people).

Tea Garden Holiday Inn *(☎ 222 8860; singles Rs 650-1200, doubles Rs 750-1300)*, near Rawana Holiday Resort, has nine clean, spacious rooms. The cheaper rooms are a bit small; the more expensive rooms share a roomy balcony. There's also a leafy communal balcony with pleasant views to the small Rawana Falls (and decent views through Ella Gap), friendly hosts and excellent food.

Ella Gap Tourist Inn *(☎ 222 8528; Passara Rd; rooms Rs 650-1350)* has a pleasant restaurant – try the *lampreis* (rice and curry wrapped and cooked in a banana leaf) for Rs 400 – but the rooms are looking tired and weren't so clean when we visited. It does have a leafy garden.

Ambiente *(☎ 222 8867; ⓔ kanta@telenett.net; Kitalella Rd; rooms Rs 1000-1800)* is at the top of a hill. There are a variety of rooms, with and without bathrooms. We didn't want to leave this place, as it seemed to have it all: gobsmacking views down Ella Gap, friendly staff, great food (spaghetti bolognaise Rs 300, rice and curry Rs 300), and a relaxed, gentle ambience. A three-wheeler from here to the train station should cost Rs 60. The pet dogs are excellent guides, and will lead you to Little Adam's Peak, Ella Rock and the Rawana Falls.

Ravana Heights *(☎ 222 8888; ⓔ jith@ravanaheights.com; singles/doubles US$18/20)*, opposite the 27km post on the Ella to Wellawaya road, has four superclean rooms in a terrific little boutique guesthouse. It's a stylish, modern home with great service and friendly owners. There's a veranda and a pretty garden. Guests can avail themselves of the various excursions organised by the hosts. The food is lovely too – if you ring ahead you can have dinner here for US$6 per person.

Grand Ella Motel *(☎ 222 8536; ⓔ chc@sltnet.lk; singles/doubles in old wing US$26/30,* *in new wing US$46/52)*, formerly the Ella Resthouse, has great views from the front lawn right through Ella Gap. It's run by a government corporation so the service can be utterly uninspired. This place pays a hefty commission to drivers, so don't be surprised if your driver suggests you stay here.

Ella Adventure Park *(☎ 228 7263; ⓔ wholiday@sri.lanka.net; standard rooms US$50, treehouses US$60)* is about 9km southeast of Ella on the Wellawaya road. This modern top-end place is different to the usual cardboard-cut-out hotel. It has log furniture, natural-toned decor, Flintstone-esque stone features and a quiet bush setting. The treehouses are especially cute. All this style doesn't come cheap though. The management organises paragliding, canoeing, rock climbing, abseiling, camping and more. Or you can relax and laugh at the people sweating through corporate team-building exercise weekends.

Places to Eat & Drink

All of the guesthouses serve food. If you want to try somewhere different, check out Ambiente or the Country Comfort Inn. You could eat at any of the smaller places, but you need to give them some advance warning.

Curd & Honey Shop *(mains Rs 60-70)* is a cheerful little eatery with unusually tasty, cheap food. It does mostly rice and curry, fried rice and noodle dishes. Try the delicious curd with lashings of *kitul* (palm) syrup.

Udayanga Restaurant *(mains around Rs 100)* has tasty rice and curry for Rs 90, as well as Western-style dishes from Rs 110. The owner is very friendly, and this place is simple and clean.

Ella View Restaurant & Bar, clad with grass matting, is a good place to have a quiet drink. If you're a solo female traveller you may get annoyed by stares.

Getting There & Away

Bus & Taxi The road to Ella diverges from the Bandarawela–Badulla road about 9km out of Bandarawela. Bus services here change schedule fairly often, and a couple of old rogues hang around asking for foreign coins and occasionally taking money from people to buy bus tickets – don't trust them.

Buses to Matara stop at Ella around every hour from about 6.30am until about 2.30pm (CTB bus Rs 60, intercity express Rs 150). The buses are likely to be quite full by the time they reach Ella, though the buses around noon are usually less busy. You can always catch a bus to Wellawaya (Rs 16) and change there for a service to the South or for Monaragala (for Arugam Bay).

If you wish to go to Kandy you must change at Badulla. Alternatively you could go to Wellawaya, catch the intercity to Nuwara Eliya and then change again for Kandy (see Wellawaya later in this chapter). Buses to Bandarawela cost Rs 10 and are fairly frequent. There are infrequent buses to Badulla, although you can always get a bus to Bandarawela and change there for Badulla. It is advisable to catch intercity express buses from Bandarawela, Wellawaya and Badulla.

It costs Rs 350 to go by taxi from Ella to to Bandarawela.

Train Ella is an hour from both Haputale and Badulla on the Colombo–Badulla line. The stretch from Haputale (through Bandarawela) is particularly lovely. About 10km north of Ella, at Demodara, the line performs a complete loop around a hillside and tunnels under itself at a level 30m lower. Ella's train station is quaint, and the fares and timetables well posted. The main trains to Colombo depart at 6.52am *(Udarata Menike)* and 10.07am *(Podi Menike)*. These trains have an observation car that should be booked ahead. Other trains to Colombo depart at 6.44am and 8.13pm (Rs 154.50 in 2nd class); to Kandy trains depart at 10.07am, 1.07pm and 6.44pm (Rs 97 in 2nd class); to Badulla departures are at 5.28am, 7.55am, 1.02pm, 2.45pm, 3.28pm (*Podi Menike*) and 6.09pm (*Udarata Menike*, Rs 12 in 2nd class).

AROUND ELLA

Some people like to visit the **Dowa Temple** from Ella. (See under Bandarawela earlier in this chapter for more information.) Others might want to visit a tea factory: **Uva Halpewaththa Tea Factory** runs tours. To get there catch a bus to Bandarawela, get off at Kumbawela junction and flag a bus going to Badulla. Get off just after the 27km post, near the Halpe temple. From here you've got a 2km walk to the factory. A three-wheeler from Ella will charge Rs 150 return.

The **Rawana Ella Falls** are about 6km down Ella Gap towards Wellawaya. The water comes leaping down the mountainside in what is claimed to be the wildest-looking fall in Sri Lanka, although some travellers aren't impressed. There are vendors selling food and trinkets and the invariable array of 'guides' wanting to point out 'the waterfall'. Buses from Ella cost Rs 6 and a three-wheeler will charge Rs 30 return including waiting time.

Further up the road and to your left as you approach Ella, a side road takes you to a little **temple** and a **cave** that is associated with the Sita–Rama story. You may visit the temple, which is part of a monastery, but remember to remove your shoes and hat, and to cover your legs and arms. Just before the temple, in a cleft in the mountain that rises to Ella Rock, is a cave said to be the very one in which the king of Lanka held Sita captive. Boys often materialise to show you where the track up to the cave starts, but the track is steep, overgrown and slippery. Most find the cave itself to be a disappointment.

Walks

Ella is a great place for walks. It would be inadvisable for women to head off walking alone; it's best to go with a companion or two.

A gentle walk will take you to what is locally dubbed **Little Adam's Peak**. Go down the Passara road until you get to the plant shop on your right, just past the 1km post. Follow the track that is on your left as you face the garden shop. Little Adam's Peak is the biggest hill on your right. Take the second path that turns off to your right and follow that to the top of the hill. Part of this path passes through a tea estate. The walk from Ella takes about 45 minutes each way.

Getting to **Ella Rock** is more demanding, and you'll pass by the small **Rawana Falls** on your way. Head along the railway tracks (towards Bandarawela) for about 2.5km until you come to the metal bridge; here you'll see the falls. Continue along the tracks to just before the 166¼km sign, where you'll see a path heading to the left. Follow this over a creek, turn left, continue around a volleyball court, pass some houses and you'll soon come to a woodland. The track continues to the top of the rock, where you'll be rewarded with stunning views. The walk takes about two hours each way.

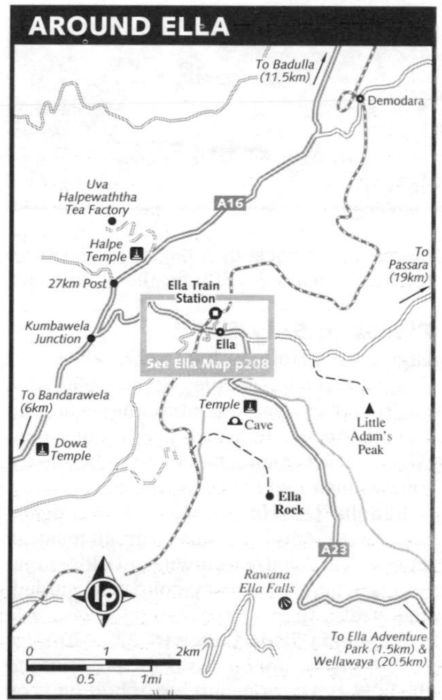

BADULLA

☎ 055 • pop 40,900

Standing at an altitude of about 680m, Badulla marks the southeast extremity of the hill country and is a gateway to the east coast. The capital of Uva Province is one of Sri Lanka's oldest towns, and has a local reputation as a base for black marketeers. The Portuguese occupied it briefly, then torched it upon leaving. For the British it was an important social centre, although the teeming roads have changed the atmosphere quite drastically today. If you are a history buff, take a look through **St Mark's Church** and peruse the old headstones. Inside the church is a plaque to the elephant hunter Major Rogers, who was killed by lightning. The railway through the hill country from Colombo and Kandy terminates here.

Information

The **post office** *(Post Office Rd)* is near the bus station. A **Bank of Ceylon** *(Bank Rd)* is along its namesake. Opposite you'll see the sign to **Cybrain Computer Systems** *(40/1 Bank Rd)*, which has Internet access for Rs 60 per hour.

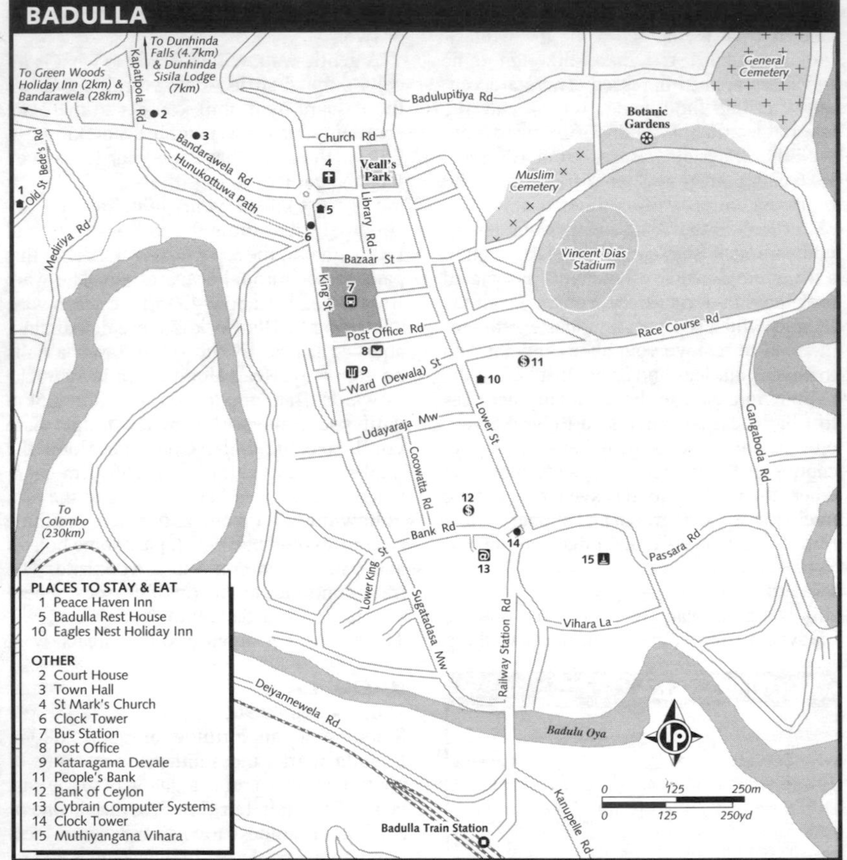

Dunhinda Falls

Five kilometres north of Badulla you'll find the 60m-high Dunhinda Falls *(admission Rs 15)*, said to be the most awe-inspiring in Sri Lanka. The best time of the year to see them is June and July but they're worth a visit anytime. It's a good spot for a picnic, but watch out for monkeys with lightning reflexes! Buses leave every 30 minutes from Badulla (Rs 12). From the bus stop the falls are about 1km along a clearly defined, sometimes rocky, path. It can be a bit of a scramble, so wear suitable shoes. There's a good observation spot at the end of the path and you can see a lower falls on the walk. There are many cold drink and snack places both on the main road and along the trail. Avoid public holidays and weekends, when the place can get packed. A three-wheeler from town will charge Rs 300 for the return trip.

Places to Stay & Eat

Eagles Nest Holiday Inn *(☎ 222 2841; 159 Lower St; singles/doubles Rs 400/550)* is a no-frills place with quaint rooms set around a courtyard. There's a bar and liquor outlet, which attracts a clientele that might make a lone woman feel uncomfortable.

Badulla Rest House *(☎ 222 2299; singles/doubles Rs 440/770)* has a great location smack in the centre of town, and old, fading rooms. There's a grassy courtyard garden, and meals are available.

Dunhinda Sisila Lodge *(☎ 223 1302, fax 23423; singles/doubles Rs 500/900)*, close to the falls, is a curious jumble of buildings by a river – one room has a tree poking through it. There's a natural swimming hole close by. To find it, follow the Dunhinda Falls road past the falls for a further 2.3km. Meals are available.

Peace Haven Inn *(☎ 222 2523; 18 Old St Bedes Rd; singles/doubles Rs 440/550, with hot water Rs 660)* is a bit out of town near some rice paddies. It's a modern place, slightly tatty but with clean sheets at least. A three-wheeler from the bus station will cost about Rs 40, or Rs 70 from the train station. Meals are available.

Green Woods Holiday Inn *(☎ 223 1358; 301 Bandarawela Rd; rooms Rs 850)* is about 3km from the centre of town. The rooms have ceiling-to-floor windows looking out to the countryside, and all have hot water. There are no mosquito nets though, and the rooms by the road are a bit noisy. Meals are available.

There are local **nosheries** along Lower St, near the intersection with Bazaar St.

Getting There & Away

Bus Buses run to Nuwara Eliya (private bus Rs 36) every 40 minutes until 4.30pm; Bandarawela (private bus Rs 17) every 20 minutes until 4.30pm; Ella (private bus Rs 15) about every two hours until 5pm; Colombo (intercity express Rs 200) until 10pm; Kandy (CTB Rs 60, intercity express Rs 125) until 2pm; and Monaragala (private bus Rs 42) every hour until 5.30pm.

Train The main daily services to Colombo leave Badulla at 5.55am (*Udarata Menike*, not to Kandy), 9.10am (*Podi Menike* via Kandy), 5.45pm (with sleeping accommodation) and 7.15pm (a slow train). Fares are Rs 60/165.50/289 in 3rd/2nd/1st class. The *Podi Menike* has a 1st-class observation car for which you pay an additional Rs 50. Fares to Kandy are Rs 38/104/181.50.

WELLAWAYA

☎ 055

By Wellawaya you have left the hill country and descended to the plains of the ancient Sinhalese kingdom of Ruhuna. Apart from the nearby Buduruwagala carvings, there's not much of interest in the area, Wellawaya being just a small crossroads town. Roads run north up past the Rawana Ella Falls and through the spectacular Ella Gap to Ella and the hill country; south to Tissamaharama and the coast at Hambantota; east to Arugam Bay on the coast via Monaragala; and west through Ratnapura to Colombo, with a branch up to Haputale in the hill country. There are branches of **Hatton National Bank** and **Bank of Ceylon** near the bus station.

Buduruwagala

About 5km south of Wellawaya a side road branches west off the road to Tissa to the rock-cut Buddha figures of Buduruwagala *(admission Rs 100)*. A small signpost points the way along a 4km road.

The name Buduruwagala is derived from the words for Buddha (Budu), images (ruva) and stone (gala). The figures are thought to date from around the 10th century, and are of the Mahayana Buddhist school, which enjoyed a brief heyday in Sri Lanka. The gigantic standing Buddha still bears traces of its original stuccoed robe, and a long streak of orange suggests it was once brightly painted.

The central of the three figures to the Buddha's right is thought to be the Mahayana Buddhist mythological figure, the Bodhisattva Avalokitesvara (the Bodhisattva of compassion). To the left of this white-painted figure is a female figure in the 'thrice bent' posture, who is thought to be his consort, Tara. The three figures on the Buddha's left appear to an inexpert eye to be of a rather different style. One is holding up the hourglass-shaped Tibetan thunderbolt symbol known as a *dorje* – an unusual example of the Tantric side of Buddhism in Sri Lanka. One of them is said to be Maitreya, the future Buddha, while another is Vishnu. Several of the figures hold up their right hands with two fingers bent down to the palm – a beckoning gesture. You may be joined by a guide who will expect a tip.

A three-wheeler from Wellawaya will cost about Rs 150 return and a taxi Rs 250 to 300 return.

Places to Stay & Eat

The Little Rose *(101 Tissa Rd; singles/doubles Rs 350/450)*, about 1km south of town opposite the road sign announcing Wellawaya, is surrounded by rice paddies. This country home has four basic rooms, cheap food (Rs 75 for breakfast) and a jolly, welcoming family. They're building some more rooms, which should be nicer but more expensive. A three-wheeler from the bus station costs about Rs 30.

Wellawaya Rest House *(☎ 227 4899; rooms Rs 715, with air-con Rs 1315)*, on the road to Ella, has basic but reasonably clean rooms with bathrooms, and an outdoor café.

Getting There & Away

Wellawaya is a major staging point between the hill country and the south and east coasts. If you can't find a through bus you can usually find a connection in Wellawaya until mid-afternoon. Buses to Haputale (Rs 21) start running at around 5am and the last bus leaves at about 5.30pm. There are regular buses to Monaragala (Rs 18.50, one hour) with the last bus leaving about 6.30pm. Buses to Ella (Rs 16) run approximately every 30 minutes until 6pm. If you want to go to Kandy you must catch a bus to Nuwara Eliya and change there. For Tissamaharama you must change at Pannegamanuwa Junction. There are also buses to Tangalla (Rs 40, three hours) and Colombo (intercity express Rs 150, seven hours).

EMBILIPITIYA

☎ 047

Embilipitiya is a good base for tours to **Uda Walawe National Park**, as it's only 21km south of the park's ticket office. It's a busy new town built to service the surrounding irrigated paddy fields and sugar-cane plantations. The bus station is in the centre of town on the main road.

Sarathchandra Rest *(☎ 223 0044; rooms Rs 900, with air-con Rs 1200)* is on the main road, about 200m south of the bus station, opposite the People's Bank. It has an assortment of clean rooms with hot water, a restaurant and a billiards table. It's a friendly, well-run spot, and offers Uda Walawe tours for Rs 1750.

Centauria Tourist Hotel *(☎ 223 0514; e centuria@sltnet.lk; rooms with air-con Rs 2090)* is about 600m south along the main road past Sarathchandra Rest, where you'll see the turn-off. It's a fine establishment, modern but with an old-fashioned, rambling air to it. The facilities are excellent – tiled floors, TVs, balconies and an inviting swimming pool. The restaurant offers buffets when tours stay, or rice and curry (Rs 192) and spaghetti bolognaise (Rs 240). Uda Walawe 4WD tours cost Rs 1750 per person. A three-wheeler to the hotel from the bus station costs Rs 50.

Getting There & Away

Buses leave regularly for most destinations from, or near, the bus station. There are CTB buses to Tangalla (Rs 21), Matara (Rs 33) and Ratnapura (Rs 32); the intercity buses cost about twice as much. Colombo intercity buses leave every 30 minutes (Rs 130).

UDA WALAWE NATIONAL PARK

The park's 30,821 hectares centre on the large Uda Walawe Reservoir, fed by the Walawe Ganga. Of all Sri Lanka's national parks, this best rivals the savanna reserves of Africa, with herds of elephants, wild buffalo, sambar deer and leopards. The entrance to the park *(all fees Rs 2573; open 6.30am-6.30pm)* is about 12km east from the turn-off on the Ratnapura–Hambantota road, and 21km from Embilipitiya. If you select a 4WD from one of the many gathered outside the gate, you can expect to pay Rs 1200 for a half day for up to eight people with driver (see the boxed text 'Snagging the Perfect Safari Tout' in The South chapter for some hints). You will also have to pay a Rs 500 'service charge' for a compulsory tracker. Last tickets are usually sold at about 5pm.

Flora & Fauna

Apart from stands of teak near the river, there's little forest. The tall *pohon* grass, which grows in place of the forest, can make wildlife-watching difficult except during dry months.

There are about 500 elephants in the park in herds of up to 100. This is a good place to see elephants, because there's an elephant-proof fence around the perimeter of the park, preventing elephants from getting out and cattle from getting in. The best time to see elephants is from 6.30am to 10am and again from 4pm to 6.30pm, usually near water.

Other creatures that call Uda Walawe home are sambar deer, wild buffaloes (their numbers have been boosted by domesticated buffaloes), mongooses, bandicoots, foxes, water monitor lizards, crocodiles, sloth bears and the occasional leopard. There are 30 varieties of snake and a wealth of birdlife; northern migrants join the residents between November and April.

Places to Stay

Walawa Park View Hotel *(☎ 047-223 3312; Tanamalwila Rd; rooms Rs 600, with air-con Rs 1320)* is a reasonably good little lodge with spacious grounds. It's about 8km from the park on the Embilipitiya road. A 4WD safari costs a reasonable Rs 1200 per half day.

Walawa Safari Village *(☎ 047-223 3201; ⓔ kinjou@dialogsl.net; RB Canal Rd; singles/doubles US$15/18, with air-con US$21/24)* is 3km south of a small junction on the road from Empilipitiya to Uda Walawe – you'll see the sign – and 10km from the park entrance. Clean and basic rooms come in a garden setting and include breakfast. Trips to the park from here also cost Rs 1200 per half day.

In the park there are three **bungalows** and two **camp sites** along the reservoir and the Walawa Ganga. You must prebook with the **Department of Wildlife Conservation** *(☎ 011-269 4241, fax 269 8556; 18 Gregory's Rd, Cinnamon Gardens, Colombo)*. The bungalows cost US$27.60 per person per night, plus a US$30 service charge per visit. You must bring your own dry rations, kerosene and linen. Camp sites cost US$6 per site per day, plus a US$5 service charge per trip. Students and children six to 12 years of age pay half price (kiddies under six stay for free).

Getting There & Away

Most people prefer to take a tour organised by their guesthouse or hotel. While this saves time, if you are counting every rupee you can organise a 4WD from one of the drivers eagerly waiting at the gate of Uda Walawe.

If you're staying at Embilipitiya, catch a bus heading to Tanamalwila (CTB Rs 28, intercity express Rs 60) and ask to be dropped at the gate to the park.

SINHARAJA FOREST RESERVE

Sinharaja *(adult/child Rs 575/290, compulsory guide Rs 300)*, the last major, undisturbed area of rainforest in Sri Lanka, occupies a broad ridge some 30km south of Ratnapura. As the heart of the island's wet zone, on most days the forest conjures rainclouds that replenish its deep soils and balance water resources for a wide area of southwestern Sri Lanka. There are several entry points, but the most relevant to travellers is either via Kudawa in the northwest or via Mederapitiya (reached from Deniyaya) in the southeast.

Sinharaja (literally 'lion king') comprises 18,899 hectares of natural and modified forest, measuring about 21km east to west and 3.7km north to south. It was once a royal reserve, and some colonial records refer to it as Rajasinghe Forest. It may have been the last redoubt of the Sri Lankan lion. The area first entered European records when the Portuguese detailed all the villages in the area, plus their timber and fruit trees, for tax collection purposes.

In 1840 the forest became Crown land under British rule and from that time efforts were made to preserve at least some of it. However, in 1971 loggers moved in and began what was called selective logging. Replanting involved replacing the logged native hardwoods with mahogany (which does not occur naturally here). Logging roads and trails snaked into the forest and a woodchip mill was built. Conservationists lobbied hard for an end to the destruction. In 1977 the government called a halt to all logging; the machinery was dismantled and taken out of the forest, the roads gradually grew over and Sinharaja was saved. In 1989 it was made a Unesco World Heritage Site. Much of the rest of Sri Lanka's rainforest stands on mountain ridges within a 20km radius of the forest.

There are 22 villages around the forest, and locals enter it to tap *kitul* palms for sap (to make *jaggery*, a hard brown sweet) – this is allowed to a limited degree – and to collect wood and leaves for fuel and for construction. Medicinal plants are collected during specific seasons. Rattan collection is of more concern as the demand for raw cane is high. Sinharaja attracts illegal gem miners too, whose abandoned open pits pose dangers to humans and animals and cause erosion. There is also some poaching of wild animals.

Flora

Sinharaja has a wild profusion of flora, which is still being studied. The canopy trees reach heights of up to 45m, with the next layer down topping about 30m. The vegetation below the canopy is not thick and impenetrable, as rumour sometimes has it. Nearly all the subcanopy trees found here are rare or endangered. More than 65% of the 217 types of trees and woody climbers endemic to Sri Lanka's rainforest are found in Sinharaja.

Fauna

The largest carnivore here is the leopard. Seldom seen, the leopard's presence can usually be gauged only by droppings and tracks. Even rarer are rusty spotted cats and fishing cats. Sambar, barking deer and wild boar can be found on the forest floor. Purple-faced langurs in groups of 10 to 14 are fairly common. There are three kinds of squirrel: the flame-striped jungle squirrel, the dusky-striped jungle squirrel and the western giant squirrel. Porcupines and pangolins waddle around the forest floor, mostly unseen. Six species of bat have been recorded here. Civets and mongooses are nocturnal, though you may glimpse the occasional mongoose darting through the foliage during the day.

There are 45 species of reptiles, 21 of them endemic. Venomous snakes include the green pit viper, which inhabits trees, the hump-nosed viper, and the krait, which lives on the forest floor. One of the most frequently found amphibians is the wrinkled frog, whose croaking is often heard at night. There is a wealth of birdlife: 147 species have been recorded, with 18 of Sri Lanka's 20 endemic species seen here.

Orientation & Information

Sinharaja is bordered by rivers: the Koskulana Ganga in the north and the Gin Ganga in the south. An old foot track that goes past the Beverley Estate marks the eastern border. The land decreases in elevation towards the west. The east has the highest peak in the forest, Hinipitigala (1171m).

Hinipitigala stands for most of the year under a constant drizzle, if not an outright downpour, as Sinharaja receives between 3500mm and 5000mm of rain annually, with a minimum in the driest months (August to September, January to early April) of 50mm. The drier months are the best times to visit. There's little seasonal variation in the temperature, which averages about 24°C inside the forest, with humidity at about 87%.

Sinharaja has leeches in abundance. It would be most unusual to walk through this forest and not attract one or more of these unpleasant little critters. In colonial times the British, Dutch and Portuguese armies rated leeches as their worst enemy when they tried to conquer the hinterland (which was then much more forested), and one British writer claimed leeches caused more casualties than all the other animals put together. These days you needn't suffer as much. See Health in the Facts for the Visitor chapter for tactics on removing the critters.

THE HILL COUNTRY

Kudawa

The main ticket office is at the Forest Department here. The department offers basic dorm-like accommodation. See Places to Stay & Eat, later, for details of some recommended guides.

Deniyaya & Around

Deniyaya is the closest base for visiting Sinharaja if coming from the south or east. Tickets to the forest reserve must be bought at Deodawa, 5km from Deniyaya on the Matara road. The entrance is near Mederapitiya (10km from Deniyaya) via Pallegama. There is a path that follows the Gin Ganga on the park's southern border.

Several travellers wrote to recommend **Sena Serasinghe** *(☎ 071 200727)* for information and tours of Sinharaja and arranging bed and breakfast accommodation.

Kotapola, 6km south of Deniyaya, has a superb early-17th-century **rock temple**. It's well worth the climb. The **Kiruwananaganga Falls**, some of the largest in Sri Lanka (60m high and up to 60m wide), are 5km east of Kotapola on the road towards Urubokka. The **Kolawenigama Temple**, 3km from Pallegama (which is 3km from Deniyaya), is of modest proportions but has a unique structure that resembles Kandy's Sri Dalada Maligawa. It was built by King Buwanekabahu VII as recognition of the protection the villagers gave to the Tooth Relic. The shrine has Kandyan-style frescoes.

Places to Stay & Eat

Kudawa & the Northwest Right on the park's boundary near Kudawa, **Martin Wijesinghe's** *(Forest View, Kudawa; rooms Rs 500)* is a congenial place. It's is about 4km from the ticket office. You can contact Martin by telegram in advance at the **Weddagala post office** *(☎ 045-225 5256)*. Martin is an expert on Sinharaja, having worked as a ranger here for years, and is a mine of information. The accommodation is basic. You can get a good rice and curry meal here – vegetarian, as there is no fridge – but if you are coming with your own vehicle it would be a courtesy to bring your own food, which the family will cook for you.

The Forest Department at Kudawa has **bungalows** with basic accommodation. Contact the **Forest Department HQ** *(☎ 011-286 6631; ⓔ forest@slt.lk; 82 Rajamalwatte Rd, Battaramulla)*, on the outskirts of Colombo, for more information.

It is far simpler and cheaper to stay with one of the guides based at Kudawa. Sunil Handuwila is one who can be contacted there, and people can stay at his house (one spare room) for Rs 300 per night.

At Koswatta, 3km from Kalawana, **Singraj Rest** *(☎ 045-225 5201; rooms Rs 1200)* is a country hotel with seven rooms, a restaurant (mains around Rs 170) and a bar – the latter is just about the only entertainment in these parts. The rooms are quite decent, though there's cold water only. Staff can arrange taxis to Sinharaja for Rs 1500 per day. A three-wheeler here from Kalawana will cost about Rs 150.

Boulder Garden *(☎ 045-225 5812; ⓔ info@bouldergarden.com; Sinharaja Rd, Koswatta; singles/doubles full board US$185/215)* is an expensive but brilliantly designed ecoresort, which somehow blends in with a series of huge boulders and streams. It runs birdwatching tours and hiking trips around 10 hectares of rainforest. There are 10 suites, painstakingly built from rock. Meals are available.

Deniyaya Staying at **Sinharaja Rest** *(☎ 041-227 3368, fax 227 3368; Temple Rd; singles/doubles Rs 500/800)* saves a lot of hassle by arranging a rainforest walk with Palitha Ratnayaka. Palitha is a certified guide and very knowledgeable about the forest. The six rooms at his home are fairly basic, but there's loads of information on Sinharaja and good home cooking. A trip to Sinharaja with Palitha costs Rs 500 per person per day, plus the Rs 575 entry and an Rs 800 per person 4WD ride up to Mederapitiya. Nonguests can take his tours too.

Deniyaya Rest House *(☎ 041-227 3600; rooms Rs 650)* has great views. Like most resthouses, this place has a plum position; in this case, overlooking the town and the countryside. The large, quaint rooms are in fair condition, and there's a bar and restaurant. Staff arrange forest tours through Sinharaja Rest.

Sathmala Ella Rest *(☎ 041-227 3481; Pallegama, Deniyaya; rooms Rs 1000-1200, hot water Rs 200 extra)* is a handsome middle-class home in a village about 3km from Deniyaya, run by a friendly family. There are nine modern rooms with bathroom. It also runs tours into the forest for Rs 500 per person, plus the Rs 575 entry fee and Rs 500 per person for transport. There's a waterfall about 2km away. A three-wheeler from Deniyaya should cost Rs 150.

Getting There & Away

Kudawa & the Northwest There are buses from Ratnapura to Kalawana (Rs 45 for an express) and from Colombo to Weddagala (4km before Kudawa). There are about four buses daily from Weddagala to Kudawa. Try to start as early as you can. The roads through these hills are often damaged by flooding.

Deniyaya There are several buses to/from Galle (CTB Rs 60), although you can always catch one of the more frequent buses to Akuressa (Rs 15 from Deniyaya) and change there. Many buses pass through Akuressa.

There's an intercity express bus to Colombo (Rs 150, 5½ hours); if you want a CTB bus you're better off going to Akuressa or Pelmadulla and changing. For Ella and Nuwara Eliya you must catch a bus to Pelmadulla and change there.

For Ratnapura there are buses roughly every hour from 6.45am until the afternoon (CTB Rs 60).

If you have a car, the road through the Hayes Tea Estate north of Deniyaya, en route to Madampe and Balangoda (for Belihul Oya, Haputale or Ratnapura), is very scenic.

SINHARAJA TO RATNAPURA

The A17 road goes northeast from Deniyaya and passes through **Rakwana**. The view from above the town gives a sweeping panorama across the plains of Uda Walawe National Park, with the escarpment of the Peak Sanctuary in the north.

The best place to stay is the **Rakwana Rest House** *(☎ 045-224 6299; rooms Rs 825)*, a modest British bungalow with four rooms (with good bathrooms), a fine veranda, dining and drinks. It is one of the nicer resthouses we visited.

From Rakwana the road reaches a southern spur of the hill (and tea) country before

Pelmadulla. Pelmadulla, between Ratnapura and Haputale, is an important junction town.

Buses between Rakwana and Ratnapura cost Rs 20 (two hours). Buses to Deniyaya cost Rs 35, but the road is in bad shape.

RATNAPURA

☎ 045 • pop 46,300

Busy Ratnapura (City of Gems), 100km southeast of Colombo, is the centre of a number of richly watered valleys between Adam's Peak and Sinharaja Forest Reserve. The climate here is wet and humid. The town has a famous daily gem market, the bazaar of the region's ancient wealth of gemstones. The rural scenery surrounding the town is underappreciated – paddy fields cloak the valley floors while rubber trees and tea bushes grow on the hills. Many villagers keep the old Sinhalese traditions, such as leaving candles outside the front door at dusk to prevent evil spirits from entering.

Ratnapura was the traditional start of the toughest pilgrimages up to Adam's Peak, and this is reputed to be the best place for views of the sacred mountain (the Hatton side is at a higher elevation).

The attractive route from Ratnapura to Haputale skirts around the southern edge of the hill country and then ascends into the hills.

Things to See & Do

The **National Museum** (*☎ 222 2451; adult/child Rs 35/25, camera Rs 135; open 9am-5pm Sat-Wed*) has the fossil remains of various animals (eg, rhinos, elephants) discovered in gem pits on display. There are items of local culture as well, including gems, fabrics and jewellery.

There's a **Gem Museum** (*Pothgulvihara Mawatha, Getangama; admission free; open 9am-4pm daily*), which is signposted from the main street where the clock tower is. There's a good display of gems as well as information on mining and polishing. A return three-wheeler trip from the centre of town should cost Rs 100 (including waiting time).

There aren't any **gem mines** catering for tourist visits but if you're interested in seeing one your guesthouse or hotel should be able to organise something. You can also watch gem merchants selling their wares in the area northeast of the clock tower.

Pompakelle Forest Park lies behind the Rest House (see Places to Stay & Eat, later). There are walking trails through this lush forest.

One of the oldest routes up Adam's Peak, the **Gilimalai para**, starts from the splendid **Maha Saman Devale** complex, 4km west of the city. Saman (aka Kataragama and Skanda), the war god, is the patron deity of the trek up the holy mountain. It's a handsome

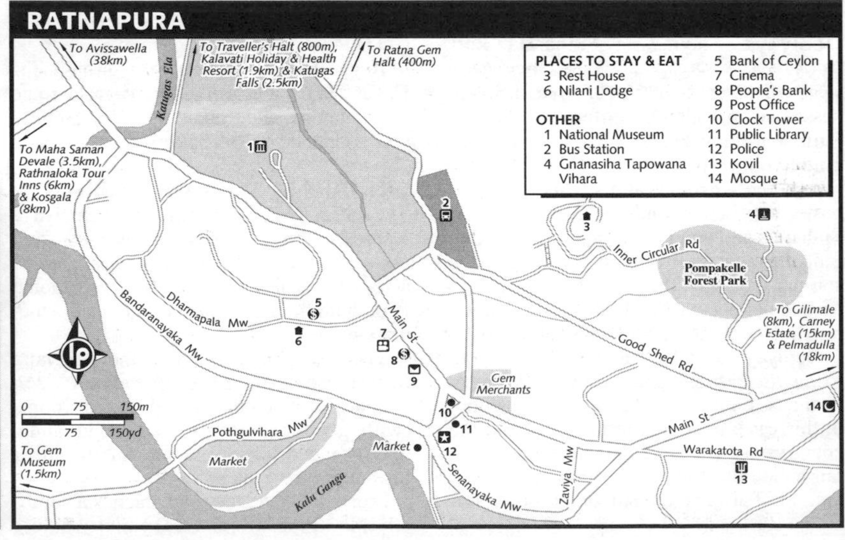

Gems

Every other person you meet in Ratnapura's streets is likely to whisper that they have an unbelievable bargain wrapped up in their pocket. If you're no expert on gemstones the bargain will be on their part, not yours. Synthetic stones are very hard to spot, even for experts.

Gems are still found by ancient methods. Gem miners look for seams of *illama*, a gravel-bearing stratum likely to hold gemstones. It's usually found in the upper reaches of newly buried riverbeds – the gems are heavier than gravel so aren't carried to the lower reaches of rivers. On the Colombo–Ratnapura road you'll see countless gem-mining operations in paddy fields beside the road, but there are many more off in the hills and fields all around. Different areas have different specialities – villages sometimes have weekly gem markets.

Gem mining is a cooperative effort, requiring men to dig out the *illama*, work the pump and wash the muddy gravel, as well as an expert to search through the pebbles. If a stone is found, the profit is divided between all the members of the coop, from the person who supplies the finances to the one up to his neck in mud and water, clad only in a tiny loincloth known as an *amudes*. Children are sometimes sent down the shafts. The mines can be vertical or horizontal depending on which way the *illama* runs.

It's a peculiarity of Sri Lankan gemming that a variety of stones is almost always found in the same pit. A stone's value depends on a number of factors including rarity, hardness and beauty. Gems are still cut and polished by hand, although modern methods are also coming into use. Some stones are cut and faceted *(en cabochon)*, while others are simply polished. The division between precious and semiprecious stones is purely arbitrary – there is no clear definition of what makes one stone a precious stone and another only semiprecious. Some of the more popular types of stone are listed here.

Corundrums are a group that includes sapphires and rubies, both precious stones and second only to the diamond in hardness. The best and most valuable rubies are red, not found in Sri Lanka in commercial quantities. You will, however, see pink rubies, which are also correctly called pink sapphires. Rubies and sapphires are the same type of stone, with gradations of colour depending on the precise proportions of the chemicals in their make-up. Star rubies and star sapphires are a feature of the Ratnapura gem industry. The stone is comparatively dull, but under light a starburst appears in the stone. Other sapphires can be yellow, orange, white and, most valuable, blue. Sri Lanka has produced three of the world's largest blue sapphires, including the Star of India (displayed at the New York Museum of Natural History). Beware of pink or blue spinels being passed off as sapphires. You can often find corundrums containing 'silk': minute inclusions that give the stone a star effect, particularly with a single light source.

Cat's-eye and alexandrite are the best known in the **chrysoberyl** group. Cat's-eyes, with their cat-like ray known as *chatoyancy*, vary from green through a honey colour to brown; look for translucence and the clarity and glow of the single ray. Alexandrite is valued for its colour change under natural and artificial light. One rip-off to watch for is tourmalines, which are far less valuable, being sold as cat's-eyes.

The best-known stone in the **beryl** group, the emerald, is not found in Sri Lanka. Aquamarine is found here, and is quite reasonably priced since it is not as hard or lustrous as other stones.

The appearance of a **zircon** can approach that of a diamond, although it is a comparatively soft stone. Zircon comes in a variety of colours, from yellow through orange to brown and green.

Quartz varies from transparent to opaque, and is usually quite well priced. Quartz also varies widely in colour, from purple amethyst to brown smoky quartz, right through to yellow or orange citron.

The moonstone, or **feldspar**, is Sri Lanka's special gem. Usually a smooth, grey colour, it can also be found with a slight shade of blue although this colouring is rarer.

Among the other precious stones, **spinels** are fairly common but are also quite hard and rather attractive. They come in a variety of colours and can be transparent or opaque. **Garnets** are a sort of poor person's ruby; light-brown garnets are often used in local rings. **Topaz** isn't found in Sri Lanka – if someone offers it to you it'll probably be quartz.

temple, with a series of broad courtyards and whitewashed buildings in the Kandyan style, with some Portuguese influence. The major festival here is a *perahera* on Esala *poya* (July/August), not so well known because it coincides with the Kandy *perahera*.

Peak-baggers and pilgrims today pick up the Gilimalai para from the roadhead at Carney Estate, 15km or one hour away by bus. It takes six to eight hours going up, and five to seven hours coming down. Leeches are a particular menace on this trail. Before the road was built, the village of **Gilimalai** ('swallowed mountain' – there's no view from here) was the first night halt or *ambalama* on the pilgrimage. The next stop at **Pallebadole** (elevation 600m) is a hill village with a dagoba and pilgrim's lodgings. Further uphill is **Nilihela**, a gorge – pilgrims tell a story of a woman named Nili who tried to save her child falling over the edge, but fell herself. Pilgrims pause to call out her name, and the eerie echoes send her answer ever more faintly. The trail winds up to Diyabetma on the saddle of a ridge, then up the steep final ascent to the footprint on the summit.

There are less arduous walks than Adam's Peak much closer to town, even right from the Rest House. Three kilometres north of town are the **Katugas Falls**, which are quite pleasant but are crowded on Sundays and public holidays. There's a full-size replica of the **Aukana Buddha** at the Gnanasiha Tapowana Vihara, on top of a hill overlooking the town; you can walk to it through Pompakelle Forest Park. About 8km from town, at Kosgala, are some **caves**.

You can also use Ratnapura as a base for a day trip to Sinharaja Forest Reserve. Expect to pay around Rs 3000 (up to four people). You'll also be offered trips to Uda Walawe National Park for Rs 4000 but it's really too long a journey to do in a day.

Monks and Poya Days

All the crucial events in the Buddha's life occurred on full moons. Strictly speaking there are four *poya* days every lunar month, at no moon, half moon, full moon and half moon. The modern holidays are for the holiest *poya*, the full moon, and it is these which are usually referred to as *poya* days.

The Buddha's rules for upholding monastic life centre on *poya* days. The Buddha arranged that on new moon and full moon days, monks had to recite the rules of conduct *(patimokka)* for the Sangha, or community of monks. One of the stricter rules was on attendance – even if a monk was sick, the rest of his community had to assemble for the ceremony at his bedside. There are 227 *patimokka* in the Theravada tradition, which are divided into different categories, from minor rules on decorum to the major sins that immediately disbar you from the Sangha. The head monk recites each class of rules, then asks three times if all the monks are pure. A monk should publicly confess any lapse. Once the confession is over, the head monk declares the Sangha to be pure. The core of the split between the different Nikayas or Buddhist orders in Sri Lanka is over slightly different lists of *patimokka*. By custom, elderly Buddhists swear to live by the Eight Precepts – the highest vows for lay people – in groups on full moon *poya* days.

Also on *poya* days, villagers visit their temple to make *puja* (prayers and offerings) to the bodhi tree or a stupa. Spirit mediums don't become possessed on *poya* days, as it is seen as bad form.

Places to Stay & Eat

Ratna Gem Halt *(☎ 222 3745, 153/5 Outer Circular Rd, doubles Rs 450)* is a family house north of town with four guest rooms. It won plaudits from readers for its hospitality, food and fine views. It's run by a gem dealer's family, who also have a gem showroom.

Travellers Halt *(☎ 222 3092; 30 Outer Circular Rd; singles/doubles Rs 500/600, with air-con Rs 900/1000)*, just over 1km out of town in the direction of Polhengoda Village, has nine rooms, three with air-con. The rooms are clean and pleasant and management are keen to arrange tours. A three-wheeler from the bus station should cost Rs 50.

Nilani Lodge *(☎ 222 2170; e hashani@sltnet.lk; 21 Dharmapala Mawatha; singles/doubles Rs 715/935, with air-con Rs 935/1340)* is a 1970s-vintage concrete building in town with clean, comfy rooms with hot water.

Rest House *(☎ 222 2299; rooms Rs 1500)* has the best site in town, right on top of the hill that dominates Ratnapura. The colonial-style rooms are large and bare, and the service is sometimes funnier than at *Fawlty Towers*. We've had several warnings about gem scams being perpetrated here. Still, the place has heaps of charm with its spacious veranda, bar and grassy garden.

Kalavati Holiday & Health Resort *(☎ 222 2465, fax 222 3657; Polhengoda Village; singles/doubles from Rs 1180/1293, with air-con Rs 1800/1910)* is an Ayurvedic centre 2.5km from the Ratnapura bus station. There is an extensive herb garden and the place itself is kitted out with antique furniture. The Ayurvedic business seems to be in a slump but the gardens help make it a pleasant place to stay. The rooms are basic and could use some treatment themselves. It has good food and quite an extensive menu. A three-wheeler from the bus station will cost about Rs 75.

Rathnaloka Tour Inns *(☎/fax 222 2455; ⓔ ratnaloka@eureka.lk; Kosgala/Kahangama; rooms US$30, deluxe rooms US$42)* is an upmarket place 6km from town built by a gem magnate. Like so many of the buildings funded with gem wealth around town, it strives to make a statement, but there's a large garden, an inviting pool and attentive service. Rooms have air-con and hot water; there are also deluxe rooms. There is a good restaurant here. A taxi from Ratnapura should cost Rs 500; a three-wheeler half as much.

There are several **eateries** in and near Main St that serve reasonable rice and curry for low prices.

Getting There & Away

There are heaps of buses to long-distance destinations, including Colombo (intercity bus Rs 75, CTB Rs 36). Any bus coming from Colombo is likely to be jam-packed. For Hatton or Nuwara Eliya, you'll have to catch a bus to Avissawella (Rs 14) and change there. For Haputale, Ella and Badulla you'll probably have to catch a bus to Balangoda (Rs 21) and change there. The CTB bus to Embilipitiya (for Uda Walawe National Park) costs Rs 32. To get to Galle you must change at Matara (Rs 75, 4½ hours).

The Ancient Cities

The ancient cities region lies north of the hill country, in one of the driest parts of the country. During the golden age of Sinhalese civilisation it was called Rajarata – the land of kings. Across 1500 years of dynasties, wars, invasions and religious missions to China and South-East Asia, increasingly ambitious dams and irrigation systems supported two great cities (Anuradhapura and Polonnaruwa) and many other magnificent reminders of the strength of the region's Buddhist culture. For almost 1000 years the jungle did its best to reclaim them, but major archaeological excavations over the past century have partially restored their past glory. For the past 100 years engineers have been patching up the irrigation system and marvelling at the skill of the original builders.

A long-running partnership between the Sri Lankan government and Unesco continues to restore ancient sites. The Cultural Triangle project centres on the old capitals of Kandy, Anuradhapura and Polonnaruwa, and tickets priced in US dollars are required (see the boxed text 'Cultural Triangle Tickets' for details).

Apart from a 1985 attack on Anuradhapura, the civil war didn't reach the ancient city sites.

Kandy (see the Hill Country chapter) is a good starting point for a visit; you can also continue up the east coast through Ampara, or inland along the fine roads of the Mahaweli irrigation scheme area.

Highlights

- Pausing to catch your breath by the saucy frescoes as you clamber up the Sigiriya rock fortress
- Taking in the view over Anuradhapura's great dagobas (Buddhist shrines) from the holy hill of Mihintale
- Cycling through the dappled shade around Polonnaruwa's stone ruins and spending time under the serene gaze of the Buddha of Gal Vihara
- Counting the Buddhas at Dambulla's beautiful cave temples
- Pausing in the shade of Sri Maha Bodhi, the sacred bodhi tree and living Buddha relic at Anuradhapura

MATALE

☎ 066 • pop 36,400

This mid-sized regional city at the heart of the island lies in a broad fertile valley at an elevation of 300m. The road to Kandy, 24km south, ascends past paddy fields, areca nut plantations and pepper vines. Other regional specialities include vanilla, rubber, cinchona and cardamom. The town's pleasant park includes a monument to the leaders of the 1848 Matale Rebellion – one of the less famous contributions to the Year of Revolutions!

Not far north of the bus stop for Kandy is an interesting Hindu temple, the **Sri Muthumariamman Thevasthanam** *(admission Rs 25)*. A priest will show you the five enormous, colourful ceremonial chariots pulled along by people during an annual festival.

A drive east through the 1500m-high Knuckles Range, east of Matale, presents some remarkable mountain views. The B38 heads uphill from the north end of town to a pass near Rattota, while other roads head southwest to the hill villages of Elkaduwa and Karagahandala before winding down to Kandy and the Victoria Reservoir. For more details of the Knuckles Range, see The Hill Country chapter.

Aluvihara

The rock monastery of Aluvihara is beside the Kandy–Dambulla road, 3km north of Matale. The monastery caves are situated among rocks that have fallen from the mountains high above the valley. It's an extremely picturesque setting. Legend has it that a giant used three of the rocks as a base for his cooking pot, and the name Aluvihara (ash temple) refers to the ashes from the cooking fire. Ancient drip ledges line the rocks above the frescoed caves, while bats rustle in sheltered corners of the rocks. The frescoed cave shrines include two reclining Buddha images. One cave is dedicated to Buddhagosa, the Indian Pali scholar who is supposed to have spent several years here.

Buddhist doctrines were first transcribed from oral and Sinhalese sources into Pali

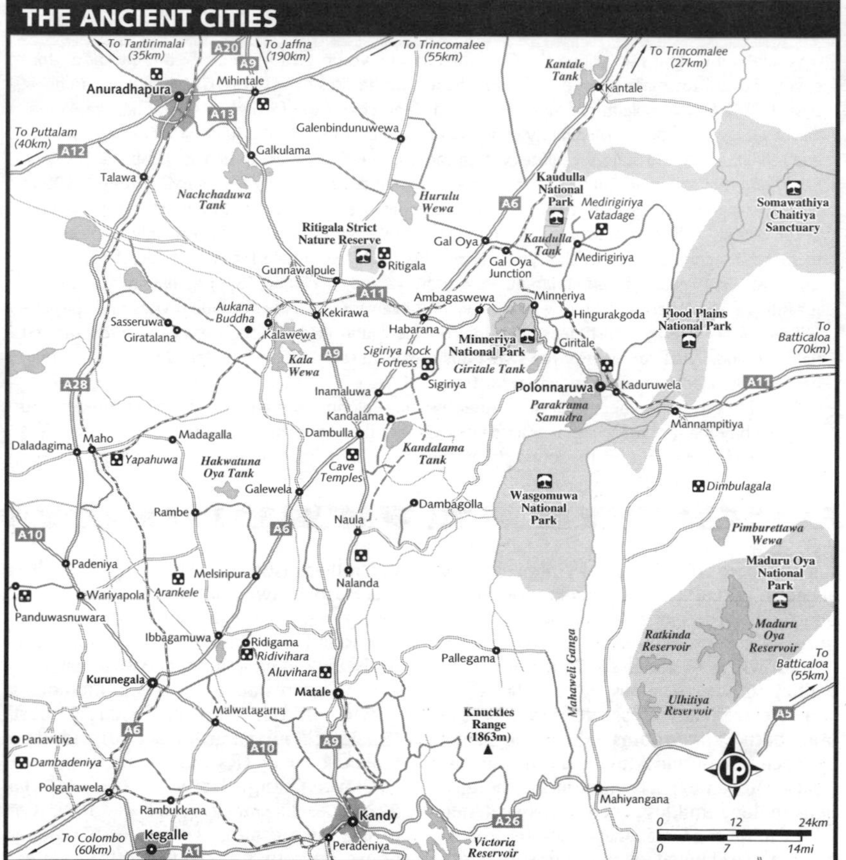

text by a council of monks held at Aluvihara in the 1st century BC. Two thousand years later the monastic library was destroyed by British troops putting down a revolt in 1848. The long process of replacing the *ola* (palm leaf) manuscripts still occupies monks, scribes and craftsmen today. You can see their **workshop** *(admission Rs 50)*; the price might include having your name inscribed on a small card of *ola*. See the boxed text 'Ola Leaves & Sinhala Script'.

One of the monastic caves contains a **horror chamber** *(admission Rs 20)*. It's money well spent if you're considering straying from the straight and narrow – the gaudy statues of devils and sinners show the inventive range of punishment meted out in the afterlife. One scene shows a sexual sinner with his skull cut open and his brains being ladled out by two demons. Another exhibit shows prostitutes being impaled. Some of the demons seem to be taking real pleasure in their work.

A three-wheeler from Matale to Aluvihara will cost about Rs 280 return plus waiting time, and a bus will cost Rs 3.50.

Matale Heritage Centre

About 2km north of Matale, the Matale Heritage Centre *(☎ 222 2404; 33 Sir Richard Aluvihara Mawatha)* draws on the rich craft traditions of the area, producing quality batik, embroidery, carpentry and brass work. It occupies a sprawling compound of bungalows, workshops and gardens. Beside selling crafts, the centre does meals for groups of

Cultural Triangle Tickets

If you intend visiting sites within the Cultural Triangle, you need to buy either a round ticket that covers most of the major sites, or individual tickets at the sites themselves. Currently a round ticket costs US$32.50 (payable in the rupee equivalent) and covers the following: Anuradhapura, Polonnaruwa, Sigiriya, Ritigala, Medirigiriya and Nalanda, plus a few sites in Kandy (but *not* the Sri Dalada Maligawa). Many Buddhist shrines within the Cultural Triangle area, such as Dambulla, Sri Maha Bodhi and Mihintale, are run by the Sangha and charge separate entry fees, varying from Rs 100 to 500. The round ticket is valid for 60 days from the date of purchase, and you must start using your ticket within 14 days of purchasing it. The ticket entitles you to one day's entry only – if you wish to spend a second day at any site, you pay the full day's fee. If paid for individually, the tickets to sites cost US$15 each for Anuradhapura, Polonnaruwa and Sigiriya; US$8 for Medirigiriya; and US$5 for Ritigala and Nalanda. All foreign nationals and even foreigners with resident visas must pay the full amount. There are no student discounts on the round ticket, though sometimes you can get half-price individual site tickets if you sweet talk the ticket seller. Children under 12 years are charged half price, while those under six get in for free.

Round tickets can be bought at the Anuradhapura, Polonnaruwa and Nalanda ticket offices. You can also buy them at the Cultural Triangle office, near the tourist office in Kandy.

For details of which sites the round ticket covers in Kandy, see Information under Kandy in The Hill Country chapter.

four or more, if you book by phone a day ahead. It costs Rs 475 per person for a banquet with three kinds of rice and up to 20 different curries. A three-wheeler here from Matale will cost about Rs 250 return plus waiting time, while a bus will cost Rs 3.

There are many **spice gardens** and several **batik showrooms** along the road between Matale and Aluvihara. The various treats you can expect on a tour of the gardens include milkless cocoa tea sweetened with vanilla and banana, and various creams and potions claimed to make hair shine or to cure flatulence. Prices at some spice garden shops are high, so check in a market before you set out so that you have something to compare prices with.

Places to Stay & Eat

Rock House Hotel (*☎ 222 3239; 17/16A Hulangamuwa Rd; singles/doubles Rs 880/1200*), set in a pretty garden, is a modern place just to the south of the Rest House (it is signposted on the main road). There are seven plain rooms sharing a broad balcony, but considering they don't have hot water they're a bit overpriced.

Matale Rest House (*☎ 222 2299; e thilanka@ids.lk; Park Rd (William Gopawala Mawatha); rooms Rs 1000, with air-con Rs 1500*) is managed by a private company. There are 14 clean doubles (with hot water) in a rather institutional building, lifted by a broad front lawn and garden centring on a lovely bodhi tree that predates the hotel. The Rest House lies south of the town centre in the old cantonment (British garrison) area. The restaurant's menu includes a lunch buffet if there are enough guests (Rs 350), a mixed grill (Rs 370) and vegetable chop suey (Rs 185).

Clover Grange Hotel (*☎ 223 1144, fax 223 0406; 95 King St; rooms Rs 1300*), west of the town centre, is a gorgeous colonial house with two elegant, spotlessly clean rooms with hot water. The hotel has a large dining room with a bar. It serves good food such as devilled beef for Rs 185 and rice and fish curry for Rs 295.

A&C Restaurant (*☎ 223 2717; 3/5 Sir Richard Aluvihara Mawatha*) is on the same turn-off as the Matale Heritage Centre, but coming from Matale take a sharp left rather than the road to the centre. With tables on a sheltered veranda, it's a decent place to stop for lunch if you're travelling by car or van. Noodle dishes cost Rs 200 to 350; rice and curry costs Rs 400. It's slightly expensive but offers good cooking with good service. It's open only for lunch daily.

Getting There & Away

Bus No 594 to Matale (Rs 25 by intercity express, Rs 14 by private bus) leaves from

Along the trail at Horton Plains, near World's End

BOTH PHOTOGRAPHS BY ANDERS BLOMQVIST

Looking down from the top of Adam's Peak at the trail and dagoba (Buddhist shrine)

NIGEL MARSH

Standing Buddha, Aukana

ANDERS BLOMQVIST

Seated Buddha, Mihintale

ANDERS BLOMQVIST

Thuparama dagoba, Anuradhapura

beside the central clock tower in Kandy. Dambulla or Anuradhapura buses from Kandy or Matale will drop you at Aluvihara or the spice gardens. There are six daily trains on the pretty 28km-long spur line between Matale and Kandy (Rs 6, 1½ hours).

NALANDA

☎ 066

There is an 8th-century *gedige* (temple) at Nalanda *(adult/child US$5/2.50)*, about 25km north of Matale and 20km before Dambulla. It is a rare example of mixed Buddhist and Hindu architecture, though to some eyes it looks oddly like a Mexican Mayan temple! It has a couple of Tantric carvings with sexual subjects, but before you get too excited, the carvings are weather-beaten – some people are disappointed. Entry is included in the Cultural Triangle round ticket (see the boxed text 'Cultural Triangle Tickets').

The site is beside a tank 1km east of the main road – a sign marks the turn-off near the 49km post. Anuradhapura buses from Kandy or Matale will drop you at the turn-off.

DAMBULLA

☎ 066

A barren town, Dambulla's only attraction is the cave temples (also known as the rock temple and golden temple). You can visit it as a day trip on public transport from Kandy, or travel through on your way to/from Sigiriya. If you decide to stay the night, the accommodation for all budgets is decent.

Cave Temples

The beautiful cave temples *(adult/child Rs 500/free; open 7am-7pm daily)* are 100m to 150m above the road in the southern part of Dambulla. The hike up to the temples begins along a vast, sloping rock face with steps in some places. The Cultural Triangle ticket isn't valid here. The ticket office is at the gate near the monstrous Buddha, and your receipt is checked at the entrance to the temples. Photography is allowed inside the caves, but you're not allowed to photograph people. There are superb views over the surrounding countryside from the level of the caves. Sigiriya, 22km northeast, is clearly visible.

Unfortunately this precinct has been distastefully commercialised with the construction of what is claimed to be the largest **Buddha statue** in the world (30m high) in the Dharmachakkra posture, and a **museum** *(adult/child Rs 100/50; open 7.30am-11.30pm daily)*. The museum contains no information in English, and only brief labels in Sinhala, but there is an **Internet café** and a Buddhist publications bookshop.

The caves' history is thought to date to around the 1st century BC when King Valagambahu, driven out of Anuradhapura, took refuge here. When he regained his throne, he had the interior of the caves carved into magnificent rock temples. Later kings made further improvements, including King Nissanka Malla who had the caves' interiors gilded, earning the place the name Ran Giri (Golden Rock).

There are five separate caves containing about 150 Buddha images. Most of the paintings in the temples date from the 19th century.

Ola Leaves & Sinhala Script

The elegant swirls and flourishes of the 58-letter Sinhala script developed partly due to the nature of the *ola* leaves used as writing material. The leaves are tough but have a distinct fibre. Straight lines and angles tend to cut the leaves lengthways, so the elegant, swirling script evolved to avoid damage. Writing paper wasn't used in early Sri Lanka, probably because *ola* leaves were so readily available. Seventeenth-century sea captain, Robert Knox, remarked on how cheap they were.

Ola leaves are prepared from the young leaves of the talipot palm. The leaves are boiled, dried, rolled and stretched. Writing is a kind of engraving done with a steel-tipped stylus; to make it legible, it has to be dyed. The leaf is washed over with a sticky blend of charcoal and *dummala* oil, made from a fossilised resin found in paddy fields. Most of the resin is wiped off to leave the blackened letters. The resin also preserves the leaves; they can last as long as 500 years. All the Sinhalese classics, the Pali Canon, the Mahavamsa and the Jataka tales were engraved on *ola* leaves.

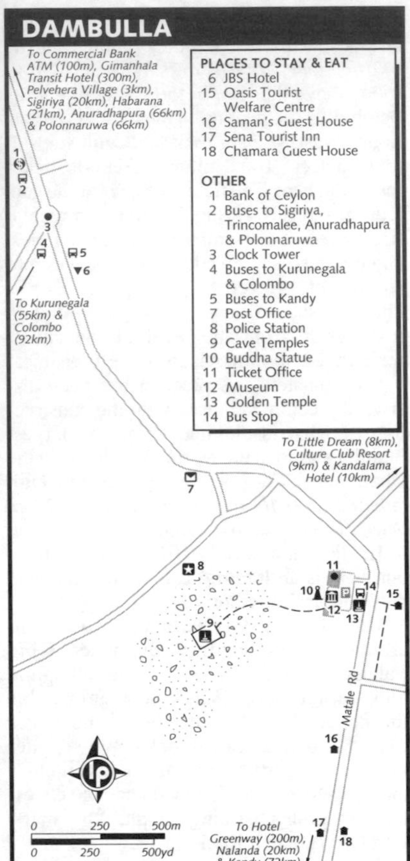

Cave I (Devaraja Viharaya) The first cave, the Temple of the King of the Gods, has a 15m-long reclining Buddha. Ananda, the Buddha's most loyal disciple, and other seated Buddhas are depicted nearby. A statue of Vishnu is held in a small shrine within the cave, but it's usually closed.

Cave II (Maharaja Viharaya) The Temple of the Great King is arguably the most spectacular. It measures 52m from east to west and 23m from the entrance to the back wall. The highest point of the ceiling is 7m. This cave is named after the two statues of kings it contains. There is a painted wooden statue of Valagamba (Vattajamini Ahhaya) on the left as you enter and another further inside of Kirti Sri Nissankamalla. The cave's main Buddha statue, which appears to have once been covered in gold leaf, is situated under a *makara torana* (ornamental archway), with the right hand raised in *abhaya mudra* (conveying protection). Hindu deities are also represented. The vessel inside the cave collects water that drips from the ceiling of the temple – even during droughts – which is used for sacred rituals. There are brilliantly coloured frescoes of Buddhism's arrival in Sri Lanka, meritorious deeds done by kings, and great battles.

Cave III (Maha Alut Viharaya) This cave, the New Great Temple, was said to have been converted from a storeroom in the 18th century by King Kirti Sri Rajasinghe of Kandy, one of the last of the Kandyan monarchs. This cave, too, is filled with Buddha statues, including a beautiful reclining Buddha, and is separated from Cave II by only a masonry wall.

Cave IV (Pachima Viharaya) The relatively small Western Cave is not the most westerly cave – that position belongs to Cave V. The central Buddha figure is seated under a *makara torana*, with its hands in *dhyana mudra* (a meditative pose in which the hands are cupped). The small dagoba (Buddhist shrine) in the centre was broken into by thieves who believed that it contained jewellery belonging to Queen Somawathie.

Cave V (Devana Alut Viharaya) This newer cave was once used as a storehouse, but it's now called the Second New Temple. It features a reclining Buddha; Hindu deities including Kataragama and Vishnu are also present.

Places to Stay & Eat

Saman's Guest House *(☎ 228 4412; Matale Rd; singles/doubles from Rs 150/300)* has rooms lining a central hallway, which is cluttered with antique stuff from the shop at the front. The rooms aren't the cleanest.

Oasis Tourist Welfare Centre *(☎ 228 4388; rooms from Rs 200)* is a cheap place almost directly opposite the entrance to the cave temple car park. It's dark and rough, but all rooms share a reasonable bathroom.

Sena Tourist Inn *(☎ 228 4421; Matale Rd; singles/doubles Rs 350/450)* has six basic rooms in a friendly family house.

Little Dream *(☎ 072 893736; singles/doubles Rs 440/660)* is a friendly, laid-back place near the Kandalama tank where you can swim in the tank, bathe in the river or snooze in a hammock. It's about 8km along the road to Culture Club Resort – a three-wheeler from the temple costs Rs 100 and about Rs 150 from the clock tower, or you can look for the guesthouse's three-wheeler.

Chamara Guest House *(☎ 228 4488; Matale Rd; singles/doubles Rs 715/825)* is a relaxed place with basic rooms and two newer rooms at the back.

Hotel Greenway *(☎/fax 228 4803; ⓔ davids@sltnet.lk; Matale Rd; singles/doubles Rs 660/900)* is a three-storey hotel block on the main road. Now under new management, it has neat and tidy rooms in one of the bigger places in town.

Gimanhala Transit Hotel *(☎ 228 4864; Anuradhapura Rd; singles/doubles Rs 1485/1980, with hot water & air-con Rs 2475/2970)*, about 800m beyond the Colombo junction on the north edge of town, is a good-value hotel. The staff are helpful, the rooms sparkle and there is a swimming pool (Rs 150 for nonguests). The restaurant's daily lunch buffet (Rs 440) is a popular stop.

Pelvehera Village *(☎ 228 4281; singles/doubles Rs 2420/3080, with air-con 2920/3580)*, 3km north of Dambulla (at Bullagala Junction) and just off the main road, is a modern place with 10 spotless, bare rooms with hot water. The restaurant serves good food too – it's a nice place to stop for a bite to eat (rice and curry from Rs 295).

For those with cash to splash, there are two top-end places several kilometres east of Dambulla on the Kandalama tank.

Culture Club Resort *(☎ 223 1822; ⓔ ccrk@sltnet.lk; doubles/triples US$93/107)* can be reached by following the Kandalama road about 3km from Dambulla and then veering left for another 6km or so, via the Kandalama tank wall. The resort is a huge, breezy complex consisting of stylish bungalows with air-con in beautiful gardens. Facilities include a swimming pool, bird-watching walks, and, just what you needed, a palm reader on weekdays. There are also 11 'eco-lodges', built with traditional materials and methods (plus solar hot water).

Kandalama Hotel *(☎ 228 4100; ⓔ ashmres@aitkenspence.lk; singles/doubles US$96/120)* is along the Kandalama road a couple of kilometres past the turn-off to the Culture Club Resort and down a dirt road (it's signposted). If you're interested in modern architecture, this place will set your heart racing. It's a huge establishment – 1km from end to end, with 162 rooms with air-con and three swimming pools – but the design beautifully complements the landscape. It offers bird-watching walks and 4WD safaris, and has its own traditional village, Puranagama.

JBS Hotel *(lunchtime buffet Rs 60)*, upstairs on the main road to Anuradhapura and next to the Singer store, serves tasty food 24 hours a day.

Getting There & Away

Dambulla is 72km north of Kandy on the road to Anuradhapura. The Colombo to Trincomalee road meets this road 2km north of the cave temple, then splits off from it a couple of kilometres further north, leading to Sigiriya and Polonnaruwa. Because Dambulla is on so many major routes, plenty of buses pass through with varying frequency. However, the nearest train station is at Habarana, 23km to the north, from where you can catch a Kandy-bound bus.

By bus it takes 1½ hours to get to Polonnaruwa (Rs 30, 66km), two hours to Anuradhapura (Rs 30, 68km), and two hours to Kandy (Rs 30). There are buses to Sigiriya (Rs 10, 40 minutes) roughly every 30 minutes. Touts will tell you otherwise to get you into a three-wheeler. The bus takes four hours to get to Colombo (normal/air-con Rs 58/130).

You can flag buses plying this busy route to go between the two parts of Dambulla, or take a three-wheeler for Rs 30.

SIGIRIYA

☎ 066

The spectacular rock fortress of Sigiriya *(Lion Rock; adult/child US$15/7.50; open 7am-5.30pm daily)*, 22km northeast of Dambulla, is among Sri Lanka's major attractions, and is part of the Cultural Triangle (see the boxed text 'Cultural Triangle Tickets' earlier in this chapter).

A leafy village lies to the southern side of the rock. Once the sun sets it becomes very dark – if you want to explore at night you'll need a torch (flashlight).

In 477 King Dhatusena of Anuradhapura was overthrown and, so one legend goes, was walled in alive by Kasyapa, his son by a palace consort. Moggallana, Dhatusena's son by his true queen, fled to India swearing revenge, so Kasyapa, fearing an invasion, decided to build an impregnable fortress on the huge rock of Sigiriya. When the long-expected invasion finally came in 491, Kasyapa didn't just skulk in his stronghold, but rode out at the head of his army on an elephant. Attempting to outflank his half-brother, Kasyapa took a wrong turn and became bogged in a swamp. He was deserted by his troops and took his own life.

Sigiriya later became a monastic refuge and in the 16th and 17th centuries it was an outpost of the Kandyan kingdom, but it fell into disrepair, and was rediscovered by archaeologists only during the British colonial era. To describe Sigiriya as merely a fortress does it no justice. Atop the 200m-high rock (377m above sea level) Kasyapa built a wet-season palace – a kind of 5th-century penthouse. Sigiriya is also a significant urban site where you can see ancient forms of architecture, engineering, urban planning, hydraulic technology, gardening and art.

Orientation & Information

The village, on the south side of the rock, is just a collection of grocery stores and small restaurants. The **Centre for Eco-Cultural Studies** *(CES; W www.cessrilanka.org)* and **Sigiriya Ecocultural Tour Guide Association (Setga)** have an information desk *(Hotel Rd; open 8am-6pm daily)* with brochures on the area's fauna. These organisations run a range of wildlife and cultural expeditions.

The Rock

Sigiriya is covered by the Cultural Triangle round ticket. Tickets are also sold near the site entrance, and at the Rest House (see Places to Stay). Hopeful guides hang around the entrance to the site and will also approach you once you're in the site. CES/Setga does a three- to four-hour tour of the royal complex for Rs 300 per person. On a relatively busy day you can overhear the commentaries given to tour groups, as long as you can find one in your language.

An **archaeological museum** *(admission free; open 8am-5pm Wed-Mon)*, near the entrance, is in poor condition. A small **bookstand** *(open 8am-4pm daily)* is outside.

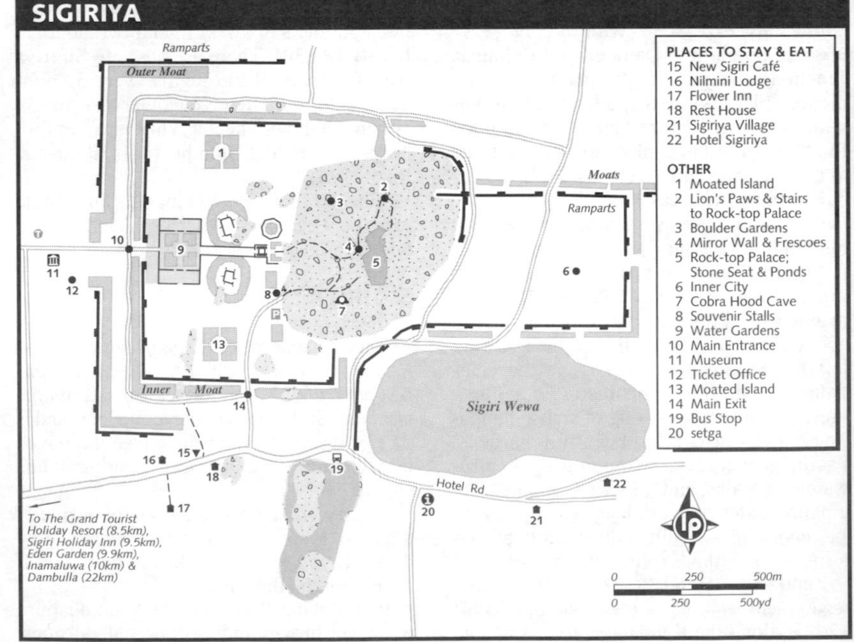

An early or late ascent of the rock avoids the main crowds and the fierce heat. Allow at least two hours for the return trip, and more on very busy days. Bring plenty of water and wear a hat (as it's often too windy near the summit to carry an umbrella). The ascent involves a very steep climb, so if you're not fit it may be tough. Beware of 'helpers' who latch onto visitors who look as if they may have difficulty. Drinks are available at stalls near the lion's paws for inflated prices.

Royal Gardens The landscaped gardens around Sigiriya consist of water gardens, boulder gardens and terraced gardens.

The usual approach to the rock is through the western (and most elaborate) gate. This takes you through Kasyapa's beautiful symmetrical **water gardens**, which extend from the western foot of the rock with royal bathing pools, little moated islands with pavilions that acted as dry-season palaces, and trees framing the approach to the rock. The rock rises sheer and mysterious from the jungle. A switchback series of steps leads up through the boulders at its foot to the western face, then ascends it steeply.

The **boulder gardens**, closer to the rock, feature rocks that once formed the bases of buildings. The steplike depressions in the sides of boulders were the foundations of brick walls and timber columns. The cistern and audience hall rocks are impressive forms in this garden.

The base of Sigiriya has been landscaped to produce the **terraced gardens**.

Cobra Hood Cave This rocky projection earned its name because the overhang resembles a fully opened cobra's hood. Generally you will pass by this cave after descending the rock on your way to the south gate and the car park. Below the drip ledge is a 2nd-century BC inscription that indicates it belonged to Chief Naguli, who would have donated it to a monk. The plastered interior of the cave was once embellished with floral and animal paintings.

Frescoes – The Sigiriya Damsels About halfway up the rock there is a modern spiral stairway that leads up from the main route to a long, sheltered gallery in the sheer rock face.

In this niche there is a series of paintings of beautiful women, believed to represent *apsaras* (celestial nymphs). They are similar in style to the rock paintings at Ajanta in India, but have a specific character in their classical realist style. These 5th-century pin-ups are the only nonreligious old paintings to be seen in Sri Lanka. Although there may have been as many as 500 portraits at one time, only 22 remain today – several were badly damaged by a vandal in 1967. Today security is quite tight on the approach to this section of the rock. Protected from the sun in the sheltered gallery, the paintings remain in remarkably good condition, their colours still glowing. They're at their best in the late afternoon light. Flash photography is not allowed.

Mirror Wall with Graffiti Beyond the fresco gallery the pathway clings to the sheer side of the rock and is protected on the outside by a 3m-high wall.

This wall was coated with a mirror-smooth glaze upon which visitors of 1000 years ago felt impelled to note their impressions of the women in the gallery above. The graffiti were inscribed between the 6th and 14th centuries, and 685 of them have been deciphered and published in a two-volume edition, *Sigiri Graffiti*, by Dr S Paranavitana (Oxford University Press). They are of great interest to scholars for their evidence of the development of the Sinhala language and script, and because they demonstrate an appreciation of art and beauty. You'll have to look hard beyond the modern mess to see the ancient messages.

One typical graffito reads:

> The ladies who wear golden chains on their breasts beckon me. As I have seen the resplendent ladies, heaven appears to me as not good.

Another, by a female scribbler, reads:

> A deer-eyed young woman of the mountain side arouses anger in my mind. In her hand she had taken a string of pearls and in her looks she has assumed rivalry with us.

Lion's Paws At the northern end of the rock the narrow pathway emerges on to the large platform from which the rock derives its name – the Lion Rock, Sigiriya. In 1898

HCP Bell, the British archaeologist responsible for an enormous amount of discovery in Sri Lanka, found two enormous lion paws when excavating here. At one time a gigantic brick lion sat at this end of the rock and the final ascent to the top commenced with a stairway that led between the lion's paws and into its mouth!

The 5th-century lion has since disappeared, apart from the first steps and the paws. To reach the top means clambering up across a series of grooves cut into the rock face. Fortunately there is a stout metal handrail.

The Summit The top of the rock covers 1.6 hectares. At one time it was covered with buildings, but only the foundations remain today. The design of this rock-top palace, and the magnificent views it commands, suggests that Sigiriya was more a palace than a fortress. A pond hewn out of the rock measuring 27m by 21m looks for all the world like a modern swimming pool, although it may have been used merely for water storage.

A smooth slab of flat stone, often referred to as the king's stone throne, faces the rising sun. You can sit and gaze across the surrounding jungle as Kasyapa probably did over 1500 years ago.

Places to Stay & Eat

Nilmini Lodge *(☎ 223 3313; rooms Rs 500)* has three smallish rooms in the family home, and a front porch from which you can watch the world go by. The hosts are friendly and the food is good. Guests can use bicycles for free.

Flower Inn *(singles/doubles Rs 400/500)*, on the same side as the Rest House and down a path, is run by such a friendly family with such a pretty garden that you can excuse the dodgy ceiling in one of the four rooms.

Rest House *(☎/fax 223 1899; rooms with breakfast US$27, with breakfast & air-con US$35)* has an unbeatable location about 400m from the side of the rock. Its clean and tasteful rooms with hot water make it one of the better-looking resthouses. There's a large, airy restaurant with friendly, but slow, service. Set menus cost from US$4.50 for rice and curry to US$7 for a four-course meal. You can buy full-price tickets to the rock here.

If you don't mind staying a little further away from the entrance, there are three places near the junction of the road leading to the village.

Sigiri Holiday Inn *(☎ 072 515210; Sigiriya Rd; doubles/family rooms Rs 660/825)* is a compact and friendly place 500m from the Inamaluwa junction on Sigiriya Rd. With spotless bathrooms and an outdoor restaurant, it's a pleasant spot.

The Grand Tourist Holiday Resort *(☎ 0777 384723; Sigiriya Rd; rooms Rs 880)* has a peaceful garden setting down a track off the road. The spacious rooms have hot water and the *cadjan*-roofed restaurant serves rice and curry and other dishes from Rs 275.

Eden Garden *(☎/fax 228 4635; Sigiriya Rd; doubles/triples Rs 1950/2230, with air-con Rs 2500/2780)* is 100m from the junction, at Inamaluwa. Despite the ugly facade, this is a good spot – large, clean rooms, some with balconies, overlook a well-kept garden. There's a pool (Rs 150 for nonguests).

Sigiriya's two top-end hotels are close together about 1km beyond the resthouse.

Sigiriya Village *(☎/fax 223 1803; ⓔ sales.svhl@lanka.ccom.lk; rooms from US$60)* has clusters of three levels of luxurious rooms in leafy landscaped grounds. The pool (Rs 100 for nonguests) has views of the rock and an organic garden supplies the hotel's kitchen. Buffet meals cost Rs 700.

Hotel Sigiriya *(☎ 228 4811; ⓔ serendib@serendib.lanka.net; singles/doubles US$58/65)* has splendid views of the rock from its dining room and pool (Rs 250 for nonguests), as well as all the usual facilities and comfortable, airy rooms. Breakfast, lunch and dinner cost US$6, $7 and $10, respectively.

New Sigiri Café *(mains Rs 80-100)*, with rice and curry from Rs 80, is a cheaper, local alternative to guesthouse menus.

Getting There & Away

Sigiriya is about 10km east of the main road between Dambulla and Habarana. The turn-off is at Inamaluwa. In the morning buses run from Dambulla about every 30 minutes from 7am (Rs 10, 40 minutes), but they are less frequent in the afternoon. The last bus back to Dambulla leaves at 7pm (but double-check this). A three-wheeler from Dambulla to Sigiriya costs about Rs 300. The paved road does not continue beyond Sigiriya, so if you want to head north you'll have to go to the junction and catch one of the many buses travelling the main highway, or change at Dambulla.

POLONNARUWA

☎ 027

For three centuries Polonnaruwa was a royal capital of both the Chola and Sinhalese kingdoms. Although nearly 1000 years old, it is much younger than Anuradhapura and generally in better repair. The monuments are arranged in a reasonably compact garden setting and their development is easier to follow. All in all, you'll probably find Polonnaruwa the easier of the two ancient capitals to appreciate. It is best to explore by bicycle, which you can rent from several places in town.

The South Indian Chola dynasty first made its capital at Polonnaruwa, after conquering Anuradhapura in the late 10th century. Polonnaruwa was a more strategic place to guard against any rebellion from the Ruhunu Sinhalese kingdom in the southeast. It also, apparently, had fewer mosquitoes! When Vijayabahu I, the Sinhalese king, drove the Cholas off the island in 1070, he kept Polonnaruwa as his capital.

King Parakramabahu I (r. 1153–86) raised Polonnaruwa to its heights, erecting huge buildings, planning beautiful parks and, as a crowning achievement, creating a 2500-hectare tank – so large that it was named the Parakrama Samudra (Sea of Parakrama). The present lake incorporates three older tanks, so it may not be the actual tank he created.

Parakramabahu I was followed by Nissanka Malla (r. 1187–96), who succeeded in virtually bankrupting the kingdom through his attempts to match his predecessors' achievements. By the early 13th century, Polonnaruwa was beginning to prove as susceptible to Indian invasion as Anuradhapura, and despite another century of efforts to stand strong, eventually it too was abandoned and the centre of Sinhalese power shifted to the western side of the island.

Orientation

Polonnaruwa has both an old town and, to its south, a sprawling new town. The main areas of ruins start on the northern edge of the old town and spread north. Accommodation is mostly in and around the old town. The main bus and train stations are in Kaduruwela, a few kilometres east of the old town on Batticaloa Rd. However, buses from anywhere except the east go through the old town on their way in, so you can get off there.

The ruins at Polonnaruwa can be conveniently divided into five groups: a small group near the Rest House on the banks of the tank; the royal palace group to the east of the Rest House; a very compact group a short distance north of the royal palace group, usually known as the quadrangle; a number of structures spread over a wide area further north – the northern group; and a small group far to the south towards the new town – the southern group. There are also a few scattered ruins outside these groups.

Information

The Cultural Triangle round ticket is valid for Polonnaruwa (see the boxed text 'Cultural Triangle Tickets' earlier in this chapter). There's an **information counter** for the ruins *(☎ 222 4850; open 7.30am-6pm daily; adult/child US$15/7.50)* at the museum, near the Rest House. You can get maps and brochures and buy tickets to the site. A well-stocked **bookshop** is near the museum entrance. Officially the site closes at 6pm, but in practice you can stay till dark. Tickets are not checked at the Rest House group or at the southern group, but the other three groups are within a single big enclosure and you have to enter at the official entrance on Habarana Rd, just north of the royal palace. Although the ticket technically allows you only one entrance, you can ask a ticket collector to sign and date your ticket so you can enter again. This way you could visit the site in the morning, take a break over midday to avoid the heat, and head back to the site in the late afternoon. Don't believe three-wheeler drivers who say you don't need a ticket if you travel with them.

The **post office** and **People's Bank** are in the centre of the old town on Batticaloa Rd, and there's also a **Seylan Bank** near the channel. You can use IDD and Internet facilities at **Sachira Communication Centre** *(70B Habarana Rd)*. In Kaduruwela, there are several banks on Batticaloa Rd within 350m of the bus station on the new town side. The **Hatton National Bank** and **Commercial Bank** have ATMs. There's Internet access at **Lucky Communication**, opposite the bus station.

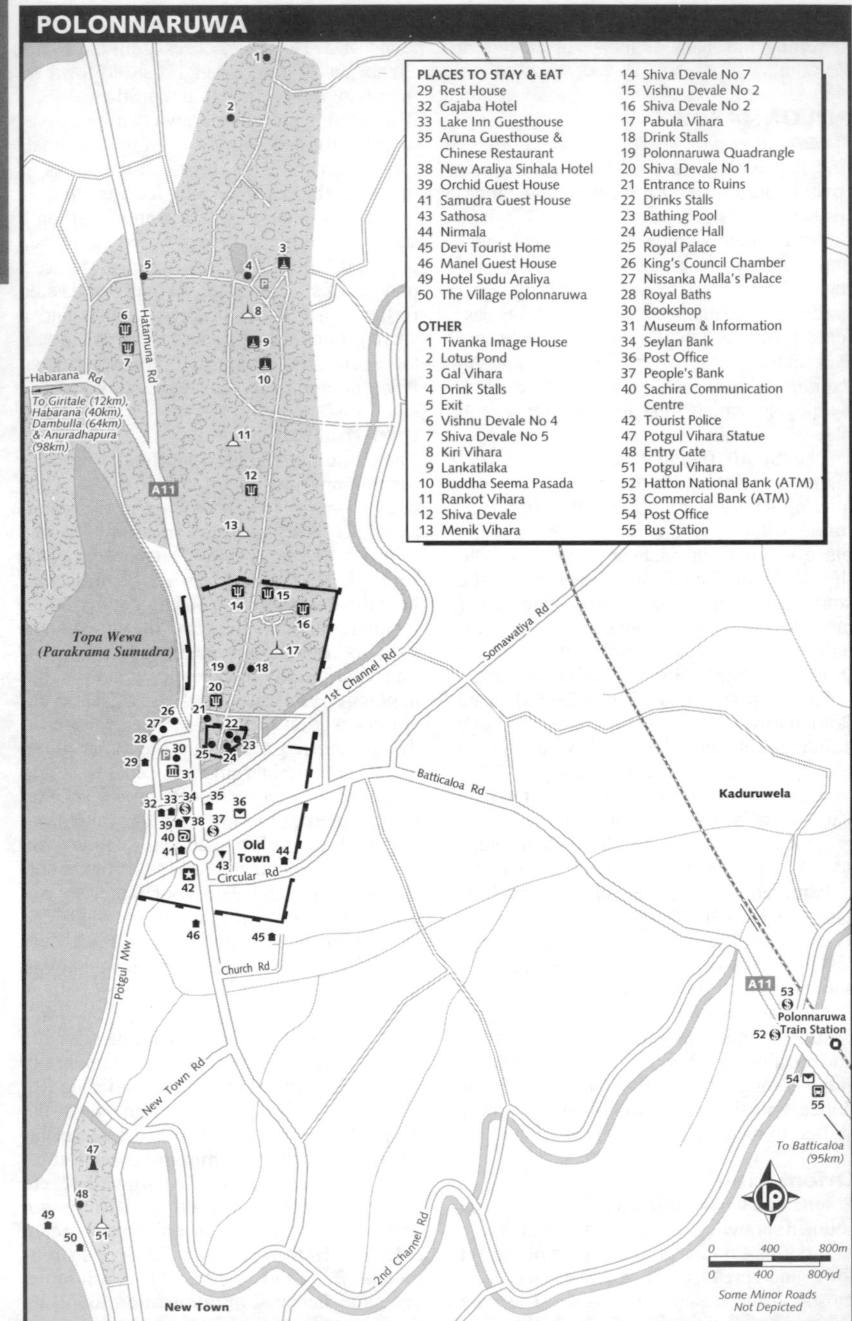
POLONNARUWA
PLACES TO STAY & EAT
29 Rest House
32 Gajaba Hotel
33 Lake Inn Guesthouse
35 Aruna Guesthouse & Chinese Restaurant
38 New Araliya Sinhala Hotel
39 Orchid Guest House
41 Samudra Guest House
43 Sathosa
44 Nirmala
45 Devi Tourist Home
46 Manel Guest House
49 Hotel Sudu Araliya
50 The Village Polonnaruwa
OTHER
1 Tivanka Image House
2 Lotus Pond
3 Gal Vihara
4 Drink Stalls
5 Exit
6 Vishnu Devale No 4
7 Shiva Devale No 5
8 Kiri Vihara
9 Lankatilaka
10 Buddha Seema Pasada
11 Rankot Vihara
12 Shiva Devale
13 Menik Vihara
14 Shiva Devale No 7
15 Vishnu Devale No 2
16 Shiva Devale No 2
17 Pabula Vihara
18 Drink Stalls
19 Polonnaruwa Quadrangle
20 Shiva Devale No 1
21 Entrance to Ruins
22 Drinks Stalls
23 Bathing Pool
24 Audience Hall
25 Royal Palace
26 King's Council Chamber
27 Nissanka Malla's Palace
28 Royal Baths
30 Bookshop
31 Museum & Information
34 Seylan Bank
36 Post Office
37 People's Bank
40 Sachira Communication Centre
42 Tourist Police
47 Potgul Vihara Statue
48 Entry Gate
51 Potgul Vihara
52 Hatton National Bank (ATM)
53 Commercial Bank (ATM)
54 Post Office
55 Bus Station
Habarana Rd
To Giritale (12km), Habarana (40km), Dambulla (64km) & Anuradhapura (98km)
Hatamuna Rd
A11
Topa Wewa (Parakrama Samudra)
1st Channel Rd
Somawatiya Rd
Batticaloa Rd
Kaduruwela
Old Town
Circular Rd
Church Rd
Potgul Mw
New Town Rd
2nd Channel Rd
New Town
Polonnaruwa Train Station
To Batticaloa (95km)
0 400 800m
0 400 800yd
Some Minor Roads Not Depicted

Museum

The museum *(open 7.30am-6pm daily)*, near the Rest House, is first class. It's designed so you walk from one end to the other, passing through a series of rooms, each dedicated to a particular theme: the citadel, the outer city, the monastery area and the periphery, and Hindu monuments. The latter room contains a wonderful selection of bronzes. Of particular interest are the scale models of buildings, including the *vatadage* (circular relic house), which show how these places may have looked in their heyday, complete with roofs. To enter you'll need a current round ticket or a one-day ticket to the site. It's worth visiting before you head out to the site.

Royal Palace Group

This group of buildings dates from the reign of Parakramabahu I. There are three main things to see.

Royal Palace Parakramabahu's palace was a magnificent structure measuring 31m by 13m, and is said to have had seven storeys. The 3m-thick walls have holes to receive the floor beams for two higher floors, but if there were another four levels, these must have been made of wood. The roof in this main hall, which had 50 rooms in all, was supported by 30 columns.

Audience Hall The pavilion used as an audience hall by Parakramabahu is notable for the frieze of elephants around its base. Every elephant is in a different position. There are fine lions at the top of the steps.

Bathing Pool In the southeast corner of the palace grounds the Kumara Pokuna, or Prince's Bathing Pool, still has two of its crocodile-mouth spouts remaining.

Quadrangle

Only a short stroll north of the royal palace ruins, the area known as the quadrangle is literally that – a compact group of fascinating ruins in a raised-up area bounded by a wall. It's the most concentrated collection of buildings you'll find in the ancient cities. As well as the following ruins, there's a recumbent image house, chapter house, Bodhisattva shrine and bodhi tree shrine.

Vatadage In the southeast of the quadrangle, the *vatadage* is typical of its kind. Its outermost terrace is 18m in diameter and the second terrace has four entrances flanked by particularly fine guard stones. The moonstone at the northern entrance is reckoned to be the finest in Polonnaruwa, although not of the same standard as some of the best at Anuradhapura. The four entrances lead to the central dagoba with its four seated Buddhas. The stone screen is thought to be a later addition to the *vatadage*, probably by Nissanka Malla.

Thuparama At the southern end of the quadrangle, the Thuparama is a *gedige*, an architectural style that reached its perfection at Polonnaruwa. This is the smallest *gedige* in Polonnaruwa but also one of the best, and the only one with its roof intact. The building shows strong Hindu influence and is thought to date from the reign of Parakramabahu I. There are several Buddha images in the inner chamber, but they're barely visible in the late afternoon light.

Gal Pota The 'Stone Book', immediately east of the *hatadage* (see below), is a colossal stone representation of an *ola* book. It measures nearly 9m long by 1.5m wide, and from 40cm to 66cm thick. The inscription on it, the longest such stone inscription (of which there are many!) in Sri Lanka, indicates that it was a Nissanka Malla publication. Much of it extols his virtues as a king but it also includes the footnote that the slab, weighing 25 tonnes, was dragged from Mihintale, nearly 100km away!

Hatadage Also erected by Nissanka Malla, this tooth-relic chamber is said to have been built in 60 days.

Latha-Mandapaya The busy Nissanka Malla was also responsible for this unique structure, which consists of a latticed stone fence – a curious imitation of a wooden fence with posts and railings – that surrounds a very small dagoba with stone pillars around it. The pillars are shaped like lotus stalks, topped by unopened buds. It is said that Nissanka Malla sat within this enclosure to listen to chanted Buddhist texts.

Satmahal Prasada This curious building, about which nearly nothing is known, has

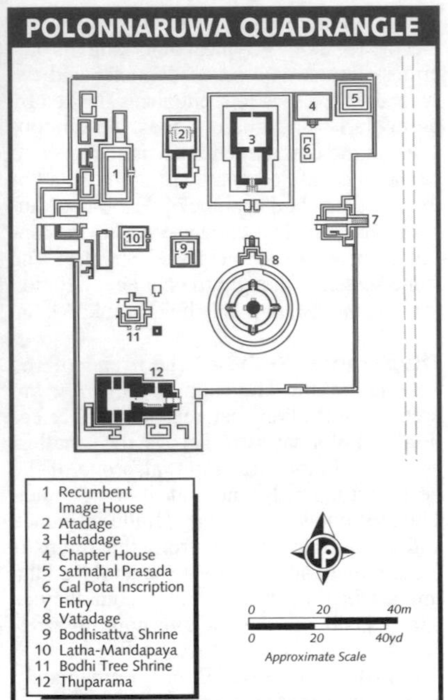

apparent Cambodian influence in its design. The construction consists of six diminishing storeys (there used to be seven) like a stepped pyramid.

Atadage This tooth-relic shrine is the only surviving structure in Polonnaruwa dating from the reign of Vijayabahu I. Like the *hatadage*, it once had a wooden upper storey.

Close to the Quadrangle

Continuing along the road leading north from the quadrangle, a gravel road branches off to the right, just before you reach the city wall. Most of the following structures are on this road, as are many others.

Shiva Devale No 1 Just south of the quadrangle, this 13th-century Hindu temple indicates the Indian influence that returned after Polonnaruwa's Sinhalese florescence. It is notable for the superb quality of its stonework, which fits together with unusual precision. The domed brick roof has collapsed, but when this building was being excavated a number of excellent bronzes, now in the Polonnaruwa museum, were found.

Shiva Devale No 2 Similar in style to Shiva Devale No 1, this is the oldest structure in Polonnaruwa and dates from the brief Chola period when the Indian invaders established the city. Unlike so many buildings in the ancient cities, it was built entirely of stone, so the structure today is seen much as it was when built.

Pabula Vihara This *vihara* (Buddhist complex), also known as the Parakramabahu Vihara, is a typical dagoba from the period of Parakramabahu I. It is the third-largest dagoba in Polonnaruwa.

Northern Group

You will need a bicycle or other transport to comfortably explore these very spread-out ruins, which are all north of the city wall. They include the Gal Vihara, probably the most famous and beautiful group of Buddha images in Sri Lanka, and the Alahana Pirivena monastic group, which is the subject of a Cultural Triangle restoration project. The Alahana Pirivena group consists of the Rankot Vihara, Lankatilaka, Kiri Vihara, Buddha Seema Pasada and other structures around them. The name of the group means 'crematory college', since it stood in the royal cremation grounds established by Parakramabahu.

Rankot Vihara After the three great dagobas at Anuradhapura this is the next biggest in Sri Lanka. There is an inscription nearby that states that Nissanka Malla watched the workmen as they constructed the dagoba. The building is in clear imitation of the Anuradhapura style, and stands 55m high. Surgical instruments found in a nearby ruined 12th-century hospital are said to be similar to those used today.

Buddha Seema Pasada This is the highest building in the Alahana Pirivena group, and it was the monastery abbot's convocation hall. This building features a fine *mandapaya* (raised platform with decorative pillars).

Lankatilaka Built by Parakramabahu, and later restored by Vijayabahu IV, this huge *gedige* has 17m-high walls, although the roof has collapsed. The cathedral-like aisle leads to a huge standing headless Buddha. The outer walls of the *gedige*, decorated with bas-reliefs, show typical Polonnaruwa structures in their original state.

Kiri Vihara The building of this dagoba is credited to Subhadra, Parakramabahu's queen. Originally known as the Rupavati Cetiya, the present name translates as 'milk-white' because, when the overgrown jungle was cleared away after 700 years of neglect, the original lime plaster was found to be in perfect condition.

Gal Vihara This group of beautiful Buddha images probably marks the high point of Sinhalese rock carving. They are part of Parakramabahu's northern monastery. The Gal Vihara consists of four separate images, all cut from one long slab of granite. At one time each was enshrined within a separate enclosure. You can clearly see the sockets cut into the rock behind the standing image, into which wooden beams would have been inserted.

The standing Buddha is 7m tall and is said to be the finest of the series. The unusual position of the arms and sorrowful facial expression led to the theory that it was an image of the Buddha's disciple Ananda, grieving for his master's departure for nirvana, since the reclining image is next to it. The fact that it had its own separate enclosure, and the later discovery of other images with the same arm position, has discredited this theory and it is now accepted that all the images are of the Buddha.

The great reclining image of the Buddha entering nirvana is 14m long, and the beautiful grain of the stone of the image's face is to many people the most impressive part of the Gal Vihara group. Notice the subtle depression in the pillow under the head and the sun-wheel symbol on the pillow end. The other two images are both of the seated Buddha. The one in the small rock cavity is smaller and of inferior quality.

Lotus Pond A track to the left from the northern stretch of road leads to the unusual Lotus Pond, nearly 8m in diameter, which has five concentric rings of eight petals each. The pool was probably used by monks.

Tivanka Image House The northern road ends at this spectacular image house which, with the Lotus Pond, is one of the few surviving structures of the Jetavanarama monastery. Its name means 'thrice bent', and refers to the fact that the Buddha image within is in a three-curve position normally reserved for female statues. The building is notable for the carvings of energetic dwarfs cavorting around the outside, and for the fine frescoes within – the only Polonnaruwa murals to have survived. Some of these date from a later attempt by Parakramabahu III to restore Polonnaruwa, but others are much older.

Southern Group

The small southern group is close to the compound of top-end hotels. By bicycle it's a pleasant ride along the bund of the Topa Wewa.

Potgul Vihara Also known as the library dagoba, this unusual structure is a thick-walled, hollow, stupa-like building that may have been used to store sacred books. It's effectively a circular *gedige*, and four smaller solid dagobas arranged around this central dome form the popular Sinhalese quincunx arrangement of five objects in the shape of a rectangle – one at each corner and one in the middle.

Statue The most interesting other structure in the southern group is the statue at the northern end. Standing nearly 4m high, it's an unusually lifelike human representation, in contrast to the normally idealised or stylised Buddha figures. Exactly whom it represents is a subject of some controversy. Some say that the object he is holding is a book and thus the statue is of Agastaya, the Indian religious teacher. The more popular theory is that it is a yoke representing the 'yoke of kingship' and that the bearded, stately figure is Parakramabahu I. The irreverent joke is that what the king is really holding is a piece of papaya.

Rest House Group

A delightful place for a post-sightseeing drink is the Rest House, situated on a small promontory jutting out into the Topa Wewa. Concentrated a few steps to the north of the Rest House are the ruins of the royal palace of Nissanka Malla, which aren't in anywhere near the same state of preservation as the Parakramabahu or royal palace group.

The royal baths are nearest the Rest House. Farthest north is the King's Council Chamber, where the king's throne, in the shape of a stone lion, once stood. It is now in the Colombo Museum. Inscribed into each column in the chamber is the name of the minister whose seat was once beside it. The mound nearby becomes an island when the waters of the tank are high; on it are the ruins of a small summer house used by the king.

Places to Stay & Eat

Devi Tourist Home *(☎ 222 3181, fax 222 3947; Lake View Watte; singles/doubles from Rs 385/550)* has spotless rooms in a shady garden. The guesthouse is about 1km south of the old town centre and down Church Rd (there's a sign on the main road). The friendly owner is one of Sri Lanka's small Malay population. Bicycles are available for Rs 150 per day.

Samudra Guest House *(☎ 222 2817; Habarana Rd; rooms Rs 150-500)*, in the old town, has a range of rooms, including a garden room and cabana at the bottom of the garden. The hosts can organise 4WD safaris to Minneriya and Kaudulla National Parks. Bicycles can be hired for Rs 100 per day.

Orchid Guest House *(☎ 222 5253; 70 Habarana Rd; singles/doubles/family rooms Rs 200/350/500)*, near the Samudra, is not the cleanest, but it's one of the cheapest options in town.

Nirmala *(☎ 222 5163; 65 Circular Rd; singles/doubles Rs 412/440, doubles with air-con Rs 880)* has rooms in the modern family home and in separate buildings.

Aruna Guesthouse & Chinese Restaurant *(☎ 222 4661; Habarana Rd; rooms Rs 400-500)* has small, boxlike rooms along a long corridor above the Chinese restaurant. The Chinese food is not bad – mains cost Rs 165 to 220.

Lake Inn Guesthouse *(☎ 222 2321; 1 Canal Rd; rooms Rs 500)*, just off the main road in the old town, has dim but passable rooms. The friendly owners hire bicycles for Rs 150 per day.

Manel Guest House *(☎ 222 2481; New Town Rd; rooms Rs 550)* is in a quiet spot just outside the old town wall. It's spacious rooms have bathrooms of different standards. Meals are served under the veranda.

Gajaba Hotel *(☎ 222 2394; singles/doubles Rs 792/1056, doubles/triples with air-con Rs 1320/1540)*, in the old town beside the tank, is a friendly and popular hotel. There's a lovely leafy garden and 23 reasonable rooms, including five with air-con and two with hot water. The restaurant has tasty food and you can hire bicycles for Rs 200 per day.

Rest House *(☎ 222 2299; ⓔ chc@sltnet.lk; doubles/family rooms US$27/40)*, on a promontory by the tank and just a short distance from the heart of the ancient city, has superb views over the water. There's a fine terrace overlooking the lake where you can sip or sup. The rooms, with hot water and some with a bathtub, are large and well enough kept. You may even be able to book the 'Queen's Room', where Queen Elizabeth II kipped in 1954. There is a bar and a restaurant with tasty food and prompt service; breakfast/lunch/dinner costs US$4/6/7.

Polonnaruwa's other upmarket accommodation is on the lakeside just over 2km south of the old town.

The Village Polonnaruwa *(☎ 222 2405, fax 222 5100; rooms Rs 1210)* has rooms around a pleasant central courtyard and rooms with air-con in ugly 1970s brick bungalows. All rooms have hot water. Nonguests may use the tiny pool if they purchase a drink or a meal.

Hotel Sudu Araliya *(☎ 222 4849; ⓔ hotelaraliya@mail.ewisl.net; singles/doubles US$38/43)* is Polonnaruwa's finest hotel. Set on the tank amid lovely landscaped gardens, all of the hotel's spacious and quality rooms have hot water, TV and air-con. There's a pool, Ayurvedic treatment centre, bicycle hire and boat trips on the tank. Breakfast/lunch/dinner costs US$4/5/6.

New Araliya Sinhala Hotel *(Habarana Rd; mains from Rs 45)*, a popular local eatery, serves breakfast, lunch and dinner, including rice and curry, and *kotthu rotty*.

The **Sathosa** store opposite the People's Bank is open 24 hours.

Getting There & Away

Bus Polonnaruwa's main bus station is actually in Kaduruwela, a few kilometres east of the old town on Batticaloa Rd. Buses to and from the west pass through the old town centre, but if you're leaving Polonnaruwa and want to make sure of a seat, it's best to start off at Kaduruwela.

CTB buses run regularly to Kandy (Rs 49). Air-con intercity buses to Kandy run until

4pm (Rs 105, four hours) via Dambulla and Habarana. If you want to get to Dambulla, catch this bus.

CTB buses for Anuradhapura leave regularly until 2.45pm (Rs 35, three hours). There are no air-con buses. Alternatively, you can go to Habarana and pick up another bus there, but a lot of people do this and seats are rare.

There are regular CTB buses to Colombo (Rs 69, six hours) until 7.15pm. The intercity air-con buses (Rs 155) leave every 30 minutes during the day.

Train Polonnaruwa is on the Colombo to Batticaloa railway line, and is about 30km southeast of Gal Oya, where the line splits from the Colombo to Trincomalee line. The train station is at Kaduruwela, near the bus station. Trains from Polonnaruwa to Colombo (six to seven hours) depart at 9.40am and 11.15pm. Tickets cost Rs 55 for a 3rd-class seat and Rs 175 in a 2nd-class sleeper (Rs 150 for a seat). To get to Trincomalee, catch the 9.40am train, then change at Gal Oya and catch the 12.25pm train from there to Trinco.

Getting Around

There are frequent buses (Rs 5) between the old town and Kaduruwela, where the bus and train stations are located. A three-wheeler costs Rs 70.

Bicycles are the ideal transport for getting around Polonnaruwa's monuments, which are surrounded by shady woodland. Bicycles with gears can be hired for about Rs 200 a day from a couple of places in the town's main street. Some guesthouses also hire bicycles (usually gearless) from Rs 100 a day.

A car and driver or three-wheeler can be hired for about three hours for around Rs 350, which is long enough to have a quick look around the ruins.

AROUND POLONNARUWA

Dimbulagala

Off the Polonnaruwa–Batticaloa road, about 8km south of Mannampitiya, a rock called Dimbulagala or **Gunners Quoin** stands out 545m above the surrounding scrub. There are hundreds of caves cut out of the rock in a Buddhist hermitage that has been occupied almost continuously since the 3rd century BC. The temple at the base of the rock is the first of 15 cave temples in the complex that adventurous visitors can explore on their way to the stupa at the top of the rock.

Giritale

☎ 027

Twelve kilometres northwest of Polonnaruwa on the Habarana road, Giritale is not the type of place you'd want to spend your honeymoon, but it's an OK base for visiting Polonnaruwa and other places nearby, especially if you have your own transport. The town is on the edge of the Giritale tank, which was built in the 7th century.

Places to Stay & Eat There are two cheapies on the busy Polonnaruwa road.

Woodside Tour Inn (*☎ 224 6307; Polonnaruwa Rd; singles/doubles Rs 550/825*) has a pretty garden setting and a huge mango tree. The 10 older rooms are bare but fine, and the five new rooms upstairs have balconies from which you can almost smell the mangoes.

Hotel Hemalee (*☎ 224 6257; Polonnaruwa Rd; singles/doubles Rs 825/1100*) has 16 rooms set around a big veranda and a grassed area. Discounts are available for stays of more than two nights.

Flashier options overlook the tank.

Giritale Hotel (*☎ 224 6311; ⓔ maya@carcumb.com; singles/doubles US$21/24*) has plain but good-value rooms with air-con and eight luxury rooms. There is a swimming pool and restaurant with great views.

The Royal Lotus (*☎/fax 224 6316; ⓔ royallotus@jinasena.com.lk; singles/doubles including breakfast US$42/54*) is an ugly 1970s monster that has rooms with air-con. Once again there's a pool and restaurant, but here each bedroom has great views of the tank. Suites with TV, minibar and bathtub cost an extra US$20. It shares some facilities with its top-end neighbour, The Deer Park.

The Deer Park (*☎/fax 224 6272; ⓔ deerpark@jinasena.com.lk; chalets US$210*), several steps up from The Royal Lotus in the posh stakes after its refurbishment, has chalets with air-con, TV, minibar, bathtub, reading material and garden views, as well as four suites and one 'presidential' suite if you want more space and features. The grounds are beautifully maintained and there's a pool, gym and squash court, but none of the rooms has views.

Medirigiriya

Near Medirigiriya, about 30km north of Polonnaruwa, is the **Mandalagiri Vihara** *(adult/child US$5/2.50)*, a *vatadage* virtually identical to the one at Polonnaruwa. Whereas the Polonnaruwa *vatadage* is crowded among many other structures, the Mandalagiri Vihara stands alone atop a low hill. Some people find it a disappointment, but the site's isolation means that it doesn't attract as many visitors as Polonnaruwa.

An earlier structure may have been built here around the 2nd century, but the one that stands today was constructed in the 7th century by Aggabodhi IV. A granite flight of steps leads up the hill to the *vatadage*, which has concentric circles of 16, 20 and 32 pillars around the central dagoba. Four large seated Buddhas face the four cardinal directions. This *vatadage* is noted for its fine ornamented stone screens. There was once a hospital next to the *vatadage* – look for the herbal medicine bath shaped like the lower half of a coffin.

This site is on the Cultural Triangle round ticket, so someone will materialise to check your ticket. Tickets are not sold at the site, so buy one from the museum in Polonnaruwa before you come.

Mandalagiri Vihara is best visited as a day trip. There are no places to stay or eat, nor are there any worth mentioning in nearby Medirigiriya.

Getting There & Away Without your own transport, getting to Medirigiriya is time consuming. It's located about 24km northeast of Minneriya village, which is on the Polonnaruwa–Habarana road. To reach Medirigiriya by bus from Polonnaruwa, Habarana or Dambulla involves at least one change at Giritale, Minneriya or Hingurakgoda, from where you can catch a bus or maybe a three-wheeler. The *vatadage* is 3km from the Medirigiriya bus stop.

NATIONAL PARKS

The national parks around Polonnaruwa and Habarana offer excellent access to elephants and other animals without the crowds of 4WDs that head into Yala West (Ruhuna) National Park. Minneriya and Kaudulla are well served by guesthouse trips. Prices range from US$30 per person including entry fees for a four-hour trip from Habarana. From Polonnaruwa and Sigiriya, you'll pay about Rs 2000 to 3000 for the 4WD, excluding entry fees. The cost of getting to either park is about the same. However, Habarana is closer to Kaudulla and Polonnaruwa is closer to Minneriya; the less time you spend travelling the longer you have in your chosen park.

Minneriya National Park

Minneriya *(adult/child US$14.40/7.20, service charge US$7.20, vehicle Rs 144)* is dominated by the ancient Minneriya Tank, but there's plenty of scrub and light forest in its 8890 hectares to provide shelter to its toque macaques, sambar deer, leopards and elephants – to name a few. The dry season, from June to September, is the best time to visit. By then, water in the tank has dried up, exposing grasses and shoots to grazing animals; elephants, in numbers up to 150, come to feed and bathe; and flocks of birds, such as little cormorants and painted storks, fish in the shallow waters.

The park entrance is along the Habarana–Polonnaruwa road, but you have to buy tickets from the Wildlife Office over at Ambagaswewa.

Kaudulla National Park

Sri Lanka's newest national park, Kaudulla *(adult/child US$7.20/3.60, service charge US$7.20, vehicle Rs 144)* was opened in 2002 around the ancient Kaudulla Tank. It established a 6656-hectare elephant corridor between Somawathiya Chaitiya and Minneriya National Parks. Just 6km off the Habarana–Trincomalee road at Gal Oya junction, Kaudulla is already a popular safari tour from Polonnaruwa and Habarana because of the good chance of getting up close and personal with elephants. In October there are up to 250 elephants in the park, including herds of juvenile males. There are also leopards, fishing cats, sambar deer, the endangered rusty spotted cat and the rarely seen sloth bear.

The best time to visit is from August to December. A catamaran is available for boat rides on the tank.

HABARANA

☎ 066

The highlights of this small village are a small tank and its central location between all the main sites. It has an upmarket hotel complex principally aimed at package tourists. It is also a good base for visits to the Minneriya and Kaudulla National Parks. Habarana has the nearest train station to Dambulla and Sigiriya.

Elephant rides around the tank can be arranged for a pricey US$20 to US$30 per person per hour. If you're spending the night here, the only free entertainment is to wander along the tank bund spotting birds.

Places to Stay & Eat

Habarana Rest *(☎ 227 0010; doubles/family rooms Rs 825/1100)* is a good cheap option just past the luxury of The Lodge on the Dambulla road. Rooms are not outstanding, but it's the only option in the price range and food is available.

Rest House *(☎ 227 0003; doubles/triples Rs 1300/1700)* has four rooms in a pleasant garden setting, but the rooms are starting to show their age. It's right on the crossroads where the buses congregate. The food is OK but overpriced.

Both of Habarana's neighbouring top-end resort hotels are part of the Keells group and offer similar services and facilities – pools, bird-watching walks, 4WD and elephant safaris, Ayurvedic treatments and views to the tank.

The Village *(☎/fax 227 0046-7; e village@keells.com; singles/doubles from US$63/75)* has spacious terraced rooms with verandas, some with air-con. The restaurant looks over the swimming pool, and there's also badminton and tennis. The lakefront setting makes for easy bird-watching before breakfast.

The Lodge *(☎/fax 227 0011-2; e lodge@keells.com; singles/doubles US$108/128)* is another step up in the luxury stakes; its spacious air-con lodges set in lush gardens have just a touch more class and the option of a TV and bathtub. If you can only afford to taste the luxury, dinner costs US$12.

Getting There & Away

Buses leave from the crossroads outside the Rest House. There are lots of departures in all directions, but if you are embarking on a long-haul trip, it's best to start as early as possible. For example, you can pick up the air-con Trinco–Colombo bus, or buses between Anuradhapura and Ampara, Batticaloa and Colombo, or Kandy (via Dambulla) and Trincomalee, but you're not guaranteed a seat.

The train station is about 1km out of town on the Trincomalee road. There are trains departing for Trincomalee at 11.49am (Rs 13/49 in 3rd/2nd class); for Polonnaruwa at 11.49am (Rs 10.50/28.50); and for Colombo at 11.22am (Rs 43.50/120).

RITIGALA

Deep inside the Ritigala Strict Nature Reserve, off the Anuradhapura–Habarana road, are the partially restored **ruins** *(adult/child US$8/4)* of an extensive monastic and cave complex. The ruins lie on a hill, which at 766m isn't exactly high, but is nevertheless a striking feature in the flat, dry landscape surrounding it. The 24-hectare site is isolated and almost deserted.

The true meaning of Ritigala remains unclear – *gala* means rock in Sinhala, but *riti* may come from the Pali *arittha*, meaning 'safety'. Thus Ritigala is probably a place of refuge, as it was for kings as long ago as the 4th century BC.

Ritigala also has a place in mythology. It's claimed to be the spot from where Hanuman (the monkey king) leapt to India to tell Rama that he had discovered where Sita was being held by the king of Lanka. Mythology also offers an explanation for the abundance of healing herbs and plants found in Ritigala. It's said that Hanuman, on his way back to Lanka with healing Himalayan herbs for Rama's wounded brother, dropped some over Ritigala.

Monks found Ritigala's caves ideal for a nonworldly existence, and more than 70 such caves have been discovered. Royals proved generous patrons, especially King Sena I, who in the 9th century made an endowment of a monastery to the *pamsukulika* (rag robes) monks.

Ritigala was abandoned following the Chola invasions in the 10th and 11th centuries, after which it lay deserted and largely forgotten until it was rediscovered by British surveyors in the 19th century. It was explored and mapped by HCP Bell in 1893.

The Site

Ritigala has none of the usual icons: no bodhi tree, relic house or Buddha images. The only embellishments are on the urinals at the forest monastery – it's been conjectured that by urinating on the fine stone carving the monks were demonstrating their contempt for worldly things.

Near the site entrance at the Archaeology Department bungalow are the remains of a *banda pokuna* (tank), which apparently fills with water during the rainy season. From here it's a scramble along a forest path via a donations hall to a ruined palace and the **monastery hospital**, where you can still see the grinding stones and huge stone baths. A restored flagstone path leads upwards; a short detour takes you to what is often described as a stone fort – or, to be more accurate, a lookout.

The next group of ruins of note are the double-platform structures so characteristic of forest monasteries. Here you can see the **urinal stones**, although they almost certainly weren't always in this exact spot. The two raised stone platforms are supported by stone retaining walls. The platform orientated to the east is rectangular, while the western one is smaller and square; unlike its counterpart, it may have had a roof of some sort. Scholars think they were used for meditation, teaching and ceremony. Someone from the Archaeology Department bungalow will accompany you (and will expect a tip, say Rs 300) but may be reluctant to take you beyond this point – although the ruins extend right up to the top – because of wild animals and dense vegetation.

You'll need at least 1½ hours to see the site properly. Entry to the ruins is included in the Cultural Triangle round ticket. Staff at the Archaeology Department bungalow sell tickets to the site and staff check all tickets, although there's no-one present after about 4pm.

Getting There & Away

Ritigala is 14km northwest of Habarana and 42km southeast of Anuradhapura. If you're coming from Habarana, the turn-off is near the 14km post. It's a further 9km to get to the Archaeology Department bungalow (2km past the turn-off at the Wildlife Department bungalow). You need your own transport to get here and the road may be impassable in the wet season (October to January). As this is a very isolated area, you are advised to go in a group of three or more people.

AUKANA

According to tradition the magnificent 12m-high standing **Aukana Buddha** *(admission Rs 150)* was sculpted during the reign of Dhatusena in the 5th century, though some sources date it to the 12th or 13th century. Kala Wewa, one of the many gigantic tanks he constructed, is only a couple of kilometres from the statue, and the road to Aukana from the Kekirawa runs along the tank bund for several kilometres. Aukana means 'sun-eating', and dawn, when the first rays light up the huge statue's finely carved features, is the best time to see it.

Note that although the statue is still narrowly joined at the back to the rock face it is cut from, the lotus plinth on which it stands is a separate piece. The Buddha's gesture or pose, *ashiva mudra*, signifies blessings, while the burst of fire above his head represents the power of total enlightenment. There's a local story that the statue was so finely carved that a drop of water from its nose would fall (without any breeze) directly between Buddha's feet. The reconstruction of the brick shelter over the statue looks like it was built by rail engineers, and detracts a little from the scene.

The Aukana Buddha is well known and often visited despite its isolation. Fewer people travel on to another image, also 12m high, although incomplete and of inferior craftwork, at **Sasseruwa**, at the site of an ancient cave monastery in the jungle. A legend relates that the two Buddhas were carved at the same time in a competition between master and student. The master's more detailed Aukana Buddha was finished first and the Sasseruwa image was abandoned by the conceding student. Buddha's gesture here is *abhaya mudra*, conveying protection. This statue, sometimes called the Resvehera Buddha, stands in a rectangular hollow in the rock. Sasseruwa is 11km west of Aukana, reached by a rough road.

Getting There & Away

It's easy to catch a bus from Dambulla or Anuradhapura to Kekirawa, and another from there to Aukana. There are five or six buses a day between Kekirawa and Aukana. Aukana is on the railway line from Colombo to Trincomalee and Polonnaruwa, and the station is just a short walk from the statue. Four trains a day (2nd and 3rd class only) stop here. A van from Kekirawa will set you back about Rs 1000 for a Kekirawa–Aukana–Kalawewa (or back to Kekirawa) circuit; a three-wheeler costs about Rs 600. From Habarana, a van will cost about Rs 1800 return.

ANURADHAPURA

☎ 025 • pop 56,600

For over 1000 years, Sinhalese kings, and occasional South Indian interlopers, ruled from the palaces of Anuradhapura. It is the most extensive and important of the Sri Lankan ancient cities, but its size and the length of its history, and equally the length of time since its downfall, make it more difficult to comprehend than younger, shorter-lived Polonnaruwa. Current-day Anuradhapura is a rather pleasant, planned city. Mature trees shade the main guesthouse areas, and the main street is orderly compared to the ugly concrete agglomerations seem in so many other regional centres.

The modern town was developed in the 20th century. In recent years a seamier side of the sacred city has emerged: the large army population (the town was a staging-post for the northern battlefields) has brought an influx of prostitutes. The town has a huge number of guesthouses, many of which cater to the rent-by-the-hour market. The ones listed in this book (hopefully) don't cater to that sort of business. The town was also a centre for war profiteering: political and business alliances conspired to loot the surrounding forests of valuable timber. Some of the timber came from areas controlled by the Liberation Tigers of Tamil Eelam (LTTE) – evidently the Tigers were happy to cooperate in return for a cut.

History

Anuradhapura first became a capital in 380 BC under Pandukabhaya, but it was under Devanampiya Tissa (r. 247–207 BC), during whose reign Buddhism reached Sri Lanka, that it first rose to great importance. Soon Anuradhapura became a great and glittering city, only to fall before a South Indian invasion – a fate that was to befall it repeatedly for over 1000 years. But before long the Sinhalese hero, Dutugemunu, led an army from a refuge in the far south to recapture Anuradhapura. The 'Dutu' part of his name, incidentally, is from 'Duttha' meaning 'undutiful', for his father, fearing for his son's safety, forbade him to attempt to recapture Anuradhapura. Dutugemunu disobeyed him, and after sent his father a woman's ornament to indicate what he thought of his father's courage.

Dutugemunu (r. 161–137 BC), set in motion a vast building program that included some of the most impressive monuments in Anuradhapura today. Other important kings who followed him included Valagambahu, who lost his throne in another Indian invasion but later regained it, and Mahasena (r. AD 276–303), the builder of the colossal Jetavanarama Dagoba, who is thought of as the last 'great' king of Anuradhapura. He also held the record for tank construction, building 16 of them in all, plus a major canal. Anuradhapura was to survive for another 500 years before finally being replaced by Polonnaruwa, but it was harassed by invasions from South India again and again – invasions made easier by the cleared lands and great roads that were a product of Anuradhapura's importance.

Orientation

The ancient city lies to the northwest of the modern town of Anuradhapura. The main road from Kandy, Dambulla and Polonnaruwa enters the town on the northeastern side then travels south to the centre, which is a spread-out affair with two bus stations – the old bus station (intercity express buses leave from nearby this station) and the new bus station 2km further south. Buses heading for the new bus station usually call at the old one on the way through, and will also let you off anywhere else along their route.

The ancient city is rather spread out. There is one important starting point for exploring it, and that is the sacred bodhi tree, or Sri Maha Bodhi, and the cluster of buildings around it. Because of roadblocks around Sri Maha Bodhi, a bicycle is the best way to explore Anuradhapura. However, you can't take a bicycle everywhere; near the bodhi tree shrine you will have to park your bike and walk. There are plenty of cold drink stalls scattered around the site – as well as plenty of people willing to act as a guide.

Remember to remove your shoes and hat before approaching a dagoba or the sacred bodhi tree.

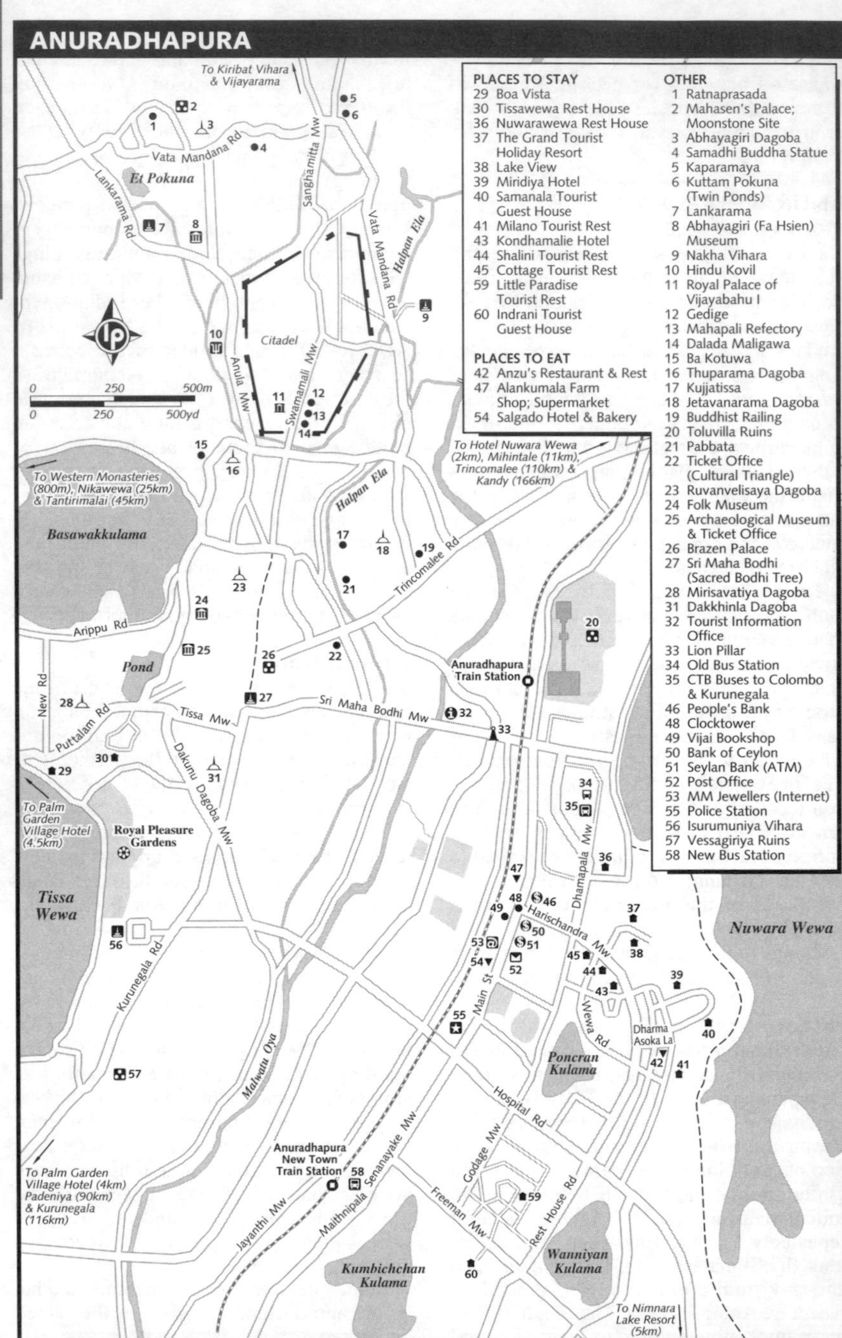
ANURADHAPURA
PLACES TO STAY
29 Boa Vista
30 Tissawewa Rest House
36 Nuwarawewa Rest House
37 The Grand Tourist Holiday Resort
38 Lake View
39 Miridiya Hotel
40 Samanala Tourist Guest House
41 Milano Tourist Rest
43 Kondhamalie Hotel
44 Shalini Tourist Rest
45 Cottage Tourist Rest
59 Little Paradise Tourist Rest
60 Indrani Tourist Guest House
PLACES TO EAT
42 Anzu's Restaurant & Rest
47 Alankumala Farm Shop; Supermarket
54 Salgado Hotel & Bakery
OTHER
1 Ratnaprasada
2 Mahasen's Palace; Moonstone Site
3 Abhayagiri Dagoba
4 Samadhi Buddha Statue
5 Kaparamaya
6 Kuttam Pokuna (Twin Ponds)
7 Lankarama
8 Abhayagiri (Fa Hsien) Museum
9 Nakha Vihara
10 Hindu Kovil
11 Royal Palace of Vijayabahu I
12 Gedige
13 Mahapali Refectory
14 Dalada Maligawa
15 Ba Kotuwa
16 Thuparama Dagoba
17 Kujjatissa
18 Jetavanarama Dagoba
19 Buddhist Railing
20 Toluvilla Ruins
21 Pabbata
22 Ticket Office (Cultural Triangle)
23 Ruvanvelisaya Dagoba
24 Folk Museum
25 Archaeological Museum & Ticket Office
26 Brazen Palace
27 Sri Maha Bodhi (Sacred Bodhi Tree)
28 Mirisavatiya Dagoba
31 Dakkhinla Dagoba
32 Tourist Information Office
33 Lion Pillar
34 Old Bus Station
35 CTB Buses to Colombo & Kurunegala
46 People's Bank
48 Clocktower
49 Vijai Bookshop
50 Bank of Ceylon
51 Seylan Bank (ATM)
52 Post Office
53 MM Jewellers (Internet)
55 Police Station
56 Isurumuniya Vihara
57 Vessagiriya Ruins
58 New Bus Station
To Kiribat Vihara & Vijayarama
Vata Mandana Rd
Et Pokuna
Lankarama Rd
Sanghamitta Mw
Halpan Ela
Citadel
Anula Mw
Swamamali Mw
0 250 500m
0 250 500yd
To Western Monasteries (800m), Nikawewa (25km) & Tantirimalai (45km)
Basawakkulama
To Hotel Nuwara Wewa (2km), Mihintale (11km), Trincomalee (110km) & Kandy (166km)
Trincomalee Rd
Arippu Rd
Pond
New Rd
Puttalam Rd
Tissa Mw
Sri Maha Bodhi Mw
Anuradhapura Train Station
Dakunu Dagoba Mw
To Palm Garden Village Hotel (4.5km)
Royal Pleasure Gardens
Tissa Wewa
Dhamapala Mw
Harischandra Mw
Nuwara Wewa
Kurunegala Rd
Main St
Wewa Rd
Dharma Asoka La
Poncran Kulama
Malwatu Oya
Hospital Rd
To Palm Garden Village Hotel (4km) Padeniya (90km) & Kurunegala (116km)
Anuradhapura New Town Train Station
Senanayake Mw
Godage Mw
Jayanthi Mw
Maithnipala
Freeman Mw
Rest House Rd
Kumbichchan Kulama
Wanniyan Kulama
To Nimnara Lake Resort (5km)

Information

The **Tourist Information Office** *(☎ 222 4546; Sri Maha Bodhi Mawatha; open 9am-4.45pm Mon-Fri, 9am-1pm Sat)* offers a rather ordinary map and a couple of brochures, but little else.

A US$15 entry ticket (or a round ticket for the Cultural Triangle – see the boxed text 'Cultural Triangle Tickets' earlier in this chapter) is required by foreigners visiting the northern areas of the ancient city. Both types of ticket can be bought at two places: the **ticket office** *(open 7am-7.30pm daily)* near the Archaeological Museum on the west side of the city, and a booth (open same hours) on Trincomalee Rd near Sri Maha Bodhi. You must also pay an extra Rs 30 for the nearby Folk Museum, and Rs 50 for the Isurumuniya Vihara. Entry to the Sri Maha Bodhi compound area costs Rs 100, but if things aren't busy perhaps no-one will approach you for the money.

The **post office** is on Main St. **MM Jewellers**, opposite the post office, has Internet facilities. **Seylan Bank** has an ATM, and **People's Bank** nearby can change travellers cheques.

The **Vijai Bookshop** *(Main St)* has a small but interesting selection of English-language titles in a back room.

Sri Maha Bodhi

The sacred bodhi tree (Sri Maha Bodhi) is central to Anuradhapura in both a spiritual and physical sense. The huge tree has grown from a cutting brought from Bodhgaya in India by the Princess Sangamitta, sister of Mahinda who introduced the Buddha's teachings to Sri Lanka, so it has a connection to the very basis of the Sinhalese religion. This sacred tree serves as a reminder of the force that inspired the creation of all the great buildings at Anuradhapura and is within walking distance of many of the most interesting monuments. The whole area around the Sri Maha Bodhi, the Brazen Palace and Ruvanvelisaya Dagoba was once probably part of the Maha Vihara (Great Temple).

The sacred bodhi tree is the oldest historically authenticated tree in the world, for it has been tended by an uninterrupted succession of guardians for over 2000 years, even during the periods of Indian occupation. There are not one but many bodhi trees here; the oldest and holiest stands on the topmost platform. The steps leading up to the tree's platform are very old, but the golden railing around it is quite modern. Railings and other structures around the trees are festooned with prayer flags. Thousands of devotees come to make offerings at weekends and particularly on *poya* (full moon) days. April is a particularly busy month as pilgrims converge on the site for *snana puja* (offerings or prayers). You must remove your shoes and your hat before entering this site.

Brazen Palace

So called because it once had a bronze roof, the ruins of the Brazen Palace stand close to the bodhi tree. The remains of 1600 columns are all that is left of this huge palace, said to have had nine storeys and accommodation for 1000 monks and attendants.

It was originally built by Dutugemunu more than 2000 years ago, but through the ages was rebuilt many times, each time a little less grandiosely. The current stand of pillars (now fenced off) is all that remains from the last rebuild – that of Parakramabahu around the 12th century.

Ruvanvelisaya Dagoba

Behind the Folk Museum, this fine white dagoba is guarded by a wall with a frieze of hundreds of elephants standing shoulder to shoulder. Apart from a few beside the western entrance, most are modern replacements for the 140 BC originals.

This dagoba is said to be Dutugemunu's finest construction, but he didn't live to see its completion. However, as he lay on his deathbed, a false bamboo-and-cloth finish to the dagoba was organised by his brother, so that Dutugemunu's final sight could be of his 'completed' masterpiece. Today, after incurring much damage from invading Indian forces, it rises 55m, considerably less than its original height. Nor is its form the same as the earlier 'bubble' shape. A limestone statue south of the great dagoba is popularly thought to be of Dutugemunu.

The land around the dagoba is rather like a pleasant green park, dotted with patches of ruins, the remains of ponds and pools, and collections of columns and pillars, all picturesquely leaning in different directions. Slightly southeast of the dagoba, you can see one of Anuradhapura's many monks' refectories. Keeping such a number of monks fed and happy was a full-time job for the lay followers.

Thuparama Dagoba

In a beautiful woodland setting north of the Ruvanvelisaya Dagoba, the Thuparama Dagoba is the oldest dagoba in Anuradhapura, if not Sri Lanka. It was constructed by Devanampiya Tissa and is said to contain the right collarbone of the Buddha. Originally in the classical 'heap of paddy rice' shape, it was restored in 1840 in a more conventional bell shape.

The dagoba stands only 19m high and at some point in its life was converted into a *vatadage*. The circles of pillars of diminishing height around the dagoba would have supported the conical roof.

Northern Ruins

There is quite a long stretch of road, which starts as Anula Mawatha, running north from the Thuparama Dagoba to the next clump of ruins. Coming back you can take an alternative route through the Royal Palace site and then visit the Jetavanarama Dagoba.

Abhayagiri Dagoba This huge dagoba (confused by some books and maps with the Jetavanarama), created in the 1st century BC, was the centrepiece of a monastery of 5000 monks. The name means 'fearless Giri' and refers to a Jain monk whose hermitage once stood at this spot. When Valagambahu fled the city before an Indian invasion, he was taunted by the monk and so, when he regained the throne 14 years later, Giri was promptly executed and this great dagoba was built over his hermitage.

After a later restoration by Parakramabahu, the dagoba may have stood over 100m high, but today it is 75m high. It has some interesting bas-reliefs, including one of an elephant pulling up a tree near the western stairway. A large slab with a Buddha footprint can be seen on the northern side of the dagoba, and the eastern and western steps have unusual moonstones made of concentric stone slabs. At the time of writing the dagoba was under further restoration.

Mahasen's Palace This ruined palace northwest of the Abhayagiri is notable for having the finest carved moonstone in Sri Lanka. Photographers will be disappointed that the railing around it makes it almost impossible to achieve an unshadowed picture. This is a peaceful wooded area full of butterflies, and makes a good place to stop and cool off during a tour of the ruins.

ANDERS BLOMQVIST

Moonstones are a striking feature of many temples in Sri Lanka's ancient cities. The animals, plants and other motifs depicted in the elaborately carved semicircular rings all have symbolic meaning.

Ratnaprasada Follow the loop road a little further and you will find the finest guardstones in Anuradhapura. Dating from the 8th century, they depict a cobra-king, and demonstrate the final refinement of guardstone design. You can see examples of much earlier guardstone design at the Mirisavatiya Dagoba.

In the 8th century a new order of *tapovana* (ascetic) monks settled in these western fringes of the city, among the lowest castes, the rubbish dumps and the burial places. These western monasteries were simple but grand structures of stone. Ornamentation was saved for toilets and urinals, now displayed at the Archaeology Museum. The monks of Ratnaprasada (Gem Palace) monastery gave sanctuary to people in trouble with the authorities: this led to a major conflict with the king of the day. When court officials at odds with the king took sanctuary in the Ratnaprasada, though, the king sent his supporters in to capture and execute them. The monks, disgusted at this invasion of a sacred place, departed en masse. The general populace, equally disgusted, besieged the Ratnaprasada, captured and executed the king's supporters and forced the king to apologise to the departed monks in order to bring the monks back to the city and restore peace.

To the south of the Ratnaprasada is the Lankarama, a 1st-century BC *vatadage*.

Samadhi Buddha Statue After your investigations of guardstones and moonstones, you can continue east from the Abhayagiri to this 4th-century seated statue, regarded as one of the finest Buddha statues in Sri Lanka.

Kuttam Pokuna (Twin Ponds) The swimming-pool like Twin Ponds, the finest ponds in Anuradhapura, are a little east of Sanghamitta Mawatha. They were probably used by monks from the monastery attached to the Abhayagiri Dagoba. Although they are referred to as twins, the southern pond, 28m in length, is smaller than the 40m-long northern pond. Water entered the larger pond through the mouth of a *makara* (mythical multispecies beast) and then flowed to the smaller pond through an underground pipe. Note the five-headed cobra figure close to the *makara* and the water filter system at the northwestern end of the ponds.

Royal Palace If you return south along Sanghamitta Mawatha, you'll pass, after about 1.5km, through the Royal Palace site. Built by Vijayabahu I in the 12th century, after Anuradhapura's fall as the Sinhalese capital, the palace is indicative of the attempts made to retain at least a foothold in the old capital.

Close to it are a deep and ancient well and the Mahapali refectory, notable for its immense trough (nearly 3m long and 2m wide) that the lay followers filled with rice for the monks. In the Royal Palace area you can also find the Dalada Maligawa, a tooth-relic temple that may have been the first Temple of the Tooth. The sacred Buddha's tooth originally came to Sri Lanka in AD 313.

Jetavanarama Dagoba

The Jetavanarama Dagoba's huge dome rises from a clearing back towards the Sri Maha Bodhi. Built in the 3rd century by Mahasena, it may have originally stood over 100m high, but today is about 70m, a similar height to the Abhayagiri, with which it is sometimes confused. It has been under reconstruction for a number of years.

The Jetavanarama Dagoba is made solidly of bricks, and an early British guidebook calculated there were enough of them to make a 3m-high wall stretching all the way from London to Edinburgh. Behind it stand the ruins of the monastery it formed part of, which housed 3000 monks. One building has door jambs over 8m high still standing, with another 3m underground. At one time, massive doors opened to reveal a large Buddha image.

Buddhist Railing

A little south of the Jetavanarama Dagoba, and on the other side of the road, there is a stone railing built in imitation of a log wall. It encloses a site 42m by 34m, but the building within has long disappeared.

Mirisavatiya Dagoba

Mirisavatiya Dagoba is one of three very interesting sites that can be visited in a stroll or ride along the banks of the Tissa Wewa. This huge dagoba, the first built by Dutugemunu after he captured the city, is almost across the road from the Tissawewa Rest House. The story goes that Dutugemunu went to bathe in the tank, leaving his ornate sceptre implanted in the bank. When he emerged he found his sceptre, which contained a relic of the Buddha, impossible to pull out. Taking this as an auspicious sign he had the dagoba built. To its northeast was yet another monks' refectory, complete with the usual huge stone troughs into which the faithful poured boiled rice.

Royal Pleasure Gardens

If you start down the Tissa Wewa bund from the Mirisavatiya, you soon come to the extensive royal pleasure gardens. Known as the Park of the Goldfish, the gardens cover 14 hectares and contain two ponds skilfully designed to fit around the huge boulders in the park. The ponds have fine reliefs of elephants on their sides. It was here that Prince Saliya, the son of Dutugemunu, was said to have met a commoner, Asokamala, whom he married, thereby forsaking his right to the throne.

Isurumuniya Vihara

This rock temple, dating from the reign of Devanampiya Tissa (3rd century BC), has some very fine carvings. One or two of these (including one of elephants playfully splashing water) remain in their original place on the rock face beside a square pool fed from the Tissa Wewa, but most of them have been moved into a small museum within the temple. Best known of the sculptures is the 'lovers', which dates from around the 5th century AD and is of the Gupta school (the artistic style of the Indian Gupta dynasty of the 4th and 5th centuries). It was probably brought here from elsewhere, since it was carved into a separate slab. Popular legend holds that it shows Prince Saliya and Asokamala.

One bas-relief shows a palace scene said to be of Dutugemunu, with Saliya and Asokamala flanking him, and a third figure, possibly a servant, behind them. There is also a fine sculpture showing a man and the head of a horse. The image house south of the pond has a reclining Buddha cut from the rock. The view over the tank from the top of the temple is superb at sunset. You can't miss the resident colony of bats. You'll be asked for a 'donation' of Rs 50.

South of the Isurumuniya Vihara are extensive remains of the Vessagiriya cave monastery complex, which dates from much the same time.

Museums

Anuradhapura's **Archaeological Museum** *(open 8am-5pm Wed-Mon, closed public holidays)* also houses a ticket office for the ancient city. It's worth visiting the museum's gorgeous old building, let alone seeing the exhibits inside. There's a restored relic chamber, as found during the excavation of the Kantaka Cetiya Dagoba at nearby Mihintale, and a large-scale model of Anuradhapura's Thuparama Vatadage as it would have been with its wooden roof.

In the museum's grounds are the carved squatting plates from Anuradhapura's western monasteries, whose monks had forsaken the luxurious monasteries of their more worldly brothers. To show their contempt for the effete, luxury-loving monks, the monks of the western monasteries carved beautiful stone squat-style toilets, with their brother monks' monasteries represented on the bottom! Their urinals illustrated the god of wealth, showering handfuls of coins down the hole.

A short distance north of the archaeological museum there's a **Folk Museum** *(admission Rs 25; open 8.30am-5pm Sat-Wed, closed public holidays)* with dusty exhibits of country life in Sri Lanka's North Central Province.

The modern, Chinese-built **Abhayagiri (Fa Hsien) Museum** *(admission free; open 10am-5pm daily)*, just to the south of the Abhayagiri Dagoba and arguably the most interesting of the museums, also has its very own collection of squatting plates. (And on the subject of toilets, there is a clean toilet block for visitors here.) In addition, you can see items of jewellery, pottery and figurines. There is a bookshop selling Cultural Triangle publications.

The Tanks

Anuradhapura has three great tanks. **Nuwara Wewa**, on the east side of the city, is the largest, covering about 1200 hectares. It was built around 20 BC and is well away from most of the old city. The 160-hectare **Tissa Wewa** is the southern tank in the old city. The oldest tank, probably dating from around the 4th century BC, is the 120-hectare **Basawakkulama** (the Tamil word for tank is *kulam*) to the north. Off to the northwest of the Basawakkulama are the ruins of the **western monasteries**, where the monks dressed in scraps of clothing taken from corpses and, it's claimed, lived only on rice (see Museums, earlier, for more details).

Places to Stay – Budget

Lake View *(☎ 222 1593; 4C4 Lake Rd; singles Rs 350-500, doubles Rs 400-550, singles/doubles with air-con Rs 800/850)* is on a lane that leads off Harischandra Mawatha, almost opposite the Cottage Tourist Rest. It's a friendly place with 10 rooms, some with hot water; the ones in the front of the building looking out towards Mihintale are best. The owners are cheerful, and guests recommend the food. Rice, curry and fish costs Rs 225. Bicycle hire is Rs 150.

Indrani Tourist Guest House *(☎ 222 2478; 745 Freeman Mawatha; singles/doubles Rs 350/ 750)* is actually down a side road south of Freeman Mawatha. It's a family home set-up with three basic rooms (three more are being built). Comments in the guestbook suggest they serve up too much food!

The Grand Tourist Holiday Resort *(☎ 223 5173; 4B2 Lake Rd; singles/doubles Rs 600/ 700)*, though grandly titled, is really a pleasant bungalow. There's an unobstructed view of Nuwara Wewa from an attractive veranda. It has four rooms. Meals are available (vegetarian rice and curry Rs 300, breakfast Rs 200). It's a quiet spot.

Samanala Tourist Guest House *(☎ 222 4321; 4N/2 Wasala Daththa Mawatha; singles/doubles Rs 550/770)* has clean rooms surrounding a courtyard, and a pretty garden fronting on to the tank. This friendly family guesthouse hires out bicycles (Rs 150 per day), and guests praise the home cooking.

Shalini Tourist Rest *(☎ 222 2425; ⓔ hotelshalini@hotmail.com; 41/388 Harischandra Mawatha; singles Rs 450-850, doubles Rs 650-1000, with air-con Rs 400 extra)* has a gingerbread-house-like annexe that has a pleasant restaurant upstairs. Rooms come with hot water. You can rent a bicycle for Rs 150 a day, or take a tour of Anuradhapura's ancient city for Rs 750 (Rs 1500 for Mihintale and Anuradhapura combined). The friendly owners will pick you up (or drop you off) for free at the bus or train station if you make arrangements in advance.

Milano Tourist Rest *(☎ 222 2364; 596/40 JR Jaya Mawatha; singles/doubles Rs 500/ 650)* has eight clean, modern and relatively spacious rooms. You can hire bicycles for Rs 200 per day.

Cottage Tourist Rest *(☎ 223 5363; 38/ 538 Harischandra Mawatha; singles/doubles Rs 450/550)*, just past the roundabout, is a cheap family-run guesthouse with Spartan rooms – it might get some street noise.

Kondhamalie Hotel *(☎ 222 2029; 42/388 Harischandra Mawatha; singles/doubles Rs 675/750)* has 32 assorted rooms. The rooms in the newest wing are good value, while rooms in the older house look worn by comparison. Bicycles can be hired for Rs 150 a day, and inexpensive food is available.

Boa Vista *(☎ 223 5052; ⓔ boavis@sltnet.lk; 142 Old Puttalam Rd; singles/doubles Rs 700/800)* is a sparsely furnished but exceptionally clean hotel run by a Canadian–Sri Lankan couple, who sometimes put people up in their modern flat if there are only a few guests. The location close to the Tissa Wewa and the Royal Pleasure Gardens is a bonus, and they offer Sri Lankan and Western meals. A three-wheeler here from town should cost Rs 60.

Nimnara Lake Resort *(☎/fax 074 580256; 21/146 Wijaya Mawatha, Attikulama; singles/doubles Rs 975/1500, with air-con Rs 1275/ 1800)* is on the banks of the Nuwara Wewa 6km south of town. It offers 11 rooms in a new building. The grounds of the guesthouse are rich in birdlife, and there are views across to Mihintale. The owners are helpful and experienced, and the food is noteworthy. There are bicycles for hire and plans to add a swimming pool. A three-wheeler from town should cost Rs 100, or you can call and they'll pick you up.

Little Paradise Tourist Rest *(☎ 223 5132; ⓔ nathol@sltnet.lk; 622/18 Godage Mawatha; singles/doubles 750/1000)* is in a hard-to-find location in a residential neighbourhood, fronting onto a rough sports field. The six rooms have balconies and fans. Call ahead and a vehicle will come to collect you.

Hotel Nuwara Wewa *(☎ 223 5339; off Anuradhapura–Mihintale road; singles/doubles Rs 550/1100)* has a charming rural location 3km from Anuradhapura, signposted on the left as you head for Mihintale. The three-storey building has nine clean rooms, plus verandas with chairs on each floor overlooking the fields and trees. It is run by an affable family, but not much English is spoken. A three-wheeler from town will cost Rs 60 (or Rs 100 from the new bus station).

Places to Stay – Mid-Range

Miridiya Hotel *(☎/fax 222 2519; e info@galway.lk; singles/doubles B&B US$26/28)* has rooms with air-con. You may share the pool with wildlife and sometimes the staff can be aloof, but there's a pretty garden running down to the tank. Nonguests may use the pool for Rs 100. This place is popular with groups.

Tissawewa Rest House *(☎ 222 2299, fax 222 3265; e hotels@quickshaws.com; singles/doubles US$24.50/29, with air-con US$27/31.50)* is a Raj-era relic with a style all its own. The Tissawewa is listed as a heritage building, and is authentic right down to the shower railings and claw-foot baths. Some consider it rundown, while others return every year. Besides high-ceiling lounge areas and verandas, it has 4.4 hectares of gardens with mahogany and teak trees. It also has the advantage of being right in there with the ruins. Since it is inside the 'sacred area' it can't sell alcohol, although you can bring your own with you. A big veranda looks out on gardens with lots of monkeys, which have no qualms about stealing your afternoon tea. The quaint rooms are mostly enormous, but there are a couple that are not, so check before you sign in. You can hire bicycles here (Rs 150 per day). As with all resthouses, the set menu is relatively pricey, but the à la carte menu is reasonably priced (mains around Rs 150 to 200). Breakfast is included in the prices given above. Guests can use the swimming pool at the Nuwarawewa Rest House. The Tissawewa is popular with groups, so it would be wise to book ahead.

Nuwarawewa Rest House *(☎ 222 2565, fax 222 3265; e hotels@quickshaws.com; New Town; singles/doubles including breakfast US$26.50/31)*, Anuradhapura's other resthouse, backs on to the Nuwara Wewa. It's pleasant even though it resembles a 1960s hospital. The rooms have air-con and cost the same whether or not they face the tank. It has a good, clean swimming pool in the garden – nonguests can splash about for Rs 200.

Palm Garden Village Hotel *(☎ 222 3961-2; e pgvh@pan.lk; Puttalam Rd, Pandulagama; singles/doubles US$83/96, suites US$108)* is Anuradhapura's top hotel, 6km west of town. Accommodation is in chalets and singles or doubles set in 38 hectares of gardens complete with tennis courts – and resident deer, peacocks and the occasional elephant. The centrepiece is a stunning swimming pool – nonguests can use it for Rs 150 per day. The suites are almost the same as the standard rooms, except for a bathtub, a TV with local channels and a four-poster bed. Meals cost US$7.50 for breakfast and US$11.50 for dinner. Foreigners with resident visas pay Rs 3500/4200 for a single/double, or Rs 4600 for a suite. A three-wheeler from town costs Rs 200.

Places to Eat

There's little in the way of eating places apart from at the places to stay.

Anzu's Restaurant & Rest *(☎ 222 5678; 394/25A Harischandra Mawatha; mains around Rs 250)*, is a relaxed house restaurant that's actually down a side street called Dharma Asoka Lane. It is run by chefs from northern China, which gives it an authenticity that sets it apart from nearly all of the Chinese restaurants out in the provinces. Sweet-and-sour pork costs Rs 275; sauteed beef with oyster sauce is Rs 225. Anzu's also has several rooms to let for Rs 400 (plus Rs 100 for a room with a bathroom).

Salgado Hotel & Bakery *(Main St)* is an old-fashioned place serving Sri Lankan breakfasts (Rs 55), short eats (around Rs 15) and biscuits.

Alankumala Farm Shop *(279 Main St, mains Rs 50-150)* is a busy spot serving Chinese lunch and dinner packets for Rs 95, rice and curry from Rs 50 and short eats. The air-con section has the usual Chinese menu: noodle dishes and mixed fried rice for Rs 80, and chicken with cashews for Rs 140. There's a **supermarket** next door.

Getting There & Away

Bus Anuradhapura has 'old' and 'new' bus stations – the old bus station is further north, closer to the train station. Private express buses leave from near the old bus station. Buses heading south start at the old bus station and call by the new bus station, whereas buses heading north to Vavuniya and east to Trincomalee start from the new bus station. It is easier to get a good seat from the starting point. There are departures to Trinco from early morning (Rs 35, 3½ hours); to Kandy (via Kekirawa and Dambulla) every hour or so until about 5pm (CTB/intercity bus Rs 70/105, three hours); and to Polonnaruwa every hour from 5.30am (Rs 35, three hours).

Kurunegala buses leave every 30 minutes from about 6am (CTB/intercity bus Rs 37/75, two hours); those to Colombo leave every 30 minutes between 5am and 8pm (CTB/intercity bus Rs 85/160, five hours). For Puttalam you may have to catch a bus to Kala Oya (private bus Rs 15), and then another bus on to Puttalam (Rs 20) from there. Buses to Kala Oya go past the road to Wilpattu National Park (get off at get off at Maragahawewa and change for Hunuwilagama).

Train Anuradhapura has two train stations; the main Anuradhapura station and the smaller Anuradhapura New Town further to the south. Trains to Colombo depart at 5am, 6.40am, 8.55am, 10.45am, 2.30pm and 11.10pm. First class seats are available on the 6.40am intercity express and the 2.30pm and 11.10pm trains. It takes four to five hours to reach Colombo, all being well. Prices are Rs 42 for a seat in 3rd class, Rs 116/141 in 2nd class for a seat/sleeper and Rs 202/277 in 1st class. For Matara (9½ hours) and Galle (8½ hours) catch the *Rajarata Rajini* at 5am. Prices to Galle are Rs 66 in 3rd class and Rs 180 in 2nd class. You can also travel between Anuradhapura and Kandy by train (any of them), changing at Polgahawela.

Getting Around

The city is too spread out to investigate on foot. A three-hour taxi trip costs about Rs 700 and a three-wheeler about Rs 500, but a bicycle (Rs 150 to 200 a day) is the nicest way to explore the ruins leisurely. There's also a terrific bike track along the bund of Nuwara Wewa. You can hire bicycles at resthouses and several guesthouses.

Numerous buses run between the old and new bus stations, via Main St.

TANTIRIMALAI

About 50km northwest of Anuradhapura, deep in the hinterland of the old Rajarata kingdom, lies a little-known 2300-year-old religious site. When Princess Sangamitta arrived with the Bodhi Tree cutting from India, her party stopped at Tantirimalai for a night as a guest of a friendly Hindu hermit. The site was honoured with a *raja maha viharaya* (royal temple) and rock-carved Buddha images, on a series of broad granite outcroppings surrounding a lotus pond. Parts of the site date from the reign of King Devanampiya Tissa in the 3rd century BC. There's no great reason to come here if time is short, but if you want to get into a little-visited corner of the country it has its rewards. There's no accommodation here, but keen cyclists could make it up and back from Anuradhapura in a day, and the indolent majority can catch a bus or hire a vehicle for the day.

The shrines and carvings are reached through the Tantirimalai Raja Maha Viharaya; entry is free. The site comprises a series of broad-backed bare rocks, one topped by an ancient bodhi tree, another by a 12m-high dagoba, behind the temple. The bodhi tree is one of the original saplings taken from the Sri Maha Bodhi. Known as the **Asthapala Bodhi**, it is a bodhi which grants wishes – the name means 'eight types of power'. After paying your respects to the bodhi tree, continue down the slope on the other side and you'll see a fine **Buddha image** in Samadhi pose carved into the side of a rock, flanked by lions and several smaller, less distinct Buddha bas-reliefs. Backtracking to the bodhi tree, turn right and head down to the beautiful lotus-filled pond backed by bare rocks. A causeway leads across the pond to the **pothgula**, or library, a small cave hewn from rock surrounded by the foundations of ancient walls.

A track leads on for 400m down a small wooded vale between rocks to the **fresco caves**, beneath a mushroom-shaped rock. The track is a little indistinct in places; follow the biggest, most likely path and you should be OK. Alas, no frescoes remain but if you look at the other side of the rock you can see carved script, possibly Brahmi, while a couple of meditation spots lie beneath nearby boulders. The mushroom-shaped rock here is probably the *tantirimalai* (Tamil for 'unclimbable rock') where the Brahmin lived.

Heading back past the *pothgula*, pop in at a simple building housing a few architectural fragments and damaged statues. The caretaker in the hut next door deserves a tip for showing you around. Continue around the base of rock on which the stupa stands to find the 15m-long, 2300-year-old **reclining Buddha** image. Part of the head and arm have been restored with concrete. The Buddha's gently rippling robes impart a wonderful sense of restfulness. It's a short walk back to the temple from here. The site is mostly bare rock that gets pretty hot in the middle of the day, so bring water and a decent hat.

Getting There & Away

There are two routes here from Anuradhapura. One route goes via the sacred city to Nikawewa. This road is asphalt right up to Nikawewa, and there's a rather rutted dirt road after that. The other route goes via Medawachchiya, then branches towards Mannar. The turn-off is about 6km past Neriyakulam on the A14 to Mannar – it's all asphalt up to the turn-off. Several buses a day (Rs 25) leave from Anuradhapura's old bus station. Hiring a car and driver for the day will cost the standard Rs 2500.

MIHINTALE

☎ 025

Thirteen kilometres east of Anuradhapura on the road to Trincomalee, Mihintale is of enormous spiritual significance to the Sinhalese because it is where Buddhism originated in Sri Lanka. In 247 BC King Devanampiya Tissa of Anuradhapura met Mahinda, son of the great Indian Buddhist emperor Ashoka, while deer hunting around the hill at Mihintale, and was converted to Buddhism.

Exploring Mihintale does involve quite a climb, so you would be wise to visit it early in the morning or late in the afternoon to avoid the midday heat. There are seven authorised guides, who charge around Rs 350 for a ton of information over two hours or so. It pays off if you have a deep interest in Buddhism and the site's history.

Each year a great festival, the Poson Poya, is held at Mihintale on the Poson full-moon night (usually in June).

The Hospital

A ruined hospital and the remains of a quincunx of buildings, laid out like the five dots on a dice, flank the roadway before you reach the base of the steps. The hospital consisted of a number of cells. A *bat oruwa* (large stone trough) sits among the ruins. The interior is carved in the shape of a human form, and into this the patient would climb to be immersed in healing oils. There are more examples of these troughs in the museum (see under Museum, later). Clay urns for storing herbs and grinding stones found at the site can be seen in the museum. Inscriptions have revealed that the hospital had its specialists – there is reference to a *mandova*, a bone and muscle specialist, and to a *puhunda vedek*, a leech doctor.

The Stairway

In a series of flights, 1840 ancient granite slab steps lead majestically up the hillside.

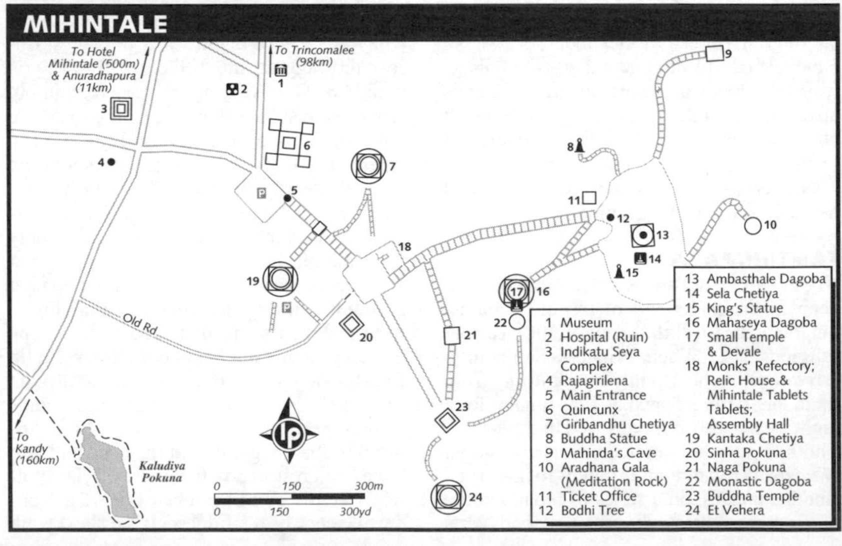

The first flight is the widest and shallowest. Higher up the steps are narrower and steeper. If you have a problem with stairs, the Old Road from the west avoids most of them.

Kantaka Chetiya

At the first landing a smaller flight of steps leads to this partly ruined dagoba off to the right. It's 12m high (originally it was higher than 30m) and 130m around its base. A Brahmi inscription found nearby records donations for the stupa. While exactly who built it is open to conjecture, Devanampiya Tissa (r. 247–207 BC) had 68 cave monasteries built, and the dagoba would have been constructed near these. King Laji Tissa (r. 59–50 BC) enlarged it. So the dagoba was built sometime in between, and is certainly one of the oldest at Mihintale. It is noteworthy for its friezes (see the boxed text 'Sculptural Symbolism'). Four stone flower altars stand at each of the cardinal points, and surrounding these are well-preserved sculptures of dwarfs, geese and other figures. Excavation on the dagoba began in 1934, at which time there was virtually no sign of it to the untrained eye. You can see a reconstruction of its interior design in the museum in Anuradhapura.

South of the Kantaka Chetiya, where a big boulder is cleft by a cave, if you look up you'll see what is thought to be the oldest inscription in Sri Lanka, predating Pali. The inscription dedicates the caves and shelters on the mountain to meditation now and for eternity. Through the cave, ledges on the cliff face acted as meditation retreats for the numerous monks once resident here. There are around 70 different sites for contemplation.

The Relic House & Monks' Refectory

At the top of the next flight of steps, on the second landing, is the monks' refectory with huge stone troughs that the lay followers kept filled with rice for the monks.

Nearby, at a place identified as the monastery's relic house, are two inscribed stone slabs erected during the reign of King Mahinda IV (r. 975–91). The inscriptions lay down the rules relating to the relic house and the conduct of those responsible for it. One inscription clearly states that nothing belonging to the relic house shall be lent or sold. Another confirms the amount of land to be given in exchange for a reliable supply of oil and wicks for lamps and flowers for offerings. Also known as the Mihintale tablets, these inscribed stones define the duties of the monastery's many servants: which servants gather firewood and cook, which servants cook but only on firewood gathered by others, and so on. There are also rules for monks: they should rise at dawn, clean their teeth, put on their robes, meditate and then go to have their breakfast (boiled rice) at the refectory, but only after reciting certain portions of the scriptures. Looking back from the relic house you get an excellent view of Anuradhapura.

Sculptural Symbolism

The four *vahalkadas* or solid panels of sculpture at the Kantaka Chetiya are among the oldest and best preserved in the country and the only ones to be found at Mihintale.

Vahalkadas face each of the four cardinal directions and comprise a series of bands, each containing some sort of ornamentation. The upper part usually contained niches in which were placed sculptures of divine beings. At either end of each *vahalkada* is a pillar topped with the figure of an animal, eg, an elephant or a lion. How or why these sculptural creations came into being is subject to speculation, but one theory is that they evolved from simple flower altars. Others suggest they were an adaptation from Hindu temple design.

The cardinal points in traditional sculptural work are represented by specific animals: an elephant on the east, a horse on the west, a lion on the north, and a bull on the south. In addition to these beasts, sculptures also feature dwarfs (sometimes depicted with animal heads), geese (said to have the power to choose between good and evil), elephants (often shown as though supporting the full weight of the superstructure), and *naga* (serpents, said to possess magical powers). Floral designs, apart from the lotus, are said to be primarily ornamental.

The Assembly Hall

On the same level as the relic house, this hall, also known as the convocation hall, is where monks met to discuss matters of common interest. The most senior monk would have presided over the discussions, and the raised dais in the middle of the hall was apparently where this person sat. Sixty-four stone pillars once supported the roof. Conservation of this site began in 1948. The main path to the Ambasthale Dagoba leads from here.

Sinha Pokuna

Just below the monks' refectory on the second landing, and near the entrance if you are coming via the old road, is a small pool surmounted by a 2m-high rampant lion, reckoned to be one of the best pieces of animal carving in the country. Anyone placing one hand on each paw would be right in line for the stream of water from the lion's mouth. There are some fine friezes around this pool.

Ambasthale Dagoba

The final steep stairway, lined with frangipani trees, leads to the place where Mahinda and the king met. The Ambasthale Dagoba *(admission Rs 250)* is built over the spot where Mahinda stood. Nearby stands a statue of the king in the place where he stood. On the opposite side of the dagoba from the statue is a cloister and behind that a large, white sitting Buddha. The stone pillars that surround the temple once supported a roof. You must remove your shoes and hat, and umbrellas aren't allowed. The shoe-minders expect a compensation of around Rs 15.

The name Ambasthale means 'mango tree' and refers to a riddle that Mahinda used to test the king's intelligence (see the boxed text 'Mahinda's Riddle').

Nearby is the **Sela Chetiya**, which has a stone rendering of the Buddha's footprint. It's surrounded by a railing festooned with prayer flags left by pilgrims who have also scattered coins here.

Mahaseya Dagoba

A stone path to the southwest of the Ambasthale Dagoba leads up to a higher dagoba (arguably the largest at Mihintale), thought to have been built to house relics of Mahinda. The bodhi tree to the left of the base of the steps is said to be one of the oldest surviving ones. From here there is a view over the lakes and trees to Anuradhapura, a horizon studded with the domes and spikes of all the massive stupas. The sunsets here are something else. A small temple at the foot of the dagoba has a reclining Buddha and technicolour modern frescoes – donations are anticipated. A room at the side is a *devale* (Hindu complex) with statues of major gods – Ganesh, Vishnu, Skanda and Saman.

Mahinda's Riddle

Before Mahinda could go ahead and initiate King Devanampiya Tissa into the new religious philosophy, he needed to gauge the king's intelligence. He decided to test the king with a riddle. Pointing to a tree he asked him the name of the tree. 'This tree is called a mango,' replied the king. 'Is there yet another mango beside this?' asked Mahinda. 'There are many mango trees,' responded the king. 'And are there yet other trees besides this mango and the other mangoes?' asked Mahinda. 'There are many trees, but those are trees which are not mangoes,' said the king. 'And are there, besides the other mangoes and those trees which are not mangoes, yet other trees?' asked Mahinda. 'There is this mango tree,' said the king, who as a result passed the test.

Mahinda's Cave

There is a path leading northeast from the Ambasthale Dagoba down to a cave where there is a large flat stone. This is said to be where Mahinda lived and the stone is claimed to be where he rested. The track to the cave is hard on tender bare feet.

Aradhana Gala (Meditation Rock)

To the east of the Ambasthale Dagoba is a steep path over sun-heated rock leading up to a point where there are great views. A railing goes up most of the way.

Naga Pokuna

Halfway back down the steep flight of steps from the Ambasthale Dagoba, a path leads to the left, around the side of the hill topped by the Mahaseya Dagoba. Here you'll find the Naga Pokuna, or 'snake pool', so called because of the five-headed cobra carved in low relief on the rock face of the pool. Its tail is said to reach down to the bottom of the pool. If you continue on from here you eventually loop back to the second landing.

Et Vehera

At an even higher elevation (309m) than the Mahaseya Dagoba are the remains of a stupa called Et Vehera (literally, the stupa of the elephant). The origin of the stupa's name is open to conjecture, but it may have been named after the monastery nearby. The Mihintale tablets mention Et Vehera and its image house. There are good views from here, especially of Kaludiya Pokuna.

Museum

There is a small museum *(admission free; open 9am-5pm Wed-Mon, closed public holidays)* on the road leading to the stairs, virtually opposite the ruins of the hospital. There are several rooms, each one dedicated to particular finds, including bronze figurines, fragments of frescoes and remnants of stone tubs from the hospital. The collection includes a replica of the interior of an 8th-century dagoba and a 9th-century gold-plated *ola* leaf manuscript. Pottery fragments from China and Persia are also on display.

Indikatu Seya Complex

Back on the road leading to the Old Rd, and strictly speaking outside of the site proper, are the remains of a monastery enclosed in the ruins of a stone wall. Inside are two dagobas, the larger known as Indikatu Seya (literally, dagoba of the needle). There is evidence to suggest that this monastery was active in fostering Mahayana Buddhism. The main dagoba's structure differs from others in Mihintale; for example, it's built on a square platform.

Nearby is a hill that's been dubbed Rajagirilena (royal cave hill) after the caves found here with Brahmi inscriptions in them. One of the caves bears the name of Devanampiya Tissa. A flight of steps leads up to the caves.

Kaludiya Pokuna

Further south along the same road is the Kaludiya Pokuna (dark water pool). This artificial pool was carefully constructed to look realistic, and features a rock-carved bathhouse and the ruins of a small monastery. It's a peaceful place.

Places to Stay & Eat

Hotel Mihintale *(☎ 226 6599; e chc@sltnet.lk; singles/doubles US$14/20)*, run by the Ceylon Hotels Corporation, is on the main road near the turn-off to the site. This is the only hotel in Mihintale. There are 10 singles or doubles with air-con, and there's slightly hapless but friendly staff. The rooms are mostly large and clean and the setting is pleasant. Moderately priced meals are available. The pavilion café at the front is a good place to pause for a cool drink and a toilet stop.

Getting There & Away

It's a fairly short bus ride (Rs 10) from Anuradhapura's new bus station out to Mihintale. A taxi there and back, with two hours to climb the stairs, costs about Rs 800; a three-wheeler is about Rs 600. It takes less than an hour to cycle here.

YAPAHUWA

This rock fortress *(admission Rs 170)* rising 100m from a plain is similar in concept to Sigiriya. Yapahuwa (pronounced yaa-pow-a), also known as Fire Rock, was built in the early 13th century as a fortress against the invading South Indian armies. Between 1272 and 1284 it was the capital of King Bhuvanekabahu I. It is believed that invading Indians carried away the sacred tooth-relic (now in Kandy) from Yapahuwa at that time, only for it to be recovered in 1288 by Parakramabahu I.

Yapahuwa's steep ornamental staircase, which led up to the ledge holding the tooth temple, is one of its finest features. (The other is the lack of tourists, unlike Sigiriya.) One of the lions near the top of the staircase appears on the Rs 10 note. The porches on the stairway had very fine pierced-stone windows, one of which is now in the museum in Colombo; the other is in the museum onsite. Reliefs of dancers, musicians and animals are evidence of South Indian influence. The view from the top of the staircase is wonderful. Climbing right up to the top of the rock is not really feasible as it's very overgrown.

There is a **museum** of sorts to the right of the site entrance. On display are stone sculptures of Vishnu and Kali, fragments of pottery and the carved stone screen, but all signs are in Sinhala. Behind the museum is something more fascinating – a **cave temple** that contains some 13th-century frescoes. The repetition of images across a geometric grid also appears in ancient Buddhist sites in India, such as Ajanta, inland from Mumbai, and Alchi in Ladakh. Also in the temple are wooden Buddha images and, interestingly, one image made of bronze. The temple is usually locked but a monk will open it for you if you ask, although you are expected to make a donation. Photography is not allowed in the temple or in the museum.

A guide will attach himself to you in anticipation of a tip.

Getting There & Away

Yapahuwa is 4km from Maho railway junction, where the Trincomalee line splits from the Colombo–Anuradhapura line, and about 5km from the Anuradhapura–Kurunegala road. It's possible to take a three-wheeler from the Anuradhapura–Kurunegala road to the site, although occasional buses do travel from here to Maho and back. A three-wheeler from Maho to the site costs Rs 150 one way. A three-wheeler from the main road and back would cost about Rs 600 with waiting time. Maho is an important rail junction, and most trains going to and from Colombo stop here.

PADENIYA

About 85km south of Anuradhapura, and 25km northwest of Kurunegala, where the Puttalam and Anuradhapura roads branch off, is the **Padeniya Raja Maha Vihara** *(donations appreciated)*, which is worth popping into if you're passing by. It's a pretty, medieval temple with 28 carved pillars and a stunning elaborate door (said to be the largest in Sri Lanka) to the main shrine. There is also a clay image house and a library, as well as a preaching hall with an unusual carved wooden pulpit.

PANDUWASNUWARA

About 17km southwest of Padeniya, on the road between Wariyapola and Chilaw, are the 12th-century remains of the temporary capital of Parakramabahu I. It's nothing on the scale of Anuradhapura or Polonnaruwa, but it's worth stopping in if you're heading past. The sprawling site, covering some 20 hectares, hasn't been fully excavated. The turn-off to the site is at Panduwasnuwara village, where there is a small **museum** *(donation expected)*. Most of the signs are in Sinhala.

Approaching the site, the first thing you'll see is the moat and the massive citadel wall. After that the road swings to the right and past the remains of the palace, where there are signs in English and Sinhala. Nearby, and indeed throughout the site, are the remains of image houses and dagobas as well as evidence of living quarters for monks. Follow the road past the school and veer left; you will shortly come to a restored tooth temple with a bodhi tree and, beyond that, the remains of a round palace (apparently once multistoreyed) enclosed in a circular moat.

There are many stories about who lived in this palace and why it was built. Legend has it that it kept the king's daughter away from men who would desire her, as it had been prophesised that if she bore a son, he would eventually claim the throne. Another story is that it was built to house the king's wives and, intriguingly, that there was once a secret tunnel that led from the king's palace and under the moat to the queens' palace. However attractive these stories are, they are merely that, and the fact remains that no-one really knows why this place was built.

Buses run between Kurunegala (via Wariyapola) and Chilaw on a regular basis, and it would be possible to be dropped off at Panduwasnuwara village and to walk the remaining 1km. However, it's far more practical to come with your own transport.

ARANKELE

This 6th-century forest hermitage, 23km east of Panduwasnuwara, is claimed to have housed the great sage, Maliyadeva, and his followers. The ruins of the hermitage include moats, stone walls, an ancient hospital that has retained its stone herbal baths and grinding stones, and an ancient sewerage system. The usual entry to the site is by the well-shaded *sakman maluwa* (stone-paved meditation walk). A hermit community of monks still lives to the west of the complex and devotees bring offerings of food, drink and other necessities daily. It's quite hard to get to by public transport – you won't miss all that much if you can't get there.

RIDIGAMA & RIDI VIHARA

Ridi Vihara *(admission Rs 100 donation)*, literally the 'Silver Temple', is so named because it was here that silver ore was discovered in the 2nd century BC. Although not on the usual beaten track, it's well worth a visit to see its wonderful frescoes and the unusual Dutch (Delft) tiles in the main cave.

Legend has it that King Dutugemunu, who reigned in the 2nd century BC, lacked the funds to finish an important dagoba in Anuradhapura. The discovery of silver ore at the place now known as Ridigama allowed him to complete the work, and as a token of his gratitude he decided to establish a temple in the cave where the ore was allegedly discovered, and to put in this cave a gold-plated statue of the Buddha. The golden statue is still in the main cave, called the **Pahala Vihara** (Lower Temple), secure inside a special case. Also within the Pahala Vihara is a 9m recumbent Buddha that rests on a platform decorated with a series of blue-and-white tiles, which were a gift from the Dutch consul. The tiles depict scenes from the Bible, including Adam and Eve being banished from the Garden of Eden, and the transfiguration of Christ. Here you can see what remains of a beautiful piece of ivory carving over the lintel. Unfortunately, this and other pieces of art have been subject to vandalism over the years.

The nearby **Uda Vihara** (Upper Temple) was built by King Kirthi Sri Rajasinghe. The entrance has a Kandyan-period moonstone. It's interesting to try to pick out some of the clever visual tricks used by the fresco artists. In one case, what appears to be an elephant at a distance reveals itself on closer inspection to be a formation of nine maidens. Hindu deities and images of the Buddha are represented in the caves.

The huge boulder that looms over the whole temple complex is attractive to the local wild bee population; you can see their nests bulging below the overhang. It's said that those who enter the temple with impure hearts will get stung, so watch out.

Just beyond the temple courtyard is what used to be a hermit's retreat. It now houses only a small shrine, but there's a skilfully carved pillared porch.

Although there are no signs banning flash photography you should, of course, refrain from using a flash inside the caves in order to preserve the frescoes. Remember, this is not an entertainment for tourists but a working temple, and you should dress and behave appropriately. Cover your shoulders and legs, remove your shoes and hat and conduct yourself as you would be expected to in a place of worship.

Outside the temple complex you can see an abandoned dagoba at the top of a smooth rocky outcrop. On the way up, to your right, is an ancient inscription in the stone, said to have been etched on King Dutugemunu's behalf. An easy 10-minute walk starts to the right of this dagoba (as you are walking up to it). Head past a modern pavilion to an abandoned bungalow; nearby, on the top of the cliff, is a slab from which you get the most magnificent views.

Getting There & Away

Ridi Vihara is south of the Kurunegala–Dambulla road. If you are coming by car from Kurunegala, the turn-off to Ridigama village is on your right just past Ibbagamuwa village. The temple is about 2km from Ridigama via Temple Junction. Buses run between Kurunegala and Ridigama village (Rs 10, approximately every 45 minutes). From the village you can take a three-wheeler to the temple (approximately Rs 300 return, including waiting time).

KURUNEGALA

☎ 037 • pop 28,300

Kurunegala is an important crossroads town on the routes between both Colombo and Anuradhapura, and Kandy and Puttalam. The town itself is not particularly interesting, but the region around Kurunegala is rich in archaeological sites and temples.

The large, smooth rocky outcrops that loom over the low-rise buildings are a striking feature of this city. Named for the animals they appear to resemble (tortoise rock, lion rock etc), the outcrops are not surprisingly endowed with mythological status. It's said that they were formed when animals that were endangering the free supply of water to the town were turned into stone.

There's a road going up **Etagala**, a large black boulder on the eastern side of the city. The views are extensive from here. On the way up you pass a small shrine, **Ibbagala Vihara**, and at the head of the road there is a **temple** named after the rock itself.

There are some pleasant lodgings around the lake. There is a **post office** *(Colombo Rd)* in town. Check your emails at **Nexus Cyber Café** *(60 Kandy Rd)*. **Seylan Bank** *(Colombo Rd)* has an ATM, as does **Commercial Bank**

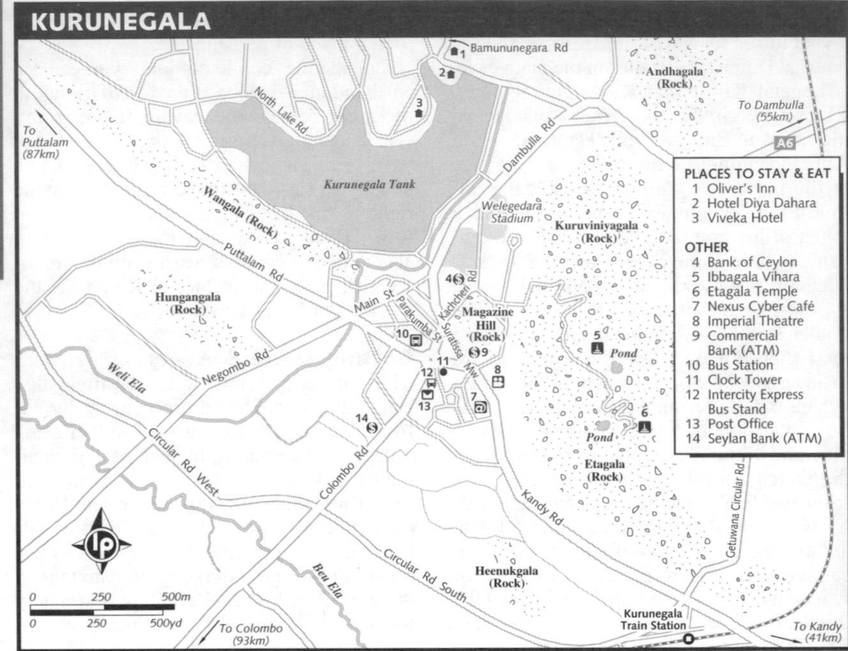

(Suratissa Mawatha), which is close to the fine old Imperial Cinema, still pulling a crowd to dramas and romance today. You can change travellers cheques at the **Bank of Ceylon**, 450m north of the post office.

Places to Stay & Eat

There are six or seven hotels around town, but the most pleasant are around the lake. A three-wheeler to these places from town should cost Rs 60, or Rs 80 to 100 from the train station.

Oliver's Inn *(☎ 222 3452, fax 222 0092; 2 Bamununegara Rd; singles/doubles Rs 300/500, with air-con Rs 800/1000)* is a 1960s suburban kit home with five rooms, one them with air-con. The manager is a friendly old chap and the staff are helpful too. It's just around the corner from Hotel Diya Dahara.

Hotel Diya Dahara *(☎ 222 3452, fax 222 0092; 7 North Lake Rd; singles/doubles Rs 825/1320)* has rooms with hot water and balcony. It's a little expensive for what they are, but there's a pretty garden, and a good restaurant beside the lake. The grandiose building across the road is under the same management, and has a honeymoon suite for Rs 3850 and large singles/doubles with air-con for Rs 1650/2200.

Viveka Hotel *(☎ 222 2897; ⓔ viveka_hotel@hotmail.com; 64 North Lake Rd; singles/doubles Rs 850/950)* is a 150-year-old villa kept up with lots of spit and polish. The elegant veranda looks over the lake to the town. The three rooms are Spartan white cubes with new bathrooms. Some interesting framed photographs grace the main room, and it has Kurunegala's most convivial bar. It sometimes hosts weddings.

Hotel Diya Dahara and the Viveka Hotel have restaurants.

Getting There & Away

A new bus station was undergoing a stop-start renovation when we visited, so CTB and the cheaper private buses were honking their way through the busy central bazaar streets. Intercity buses depart from a yard behind the clock tower. You may be dropped here when you arrive.

Intercity express buses to Anuradhapura leave every 30 minutes between 6am and 5.30pm (CTB Rs 37, express Rs 75, two hours). CTB buses to Chilaw leave every 30 minutes between 6am and 7pm (Rs 21.50, 2½ hours). There are regular CTB and express buses to Colombo (Rs 60, express, four to five hours) and Kandy (Rs 40, express, one hour). There are also buses to Negombo (Rs 44, 3½ hours).

The train station, 2km from the town centre, sees frequent visits from trains on the Northern Line. There are eight trains between Kurunegala and Colombo daily (Rs 55/ 95 for 2nd/1st class seats, two to three hours) and four trains daily to Anuradhapura (Rs 63/110, three hours).

DAMBADENIYA

For a short time in the mid-13th century this small town was the site of the capital of Parakramabahu II (r. 1236–70). There is little to see in terms of palace remains, except for six ponds. About 400m east of the centre of town is a **temple** (Vijayasundarama) with wall paintings said to date from when Dambadeniya served as a capital (but there are swathes of recent 'restorative' paint work). It is also where the tooth relic was exhibited. More archaeological excavation work in this area has been scheduled.

If you have your own transport you may enjoy a detour to a little-visited site called **Panavitiya**, where a small resting place (called *ambalama*, which means 'rest hall') was built in the 18th century. The *ambalama* belonged to an era when people travelled long distances on foot. The structure is very simple. A stone platform (4m by 3m) supports a wooden pillar frame, with raised planks running around the sides, so people could (and still can, actually) sit facing into the centre.

The 26 carved wooden pillars support a modern tiled roof. The original also had a roof, judging by the tile fragments that were discovered buried in the ground. Unfortunately white ants have invaded some of the pillars. The carvings depict lotus flowers, wrestlers, two women greeting one another, snakes in combat, dancers, deer, and men chatting.

To get to Panavitiya, look carefully for the Quinco Highland Sales Outlet sign (there's a white milk bottle with the sign) 4km north of Dambadeniya. The turn-off is opposite this sign. Panavitiya is 3km down this road, near a temple.

The East

Long white beaches, a turquoise sea, great surf, colourful towns and shrubby parks teeming with wildlife make the multiethnic East an area ripe for exploration. In the post-war environment this region is set to boom: the government is promoting tourism in the East, and hotel groups have plans to develop resort-style hotels.

The East extends from Yala East National Park and Arugam Bay in the south, along the beaches, lagoons and fishing villages of the east coast, to Nilaveli beach in the north. Inland, enormous reservoirs and Maduru Oya and Gal Oya National Parks form the western boundary. In between are vast paddy fields, ruins from ancient kingdoms and abundant bird and animal life.

This region had its fair share of tragedy during the war, but has not seen the type of full-blown military operations common in the North during the 1990s, so its major towns are further along the road to reconstruction. However, there are still moving reminders of the destructive war, especially along the coast. At the time of research, some areas were under the control of the Liberation Tigers of Tamil Eelam (LTTE) and not all roads were open. It is possible to travel around by public transport – if you're patient. If you have a long-distance destination, get going early in the morning, as most services are more frequent at this time.

Conveniently, the region is at its best climatically from about May to September, when the monsoon is making things unpleasant on the west and south coasts. With train lines reopening, national parks becoming safe to visit and accommodation beginning to mushroom, it's definitely time to go east.

Highlights

- Snorkelling around Pigeon Island just off the beautiful Nilaveli beach
- Catching waves, rays and the party scene at Arugam Bay
- Spotting abundant animal and birdlife while moving through the district
- Venturing into the wilds of little-visited Yala East National Park

TRINCOMALEE

☎ 026 • pop 57,000

Trincomalee (or Trinco as it's called) is the gateway to some of the finest beaches in Sri Lanka: Uppuveli and Nilaveli. With one of the world's best deep harbours, it is the East's largest industrial centre and naval base, and a potential economic centre post-war. There are a handful of things to see in town and pretty views across the three main bays, but many people pass through on their way to the beach.

During the recent war the area continued to attract some travellers, and when the 2002 cease-fire came into effect the town and beaches were flooded with Sri Lankans from the South taking the first opportunity in many years to appreciate the fine, white-sand beaches. There isn't much accommodation in the town, but guesthouses are reopening along the Uppuveli and Nilaveli beaches.

Trincomalee has the most convoluted colonial history in Sri Lanka. The Dutch (or rather the Danes, because Danish ships were used in the Dutch-sponsored visit) first turned up in 1617, but their visit was a brief one. The Portuguese arrived in 1624 and built a small fort. It changed hands between the Dutch, the king of Kandy, the Dutch, French, Dutch, British, French and Dutch – and all this before 1795!

In 1795 the British were back again, and after a four-day bombardment they kicked the Dutch out. When Singapore fell to the Japanese in WWII, Trincomalee became strategically important to the British, thereby opening itself up to become a military target. It was bombed in 1942 by the Japanese but the naval base remained in British hands until 1957, when a defence agreement with the British ended. Trinco's fortune rose and fell with the war, and some now have high hopes for its economic future and development.

Orientation & Information

Trinco's commercial centre is concentrated in the middle of the peninsula. The military occupies the hilly tip of the peninsula, and it's not possible to enter this area.

You'll have no problem changing money. The **Commercial Bank** *(193 Central Rd)*, **Hatton National Bank** *(59 Ehamparam Rd)* and **Bank of Ceylon** *(9 Main St)* are all close to the bus station. The Commercial Bank and the Hatton National Bank have ATMs.

Trinco must have the highest concentration of Internet cafés in Sri Lanka: there are three within about 50m on Court Rd, all open long hours daily. **PC Home** *(358 Court Rd)* has the biggest set-up and the cheapest rates (Rs 60 per hour). **Comet Internet Browsing Spot** *(325 Court Rd)* has air-con. Comet and **JSP Internet Cafe** *(380 Court Rd)* charge Rs 5 per minute.

Fort Frederick

Originally built by the Portuguese, Fort Frederick, on the spit of land pointing east into the sea, is a military camp, but visitors are allowed to walk through the fort in order to visit the Koneswaram Kovil, a temple at the end of the spit. At the time of research, you were not allowed to bring a camera or photograph the fort. The views of the harbour from the road leading up to the temple are spectacular. Close to the fort's gate is a **stone slab** inscribed with the double-fish emblem of the South Indian Pandyan empire and a prediction of the 'coming of the Franks'. You have to search to find it, as it is built into the fort's entrance arch on the right- and left-hand sides and has been painted over with traffic symbols.

Koneswaram Kovil & Swami Rock

At the end of the road veering left up through the fort is Swami Rock, also known as 'lover's leap', which drops sharply about 130m to the sea below. A Hindu temple, the Koneswaram Kovil, occupies the end of the spit; you must leave your shoes at the foot of the steps leading to the temple itself. When the Portuguese arrived in 1624 there was an important Hindu temple perched atop the rock, so with typical religious zeal they levered it over the edge. The base of a pillar of the original temple can be seen under the decorated tree at the end of the rock. Scuba divers have found traces of the old temple under the waters below, and recovered the temple lingam (phallic symbol of Shiva), which is now mounted in the new temple precincts. Arthur C Clarke describes the first diving discovery in *The Reefs of Taprobane*.

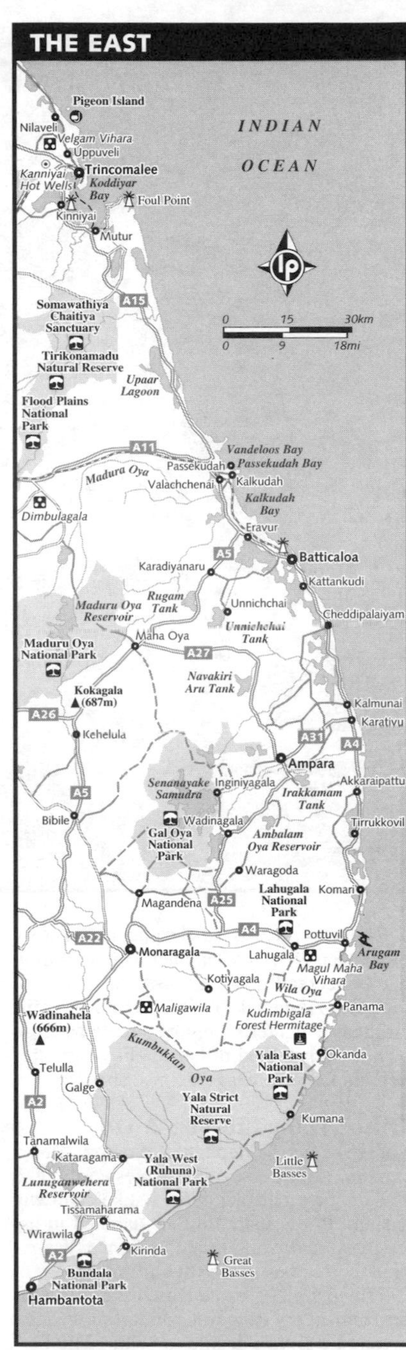

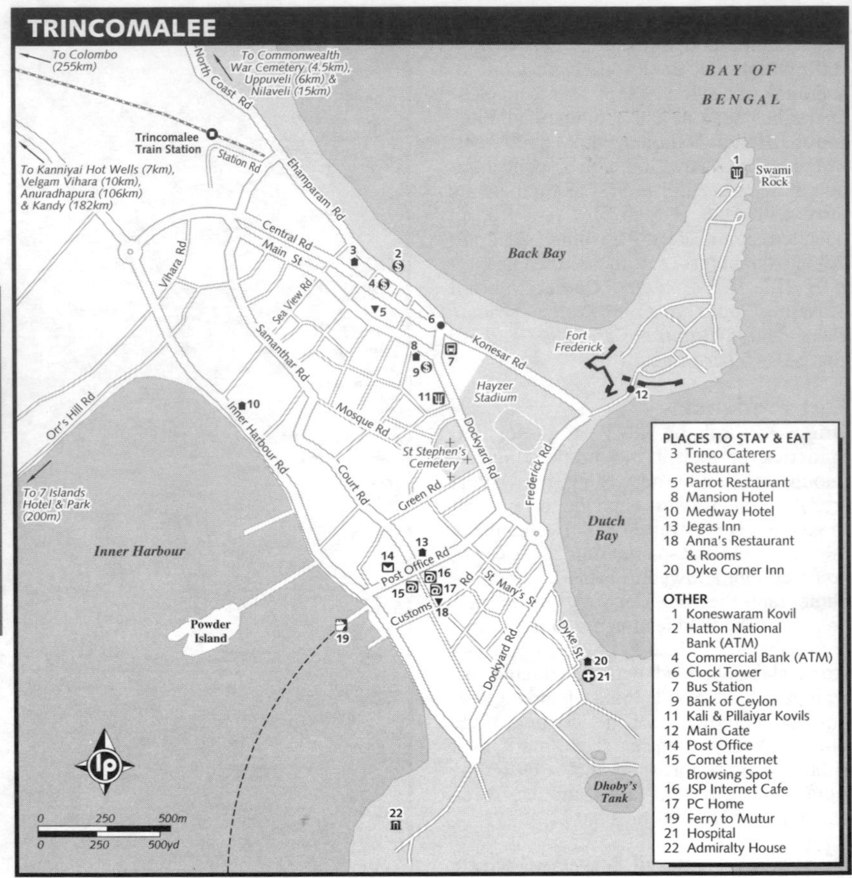

The 'lover's leap' label came from a story of a Dutch official's daughter who, watching her fiance sail away, decided to make the fatal leap. In fact the official erected the pillar in his daughter's memory simply because he was rather fond of her; eight years after her supposed romantic demise she married.

Other Things to See & Do

Somewhere in **St Stephen's Cemetery** *(Dockyard Rd)* is the grave of PB Molesworth, who was the first manager of Sri Lanka's railway system. In his spare time he dabbled in astronomy, and while living in Trinco discovered the famous Red Spot on Jupiter.

Trinco's picturesque **Dutch Bay** can suffer from a very dangerous undertow, so take great care if you decide to swim. The best beaches in the Trinco area are north of the city, particularly at Nilaveli (see Uppuveli & Nilaveli later in this chapter).

Places to Stay & Eat

Some of the budget places in Trinco are not much fun for women travellers, but there are a few acceptable options. Uppuveli and Nilaveli have a greater range.

There are four budget options on Dyke St, with their back rooms facing the sea. **Dyke Corner Inn** *(☎ 222 0318; 210/1 Dyke St; doubles/triples with shared bathroom Rs 300/400)*, near the general hospital, is the best of this bunch. The rooms and bathrooms are clean and it seems a neat, well-run place. There are no mosquito nets and no food is served.

Mansion Hotel *(☎ 222 2745; 23 Main St; singles/doubles from Rs 400/500)* is a passable option. There are some singles/doubles with air-con for Rs 1300/1500.

Jegas Inn *(☎ 222 7272, 071 294694; 108 Post Office Rd; rooms Rs 500, with bathroom Rs 750)* has OK doubles and triples (no nets) in a relatively new house. The whole house, including the kitchen, can be rented for Rs 2500 per night.

Trinco Caterers Restaurant *(☎ 222 7759; 238 Central Rd; singles/doubles with shared bathroom Rs 300/400)* has small, boxlike rooms (no nets) upstairs in an area off the restaurant. This is also a new, popular lunch and dinner spot. Lunch packets cost Rs 45, rice and curry is Rs 60 and mixed fried rice is Rs 150.

Medway Hotel *(☎ 222 7655, fax 222 2582; 250 Inner Harbour Rd; e jrstrinc@slt.lk; rooms Rs 3000)* was the only nonbudget place in town at the time of research. It has eight clean, spacious new doubles with air-con, hot water and harbour views. An extra mattress in the room costs Rs 500.

7 Islands Hotel & Park *(☎ 222 2373)* was being transformed into a large air-con hotel with magnificent harbour views at the time of research. Follow Orr's Hill Rd to the end of the promontory, where a sign indicates the turn-off. The driveway up to the hilltop hotel is very steep.

Anna's Restaurant & Rooms *(☎ 222 4828; 276 Court Rd; mains Rs 60-80)* is a spotless, upstairs restaurant. Rice and curry or vegetable fried rice will set you back Rs 60. Anna has four rooms (no nets) with bathroom being built. If they're as clean as her restaurant, these could be among the best cheap rooms in town.

Parrot Restaurant *(96 Main St)* is welcoming and serves standard rice and noodle dishes, and rice and curry.

There are also a few basic **eateries**, mostly near the bus station.

Getting There & Away

Bus There are several private and CTB buses from Trinco to all over the island. Private buses have more frequent services to Colombo, Batticaloa, and Nilaveli.

Ordinary private buses to Colombo leave Trinco from 5.30am to 5pm and from 9pm to midnight (Rs 90, seven hours), and air-con buses leave approximately every 45 minutes until midnight (Rs 180, six hours). You can catch these air-con buses to anywhere en route (eg, Habarana, Dambulla or Kurunegala).

For Anuradhapura, there are buses between 10am and 1pm (Rs 37, three hours). Ordinary private buses run every two to three hours to Kandy (six hours). To head north, there are CTB buses in the morning and at 4pm to Vavuniya (Rs 53, 3½ hours), and three go daily to Mannar (Rs 82, six hours).

For Batticaloa, there's one CTB bus at 6.30am (Rs 76, four hours), and a few private buses during the day (Rs 140). At the time of research these buses travelled via Habarana and Polonnaruwa because the road from Trinco to Mutur and south from Mutur to Batticaloa was closed.

Train There are two trains daily between Trinco and Colombo Fort via Habarana, leaving at 8.45am (arriving at Fort at 4.45pm) and 8pm (arriving at 5.15am). Fares are Rs 61 in 3rd class and Rs 168 in 2nd class (sleeper Rs 193). For Polonnaruwa and Batticaloa change at Gal Oya.

AROUND TRINCOMALEE

Commonwealth War Cemetery

This cemetery, about 4.5km north of Trinco on Nilaveli Rd, is the last resting place for many servicemen who died at Trinco during WWII. It's beautifully maintained and the friendly caretaker, who lives next door, can show you a record of exactly who's buried where. He'll also show you photographs of Princess Anne planting a tree in 1995 to mark the replacement of several headstones that were damaged during fighting in the late 1980s.

Kanniyai Hot Wells

Kanniyai's hot wells *(admission Rs 2, car parking Rs 10)*, 7km northwest of Trinco, are a popular place for a slosh with buckets of warm water. According to legend the wells were created by Vishnu to distract king Rawana, who named them after his mother, thinking that she had died. The water flows up into tiled structures, and there are changing rooms for men and women. If you haven't had a hot shower for a while, it's a pleasant place for a splash, wrapped in your lungi or sarong.

Velgam Vihara

This isolated complex of Buddhist ruins about 10km northwest of Trinco dates from at least the 2nd century AD, and is a rare example of a Buddhist shrine used by Tamils. The temple was maintained by the Cholas after their conquest in the 10th century and inscriptions in Tamil show that it was named after one of the Chola kings, Rajaraja I. It was popularly called Natanar Kovil.

The two major ruins at the site are a stupa and an image house. The image house was redecorated with Chola architectural styles during their reign, including the use of Dravidian mouldings at the base. The most striking feature at the complex is the carved standing Buddha figure.

A new Buddhist temple is being rebuilt near the site, and the resident monk may show you photographs of Sinhalese victims of an LTTE attack in 2000.

The ruins are off Nilaveli Rd, and the best access road is off the A12 to Anuradhapura past Kanniyai.

Mutur

Across Koddiyar Bay from Trinco, the mostly Muslim town of Mutur is an outing off the well-trodden track to the beaches north of town. At the time of research the road from Trinco to Mutur through Kinniyai (not Kanniyai near the hot wells) was closed, so the ferry was the only link between the two towns.

Just west of Mutur, Sri Lanka's largest river, the **Mahaweli Ganga**, which starts near Adam's Peak and flows through Kandy, reaches the sea.

Near Mutur a stone at the foot of an **old tree** once announced:

> This is the White Man's Tree, under which Robert Knox, Captain of the ship *Ann* was captured AD 1660. Knox was held captive by the Kandyan king for 19 years. This stone was placed here in 1893.

In fact it was Robert Knox's father (Robert Knox Senior) who was captain of the *Ann* and Robert Knox Junior who spent 19 years in Kandy (see Books in the Facts for the Visitor chapter). The stone has disappeared, but elderly people in Mutur can direct you to 'Knox tree'.

Two ferries accommodating 100-plus passengers, one a 24-year-old rust-bucket and the other a year 2000 model, run between Trinco and Mutur, departing from Trinco at 7.45am, 10.45am and 2.30pm (Rs 32). The last ferry returns from Mutur at 5pm.

UPPUVELI & NILAVELI

☎ 026

The wide, fine-white-sand beaches and turquoise-coloured waters of Sri Lanka's east coast are arguably at their best here. The beaches stretch uninterrupted towards the horizon and the hotel development hasn't (yet) made it onto the sand, but there are enough guesthouses and hotels to offer a range of accommodation.

Heading north from Trincomalee, the road cuts through marshes to Uppuveli and on to Nilaveli. The beach stretches 6km to Uppuveli, continues to Nilaveli village, 15km north of Trincomalee, and halts at a lagoon mouth about 4km further north. Beware of the currents near the lagoon mouth and all along the beach. It may be too dangerous to swim during December and January.

Diving & Snorkelling

A couple of places on this stretch of coast will take you to **Pigeon Island**, not far north of the Nilaveli Beach Hotel, to snorkel for coral and fish. Nilaveli Beach Hotel charges Rs 550 to drop up to two guests at the island. French Garden Pragash Guest House will take up to six passengers in a boat for Rs 1600 for the day. It hires snorkelling equipment for Rs 150 per day.

Nilaveli Beach Hotel has a diving centre in the season (from about May to September) where you can organise dives. See the boxed text 'Responsible Diving & Snorkelling' under Hikkaduwa in the West Coast chapter for some advice.

Places to Stay & Eat

When you visit Uppuveli and Nilaveli there will probably be twice as many places as those mentioned here – things are moving fast. The following places are listed in order from south to north. They are all signposted from the main road and all serve food.

Uppuveli The 57-room **Hotel New Sea Lord** *(☎ 222 2396; 3rd Mile Post; rooms from Rs 850, with air-con Rs 2200)* has started to reopen (no nets). The older rooms are cheaper and closer to the beach; the newer rooms have air-con. Newer standard rooms (including triples) cost Rs 1320.

Anton Tourist Guest House *(☎ 222 1705; rooms Rs 300)*, run by the French Garden Pragash Guest House owner's brother, has basic rooms in a garden setting. They're back from the beach, but are pretty good value.

French Garden Pragash Guest House *(☎ 222 1705; rooms Rs 400-600)* is a laid-back, friendly spot with a great position right on the beach. The rooms are basic, but clean enough. Beach-front rooms are at the upper end of the price range; add Rs 1000 for the air-con room. This is probably the only place in Sri Lanka that charges Sri Lankans a higher rate than foreigners (see the boxed text 'Reversing the Rates').

Nema Beach House *(☎ 222 7613; rooms with breakfast Rs 2200)* has four sunny rooms close to the road.

Lily Motel *(☎ 222 7422; singles/doubles Rs 250/400, with bathroom Rs 350/500)* is probably the best-value budget place in the area. It's reopened after 18 years with basic rooms in a large house. Although it's on the inland side of the road, the front garden is filled with hibiscus trees, making this a haven away from the beach. Rates include breakfast, and other meals are cheap (mains Rs 125 to 150).

Golden Beach Cottages *(☎ 222 2334; rooms Rs 500)* has simple, straightforward rooms alongside a sandy front garden and flower beds. Food is available on order.

Hotel Club Oceanic *(☎ 222 2307, fax 222 7532; Sampaltive Post; singles/doubles half board US$30/45)*, about 3km north of Trinco, has been transformed from a tired-looking resort hotel to a swish upmarket place with standard and superior rooms as well as luxury chalets. There's a pool and all the usual top-end touches.

Nilaveli A couple of hundred metres before Nilaveli village, **Hotel Coral Bay** *(☎ 223 2272, fax 223 2202; 389 Fishermans Lane; singles/doubles Rs 825/1650, with air-con Rs 1100/2200)* has 10 rooms with hot water and beach views from their front verandas. The owners are planning a swimming pool.

Hotel Sea Yard *(10th Mile Post; rooms Rs 770)* has pleasant, clean rooms set around a garden and is close to the beach. A family room has two bedrooms, a kitchen and bathroom.

Reversing the Rates

You've seen the price lists at entrances to Sri Lanka's most famous attractions: Foreigners Rs 575, Locals Rs 25. What's not so obvious to visitors is the dual-pricing system in place for foreigners and Sri Lankans at resort hotels. Sri Lankans generally pay about half the rate charged to foreigners.

There's one guesthouse owner who has reversed this practice. Raj at French Garden Pragash Guest House in Uppuveli has gained national publicity over his decision to charge his fellow Sri Lankans at least Rs 150 more for a room. Raj's logic is simple: foreigners continued to patronise his guesthouse throughout the ethnic conflict, so they should be rewarded for their commitment to Sri Lanka (and his business).

Sinhalese Sri Lankans rarely ventured to Trinco or its beaches over the past 20 years, because of the perceived danger of visiting the area. That all changed in 2002, when an estimated 10,000 people descended on Nilaveli and Uppuveli for the Wesak long weekend. The guesthouses overflowed, local residents let out their rooms and slept on the floor, and other visitors stayed on the beach. And those who could find accommodation at Raj's guesthouse paid more for the privilege than foreign guests.

Shahira Hotel *(☎ 223 2224; rooms Rs 880)* has reopened, boasting spotless rooms with individual colour schemes around a garden. There's a bar (Lion lager Rs 110), TV, indoor games and, coming soon, a small swimming pool.

H & U *(☎ 222 6254, 0777 54390; 11th Mile Post,.1 Beach Rd; rooms Rs 550)*, on the road to the Nilaveli Beach Hotel, is a backpacker-friendly place. Its big, basic rooms accommodate up to four people at a fixed room rate. You can access the Internet (Rs 10 per minute), and the owner has big plans for a TV, reception and sitting area. Candlelit barbecues (Rs 350) can be organised.

Hotel Nilaveli Garden Inn *(☎/fax 223 2228; e viptours@lankacom.net; rooms from Rs 990, with air-con Rs 1650)*, next to Nilaveli Beach Hotel but back from the beach, has big new rooms with bright bathrooms for Rs 1320. The older rooms are fine too.

Nilaveli Beach Hotel *(☎ 223 2295-6; ⓔ tangerinetours@eureka.lk; singles/doubles from US$32/35, with air-con from US39/42)*, 18km from Trinco, stayed open throughout the war. The resort-style hotel is friendly and well run, and has an excellent position on the beach and a swimming pool. There is a range of rooms with different views, including three suites with hot water, TV and minibar. The food is good, with buffets available (US$7/8/9 for breakfast/lunch/dinner).

Getting There & Away

A private bus (more like a van) runs from Trincomalee to Nilaveli (via Uppuveli) every 30 minutes (Rs 15). The guesthouses near the Nilaveli Beach Hotel are closer to Erakkandy than Nilaveli, so you're better off catching a bus to this village. A three-wheeler from Trinco to Uppuveli costs Rs 100; to Nilaveli it's about Rs 250.

KALKUDAH & PASSEKUDAH

☎ 065

The long, wide, fine-white-sand beaches around Kalkudah Bay stretch south for kilometres, while the curved Passekudah Bay is more compact but still impressively vast. The Kalkudah headland juts out to separate Kalkudah beach from the sweep of Passekudah, where the reef turns the bay into a calm, blue, shallow swimming area.

Situated about 30km north of Batticaloa, Kalkudah and Passekudah were once the most developed tourist areas on the east coast. However, the war has devastated tourist infrastructure, and the early signs are that it will be slower to recover than Nilaveli and Uppuveli.

Places to Stay & Eat

At the time of research there were just a couple of guesthouses operating in the area. Neither had mosquito nets.

Simla Inn *(☎ 225 7184; rooms with shared bathroom Rs 400)* is the longest-running guesthouse in this area and the only one in Kalkudah at the time of research (see the boxed text 'Simla Survivors'). It's nothing flash, but the four rooms and bathrooms are clean, and the stay will give you a taste of village life. Victoria makes her curries with vegetables fresh from the lush garden. Simla Inn is on the road to Kalkudah, just after the turn-off to Passekudah.

Ethan Inn *(☎ 222 6317, 0777 434021; singles/doubles Rs 500/600)* is a new, bare place near the Passekudah shops and post box. It has three rooms and a veranda offers some shade. Meals are available (Rs 50 for rice and curry and Rs 100 for fried rice).

Ask at **Akshana Restaurant** *(☎ 225 7484; rooms Rs 300)*, one of the shops in Kalkudah, about the room in the family home.

Getting There & Away

Kalkudah and Passekudah are about 5km from Valachchenai, the closest train station. Two daily trains run from Valachchenai to Colombo via Polonnaruwa, Gal Oya and Maho, departing Valachchenai at 7.40am (arriving in Colombo Fort at 4.45pm) and 7.15pm (arriving at 5.15am in Colombo). The fare to Colombo is Rs 83/206/390 in 3rd class/2nd class/sleeper.

Buses from Valachchenai and Batticaloa run to Kalkudah, though only every few hours, and you can also get a three-wheeler at Valachchenai.

BATTICALOA

☎ 065

The east coast is indented with many lagoons and Batticaloa (Batti to its friends) is almost surrounded by one of the largest – you must cross bridges and causeways to enter or leave the town. In 1602 Batti became the first Dutch foothold on the island. It's the second-biggest town on the east coast and was an LTTE stronghold until the government retook it in 1991. So secure did the Tigers feel here at one time that they even started building their own monuments, one of which has now been turned into a clock tower.

Orientation & Information

There are three main parts to Batti. On the 'mainland' you find the suburb of Kallady and two of the good guesthouses; if you're coming in to Batti from Kalmunai you'll hit this area first. Crossing the Kallady bridge from east to west takes you to the landmass called Koddamunai, where you'll find the train station and many businesses. Crossing the Koddamunai bridge to the south will bring you to the commercial centre of Batti, where there are banks and the bus station.

The **Bank of Ceylon** is on Covington Rd south of the bus station and the narrow

Simla Survivors

Amid the deserted guesthouses and hotels lining the road to Kalkudah Bay, Simla Inn stands testament to the devotion of one family and the suffering of the local tourist industry. Victoria and Thomas opened Simla Inn in 1978, just months before a devastating cyclone hit the region. They reopened in 1981, two years before the war in the North and East started. But Simla Inn stayed open, and a few foreign tourists trickled into the area. Thomas operated a small *kade* (shop), and Victoria reared chickens and ran a small catering business to supplement the dwindling guesthouse income.

Some of their guests experienced first-hand the impact of the conflict. Thomas and Victoria recall the day of 11 June 1990, when fighting between government forces and the Liberation Tigers of Tamil Eelam (LTTE) next to the house forced their German guests to crouch in a corner for protection. Thomas hid in the outside bathroom, and listened to bullets hit the walls.

Proud Methodists, they say they have prayed for peace every day and now look forward to hosting increasing numbers of tourists. They're patching up the bullet holes and cracks caused by the vibration of artillery fire nearby, and wait for a new generation of visitors to discover the beautiful beaches of Kalkudah and Passekudah.

bridge connecting the two landmasses. The **Hatton National Bank** (with ATM) is on Central Rd, which is the extension of the Koddamunai bridge. There's a **post office agency** on Lloyds Ave near the Hamsha Restaurant, and Internet access at **Riviera Enterprises** *(19 Boundary Rd; open 8.30am-6pm Mon-Sat)*, 150m off Trinco Rd.

Things to See & Do

Batti has an interesting little **Dutch fort**. At the time of research areas around the fort were occupied by the army, but you could walk freely into the fort, through the gate under the 6m-thick walls, and into the *kachcheri* (registrar office). Above the fort gate facing the lagoon, you can make out the date 1682 and the VOC (Verenigde Oostindische Compagnie – Dutch East India Company) symbol.

The town is most famous for its **singing fish**. Between April and September a distinct, deep note (described as the type of noise produced by rubbing a moistened finger around the rim of a wine glass) can be heard from the depths of the lagoon. It is strongest on full-moon nights. Theories about its cause range from shoals of catfish to clusters of shellfish.

Places to Stay & Eat

There's not much passable accommodation in Batti, but the following places are good options.

Lake View Inn *(☎ 222 2339; 6B Lloyds Ave; rooms Rs 165, with bathroom Rs 550, singles/doubles with air-con & bathroom Rs 1100/1320)* is the best place in the town. It's across the lagoon from the bus stand and has good sunset views from its rooftop. The restaurant attracts many locals. The tasty curries, excellent *pittu* (steamed rice flour and coconut) and string *hoppers* cost Rs 75; rice and curry is Rs 90.

Subaraj Inn *(☎ 222 5983; 6/1 Lloyds Ave; rooms from Rs 550)* is a popular new place behind the Lake View Inn. It has a TV room, and good food served in an outdoor eating area.

Riviera Resort *(☎ 222 2165; ⓔ riviera@sltnet.lk; New Dutch Bar Rd, Kallady; rooms Rs 600)*, is a peaceful and well-run place in Kallady, on the lagoon about 1.5km from town. As well as the clean and neat doubles, there is a cute single (Rs 400) atop the water tower. There's a tennis court, boat rides and singing-fish tours on the lagoon. Book in advance as this established place attracts embassy and NGO staff. A three-wheeler from town costs Rs 50.

Bridge View Restaurant *(☎ 222 3723; 63/24 New Dutch Bar Rd, Kallady; rooms Rs 660, with air-con Rs 1320)*, just around the corner from the Riviera, doesn't have a view of the Kallady bridge, but does have its own ornamental bridge. It's new and clean, with a garden setting and a restaurant in a round building.

Hamsha Restaurant *(4 Lloyds Ave; mains Rs 60-125)*, next to the Lake View Inn, serves Indian and Chinese food (cooked with sesame oil and soy sauce!), as well as good short eats. Vegetable biryani costs Rs 60; beef or chicken biryani and mixed fried rice cost Rs 100. Pizzas will soon be on the menu.

Getting There & Away

There are CTB buses from Batticaloa to Colombo, the hill country and all over the East and North. There are twice-daily services to Colombo (Rs 95, seven hours), Badulla (Rs 67, 5½ hours), Vavuniya (Rs 77, seven hours) and Trinco. There's one daily trip to Mannar (Rs 105, 9½ hours) and Pottuvil (for Arugam Bay; Rs 36, four hours). There are frequent buses from about 5.30am to 5.30pm to Kalmunai (Rs 16, 1½ hours) and Valachchenai (Rs 12, 1½ hours).

Private agencies running long-haul semi-luxury bus services to the North and South are springing up; look for the sandwich boards on the footpaths opposite the bus station.

In early 2003 the rail line between Valachchenai and Batticaloa reopened. There are two services daily between Colombo Fort and Batticaloa, via Polonnaruwa. The fast passenger service leaves Colombo at 6.15am and arrives about 4pm, and the slower train departs at 8pm and arrives in Batti at about 6am. There are departures from Batti to Colombo at 6.40am and 6.20pm.

AMPARA

☎ 063

One of the East's district capitals, Ampara is a transport hub between the East, the hill country, ancient cities and the South. However, as with Monaragala further south, you don't want to get stuck here.

There are several **banks** on the right-hand side of DS Senanayake Vidiya, the main road into town from the west. The **Commercial Bank** and **Hatton National Bank** have ATMs. There's a post office agency, **Shalika**, on the left-hand side of the main road before the clock tower, close to the bus station.

Places to Stay & Eat

Rest House *(☎ 222 3612; Dutugemunu Rd; rooms Rs 330)* has acceptable rooms if you have to stay. There are also dorm-style rooms sleeping five for Rs 560. Meals are available; rice and curry lunch costs Rs 85. Take the lakeside road north of the bus stop and turn right before the playground.

New Araliya Guest House *(☎ 222 2377; Dewasthana Mawatha; rooms from Rs 1045)* has a pleasant garden setting but disappointingly grubby rooms with air-con. Western breakfast costs Rs 75, and rice and curry lunch or dinner is Rs 135. Turn left into the street after the Rest House to get here.

Getting There & Away

CTB and private buses operate from the bus stop, near the clock tower. There's an air-con intercity bus to Kandy every 45 minutes from 6.15am till 1.30pm (Rs 200, 4½ hours) and normal buses before mid-morning (Rs 98, six hours). Private buses to Colombo leave between 4pm and 8pm (Rs 176, 10 hours) and there are two CTB buses each day. Two buses to Anuradhapura leave in the early morning (Rs 145, eight hours) and one CTB bus travels to Galle (Rs 115).

To get to Pottuvil (for Arugam Bay) take a regular bus to Akkaraipattu (Rs 16). For Batticaloa, go to Kalmunai (Rs 16). CTB has a 7.15am bus to Trincomalee (Rs 145, nine hours) via Polonnaruwa and Habarana.

GAL OYA NATIONAL PARK

The 62,936 hectares of Gal Oya park, to the west of Ampara, is made up of the catchment of the largest tanks in Sri Lanka, the Senanayake Samudra. March to July is the best time to see wildlife. The beloved jumbo is the star attraction – around 150 elephants have been spotted at one time – with the best viewing from 6.30am to 9.30am and 4.30pm to 6pm. The usual way of seeing Gal Oya is to hire a small motor boat around the lake (Rs 500 to 1000), watching the animals and birds on the shore and drifting in close to herds of elephants. Gal Oya doesn't attract many visitors, but this may soon change.

There's a wildlife bungalow beside the Ekgal Aru tank, east of the park. Book through the **Department of Wildlife Conservation** *(☎ 011-269 4241, fax 269 8556; 18 Gregory's Rd, Cinnamon Gardens)*.

Safari Inn Hotel & Restaurant *(☎ 063-224 2147; rooms Rs 500)* has miserable and dirty rooms with bathroom outside, but is building 10 new double rooms with bathroom. It does have a pleasant restaurant setting and bar (rice and curry costs Rs 55). Ask about organising trips into the park.

To enter Gal Oya, you'll need to go to Inginiyagala (23km from Ampara). If you're coming from the south, you can take the turn-off (to Inginiyagala) near the 27km post before you reach Ampara. You may need a 4WD on this route.

MONARAGALA

☎ 055

This small town, also known as Peacock Rock, is a junction point between the hill country, the South and the east coast. Its only real attraction is as the closest major town to Maligawila (see following). Anyone heading to/from Arugam Bay from the South or hill country must pass through here.

There's a **Hatton National Bank** opposite the post office on the Wellawaya side of town. The **Bank of Ceylon** is around 1km from the centre of town on Wellawaya Rd. You can access the Internet at **Lanka Photo** *(36 Main St)*.

Places to Stay & Eat

If you get stuck in Monaragala, there are a handful of places to stay on the main road. They are listed in order from the Wellawaya end of town.

Victory Inn *(☎/fax 227 6100; 65 Wellawaya Rd; singles/doubles Rs 450/600)*, opposite the Rest House, will have the best rooms in town when its new, upstairs extension is complete. Its older rooms are basic but OK; the new rooms have tiled floors (one will have air-con) and balconies to an indoor garden and outside. The new rooms will be pricier. The young owner has a good knowledge of the area; ask him about ruin sites.

Wellassa Inn Rest House *(☎ 227 6815; rooms Rs 550)* has a pleasant garden setting and sitting area. The room with air-con costs Rs 990. This is one of the better places for rice and curry (from Rs 130). It's about 500m from the bus station, in the direction of Wellawaya.

Apart from these places there are a few basic **eateries** near the bus station at the Pottuvil end of town. **New Thaj Hotel** *(42 Pottuvil Rd)* has tasty rice and curry for Rs 40.

Getting There & Away

Buses running to Arugam Bay (via Pottuvil) leave Monaragala at 9.30am, 11.15am and 12.30pm (Rs 40, three hours). There are regular buses to Ampara (Rs 50, 3½ hours) between 6.30am and 3.30pm. Colombo-bound intercity buses run every 45 minutes until late (Rs 220, seven hours) and there's an hourly air-con intercity bus to Matara (Rs 150, 4½ hours). To get to the hill country, take a bus to Wellawaya (Rs 22, 45 minutes), a transport hub. Heading south, there are buses to Kataragama at 1.15pm and 4pm.

MALIGAWILA

At Maligawila, about 15km south of Monaragala via Okkampitiya, stand two huge, ancient **statues** *(admission by donation)* in a peaceful and shady forest glade. Combined with Buduruwagala, the Maligawila statues make this corner of Sri Lanka fertile ground for monument hunters. One of the statues, an 11m-high Buddha, is reckoned to be the world's largest free-standing Buddha figure. The other, 1km away, is a 10m-high Avalokitesvara. Thought to date from the 6th or early 7th century, and attributed to King Aggabodhi, the statues had lain fallen for centuries before being unearthed in the 1950s, and were raised and restored from 1989 to 1991. The Avalokitesvara had been broken into more than a hundred pieces. Both statues are made of crystalline limestone.

From the car park, it's about a 10-minute walk to the Buddha statue, and about a five-minute walk to the Avalokitesvara. Buses run regularly to/from Monaragala (Rs 15, 1¼ hours).

ARUGAM BAY

☎ 063

Arugam Bay is a tiny fishing village 3km south of the small town of Pottuvil at the remote southern end of the east coast. It has probably the best surf in Sri Lanka, and because of this it has developed into a hang-out for low-budget travellers and, increasingly, mid-range visitors. With much easier access since the cease-fire, it's developing into a hot party spot on the east coast. There's a wide, sweeping beach in front of the village that is good for swimming virtually year-round. South of the surf promontory a long, deserted beach leads down to 'Crocodile Rock', from where wild elephants can quite often be seen.

The best surfing is between April and September and during this 'season' the number of travellers – many of whom are die-hard surfers – visiting the area increases. When the surf season finishes some guesthouses and restaurants shut up shop, and the fishing season starts. At the time of writing, a new fishing village was being built near Crocodile Rock, and fishermen from Arugam Bay were to be relocated there.

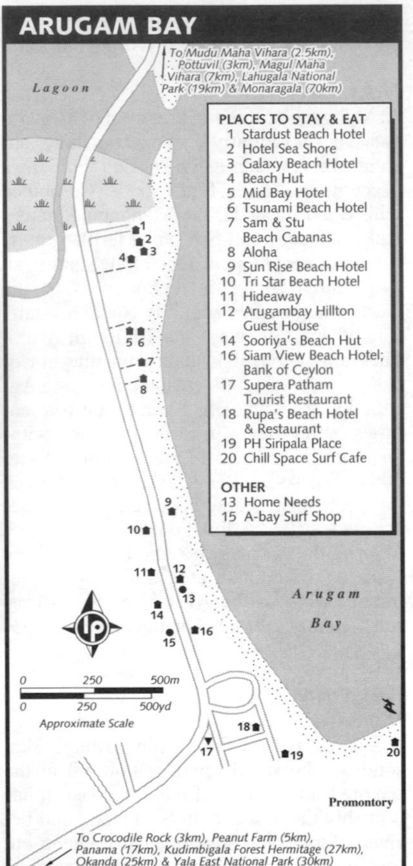

Information

The **Bank of Ceylon** *(open 10am-10pm daily)* has a foreign-exchange office next to the Siam View Beach Hotel. An ATM is planned. There's also a branch on Main St in Pottuvil.

The nearest **post office** is a new pink building on the Arugam Bay side of Pottuvil. During the season there are a couple of communication centres in Arugam Bay. You can use the Internet facilities at Siam View Beach Hotel and Arugambay Hillton (see Places to Stay, later).

Things to See

A walk to **Crocodile Rock** and **Elephant Rock**, about 3km south of Arugam Bay, will give you an appreciation of the extent of the beautiful beaches. This is a popular surfing spot, and in the early morning or evening you may see elephants roaming nearby. You can cycle or take a three-wheeler (Rs 300) part of the way. Take the road to the next village, Pasarichenai, and take the second dirt track in the village (or ask someone).

The ancient ruins of **Mudu Maha Vihara** on the edge of Pottuvil feature a 3m-high standing Buddha statue facing two smaller Bodhisattva figures.

Surfing

Arugam Bay offers consistent surf from April to September, with some good days extending to November. The surf does not produce high-performance waves, but there are good all-round right-breaking waves of up to 1.6m, and it's a good place to learn to surf. With a water temperature of 24°C to 28°C year-round, you don't need a wet suit. The best surf spots are at Pottuvil Point to the north of Arugam Bay, the main promontory south of the bay, Crocodile Rock (3km south of Arugam Bay), and Peanut Farm further south.

A-bay Surf Shop rents boards for Rs 300 per day or Rs 1500 per week.

Organised Tours

See the boxed text 'Restoring the Natural Cycle' for information about the Pottuvil Lagoon ecotour.

Some of the guesthouses in town will organise jeep safaris to Yala East National Park and boat trips for dolphin-spotting. Ask at Arugambay Hillton, Siam View or Tri Star.

Places to Stay

Many of Arugam Bay's guesthouses are very similar, but at the time of research several were planning extensions. Most places have cabanas with varying levels of comfort, as well as rooms. All the spots to the east of the main road have prime views of the beachfront. There are sometimes power cuts, so come prepared with a torch (flashlight).

Places to Stay – Budget

Beach Hut *(☎ 224 8202; cabanas Rs 150, singles/doubles Rs 200/300)* is a popular place for the budget-conscious – the cheapest option is a basic cadjun hut for Rs 60 and the latest addition is a beach-front room with mezzanine-level bed for Rs 450. Some of

Restoring the Natural Cycle

The Pottuvil Lagoon ecotour will give you two hours of calm paddling and an insight into the importance of mangrove ecosystems to the area. Local fishermen drive fibreglass canoes with two passengers through the mangroves, stopping off at the sandbar on the ocean and then at a mangrove nursery. You might see wild elephants, and you'll definitely see lots of bird and animal life.

The tour was set up as part of a mangrove conservation project by the local Hidayapuram Fisheries Cooperative Society and the Sri Lankan NGO Sewa Lanka Foundation. Since the 1990s more than half the mangroves in Pottuvil Lagoon have been destroyed. They were cut back for security reasons and are also under threat from local farmers who want to increase their cultivation area. The destruction of the mangroves affects the fishing potential of the area and local livelihoods. Proceeds from the tour go to the boat driver and the society, which puts the money back into replanting mangrove trees.

The tour costs Rs 1200, including return three-wheeler transport from Arugambay Hillton Guest House and the lagoon, and can be booked at Arugambay Hillton Guest House.

the rooms and cabanas share a bathroom. It's simple, family-run accommodation – and you can't complain about the prices. Guests have free use of bicycles.

Sooriya's Beach Hut *(☎ 224 8232; rooms from Rs 150)* is a good, cheap option. It has no-frills treehouses and rooms – all with shared bathroom – including a family tree house for Rs 400. It's blessed with a long, rambling garden.

Rupa's Beach Hotel & Restaurant *(☎ 224 8258; singles/doubles with shared bathroom Rs 250/350)* has ordinary huts but is building bigger and better rooms. These will cost Rs 1000.

PH Siripala Place *(☎ 224 8251; rooms & cabanas with shared bathroom Rs 350-500)* is a friendly family place. There are four rooms and three cabanas.

Sun Rise Beach Hotel *(☎ 224 8200; singles/doubles Rs 330/440)* has five basic but slightly small rooms. There's a beachside restaurant in the season.

Arugambay Hillton Guest House *(☎/fax 224 8189; ⓔ raheemhillton@yahoo.com; rooms Rs 400-700)* has a friendly owner, rooms around a garden and unique bed linen: if you want to sleep on hot pink sheets, this is the place! The more expensive rooms have bathrooms and spring mattresses. Five new rooms will feature private balconies and sea views.

There is a clutch of newer places just south of the bridge.

Hotel Sea Shore *(☎ 224 8410; singles/doubles Rs 800/1000, single/family cabana Rs 600/1000)* is a new place with a big sandy front garden, four rooms and two cabanas. The rooms have verandas and sitting areas. The restaurant has good sea views.

Galaxy Beach Hotel *(☎ 224 8415; cabanas with shared bathroom Rs 220, singles/doubles Rs 220/440)*, on the beach, has a barren front garden, but offers good-value rooms with verandas.

Mid Bay Hotel *(☎ 224 8390; ⓔ surfcity@itmin.com; single/double cabanas with shared bathroom Rs 330/550, singles/doubles Rs 550/880)* has simple rooms, large bathrooms, and a lush garden just back from the beach.

Tsunami Beach Hotel *(☎ 224 8038; singles/doubles Rs 400/700, with bathroom Rs 700/1000)*, on the beach, has art adorning its walls and friendly staff.

Sam & Stu Beach Cabanas *(☎ 224 8341; cabanas with shared bathroom from Rs 500)* has roomy cabanas, some with a shared outdoor sunken shower. Watch out for the cactus in front of the beach-front fence.

Aloha *(☎/fax 224 8379; ⓔ johnsonratna@yahoo.co.uk; singles/doubles Rs 400/600, with bathroom Rs 900/1100)* is a new place with a range of spacious cabanas, some of which have garden bathrooms and an upstairs outdoor terrace for sleeping in the sea breeze. No food is served.

Places to Stay – Mid-Range

Siam View Beach Hotel *(☎ 224 8195; ⓔ arugambay@aol.com; rooms Rs 250, with bathroom from Rs 350, suites Rs 5000)* has an assorted mix of rooms and cabanas to suit just about any budget. There's a family room (Rs 2000), a beach house with two rooms sleeping eight people (Rs 2500), and a suite with Jacuzzi and laptop connection being built. Some of the rooms have hot water. Siam View is proud of its environmental policies; among its initiatives is the use of recycled plastic water bottles as sealed unit roof insulation. The restaurant has a good international menu (see Places to Eat, later).

Chill Space Surf Cafe *(doubles Rs 1500 with breakfast)* is a new place with two good-sized rooms in a good location on the surf point. The rooms have direct sea views.

Hideaway *(☎ 224 8259; ⓔ tissara@eureka.lk; doubles/triples Rs 935/1155, double/triple cabanas Rs 1100/1375)* is a character-filled gem. It has four cabanas in the large front garden and five rooms upstairs in a big, old house. All are spacious and clean and have some special little decorative touches.

Stardust Beach Hotel *(☎ 224 8191; ⓔ starcom@lankacom.net; double huts Rs 1650, single/double cabanas Rs 1180/2250, luxury rooms Rs 4100)* is the first place you reach after leaving Pottuvil. It's a Danish-owned, stylish place with a pretty garden. There are two types of cabanas: simple grass huts and fancy cabanas. Also available are single rooms and 'luxury' rooms (if luxury means no hot water or air-con). The food is to die for (see Places to Eat, later).

Tri Star Beach Hotel *(☎ 224 8404; ⓔ tristar3@sltnet.lk; rooms with breakfast Rs 1500)* has smart, clean adjoining rooms in blocks of two. Tri Star is about to replicate the design with 10 upmarket rooms withy air-con, and Arugam Bay's first swimming pool. The new rooms will have all mod cons and a price tag in the thousands of rupees.

Places to Eat

There are several local **eateries** on the main road. A vegetable *rotty* costs Rs 10.

Supera Patham Tourist Restaurant *(mains Rs 50-75)* is a popular local place that's open year-round. It serves rice and curry and fried rice.

Stardust Beach Hotel *(☎ 224 8191; ⓔ starcom@lankacom.net; mains Rs 300-510)* has a mouthwatering menu. The palmyra ice cream gets rave reviews and the Danish-style burger (Rs 425 at lunch, Rs 520 at dinner) or the chicken salad (Rs 420) are a pleasant change from usual guesthouse fare.

Siam View Beach Hotel *(☎ 224 8195; ⓔ arugambay@aol.com; mains Rs 230-375)* has a Thai cook whipping up green curries (Rs 375) and other Thai dishes, and a Chinese chef. Its menu includes a platter of local cheeses (Rs 165), pizza (from Rs 245) and a daily buffet from 11am to 4pm (Rs 365).

Entertainment

Arugam Bay is small so you'll soon get a feel for where the happening party places are. Ask other travellers and cruise along the beach.

Siam View Beach Hotel is one of Arugam Bay's party places: there's a billiard table, Internet facilities, booze, games and nightly videos. Some of Thailand's full-moon parties are being relocated to Siam View.

Arugambay Hillton Guest House has full-moon parties and an easy-going owner so you could even organise your own party.

Getting There & Around

CTB buses to Colombo depart Pottuvil at 6.45am and 5pm daily (Rs 170, 10 hours) and the daily bus to Badulla leaves at 1pm. You can get to Monaragala on either of these buses.

There are two buses daily to Batticaloa, a six-hour trip. More frequent buses run to Akkaraipattu (Rs 18, 1½ hours).

Buses from Pottuvil to Panama leave at 8am, 10am and 1.30pm and will drop you at Arugam Bay for Rs 3. In the other direction, buses leave Panama at 9am, 11am and 2.30pm and pass through Arugam Bay about 15 to 30 minutes later. A three-wheeler one way from Pottuvil to Arugam Bay costs about Rs 50. You can hire a three-wheeler for the day for about Rs 1500.

Home Needs grocery store hires bicycles for Rs 20 per hour or Rs 150 per day. Siam View Hotel rents out quad bikes for Rs 250 per hour.

AROUND ARUGAM BAY

Lahugala National Park

About 16km inland from Pottuvil, tiny Lahugala National Park (1554 hectares) has a superb variety of birdlife and lies on an 'elephant corridor'. The attraction for elephants is the *beru* grass, which grows in the pastures around the three tanks in the park (Lahugala, Kitulana and Sengamuwa). Around August, when surrounding areas are dried out, the elephants start to move in. With the October rains most of them drift back to their regular haunts. You may see elephants from the Monaragala–Pottuvil road, which runs through the park.

At the time of research, there were plans to build a bungalow in the park and develop the road system before opening the park to visitors.

Magul Maha Vihara

East of Lahugala National Park, about 4km from Pottuvil, lies an evocative 'lost-in-the-jungle' ruin called the Magul Maha Vihara *(admission by donation)*. Some people will tell you that this was where King Kavantissa married Viharamahadevi, but this took place at the site of the same name in Yala West (Ruhuna) National Park. The ruins feature a *vatadage* (circular relic house), a dagoba (Buddhist monument) and numerous guardstones and moonstones. A kilometre south of the ruins you can see the remains of a circular structure that may have been an elephant stable. The site was partially restored in the 1960s.

Okanda

The village of Okanda has an important Hindu temple, an isolated Buddhist forest hermitage, and a surf point off a sweeping white beach. The beach attracts surfers from May to August. You may see elephants on the road, particularly in October.

The **Hindu kovil** is a key pick-up point for the Pada Yatra pilgrimage to Kataragama in the annual July/August *perahera* season (see the boxed text 'The Long Walk to Kataragama' in The South chapter). Hundreds of pilgrims gather here to join the 45-day walk from Jaffna and Mullaitivu to Kataragama for the last five-day leg. Up on the rocks behind the temple is a series of small pools in which pilgrims bathe before making offerings. There are excellent views of the coast towards Arugam Bay.

A few kilometres back north towards the town of Panama, the **Kudimbigala forest hermitage** (4700 hectares) was established in the 1st century BC by Buddhist priests. The rock caves and brick buildings are said to date from this period, and an inscription above one of the first rock temples you see on your ascent features a 1st-century BC inscription over the arch. There are 225 known caves in the area. It was abandoned during the war and used by the LTTE as a hide-out, but was resettled by Buddhist monks in 2002. There are plans to develop the hermitage into an international meditation centre. You need to allow about two hours to explore the area and to make it to the top of the rock for spectacular views as far as Kataragama. From the car park, take the path on the right-hand side of the white building.

The road from Arugam Bay to Panama is low in places and may be under water in the wet season. If it's not too bad, you can make the trip in a three-wheeler (Rs 1000 for the round trip or Rs 1500 for the day).

Yala East National Park

This park (18,149 hectares) was rarely visited during the war, but is set to become a less visited alternative to its busy neighbour Yala West (Ruhuna). Yala East is entered at Okanda, about 30km down the coast track south of Arugam Bay via the small town of Panama. It has large numbers of water birds, particularly further south in the Kumana mangrove swamp (200 hectares), where many nest in May and June. Common birds include pelicans, painted storks, spoonbills, white ibis, open billed storks, herons, egrets, Indian darters and little cormorants. One of Sri Lanka's rarest birds, the black-necked stork, may be seen. The other fauna is similar to what you'll spot in Yala West, namely elephants and leopards.

Some guesthouses in Arugam Bay run 4WD safaris. A full-day trip to Kumana will cost Rs 6000 to 7000, or you could organise a two-day camping trip further into the park.

Jaffna & the North

The North holds an appeal that almost 20 years of civil war have failed to extinguish. With significant Hindu, Christian and Buddhist sites, many beautiful *kovils* (Hindu temples), interesting topography, a group of charming islands, and now, some Liberation Tigers of Tamil Eelam (LTTE) war memorials, the North is a fascinating place to spend some time.

Before the troubles escalated with the 1983 riots, about 750,000 people lived on the Jaffna peninsula, with about 118,000 in Jaffna town. Thousands of people fled from fighting during the war, seeking refuge in the Vanni, neighbouring India, or other parts of Sri Lanka, and thousands were killed. When the government reclaimed the peninsula in 1995, people trickled back in, and since the 2002 cease-fire, thousands have returned to the North and to the peninsula.

The North is made up of two distinct areas: the low-lying Jaffna peninsula and the islands surrounding it, and the vast Vanni, a flat scrubby area, most of which is under the control of the LTTE. These are joined by a narrow strip of land, Elephant Pass, which has been a military strategic point during the war and a bloody battleground. Although some of the peninsula is inaccessible because it forms High Security Zones occupied only by the military, you can travel relatively freely elsewhere. But be prepared for checkpoints and blocked roads. In the Vanni region, travel is pretty much limited to up and down the A9 Hwy (the land east and west of the A9 Hwy is mined), and on major roads such as those to Mannar.

Most of the year the region is dry, but after the northeastern monsoon, from October to January, the greenery erupts. The Jaffna peninsula is renowned for its rich agriculture – potatoes, chillies, onions – aided by irrigation from limestone wells, and farmers are now returning to commercial volumes of production. The region is also famous for its distinctively tasty mangoes. The shallow lagoons around the peninsula are home to abundant birdlife and it doesn't take much effort to see many different species.

All the national parks in the North are closed and it's not advisable to visit them due to the presence of poachers and other people you wouldn't want to run into. Contact the **Ceylon Tourist Board** (ⓔ *tourinfo@sri.lanka.net)* for the latest details.

Highlights

- Witnessing the rebuilding of Jaffna's bustling bazaars and thriving community
- Attending a punctual *puja* (offerings or prayers) at the Nallur Kandaswamy Kovil
- Cruising across to Nainativu island to walk in the steps of the Buddha and mythical Hindu characters
- Pausing to ponder at the now-silent battlefields of the Vanni

It would be easy to think of the North as a difficult destination, 'another country' a world away from Colombo. In many ways this is true, and the challenges for resettlement and rebuilding are enormous (see the boxed text 'Rebuilding the North & East', later). However, for the astute traveller the hardships are few and the rewards are many. Although there are hardly any places to stay and eat outside Jaffna, the town itself has everything you'll need: banks, plenty of basic guesthouses, restaurants, markets, organised public and private bus networks, and very friendly and helpful hosts.

JAFFNA

☎ 021 • pop 120,000

Once Sri Lanka's 'second' major city and the industrious capital of the North, Jaffna is now much diminished. Held by the government, the LTTE and the Indian Peace Keeping Force (IPKF) since the war began in 1983, it's been a key conflict point, with visible and subtle impacts – the substantial buildings in the streets facing the lagoon sustained heavy damage. The population make-up has also changed: Muslims were driven out by the LTTE in 1990 and now Hindus are an absolute majority, with Christians making up the second-biggest religious community.

But Jaffna is a town on the move. Cut off from the rest of Sri Lanka for years, it's now one of *the* places to visit for Sri Lankans. In

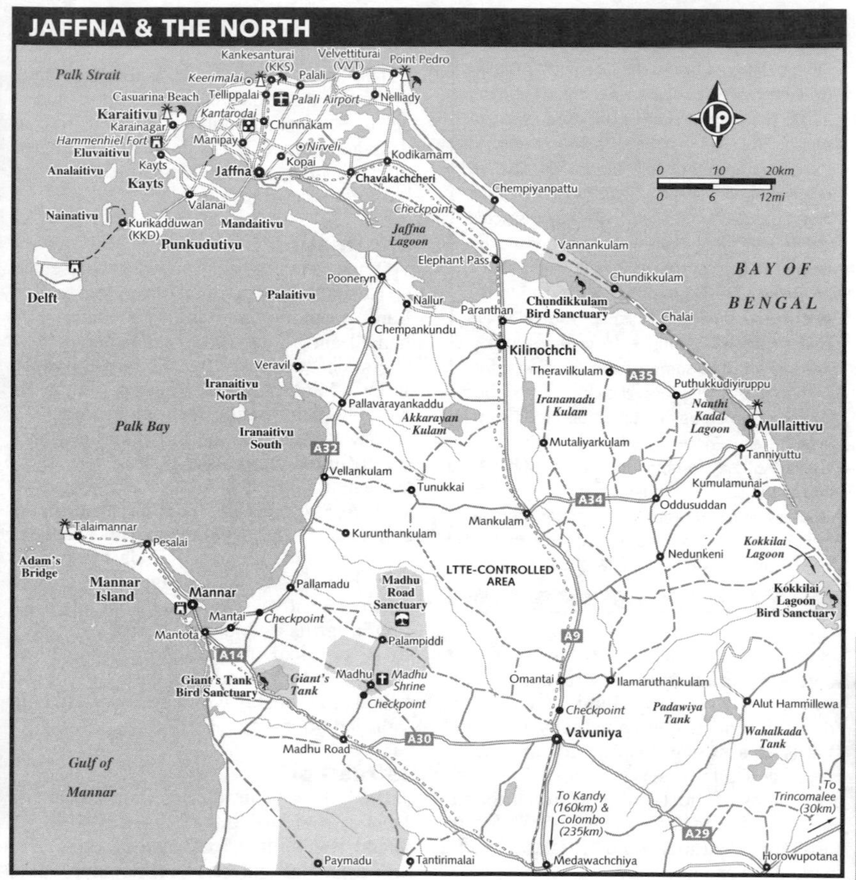

fact, many hope that stronger links between northern Tamils and southern Sinhalese will increase resistance to any potential resumption of the war. The economic blockade has lifted and the local economy is opening up to goods from the South and from India. The bazaar buzzes and Jaffna's leafy residential streets hum with the activities of a community returning to normalcy. New government buildings are appearing and there is a cautious optimism that the city's fortune could be turning around. For the moment though, Jaffna feels like an occupied city: army camps and posts occupied by Sinhalese Sri Lankan Army (SLA) troops are placed at strategic locations and restrict access. The language barrier between Tamil residents and Sinhalese police officers makes for an uneasy relationship. And there are still signs that time has stood still here: old cars in relatively good condition cruise the streets as private vehicles and taxis.

The Portuguese, who arrived in Sri Lanka in the 16th century, took over the Tamil kingdom centred on Jaffna, just as they took over other coastal kingdoms. Jaffna was the longest-lasting Portuguese stronghold on the island, and only surrendered to the Dutch after a bitter three-month siege in 1658. Portuguese and Dutch fortifications are dotted around the peninsula, though most of the forts are occupied by military forces.

In 1795 the British took over Jaffna from the Dutch. The British period of colonial rule

Changing Times

Things changed fast in the North after the introduction of Sri Lanka's cease-fire in February 2002. The pace of change surprised even optimistic Sri Lanka watchers: the A9 opened to civilian traffic and people and goods travelled relatively freely, civilian flights between Jaffna and Colombo multiplied, bans on restricted goods were lifted and checkpoints became inactive. All this meant massive changes to the lives of people living in the North, and to the goods and services available. The signs are that things will continue to change quickly, and, as a result, some of the practical information in this chapter will change – new bus routes will open up and timetables will be updated, train services to Jaffna and Kankesanturai (KKS) may resume, the logistics of the A9 trip to the South will change, and new guesthouses and restaurants will spring up. Double-check information before assuming that all important bus is running at 6.30am.

shaped the future of the city in significant ways. The introduction of Christian mission schools, coupled with a Tamil emphasis on education and career, put many northern Tamils in a strong position for university places and public service jobs. Sinhalese perceptions of the Tamils' disproportionate representation in these areas contributed to anti-Tamil sentiment and legislation, and sparked the ensuing war.

Since the early 1980s – in a period surely worse than any other in its history – Jaffna has been fought over by Tamil guerrillas, SLA troops and the IPKF. The government took Jaffna town from the LTTE in late 1995, and has held it since, though the LTTE continues to have economic and political influence.

Orientation

Jaffna's bustling commercial district is centred on Hospital Rd (where you'll find banks, the bus station, taxis and three-wheelers, and market) and Stanley Rd (airline offices). Guesthouses are concentrated around the pleasant residential areas on Kandy Rd and Temple Rd. Street numbering on Jaffna's roads has changed and not all places have put up new numbers – if the system seems confusing, persist in your search and ask.

The area southeast of the fort was once the focus of Jaffna's civic life, but is now a desolate wreck. People continue to live in damaged homes in this area. At the time of research many of the 'Cross' streets were blocked off at Beach Rd.

Information

Sri Lanka's major banks are well represented on Hospital Rd. The Bank of Ceylon, Seylan Bank, Commercial Bank and Hatton National Bank all have ATMs and change travellers cheques. At the time of research Jaffna's Internet access was slow, but possible, at the **Information Technology Park** *(272 Stanley Rd)* and, just north of the town centre, at **Global Informatics** *(379 Kasturiya Rd)*.

Ceylinco Travels & Tours *(☎ 222 5063; Seylan Bank Bldg, 560 Hospital Rd)* is an agent for SriLankan Airlines and reconfirms tickets.

Street lights are few and Jaffna people have been living with a night-time curfew during recent years, so there's not much action in Jaffna after dark. There's also likely to be political instability for some time. Don't wander around after dark – if you get lost, there probably won't be anyone to help you find your way.

Jaffna Fort

Jaffna's fort, centrally positioned near the lagoon-front beside the causeway to Kayts island, was built in 1680 by the Dutch, over an earlier Portuguese fort (the outer works were not built until 1792). The fort has seen much fighting during the recent unrest, and in 1990 the LTTE, which controlled the rest of Jaffna, forced government forces out after a 107-day siege.

Architecturally, this is probably the best Dutch fort in Asia. The star-shaped fort, built on a grass-covered mound and surrounded by a moat, is 22 hectares in area and grander than the Dutch headquarters fort in Jakarta, Indonesia. Today it is again home to a military garrison and is strictly off-limits. It is believed that the King's House, the onetime residence of the Dutch commander and an excellent example of Dutch architecture of the period, and the 1706 Dutch church, Groote Kerk, located inside the fort, are ruined. On the outer wall there used to be a small British-period house in which the writer Leonard Woolf, Virginia Woolf's husband, lived for some time. It features in his autobiography *Growing*.

Nallur Kandaswamy Kovil

Located about 2km north of the town centre, this is one of Jaffna's best known and most significant Hindu *kovils*, mainly because of its punctual *pujas* (offerings) and spectacular juggernaut festival. Its sacred deity, Murugan the protector (or Skanda), is paraded around the temple during the 25-day festival in July/August. The original Murugan temple was built in the 15th century and destroyed by the Portuguese in the 17th century. The current building was constructed in 1734. The beautifully maintained large and airy complex has shrines to several Hindu deities around the central sanctum, decorative brasswork, larger-than-life murals, pillared halls and colourful *gopurams* (gateways). *Pujas* are held at 4.30am, 5am, 10am, noon, 4pm, 4.30pm and 5pm daily. The temple is closed from 12.15pm to 3pm, and after 5pm.

Men must remove their shirts (as well as shoes) before entering the temple. Prime Minister Ranil Wickremasinghe's visit to the temple during the cease-fire in 2002 was seen as a symbolic step towards intercommunal peace.

Other Places of Worship

Jaffna has countless **Hindu temples** ranging from sprawling complexes with towering *gopurams*, *mandapams* (pillared pavilions) and extensive grounds, to tiny roadside shrines. Most are characterised by vertical red-and-white stripes on the external walls.

Before the war, Christians made up about 12% of Jaffna's population. Today's Christians worship in a number of substantial churches around town. The biggest is the Roman Catholic cathedral, **St Mary's** *(Cathedral Rd)*, which was dedicated in 1982. Like other Catholic churches in town, it contains a statue of the crucified Christ covered in a shroud lying inside a glass case. **St John the Baptist Church** *(Main St)*

Rebuilding the North & East

No-one knows exactly how many land mines and unexploded ordnances (UXOs) are dotted around the North and East, nor where they are all located. One estimate is 1.5 million in the Vanni, and another 500,000 in the rest of the North and East.

Many land mines were laid in strict military textbook style in defensive positions, bordered with low-entanglement barbed wire and fenced off (eg, around the fort in Jaffna). But many others were not, and these are now a threat to the thousands of refugees (known as internally displaced persons – IDPs) returning to their former homes and attempting to resume a 'normal' life. Every month 15 to 25 people in Jaffna and the Vanni sustain UXO- or mine-related injuries. Half of these victims are boys who have found something curious to play with; the other half are mostly men who step on mines when farming. The government's mine action office in Jaffna is surveying, marking and fencing mined areas, and there are teams clearing the mines. In the meantime, the office is working with nongovernmental organisations (NGOs) to raise mine awareness, rehabilitate victims, help victims develop other skills with which they can make their living, or provide credit to establish new enterprises.

United Nations High Commissioner for Refugees (UNHCR) estimates put the number of people displaced during the war at 800,000. Of this number, 100,000 fled to India and 64,000 were living in government camps there at the time of research. Another 100,000 people lived in 'welfare centres' (refugee camps) in Sri Lanka. On the positive side, 12 months into the cease-fire, more than 271,000 had returned to settle. Some returned to find their homes relatively undamaged; others found their homes destroyed, or occupied by other refugees who needed somewhere to live. This has created property disputes difficult to resolve, because titles have been lost or identifying objects have been destroyed.

This is just the start of the long road to recovery. The region needs new public and private buildings, hospitals and schools, roads, telephone and electricity services, and economic opportunities. The government has held donor conferences with the international community seeking pledges, and it will be judged on its delivery of real change to the people of the North and the East.

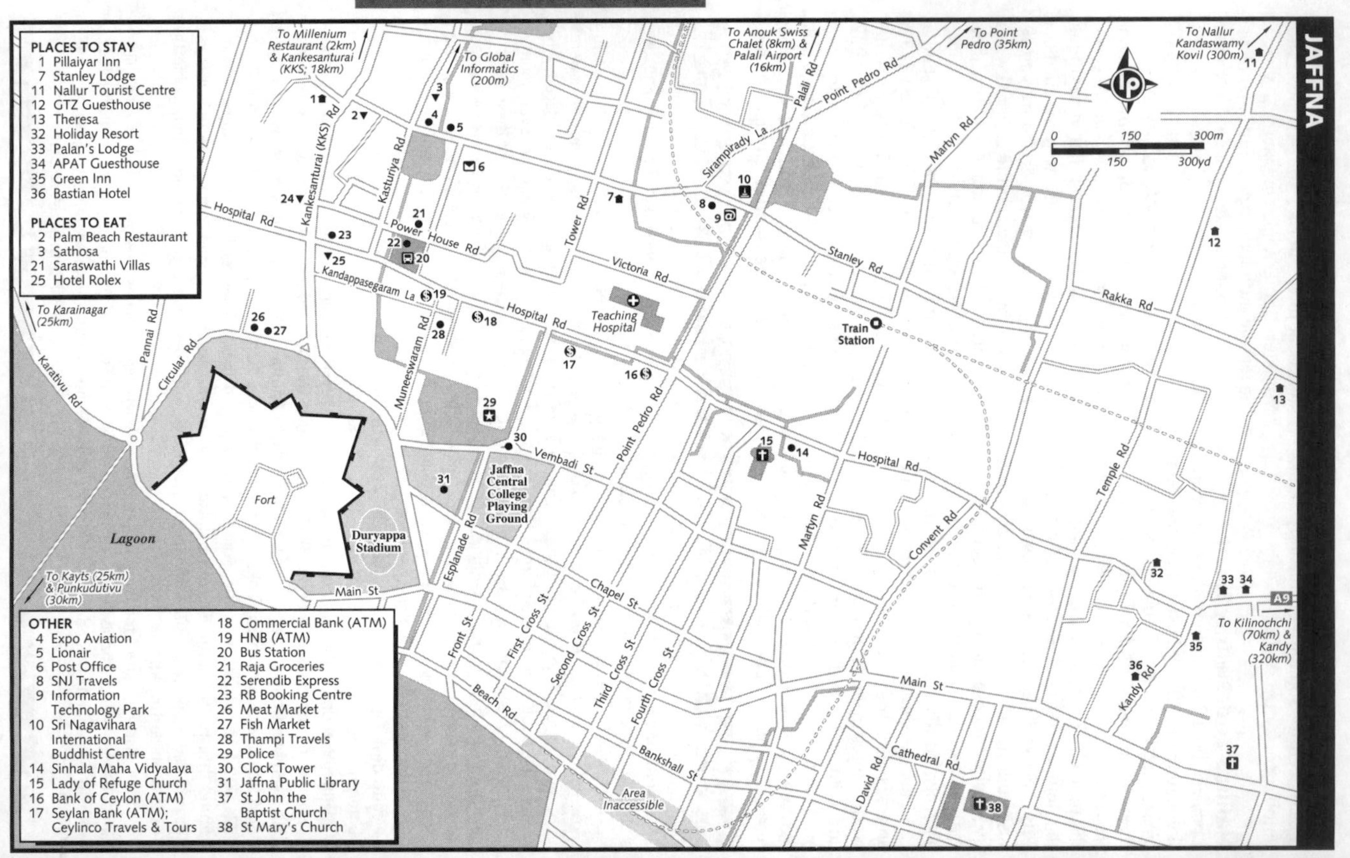
JAFFNA
PLACES TO STAY
1 Pillaiyar Inn
7 Stanley Lodge
11 Nallur Tourist Centre
12 GTZ Guesthouse
13 Theresa
32 Holiday Resort
33 Palan's Lodge
34 APAT Guesthouse
35 Green Inn
36 Bastian Hotel
PLACES TO EAT
2 Palm Beach Restaurant
3 Sathosa
21 Saraswathi Villas
25 Hotel Rolex
OTHER
4 Expo Aviation
5 Lionair
6 Post Office
8 SNJ Travels
9 Information Technology Park
10 Sri Nagavihara International Buddhist Centre
14 Sinhala Maha Vidyalaya
15 Lady of Refuge Church
16 Bank of Ceylon (ATM)
17 Seylan Bank (ATM); Ceylinco Travels & Tours
18 Commercial Bank (ATM)
19 HNB (ATM)
20 Bus Station
21 Raja Groceries
22 Serendib Express
23 RB Booking Centre
26 Meat Market
27 Fish Market
28 Thampi Travels
29 Police
30 Clock Tower
31 Jaffna Public Library
37 St John the Baptist Church
38 St Mary's Church
To Millenium Restaurant (2km) & Kankesanturai (KKS; 18km)
To Global Informatics (200m)
To Anouk Swiss Chalet (8km) & Palali Airport (16km)
To Point Pedro (35km)
To Nallur Kandaswamy Kovil (300m)
To Karainagar (25km)
To Kayts (25km) & Punkudutivu (30km)
To Kilinochchi (70km) & Kandy (320km)
A9
0 150 300m
0 150 300yd
Kankesanturai (KKS) Rd
Kasturiya Rd
Hospital Rd
Power House Rd
Tower Rd
Victoria Rd
Kandappasegaram La
Muneeswaram Rd
Teaching Hospital
Sirampirady La
Palali Rd
Point Pedro Rd
Martyn Rd
Stanley Rd
Rakka Rd
Train Station
Pannai Rd
Circular Rd
Karativu Rd
Fort
Lagoon
Duryappa Stadium
Main St
Vembadi St
Jaffna Central College Playing Ground
Esplanade Rd
Front St
First Cross St
Second Cross St
Third Cross St
Fourth Cross St
Chapel St
Beach Rd
Bankshall St
Area Inaccessible
Convent Rd
Temple Rd
Kandy Rd
David Rd
Cathedral Rd

was the first Anglican church in Sri Lanka, established in the early 19th century. The current building, built later in the 19th century, looks like it could have been plucked out of an English village.

After the government retook Jaffna in 1995, the **Sri Nagavihara International Buddhist Centre** *(Stanley Rd)* was quickly rebuilt. It caters for a community of Tamil Buddhists, most of whom converted from Hinduism, and visitors from the South. The dagoba (Buddhist shrine) contains a relic from Kataragama, placed inside in 2002. A separate building in the front of the grounds contains golden statues of Hindu deities.

Markets

Jaffna's bustling markets and bazaars are worth visiting for the atmosphere as much as for perusing or purchasing what's actually on sale. The peninsula is renowned for its tasty mangoes, and the **fruit and vegetable market** is where you'll be able to buy your fill. The newly built **fish market** and **meat market** on Circular Rd are worth a look. Shops around town sell products made from woven palmyra. Moving up the price range, there are gorgeous saris from India and 22-carat gold jewellery in a strip of Kasturiya Rd.

Organised Tours

Lionair *(1T Stanley Rd)* offers a day trip and a two-day trip from Colombo to Jaffna. The day trip involves flying from Colombo at 7.30am and includes visits to the new library, Nallur Kandaswamy Kovil, and a trip to Chavakachcheri, a place on the peninsula that was hard hit by the recent war. The two-day trip on Saturday and Sunday covers this itinerary plus a trip to Nainativu and Keerimalai. Tours are for a group of at least six people.

Places to Stay

Most of Jaffna's accommodation is pretty basic and clean, and several places have rooms with air-con. Unless otherwise stated, the following places have shared bathrooms and also serve meals.

Places to Stay – Budget

Stanley Lodge *(☎ 222 5371; 218 Stanley Rd; rooms Rs 500)* is centrally located on Stanley Rd. Basic but clean, it's not a bad option in this price range.

Green Inn *(☎ 222 3898, fax 222 2298; 60 Kandy Rd; rooms with/without bathroom Rs 1320/880, with air-con Rs 2420)* has some oddly shaped rooms with plastic partitions, but is neat and tidy. The garden can be used to park the car, and there's a large restaurant.

Bastian Hotel *(☎/fax 222 2605; 37 Kandy Rd; singles/doubles Rs 550/1100, doubles/triples with bathroom & air-con Rs 2200/2750)* is an established guesthouse with a restaurant and bar in a shady setting. Only the rooms with air-con have bathrooms (of varying standards), but the shared bathrooms are basic but OK. There are no mosquito nets.

Holiday Resort *(859/15 St John's Lane; doubles/family room Rs 800/1000)* has two rooms with high ceilings inside a main house, and smaller rooms with a new shared bathroom behind the house. The family room has its own bathroom. With a large back veranda and garden, and rooms with air-con and a children's pool planned, this has the potential to be a pleasant and friendly spot. There's no restaurant, but meals can be organised.

Theresa *(☎ 222 2597; e brendonj@sltnet.lk; 72A Rakka Rd; rooms Rs 1500, family room with bathroom Rs 2000)* has three rooms with air-con above the family home and communications business – and the advantage of on-the-spot Internet access (Rs 8 per minute at night). One of the rooms has a balcony, a plus in this pleasant residential area.

APAT Guesthouse *(☎ 0777 738221; Kandy Rd; singles/doubles Rs 385/825)* has a shady front yard and rooms set around a dining and lounge area.

Palan's Lodge *(☎/fax 222 3248; 71 Kandy Rd; doubles/triples Rs 500/750)* has a range of rooms and bathroom facilities. The bathrooms are spotless and there is a pleasant front garden. There are no mosquito nets or food, but there's a communications centre, Internet and phone in the front office, and bottled water for sale.

Nallur Tourist Centre *(☎ 0777 170072; 431 Temple Rd; doubles/triples/quads Rs 500/750/1000)* is big, bare and basic. Some of the shared bathrooms have squat toilets, and there are no mosquito nets. Meals are available, although they're not prepared here.

GTZ Guesthouse *(☎ 222 2203; 114 Temple Rd; rooms per person Rs 1000)* is spotless, and you may rub shoulders with NGO and aid-agency staff.

The Fall & Rise of the Jaffna Library

Symbolically, one of the first major public buildings to be completed after the 2002 cease-fire was the Jaffna Public Library. The earlier library had been burnt by pro-government mobs (some say forces) after violence-ridden Jaffna District Council elections in July 1981. As an important Tamil cultural centre and historic institution (it was inaugurated in 1841), Jaffna's library was of great significance, and its destruction was interpreted as an act of cultural genocide in some quarters. The world-renowned library held almost 100,000 volumes and was said to have one of the best collections in South Asia. Irreplaceable single-copy books were destroyed, including *Yalpanam Vaipavama*, a history of Jaffna. Manuscripts by the philosopher, artist and author Ananda Kumaraswamy, and intellectual Professor Isaac Thambaiya, were also lost. Memoirs of writers who had significantly contributed to Tamil culture went up in smoke.

The reconstruction was initiated in 1999 by the People's Alliance–led government, which sought donations of books and building materials. The new United National Party–led government continued the Rs 120 million project, and Unesco and the Ford Foundation have donated books to stock the shelves. Architects kept true to the Mughal-style design of the previous building, constructed in 1950, but the new building will modernise with the electronic age.

At the time of writing, the library was still waiting to be officially opened because of division among Tamil political groups.

Places to Stay – Mid-Range & Top End

Pillaiyar Inn *(☎/fax 222 2829; 31 Manipay Rd; rooms US$22, with bathroom & air-con US$33)*, behind Pillaiar Stores, has six rooms in a small building, and there is a three-storey building being developed behind. It's a pleasant spot with landscaped gardens and excellent views from the rooftop. However, some of the rooms in the front building are divided by less-than-full-length partitions and there's a dual-pricing policy here (Sri Lankans pay about half-price).

Anouk Swiss Chalet *(☎ 0777 733317; Palali Rd; rooms with air-con & breakfast Rs 5400)*, a charming traditional Jaffna home 9km from town, is popular with diplomats and expats. The four rooms with air-con are set around an inner courtyard and sitting area (complete with a length of rail from the Jaffna–Vavuniya track now serving as a pylon) and have large open-air bathrooms. Three of the rooms have a spacious dressing area. Good-quality Western and Sri Lankan meals are available for guests ordering in advance; rice and curry costs from Rs 250.

Places to Eat

Hotel Rolex *(340 Hospital Rd; mains Rs 60-100)* is a busy local eating house serving a range of food for breakfast, lunch and dinner. Short eats cost from Rs 6, while chicken biryani is Rs 100.

Saraswathi Villas *(195 KKS Rd; mains Rs 35-50)* serves typical vegetarian Tamil food: short eats, *dosa* (wafer-like pancakes), *pittu* (steamed rice flour and coconut), and rice and curry. Takeaway lunch packets for Rs 35 are also available.

Millennium Restaurant *(76/60 Ramanathan Rd; mains Rs 45-135)*, about 2km from the centre of town off KKS Rd, is a local drinking spot that has a landscaped garden with a heavy emphasis on concrete. It's not the most salubrious place, but it's functional. Lion lager costs Rs 95 and Carlsberg is Rs 115.

Palm Beach Restaurant *(☎ 0777 153889; 49 Stanley Rd; mains Rs 100-150)* is one of Jaffna's best-looking restaurants. It serves North and South Indian food, including tandoori, *dosa* and *puri* (deep-fried dough puffs), in air-conditioned comfort. Although the Palm Beach's subtitle is 'chicken and pizza restaurant', the pizza hasn't yet made it into the repertoire and chicken is not always available.

For self caterers, the national government supermarket, **Sathosa**, *(583 Kasturiya Rd)* is open Monday to Friday.

Getting There & Away

Air Three domestic airlines fly between Colombo and Jaffna and each has at least one flight daily from Jaffna back to Colombo (early morning, mid-afternoon or evening).

Lionair also offers day and two-day trips for groups from Colombo (see Organised Tours, earlier).

Expo Aviation (☎/fax 222 3891, 0777 730555, ⓔ jaffna@expoavi.com) 1E Stanley Rd. Expo has one flight daily except Thursday and two flights on Monday and Saturday for Rs 2425/4550 one way/return.

Lionair (☎ 222 3891, ⓔ lionairsales@sierra.lk) 1T Stanley Rd. The biggest and most respected airline serving Jaffna has three flights daily except Wednesday for Rs 4000/6950 one way/return. **Thampi Travels** (☎ 222 2040) Kandappasegaram Lane, is Lionair's busy handling agent. It's open daily.

Serendib Express (☎ 222 3916, 0777 801038) 13 Power House Rd. Serendib has two flights daily, except Tuesday and Thursday (one flight) and Friday (no flight), for Rs 2425/4550 one way/return.

When flying out of Jaffna, passengers meet at the **Sinhala Maha Vidyalaya** grounds (a block of land next to the Lady of Refuge Church) at least 2½ hours before departure. Here, your bags will be searched by Sri Lankan police before you board the airline bus for the 17km drive to Palali Airport. There are further bag and body searches at Palali. Until 2002 Palali was a military airport, so facilities are basic. There is nowhere to buy food or drinks and nonpassengers are not allowed into the airport.

Bus There are several private buses from Jaffna to Colombo daily (see the boxed text 'Up & Down the A9'), and an extensive Central Transport Board (CTB) and private bus network around the peninsula. Around the peninsula, no bus trip will cost you more than Rs 20, and services run from about 6.30am to 7pm. Some services are infrequent; check before you head out so you don't get stranded.

Some of the businesses that run the Rs 1000 van or bus services to Colombo also send buses to towns in the East. Ask at **RB Booking Centre** *(15 Grand Bazaar)*.

Taxi It should be easy to hire a taxi for three hours for about Rs 1000, or it will cost about Rs 3000 for a full-day tour of the peninsula of up to 75km. Private travel agencies will also charge about Rs 3000 for a full-day trip.

Getting Around

To/From the Airport Palali Airport is about 17km north of Jaffna near KKS. At the time of research, this was in a High Security Zone, so the domestic airlines provided transport to and from the airport (see Getting There & Away earlier for information on this process).

Taxis & Three-Wheelers Taxis and three-wheelers queue neatly in the centre of Hospital Rd. A three-wheeler from Hospital Rd in the centre of town to the guesthouses near Kandy Rd will cost about Rs 70.

AROUND JAFFNA

The Jaffna peninsula is almost an island; only the narrow neck of land occupied by **Chundikkulam Bird Sanctuary** (currently inaccessible), and the causeway known as **Elephant Pass** (elephants once waded across the shallow lagoon, but it's now more famously known as a battleground), connect it to the rest of Sri Lanka. The terrain is low lying, and much of it is covered by shallow lagoons; there are a number of islands off the western side of the Jaffna peninsula.

The places of interest on the peninsula could all be visited from Jaffna in one day if you have your own transport. The islands (except Delft), though, would require another day.

Staying Safe

The North may be changing fast, but there are still several precautions you should take when travelling here.

With hundreds of thousands of land mines and tonnes of unexploded ordnance around the peninsula, be careful where you put your precious feet. Walk only on roads or very well-trodden paths. Do not wander off roads or on deserted beaches. If you see something suspicious-looking on the side of the road, do not touch it.

Peace on the peninsula has been uneasy in some quarters, most notably between the Liberation Tigers of Tamil Eelam (LTTE) and the Eelam People's Democratic Party (EPDP). Avoid political gatherings or large meetings; situations can turn dangerous dramatically and instantly.

Up & Down the A9

When the A9 Hwy from Vavuniya to Jaffna reopened to traffic in April 2002 after 12 years, hundreds of vehicles made the trip each day. Goods banned during the war because of their possible use to the LTTE flooded through the Vanni to the Jaffna peninsula. Tamils returned to meet relatives and see the land they hadn't seen for years, and Sinhalese visited what had almost become a different country.

Because the A9 passes through LTTE-controlled territory, there are no CTB buses plying this route. You can take a CTB or private bus to Omantai, the southern Forward Defence Line (FDL), pass through the LTTE and army checkpoints, then board a 'LTTE bus' to travel to the northern FDL, go through more LTTE and army checkpoints, and take another bus from here to Jaffna town. The fastest and easiest alternative is to book a seat in a bus or van that leaves from one of the many businesses on Galle Rd in Wellawatta, Colombo (see Bus under Getting There & Away in the Colombo chapter). These vehicles make the trip every day except Sunday, when the FDLs are closed, and the drivers know the ins and outs of the registration procedures at both ends.

The FDLs were set up under the cease-fire agreement, but the specifics of the process seem to change by the day. At the time of research, there was no fee to enter or leave LTTE territory, though the LTTE imposed a 'duty' of 20% to 30% on goods being taken to the Vanni or peninsula for sale. Vehicles, people and bags are searched, though if you're not Sri Lankan the searches by both the army and LTTE may not be as rigorous. The trip could take anything from 10 to 16 hours, depending on the length of queues at checkpoints, how many times you stop for food or tea, and whether you get a flat tyre! Travelling in a smaller vehicle with fewer passengers and luggage may speed up the trip, but you also feel the bumps more.

From Jaffna, vehicles leave in the morning so there's plenty of time to cross the FDLs. **SNJ Travels** *(☎ 222 2837; 240 Stanley Rd)* has an air-con coach from Jaffna three times a week. **RB Booking Centre** *(15 Grand Bazaar)* has two services from Jaffna to Colombo daily (except Sunday). A bus leaves at 6.30am and a van departs at 10.30am. **Raja Groceries** *(153 Power House Rd)* has a van leaving in the morning – look for the green-coloured building opposite the bus station. These services cost Rs 1000.

With the Asian Development Bank funding rebuilding of the highway, and successful peace talks, travel up and down the A9 is likely to become much smoother – in more ways than one.

LTTE Sites

With the cease-fire in 2002, some of the significant LTTE sites on the peninsula have taken on a new lease of life. There are several sites easily accessible from Jaffna, and these could be visited in a half-day trip or as part of a day trip around the peninsula.

Kopai Cemetery The **Mavira Thuyilim Illam** (Martyrs' Sleeping House) at Kopai, about 8km northeast of Jaffna, is a sobering reminder of the enormous loss of life in the war. With 2350 graves in numbered plots, this is the largest LTTE cemetery on the peninsula. It was bombed in 1995 when government forces retook the peninsula and graves are now being rebuilt, along with a large entrance gate and central podium. The graves include that of Malathi, the first female LTTE cadre to die in the conflict in a confrontation with the IPKF at Kopai on 10 October 1987. Headstones state the names of the cadres, their home villages, and the date of their death.

Nelliady Shrine About 26km northeast of Jaffna, a golden statue of Captain Miller commemorates the first Black Tiger (suicide bombing) attack at Nelliady. Hero or villain, Captain Miller died, with at least 200 SLA soldiers, on 5 July 1987 when he drove an explosives-laden truck into the Nelliady school, which was an army camp at the time. The shrine, about 200m along the road heading north from the town's junction, was rebuilt in 2002.

Valvedditturai Before the war Valvedditturai (VVT), 30km from Jaffna on the north coast, had a reputation as a wealthy village because of its income from smuggling operations across the Palk Strait. These days it's better known as the birthplace and home town of LTTE leader Vellupillai Prabhakaran, and you can visit the **Prabhakaran family house**. A modest painted sign on the front fence declares Prabhakaran as 'The President of Tamil Eelam'. The green, five-roomed house has escaped major damage, apart from a damaged tile roof. The graffiti in Tamil and English by countless praising visitors makes for an interesting read, and reminds one of Jim Morrison's grave!

Locals can also take you to the *kovil* that the Prabhakaran family attended. This Shiva temple shows evidence of the town's wealth: temple juggernauts are mounted on the back of mechanical car bodies, including a Commer! The temple is just west of the centre of VVT, on the KKS Rd, and Prabhakaran's family house is about 500m further west. Ask for directions.

Beaches

Much of the peninsula's coastline has served as a battleground. Deserted beaches may contain land mines or UXOs; do not walk on the beaches. The following recommended beaches are exceptions.

About 2km east of the **Point Pedro** lighthouse and the fishing boats, a white sandy beach gives way to a safe, but deep, swimming spot. Regular visitors say it's a good place to body-surf and meet villagers. There are bunkers on the ridge facing the coast. It takes about one hour to drive here from Jaffna: turn right at the main junction in Point Pedro, before the bus stop, and head under the old Dutch tollgate. Buses to Point Pedro leave Jaffna every 30 minutes.

Palm Beach at KKS, 18km north of Jaffna, was a popular beach before the war, but at the time of research it was still in one of the controversial High Security Zones and was inaccessible.

Springs

Jaffna's famous agricultural produce is fuelled by the water drawn from wells drilled into the limestone shelf that forms the peninsula. **Nirveli spring**, a natural well, can be seen about 2km northeast of Kopai. The water is fresh for the first 15m or so, but salt for the rest of its 45m depth. It's only worth a visit if you happen to be driving past.

The **Keerimalai spring**, on the coast near KKS, is said to contain healing waters. These waters cured a horse-faced princess of her equine characteristics. At the time of research, Keerimalai spring was in a High Security Zone, but visitors were allowed access after searches and with an armed army escort.

Islands

Kayts, Karaitivu and Punkudutivu are joined to the mainland by causeways over the shallow waters around the peninsula. Buses run to all these islands from Jaffna. These flat, sparsely populated islands are great places to observe local life and explore. One of the most popular trips is to take a bus to Kurikadduwan (KKD) on Punkudutivu, catch the ferry across to Nainativu, then return via the same route.

Karaitivu Also known as Karainagar, after its main town, this island has a beach on its northern shore that is popular with locals. However, the most appealing thing about **Casuarina Beach** are the casuarina trees: it is littered with rubbish and the water is shallow. There are ferries from Karainagar jetty, on the southern tip of the island, to Kayts at 8.15am, noon, 2.45pm and 4.30pm.

Hammenhiel Fort Between the islands of Kayts and Karaitivu stands the island fort of Hammenhiel, now a navy camp. The name means 'heel-of-the-ham' – the Dutch thought that Sri Lanka was shaped like a ham. The fort used to be accessible by boat from Kayts.

Kayts The largest of the islands, Kayts is dotted with Roman Catholic shrines and large churches. From the town of Kayts on the northern tip, you can see Hammenhiel fort. There are buses from Jaffna to Kayts town every two hours. Ferries from Kayts to Karainagar on Karaitivu leave at 8.30am, 1pm, 3pm and 5.15pm.

Punkudutivu The island of Punkudutivu hosts the main ferry port, Kurikadduwan (KKD), between the islands of Nainativu and Delft. The bus that crosses the island will probably stop at a *kovil* en route, allowing the priest to board and distribute sacred ash in exchange for small donations. Buses from Jaffna depart for KKD approximately every 1½ hours. Ferries from KKD leave for Nainativu (Rs 10, 20 minutes) at 9am, 10am,

11.30am, 1.30pm, 3.30pm, 4.30pm and 6pm, or for Delft (Rs 20, one hour) at 10.30am and 3.30pm.

Nainativu This island, also referred to as Nagadipa, attracts both Buddhist and Hindu pilgrims and has strong links with *naga* (serpent deity) figures. After the A9 reopened in 2002, Nainativu was flooded with thousands of Sinhalese tourists visiting the site where the Buddha is believed to have set foot.

Nagadipa temple is built on one of the sites the Buddha visited during his second trip to Sri Lanka. It is said that he came here to prevent war breaking out between a *naga* king and his nephew over the ownership of a chair studded with gems. The oldest temple currently on the site, it was built in the 1930s. There has been a long Buddhist presence on this island.

The large, airy complex of **Naga Pooshani Amman Kovil** is dedicated to the *naga* goddess, Meenakshi, the wife of Shiva. Women trying to conceive come seeking blessings, then bring their babies to the temple to fulfil their vows. Several other Hindu deities are represented, and the temple is exquisitely decorated with bronze and silver decorative metalwork. Men must remove their shirts before entering.

The temple is associated with a story about a dispute between a serpent and vulture over the serpent's offerings to the temple. A passing merchant gave up his wealth to resolve the dispute, only to return home to find his house full of treasures. Two stones on the north side of the island are believed to represent the serpent and vulture. The annual 18-day festival is held from 1 to 18 June and culminates with the temple car parade, the water-cutting ceremony, and the parading of the temple deity in a boat on the waters off the island.

Ferries from Nainativu's jetty leave for KKD (20 minutes) at 7.30am, 8.45am, 10am, 12.30pm, 2.30pm, 3.30pm and 5.30pm.

Delft Named after the Dutch ceramics town, Delft is 10km off Punkudutivu and accessible only by ferry from KKD. The island bears traces of the Portuguese and Dutch eras (such as the Dutch garrison-captain's country house with a stone pigeoncote) and is known for its bleak, windswept beauty.

The small **Dutch fort** is a short walk from the ferry dock. Behind that is a beach with many exquisite shells, but don't be tempted to souvenir them. On the island are hundreds of walls which, like the Dutch fort, are made of huge, beautiful chunks of the brain and fan coral from which the island is composed. The island is also known for the locally bred Delft ponies, descended from Dutch mounts.

Ferries from KKD leave for Delft (one hour) at 10.30am and 3.30pm, and from Delft to KKD at 7am and 1.30pm.

Dhurkai Amman Kovil

This Hindu temple at Tellippalai, about 4km south of KKS, is also known as Sri Durga Devi temple, and is popular with women who come to worship the goddess on Tuesday. It's a vast complex, with a central shrine area surrounded by a veranda, pillared halls and other shrines. *Pujas* are performed at 7.30am, 11.30am and 4.30pm. In August the temple hosts a 12-day festival. Men must remove their shirts before entering.

Kantarodai Ruins

At Kantarodai, about 3km west of Chunnakam between Jaffna and KKS, lies **Purana Rajamaha Viharaya**, where nearly 100 miniature dagobas are crammed into a tiny area not much bigger than a hectare. About 20 dagobas are clearly visible, ranging in size from about 1m to 4m in diameter, and of another 20 or so only the foundations remain. Others lie still buried under the site. Discovered in 1916, they are thought to be over 2000 years old.

The site is south off the Chunnakam–Chankanai Rd, but it's hidden behind several twists and turns in the road so ask for directions.

KILINOCHCHI

Serving as the headquarters of the LTTE, Kilinochchi has been under their control for several years. At the time of research the area was noticeably free of a SLA presence: no checkpoints, no armed soldiers at strategic points and no barbed wire. There is an LTTE-run guesthouse in town, the **Vanni Inn**.

If you're travelling by 'public transport' between Colombo and Jaffna, theoretically you could get off the LTTE bus at Kilinochchi. If you're on a private bus, you should ask the booking agent whether you can set down at Kilinochchi.

VAVUNIYA

☎ 024

The town of Vavuniya (pronounced Vow-nya) is best known as the northernmost town maintained under government control during the war. The rail line stops here and it's a hub for bus links between the East, the North, the South, and Mannar in the west. There are several banks on Kandy Rd near the bus station, including a Commercial Bank with an ATM.

Accommodation is limited and it's not really a place to linger. If you have some time to spare, there's a small **archaeological museum** *(admission free; open 8am-5pm Wed-Mon)* featuring Buddhist statues from the 8th to 10th centuries, found in the North. The museum is opposite an English-looking stone church at the Jaffna road junction, north of the bus station. South of the lodges on Kandy Rd, an **IPKF squash court** dated 1988 lies in ruins. **Bazaar St**, in the town centre, is a hive of commercial activity.

Places to Stay & Eat

Unless otherwise stated, the following places have shared bathroom.

Vanni Inn *(☎ 222 1406, fax 223 3074; Gnanavairavar Kovil Lane; rooms Rs 400, doubles/triples with air-con Rs 800/1000)* is the best of an ordinary bunch of places to stay. Located off 2nd Cross St, which runs off Kandy Rd at the Commercial Bank, it's clean enough and has a restaurant.

Two places opposite the bus station are a bit bleaker. **SVS Lodge** *(☎ 222 1535; 149A Kandy Rd; rooms with/without bathroom Rs 350/300)* has passable rooms and OK bathrooms. **Hotel Vashantham** *(☎ 222 2366; 40 Kandy Rd; rooms Rs 385, with air-con Rs 1430)*, south from SVS Lodge, has clean rooms but filthy bathrooms.

Rest House *(☎ 222 2299; Station Rd; singles/ doubles Rs 450/500, with air-con Rs 750/800)*, near the train station, gets more use as a local drinking spot than as a resthouse. Women travellers may not feel safe here. It serves meals, including rice and curry from Rs 55.

There are several local **eateries** on Kandy Rd and on bustling Bazaar St.

Getting There & Away

Bus Private intercity air-con buses leave for Colombo every 30 minutes until 7.30pm (Rs 190, six hours) and every 30 minutes for Kandy until 4pm (Rs 135, four hours). These depart from a stop opposite the CTB bus station on Kandy Rd. CTB buses frequently travel to Omantai (Rs 15, 30 minutes), Mannar (Rs 28, 2½ hours) and Trincomalee (Rs 48, three hours). There are buses in the morning to Kandy (Rs 65, five hours) via Dambulla and Matale, Anuradhapura (Rs 16, two hours) and Colombo (Rs 71, six hours), and two to Batticaloa at 6am and 1.30pm (Rs 77, seven hours) via Polonnaruwa (Rs 56, five hours).

Train The northern line from Colombo to Vavuniya via Anuradhapura has four daily trains that take five to seven hours, depending on the type of service. The quickest is the intercity express, which departs Colombo Fort at 4.30pm daily. Other trains depart at 5.45am, 2pm and 9.30pm. Fares are Rs 52.50/144/251.50 in 3rd/2nd/1st class. To Anuradhapura or Colombo, there are trains departing Vavuniya at 3.15am, 5.45am, 1.15pm and 9.30pm.

MADHU SHRINE

The statue of **Our Lady of Madhu**, about 45km from Mannar, attracts hundreds of thousands of pilgrims for its major festival on 15 August. It has also been a site of conflict during the war, and a place of refuge. The Portuguese-style church stands in peaceful grounds large enough to accommodate the festival visitors.

Construction of the existing building began in 1872, but the statue has been here since 1670, when Catholics at Mantai, near Mannar, faced persecution by the Dutch and travelled to Kandy and around the Vanni before settling at Madhu.

Around this time, Our Lady of Madhu became well known in other parts of Sri Lanka as a protector against snakebite, and earth taken from Madhu was also thought to be a protection. Madhu has been a place of pilgrimage for Christians and also non-Christians ever since. In 1924 the statue was crowned by a papal legate in front of a crowd of 150,000.

During the war, tens of thousands of people sought refuge at the church where the

Open Relief Centre (ORC) was being operated by the government and the UNHCR. In 1999, 37 of these refugees were killed in shelling between the SLA and the LTTE.

During the 2002 cease-fire, an estimated 500,000 people attended the August festival, when the statue is paraded. The statue is also taken out for the festival on 2 July and other festivals are held on 1 January, 2 February, 10 and 15 March, the first Sunday of May, 8 September, first Saturday of October and 8 December.

At the time of research, the Madhu shrine was in an area under LTTE control, so it was necessary to pass through government and LTTE checkpoints and fill in a registration form at the LTTE point.

MANNAR ISLAND

☎ 023

Mannar is a dry, relatively barren island hit hard during the war. With a big population of donkeys, a few African baobab trees, and a former international ferry port just kilometres from India, it sounds an exotic destination, but there's very little to see or do. Interestingly, Mannar district has the largest proportion of Roman Catholics in the country: 40%.

Life on Mannar changed dramatically during the war. Because of its location, it was a major exit and entry point to and from India, and became a major host of refugees. The island's large Muslim population was driven out by the LTTE in 1990, and the land has been mined. There are large welfare centres housing internally displaced persons (IDPs) and refugees are now returning from other parts of the Vanni.

The island has one major town, Mannar, at the southern end, joined to the mainland by a 3km causeway. It isn't particularly interesting, apart from its picturesque **Portuguese/Dutch fort** at the end of the causeway, which became an army camp during the war. A huge **baobab tree** is the town's other point of interest. The island once featured many of these trees, probably introduced centuries ago from Africa by Arab traders.

Mannar town has a **Hatton National Bank** *(Our Lady of Madhu Veethya)* and ATM.

The town also has the only guesthouse on the island. **Star Guest House** *(☎ 223 2177; Moor St; singles/doubles Rs 300/350, with bathroom & air-con Rs 900)* has a range of rooms in a large house. There are only two rooms with bathroom; if you want one of these, book ahead. Women travellers may not feel comfortable with the common bathrooms and toilets.

Talaimannar, near the western end of the island, is about 3km from the pier that was the arrival and departure point of the ferry to Rameswaram, which operated until 1984. A little further west, an abandoned lighthouse marks the start of **Adam's Bridge**, the chain of reefs, sandbanks and islets that almost connects Sri Lanka to India. In the Ramayana, these are the stepping stones that Hanuman, the monkey king, leapt across when following Rawana, the demon king of Lanka, in his bid to rescue Sita. Talaimannar sustained heavy damage during the war and there are uncleared land mines around the town. At the time of research the town was like a ghost town and the navy occupied the tip of the island near the lighthouse.

There are regular CTB buses between Mannar and Talaimannar (Rs 18, one hour) and also Vavuniya (Rs 28, two hours). Four CTB buses head to Colombo daily (Rs 100, seven hours), and there are almost hourly private services from 5.30am to 11pm (Rs 166, six hours). There's one CTB bus to Trincomalee daily (Rs 86, five hours) as well as a couple of private buses in the early morning, and one CTB bus to Batticaloa (Rs 103, eight hours) via Polonnaruwa.

Language

Sinhala and Tamil are both national languages, with English commonly described as a linking language. It's easy to get by in Sri Lanka with English, and the Sri Lankan variety has its own unique characteristics – 'You are having a problem, isn't it, no?'. While English may be widely spoken in the main centres, off the beaten track its spread thins. In any case, even a few words of Sinhala or Tamil will win you smiles. People really appreciate the effort when they meet foreigners willing to greet them in their own language.

Sinhala

Sinhala is somewhat simplified by the use of many *eka* words. Eka is used more or less similarly to the English definite article 'the' and *ekak* is used like 'a' or 'any'. English words for which there is no Sinhala equivalent have often been incorporated into Sinhala with the simple addition of *eka* or *ekak*. So, if you're in search of a telephone it's simply *telifoon ekak* but if it's a specific telephone then you should say *telifoon eka*. Similarly, English definitions of people have been included in Sinhala simply by adding *kenek* – if you hire a car the driver is the *draiwar kenek*.

Two useful little Sinhala words are *da* and *ge*. *Da* turns a statement into a question – thus if *noona* means a lady then *noona-da* means 'This lady?' or 'Is this the lady?'. *Ge* is the Sinhala equivalent of an apostrophe indicating possession; thus 'Tony's book' in Sinhala is *Tony-ge pota*. *Ta* is like the English preposition 'to' – if you want to go 'to the beach' it's *walla-ta*.

As in many other Asian countries, Sri Lankans do not use the multitude of greetings that you find in English ('Hello', 'Good morning', 'How are you', 'Goodbye'). Saying *aayu-bowan* more or less covers them all. Similarly, there isn't really a Sinhala word for 'Thank you'. You could try *stuh-tee* but it's a bit stiff and formal – a simple smile will often suffice. Appreciation of a meal can be expressed by *bohomạ rahay*, which is both a compliment and an expression of appreciation. *Hari shook* translates as 'wonderful', 'terrific' or even 'fine'. A side-to-side wiggle of the head often means 'yes' or 'OK'.

For a more comprehensive guide to the language, pick up a copy of Lonely Planet's *Sinhala phrasebook*.

Forms of Address

In Sinhala there are more than 20 ways to say 'you' depending on the person's age, social status, sex, position and even how well you know them. The best solution is to simply avoid saying 'you'. The word for Mr is *mahaththeya* – 'Mr Jayewardene' is *Jaye-wardene mahaththeya*. The word for 'Mrs' is *noona* and it also comes after the person's name. Any non-Eastern foreigner is defined as white *(sudha)*, so a male foreigner is a *sudha mahaththeya*.

Sinhala is officially written using a cursive script and there are about 50 letters in the alphabet.

Pronunciation

The transliteration system used in this guide to represent the sounds of Sinhala uses the closest English equivalents – they are approximations only. Listening to Sri Lankans is the best way to learn Sinhala pronunciation.

When consonants are doubled they should be pronounced very distinctly, almost as two separate sounds belonging to two separate words. The letters **t** and **d** are pronounced less forcefully than in English, and **g** is pronounced as in 'go', not as in 'rage'. The letter **r** is more like a flap of the tongue against the roof of the mouth – it's not pronounced as an American 'r'.

Vowels

a as the 'u' in 'cup'; **aa** is pronounced more like the 'a' in 'father'
e as in 'met'
i as in 'bit'
o as in 'hot'
u as in 'put', not as in 'hut'

Vowel Combinations

ai as the word 'eye'
au as the 'ow' in 'how'

Greetings & Civilities

Hello.	*hello*
Goodbye.	*aayu-bowan*
Yes.	*owu*
No.	*naeh*
Please.	*karuna kara*
Thank you.	*stuh-tee*
Excuse me.	*sama venna*
Sorry/Pardon.	*kana gaatui*
Do you speak English?	*oyaa in-ghirisih kata karenawa da?*
How much is it?	*ehekka keeyada?*
What's your name?	*oyaaghe nama mokka'da?*
My name is …	*maaghe nama ...*

Getting Around

When does does the next … leave/arrive?
meelanga ... pitat venne/peminenne?

boat	*bohtuwa*
bus (city)	*bas eka*
bus (intercity)	*bas eka (nagaraantara)*
train	*koh-chiya*
plane	*plane eka*

I want to get off.	*mama metina bahinawa*
I'd like a one-way ticket.	*mata tani gaman tikat ekak ganna ohna*
I'd like a return ticket.	*mata yaam-eem tikat ekak ganna ohna*

1st class	*palamu veni paantiya*
2nd class	*deveni paantiya*
3rd class	*tunveni paantiya*
timetable	*kaala satahana*
bus stop	*bas nevatuma/ bas hohlt eka*
train station	*dumriya pala*
ferry terminal	*totu pala*

Where is (a/the) ...?	*... koheda?*
Go straight ahead.	*kelinma issarahata yaanna*
Turn left.	*wamata herenna*
Turn right.	*dakunata herenna*
near	*lan-ghai*
far	*durai*

I'd like to hire ...	*mata ... ekak bad-data ganna ohna*
a car	*kar*
a bicycle	*baisikel*

Signs – Sinhala

Entrance	
etul veema	ඇතුල්වීම
Exit	
pita veema	පිටවීම
Information	
toraturu	තොරතුරු දැන්වුම
Open	
virutai etta	විවෘතව ඇත.
Closed	
vasaa etta	වසා ඇත.
Prohibited	
tahanam	තහනම් වෙ.
Police Station	
polis staaneya	පොලිස් ස්ථානය
Rooms Available	
kamara etta	කාමර ඇත.
No Vacancies	
ida netu	කාමර නැත.
Toilets	
wesikili	වැසිකිළි
Men *purusha*	පුරුෂ
Women *sthree*	ස්ත්‍රී

Around Town

bank	*benkuwa*
chemist/pharmacy	*faamisiya*
... embassy	*... embasiya*
my hotel	*mang inna hotalaya*
market	*maakat eka*
newsagency	*patara ejensiya*
post office	*tepal kantohruwa*
public telephone	*podu dura katanayak*
stationers	*lipi dravya velendoh*
tourist office	*sanchaaraka toraturu karyaalayak*

What time does it open/close?	*ehika kiyatada arinne/vahanne?*

Accommodation

Do you have any rooms available?	*kaamara tiyanawada?*
for one person	*ek-kenek pamanai*
for two people	*den-nek pamanai*
for one night	*ek rayak pamanai*
for two nights	*raya dekak pamanai*
How much is it per night?	*ek ra-yakata kiyada*
How much is it per person?	*ek keneh-kuta kiyada*
Is breakfast included?	*udeh keh-emat ekkada?*

hotel	*hotel eka*
guesthouse	*gesthaus eka*
youth hostel	*yut-hostel eka*
camping ground	*kamping ground eka*

Some Useful Words

big	*loku*
small	*podi, punchi*
bread	*paan*
butter	*batah*
coffee	*koh-pi*
egg	*bit-taraya*
fruit	*palaturu*
ice	*ais*
medicine	*beh-yit*
milk	*kiri*
rice (uncooked)	*haal*
rice (cooked)	*baht*
sugar	*seeni*
tea	*te-eh*
vegetables	*elavalu*
water	*watura*

Time & Days

What time is it?	*velava keeyada?*
day	*davasa*
night	*reh*
week	*sumaaneh*
month	*maaseh*
year	*awurudeh*
today	*ada*
tomorrow	*heta*
yesterday	*ee-ye*
morning	*udai*
afternoon	*havasa*

Monday	*sandu-da*
Tuesday	*angaharuwaa-da*
Wednesday	*badaa-da*
Thursday	*braha-spetin-da*
Friday	*sikuraa-da*
Saturday	*senasuraa-da*
Sunday	*iri-da*

Numbers

0	*binduwa*
1	*eka*
2	*deka*
3	*tuna*
4	*hatara*
5	*paha*
6	*haya*
7	*hata*
8	*a-teh*
9	*navaya*
10	*dahaya*

Emergencies – Sinhala

Help!	*aaneh!/aayoh!/ amboh!*
Call a doctor!	*dostara gen-nanna!*
Call the police!	*polisiyata kiyanna!*
Leave me alone!	*mata maghe paduweh inna arinna!*
Go away!	*metanin yanna!*
I'm lost.	*maa-maa nativelaa*

100	*seeya*
200	*deh seeya*
1000	*daaha*
2000	*deh daaha*
100,000	*lakshaya*

one million	*daseh lakshaya*
10 million	*kotiya*

Tamil

The vocabulary of Sri Lankan Tamil is pretty much the same as that of South India – words have the identical written form in the traditional cursive script – but there are marked differences in pronunciation between speakers from the two regions. The transliteration system used in this guide is intended to represent the sounds of Sri Lankan Tamil using the roman alphabet – as with all such systems it is an approximate guide only. The best way to improve your pronunciation is to listen to the way Sri Lankans themselves speak the language.

Pronunciation

Vowels

a	as the 'u' in 'cup'; **aa** is pronounced as the 'a' in 'father'
e	as in 'met'
i	as in 'bit'
o	as in 'hot', eg, *rotty* (bread)
u	as in 'put', eg, *ulluh* (seven)

Vowel Combinations

ai	as in 'eye'
au	as in 'how'

Consonants

Most consonants are fairly similar to their English counterparts. The following are a few that may cause confusion:

dh one sound, as the 'th' in 'then' (not as in 'thin')
g as in 'go'
r a flap of the tongue against the roof of the mouth – not pronounced as an American 'r'
s as in 'sit'
th one sound, as in 'thin'

Greetings & Civilities

Hello.	*vanakkam*
Goodbye.	*poytu varukirehn*
Yes.	*aam*
No.	*il-lay*
Please.	*tayavu saydhih*
Thank you.	*nandri*
That's fine, you're welcome.	*naladu varuheh*
Excuse me.	*mannikavum*
Sorry/Pardon.	*mannikavum*
Do you speak English?	*nin-gal aangilam paysu-virhalaa?*
How much is it?	*ahdu evvalah-vur?*
What's your name?	*ungal peyr en-na?*
My name is …	*en pay-yehr ...*

Getting Around

What time does the next … leave/arrive?
eppohlidur arutur ... sellum/vahrum?

boat	*padadur*
bus (city)	*baas (naharam/ul-loor)*
bus (intercity)	*baas (veliyoor)*
train	*rayill*
I want to get off.	*iranga po-orem*
I'd like a one-way ticket.	*enakku oru vahlay tikket vaynum*
I'd like a return ticket.	*enakku iru vahlay tikket vaynum*
1st class	*mudalahaam vahuppur*
2nd class	*irandaam vahuppur*
luggage lockers	*vai-dhu pehna saamaan*
timetable	*haala attavanay*
bus/trolley stop	*baas nilayem*
train station	*rayill nilayem*
Where is it?	*un-ghe irukkaradhur?*
Where is a/the ...?	*... un-ghe?*
Go straight ahead.	*neraha sellavum*
Turn left.	*valadhur pakkam tirumbavum*
Turn right.	*itadhur pakkam tirumbavum*

Signs – Tamil

Entrance
vahli ullay வழி உள்ளே
Exit
vahli veliyeh வழி வெளியே
Information
tahavwel தகவல்
Open
turandul-ladur திறந்துள்ளது
Closed
adek-kappatulladur
அடைக்கப்பட்டுள்ளது
Prohibited
anumadee-illay அனுமதி இல்லை
Police Station
kaav'l nilayem காவல நிலையம்
Rooms Available
arekahl undu அறைகள் உண்டு
Full, No Vacancies
illay, kaali illay
நிரம்பியுள்ளது, காலி இல்லை
Toilets
kahlippadem மலசலகூடம்
Men *aan* ஆண்
Women *pen* பெண

near	*aruhil*
far	*tu-rahm*
I'd like to hire ...	*enakku ... varaykhur vaynum*
a car	*kaa*
a bicycle	*sai-kul*

Around Town

bank	*vanghee*
chemist/pharmacy	*marunduh kadhai-karehr*
... embassy	*... tudharahem*
my hotel	*en udehr hotehl*
market	*maarket*
newsagency	*niyuz ejensee*
post office	*tavaal nilayem*
public telephone	*podhu tolai-pessee*
stationers	*eludhuporul vanihehr*
tourist office	*toorist nilayem*
What time does it open/close?	*et-thana manikka tirakhum/mudhum?*

Accommodation

Do you have any rooms available?	*arekil kidhekkumaa?*

for one/two people	*oruvah/iruvah ukku*
for one/two nights	*oru/irandu iravukku*
How much is it per night/per person?	*oru iravukku/oru naba-rukku evvalavur?*
Is breakfast included?	*kaaleh setrundeen sehrtoh?*
hotel	*hotehl*
guesthouse	*virun-dhinar vidhudheh*
youth hostel	*ilainar vidhudheh*
camping ground	*tan-gum idahm*

Some Useful Words

big	*periyeh*
small	*siriyeh*
bread	*rotti/rotty*
butter	*ven-nay*
coffee	*kahpee*
egg	*muh-tay*
fruit	*paadham*
ice	*ais*
medicine	*marunduh*
milk	*paal*
rice	*areesee*
sugar	*seeree*
tea	*teh-neer*
vegetables	*kaay-karahil*
water	*neer*

Time & Days

What time is it?	*mani eh-tanay?*
day	*pahel*
night	*iravu*
week	*vaarem*
month	*maadhem*
year	*varudem*
today	*indru*
tomorrow	*naalay*
yesterday	*neh-truh*
morning	*kaalai*
afternoon	*matiya-nem*
Monday	*tin-gal*
Tuesday	*sevvaay*
Wednesday	*budahn*
Thursday	*viyaalin*
Friday	*vellee*
Saturday	*san-nee*
Sunday	*naayru*

Numbers

0	*saidhu*
1	*ondru*
2	*iranduh*
3	*muundruh*

Emergencies – Tamil

Help!	*udavi!*
Call a doctor!	*daktarai kuppa-ravum!*
Call the police!	*polisai kupparavum!*
Leave me alone!	*enna taniyaahu irukkaviduh!*
Go away!	*pohn-goh!/ tolandu po!* (informal)
I'm lost.	*naan valee tavuree-vittehn*

4	*naan-guh*
5	*ainduh*
6	*aaruh*
7	*ulluh*
8	*uttu*
9	*onbaduh*
10	*pat-tuh*
100	*nooruh*
1000	*aayirem*
2000	*irundaayirem*
100,000	*lah-chem*
one million	*pattuh lah-chem*
10 million	*kohdee*

Sri Lankan English

Like every other country where English is spoken, Sri Lanka has its own peculiar versions of some words and phrases. Life can be a bit confusing if you don't have a grasp of some of the essentials of Sri Lankan English.

Greetings & Questions

Go and come – farewell greeting, similar to 'see you later', not taken literally
How? – How are you?
Nothing to do – Can't do anything
What to do? – What can be done about it?; more of a rhetorical question
What country? – Where are you from?

People

batchmate – university classmate
baby/bubba – used for any child up to about adolescence
to gift – to give a gift
paining – hurting

peon – office helper
uncle/auntie – term of respect for elder

Getting Around

backside – part of the building away from the street
bajaj – three-wheeler
bus halt – bus stop
coloured lights – traffic lights
down south – the areas south of Colombo, especially coastal areas
dropping – being dropped off at a place by a car
get down (from bus/train/three-wheeler) – to alight
hotel – a small, cheap restaurant without accommodation
normal bus – not a private bus
outstation – place beyond a person's home area
petrol shed – petrol/gas station
pick-up (noun) – 4WD utility vehicle
seaside/landside – indicates locations, usually in relation to Galle Rd
two-wheeler – motorcycle
up and down – return trip
up country/hill country – Kandy and beyond, tea plantation areas
vehicle – car

Food

bite – snack usually eaten with alcoholic drinks
boutique – a small, hole-in-the-wall shop, usually selling small, inexpensive items
cool spot – traditional, small shop that sells cool drinks and snacks
lunch packet/rice packet – portion of rice and curry wrapped in plastic and newspaper and taken to office/school for lunch
short eats – snack food

Money

buck – rupee
purse – wallet
last price – final price when bargaining

Place Names

Sri Lanka's often fearsome-looking place names become much simpler with a little analysis. See the boxed text 'Understanding Place Names' in the Facts for the Visitor chapter.

Pronunciation

Pronounce each name as a series of clearly defined syllables (stress generally falls on the second last syllable), eg, Anuradhapura (a-nu-ra-da-**pu**-ra), Polonnaruwa (poh-loh-na-**ru**-wa).

GAZETTEER

English Sinhala	Tamil
Adam's Peak	
ශ්‍රීපාදය	சிவனொலிபாதம்
Aluthgama	
අළුත්ගම	அளுத்கம
Ambalangoda	
අම්බලන්ගොඩ	அம்பலாங்கொடை
Anuradhapura	
අනුරාධපුරය	அனுராதபுரம்
Arugam Bay	
ආරුගම්බේ	அறுகம் முனை
Aukana	
අව්කන	அக்குறணை
Badulla	
බදුල්ල	பதுளை
Bandarawela	
බන්ඩාරවෙල	பண்டாரவளை
Batticaloa	
මඩකලපුව	மட்டக்களப்பு
Belihul Oya	
බෙලිහුල්ඔය	பெலிகுல் ஓய
Bentota	
බෙන්තොට	பெந்தோட்டை
Beruwela	
බේරුවල	பேருவலை
Bundala National Park	
බූන්දල අභයභූමිය புந்தள	
Chilaw	
හලාවත	சிலாபம்
Colombo	
කොළඹ	கொழும்பு
Dambadeniya	
දඹදෙණිය	தம்பதெனிய
Dambulla	
දඹුල්ල	தம்புல்லை
Dimbulagala	
දිඹුලාගල	திம்புளகல
Ella	
ඇල්ල	எல்ல
Gal Oya National Park	
ගල්ඔය අභයභූමිය கல் ஓயா	

Galle
ගාල්ල காலி
Giritale
ගිරිතලේ கிரித்தல
Habarana
හබරණ ஹபறண
Hambantota
හම්බන්තොට ஹம்பாந்தோட்டை
Haputale
හපුතලේ ஹப்புத்தளை
Hikkaduwa
හික්කඩුව ஹிக்கடுவை
Horton Plains National Park
හෝර්ටන් තැන්න අභයභූමිය
ஹோட்டன் பிளெயின்ஸ்
Induruwa
ඉඳුරුව இந்துறுவ
Jaffna
යාපනය யாழ்ப்பாணம்
Kalpitiya
කල්පිටිය கற்பிட்டி
Kalutara
කළුතර களுத்துறை
Kandy
මහනුවර கண்டி
Kataragama
කතරගම கதிர்காமம்
Kitulgala
කිතුල්ගල கித்துள்கல
Kurunegala
කුරුණෑගල குருநாகல்
Lahagula National Park
ලාහුගල අභයභූමිය
Mannar Island
මන්නාරම් දූපත් மன்னார் தீவு
Matara
මාතර மாத்தறை
Medirigiriya
මැදිරිගිරිය மதிரிகிரிய
Mihintale
මිහින්තලය மிகிந்தலை
Minneriya National Park
මින්නේරිය අභයභූමිය
Mirissa
මිරිස්ස மிரிஸ்ஸ
Monaragala
මොණරාගල மொனறாகலை

Mulkirigala
මුල්ගිරිගල முல்கிரிகல
Negombo
මීගමුව நீர்கொழும்பு
Nilaveli
නිලාවෙලි நிலாவெளி
Nuwara Eliya
නුවර එළිය நுவரேலியா
Padeniya
පාදෙනිය பாடெனிய
Panduwasnuwara
පඬුවස්නුවර பண்டுவஸ் நுவர
Polonnaruwa
පොළොන්නරුව பொலன்னறுவை
Puttalam
පුත්තලම புத்தளம்
Ratnapura
රත්නපුරය இரத்தினபுரி
Ritigala
රිටිගල றித்திகல
Sigiriya
සීගිරිය சீகிரிய
Sinharaja
සිංහරාජ சிங்ஹராஜ
Tangalla
තංගල්ල தங்காலை
Tissamaharama
තිස්සමහාරාමය திசமஹாறம
Trincomalee
ත්‍රිකුණාමළය திருகோணமலை
Uda Walawe National Park
උඩ වලවේ අභයභූමිය
உடவளவ்வை
Unawatuna
උණවටුන உணவட்டுன
Uppuveli
උප්පුවෙල உப்புவெளி
Weligama
වැලිගම வெலிகம
Wellawaya
වැල්ලවාය வெல்லவாய
Wilpattu National Park
විල්පත්තු ජාතික වනෝද්‍යානය
வில்பத்து தேசிய புகல் அரண்
Yala (Ruhuna) National Park
යාල (රුහුන) අභයභූමිය
Yapahuwa
යාපහුව யாப்பஹுவ

Glossary

aluva – rice flour, treacle and cashew-nut fudge
ambalama – wayside shelter for pilgrims
ambul thiyal – a pickle usually made from tuna; translates literally as 'sour fish curry'
amudes – loincloths worn by gem miners
arrack – distilled *toddy*, often very potent
Aurudu – Sinhalese and Tamil New Year, celebrated on 14 April
Avalokitesvara – the *Bodhisattva* representing compassion
Ayurveda – traditional system of medicine using herbs and oils to heal and rejuvenate

bailas – folk tunes (often love songs) based on Portuguese, African and local elements
baobab – water-storing tree *(Adansonia digitata)*, probably introduced to Mannar Island and the Vanni in northern Sri Lanka by Arab traders
bed tea – early morning cuppa served to you in bed
Bhikku – Buddhist monk
Bhikkuni – Buddhist nun
biryani – delicate North Indian dish of spiced rice with meat, hard-boiled egg and pickles
bodhi tree – large spreading tree *(Ficus religiosa)*; the tree under which the Buddha sat when he attained enlightment, and the many descendants grown from cuttings of this tree
Bodhisattva – divine being who, although capable of attaining *nirvana,* chooses to reside on the human plane to help ordinary people attain salvation
bonda – deep-fried potato and lentil ball in lentil flour batter
boutique – naturalised Portuguese word for a street stall or small shop
Brahmi – early Indian script used from the 5th century BC
bund – built-up bank or dyke surrounding a *tank*
Burgher – Sri Lankan Eurasian, generally descended from Portuguese-Sinhalese or Dutch-Sinhalese intermarriage

cadjan – coconut fronds woven into mats and used as building material
Ceylon – British colonial name for Sri Lanka
chena – shifting cultivation whereby land is cultivated until its fertility diminishes; it is then abandoned until it is restored naturally. This usually damages the environment
chetiya – Buddhist shrine
Chinese rolls – deep-fried pastry rolls filled with vegetables or meat
Chola – powerful ancient South Indian kingdom that invaded Sri Lanka on several occasions
coir – mat or rope made from coconut fibres
copra – dried coconut kernel used to make cooking oil and also exported for use in the manufacture of confectionery
crore – 10 million of anything, but most often rupees
CTB – Central (formerly Ceylon) Transport Board, the state bus network
Culavamsa – the 'Minor Chronicle', which continues the history commenced in the *Mahavamsa* up to 1758
curd – buffalo-milk yogurt
curd vadai – deep-fried lentil patty with yogurt
cutlets – deep-fried meat or fish balls

dagoba – Buddhist monument composed of a solid hemisphere containing relics of the Buddha or a Buddhist saint; also called *stupa*
devale – a complex designed for worshipping a Hindu or Sri Lankan deity; devales are sometimes found near Buddhist shrines
dhal – thick soup made of split lentils; in Sinhala, *parripu*
dharma – the word used by both Hindus and Buddhists to refer to their respective moral codes of behaviour
dorje – hourglass-shaped Tibetan thunderbolt symbol
dosa/dosai – wafer-like pancakes
Dravidian – South Indian group of peoples and languages; Tamils are included within this grouping

Eelam – Tamil word for precious land
EPDP – Eelam People's Democratic Party

gala – rock
ganga – river
gaw – old Sinhalese unit of distance
gedige – hollow temple with extremely thick walls and a corbelled roof

geta bera – Kandyan double-ended drum
gopuram – soaring pyramidal gateway of a Hindu temple; a style of *Dravidian* architecture found principally in South India
guardstones – carved ornamental stones that flank doorways or entrances to temples
gurulu – legendary bird that preys on snakes, used as an image in carved *raksha* masks

hodhi – curry with a thin gravy
hopper – popular Sri Lankan snack or meal; a regular hopper is like a small, bowl-shaped pancake, fried over a high flame, while string hoppers are made of tangled circles of steamed noodles
howdah – seat for carrying people on an elephant's back
Hanuman – the monkey king, character from the *Ramayana*

idli – South Indian rice dumpling
illama – a gravel-bearing stratum likely to hold gemstones
IPKF – Indian Peace Keeping Force; the Indian Army contingent present in northern Sri Lanka from 1987 to 1990

jaggery – hard, brown sweet made from *kitul*
Jataka tales – stories of the previous lives of the Buddha
juggernaut – huge, extravagantly decorated temple cart, dragged through the streets during Hindu festivals (sometimes called a 'car')
JVP – Janatha Vimukthi Peramuna or the People's Liberation Army; a Sinhalese Marxist revolutionary organisation that rose up in 1971 and again in the late 1980s

kalu dodol – coconut milk, *jaggery* and cashew-nut sweet
Karavas – fisherfolk of Indian descent
karma – Hindu-Buddhist principle of retributive justice for past deeds
kavun – spiced flour and treacle batter-cake fried in coconut oil
kiri bath – a dessert of rice cooked in milk; it also has ritual significance
kitul – sap from the *kitul* palm drawn off from the tree; in liquid form it's known as treacle, and when boiled down as *jaggery*
kolam – costume or guise; used to refer to masked dance-drama; also rice-flour designs that adorn thresholds of buildings in Tamil areas
kool – a speciality of Jaffna consisting of a boiled-and-fried vegetable combination dried in the sun
korma – curry-like braised dish
kotthu rotty – *rotty* chopped up and mixed with vegetables, eggs or meat
kovil – Hindu temple; most Sri Lankan *kovils* are dedicated to the worship of Shiva
kul – spicy chowder dish, popular in Jaffna
kulam – Tamil word for *tank*

lakh – 100,000; a standard unit of measurement in Sri Lanka and India
Laksala – government-run arts and handicrafts shop
lamprais – rice and curry wrapped up and cooked in a banana leaf; a Dutch word that literally means 'lump rice'
lingam – phallic symbol; symbol of Shiva
LTTE – Liberation Tigers of Tamil Eelam, also known as the Tamil Tigers; separatist group fighting for an independent Tamil Eelam in the north and east

Maha – the northeast monsoon season
Mahavamsa – the 'Great Chronicle', a written Sinhalese history running from the arrival of Prince Vijaya from India in the 6th century BC, through the meeting of King Devanampiya Tissa with *Mahinda*, and on to the great kings of Anuradhapura
Mahaweli Ganga – Sri Lanka's biggest river, which starts in the hill country near Adam's Peak, flows through Kandy and eventually reaches the sea near Trincomalee
Mahayana – a later form of Buddhism prevalent in Korea, Japan and China, which literally means 'greater vehicle'. It emphasises the *Bodhisattva* ideal, which teaches the renunciation of *nirvana* to help other beings to reach enlightenment
Mahinda – son of the Indian Buddhist emperor Ashoka, credited with introducing Buddhism to Sri Lanka
mahout – elephant rider or master
Maitreya – future Buddha
makara – mythical beast that is a cross between a lion, a pig and an elephant, commonly carved in the balustrade of temple staircases
makara torana – ornamental archway
mallung – shredded green leafy vegetable mixed with grated coconut and lightly stir-fried, eaten as an accompaniment to rice and curry

mandapaya – a raised platform with decorative pillars
masala – mix (often spices)
masala dosa – curried vegetables inside a lentil and rice-flour pancake
mawatha – avenue or street; abbreviated to 'Mw'
moonstone – semiprecious stone; also a carved stone 'doorstep' seen at temple entrances
mudra – symbolic hand position of a Buddha image

naga – snake; also applies to snake deities and spirits
naga raksha – a *raksha* mask featuring a 'coiffure' of writhing cobras
Nikaya – an order of Buddhist monks (a division of the *Sangha*)
nirvana – the ultimate aim of Buddhists, final release from the cycle of existence
nuwara – city

ola – palm leaf used in manuscripts and traditional books
oruva – outrigger canoe
oya – stream or small river

PA – People's Alliance; a coalition including the *SLFP* founded in 1994
paddy – unhusked rice
padma – lotus flower
Pali – the language in which the Buddhist scriptures were originally recorded
palmyra – tall palm tree found in the dry northern region
pappadam – thin, round, crisp bread eaten with curries or as a snack
parripu – red-lentil *dhal*
perahera – a procession, usually with dancers, drummers and elephants
pirivena – centre of learning attached to monastery
pittu – steamed mixture of rice flour and grated coconut, sometimes made with slightly roasted wheat flour
plantain – banana; there are many different varieties in Sri Lanka, some of which are eaten as an everyday fruit while others are reserved for special occasions
pokuna – artificial pond
pol – Sinhala word for 'coconut'
poya – full-moon holiday
puja – literally meaning 'respect'; offering or prayers

rajakariya – literally 'workers for the king', the tradition of feudal service
raksha – type of mask used in parades and festivals
Rakshasas – legendary rulers of Sri Lanka, led by *Rawana*
Ramayana – ancient story of Rama and Sita and their conflict with *Rawana*
rasa-kavili – sweets
Rawana – the 'demon king of Lanka' who abducts Rama's beautiful wife Sita in the Hindu epic the *Ramayana*
red rice – partly hulled rice
relic chamber – chamber in a *dagoba* housing a relic of the Buddha or a saint and representing the Buddhist concept of the cosmos
rotty – elasticated, doughy pancake; also a small parcel of vegetables or meat wrapped up in a *rotty*
Ruhunu – ancient southern centre of Sinhalese power near Tissamaharama; it continued to stand even when Anuradhapura and Polonnaruwa fell to Indian invaders; also spelt *Ruhuna*

sambol – chilli side dish, often made with coconut or onion; the general name for any spicy-hot dish
samudra – large *tank* or inland sea
Sangamitta – sister of *Mahinda* who brought the sapling from Bodhgaya in India from which the sacred bodhi tree at Anuradhapura grew
sanni – devil-dancing mask
Sangha – the community of Buddhist monks; in Sri Lanka, an influential group divided into several *Nikayas* or orders
Sanskrit – ancient Indian language, the oldest known member of the family of Indo-European languages
sari – traditional garment worn by women
school pen – ballpoint pen, often requested (or demanded!) from tourists by Sri Lankan children
short eats – plates of small pastries and savouries, such as *bonda*, *Chinese rolls* and *vadai*, served at tea shops
sikhara – a dome- or pyramid-shaped structure rising above the shrine room of a Hindu *kovil*
Sinhala – language of the Sinhalese people
Sinhalese – the majority population of Sri Lanka, principally Sinhala-speaking Buddhists

SLFP – Sri Lanka Freedom Party
stupa – see *dagoba*

Tamils – a people of South Indian origins comprising the largest minority population in Sri Lanka
tank – artificial water-storage lake or reservoir; many of the tanks in Sri Lanka are very large and ancient
Tantric Buddhism – Tibetan Buddhism with strong sexual and occult overtones
thali – South Indian meal consisting of rice with vegetable curries and *pappadams*
thambili – an orange-coloured drinking coconut, also known as the king coconut
Theravada – orthodox form of Buddhism practised in Sri Lanka and Southeast Asia, which is characterised by its adherence to the *Pali* canon
tiffin – colonial English expression for lunch
toddy – mildly alcoholic drink tapped from coconut palms
toddy tappers – people who perform acrobatic feats to tap *toddy* from the tops of coconut palms
TULF – Tamil United Liberation Front

UNP – United National Party, the first political party to hold power in Sri Lanka after independence
UXO – unexploded ordinance

vadai – deep-fried lentil or flour patty
vahalkada – solid panel of sculpture
vatadage – circular relic house consisting of a small central *dagoba* flanked by Buddha images and encircled by columns
Vedas – Hindu sacred books; a collection of sacred hymns composed in preclassical Sanskrit during the 2nd millennium BC and divided into four books: Rig-Veda, Yajur-Veda, Sama-Veda and Atharva-Veda
Veddahs – the original people of Sri Lanka prior to the arrival of the Sinhalese; also called the *Wanniyala-aetto*
vel – trident; Skanda, a god associated with war in Hindu legend, is often depicted carrying a *vel*
vihara, viharaya – Buddhist complex, including a shrine containing a statue of the Buddha, a congregational hall and a monks' house

Wanniyala-aetto – see *Veddahs*
wattalappam – popular dessert of Malay origin, made with *jaggery*, eggs, coconut milk and cardamom
wewa – irrigation tank, artificial lake

yak bera – double-ended drum used in the southern regions
Yala – the southwest monsoon season
YMBA – Young Men's Buddhist Association

Thanks

Many thanks to the travellers who used the last edition and wrote to us with helpful hints, useful advice and interesting anecdotes.

Keith Acker, Julian Adams, Reena Aggarwal, Magnus Ahlstrom, Samantha Andrews, Steve Andrews, Michael Anema, Penny Anson, Melvyn Appleby, Suttipong Aramkun, Pim Arntzen, Santiago Asensio-Merino, M Aubort, Anders Backstrom, Trevor Badger, Alan & Margaret Baker, Richard Baker, Rachel Ball, Mark Ballard, Bridget Band, Mark & Dianne Barber-Riley, G R Barker, Mannilla Bartels, Angelique Baselier, Drew Bassett, M & M P Bateson, Johannes Baumann, Vlady Beckerman, Christine Beerens, Heike Beermann-Landry, Patty Benjamin, Dale Benson, Eli Berg, Henrik Berlin, Mink & Jeannette Bijlsma, Jennie Billson, Carly Bishop, Helen Black, Renate Bleeken, Caroline Bone, Evert Bos, Lee Bowdidge, Rick Bowlby, Edwin Braacx, Clare Braddock, Marco Brand, Keri Bridgwater, Cornelius Briel, Kathryn Brierley, Jonathan Bromberg, Barbara Brons, Tracey Brown, Bob Buchanan, Diana Buff, Earl Bunting, Laura Burden, Vicky Buser, Ben Buston, Mike & Beryl Butcher, Gill Butterwick, Trevor Cale, Sarah Capewell, Judith Carty, Andy Catlin, Chris & Lilian Cheyenne, Progga Choudhury, Eleanor Church, Alex Clark, C A Clarke, Grahame Coggins, Kim Cole, Simon Cole, Alison Collins, Paul Compton, Steve Coney, Richard Connah, Glyn Constant, Mike Corp, Robina Cosser, Charlotte Cox, Elisabeth Cox, John Cox, Colin Currie, Jan-Hendrik Damerau, W Dasanayake, Robin Daus, Adam Davies, Derek Davies, Pri de Silva, Rene & Marlese de Villiers, Bruce Deane, Solveig Deane-Johns, Jean-Paul Degen, Ruud den Boer, Gary Denness, Delphine Derniaux, Robert Desprez, John Devlin, Carol Dezateux, Jacqueline Diffey, Joanne Dissanayake, Frank Dittberner, Tom Donald, Kelly Douglas, Magdalena Dral, Simon Drury, Bram Dumolin, Fiona Dunn, Jeremy Durston, Colin Dyer, Katarzyna Dziedzina, Alistair Eastwood, Sabine Effenberger, Astrid Elksnet, Katie Enock, Clive Essame, Sarah Evans, Dr M J Everett, E M Everett, Guido Faes, Warren Feagins, Marta Fernández Olmos, Victoria Finlay, Andrew Fischer, Nicola Flint, Lars Forchhammer, Michael Fox, Avery Freed, Juergen Friebe, Hilvie & Georg Fries, Carlo Galeotti, Janne Geraets, David Gero, Christiane Gertz, Howard Gibson, Joyce & Gale Gibson, Julie Gibson, Werner Giese, Quentin Given, Daragh Glynn, Mason & Ray Gold, Callum Gordon, Miquel Graboleda, Jennifer Grebe, Alison Grimshaw, Mariska Groen, Justin Haccius, Ruediger Hahn, David Hall, David Handley, Bruno Hannud, Richard Harding, Christopher Hart, Richard Hartling, Rowan Harvey, Greg Hassall, Conrad Hatch, Bernhard Heinrich, Georges Helbling, Joe Higham, John Hill, Simon Hill, E Hodges, Kirsty Hogg, Howard R Houck, Franziska Hucht, Danielle Hughes, Mike & Li Hughes, Lily Humphries, Karen Humphreys, Richard Hutchinson, Futaba Iwase, Ronald Izendooren, Andrew Jacob, So Janchoen, Neil Jebb, Felicity Jenni, Tony Jenni, Anne & I Johnson, Stephanie Johnston, Richard Jones, Louise Jorgensen, Stanislav Kadlec, Haemish Kane, Judith Karena, Pius Karena, Leanne Kearney, Martin Kennard, Yvonne Kennett, Hubert Kerstens, Albert Kleinjan, Maureen Klimaszewski, Diedrich Koehn, Deanne Koelmeyer, Thomas Korostenski, Caroline Kozaka, Ger Kraan, Julia Krivachy, Wendy Ladage, Veronique Laloe, Mia Lambregts, Etinne Larock, Yvonne Lazarowicz, Jane Lewis, Keith Liker, J Alfred Lindegger, Ben Line, Andy & Petra Linsinger, N Logan, Deborah Lomond, Ruby Long, Geoff Lucas, Sonny Lundmark, Al Lunemann, Pamela Luther, Tony Lynch, Yvonne Lyth, Camilla Madsen, Pirotte Magaly, Nigel Maggs, Gehan Mahendren, Kevin Mannens, Ariel Maor, Nicola & William Marsden, Mary Mathisen, Martin Matthiak, Chris Maund, Cullum McAlpine, Jenny McMullen, Manfred Meiners, David Menhinick, Neil Metcalfe, Marc Middendorp, Marlies Mik, Connie Miller, Grzegorz Mlynarczyk, Fiona Molligoda, Vinod Moonesinghe, Jim & Jill Moore, Peter Moorfield, David Moreton, R Morgan, Lauren Morley, Sarah-Jane Morley, Richard Moss, Peter & Richard Mountain, Christiane Mueller, Janine Murphy, Crystal Myles, Corrado Nai Fovino, Osnat Naor, Jeanette Nelson, Kathleen Ng, Brian Nicholls, Bert Nicolaes, Udi Nir, Claude Nobus, Par Noren, Ben Oofana, Patrick Ooms, Anne O'Reilly, Cornelis & Laura Ouwersloot, Steve Ozanne, Paul Page, Ian Parker, Julie Parker, Lisa Peake, James Peiris, John Pereira, Sunil Perera, Peter Phillips, Charles Philpott, Eva-Marie & Frank Pinon, Walter Poeschl, Francesca Poglia, Pat Poore, Viva Sara Press, Henry Pringle, Alice Prior, Judi Pulsford, Brian Quinn, Leah Ramet, Dainee Ranaweera, Ian Randell, Tom Ratcliffe, Catherine Rawlingson, Hila Raz, D I Reid, Robert Reid, Annette & Dick Reijersen, Lorna Reith, Neil Rimmer, Stefania Rinaldi, Trisha & Dave Rissas, Duncan Robertson, Ian Robertson, David Robson, John

Robson, MS Rodrigo, Bandula Rodrigp, Joanne Rollier, Astrid Rose, Cynthia Rosenfeld, John & Carol Ross, Jens Roth, Peter Roth, Jonathan Ryan, Henryk Sadura, Willem Saher, Femke Schaap, Markus Schafer, Stefan Schmied, Guido Schott, Anne-Marie Schweingruber, Paul Scrobohaci, Nadira Seeram, Louise Selby, Stephanie Selhorst, Johann Selvarajah, Mary Seppi, Nargis Shaheen, M Sharp, Katie Shilcock, Daniel Silve, Annarosa Sinopoli, Paul Smart, Colette Smith, Mike Smith, Russell Smith, Alfonso Solideal Colombo, Steph Southgate, Eve Spence, Ron Stanley, Sabine Stegemann, Arend & Mirjam Steunenberg, Chantal Steuten, Kenneth Stewart, Dominic & Emma Stoppani, Martin Streimelweger, Heike Sturm, Teoh Suchin, Aity Sukidjo, Krista Sullivan, Alison Swan, Kazuhiro Takabatake, Navot Tamari, Emmanuel Teitelbaum, Emily Thomas, Jeff Thompson, Michael Trainer, Peter Treacher, Darius Tremtiaczy, Dr & Mrs D Trump, Fredrik Tukk, Steven Tyerman, Olly Tyler, Gunther Ullrich, Elizabeth Utri, Martina van den Berg, Caroline & Herman van den Wall Bake, A W Van Der Kuip, Ivy van Eer, Frits van Ens, Joost van Hovell, Jantine van Leeuwen, Mantijn van Leeuwen, Peter van Spall, Levien van Zon, Patrick Vanier, A N Varghese, Jac Vidgen, Neil Vincent, Rebecca Vincenzi, Felicia Violi, Marshal Walker, Caroline Walters, Tim Wand, Lizzie Warrener, Walter Webler, Asoka Weerasinghe, Fred Wegley, Sabine Weishaupt, Roland Wenzlhuemer, Krista Westert, Ruchira Wickramasinghes, Kanchana Wickremasinghe, Luchiano Wijesuriya, Leonoor Wijnans, Richard & Ayoma Wilen, Aled Williams, Glyn Wilson, Jori Wolf, Paula Wood, Richard Woollacott, Ron Wyatt, Jayne Yates, Arco Zaanen, Alenka Zalaznik, Suki Zoe, Anat Zverdling

Index

Text

Bold indicates maps.

Boxed Text

Bold indicates maps.

MAP LEGEND

CITY ROUTES

- Freeway — Freeway
- Highway — Primary Road
- Road — Secondary Road
- Street — Street
- Lane — Lane
- Roadblocks
- Unsealed Road
- One-Way Street
- Pedestrian Street
- Stepped Street
- Tunnel
- Footbridge

REGIONAL ROUTES

- Tollway, Freeway
- Primary Road
- Secondary Road
- Minor Road
- Unsealed Road

BOUNDARIES

- International
- State
- Disputed
- Fortified Wall
- Suburb

HYDROGRAPHY

- River, Creek
- Swamp
- Lake, Tank
- Dry Lake, Salt Lake
- Spring, Rapids
- Waterfalls

TRANSPORT ROUTES & STATIONS

- Rail, Train Station
- Non operational Rail
- Tramway
- Bus Route
- Monorail
- Cable Car, Chairlift
- Ferry
- Path in Park
- Walking Trail
- Walking Tour

AREA FEATURES

- Building
- Park, Garden
- Forest
- Market
- Beach
- Rock
- Cemetery
- Urban

MAP SYMBOLS

- CAPITAL — National Capital
- City — City, Large Town
- Town — Town
- Village — Village
- Place to Stay
- Place to Eat
- Point of Interest
- Airfield
- Airport
- Bank
- Bird Sanctuary
- Buddhist Temple
- Bus Station, Stop
- Camping Ground
- Cathedral, Church
- Cave
- Cinema
- Dive Site
- Embassy, Consulate
- Garden
- Golf Course
- Gompa
- Hindu Temple
- Hospital
- Internet Café
- Lighthouse
- Lookout
- Monument
- Mosque
- Mountain, Hill
- Mountain Range
- Museum, Gallery
- National Park
- Parking Area, Pass
- Petrol/Gas Station
- Police Station
- Post Office
- Pub, Bar
- Ruins
- Shopping Centre
- Snorkelling
- Spring
- Stately Home
- Stupa
- Surf Beach
- Swimming Pool
- Synagogue
- Taxi
- Transport (General)
- Telephone
- Theatre
- Toilet
- Tomb
- Tourist Information
- Vihara
- Zoo

Note: not all symbols displayed above appear in this book

LONELY PLANET OFFICES

Australia
Locked Bag 1, Footscray, Victoria 3011
☎ 03 8379 8000 fax 03 8379 8111
email: talk2us@lonelyplanet.com.au

UK
72-82 Rosebery Ave, London, EC1R 4RW
☎ 020 7841 9000 fax 020 7841 9001
email: go@lonelyplanet.co.uk

USA
150 Linden St, Oakland, CA 94607
☎ 510 893 8555 TOLL FREE: 800 275 8555
fax 510 893 8572
email: info@lonelyplanet.com

France
1 rue du Dahomey, 75011 Paris
☎ 01 55 25 33 00 fax 01 55 25 33 01
email: bip@lonelyplanet.fr
www.lonelyplanet.fr

World Wide Web: www.lonelyplanet.com ***or*** **AOL keyword: lp**
Lonely Planet Images: www.lonelyplanetimages.com